Lecture Notes in Computer Science 12437

More information about this series at http://www.springer.com/series/7412

Yipeng Hu · Roxane Licandro ·
J. Alison Noble · Jana Hutter ·
Stephen Aylward · Andrew Melbourne ·
Esra Abaci Turk · Jordina Torrents Barrena (Eds.)

Medical Ultrasound, and Preterm, Perinatal and Paediatric Image Analysis

First International Workshop, ASMUS 2020
and 5th International Workshop, PIPPI 2020
Held in Conjunction with MICCAI 2020
Lima, Peru, October 4–8, 2020
Proceedings

Editors
Yipeng Hu
University College London
London, UK

Roxane Licandro
TU Wien and Medical University of Vienna
Vienna, Austria

J. Alison Noble
University of Oxford
Oxford, UK

Jana Hutter
King's College London
London, UK

Stephen Aylward
Kitware Inc.
New York, NY, USA

Andrew Melbourne
King's College London
London, UK

Esra Abaci Turk
Harvard Medical School
and Children's Hospital
Boston, MA, USA

Jordina Torrents Barrena
Hewlett Packard
Barcelona, Spain

Universitat Pompeu Fabra
Barcelona, Spain

ISSN 0302-9743 ISSN 1611-3349 (electronic)
Lecture Notes in Computer Science
ISBN 978-3-030-60333-5 ISBN 978-3-030-60334-2 (eBook)
https://doi.org/10.1007/978-3-030-60334-2

LNCS Sublibrary: SL6 – Image Processing, Computer Vision, Pattern Recognition, and Graphics

This Springer imprint is published by the registered company Springer Nature Switzerland AG
The registered company address is: Gewerbestrasse 11, 6330 Cham, Switzerland

Editors
Yipeng Hu
University College London
London, UK

J. Alison Noble
University of Oxford
Oxford, UK

Stephen Aylward
Kitware Inc.
New York, NY, USA

Esra Abaci Turk
Harvard Medical School
and Children's Hospital
Boston, MA, USA

Roxane Licandro
TU Wien and Medical University of Vienna
Vienna, Austria

Jana Hutter
King's College London
London, UK

Andrew Melbourne
King's College London
London, UK

Jordina Torrents Barrena
Hewlett Packard
Barcelona, Spain

Universitat Pompeu Fabra
Barcelona, Spain

ISSN 0302-9743 ISSN 1611-3349 (electronic)
Lecture Notes in Computer Science
ISBN 978-3-030-60333-5 ISBN 978-3-030-60334-2 (eBook)
https://doi.org/10.1007/978-3-030-60334-2

LNCS Sublibrary: SL6 – Image Processing, Computer Vision, Pattern Recognition, and Graphics

This Springer imprint is published by the registered company Springer Nature Switzerland AG
The registered company address is: Gewerbestrasse 11, 6330 Cham, Switzerland

Yipeng Hu · Roxane Licandro ·
J. Alison Noble · Jana Hutter ·
Stephen Aylward · Andrew Melbourne ·
Esra Abaci Turk · Jordina Torrents Barrena (Eds.)

Medical Ultrasound, and Preterm, Perinatal and Paediatric Image Analysis

First International Workshop, ASMUS 2020 and 5th International Workshop, PIPPI 2020 Held in Conjunction with MICCAI 2020 Lima, Peru, October 4–8, 2020 Proceedings

Preface ASMUS 2020

Advances in Simplifying Medical UltraSound (ASMUS 2020) is an international workshop that provides a forum for research topics around ultrasound image computing and computer-assisted interventions and robotic systems that utilize ultrasound imaging. In its inaugural form, advice and experience was received from the team of enthusiastic organizers, in particular, those previously involved in the highly successful MICCAI POCUS workshop series (Point-of-Care Ultrasound: Algorithms, Hardware and Applications).

We were pleased to see the high quality of submissions, evidenced by reviewer feedback and the fact that we had to reject a number of papers with merit due to the competitive nature of this workshop. The 19 accepted papers were selected based on their scientific contribution, via a double-blind process involving written reviews from at least two external reviewers in addition to a member of the committee. Partly due to the focused interest and expertise, we received a set of exceptionally high-quality reviews and consistent recommendations.

The published work includes reports across a wide range of methodology, research, and clinical applications. Advanced deep learning approaches for anatomy recognition, segmentation, registration, and skill assessment are the dominant topics, in addition to ultrasound-specific new approaches in augmented reality and remote assistance. An interesting trend revealed by these papers is the merging of ultrasound probe and surgical instrument localization with robotically assisted guidance to produce increasingly intelligent systems that learn from expert labels and incorporate domain knowledge to enable increasingly sophisticated automation and fine-grained control.

We would like to thank all reviewers, organizers, authors, and our keynote speakers, Emad Boctor and Lasse Lovstakken, for sharing their research and expertise with our community. and we look forward to this workshop inspiring many exciting developments in the future in this important area.

August 2020

Yipeng Hu
Alison Noble
Stephen Aylward

Preface PIPPI 2020

The application of sophisticated analysis tools to fetal, neonatal, and paediatric imaging data is of interest to a substantial proportion of the MICCAI community. It has gained additional interest in recent years with the successful large-scale open data initiatives, such as the developing Human Connectome Project, the Baby Connectome Project, and the NIH-funded Human Placenta Project. These projects enable researchers without access to perinatal scanning facilities to bring in their image analysis expertise and domain knowledge. Advanced medical image analysis allows the detailed scientific study of conditions such as prematurity, and the study of both normal singleton and twin development, in addition to less common conditions unique to childhood. This workshop will complement the main MICCAI 2020 conference by providing a focused discussion of perinatal and paediatric image analysis that is not possible within the main conference.

It provides a focused platform for the discussion and dissemination of advanced imaging techniques applied to young cohorts.

Emphasis is placed on novel methodological approaches to the study of, for instance, volumetric growth, myelination and cortical microstructure, and placental structure and function. Methods will cover the full scope of medical image analysis: segmentation, registration, classification, reconstruction, atlas construction, tractography, population analysis, and advanced structural, functional, and longitudinal modeling, with an application to younger cohorts or to the long-term outcomes of perinatal conditions.

Challenges of image analysis techniques as applied to the preterm, perinatal, and paediatric setting are discussed, which are confounded by the interrelation between the normal developmental trajectory and the influence of pathology. These relationships can be quite diverse when compared to measurements taken in adult populations and exhibit highly dynamic changes affecting both image acquisition and processing requirements.

August 2020

Roxane Licandro
Jana Hutter
Esra Abaci Turk
Jordina Torrents
Andrew Melbourne

Organization

Organization Chairs

Yipeng Hu	University College London, UK
Alison Noble	University of Oxford, UK
Stephen Aylward	Kitware Inc., USA

Organisation Committee ASMUS 2020

Purang Abolmaesumi	University of British Columbia, Canada
Gabor Fichtinger	Queen's University, Canada
Jan d'Hooge	KU Leuven, Belgium
Chris de Korte	Radboud University, The Netherlands
Su-Lin Lee	University College London, UK
Nassir Navab	Technical University of Munich, Germany
Dong Ni	Shenzhen University, China
Kawal Rhode	King's College London, UK
Russ Taylor	Johns Hopkins University, USA

Program Chair ASMUS 2020

Alexander Grimwood	University College London, UK

Demonstration Chair ASMUS 2020

Zachary Baum	University College London, UK

Program Committee ASMUS 2020

Rafeef Abugharbieh	University of British Columbia, Canada
Ester Bonmati	University College London, UK
Qingchao Chen	University of Oxford, UK
Richard Droste	University of Oxford, UK
Aaron Fenster	Robarts Research Institute, Canada
Yuan Gao	University of Oxford, UK
Samuel Gerber	Kitware Inc., USA
Nooshin Ghavami	King's College London, UK
Alberto Gomez	King's College London, UK
Ilker Hacihaliloglu	Rutgers University, USA
Lok Hin Lee	University of Oxford, UK
Jianbo Jiao	University of Oxford, UK
Bernhard Kainz	Imperial College London, UK

Lasse Løvstakken	Norwegian University of Science and Technology, Norway
Terence Peters	Western University, Canada
Bradley Moore	Kitware Inc., USA
Tiziano Portenier	ETH Zurich, Switzerland
João Ramalhinho	University College London, UK
Robert Rohling	University of British Columbia, Canada
Harshita Sharma	University of Oxford, UK
Tamas Ungi	Queens University, Canada
Qianye Yang	University College London, UK
Lin Zhang	ETH Zurich, Switzerland
Veronika Zimmer	King's College London, UK

Committee PIPPI 2020

Roxane Licandro	TU Wien and Medical University of Vienna, Austria
Jana Hutter	King's College London, UK
Andrew Melbourne	King's College London, UK
Jordina Torrents Barrena	Hewlett Packard, Spain
Esra Abaci Turk	Boston Children's Hospital, USA

Sponsors

MGI Tech Co., Ltd.

Wellcome/EPSRC Centre for Interventional and Surgical Sciences (WEISS)

Contents

Diagnosis and Measurement

Segmentation, Captioning and Enhancement

Localisation and Guidance

Robotics and Skill Assessment

PIPPI 2020

Diagnosis and Measurement

Remote Intelligent Assisted Diagnosis System for Hepatic Echinococcosis

Haixia Wang[1,2], Rui Li[1,2], Xuan Chen[3], Bin Duan[3], Linfewi Xiong[4], Xin Yang[5], Haining Fan[6], and Dong Ni[1,2](✉)

[1] School of Biomedical Engineering, Shenzhen University, Shenzhen, China
[2] Medical UltraSound Image Computing (MUSIC) Lab, Shenzhen University, Shenzhen, China
nidong@szu.edu.cn
[3] Shenzhen BGI Research, Shenzhen, China
[4] Shenzhen MGI Tech Co., Ltd., Shenzhen, China
[5] Department of Computer Science and Engineering, Chinese University of Hong Kong, Hong Kong, China
[6] Qinghai University Affiliated Hospital, Qinghai, China

Abstract. Hepatic echinococcosis (HE) is a serious parasitic disease. Because of its high efficiency and no side effects, ultrasound is the preferred method for the diagnosis of HE. However, HE mainly occurs in remote pastoral areas, where the economy is underdeveloped, medical conditions are backward, and ultrasound specialists are inadequate. Therefore, it is difficult for patients to receive timely and effective diagnosis and treatment. To address this issue, we propose a remote intelligent assisted diagnosis system for HE. Our contributions are twofold. First, we propose a novel hybrid detection network based on neural architecture search (NAS) for the intelligent assisted diagnosis of HE. Second, we propose a tele-operated robotic ultrasound system for the remote diagnosis of HE to mitigate the shortage of professional sonographers in remote areas. The experiments demonstrate that our hybrid detection network obtains mAP of 74.9% on a dataset of 2258 ultrasound images from 1628 patients. The efficacy of the proposed tele-operated robotic ultrasound system is verified in a remote clinical application trial of 90 HE patients with an accuracy of 86.7%. This framework provides an accurate and automatic remote intelligent assisted diagnostic tool for HE screening and has a good clinical application prospect.

Keywords: Neural architecture search · Robotic ultrasound · Intelligent assisted diagnosis

1 Introduction

Echinococcosis is a global parasitic disease found on pastoral areas of every continent except Antarctica [1], with a high prevalence rate of 5%–10% in parts of South America, Africa and Asia [2,3]. Among them, people in Western China, especially the Tibetan Plateau, have the highest prevalence rate of

Y. Hu et al. (Eds.): ASMUS 2020/PIPPI 2020, LNCS 12437, pp. 3–12, 2020.
https://doi.org/10.1007/978-3-030-60334-2_1

human echinococcosis. It is reported that the areas with higher grassland area ratio and lower economic level exhibit higher incidence of echinococcosis [4]. These areas are often characterized by poor economy, harsh environment, lack of specialists. Therefore, a large number of patients infected by echinococcosis can not get timely and effective treatment. As a result, remote intelligent assisted diagnosis of echinococcosis is highly expected to assist clinicians in echinococcosis screening in remote areas.

Hepatic echinococcosis (HE) refers to echinococcosis in the liver, accounting for 75% of echinococcosis cases [5]. Ultrasound is the preferred method for the diagnosis of HE due to its low cost, high efficiency and no side effects [6]. The World Health Organization proposed classification criteria for echinococcosis based on ultrasonic image characteristics. According to the criteria, HE mainly categorized by cystic echinococcosis (CE) and alveolar echinococcosis (AE), which are caused by Echinococcus granulosus and multilocularis, respectively. Meanwhile, CE is divided into five sub-types including CE1–CE5 [7], and AE is divided into three sub-types including AE1–AE3 [8]. In addition, cystic lesion (CL) referrers to the lesion requires further diagnosis [7].

Intelligent assisted diagnosis of HE from ultrasound images remains challenging for two reasons (Fig. 1). First, lesions often possess high intra-class variation caused by various factors between different devices, like contrast preferences, imaging artifacts of acoustic shadows and speckles. Second, lesions vary in size greatly. Third, the boundary between AE lesions and surrounding tissues is blurred, which makes it difficult to locate and classify the lesions.

To better assist clinicians in HE diagnosis, we proposed a hybrid detection network based on NAS. In order to meet the requirements of HE screening in remote areas, we proposed a tele-operated robotic ultrasound system. The tele-operated robotic ultrasound system equipped with hybrid detection network can be used to realize intelligent auxiliary diagnosis of HE remotely.

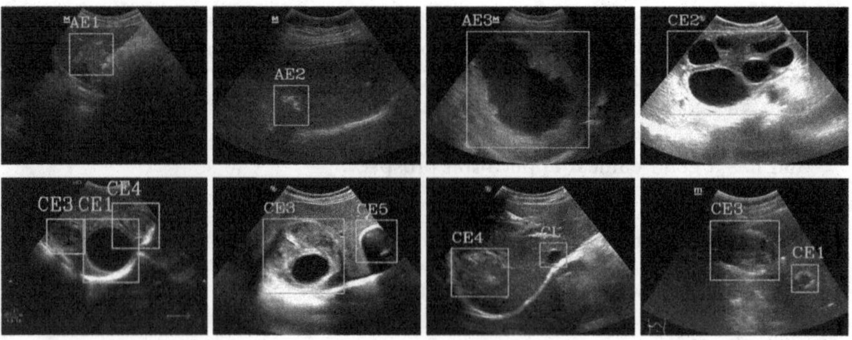

Fig. 1. Examples of HE ultrasound images. The locations and types of HE lesions are indicated by the green boxes and texts, respectively.

2 Related Works

2.1 Neural Architecture Search

Compared to classic machine learning methods, Convolutional neural network (CNN) automates the learning of features, feature hierarchy, and mapping function. Recent advances in CNN mainly focused on crafting the architecture of CNN models to improve the performances [9]. However, it requires a lot of time and efforts to perform extensive experiments on selection of network structure and hyper-parameters. Neural architecture search (NAS) addresses the aforementioned issues by automatically generating an effective and compact network architectures [10]. Generally, NAS searches for an optimal network by conducting a search strategy in a search space that includes all possible network architectures or network components.

Zoph et al. [11] proposed a NAS method that can automatically find architecture. Liu et al. [12] proposed the differentiable architecture search, which constructed networks by stacking basic network cells. Woong et al. [13] proposed a NAS framework that revisited the classic U-net. Whereas, their search space is mainly limited around several 2D and 3D vanilla convolutional operators.

In this study, we propose a novel hybrid detection network to encode expert's knowledge through NAS. It also adopts a mixed depthwise convolution operator to decrease the backbone parameters while boosting performance.

2.2 Robotic Ultrasonic System

Gourdon et al. [14] designed a master/slave system used for ultrasound scanning. Courreges et al. [15] presented a robotic teleoperated system for ultrasound scanning. Similar systems can be found in [16–19]. Most of the previous research in this field focused only on robot design and control, whereas the operating efficiency, ultrasound system control and audio-video communication were often ignored. Scott et al. [20] proposed a commercial tele-robotic ultrasound system, which allows the communication between doctor-side and patient-side via a video conference system. However, this system can only achieve three degrees of freedom (DOFs) robot control, which greatly reduces the doctor's operating efficiency.

In this study, we describe a novel tele-operated robotic ultrasound system. In addition to tele-operation of the ultrasound probe, our system provides ultrasound system control and audio-video communication as well. Our system allows doctor to conduct a real ultrasound examination and diagnosis. Although the concept of tele-operated robotic ultrasound scanning is not new, we have greatly eased use of tele-operated robotic ultrasound system. Through the combination of sensors, we created a novel console that allows the doctor to operate like a real ultrasound scan. In order to allow the robot to accurately reproduce the doctor's movement while maintaining flexible contact with the patient, an integrative force and position control strategy was applied.

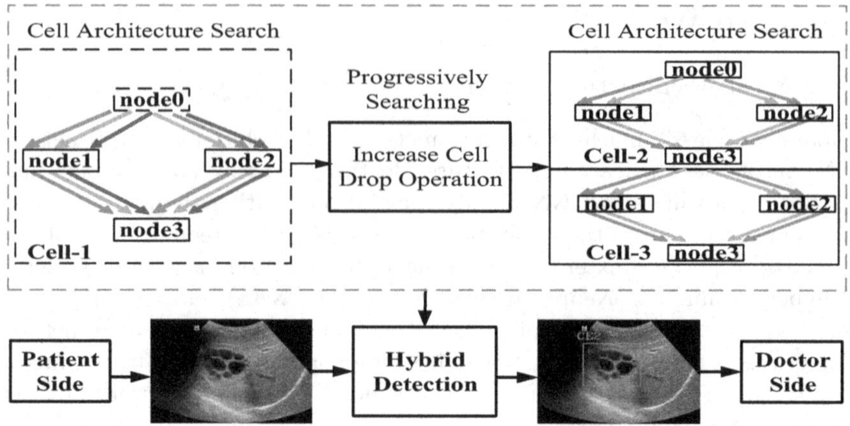

Fig. 2. A schematic of the proposed remote intelligent assisted diagnosis system.

3 Method

In this study, we proposed a remote intelligent assisted diagnosis system (Fig. 2). Specially, we first explored a classification model based on NAS, which can learn to customize optimal network architecture for HE classification tasks. Further more, based on this classification model, we proposed a hybrid detection network to obtain better detection and classification performance for HE diagnoisis. Moreover, we also proposed a tele-operated robotic ultrasound system to assist ultrasonic scanning of HE in remote areas. Finally, we combined the hybrid detection network and the tele-operated robotic operating system to realize the remote intelligent assisted diagnosis of HE.

3.1 The Hybrid Classification Model

The proposed hybrid classification model is trained through the cell searching stage and the evaluation stage. At the cell searching stage, it searches the most suitable cell by learning the operations on its edge using a bi-level optimization. At the evaluation stage, it updates the parameters based on a training scheme similar to the fine-tuning process.

Cell Architecture Search. A cell is consisted of operations, where an ordered sequence of N nodes $x_1, \ldots, x_N$ (latent representation, e.g. feature map) are connected by directed edges (i, j) (represents operations $o(\cdot) \in O$). The NAS process boils down to find the optimal cell structure. More formally, each internal node is computed as the sum of all its predecessors within a cell:

$$x_j = \sum i \leq jO^{(i,j)(x_i)} \tag{1}$$

The architecture parameters α and the weights of the network ω can be learned through the bi-level optimization problem:

$$\begin{aligned} \min_{\alpha} \quad & L_{val}(\omega^*(\alpha), \alpha), \\ s.t. \quad & \omega^*(\alpha) = \arg\min_{\omega} L_{train}(\omega, \alpha). \end{aligned} \tag{2}$$

where L_{train} is the training loss and L_{val} is the validation loss. The final architecture is then derived by:

$$o^{(i,j)} = \underset{o \in O, o \neq zero}{\arg\max} \frac{\exp(\alpha_o^{(i,j)})}{\sum_{o' \in O} \exp(\alpha_{o'}^{(i,j)})}. \tag{3}$$

To reduce the search space, only two types of cells are learned: the normal cell and the reduction cell. They both share the same candidate operations. The difference is that the reduction cell reduces the image size by a factor of 2 using stride 2. To further compress the model and improve the performance, we introduce the MixConv layer into the candidate operations. For example, a MixConv35 layer combines the convolutional kernels of sizes $[3 \times 3]$ and $[5 \times 5]$ to fuse the features extracted from different receptive fields.

Progressively Searching. Besides selecting different operations for each node, setting an optimal network depth is crucial in designing architectures. To allow learn-able depth, our model uses a progressively searching strategy proposed in [21]. The cell architecture searching is divided into K stages. The number of stacked cells is gradually increased in each stage and the candidate operations are gradually dropped into the target one-hot like structure. The final architecture is obtained by evaluating the final scores and removing the none operation.

The Network Architecture. We choose the network Darknet53 [22] as the baseline architecture, and modify it with stacking of NAS cells to build a hybrid classification model. We replaced the stage 4 and 5 in Darknet53 with cells, and searched for the optimal network using the target medical image dataset, to obtained the optimal classification result. The hybrid classification model based on the NAS method avoids the complexity of manually designing the network, and at the same time can effectively extract the data-specific features from the target data set. Therefore, the hybrid classification network is suitable for intelligent diagnosis of HE, which is an under-explored field in the community of machine learning.

3.2 The Hybrid Detection Network

The proposed hybrid detection network adopts the successful detection network YOLOv3 [22], but makes the modification on the backbone Darknet53. The searched hybrid classification model was transplanted to the hybrid detection network as the backbone to obtain the final detection and classification results. We find that the proposed hybrid detection network can not only utilizes the power of NAS but also leverages the pre-trained models on special medical image datasets in an adjustable manner.

3.3 Tele-remoted Robotic Ultrasound System

Our tele-operated robotic ultrasound system consists of two parts: a doctor-side sub-system (Fig. 3a) and a patient-side sub-system (Fig. 3b). The system realizes remote robot control, ultrasound control and audio-video communication.

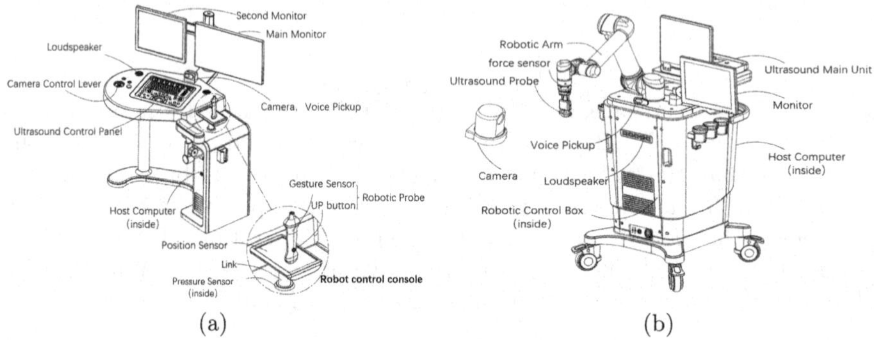

Fig. 3. (a) Components of doctor-side subsystem. (b) Components of patient-side subsystem.

Doctor-Side Subsystem. As shown in Fig. 3a, the doctor could manipulate a robot control console to control the remote robotic arm. The console has six DOFs. The gesture sensor inside the robotic probe corresponds to three DOFs for rotation, the position sensor located corresponds to two DOFs for the movement on horizontal plane, and the "UP button" and pressure sensor correspond to one DOF for the up and down movement. First, the gesture and position from doctor side should be transformed to the robot coordinate system. The gesture and position in the robot coordinate system can be calculated by:

$$R_{robot} = R_{console\_to\_robot}\; R_{console}\; R_{robot\_to\_console}, \tag{4}$$

$$p_{robot} = R_{console\_to\_robot}\; p_{console}, \tag{5}$$

where R_{robot} is a 3×3 rotation matrix in the robot coordinate system, p_{robot} is a 3×1 position vector in the robot coordinate system, $R_{console\_to\_robot}$ is the transformation matrix of console coordinate system with regard to robot coordinate system, $R_{robot\_to\_console}$ is the trans formation matrix of robot coordinate system with regard to console coordinate system, and $R_{console}$ and $p_{console}$ are the rotation matrix and the position vector in the console coordinate system respectively.

Patient-Side Subsystem. An ultrasound control panel included in our doctor-side sub-system is designed to control the ultrasound main unit included in our patient-side sub-system remotely. The screen interface of the ultrasound main unit is captured by a video capture card and then transferred to doctor-side through internet. The control signal for the ultrasound main unit is sent out from the ultrasound control panel to the ultrasound main unit following the control protocol. From Fig. 3, we can see that camera and voice pickup are also included in each subsystem. Through audio-video transmission technology, remote audio-video communication could also be achieved.

4 Experimental Results

In this study, we implemented our method in PyTorch on three 2080Ti GPUs with batch size equals to 32. We trained the network with SGD optimizer [23]. Totally, we spent about 6 h searching the hybrid classification model and 24 h training the hybrid detection network. Moreover, the inference time for per ultrasound image is less than 50 ms.

The HE ultrasound images were collected from hospitals in Qinghai province and Tibet Autonomous Region, and annotated by experts from Affiliated Hospital of Qinghai University. The dataset consisted of 9112 HE ultrasound images from 5028 patients. We randomly selected 6854 images from 3400 patients as training data and the rest are kept as test data. In addition, 90 extra cases were used in the clinical application experiment of robotic remote intelligent assisted diagnosis.

4.1 Results on the Classification Model

Table 1. Comparative results on classification experiments of different methods.

Method	Parameter (Million)	Size (MB)	Precision (%)	Recall (%)	F1-score (%)
DarkNet53	41.61	333.2	85.76	85.71	85.65
Hybrid DarkNet53	20.28	162.7	86.18	86.08	86.04
Hybrid+Mixconv	**17.91**	**137.3**	**86.73**	**86.67**	**86.64**

Table 1 presents the precision, recall, and F1-score achieved by different models. From the top to the bottom, "Darknet53" represents the original Draknet53, "Hybrid Darknet53" stands for the combination of Darknet53 with cells obtained by the NAS method, and "Hybrid+Mixconv" is embedding the mixconv operation into hybrid Darknet53. The result shows that the hybird Darknet53 with mixconv operation achieved the best performance while reducing computational resource consumption by more than a half.

4.2 Results on the Hybird Detection Network

Table 2 is the comparative results on detection experiments of different methods. "Baseline" represents the detection result of the vanilla YOLOv3 [22]. "Proposed" demonstrates the result of the proposed hybird detection network. The experimental result shows that the proposed method can greatly improve the detection performance of most categories.

Table 2. Comparative results on detection experiments of different methods.

Method	Types	AE1	AE2	AE3	CE1	CE2	CE3	CE4	CE5	CL	Avg
Baseline	mAP50	62.5	**67.6**	**73.0**	71.6	71.8	70.5	84.0	72.7	**83.6**	73.0
Proposed	mAP50	**68.0**	60.0	72.8	**74.8**	**78.6**	**73.5**	**85.0**	**79.9**	81.7	**74.9**

4.3 Results on the Remote Robotic US Images

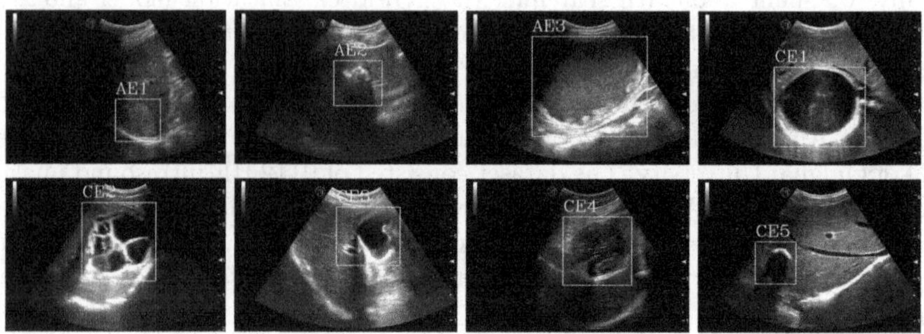

Fig. 4. Examples of HE ultrasound images obtained by the tele-remoted robotic ultrasound system. The yellow boxes and texts on the images indicate the locations and categories of the HE lesions predicted by the hybrid detection network. (Color figure online)

The clinical application trial of the remote intelligent assisted diagnosis system was carried out in Luohu People's Hospital (Shenzhen, Guangdong) and Qinghai University Affiliated Hospital (Xining, Qinghai). In the trial, ultrasonic operators on the doctor-side remotely located in Shenzhen control the robot on the patient-side located in Xining to acquire ultrasonic images of the livers. Then we use the hybrid detection network to analyse these images and produce auxiliary diagnostic results (Fig. 4). The result is considered correct if it is consistent with expert diagnosis. The accuracy of the test on 90 subjects suspected of being infected with HE is 86.7%. Results show that the proposed remote intelligent assisted diagnosis system is safe and effective.

5 Conclusions

In this work, we propose an effective remote intelligent assisted diagnosis system for HE. First, we propose a hybrid classification model by combining a pre-trained model with the search architecture, and obtain better performance on the classification of HE. Then, we propose a hybrid detection network by embedding the hybrid model into the general detection network. Finally, a tele-operated robotic remote operating system is used to realize remote intelligent auxiliary diagnosis for HE. The experimental results show that the combined framework of remote robotic ultrasound and artificial intelligence can be effectively applied to assist intelligent diagnosis of HE.

References

1. Bhutani, N., Kajal, P.: Hepatic echinococcosis: a review. Ann. Med. Surg. **36**, 99–105 (2018)
2. Torgerson, P.R., Keller, K., Magnotta, M., Ragland, N.: The global burden of alveolar echinococcosis. PLoS Negl. Trop. Dis. **4**(6), e722 (2010)
3. Liu, L., et al.: Geographic distribution of echinococcosis in tibetan region of Sichuan Province, China. Infect. Dis. Poverty **7**(1), 1–9 (2018)
4. Huang, D., et al.: Geographical environment factors and risk mapping of human cystic echinococcosis in Western China. Int. J. Environ. Res. Public Health **15**(8), 1729 (2018)
5. Nunnari, G., et al.: Hepatic echinococcosis: clinical and therapeutic aspects. World J. Gastroenterol. WJG **18**(13), 1448 (2012)
6. Fadel, S.A., Asmar, K., Faraj, W., Khalife, M., Haddad, M., El-Merhi, F.: Clinical review of liver hydatid disease and its unusual presentations in developing countries. Abdom. Radiol. **44**(4), 1331–1339 (2019)
7. WHO Informal Working Group, et al.: International classification of ultrasound images in cystic echinococcosis for application in clinical and field epidemiological settings. Acta Trop. **85**(2), 253–261 (2003)
8. Eckert, J., Gemmell, M.A., Meslin, Z.S., World Health Organization, et al.: WHO/OIE manual on echinococcosis in humans and animals: a public health problem of global concern (2001)
9. Ronneberger, O., Fischer, P., Brox, T.: U-Net: convolutional networks for biomedical image segmentation. In: Navab, N., Hornegger, J., Wells, W.M., Frangi, A.F. (eds.) MICCAI 2015. LNCS, vol. 9351, pp. 234–241. Springer, Cham (2015). https://doi.org/10.1007/978-3-319-24574-4_28
10. Elsken, T., Metzen, J.H., et al.: Neural architecture search: a survey. arXiv preprint arXiv:1808.05377 (2018)
11. Zoph, B., Le, Q.V.: Neural architecture search with reinforcement learning. arXiv preprint arXiv:1611.01578 (2016)
12. Liu, H., Simonyan, K., et al.: Darts: differentiable architecture search. arXiv preprint arXiv:1806.09055 (2018)
13. Bae, W., Lee, S., et al.: Resource optimized neural architecture search for 3D medical image segmentation. arXiv preprint arXiv:1909.00548 (2019)
14. Gourdon, A., Poignet, P., Poisson, G., Vieyres, P., Marche, P.: A new robotic mechanism for medical application. In: 1999 IEEE/ASME International Conference on Advanced Intelligent Mechatronics (Cat. No. 99TH8399), pp. 33–38. IEEE (1999)
15. Courreges, F., Vieyres, P., Istepanian, R.S.H.: Advances in robotic tele-echography services-the Otelo system. In: The 26th Annual International Conference of the IEEE Engineering in Medicine and Biology Society, vol. 2, pp. 5371–5374. IEEE (2004)
16. Arbeille, Ph., et al.: Realtime tele-operated abdominal and fetal echography in 4 medical centres, from one expert center, using a robotic arm & ISDN or satellite link. In: 2008 IEEE International Conference on Automation, Quality and Testing, Robotics, vol. 1, pp. 45–46. IEEE (2008)

17. Fonte, A., et al.: Robotic platform for an interactive tele-echographic system: the prosit ANR-2008 project. In: The Hamlyn Symposium on Medical robotics, pp. N-A (2010)
18. Mathiassen, K., Fjellin, J.E., Glette, K., Hol, P.K., Elle, O.J.: An ultrasound robotic system using the commercial robot UR5. Front. Robot. AI **3**, 1 (2016)
19. Stańczyk, B., Kurnicki, A., Arent, K.: Logical architecture of medical telediagnostic robotic system. In: 2016 21st International Conference on Methods and Models in Automation and Robotics (MMAR), pp. 200–205. IEEE (2016)
20. Adams, S.J., et al.: Initial experience using a telerobotic ultrasound system for adult abdominal sonography. Canad. Assoc. Radiol. J. **68**(3), 308–314 (2017)
21. Chen, X., Xie, L., et al.: Progressive differentiable architecture search: bridging the depth gap between search and evaluation. arXiv preprint arXiv:1904.12760 (2019)
22. Redmon, J., Farhadi, A.: Yolov3: an incremental improvement. arXiv preprint arXiv:1804.02767 (2018)
23. Bottou, L.: Large-scale machine learning with stochastic gradient descent. In: Lechevallier, Y., Saporta, G. (eds.) Proceedings of COMPSTAT 2010, pp. 177–186. Springer (2010)

Calibrated Bayesian Neural Networks to Estimate Gestational Age and Its Uncertainty on Fetal Brain Ultrasound Images

Lok Hin Lee[1(✉)], Elizabeth Bradburn[2], Aris T. Papageorghiou[2], and J. Alison Noble[1]

[1] Institute of Biomedical Engineering, Department of Engineering Science, University of Oxford, Oxford, UK
lokhin.lee@eng.ox.ac.uk

[2] Nuffield Department of Women's and Reproductive Health, University of Oxford, Oxford, UK

Abstract. We present an original automated framework for estimating gestational age (GA) from fetal ultrasound head biometry plane images. A novelty of our approach is the use of a Bayesian Neural Network (BNN), which quantifies uncertainty of the estimated GA. Knowledge of estimated uncertainty is useful in clinical decision-making, and is especially important in ultrasound image analysis where image appearance and quality can naturally vary a lot. A further novelty of our approach is that the neural network is not provided with images pixel size, thus making it rely on anatomical appearance characteristics and not size.

We train the network using 9,299 scans from the INTERGROWTH-21st [22] dataset ranging from $14 + 0$ weeks to $42 + 6$ weeks GA. We achieve average RMSE and MAE of 9.6 and 12.5 days respectively over the GA range. We explore the robustness of the BNN architecture to invalid input images by testing with (i) a different dataset derived from routine anomaly scanning and (ii) scans of a different fetal anatomy.

Keywords: Fetal ultrasound · Bayesian Neural Networks · Uncertainty in regression · Gestational age estimation

1 Introduction

Knowledge of gestational age (GA) is important in order to schedule antenatal care, and to define outcomes, for example on whether a newborn is term or preterm [24]. Charts or formulas are used to estimate GA from ultrasound-based fetal measurements [21]. Fetal measurements are taken in standard imaging planes [24], which in the case of the head biometry plane, rely on the visibility of specific fetal brain structures. Classic GA estimation in a clinical setting relies on manual ellipse fitting by a trained sonographer, which has both significant intra-observer variability and skilled labour requirements [28].

Y. Hu et al. (Eds.): ASMUS 2020/PIPPI 2020, LNCS 12437, pp. 13–22, 2020.
https://doi.org/10.1007/978-3-030-60334-2_2

In this paper we set out to assess the feasibility of estimating GA directly from image appearance rather than geometric fitting of ellipses of lines which is known to be difficult to automate across gestation. GA estimation based directly on image appearance would reduce the need for human interaction of automated biometry after image capture. Further, significant progress has been made in automatic plane finding [2,12], meaning that our algorithm might, in the future, be incorporated in a fully automated ultrasound-based GA estimation solution for minimally trained healthcare professional in a global health setting [23].

There have been previous attempts to automate GA estimation. These include GA estimation methods based on automating ellipse-fitting on fetal head images. Ciurte et al. [3] formalize the segmentation as a continuous min cut problem on ultrasound images represented as a graph. However, the method is semi-supervised and requires sonographer intervention. [10] directly estimate HC, but rely on predetermined ultrasound sweep protocols. [26] use a multi-task convolutional neural network to fit an ellipse on a fetal head image. However, all the methods above rely on clinical fetal growth charts for conversion of fetal measurements to GA, and therefore are subject to the same uncertainties.

Namburete et al. [18] and [19] use regression forests with bespoke features and convolutional neural networks to directly regress GA from 3D ultrasound data without regressing from fetal measurements. However, such models only provide point estimates of GA without taking into account uncertainties caused by anatomical or image variations, and rely on costly 3D ultrasound volumes and probes.

We therefore use a Bayesian Neural Network (BNN) [16] to perform regression directly on two dimensional fetal trans-thalamic (TT) plane images in both the second and third trimesters. A Bayesian Neural Network learns the distribution across each individual trainable parameter. This allows the BNN to predict probability distributions instead of point estimates, which allows the calculation of uncertainty estimates that can further inform clinical decision making. BNNs have been used in medical disease classification [6,15] and brain segmentation [17,25].

Contributions. We use a Bayesian Neural Network (BNN) trained on fetal trans-thalamic (TT) plane images for GA estimation. Firstly, we directly estimate GA from images of the fetal TT plane. Secondly, we train the BNN and an auxiliary isotonic regression model [13] to predict calibrated aleatoric and epistemic uncertainties (definitions of these terms are given in Sect. 1.1). Thirdly, we show that the Bayesian treatment of inference allows for automatic detection against unexpected and out-of-distribution data. Specifically, we test the trained BNNs on datasets outside of the training distribution; (i) a test dataset of TT planes taken with a different ultrasound machine and (ii) a test dataset of fetal US images other than the TT plane on the original ultrasound machine.

1.1 Neural Network Architecture

Due to computer memory limitations, we investigate the use of VGG-16 [9] as the backbone of a Bayesian Neural Network in a regression context as a proof of concept (See Fig. 1.). Other backbones e.g. ResNets [] could also be used.

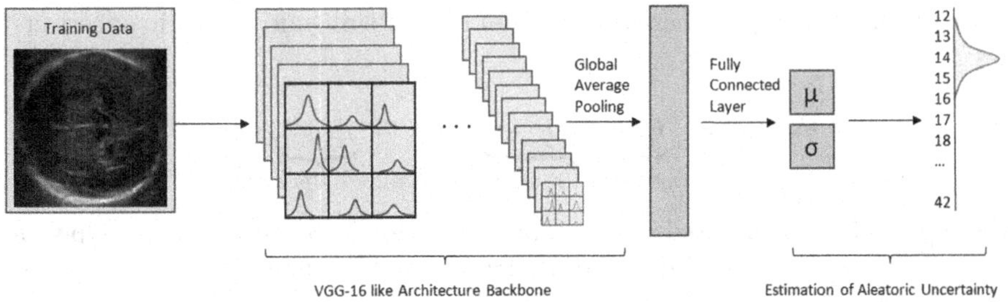

Fig. 1. The overview of the Bayesian Neural Network. The VGG-like backbone consists of five convolutional blocks and a global average pooling layer at the top to act as a regression layer. Each convolutional block CB consists of two convolutional layers, a batch normalization layer and a max pooling layer. Each $CB^{\,f,sz,st}$ was parameterized by the shared filter size, kernel size and stride respectively. The VGG-16 like backbone, in this notation, is $CB^{\,64,3,2}$ - $CB^{\,128,3,2}$ - $CB^{\,256,3,2}$ - $CB^{\,512,3,2}$ - $CB^{\,512,3,2}$

Epistemic and Aleatoric Uncertainties. We can break down uncertainty estimates into uncertainty over the network weights (epistemic uncertainty) and irreducible uncertainties over the noise inherent in the data (aleatoric uncertainty) [11]. As training data size increases, in theory epistemic uncertainty converges to zero. This allows us to discern between uncertainties where more image data would be useful and uncertainties that are inherent in the model population. Research has also found that predicted uncertainty estimates from BNNs may be mis-calibrated to actual empirical uncertainty [8,14]. A well calibrated regressive model implies that a prediction y with a predicted p confidence interval will lie within the confidence interval p of the time for all $p \in 0, 1$. We therefore additionally perform calibration [13] of uncertainty estimates.

Probabilistic Regression. We use a probabilistic network in order to estimate the aleatoric and epistemic uncertainties in image-based prediction.

To estimate epistemic uncertainty, we use mean-field variational inference [7] to approximate learnable network parameters with a fully factorized Gaussian posterior $q(\boldsymbol{W}) \sim N(\mu, \sigma)$, where $\boldsymbol{W}$ represents learnable weights, μ represents the parameter mean and σ represents the standard deviation of the parameter.

Gaussian posteriors and priors both reduce the computational cost of estimating the evidence lower bound (ELBO) [27], which is required as the prior $p(\boldsymbol{W})$ is computationally intractable. The use of mean-field variational inference doubles the network size for each backbone network, as each weight is parameterized by the learned means and standard deviation weights.

To estimate aleatoric uncertainty, a network is trained to minimize the negative log likelihood between the ground truth GA and a predicted factorized Gaussian, which is used as an approximation of the aleatoric uncertainty. During the forward pass, samples are drawn from the parameterized network weight distributions. The variation in the mean predicted GA from model weight perturbations can then be used as an estimate of epistemic uncertainty. The total predictive uncertainty is therefore the sum of epistemic and aleatoric uncertainties:

$$Var(y) \approx \underbrace{E(\hat{y}^2) - E(\hat{y})^2}_{\text{Epistemic Uncertainty}} + \underbrace{E(\hat{\sigma}^2)}_{\text{Aleatoric Uncertainty}} \tag{1}$$

where $\hat{y}$ represents the predicted mean, $\hat{\sigma}^2$ the predicted variance and expectations are sampled using Monte Carlo inference at test time.

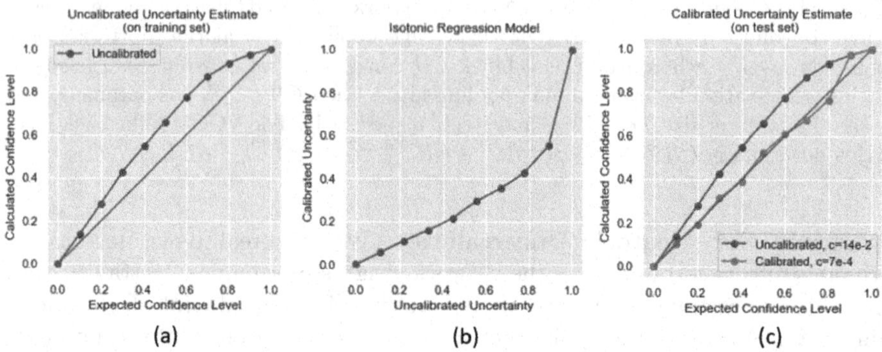

Fig. 2. An overview of the uncertainty calibration results, here on a trained VGG-16 network with cyclical KL annealing. (a) is the uncalibrated uncertainty interval plot on the training set, (b) is the predicted auxiliary regression model, and (c) shows the final calibrated uncertainty on the test set with reduced calibration error.

Uncertainty Calibration. Intuitively, for every predicted confidence interval, the predicted GA should be within the interval with the predicted probability p_j. However, the use of variational inference and approximate methods means that predicted uncertainties may not accurately reflect actual empirical uncertainties [13]. We therefore calibrate uncertainty predictions using an auxiliary isotonic regression model trained on the training set (Fig. 2). We quantify the quality of the uncertainty calibration using the calibration error:

$$Err = \frac{1}{m} \sum_{m} (p_j - \hat{p}_j)^2 \tag{2}$$

where p_j and $\hat{p}_j$ are the predicted confidence level and actual confidence levels respectively, and m is the number of confidence levels picked. In this paper, we pick m = 10 intervals with p_j confidence intervals equally distributed between [0, 1]. Confidence intervals were calculated based on a two-sided confidence interval test of the predicted Normal distribution.

Implementation Details. Both networks were trained from scratch with learnable parameters initialized from a $N(0,1)$ distribution. The network architecture is outlined in Fig. 1. The loss function therefore takes the term:

$$\mathcal{L}_{total} = \frac{1}{N}\sum_{n} -\frac{1}{2}\left(\frac{y-\mu_i}{\sigma_i}\right)^2 + \lambda(epoch)\mathcal{L}_{KL} \quad (3)$$

where y is the ground truth GA, μ_i and σ_i indicates the predicted mean GA and scale of the aleatoric uncertainty, $\mathcal{L}_{KL}$ is the Kullback-Leibler loss of the weight parameters.

Networks empirically do not successfully converge with a $\lambda(epoch) = k$ if k is constant. We therefore explore two annealing schedules such that $\lambda(epoch)$ is (i) either a monotonic function that starts at zero at the first epoch and scales linearly to one by the hundredth epoch [1] or a (ii) cyclical annealing schedule with $\lambda(epoch)$ cyclically annealing between 0 and 1 every 100 epochs [5].

Networks were trained with the Adam optimizer under default parameters with a batch size of 50, and trained for a minimum of 300 epochs until validation loss stopped decreasing. All networks were implemented using Tensorflow Probability [4], and trained on a Intel Xeon E5-2630 CPU with a NVIDIA GTX 1080 Ti GPU.

2 Dataset

We use three clinical ultrasound datasets, designated Dataset A, B and C. Dataset A was used to train and validate the network, whilst Dataset B and C were only used during external testing.

Dataset A. In Dataset A, derived from the INTERGROWTH-21st study [22], ultrasound scans of enrolled women were performed every 5 ± 1 weeks of gestation, leading to ultrasound image scans from GAs ranging from $14 + 0$ weeks to $41 + 6$ weeks. We used the TT plane image to regress to find the GA, as the plane shows features that vary in anatomical appearance as the fetus grows [20].

Ground truth GAs for Dataset A are defined as the date from the last menstrual period (LMP) and further validated with a crown-rump measurement in the first trimester that agreed with the LMP to within 7 days. Images were captured using the Philips HD-9 (Philips Ultrasound, Bothell, WA, USA) with curvilinear abdominal transducers (C5-2, C6-3, V7-3).

Using a 90/1/9 train/validation/test split on the subjects, we generated a training set (8369/3016 images/subjects), validation set (91/35) and test set (849/300) (Fig. 3).

Dataset B. This dataset consists of routine second and third trimester scansUltrasound scans had been acquired using a Voluson E8 version BT18 (General Electric Healthcare, Zipf, Austria) which had different imaging characteristics and processing algorithms to the machine used for Dataset A. We extracted

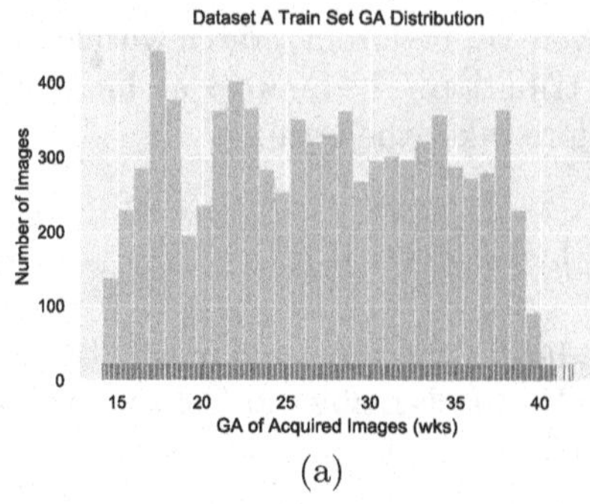

(a)

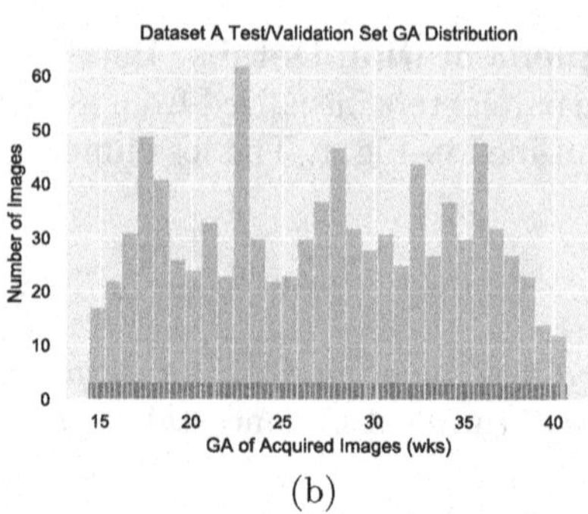

(b)

Fig. 3. An overview of the GA distribution in Dataset A for (a) train and (b) validation and test sets.

N = 20 TT planes from clinical video recordings from different subjects. GAs inferred from growth charts ranged from 18 + 6 weeks to 22 + 1 weeks.

Dataset C. This dataset consists of 6,739 images taken with the same image acquisition parameters and GA ranges as dataset A. However, the images were of the fetal femur plane instead of the TT plane.

Dataset Pre-Processing and Augmentation. All images had sonographer measurement markings removed using automated template matching and a median filter, and were resized to 224×224 pixels. Images were then further visually checked to be satisfactory TT plane images by an independent sonographer. Pixel intensities were normalized to $[-1, 1]$. During training, we augment the dataset by randomly flipping the image horizontally, random resizing of the image by $\pm 10\%$ and by shifting the image by up to 20 pixels vertically and horizontally. We find this reasonable, as variation in TT plane image appearance in each dataset for the same GA exceed this range. We also normalize GA to $[-1, 1]$. However, we do not give pixel size information to the network to reduce the impact of biometric measurement information.

3 Results

We present the results of both BNNs on the datasets separately.

Dataset A. The results for networks with both annealing functions are summarized in Table 1. The network that trained with cyclical Kullback-Leibler annealing outperformed monotonic annealing. This may be due to the fact that setting $\lambda(epoch)$ to zero dramatically changes the hyper surface of the loss function, whilst the monotonic annealing creates a smoother change of the hyper surface which the network can get comfortable with especially in local minima.

Table 1. Regression metrics for the investigated BNNs backbone architectures. Best results for each metric for 2D images are in bold. RMSE and MAE Metrics are calculated with the maximum likelihood for both aleatoric and epistemic uncertainties. For completeness, we include the results of [19] as a comparison. However, our results are based on regression on a single 2D ultrasound image, compared to a 3D ultrasound volume in their work.

	μ RMSE (days)	μ MAE (days)	Calibration error	No. of parameters
VGG-16 with KL Cycling	**9.6**	**12.5**	0.24/**7.4e-4**	18.8 M
VGG-16 with KL Annealing	12.2	15.4	**0.21**/1.2e-3	18.8 M
VGG-16 (Deterministic)	11.9	14.5	N/A	9.4 M
3D Convolutional Regression Network [19]		7.72	N/A	6.1 M

During inference, we estimate epistemic uncertainty with Monte Carlo iterations of n = 100. We find that the network tends to overestimate predictive uncertainties, leading to high uncertainty calibration error (Fig. 2). However, the errors are consistent and therefore lend themselves to easy calibration, significantly reducing uncertainty error once calibrated.

Plotting predictive uncertainty against GA shows that uncertainty increases with increasing gestational age (Fig. 4). This may be because biological variation increases with increasing fetal growth. This is observed in clinical fetal growth charts. This is also supported by the higher slope that aleatoric uncertainty has with increasing GA compared to epistemic uncertainty.

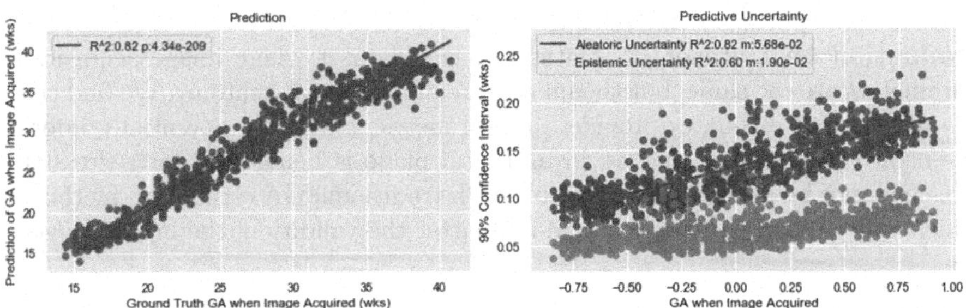

Fig. 4. An overview of the results of the model trained with Kullback-Leibler cyclical annealing. On the left, we show a scatterplot of the overall predicted GA against GT GA with r^2 of 0.8. On the right, we plot uncertainties against GT GA, and find that aleatoric uncertainty greater than epistemic uncertainty as a function of GA, where m refers to the gradient of the best fit line.

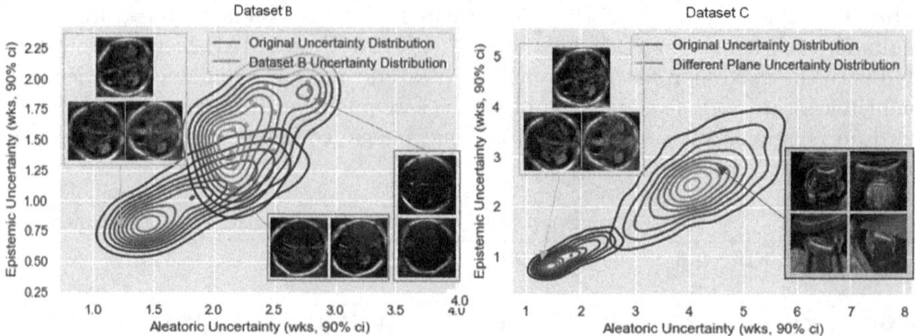

Fig. 5. An overview of kernel density estimates of the aleatoric and epistemic confidence intervals (ci) for out of distribution datasets. Images enclosed in yellow are from the dataset A test set, green from the external Dataset B imaging the same anatomy, and purple from the dataset A(FL). Figure is best viewed digitally.

Evaluation on Dataset B. We evaluate the performance of the model on Dataset B, where the image is taken on a different ultrasound machine and in a different context, but the image is of the TT plane. We find that the distribution of uncertainties is higher than the original test dataset (Fig. 5).

We empirically find that the images from the dataset B with higher image contrast and a more visible CSP or midline have reduced predictive uncertainties compared with images that do not. This is in line with the observation that the images with i) clearly visible brain anatomical structures and ii) low GAs tend to have lower predictive uncertainties in the test dataset A. The MSE and RMSE of GA of images in Dataset B are 19.6 and 18.1 days respectively. However, this is expected, as the "ground truth" gestational ages for Dataset B were taken from fetal growth charts using HC measurements, compared to the gold standard LMP ground truth available in the Dataset A. A fetus with a HC-measurement based GA of 24 weeks has a clinical 90% confidence interval of 1.4 weeks [21].

Evaluation on Dataset C. Dataset C is a dataset where image acquisition parameters are the same, but the images are of a different anatomy. We find that the uncertainty estimates provide a useful metric which can potentially inform the health professional that an invalid fetal plane is being used for regression. This may not be as obvious or possible with traditional GA estimation methods, which will predict a gestational age no matter the validity of the input image.

4 Conclusion

In this paper, we have described a Bayesian Neural Network framework with calibrated uncertainties to directly predict gestational age from a TT plane image across a wide range of GA. This was done without knowledge of pixel size. The best performing network achieved a RMSE of 9.6 days across the entire gestational age range. We demonstrated that the biased predictive uncertainties from variational inference can be calibrated, and are useful to detect images that are not within the network's training. This is potentially a useful feature to prevent the model from being used out of the intended in a real world setting.

References

1. Bowman, S.R., Vilnis, L., Vinyals, O., Dai, A.M., Jozefowicz, R., Bengio, S.: Generating sentences from a continuous space. Technical report (2016)
2. Cai, Y., Sharma, H., Chatelain, P., Noble, J.A.: Multi-task SonoEyeNet: detection of fetal standardized planes assisted by generated sonographer attention maps. In: Frangi, A.F., Schnabel, J.A., Davatzikos, C., Alberola-López, C., Fichtinger, G. (eds.) MICCAI 2018. LNCS, vol. 11070, pp. 871–879. Springer, Cham (2018). https://doi.org/10.1007/978-3-030-00928-1_98
3. Ciurte, A., et al.: Semi-supervised segmentation of ultrasound images based on patch representation and continuous min cut. PLoS One **9**(7), e100972 (2014)
4. Dillon, J.V., et al.: TensorFlow Distributions, November 2017
5. Fu, H., Li, C., Liu, X., Gao, J., Celikyilmaz, A., Carin, L.: Cyclical annealing schedule: a simple approach to mitigating KL vanishing. In: NAACL, pp. 240–250. Association for Computational Linguistics, Minneapolis, June 2019
6. Gill, R.S., Caldairou, B., Bernasconi, N., Bernasconi, A.: Uncertainty-informed detection of epileptogenic brain malformations using Bayesian neural networks. In: Shen, D., et al. (eds.) MICCAI 2019. LNCS, vol. 11767, pp. 225–233. Springer, Cham (2019). https://doi.org/10.1007/978-3-030-32251-9_25
7. Graves, A.: Practical variational inference for neural networks. In: NIPS (2011)
8. Guo, C., Pleiss, G., Sun, Y., Weinberger, K.Q.: On calibration of modern neural networks. In: ICML, vol. 3, pp. 2130–2143 (2017)
9. He, K., Zhang, X., Ren, S., Sun, J.: Deep residual learning for image recognition. In: CVPR, vol. 2016, pp. 770–778. IEEE Computer Society, December 2016
10. van den Heuvel, T.L.A., Petros, H., Santini, S., de Korte, C.L., van Ginneken, B.: Automated fetal head detection and circumference estimation from free-hand ultrasound sweeps using deep learning in resource-limited countries. Ultrasound Med. Biol. **45**(3), 773–785 (2019)
11. Kendall, A., Gal, Y.: What uncertainties do we need in Bayesian deep learning for computer vision? In: NIPS 2017, pp. 5580–5590. Curran Associates Inc., Long Beach, December 2017
12. Kong, P., Ni, D., Chen, S., Li, S., Wang, T., Lei, B.: Automatic and efficient standard plane recognition in fetal ultrasound images via multi-scale dense networks. In: Melbourne, A., et al. (eds.) PIPPI/DATRA 2018. LNCS, vol. 11076, pp. 160–168. Springer, Cham (2018). https://doi.org/10.1007/978-3-030-00807-9_16
13. Kuleshov, V., Fenner, N., Ermon, S.: Accurate uncertainties for deep learning using calibrated regression. In: ICML, vol. 6, pp. 4369–4377 (2018)
14. Lakshminarayanan, B., Pritzel, A., Blundell, C.: Simple and scalable predictive uncertainty estimation using deep ensembles. In: NIPS, vol. 2017, pp. 6403–6414, December 2017
15. Leibig, C., Allken, V., Ayhan, M.S., Berens, P., Wahl, S.: Leveraging uncertainty information from deep neural networks for disease detection. Sci. Rep. **7**(1), 1–14 (2017)

16. MacKay, D.J.C.: A practical Bayesian framework for backpropagation networks. Neural Comput. **4**(3), 448–472 (1992)
17. McClure, P., et al.: Knowing what you know in brain segmentation using Bayesian deep neural networks. Front. Neuroinform. **13**, 67 (2019)
18. Namburete, A.I., Stebbing, R.V., Kemp, B., Yaqub, M., Papageorghiou, A.T., Noble, J.A.: Learning-based prediction of gestational age from ultrasound images of the fetal brain. Med. Image Anal. **21**(1), 72–86 (2015)
19. Namburete, A.I.L., Xie, W., Noble, J.A.: Robust regression of brain maturation from 3D fetal neurosonography using CRNs. In: Cardoso, M.J., et al. (eds.) FIFI/OMIA-2017. LNCS, vol. 10554, pp. 73–80. Springer, Cham (2017). https://doi.org/10.1007/978-3-319-67561-9_8
20. Paladini, D., Malinger, G., Monteagudo, A., Pilu, G., Timor-Tritsch, I., Toi, A.: Sonographic examination of the fetal central nervous system: guidelines for performing the 'basic examination' and the 'fetal neurosonogram', January 2007
21. Papageorghiou, A.T., Kemp, B., et al.: Ultrasound-based gestational-age estimation in late pregnancy. Ultrasound Obstet. Gynecol. **48**(6), 719–726 (2016). https://doi.org/10.1002/uog.15894
22. Papageorghiou, A.T., et al.: The INTERGROWTH-21 st fetal growth standards: toward the global integration of pregnancy and pediatric care. Am. J. Obstet. Gynecol. **218**(2), S630–S640 (2018)
23. Papageorghiou, A.T., et al.: International standards for fetal growth based on serial ultrasound measurements: the fetal growth longitudinal study of the INTERGROWTH-21st project. Lancet **9946**, 869–879 (2014). https://doi.org/10.1016/S0140-6736(14)61490-2
24. Salomon, L.J., et al.: ISUOG practice guidelines: ultrasound assessment of fetal biometry and growth. Ultrasound Obstet. Gynecol. **53**(6), 715–723 (2019)
25. Sedai, S., et al.: Uncertainty guided semi-supervised segmentation of retinal layers in OCT images. In: Shen, D., et al. (eds.) MICCAI 2019. LNCS, vol. 11764, pp. 282–290. Springer, Cham (2019). https://doi.org/10.1007/978-3-030-32239-7_32
26. Sobhaninia, Z., et al.: Fetal ultrasound image segmentation for measuring biometric parameters using multi-task deep learning. In: EMBC, pp. 6545–6548. IEEE, Berlin, July 2019
27. Wen, Y., Vicol, P., Ba, J., Tran, D., Grosse, R.: Flipout: efficient pseudo-independent weight perturbations on mini-batches. In: ICLR (2018)
28. Zador, I.E., Salari, V., Chik, L., Sokol, R.J.: Ultrasound measurement of the fetal head: computer versus operator. Ultrasound Obstetr. Gynecol. Offic. J. Int. Soc. Ultrasound Obstetr. Gynecol. **1**(3), 208–211 (1991)

Automatic Optic Nerve Sheath Measurement in Point-of-Care Ultrasound

Brad T. Moore[1](✉), Sean P. Montgomery[2], Marc Niethammer[3], Hastings Greer[1], and Stephen R. Aylward[1]

[1] Kitware, Inc., Carrboro, NC 27510, USA
brad.moore@kitware.com
[2] Duke University, Durham, NC 27710, USA
[3] University of North Carolina, Chapel Hill, NC 27599, USA

Abstract. Intracranial hypertension associated with traumatic brain injury is a life-threatening condition which requires immediate diagnosis and treatment. The measurement of optic nerve sheath diameter (ONSD), using ultrasonography, has been shown to be a promising, non-invasive predictor of intracranial pressure (ICP). Unfortunately, the reproducibility and accuracy of this measure depends on the expertise of the sonologist- a requirement that limits the broad application of ONSD. Previous work on ONSD measurement has focused on computer-automated annotation of expert-acquired ultrasound taken in a clinical setting. Here, we present a system using a handheld point-of-care ultrasound probe whereby the ONSD is automatically measured without requiring an expert sonographer to acquire the images. We report our results on videos from ocular phantoms with varying ONSDs. We show that our approach accurately measures the ONSD despite the lack of an observer keeping the ONSD in focus or in frame.

Keywords: Optic nerve sheath diameter · Ocular ultrasound · Intracranial pressure

1 Introduction

The ability to monitor and manage intracranial pressure (ICP) in traumatic brain injury (TBI) patients is vital [1]. Invasive ICP techniques such as external ventricular drains (EVD) and intraparenchymal monitors (IPM) have been a clinical gold standard in measurement, but these are highly invasive procedures with the risk of severe complications [2]. Measurement of the optic nerve sheath diameter (ONSD) via ultrasonography has emerged as a promising non-invasive method for detecting elevated ICP [1, 3–5].

The typical ONSD procedure is as follows. A sonographer takes B-mode (or possibly 3D) ultrasound by placing the probe in transverse orientation over a closed eyelid. The ONSD is measured at 3 mm behind the optic bulb. A threshold value is defined that corresponds to an ICP of 20 mmHg, and if the ONSD exceeds that threshold it is considered positive for elevated ICP. Mixed results have been published regarding the appropriate threshold and the accuracy of ONSD as a measure of ICP [1, 5]. Several meta-analyses have concluded that confounding factors are: whether EVD or IPM monitors

Y. Hu et al. (Eds.): ASMUS 2020/PIPPI 2020, LNCS 12437, pp. 23–32, 2020.
https://doi.org/10.1007/978-3-030-60334-2_3

were used, whether racial, age, and other demographics factors affect ONSD, the expert's accuracy at manually measuring ONSD, and the potential condition (e.g. TBI, liver failure) causing the underlying elevated ICP [6, 7]. Despite this, a recent study found ONSD to be the single strongest correlated ultrasound-based method for diagnosing elevated ICP in severe traumatic brain injury patients [3].

There are existing methods for the automatic estimation of ONSD. Meiburger et al. [8] developed a dual-snake method for segmenting both the optic nerve and the optic nerve sheath in single images taken by a sonographer. Their approach was compared with that of expert manual measurements, and they reported a correlation coefficient of .61–.64. Soroushmehr et al. [9] used super-pixel segmentation to label the ONS and calculated the ONSD as the difference between super-pixel peaks in a pixel row 3 mm below the ocular bulb. They reported the median ONSD from frames of ultrasound video of de-identified TBI patients. They reported an average error of 5.52% between their algorithm and the manual annotations by two experts. Gerber et al. [10] used the distance transform and affine registration with a binary ellipse to identify the eye. A binary image of two parallel lines was then registered to identify the ONS. They reported good correlation (R^2 of .82–.91) with manual experts on a 24 image dataset gathered from literature. They also reported results on a homemade ocular phantom similar to what we use here (though we use a custom 3D-printed mold for the ocular orb). However, their method required an observer to keep the ONS in frame.

Here we present an algorithm for estimating the ONSD from video taken by rocking a point-of-care ultrasound probe above the eye (Fig. 1). The goal is to allow automatic measurements of ONSD to be taken by emergency personnel untrained in ultrasound. The algorithm automatically determines if the eye and ONS are present in a frame and if present, it estimates the ONSD using a regularized sampling of the frame along the nerve. The algorithm then determines the high-quality ONS frames and ONSD measures in an entire video sequence and returns the median ONSD measure from those high-quality frames. We report our results on an ocular phantom with a series of known ONSD diameters.

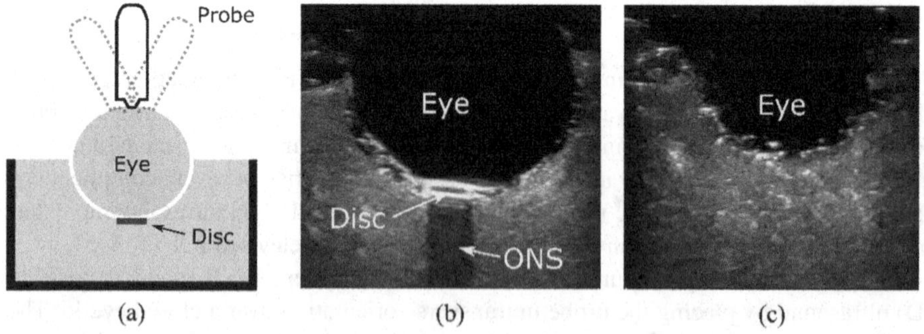

Fig. 1. (a) Schematic of the gelatin eye phantom and probe position. The disc causes a shadow from the ultrasound probe simulating the optic nerve sheath. (b) A frame from a video of the phantom study with the ONS in focus. (c) An example where the ONS is not within frame and the eye is out of focus.

2 Algorithm

The algorithm consists of three steps and is summarized as follows (Fig. 2). Individual video frames are processed independently. Step 1, the eye is detected using an elliptical RANSAC procedure [11, 12]. If the eye is detected, a search region for the nerve is defined around the lower part of the eye. A seed point for the nerve detection is a dark peak within the search region (Fig. 3a). The image is then segmented using the watershed algorithm [13], and the segmented region containing the seed point is considered the rough nerve segmentation (Fig. 3b). Step 2, for frames with an eye and nerve detected, the medial axis of the rough nerve region is then calculated, and a medial-axis-aligned image of the nerve is created (Fig. 3c). The distance between the maximal gradients in the $+y$ and $-y$ directions are calculated along the longitudinal axis (Fig. 3d). The values of the maximal gradients are recorded as a measure of how "in focus" the nerve is. The median distance is considered the ONSD estimate for the individual frame. Step 3, each frame is ranked by its maximal ONS gradient value, and the median ONSD of an upper percentile of frames is reported as the final ONSD measurement.

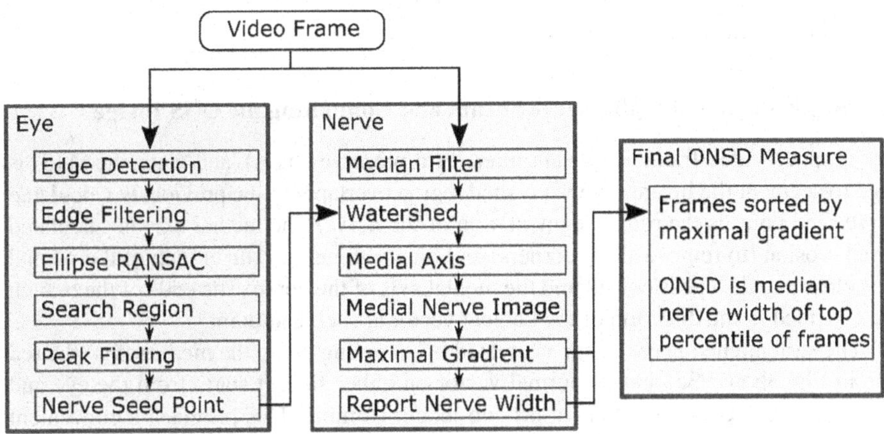

Fig. 2. Algorithm overview.

The source code is available at [26]. The code was developed in Python, using ITK [14] and its latest integration with Numpy [15, 16], as well as skimage [17], and scikit-learn [18].

Details of the steps of the algorithm are given next. Please refer to the source code for specific parameter values, e.g., for the standard deviation used with Gaussian blurring functions. Such values were held constant for all experiments here presented.

2.1 Identification of Ocular Orb and Nerve Search Region

The input video frame is first cropped at a fixed size to remove artifacts near and at the edges of the ultrasound transducer. The image is then blurred with a recursive gaussian filter and downsampled. The gradient of the image is calculated with derivative kernels and edge points are identified with a Canny edge filter [19]. Edge points are filtered by the angle of the gradient (between 10° and 170° upwards) as vertical edges are likely streaking artifacts from the probe not maintaining contact with the round eye. The remaining edge points are input to a RANSAC algorithm with an algebraic fit elliptical model [11, 12]. Bad models in the RANSAC algorithm are defined as ellipses whose widths and heights are outside of 16 and 42 mm.

A strip following the curve of the ellipse and the bottom of the orb is collapsed to a 1D signal, and a peak finder is used to find the seed point for the nerve (scipy.signal.find_peaks with a fixed prominence threshold). Let the transform e, define a new space $(x, y) = e(t, a, b, \theta, x_c, y_c)$ based on the fit of an elliptical model of the eye to a frame, where t, a, b, θ, x_c, y_c are the elliptical angle coordinate, half the width, half the height, the angle of rotation, and the center coordinates of the ellipse, respectively. Let t_0 and t_n be the elliptical coordinates of the leftmost and rightmost inlier point from RANSAC (e.g. the pink points in Fig. 3a). Let d_0 and d_m be the parameters that define the distance of the strip from the eye and its thickness. The strip image is defined as $(x_i, y_j) = e(t_i, a + d_j, b + d_j, \theta, x_c, y_c)$ where $t_0 \leq t_i \leq t_n$ and $d_0 \leq d_j \leq d_m$. The 1D signal is $s_i = \sum_j I(x_i, y_j)$ where $I(x_i, y_j)$ is the intensity of the B-mode image interpolated at (x_i, y_j).

2.2 Segmentation of Optic Nerve Sheath and Computing the ONS Image

The cropped video frame is median filtered (to preserve edges), and watershed [13] is used to segment the image. The watershed region overlapping the previously calculated nerve seed point is the rough segmentation of the nerve. The medial axis is calculated by an erosion (to remove sharp corners) and binary thinning. The branch of the medial axis closest to the eye is considered the medial axis of the nerve. The ends of the branch are extended in the direction of the tangent vector at each end point.

The straightened nerve image is created by sampling along the medial axis (the red line in Fig. 3b and 3c) and its normal vector on either side. It starts from the eye and is sampled in a fixed width (12 mm) and length (6 mm). This provides a convenient coordinate system for examining the boundary of the ONS along the nerve.

2.3 Estimation of Optic Nerve Sheath Diameter

The gradient along the nerve width is then computed using the straightened nerve image. The distance between the maximal gradient points on either side of the medial axis is computed (Fig. 3d). Note, at 3 mm this is similar to the single manual measurement a sonographer would make perpendicular to the optic nerve [5]. The median value of this distance along the nerve is recorded as the ONSD estimate for the particular video frame. Similarly, the median absolute value of the maximal gradient points is recorded as a measure of how in-focus the ONS is within the frame.

The ONSD estimate for a collection of frames is the median ONSD value of the frames with the greatest maximal gradient values. We exclude all frames falling outside of a 90–98th percentile window of maximal gradient values and report the median of the remaining frames.

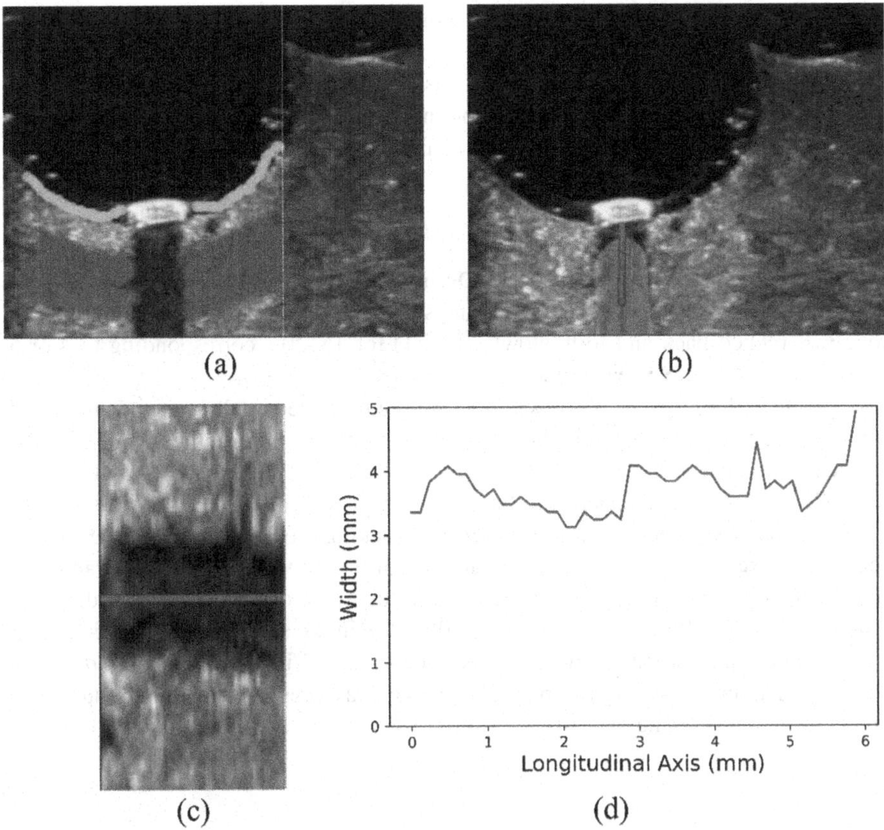

Fig. 3. (a) Results of eye detection and initial nerve seed point. Points along the eye socket are in pink, the region to search for the nerve in green, the seed point in blue. (b) Initial watershed segmentation of the nerve (in light blue), the portion of the extend medial axis corresponding to the center of the nerve image (in red), and the unsampled portion of the medial axis (thin purple line below red line). (c) The image resampled along the medial axis of the nerve with the left of the image starting at the eye and the medial axis highlighted in red. (d) The distance between maximal gradients along the medial axis (disc size is 4 mm). (Color figure online)

3 Results

3.1 Gel Phantom

The gelatin-based ocular phantom was made according to [10, 20]. This phantom has been previously used to train sonographers on the ONSD technique, as well as study the intra- and inter-observer variability of manual ONSD measurement [20]. A similar gelatin-based model was shown to be relatively indistinguishable from *in vivo* ONS ultrasound images [24]. Briefly, 350 mL of water and 21 g (3 packets) of gelatin were boiled and set to make the ocular orb. Similarly, 350 mL of water, 21 g of gelatin, and 14.3 g (1 tbs) of Metamucil were boiled and set to make the eye socket. We 3D-printed molds for the orb and socket (available here [26]) in Nylon 12 (Versatile Plastic,

Shapeways Inc., finishing). The ocular orb mold dimensions were 24.2 mm (transverse) × 23.7 mm (sagittal) × 23.4 mm (axial) according to the mean adult eye shape reported in Bekerman et al. [21]. The phantom is constructed by placing a 3D-printed disc (of varying diameter) in the socket, a small amount of water, and then the ocular orb on top (Fig. 1). Ultrasound gel is placed on the orb, and the probe is applied.

3.2 Phantom Study

A single ocular gel phantom was created. During the session, discs of varying size (3, 4, 5, 6, 7 mm) were placed between the orb and socket. To acquire a video, the ultrasound probe was rocked back and forth slowly (Fig. 1) for 15–20 s corresponding to 4 or 5 sweeps across the ONS in each video.

In practice, the probe operator will not observe the videos as they are acquired and will begin scanning from the temporal area of the upper eyelid. For the phantom study, a novice technician first confirmed the location of the disc in the phantom (unlike the real ONS, the disc was unattached to the gelatin eye and could slide out of the socket). The technician was then instructed to perform a rocking motion with the probe. As the probe was rocked, the optic nerve sheath and ocular orb moved in-and-out of frame and focus, with no particular care to capture an in-focus frame of the nerve. Each disc was recorded a total of 10 times (for a total of 50 videos in the study), with the orientation of the phantom and probe changed between recordings. Videos were acquired with a Clarius L7 HD probe (24 frames per second, "Ocular" preset). The entire dataset has been made publicly available [26].

3.3 Accuracy

Figure 4 shows a scatter plot of the estimated ONSD versus the printed disc size. Each point is the result from a single video. We performed simple linear regression with the estimated ONS as the independent variable and the disc size as the dependent variable. The result is a slope and intercept of 1.12 and −0.22, respectively, and an R^2 of 0.977. The root-mean-square deviation (RMSD) of the model is 0.22 mm. This is an improvement over the 0.6 mm–1.1 mm deviations reported by Gerber et al. on a similar phantom study [10].

Previous work used ultrasound images and video taken by experts who assessed image quality while acquiring that data and then manually selected the frames to be measured. We examined whether our accuracy would be improved by having an expert hand-selecting "good" ONS frames from each video. Approximately 3 frames per video were manually selected with the ONS in focus. Our ONSD algorithm was then run on those frames (with the modification that the maximal gradient percentile filtering was removed). The simple linear regression was repeated and resulted only in relatively minor improvements to accuracy (R^2 of 0.978 and RMSD of 0.20 mm). This result shows that our algorithm is robust to the portions of the video that either lack the ONS completely or have a poor view of it.

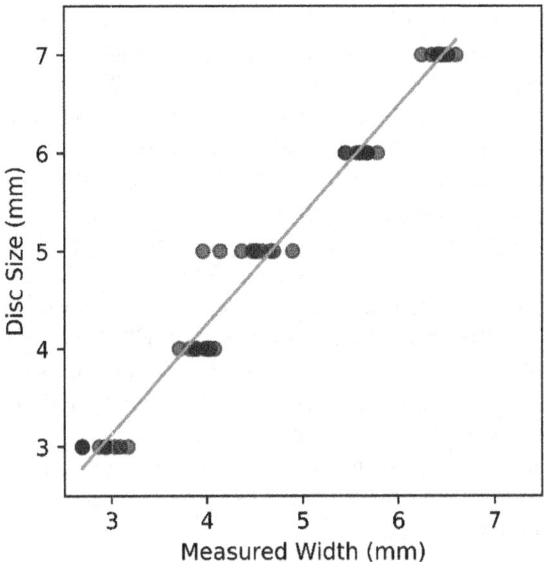

Fig. 4. Phantom study results. Purple dots are individual videos from the phantom study. Orange line is linear regression. (Color figure online)

4 Discussion

A major obstacle to the non-invasive measurement of elevated ICP at the point-of-care is the requirement of a trained sonographer. We have presented an ONSD estimation algorithm designed to operate on videos taken by emergency personnel untrained in ultrasonography. Our method is robust to frames where the ONS is missing or out of focus, and our RMSD of 0.22 mm is similar to previously reported intra-observer reliabilities of 0.1–0.5 mm [22]. Of the previously published automatic ONSD methods, Gerber et al. [10] and Soroushmehr et al. [9] both considered applying their methods to video. In both papers, however, a sonographer maintained the ONS during the video.

We have validated our algorithm using a realistic [20] ocular phantom model and our next step is to apply our method in an upcoming human study with healthy volunteers and TBI patients. There are several open questions to the clinical application of ONSD for TBI patients. For example, despite promising sensitivity and specificity of ONSD for detecting elevated ICP in individual studies [5], a consistent method for determining the ONSD threshold remains elusive [1]. Reported thresholds for ONSD have ranged anywhere from 4.1–5.7 mm for indicating elevated ICP [6]. A number of explanations for this heterogeneity have proposed, such as whether ONSD measurements were averaged between eyes, which plane the ONSD was measured in (transverse or sagittal), or whether there are other confounding patient demographics (e.g., age, sex, BMI) [25].

Our approach gives several advantages for pursuing these clinical challenges. First, our automatic method removes the error and biases of manual measurement. Second, the parameters of our algorithm should be robust in the transition from phantom to clinical data. The preprocessing parameters such as blurring and edge detection are dependent on the ultrasound device settings (which will be controlled) and not the anatomical sizes of the ocular orb and ONS. Since we identify the ocular orb as an intermediate step, we will be able to apply a recently suggested normalization of the ONSD by the transverse orb diameter [23]. Finally, the ONSD measurement presented here is based off of the medial transformation of the sinuous ONS (i.e. the straightened nerve image). Anatomically, the ability of the ONS to distend with elevated ICP is dependent on the density of a fibrous trabecular network along its length. While the manual measurement of ONSD is typically done at a single point of maximal dilation 3 mm distal to the orb, our method can measure the ONSD at any point along the length. Ohle et al. [25] conjectured that multiple measurements along the ONS may be a useful way to normalize an individual's trabecular density, thereby improving the prediction of ICP.

The requirement of a sonographer to acquire and manually measure ONSD prevents the broad application of the method at the point-of-care. We have presented an automated method for measuring ONSD that does not require a trained sonographer to acquire the ultrasound data. Furthermore, this method will allow us to pursue important clinical questions regarding the relationship between ONSD and elevated ICP in TBI patients in an upcoming human study.

Acknowledgements. This effort was sponsored by the Government under Other Transactions Number W81XWH-15-9-0001/W81XWH-19-9-0015 (MTEC 19-08-MuLTI-0079). The views and conclusions contained herein are those of the authors and should not be interpreted as necessarily representing the official policies or endorsements, either expressed or implied, of the U.S. Government.

References

1. Changa, A.R., Czeisler, B.M., Lord, A.S.: Management of elevated intracranial pressure: a review. Curr. Neurol. Neurosci. Rep. **19**(12), 1–10 (2019). https://doi.org/10.1007/s11910-019-1010-3
2. Tavakoli, S., Peitz, G., Ares, W., Hafeez, S., Grandhi, R.: Complications of invasive intracranial pressure monitoring devices in neurocritical care. Neurosurg. Focus **43**(5), 1–9 (2017). https://doi.org/10.3171/2017.8.FOCUS17450
3. Robba, C., Cardim, D., Tajsic, T., Pietersen, J., Bulman, M., Donnelly, J., Lavinio, A., et al.: Ultrasound non-invasive measurement of intracranial pressure in neurointensive care: a prospective observational study. PLoS Med. **14**(7) (2017). https://doi.org/10.1371/journal.pmed.1002356
4. Koskinen, L.-O.D., Malm, J., Zakelis, R., Bartusis, L., Ragauskas, A., Eklund, A.: Can intracranial pressure be measured non-invasively bedside using a two-depth Doppler-technique? J. Clin. Monit. Comput. **31**(2), 459–467 (2016). https://doi.org/10.1007/s10877-016-9862-4
5. Dubourg, J., Javouhey, E., Geeraerts, T., Messerer, M., Kassai, B.: Ultrasonography of optic nerve sheath diameter for detection of raised intracranial pressure: a systematic review and meta-analysis. Intensive Care Med. **37**(7), 1059–1068 (2011). https://doi.org/10.1007/s00134-011-2224-2
6. Jeon, J.P., et al.: Correlation of optic nerve sheath diameter with directly measured intracranial pressure in korean adults using bedside ultrasonography. PLoS ONE **12**(9), 1–11 (2017). https://doi.org/10.1371/journal.pone.0183170

7. Rajajee, V., Williamson, C.A., Fontana, R.J., Courey, A.J, Patil, P.G.: Noninvasive intracranial pressure assessment in acute liver failure (published correction appears in Neurocrit Care. **29**(3), 530 (2018)). Neurocrit Care **29**(2), 280–290 (2018). https://doi.org/10.1007/s12028-018-0540-x
8. Meiburger, K.M., et al.: Automatic optic nerve measurement: a new tool to standardize optic nerve assessment in ultrasound b-mode images. Ultrasound Med. Biol. **46**(6), 1533–1544 (2020). https://doi.org/10.1016/j.ultrasmedbio.2020.01.034
9. Soroushmehr, R., et al.: Automated optic nerve sheath diameter measurement using super-pixel analysis. In: Proceedings of the Annual International Conference of the IEEE Engineering in Medicine and Biology Society (EMBS), pp. 2793–2796 (2019). https://doi.org/10.1109/embc.2019.8856449
10. Gerber, S., et al.: Automatic estimation of the optic nerve sheath diameter from ultrasound images. In: Cardoso, M.J., et al. (eds.) BIVPCS/POCUS -2017. LNCS, vol. 10549, pp. 113–120. Springer, Cham (2017). https://doi.org/10.1007/978-3-319-67552-7_14
11. Halir, R., Flusser, J.: Numerically stable direct least squares fitting of ellipses. In: 6th International Conference in Central Europe on Computer Graphics and Visualization WSCG 98, pp. 125–132 (1998)
12. Fischler, M.A., Bolles, R.C.: Random sample consensus: a paradigm for model fitting with applications to image analysis and automated cartography. Commun. ACM **24**(6), 381–395 (1981). https://doi.org/10.1145/358669.358692
13. Beare, R., Lehmann, G.: The watershed transform in ITK - discussion and new developments. Insight J. **6**, 1–24 (2006)
14. Johnson, H.J., McCormick, M., Ibáñez, L., Consortium, T.I.S.: The ITK Software Guide, 4th edn. Kitware, Inc., New York (2018)
15. Oliphant, T.E.: A Guide to NumPy. Trelgol Publishing, USA (2006)
16. Van der Walt, S., Colbert, S.C., Varoquaux, G.: The NumPy array: a structure for efficient numerical computation. Comput. Sci. Eng. **13**, 22–30 (2011). https://doi.org/10.1109/MCSE.2011.37
17. Van der Walt, S., et al.: Scikit-image: Image processing in Python. PeerJ **2**, e453 (2014). https://doi.org/10.7717/peerj.453. (the scikit-image contributors)
18. Pedregosa, F., Varoquaux, G., Gramfort, A., Michel, V., Thirion, B., Grisel, O., et al.: Scikit-learn: Machine learning in python. J. Mach. Learn. **12**, 2825–2830 (2011). https://doi.org/10.5555/1953048.2078195
19. Canny, J.: A computational approach to edge detection. IEEE Trans. Pattern Anal. Mach. Intell. **8**(6), 679–698 (1986). https://doi.org/10.1109/TPAMI.1986.4767851
20. Zeiler, F.A., et al.: A unique model for ONSD Part II: Inter/Intra-operator variability. Can. J. Neurol. Sci. **41**(4), 430–435 (2014). https://doi.org/10.1017/S0317167100018448
21. Bekerman, I., Gottlieb, P., Vaiman, M.: Variations in eyeball diameters of the healthy adults. J. Ophthalmol. (2014). https://doi.org/10.1155/2014/503645
22. Moretti, R., Pizzi, B., Cassini, F., Vivaldi, N.: Reliability of optic nerve ultrasound for the evaluation of patients with spontaneous intracranial hemorrhage. Neurocrit. Care **11**, 406–410 (2009)
23. Du, J., Deng, Y., Li, H., Qiao, S., Yu, M., Xu, Q., et al.: Ratio of optic nerve sheath diameter to eyeball transverse diameter by ultrasound can predict intracranial hypertension in traumatic brain injury patients: A prospective study. Neurocrit. Care **32**(2), 478–485 (2020). https://doi.org/10.1007/s12028-019-00762-z
24. Murphy, D.L., Oberfoell, S.H., Trent, S.A., French, A.J., Kim, D.J., Richards, D.B.: Validation of a low-cost optic nerve sheath ultrasound phantom: An educational tool. J. Med. Ultrasound (2017). https://doi.org/10.1016/j.jmu.2017.01.003

25. Ohle, R., McIsaac, S.M., Woo, M.Y., Perry, J.J.: Sonography of the optic nerve sheath diameter for detection of raised intracranial pressure compared to compute tomography: a systematic review and meta-analysis. J. Ultrasound Med. **24**, 1285–1294 (2015). https://doi.org/10.7863/ultra.34.7.1285
26. Moore, B.T., Montgomery, S.P., Niethammer, M., Greer, H., Aylward, S.R.: Source code, data, and 3D model (2020). https://github.com/KitwareMedicalPublications/2020-MICCAI-ASMUS-Automatic-ONSD

Deep Learning for Automatic Spleen Length Measurement in Sickle Cell Disease Patients

Zhen Yuan[1(✉)], Esther Puyol-Antón[1], Haran Jogeesvaran[2], Catriona Reid[2], Baba Inusa[2], and Andrew P. King[1]

[1] School of Biomedical Engineering and Imaging Sciences, King's College London, London, UK
zhen.1.yuan@kcl.ac.uk

[2] Evelina Children's Hospital, Guy's and St Thomas' NHS Foundation Trust, London, UK

Abstract. Sickle Cell Disease (SCD) is one of the most common genetic diseases in the world. Splenomegaly (abnormal enlargement of the spleen) is frequent among children with SCD. If left untreated, splenomegaly can be life-threatening. The current workflow to measure spleen size includes palpation, possibly followed by manual length measurement in 2D ultrasound imaging. However, this manual measurement is dependent on operator expertise and is subject to intra- and inter-observer variability. We investigate the use of deep learning to perform automatic estimation of spleen length from ultrasound images. We investigate two types of approach, one segmentation-based and one based on direct length estimation, and compare the results against measurements made by human experts. Our best model (segmentation-based) achieved a percentage length error of 7.42%, which is approaching the level of inter-observer variability (5.47%–6.34%). To the best of our knowledge, this is the first attempt to measure spleen size in a fully automated way from ultrasound images.

Keywords: Deep learning · Sickle Cell Disease · Spleen ultrasound images

1 Introduction

Sickle Cell Disease (SCD) is one of the most common genetic diseases in the world, and its prevalence is particularly high in some parts of the developing world such as sub-Saharan Africa, the Middle East and India [4,7,13]. In the United States, 1 in 600 African-Americans has been diagnosed with SCD [1,2], and it was reported that 1 in every 2000 births had SCD during a newborn screening programme in the United Kingdom [11,18]. This multisystem disorder results in the sickling of red blood cells, which can cause a range of complications such as micro-vascular occlusion, haemolysis and progressive organ failure [4,8,14].

Y. Hu et al. (Eds.): ASMUS 2020/PIPPI 2020, LNCS 12437, pp. 33–41, 2020.
https://doi.org/10.1007/978-3-030-60334-2_4

The spleen is an essential lymphatic organ of the human body, which plays the role of a filter that cleans blood and adapts immune responses against antigens and microorganisms. Splenomegaly (abnormal enlargement of the spleen) is frequent among children with SCD. Splenomegaly, if left untreated, can be a serious and life-threatening condition, and so SCD patients typically have their spleen size measured at routine clinical appointments [3].

The typical workflow for measuring the size of the spleen includes palpation, possibly followed by manual length measurement from a 2D ultrasound examination. However, this workflow suffers from a number of drawbacks. First of all, palpation is relatively crude and non-quantitative, and only allows the clinician to make a preliminary judgement as to whether further ultrasound examination is required. Second, spleen measurement from ultrasound requires sonographer expertise and is subject to significant intra- and inter-observer variability [16]. Furthermore, in parts of the developing world, where there is a high prevalence of SCD, there is often a shortage of experienced sonographers to perform this task.

In recent years, deep learning models have been proposed for automatic interpretation of ultrasound images in a number of applications [6,9,12]. In [6], the EchoNet model was proposed for segmentation of the heart's anatomy and quantification of cardiac function from echocardiography. In [12], a Convolutional Regression Network was used to directly estimate brain maturation from three-dimensional fetal neurosonography images. Recently, [9] developed a model based on ResNet to estimate kidney function and the state of chronic kidney disease from ultrasound images. However, although automatic spleen segmentation has been attempted from magnetic resonance and computed tomography images [10], automatic interpretation of ultrasound images of the spleen remains challenging due to the low intensity contrast between the spleen and its adjacent fat tissue. To the best of our knowledge, there is no prior work on automated spleen segmentation or quantification from ultrasound. In this paper, we propose the use of deep learning for automatic estimation of the length of the spleen from ultrasound images. We investigate two fully automatic approaches: one based upon image segmentation of the spleen followed by length measurement, and another based on direct regression against spleen length. We compare the results of these two methods against measurements made by human experts.

2 Methods

Two types of approach were investigated for estimating the length of the spleen from the images, as illustrated in Fig. 1. The first type (network outside the dotted frame in Fig. 1(a)) was based on an automated deep learning segmentation followed by length estimation (see Sect. 2.1). In the second type of approach (see Sect. 2.2) we estimated length directly using deep regression models. Two different techniques for length regression were investigated (dotted frame in Fig. 1(a) and Fig. 1(b)).

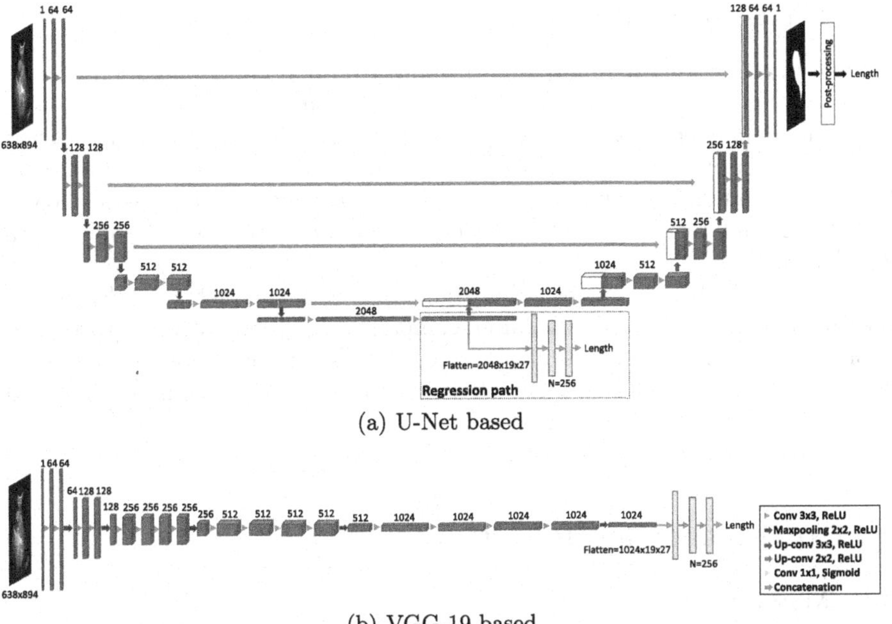

(a) U-Net based

(b) VGG-19 based

Fig. 1. Diagram showing the architectures for the three proposed models. (a) The first model is based upon a U-Net architecture, which performs a segmentation task. This is followed by CCA/PCA based postprocessing to estimate length. The encoding path of the U-net is also used in the second model, and combined with the extra fully connected layers within the dotted frame, which perform direct regression of spleen length. Note that this model does not include the decoding path of the U-net. (b) In the third model the same fully connected layers as in (a) are added at the end of a VGG-19 architecture to estimate length.

2.1 Segmentation-Based Approach

We used a U-Net based architecture [15] to automatically segment the spleen. Because of the size of our input images, we added an additional downsampling block to further compress the encodings in the latent space compared to the original U-Net. We applied dropout with probability 0.5 to the bottle-neck of our network. Each convolutional layer was followed by batch normalisation. We used the ReLU activation function for each convolutional layer and the sigmoid activation function in the output layer to classify each pixel as either spleen or background. A Dice loss function was used to penalise the difference between predicted labels and ground truth labels.

Based on the segmentation output of the U-net, we performed connected components analysis (CCA) to preserve the largest foreground (i.e. spleen) region. We then applied principle components analysis (PCA) on the coordinates of the identified spleen pixels to find the longest axis. The spleen length was then computed as the range of the projections of all spleen pixel coordinates onto this axis.

2.2 Regression-Based Approach

We investigated two different models for direct estimation of spleen length.

In the first model the encoding part of the U-net was used to estimate a low-dimensional representation of spleen shape. We then flattened the feature maps in the latent space and added two fully connected layers (dotted frame in Fig. 1(a)) with number of nodes N = 256. Each fully connected layer was followed by batch normalisation. Note that this model does not include the decoding path of the U-net.

We compared this model to a standard regression network (Fig. 1(b)), the VGG-19 [17]. To enable a fairer comparison between the two regression approaches, the same number of nodes and layers were used for the fully connected layers in the VGG-19 as were used for the first regression network. Batch normalisation was applied after each layer.

The mean square error loss was used for both models.

3 Experiments and Results

3.1 Materials

A total of 108 2D ultrasound images from 93 patients (aged 0 to 18) were used in this study. All patients were children with SCD and received professional clinical consultation prior to ultrasound inspection. Up to 4 ultrasound images were obtained from each patient during a single examination. Ultrasound imaging was carried out on a Philips EPIQ 7. During the process of imaging, an experienced sonographer followed the standard clinical procedure by acquiring an ultrasound plane that visualised the longest axis of the spleen and then manually marked the starting and ending points of the spleen length on each image. To remove the manual annotations on the acquired images, we applied biharmonic function-based image inpainting on all images [5]. The images were then manually cropped to a 638 $\times$ 894 pixel region of interest covering the entire spleen.

In addition to the manual length measurements made by the original sonographer (E1), manual measurements were made from the acquired ultrasound images (with annotations removed) by two further experts (E2 and E3) in order to allow quantification of inter-observer variability. Due to variations in pixel size between the images, all manual spleen length measurements (in millimetres) were converted to pixels for use in training the regression models.

To train the segmentation-based approach, the spleen was manually segmented in all images by a trained observer using ITK-SNAP [19].

3.2 Experimental Setup

Data augmentation was implemented in training all models, consisting of intensity transformations (adaptive histogram equalisation and gamma correction) and spatial transformations (0 to 20 degree random rotations). We intensity-normalised all images prior to using them as input to the networks. For evaluation, we used a three-fold nested cross-validation. For each of the three folds of the main cross-validation, the 72 training images were further separated into three folds, and these were used in the nested three-fold cross-validation for hyperparameter optimisation (weight decay values 10^{-6}, 10^{-7} and 10^{-8}). The model was then trained on all 72 images based on the best hyperparameter and tested on the remaining 36 images in the main cross-validation. This process was repeated for the other two folds of the main cross-validation.

For the second model (i.e. direct estimation using the U-net encoding path), we investigated whether performance could be improved by transferring weights from the U-net trained for the segmentation task. Therefore, in our experiments we compared four different techniques based on the three models outlined in Fig. 1:

1. Segmentation-based approach followed by postprocessing (SB).
2. Direct estimation based on the encoding path of the U-net, without weight transfer from the U-net trained for segmentation (DE).
3. The same direct estimation approach with weight transfer from the segmentation U-net (DEW).
4. The VGG-19 based direct estimation approach (VGG).

3.3 Implementation Details

The proposed models were all implemented in PyTorch and trained using an NVIDIA TITAN RTX (24 GB). The learning rate was set to 10^{-5} for all models. All models were trained using the Adam optimiser, with a batch size of 4 due to memory limitations.

3.4 Results

The results are presented in Table 1. This shows the following measures:

- PLE (Percentage Length Error): The percentage error in the length estimate compared to the ground truth.
- R: The Pearson's correlation between length estimates and the ground truth.
- Dice: For SB only, the Dice similarity metric between the ground truth segmentation and the estimated segmentation.
- HD (Hausdorff Distance): For SB only, the general Hausdorff distance between estimated and ground truth segmentations.

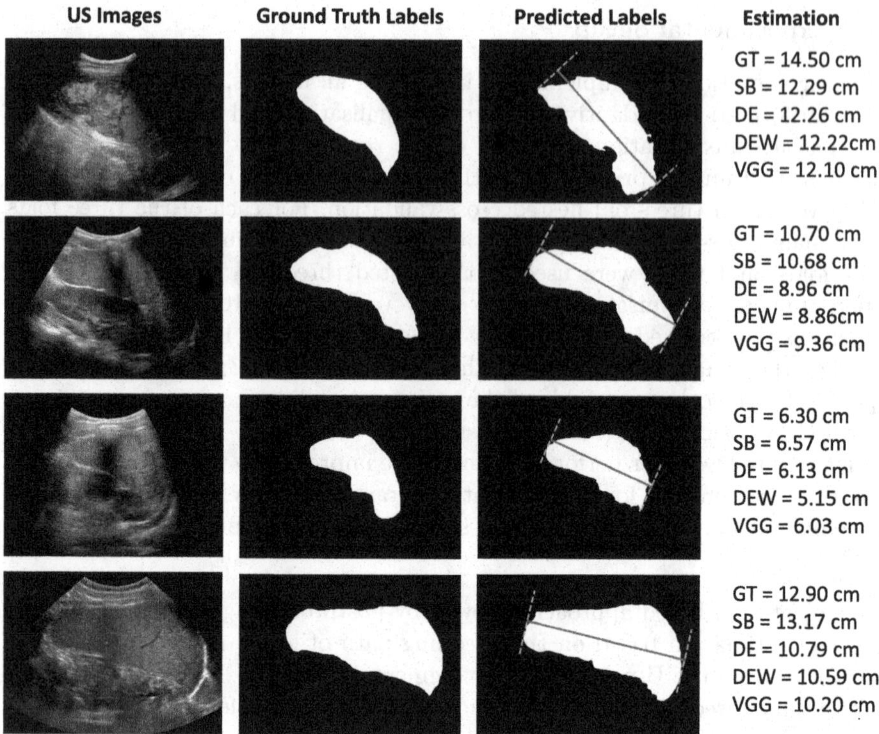

Fig. 2. Visualisations of ultrasound images, ground truth labels (i.e. segmentations) and predicted labels after CCA. The blue line segments in the predicted labels indicate the PCA-based length estimates. Ground truth lengths and estimated lengths made using the different approaches are presented in the fourth column. Each row represents a different sample image. (Color figure online)

For all measures, the ground truth was taken to be the original manual length measurement made by E1 and the measures reported in the table are means over all 108 images. We present some examples of images and segmentations in Fig. 2, along with ground truth lengths and estimations made by the different models.

Table 1 also shows the agreement between the length measurements made by the three human experts (E1, E2 and E3).

The results show that the segmentation-based approach outperformed the other three approaches and its performance is close to the level of inter-observer variability between the human experts. The direct estimation methods perform less well, and we find no improvement in performance from weight transfer.

Table 1. Comparison between results for segmentation-based estimation (SB), direct estimation (DE), direct estimation with weight transfer (DEW) and VGG-19 based direct estimation (VGG). PLE: Percentage Length Error, R: Pearson's correlation, Dice: Dice similarity metric, HD: general Hausdorff Distance. All values are means over all 108 images. The final three columns quantify the level of inter-observer variability between the three experts E1, E2, and E3.

Methods	SB	DE	DEW	VGG	E1 vs E2	E1 vs E3	E2 vs E3
PLE	7.42%	12.80%	12.88%	12.99%	5.47%	5.52%	6.34%
R	0.93	0.86	0.87	0.88	0.94	0.97	0.93
Dice	0.88	–	–	–	–	–	–
HD (mm)	13.27	–	–	–	–	–	–

4 Discussion and Conclusion

In this work, we proposed three models for automatic estimation of spleen length from ultrasound images. To the best of our knowledge, this is the first attempt to perform this task in a fully automated way. We first adjusted the U-Net architecture and applied post-processing based on CCA and PCA to the output segmentation to estimate length. We also proposed two regression models, one based on the U-Net encoding path and one based on the well-established VGG-19 network.

Our results showed that the segmentation-based approach (SB) had the lowest PLE and the highest correlation. The performance of this approach was close to the level of human inter-observer variability. The PLE and correlation for the first direct estimation approach with or without weight transfer (DE and DEW) were similar. This indicates that weights learned from the segmentation task do not help to improve the performance of the direct estimation task. This is likely due to a strong difference between the optimal learnt representations for segmentation and length estimation tasks. The results produced by the two regression-based models (DE/DEW and VGG) are also similar. However, compared to the U-Net encoding path direct estimation network (DE, DEW), VGG-19 has a relatively small number of parameters (178,180,545 vs. 344,512,449) but achieves similar results, which demonstrates the potential of the VGG-19 model for this length estimation task.

Although we have achieved promising results in this work, there are some limiting factors that have prevented the results from being even better. The first is that some of our training data suffer from the presence of image artefacts. The second is that the spleen and its adjacent fat have quite low intensity contrast. These two factors combined make measuring the length of the spleen very challenging, and it is likely that human experts use knowledge of the expected location and anatomy of the spleen when making manual measurements to overcome a lack of visibility of the spleen. Finally, we have a limited amount of data (108 images). In the future, we aim to obtain more ultrasound images. With a larger database of training images, we believe the performance of the segmentation-based approach has the potential to reach or surpass that of human experts. We also plan to investigate alternative architectures to exploit possibly synergies between the segmentation and length estimation tasks.

Acknowledgements. This work was supported by the Wellcome/EPSRC Centre for Medical Engineering [WT 203148/Z/16/Z]. The support provided by China Scholarship Council during PhD programme of Zhen Yuan in King's College London is acknowledged.

References

1. Angastiniotis, M., Modell, B.: Global epidemiology of hemoglobin disorders. Ann. New York Acad. Sci. **850**(1), 251–269 (1998)
2. Biswas, T.: Global burden of sickle cell anaemia is set to rise by a third by 2050. BMJ **347**, f4676 (2013)
3. Brousse, V., Buffet, P., Rees, D.: The spleen and sickle cell disease: The sick (led) spleen. British J. Haematol. **166**(2), 165–176 (2014)
4. Chakravorty, S., Williams, T.N.: Sickle cell disease: A neglected chronic disease of increasing global health importance. Archives Dis. Child. **100**(1), 48–53 (2015)
5. Damelin, S.B., Hoang, N.: On surface completion and image inpainting by biharmonic functions: Numerical aspects. Int. J. Math. Math. Sci. **2018**, 8 p. (2018)
6. Ghorbani, A., et al.: Deep learning interpretation of echocardiograms. NPJ Digital Med. **3**(1), 1–10 (2020)
7. Grosse, S.D., Odame, I., Atrash, H.K., Amendah, D.D., Piel, F.B., Williams, T.N.: Sickle cell disease in africa: A neglected cause of early childhood mortality. Am. J. Prev. Med. **41**(6), S398–S405 (2011)
8. Inusa, B., Casale, M., Ward, N.: Introductory chapter: Introduction to the history, pathology and clinical management of sickle cell disease. In: Sickle Cell Disease-Pain and Common Chronic Complications. IntechOpen (2016)
9. Kuo, C.C., et al.: Automation of the kidney function prediction and classification through ultrasound-based kidney imaging using deep learning. NPJ Digital Med. **2**(1), 1–9 (2019)
10. Mihaylova, A., Georgieva, V.: A brief survey of spleen segmentation in MRI and CT images. Int. J. **5**(7), 72–77 (2016)
11. Modell, B., et al.: Epidemiology of haemoglobin disorders in Europe: an overview. Scand. J. Clin. Lab. Invest. **67**(1), 39–70 (2007)
12. Namburete, A.I.L., Xie, W., Noble, J.A.: Robust regression of brain maturation from 3D fetal neurosonography using CRNs. In: Cardoso, M.J., et al. (eds.) FIFI/OMIA -2017. LNCS, vol. 10554, pp. 73–80. Springer, Cham (2017). https://doi.org/10.1007/978-3-319-67561-9_8
13. Piel, F.B., et al.: Global epidemiology of sickle haemoglobin in neonates: a contemporary geostatistical model-based map and population estimates. Lancet **381**(9861), 142–151 (2013)
14. Piel, F.B., Steinberg, M.H., Rees, D.C.: Sickle cell disease. N. Eng. Med. **376**(16), 1561–1573 (2017)
15. Ronneberger, O., Fischer, P., Brox, T.: U-Net: Convolutional networks for biomedical image segmentation. In: Navab, N., Hornegger, J., Wells, W.M., Frangi, A.F. (eds.) MICCAI 2015. LNCS, vol. 9351, pp. 234–241. Springer, Cham (2015). https://doi.org/10.1007/978-3-319-24574-4_28

16. Rosenberg, H., Markowitz, R., Kolberg, H., Park, C., Hubbard, A., Bellah, R.: Normal splenic size in infants and children: Sonographic measurements. AJR Am. J. Roentgenol. **157**(1), 119–121 (1991)
17. Simonyan, K., Zisserman, A.: Very deep convolutional networks for large-scale image recognition (2014). arXiv preprint arXiv:1409.1556
18. Streetly, A., Latinovic, R., Hall, K., Henthorn, J.: Implementation of universal newborn bloodspot screening for sickle cell disease and other clinically significant haemoglobinopathies in england: screening results for 2005–7. J. Clin. Pathol. **62**(1), 26–30 (2009)
19. Yushkevich, P.A., et al.: User-guided 3D active contour segmentation of anatomical structures: significantly improved efficiency and reliability. Neuroimage **31**(3), 1116–1128 (2006)

Cross-Device Cross-Anatomy Adaptation Network for Ultrasound Video Analysis

Qingchao Chen[1(✉)], Yang Liu[1], Yipeng Hu[3], Alice Self[2], Aris Papageorghiou[2], and J. Alison Noble[1]

[1] Department of Engineering Science, University of Oxford, Oxford, UK
{qingchao.chen, yang.liu, alison.noble}@eng.ox.ac.uk
[2] Nuffield Department of Women's and Reproductive Health, University of Oxford, Oxford, UK
{alice.self, aris.papageorghiou}@wrh.ox.ac.uk
[3] Wellcome/EPSRC Centre for Interventional Surgical Sciences, University College London, London, UK
yipeng.hu@ucl.ac.uk

Abstract. Domain adaptation is an active area of current medical image analysis research. In this paper, we present a cross-device and cross-anatomy adaptation network (CCAN) for automatically annotating fetal anomaly ultrasound video. In our approach, deep learning models trained on more widely available expert-acquired and manually-labeled free-hand ultrasound video from a high-end ultrasound machine are adapted to a particular scenario where limited and unlabeled ultrasound videos are collected using a simplified sweep protocol suitable for less-experienced users with a low-cost probe. This unsupervised domain adaptation problem is interesting as there are two domain variations between the datasets: (1) cross-device image appearance variation due to using different transducers; and (2) cross-anatomy variation because the simplified scanning protocol does not necessarily contain standard views seen in typical free-hand scanning video. By introducing a novel structure-aware adversarial training module to learn the cross-device variation, together with a novel selective adaptation module to accommodate cross-anatomy variation domain transfer is achieved. Learning from a dataset of high-end machine clinical video and expert labels, we demonstrate the efficacy of the proposed method in anatomy classification on the unlabeled sweep data acquired using the non-expert and low-cost ultrasound probe protocol. Experimental results show that, when cross-device variations are learned and reduced only, CCAN significantly improves the mean recognition accuracy by 20.8% and 10.0%, compared to a method without domain adaptation and a state-of-the-art adaptation method, respectively. When both the cross-device and cross-anatomy variations are reduced, CCAN improves the mean recognition accuracy by a statistically significant 20% compared with these other state-of-the-art adaptation methods.

Y. Hu et al. (Eds.): ASMUS 2020/PIPPI 2020, LNCS 12437, pp. 42–51, 2020.
https://doi.org/10.1007/978-3-030-60334-2_5

1 Introduction

Although ultrasound (US) imaging is recognized as an inexpensive and portable imaging means for prenatal care, training skilled sonographers is time-consuming and costly, resulting in a well-documented shortage of sonographers in many countries including the UK and the US. 99% of world-wide maternal deaths occur in low-and-middle-income (LMIC) countries where the access to ultrasound imaging is even more limited [7]. To address this challenge, recent academic research on solutions for LMIC setting has proposed a three-component approach: i) the adoption of inexpensive and portable US equipment, ii) designing simple-to-use US scanning protocols, e.g. the obstetric sweep protocol (OSP) [1] and iii) innovating intelligent image analysis algorithms [6,9,10]. Arguably, the third innovation plays a bridging role in this approach, enabling the other two cost-effective components of the solution.

Whilst simplified scanning protocols are less-dependent on user skills, they generate diagnostic images that deviate in appearance to those acquired using the standardized protocols used in fetal assessment. Even experienced sonographers can struggle to interpret and analyze data obtained using simple protocols on inexpensive machines, which are often equipped with older generation transducers and processing units. Furthermore this data degrades modern machine learning models compared to those developed with well-curated datasets [4,5,9]. Refining these existing models trained with site-specific data is an option, but requires additional data to be acquired and manually annotated, which may present substantial logistic challenges in expertise and cost.

As an alternative, in this work, we propose an unsupervised domain adaptation approach to train and adapt deep neural networks, learning from a ***source domain*** of high-end ultrasound machine images and expert annotations to classify a ***target domain*** of unpaired unlabeled images. As illustrated in Fig. 1a, in the fetal anomaly examination application of interest, as an "instructor" dataset, the source-domain images are acquired by experienced sonographers following an established fetal anomaly screening free-hand ultra-sound protocol [8], hereafter referred to as the ***free-hand dataset***. The target-domain dataset is ultrasound video acquired using a simplified single-sweep protocol [10], also illustrated in Fig. 1b, hereafter referred to as the ***single-sweep dataset***. Classifying video frames in such single-sweep data into multiple anatomical classes is useful for assisting a range of clinical applications, including anomaly detection, gestational age estimation and pregnancy risk assessment [9].

The proposed unsupervised domain adaptation approach in this paper addresses two unique and specific dataset variations: 1) the variations of anatomical appearance between the source and target training images attributed to acquiring data with two different ultrasound devices (the ***cross-device variation***); and 2) the variations between anatomical class labels where the target domain label set is a smaller subset of the source domain label set (the ***cross-anatomy variation***). We argue that the cross-anatomy variation is common, since there exists richer anatomical structures and a larger anatomical label set in the free-hand dataset (source domain) compared with the single-sweep dataset (target domain). More specifically, we propose a novel structure-aware adversarial domain adaptation network with a selective adaptation module to reduce two types of variations, such that, the model trained using the free-hand dataset with four anatomical-class-labels can be used to effectively classify a single-sweep dataset with two classes.

The contributions of this paper are summarized as follows: 1) for the first time, we propose a Cross-device and Cross-anatomy Adaptation Network (CCAN) to reduce cross-device and cross-anatomy variations between two datasets, as described in Sect. 2; 2) we propose a novel structure-aware adversarial training strategy based on multi-scale deep features to effectively reduce cross-device variations; 3) we propose a novel anatomy selector module to reduce cross-anatomy variations; 4) we demonstrate the efficacy of the proposed approaches with experiment results on two sets of clinical data.

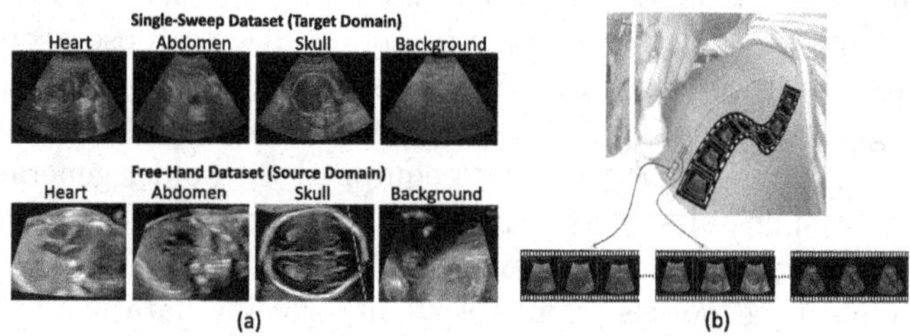

Fig. 1. (a) Example frames illustrating the cross-device variations between free-hand and single-sweep datasets. (b) Illustration of the single-sweep protocol.

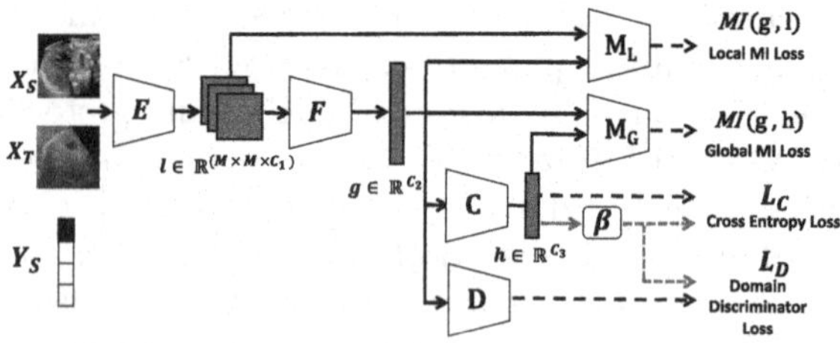

Fig. 2. Architecture of a Cross-Device Cross-Anatomy Adaptation Network.

2 Methods

2.1 Cross-Device and Cross-Anatomy Adaptation Network

We assume that the source image X_S with the discrete anatomy label Y_S are drawn from a source domain distribution $P_S(X, Y)$, and that the target images

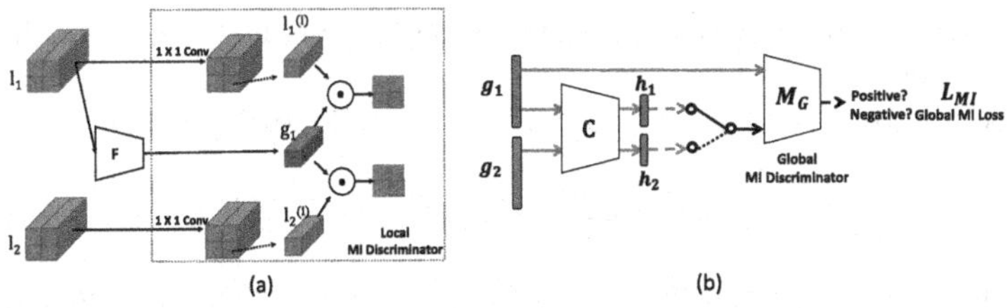

Fig. 3. Architecture and implementation of (a) local and (b) global MI estimation.

X_T are drawn from the target domain distribution $P_T(X, Y)$ without observed labels Y_T. In our application, the source and target distributions are represented by the free-hand and single-sweep datasets, respectively. Since direct supervised learning using the target labels is not possible, CCAN instead learns an anatomy classifier driven by source labels only, and then adapts the model for use in the target domain.

As illustrated in the modules connected by black lines in Fig. 2, the proposed CCAN includes an encoder E, projection layer F, the anatomy classifier C, the domain classifier D and two Mutual Information (MI) discriminators M_L and M_G. Specifically, the source images are first mapped by the encoder E to the convolutional feature $E(X_S)$, and then projected to a latent global feature representation $F(E(X_S))$. Then the anatomy classifier C minimizes a cross-entropy loss L_C, between the ground-truth Y_S and the predicted source labels $C(F(E(X_S)))$, i.e., $\min_{E,F,C} \mathcal{L}_C$. We adopt the adversarial training loss L_D [5] to learn domain invariant features, where the domain classifier D tries to discriminate between features from the source and target domain, while E and F tries to "confuse" D, i.e. $\max_{E,F} \min_{D} \mathcal{L}_D$.

However, facing the large anatomical variations, it is still an open question as to which levels of deep features to align and which should be domain-invariant. To answer this question, and referring to the notation in Fig. 2, we propose to align the *distribution of multi-scale deep features* in adversarial training by compressing information from local convolutional feature maps l, and the classifier prediction h into a unified global semantic feature g and to reduce cross-domain variations of g. More specifically, we maximize the *local* and *global* MI losses, $MI(g, l)$ and $MI(g, h)$, between two feature pairs, (g, l) and (g, h) respectively. The MI estimation [2] is achieved by two binary classification losses, distinguishing whether two features are a positive or negative pair from the same image, as shown in Fig. 3. Taking $MI(g, h)$ as an example, it relies on a sampling strategy that draws positive and negative samples from the joint distribution $P(g, h)$ and from the marginal product $P(g)P(h)$ respectively. In our case, the positive samples (g_1, h_1) are features of the same input, while the negative samples (g_1, h_2) are obtained from different inputs. That is, given an input g_1 and a set of positive and negative pairs from a minibatch, the global MI discriminator M_G aims to distinguish whether the other input h_1 or h_2 from the same input image as g_1 or not, as shown in Fig. 3.

The overall objective can be summarized by the following minimax optimization:

$$\min_{E,F,C} \max_{D} \; -\mathcal{L}_C + \alpha\mathcal{L}_D + \gamma(MI(g,l) + MI(g,h)) \tag{1}$$

where α and γ are the weights of $\mathcal{L}_D$ and MI losses respectively. In this work, the hyper-parameters are set empirically (via grid-searching from the evaluation set) to weight between the classification loss $\mathcal{L}_C$, the domain classification loss $\mathcal{L}_D$ and MI loss $MI(g,l) + MI(g,h)$. The detailed domain discriminator loss $\mathcal{L}_D$ and MI losses therefore, are given by the Eqs. (2)–(5). Note that before the inner-product operation in Eq. (3), we used two projection layers W_h and W_l for classifier prediction h and local feature map l respectively.

$$\mathcal{L}_D = -\frac{1}{N_S}\sum_{j=1}^{N_S} log(D(F(E(x_S^j)))) - \frac{1}{N_T}\sum_{i=1}^{N_T} log(1 - D(F(E(x_T^i)))), \tag{2}$$

$$M_G(g,h) = g^T W_h h, \; M_L(g,l) = \frac{1}{M^2}\sum_{i}^{M^2} g^T W_l l^{(i)}, \tag{3}$$

$$MI(g,h) = \mathbb{E}_{X_P}[log\sigma(M_G(g_1,h_1))] + \mathbb{E}_{X_N}[log(1 - \sigma(M_G(g_1,h_2)))] \tag{4}$$

$$MI(g,l) = \mathbb{E}_{X_P}[log\sigma(M_L(g_1,l_1))] + \mathbb{E}_{X_N}[log(1 - \sigma(M_L(g_1,l_2)))] \tag{5}$$

2.2 Selective Adaptation Module for Cross-Anatomy Variations

Due to different scanning protocols used to acquire the free-hand and single-sweep datasets, the available anatomical categories of the source domain Y_S often do not correspond to those of the target domain label Y_T. Often, the anatomical class set of source domain C_S may contain classes outside of the one in target domain C_T which henceforth we refer to as the outlier. When this large cross-anatomy variation exists, the network training described in Sect. 2.1 still aims to match *identical* class categories between source and target domain, leading to a trained network prone to cross-anatomy misalignment of the label space. For example, if we directly adapt a source domain model trained using four-class data X_S to the three-class (shared anatomy) target domain data X_T, mismatch may occur between the three-class features and the four-class ones, due to the lack of anatomically paired features. As a result, some features in the target domain may be randomly aligned with the features from the outlier anatomy class, possibly due to the indiscriminative marginal feature distribution.

In this work, we investigate the case where categories of Y_T are a subset of the class categories of Y_S, as the single-sweep dataset contains a smaller number of anatomical classes than the free-hand dataset. We propose CCAN-β, a variant of CCAN with a small modification, shown as the highlighted red β module in Fig. 2 to selectively adapt the model training, focusing on the shared anatomical categories $C_S \cap C_T$ while defocusing from the outlier class $C_S \setminus C_T$.

As shown in Fig. 2, β is an anatomy-wise weighting vector with the length of the source domain class categories $|C_S|$, with its kth element indicating the contribution of the kth source domain class. Ideally, β functions to down weight the classes from the outlier anatomy class $C_S \setminus C_T$ and promoting the shared anatomy classes in the set $C_S \cap C_T$. Based on this principle, we calculate β simply using the average of target classification predictions $C(F(E(X_T)))$, $\hat{\beta} = \frac{1}{N_T}\sum_{i=1}^{N_T} C(F(E(x_T^i)))$, where β is the normalized vector of $\hat{\beta}$, $\beta = \frac{\hat{\beta}}{\max(\hat{\beta})}$. N_T and x_T^i are the total number of target domain samples and individual target samples, respectively. For the shared class k_s in $C_S \cap C_T$, its weight $\beta[k_s]$ should be relatively larger than the $\beta[k_o]$ of the outlier anatomy class k_o, where k_o belongs to the set $C_S \setminus C_T$. The reason is due to the fact that $C(F(E(x_T^i)))$ are the class predictions of the target domain from the shared class categories, which should have higher probabilities and higher values in relevant positions of β.

Using β as the weighting vector with the previous loss functions $\mathcal{L}_C$ and $\mathcal{L}_D$ leads to two new loss functions, selectively focusing on the anatomy classifier C and domain classifier D on the samples from $C_S \cap C_T$, as follows:

$$\mathcal{L}_C = \frac{1}{N_S}\sum_{j=1}^{N_S} \beta_{y_s^j} \mathcal{L}_C(C(F(E(x_s^j))), y_s^j) \tag{6}$$

$$\mathcal{L}_D = -\frac{1}{N_S}\sum_{j=1}^{N_S} \beta_{y_s^j} log(D(F(E(x_s^j)))) - \frac{1}{N_T}\sum_{i=1}^{N_T} log(1 - D(F(E(x_T^i)))). \tag{7}$$

3 Experiment and Results

3.1 Implementations

We used the ResNet50 as the encoder design and the F is a Fully-Connect (FC) layer with the output dimension of 1024. The domain discriminator consists of three FC layers, with the hidden layer sizes of 512 and 512 respectively. The global MI discriminator consists of two FC layers and the local MI discriminator uses a two single 1×1 convolutional layer. When updating the classifier weight β, it is performed after each epoch.

Two datasets were used for this study to evaluate the CCAN. The first free-hand dataset (50-subjects) was acquired during a fetal anomaly examination using a GE Voluson E8 with a convex C2-9-D abdominal probe, carried out at the maternity ultrasound unit, Oxford University Hospitals NHS Foundation Trust, Oxfordshire, United Kingdom. The four class labels "Heart", "Skull", "Abdomen" and "Background", with 78685, 23999, 51257 and 71884 video frames, respectively, were obtained and annotated by experienced senior reporting sonographers. The single-sweep POCUS dataset were acquired using a Philips HD9 with a V7-3 abdominal probe, which follows the single-sweep scanning protocol [1] also shown in Fig. 1(b). The single-sweep dataset were also labeled with the same four classes, with 4136, 5632, 10399 and 17393 video frames respectively. It is important to note that the background class is clinically defined as image frames obtained during the scouting at the beginning of the procedure and transition periods between localizing other anatomical regions of interest (i.e. the foreground classes). Therefore, the background classes in the free-hand dataset may contain different anatomical contents. The target domain single-sweep dataset was split into 70% training, 10% evaluation and 20% unseen test datasets, whilst the 80% and 20% of the source domain free-hand dataset were used for training and evaluation, respectively. The mean recognition accuracy is reported on the test target domain data. In addition, the A-distance is also reported to measure the distribution discrepancy (d_A) [3]. The smaller the A-distance, the more domain-invariant the features are, in general, which suggests a better adaptation method to reduce the cross-domain divergence.

3.2 Cross-Device Adaptation Results

To evaluate the ability of CCAN to reduce cross-device variation, we compare CCAN with the method trained using source-domain data only and the benchmark domain adversarial neural network (DANN) [5]. In this work, the ResNet-50 network was pre-trained using ImageNet and fine-tuned using the source domain free-hand dataset only, which was used as the *No-Adaptation* model. For comparison, the no-adaptation recognition accuracy was obtained by directly classifying the single-sweep dataset using this model. For the three compared models, we perform two adaptation tasks: ***Exp1)*** using all samples from three anatomical classes, excluding the back-ground classes in both datasets (as they may contain different anatomical features described in Sect. 1 and 3); ***Exp2)*** using all samples from the four classes in both source and target datasets.

As shown in Table 1, compared to the no-adaptation model, statistically significant improvement (on an average of 23%) in recognition accuracy was observed by using the adaptation techniques (DANN and CCAN), with both p-values < 0.001 based on a pairwise Wilcoxon signed-rank test at a significance level of $\alpha = 0.05$ (used for all the p-values reported in this study unless otherwise indicated). Compared with the DANN, our CCAN increased the mean recognition accuracy by 9.3% in Exp1 and in particular, when considering the challenging 4-class adaptation, CCAN outperforms DANN by 19.0%. These two results are both statistically significant, with the p-values < 0.001.

The confusion matrices of CCAN using four-class and three-class adaptation are shown in Table 2, summarizing the recognition accuracies on a per-class basis. In ***Exp2***'s confusion matrix, recognition accuracies of 26.9% and 57.6% were obtained for the fore-ground heart and abdominal classes, respectively. We hypothesized that it is challenging for both DANN and CCAN that the images from free-hand dataset background class may include more diverse and unknown anatomical structures compared to the background class for the single-sweep dataset, as shown in Fig. 1(a) and Sect. 3.1. This also motivated the selective adaptation module proposed in Sect. 2.2, with its results presented in Sect. 3.3.

3.3 Cross-Anatomy Adaptation Results

As described in Sect. 2.2, the proposed CCAN-β reduces cross-anatomy variations, such that a network trained with a source domain dataset can be adapted to a target domain dataset with only a subset of the classes defined in the source domain. In our application, the free-hand dataset with the four classes were used in the training, while two experiments in which the subset classes from the single-sweep dataset were tested. The first experiment (***Exp3***) uses three foreground classes of heart, abdominal and skull and the second experiment (***Exp4***) uses two classes of heart and background in the single-sweep dataset. The recognition accuracies are compared in the two experiments, between the four models, the no-adaptation, the DANN, the CCAN and the CCAN-β with the selective adaptation module.

Tables 1(c), (d) summarises the results from Exp3 and Exp4. Without the selective adaptation module, CCAN significantly outperforms the no-adaptation and the DANN results by 11.7% and 6.2%, respectively in Exp3 (p-values < 0.001). The outperformance of CCAN-β was further boosted to 27.2% using the proposed selective adaptation module, achieving a mean recognition accuracy of 73.5%. The results from Exp4 are summarized in Table 1(d), which indicate statistically significant outperformances of 6.9%, 9.7% and 12.5% using CCAN-β in mean recognition accuracy (p-value < 0.001), compared to CCAN, DANN and no-adaptation respectively.

Table 2(c) reports the per-class accuracies of Exp3 and we can observe a considerable impact due to the anatomy variation being selectively adapted by the proposed β module. For example, the misclassifications of the three anatomical classes to the outlier anatomy class (the background class in free-hand dataset) are below 5%. Still, we can observe that 66.4% of abdomen class samples are misclassified to the heart class, potentially due to very similar image appearance between the abdomen in the single-sweep dataset and the heart in the free-hand dataset.

Table 1. Recognition rates (%), statistics and A-distance (d_A) of cross-device adaptations in (a) and (b), cross-anatomy adaptations in (c) and (d).

(a) Exp1

Methods	Acc.	Median,[1st,3rd] Quartile	d_A
No-Adaptation	60.9	73.7,[25.1,100.0]	1.96
DANN [5]	79.2	88.9,[25.1,100.0]	1.85
CCAN(Ours)	**88.5**	95.2,[73.4, 100.0]	1.64

(b) Exp2

Methods	Acc.	Median,[1st,3rd] Quartile	d_A
No-Adaptation	55.0	0.0,[0.0,61.5]	1.98
DANN [5]	62.6	14.0,[4.0,79.7]	1.94
CCAN(Ours)	**81.6**	76.3,[39.6, 97.8]	1.77

(c) Exp3

Methods	Acc.	Median,[1st,3rd] Quartile	d_A
No-Adaptation	34.6	6.4,[0.0,94.8]	1.99
DANN [5]	40.1	0.0,[0.0,94.8]	2.00
CCAN(Ours)	46.3	26.2,[0.0,72.5]	1.95
CCAN-β(Ours)	**73.5**	96.1,[23.0, 100.0]	1.88

(d) Exp4

Methods	Acc.	Median,[1st,3rd] Quartile	d_A
No-Adaptation	77.1	100.0,[0.0,100.0]	1.84
DANN [5]	78.9	94.5,[42.6,100.0]	1.85
CCAN(Ours)	82.5	100.0,[46.0, 100.0]	1.79
CCAN-β(Ours)	**89.6**	98.7, [79.3, 100.0]	1.55

Table 2. Confusion matrix (%) of using CCAN for Exp1 (88.5%), Exp2 (81.6%) and Exp3 (73.5%). H, A, S, B stand for heart, abdomen, skull and background.

(a) Exp1

		Predicted Class		
		H	A	S
Actual	H	77.4	22.6	0.0
	A	12.2	84.5	3.3
	S	0.3	0.6	99.1

(b) Exp2

		Predicted Class			
		H	A	S	B
Actual	H	26.9	4.2	0.4	68.5
	A	0.3	57.6	4.7	47.4
	S	0.0	0.0	91.8	8.2
	B	0.0	0.0	0.7	99.3

(c) Exp3

		Predicted Class			
		H	A	S	B
Actual	H	95.6	0.0	0.0	4.4
	A	66.4	29.0	2.3	2.3
	S	5.0	0.0	92.3	2.7

4 Conclusions

In this paper, we presented a cross-device and cross-anatomy adaptation network to classify an unlabelled single sweep video dataset guided by knowledge of a labelled freehand scanning protocol video dataset. The proposed novel CCAN approach significantly improved the automated image annotation accuracy on the single sweep video dataset, compared to the benchmark domain adaptation methods, by reducing both the cross-device and cross-anatomy variations between the clinical dataset domains.

Acknowledgement. The authors gratefully acknowledge the support of EPSRC grants EP/R013853/1, EP/M013774/1 and the NIHR Oxford Biomedical Research Centre.

References

1. Abuhamad, A., et al.: Standardized six-step approach to the performance of the focused basic obstetric ultrasound examination. Am. J. Perinatol. **2**(01), 090–098 (2016)
2. Belghazi, M.I., et al.: Mine: mutual information neural estimation. arXiv preprint arXiv:1801.04062 (2018)
3. Ben-David, S., et al.: A theory of learning from different domains. Mach. Learn. **79**, 151–175 (2009). https://doi.org/10.1007/s10994-009-5152-4
4. Chen, Q., Liu, Y., Wang, Z., Wassell, I., Chetty, K.: Re-weighted adversarial adaptation network for unsupervised domain adaptation. In: 2018 IEEE/CVF Conference on Computer Vision and Pattern Recognition, pp. 7976–7985 (2018)
5. Ganin, Y., et al.: Domain-adversarial training of neural networks. J. Mach. Learn. Res. **17**(1), 1–35 (2016)
6. Gao, Y., Alison Noble, J.: Detection and Characterization of the fetal heartbeat in free-hand ultrasound sweeps with weakly-supervised two-streams convolutional networks. In: Descoteaux, M., Maier-Hein, L., Franz, A., Jannin, P., Collins, D.L., Duchesne, S. (eds.) MICCAI 2017. LNCS, vol. 10434, pp. 305–313. Springer, Cham (2017). https://doi.org/10.1007/978-3-319-66185-8_35

7. van den Heuvel, T.L.A., Petros, H., Santini, S., de Korte, C.L., van Ginneken, B.: Combining automated image analysis with obstetric sweeps for prenatal ultrasound imaging in developing countries. In: Cardoso, M.J., et al. (eds.) BIVPCS/POCUS 2017. LNCS, vol. 10549, pp. 105–112. Springer, Cham (2017). https://doi.org/10.1007/978-3-319-67552-7_13
8. Kirwan, D.: NHS Fetal Anomaly Screening Programme: 180 to 20+6 Weeks Fetal Anomaly Screening Scan National Standards and Guidance for England. NHS Fetal Anomaly Screening Programme (2010)
9. Maraci, M.A., et al.: Toward point-of-care ultrasound estimation of fetal gestational age from the trans-cerebellar diameter using cnn-based ultrasound image analysis. J. Med. Imaging **7**(1), 014501 (2020)
10. Maraci, M.A., Bridge, C.P., Napolitano, R., Papageorghiou, A., Noble, J.A.: A framework for analysis of linear ultrasound videos to detect fetal presentation and heartbeat. Med. Image Anal. **37**, 22–36 (2017)

Segmentation, Captioning and Enhancement

Guidewire Segmentation in 4D Ultrasound Sequences Using Recurrent Fully Convolutional Networks

Brian C. Lee(✉), Kunal Vaidya, Ameet K. Jain, and Alvin Chen

Philips Research North America, Cambridge, MA 02141, USA
brian.c.lee@philips.com

Abstract. Accurate, real-time segmentation of thin, deformable, and moving objects in noisy medical ultrasound images remains a highly challenging task. This paper addresses the problem of segmenting guidewires and other thin, flexible devices from 4D ultrasound image sequences acquired during minimally-invasive surgical interventions. We propose a deep learning method based on a recurrent fully convolutional network architecture whose design captures temporal information from dense 4D (3D+time) image sequences. The network uses convolutional gated recurrent units interposed between the halves of a VNet-like model such that the skip-connections embedded in the encoder-decoder are preserved. Testing on realistic phantom tissues, ex vivo and human cadaver specimens, and live animal models of peripheral vascular and cardiovascular disease, we show that temporal encoding improves segmentation accuracy compared to standard single-frame model predictions in a way that is not simply associated to an increase in model size. Additionally, we demonstrate that our approach may be combined with traditional techniques such as active splines to further enhance stability over time.

1 Introduction

Cardiovascular and peripheral vascular disease are among the leading causes of morbidity and mortality worldwide, with a combined global prevalence of >600 million [1,2]. Minimally-invasive surgical techniques, typically involving the endovascular navigation of guidewires under image guidance, have been introduced to treat these diseases. Ultrasound (US) imaging provides a promising means for guiding such interventions due to its capacity to visualize soft-tissue anatomy and moving devices in real-time, with new advancements in US transducer technology leading to the emergence of volumetric 4D US imaging at high spatial and temporal resolutions. Unfortunately, human interpretation of dynamic 4D data is challenging, particularly when structures are thin, flexible,

---

Electronic supplementary material The online version of this chapter (https://doi.org/10.1007/978-3-030-60334-2_6) contains supplementary material, which is available to authorized users.

Y. Hu et al. (Eds.): ASMUS 2020/PIPPI 2020, LNCS 12437, pp. 55–65, 2020.
https://doi.org/10.1007/978-3-030-60334-2_6

deforming, and dominated by background. Rather than inferring from static frames, human experts are trained to recognize complex spatiotemporal signatures, for instance by moving devices back and forth or by looking for characteristic motions.

Our Contributions. This paper demonstrates in surgical interventional procedures performed on phantom, ex vivo, human cadaver, and live animal models, that segmenting guidewires and other devices from 4D (3D+t) US volume sequences is feasible with millimeter accuracy. We describe a deep learning method for 4D segmentation that makes use of temporal continuity to resolve ambiguities due to noise, obstructions, shadowing, and acoustic artefacts typical of US imaging. The proposed spatiotemporal network incorporates convolutional gated recurrent nodes into the skip connections of a VNet-inspired model [3]. The novelty of the architecture is in the preservation and memory of a series of multi-resolution encoded features as they pass through the recurrent nodes and are concatenated via skip connections to subsequent time points, thereby temporally propagating the learned representation at all scales. Furthermore, as a post-processing step, a continuous thin spline is adapted onto the network's logit predictions to constrain the final segmentation onto a smooth 3D space-curve.

Additional contributions of the paper: (1) We apply our method to the complex task of segmenting very thin (<nearly single-voxel (0.5 mm) thickness), flexible, and rapidly deforming guidewires moving in and out of obscurity in noisy 4D US sequences of peripheral and cardio-vascular anatomy. (2) We demonstrate state-of-art accuracy and generalizability on challenging and diverse surgical intervention datasets. (3) We show that our approach may be combined with traditional segmentation techniques such as active contours to enhance stability over time. (4) Finally, we compare performance to equally-sized networks operating on individual 3D volumes and observe improvements which are not simply due to an increase in the number of model parameters.

Comparison to Prior Work. Deep learning approaches based on fully convolutional networks have been actively studied for segmentation of thin structures in medical images [4–6]. Incorporating the time dimension, prior work on spatiotemporal segmentation using deep learning fall into one of three categories:

1. Methods operating on the entire 2D+t or 3D+t video sequence, for instance by using 3D recurrent fully convolutional networks to segment 2D US sequences [11,12] or 4D networks to segment 3D sequences [13,14]. Typically, these methods make use of bidirectional recurrent operators, which are more suited for offline sequence processing than unidirectional (online) inference. Furthermore, because these models require the entire sequence to be available, they are more applicable to short video sequences; segmenting an extended 4D US sequence of thousands of frames would not be feasible without significant computational resources.

2. Methods that split segmentation and temporal modeling into separately trained streams or utilize pre-processed temporal input features such as optical flow vectors or deformable motion fields [15,16]. In contrast, our approach requires only the raw image stream and learns temporal features in an end-to-end manner within the recurrent skip-connections.
3. Methods that introduce recurrent nodes directly into the encoder-decoder path [17–19]. Our approach differs by incorporating the recurrent nodes into skip-connections rather than the main path. We posit that this structural change allows clearer separation of spatial and temporal encodings, minimizes depth-wise disruption of back-propagated gradients, and ensures preservation of fine-grain details flowing into the decoder. Placing the recurrent nodes in their own dimension, separated from the encoder, also allows the spatial layers and recurrent temporal layers to be trained separately as a form of implicit regularization.

2 Methods

Network Architecture. The model consists of a recurrent neural network interposed between the halves of a VNet-like encoder-decoder, such that the skip connections of each encoder-decoder layer within the VNet are preserved as they pass through the recurrent nodes (Fig. 1). Unlike [15,17,20,21], we employ a multi-scale set of convolutional gated recurrent units (ConvGRU) [22] which are more efficient (fewer parameters and less complexity) than LSTM units, and additionally, the multi-scale recurrent units are specifically placed between the encoder and the decoder such that recurrence is not applied between scales. Within the ConvGRU, encoded features are concatenated with features from previous time steps before being passed to decoders; this exposes the recurrent node to every previous time point and encoder layer before making a prediction on the current timepoint. We use PReLU nonlinear activations, as well as resize-up-convolutions [23] in the decoder to reduce checkerboard artifacts.

Refinement by Spline Fitting. Predicted segmentations can be refined by using an active-contour-like algorithm to warp piecewise splines onto the image (Fig. 2). Active contours are justified for thin structure segmentation based on previous work first applied to vessel segmentation with curves [24,25] and adopted for surgical device guidance [26,27]. Because the presented data is a time-series and a precomputed device likelihood is available as a data attachment energy, a deformable snake-like model is a natural extension. We use the probability map from the network output as the contour external image energy (E_{match}) and regularize by the L2 norm of the 2nd derivative of the spline (E_{smooth}), as given by Eq. (1). Here, v are the positions of the control points of the spline and H is a function which samples the probability map at v. Using a grid search, we found $a = 1.5$ and $B = 0.15$ to work well for all models. An additional 3D VNet is trained to segment the tip of the device (VNet-small, detailed below). The output is used as a third external energy term whose values $G(x)$ for

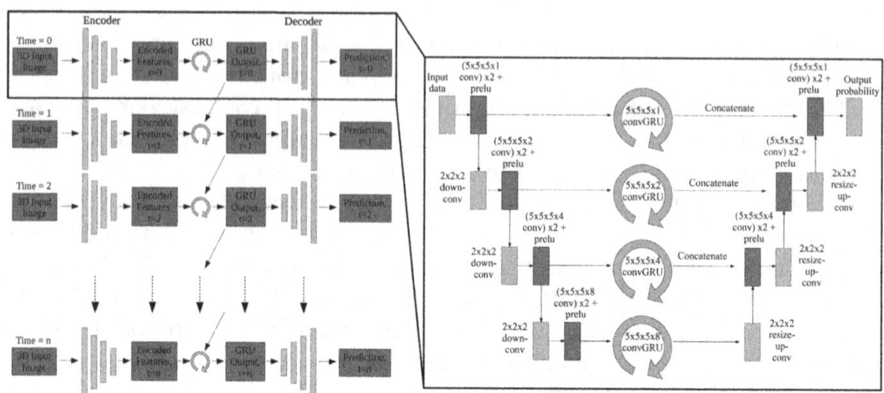

Fig. 1. Recurrent-VNet architecture. Convolutional layers denoted $(5 \times 5 \times 5 \times \mathrm{C}) \times \mathrm{D}$, with C the number of output channels and D the number of convolutional layers.

position x denote the probability of a pixel being the device tip, where $v(0)$ is a spline endpoint. Fixing the other endpoint to the image boundary (by applying L2 penalty to deviations from the boundary), the warp follows minimization of the following objective, where the gradient can be solved with respect to v:

$$E(v) = E_{image} + E_{smooth} + E_{tip} = \alpha H(v) + \beta \left|\left| \frac{d^2 v}{dx^2} \right|\right|^2 + G(v(0)) \tag{1}$$

In this formulation, the first term controls the fit of the spline to the image, the second controls the spline smoothness, and the third controls the position of the spline endpoint. While global tip predictions could be inaccurate due to the propensity of false positives, they provide good local positioning so long as the spline endpoint is initialized near the local minimum around the tip. The spline at each timepoint can be initialized by predictions from the previous timepoint. The result is a piecewise 3D spline mapped to the network predictions.

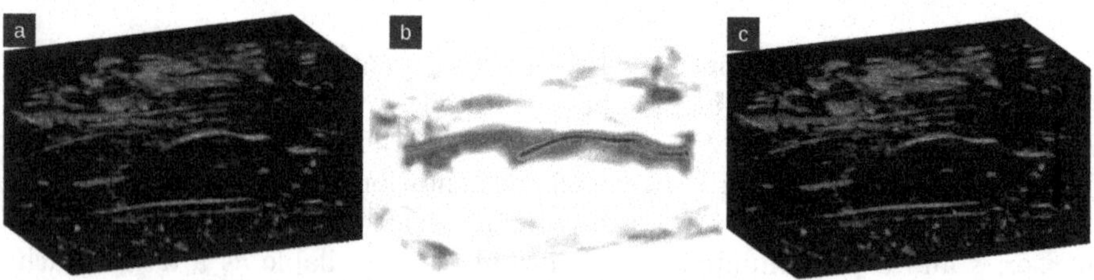

Fig. 2. Spline fit post-processing step. a) Sample 3D US volume (cropped and normalized for visualization). b) Mapped spline shown on external energy map produced by network logit predictions. c) Mapped spline shown on US volume.

Datasets. The models were trained and tested on 4D US sequences collected during endovascular surgical intervention procedures carried out on in vitro phantom models, ex vivo tissues, perfused human cadaver specimens with severe vascular disease, and in vivo beating heart swine models (Table 1). Acquisition frame rate varied but was around 2 Hz. In procedures performed on peripheral vascular anatomy, a guidewire (0.45 mm diameter) was navigated through perfused 3–6 mm diameter arterial vessels at a speeds of 2–10 cm/s, and 4D sequences were collected using a 3D linear US transducer (Philips XL14-3, 3–14 MHz bandwidth). These included in vitro and ex vivo data collected by researchers, as well as vascular disease cadaver data collected by a surgeon while navigating the guidewire through tortuous and diseased arterial vasculature. Meanwhile, in procedures on cardiovascular anatomy, including in the live (beating heart) swine model, a cardiac surgeon performed a trans-septal puncture procedure and navigated a guidewire to the mitral valve under continuous imaging with a 3D trans-esophageal transducer (Philips X8-2T, 2–8 MHz bandwidth). In all sequences, we observed substantial concurrent device and transducer motion. To assess generalizability, we trained only on the peripheral vascular ex vivo data and cardiac in vivo swine data. Meanwhile, data collected from in vitro peripheral vascular phantoms, in vitro cardiovascular phantoms, and human cadavers were left for testing. Additional details about the datasets and experimental procedures are described in Supplementary Fig. 1.

Table 1. Summary of acquired data sets. Separate models were developed for the peripheral and cardio-vascular data. All train/val/test splits were by subject.

Data set	Samples—	Sequences—	Frames	Train/Val/Test %
Peripheral vascular				
Ex vivo tissue with vessels	4	24	800	50/25/25
In vitro perfused vessel phantom	1	4	100	0/0/100 (test only)
Human cadaver with vessels	2	3	61	0/0/100 (test only)
Cardiovascular				
In vivo swine beating heart	1	6	448	50/25/25
In vitro dynamic heart phantom	1	7	396	0/0/100 (test only)

Semi-Automated Annotation Model. To estimate probability H of ground-truth segmentations, we used a simple 3D triangular convolutional filter approximating the hyperechoic appearance of thin devices in US (Supplementary Fig. 2). We then refined the segmentations using a formulation similar to Eq. (1):

$$E(v) = E_{image}(v) + E_{smooth}(v); \quad E_{image}(v) = \alpha H(v); \quad E_{smooth}(v) = \beta \left|\left|\frac{d^2 v}{dx^2}\right|\right|^2 \tag{2}$$

We constrained (with L2 penalty) one endpoint of the spline to ground-truth wire tip positions measured with an embedded tracking sensor. Voxel-wise annotations were produced by extracting the voxels intersecting the spline curve.

Training. Separate networks were trained and evaluated for the peripheral vascular (PV) and cardiovascular (CV) cases, with 50/25/25% splits (by subject) for training, validation, and testing (Table 1). The training data was split into sub-sequences consisting of 10 consecutive frames (3 sub-sequences per batch). Images varied in size but were approximately $200 \times 275 \times 100$ voxels ($0.168 \times 0.168 \times 0.189$ mm resolution) for the PV data and $200 \times 200 \times 200$ ($0.682 \times 0.675 \times 0.629$ mm resolution) for CV data. In each training epoch, six random augmentations (rotations, translations, and scaling) were applied to each sub-sequence to obtain varying $80 \times 80 \times 80$ patches for input into the networks. All training was carried out with k-fold cross-validation using weighted cross-entropy loss and learning rate decay.

Evaluation. We compared the proposed recurrent model (**VNet-RNN**, 377719 parameters) to two traditional VNet models trained on the same data - one identical to the proposed model with the recurrent node removed (**VNet-small**, 122629 parameters), and one designed to match the number of parameters of **VNet-RNN** by adding a $(5 \times 5 \times 5 \times 16) \times 1$ layer and changing the third layer to $(5 \times 5 \times 5 \times 4) \times 3$ (**VNet-large**, total 380789 parameters). We evaluated accuracy using Dice coefficient and mean modified Hausdorff distance (MHD) [28]

$$\text{MHD}(A,B) = \max(d(A,B), d(B,A)), d(A,B) = \frac{1}{N_a} \sum_{a \in A} d(a,B) \qquad (3)$$

where d is a distance between two point sets A and B and N_a is the number of points in a spline a. Whereas Dice provides a measure of pixel overlap, MHD allows a direct evaluation of accuracy in physical (mm) distances.

3 Results

Guidewire Segmentation in Peripheral Vascular Intervention. Table 2 summarizes segmentation accuracies, as measured by MHD and Dice scores, across datasets and methods. Figure 3 presents visual comparisons. The low errors on the test-only data (in vitro vessel phantoms and human cadaver), which were not included in training/validation, suggest the generalizability of all models to different tissues, anatomies, and motions. Meanwhile, in all three data sets (ex vivo, in vitro, and cadaver), we saw significant accuracy improvements using the spatiotemporal model (**VNet-RNN**) compared to VNet models operating on single volumes. Differences were more dramatic ex vivo than in vitro; we hypothesize this is because the spatiotemporal model was better at dealing with noise, ambiguity, and sudden changes in device appearance that were more common in the ex vivo tissues. The spline fitting model (**VNet-RNN+Spline**) described in Eq. (1) further reduced the average error compared to spatiotemporal network predictions without spline fitting (Fig. 2).

On the other hand, comparing the smaller single-frame VNet (**VNet-small**) with the larger model (**VNet-large**), a three-fold increase in the number of network parameters gave no appreciable improvement in segmentation accuracy (and in fact showed worse generalization on test-only data). This suggests that the improved accuracy of the spatiotemporal network, which had a similar number of parameters as **VNet-large**, was not due simply to larger model size.

Guidewire Segmentation in Cardiac Intervention. Similar comparisons were made on cardiovascular data (Table 2). Because **VNet-large** showed worse generalization than **VNet-small** previously, we did not retrain the larger models on the cardiac data. However, consistent with the earlier observations, accuracy improved using the spatiotemporal models (**VNet-RNN** and **VNet-RNN+Spline**) compared to the single-frame models. More apparent examples were again cases where the wire was obscured in a one frame but reappeared with motion. The improvement was most pronounced in vivo (Fig. 3d), likely due to the more challenging in anatomy, reinforcing the idea that temporal information plays a larger role as spatial information becomes degraded.

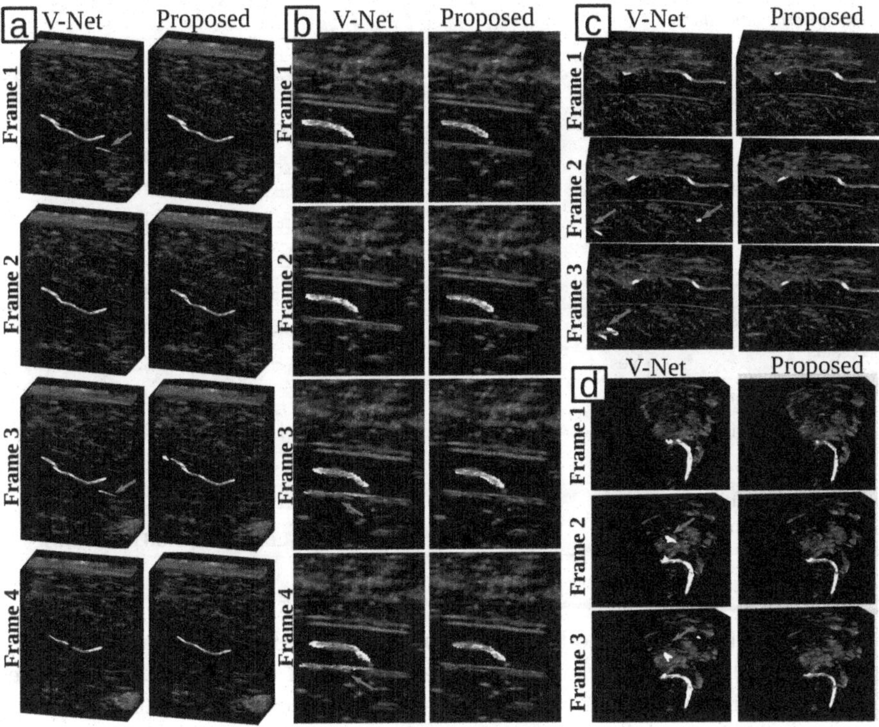

Fig. 3. Selected video frame sequences comparing spatiotemporal network predictions to single-frame **VNet-small**. a&b) Misegmentation of vessel wall, c&d) Misegmentation of echo noise. In both, errors are corrected by the spatiotemporal model.

4 Discussion

This work demonstrates the influence of temporal feature encoding on segmentation of challenging 4D medical image sequences. In particular, we focused on the scenario of very thin (submillimeter), flexible devices (guidewires) moving in and out of obscurity in noisy 4D US sequences, where large segments of the wire are invisible in any single frame. Despite the substantially increased difficulty of the described scenario, our results compare favorably to recent work by other groups, where reported Dice scores fall in the range of 0.53 to 0.57 for in vivo catheter segmentation in 3D cardiac ultrasound [30] and 0.55 for catheter segmentation in 2D X-ray fluoroscopy images [31]. Our results indicate that segmentation using fully convolutional networks may be enhanced with recurrent operations that embed spatial information from previous time points. Furthermore, we demonstrate that the models generalize well to entirely different specimens, anatomy, and tissue sources than those used for training.

Table 2. Segmentation accuracy across datasets and methods.

Data set	Test only	Model	MHD (mm)	Dice
Peripheral vascular				
Ex vivo tissue with vessels	No	VNet-small	2.212 ± 1.895	0.534 ± 0.0769
	No	VNet-large	2.128 ± 2.696	0.519 ± 0.0795
	No	VNet-RNN	1.304 ± 2.102	0.550 ± 0.0848
	No	VNet-RNN+Spline	**0.901 ± 0.727**	**0.596 ± 0.067**
In vitro perfused vessel phantom	Yes	VNet-small	1.783 ± 2.661	0.485 ± 0.100
	Yes	VNet-large	1.904 ± 2.745	0.483 ± 0.086
	Yes	VNet-RNN	1.277 ± 1.509	0.553 ± 0.085
	Yes	VNet-RNN+Spline	**0.864 ± 1.401**	**0.622 ± 0.061**
Human cadaver with vessels	Yes	VNet-small	4.012 ± 2.005	0.492 ± 0.068
	Yes	VNet-RNN	**3.210 ± 1.166**	**0.553 ± 0.048**
Cardiovascular				
In vivo swine (beating heart)	No	VNet-small	5.756 ± 6.094	0.525 ± 0.050
	No	VNet-RNN	**4.100 ± 2.776**	**0.564 ± 0.046**
In vitro dynamic heart phantom	Yes	VNet-small	4.185 ± 1.594	0.583 ± 0.038
	Yes	VNet-RNN	**3.136 ± 3.363**	**0.631 ± 0.031**

Comparisons to VNet models of varying size showed that the improvements were not simply due to an increase in the number of parameters. Rather, we posit that the improvements were due to a feature space weighted moving average effect, allowing stability in predictions where single-frame spatial features are insufficient. Single-frame segmentations were noticeably compromised in frames where the wire was obscured by surrounding anatomical structures, while exposing the models to entire sequences helped to correct these errors. On the other hand, while the temporal encodings generally provide stability on noisy data, it appears possible to also propagate noise over time. In our work, added improvements to stability and accuracy were introduced by constraining the segmentations to a single 3D space curve as a post-processing step. We suspect that future improvements could involve directly incorporating these geometric constraints into the learning process. Finally, our overall observations suggest that temporal encoding will be even more important in real clinical procedures typified by unconstrained device behavior, probe motion, anatomical variability, and physiological complexities resulting from the presence of disease.

Acknowledgements. The authors would like to thank Doug Stanton for the development of the phantom models used in the study. We would like to acknowledge Vipul Pai Raikar, Mingxin Zheng, and Sibo Li for their assistance with the data acquisition setup. We thank Shyam Bharat for reviewing the manuscript.

References

1. Shu, J., Santulli, G.: Update on peripheral artery disease: epidemiology and evidence-based facts. Atherosclerosis **275**, 379–381 (2018)
2. Roth, G.A., Johnson, C., Abajobir, A., et al.: Global, regional, and national burden of cardiovascular diseases for 10 causes, 1990 to 2015. J. Am. Coll. Cardiol. **70**(1), 1–25 (2017)
3. Milletari, F., Navab, N., Ahmadi, S.: V-Net: fully convolutional neural networks for volumetric medical image segmentation. In: 4th International Conference on 3D Vision (2016)
4. Mishra, D., Chaudhury, S., Sarkar, M., Soin, A.: Ultrasound image segmentation: a deeply supervised network with attention to boundaries. IEEE TMBE (2018)
5. Tetteh, G., et al.: DeepVesselNet: vessel segmentation, centerline prediction and bifurcation detection in 3D angiographic volumes. arXiv:1803.09340 [cs.CV] (2018)
6. Merkow, J., Marsden, A., Kriegman, D., Tu, Z.: Dense volume-to-volume vascular boundary detection. In: Ourselin, S., Joskowicz, L., Sabuncu, M.R., Unal, G., Wells, W. (eds.) MICCAI 2016. LNCS, vol. 9902, pp. 371–379. Springer, Cham (2016). https://doi.org/10.1007/978-3-319-46726-9_43
7. Yurdakul, E., Yemez, Y.: Semantic segmentation of RGBD videos with recurrent fully convolutional neural networks. In: Proceedings of the ICCV 2017. IEEE (2017)
8. Tokmakov, P., Alahari, K., Schmid, C.: Learning video object segmentation with visual memory. In: Proceedings of the IEEE ICCV 2017, pp. 4491–4500. IEEE (2017)
9. Valipour, S., Siam, M., Jagersand, M., Ray, N.: Recurrent fully convolutional networks for video segmentation. In: Proceedings of the IEEE WACV 2017. IEEE, Santa Rosa (2017)
10. Oh, S.W., Lee, J.Y., Xu, N., Kim, S.J.: Video object segmentation using space-time memory networks. In: Proceedings of the ICCV 2019. IEEE (2019)
11. Tong, Q., et al.: RIANet: recurrent interleaved attention network for cardiac MRI segmentation. Comput. Biol. Med. **109**, 290–302 (2019)
12. Chen, J., Yang, L., Zhang, Y., Alber, M., Chen, D.Z.: Combining fully convolutional and recurrent neural networks for 3D biomedical image segmentation. In: Proceedings of the NIPS 2016, pp. 3036–3044. Curran (2016)

13. Myronenko, A., et al.: 4D CNN for semantic segmentation of cardiac volumetric sequences. In: Pop, M., et al. (eds.) STACOM 2019. LNCS, vol. 12009, pp. 72–80. Springer, Cham (2020). https://doi.org/10.1007/978-3-030-39074-7_8
14. Sun, C., et al.: Segmentation of 4D images via space-time neural networks. In: Proceedings of the SPIE Medical Imaging 2020. SPIE (2020)
15. Kang, J., Samarasinghe, G., Senanayak, U., Conjeti, S., Sowmya, A.: Deep learning for volumetric segmentation in spatio-temporal data: application to segmentation of prostate in DCE-MRI. In: Proceedings of the ISBI 2019, pp. 61–65. IEEE (2019)
16. Cheng, J., Tsai, Y., Wang, S., Yang, M.S.: SegFlow: joint learning for video object segmentation and optical flow. In: Proceedings of the ICCV (2017)
17. Gao, Y., Phillips, J., Zheng, Y., Min, R., Fletcher, P., Gerig, G.: Fully convolutional structured LSTM networks for joint 4D medical image segmentation. In: Proceedings of the ISBI 2019, pp. 1104–1108. IEEE (2019)
18. Milletari, F., Rieke, N., Baust, M., Esposito, M., Navab, N.: CFCM: segmentation via coarse to fine context memory. In: Frangi, A.F., Schnabel, J.A., Davatzikos, C., Alberola-López, C., Fichtinger, G. (eds.) MICCAI 2018. LNCS, vol. 11073, pp. 667–674. Springer, Cham (2018). https://doi.org/10.1007/978-3-030-00937-3_76
19. Arbelle, A., Raviv, T.R.: Microscopy cell segmentation via convolutional LSTM networks. In: Proceedings of the ISBI (2019)
20. Mathai, T., Jin, L., Gorantla, V., Galeotti, J.: Fast vessel segmentation and tracking in ultra high-frequency ultrasound images. arXiv:1807.08784 [cs.CV] (2019)
21. Fehling, M.K., Grosch, F., Schuster, M.E., Schick, B., Lohscheller, J.: Fully automatic segmentation of glottis and vocal folds in endoscopic laryngeal high-speed videos using a deep Convolutional LSTM Network. PLoS One **15**(2), e0227791 (2020)
22. Ballas, N., Yao, L., Pal, C., Courville, A.: Delving deeper into convolutional networks for learning video representations. arXiv:1511.06432 [cs.CV] (2015)
23. Odena, A., Dumoulin, V., Olah, C.: Deconvolution and checkerboard artifacts (2016). http://distill.pub/2016/deconv-checkerboard/
24. Lesage, D., Angelini, E.D., Bloch, I., Funka-Lea, G.: A review of 3D vessel lumen segmentation techniques: models, features and extraction schemes. Med. Image Anal. **13**(6), 819–845 (2009)
25. Zhao, F., Chen, Y., Hou, Y., He, X.: Segmentation of blood vessels using rule-based and machine-learning-based methods: a review. Multimedia Syst. **25**(2), 109–118 (2017). https://doi.org/10.1007/s00530-017-0580-7
26. Slabaugh, G., Kong, K., Unal, G., Fang, T.: Variational guidewire tracking using phase congruency. In: Ayache, N., Ourselin, S., Maeder, A. (eds.) MICCAI 2007. LNCS, vol. 4792, pp. 612–619. Springer, Heidelberg (2007). https://doi.org/10.1007/978-3-540-75759-7_74
27. Chang, P., Rolls, A., Praetere, H., Poorten, E.: Robust catheter and guidewire tracking using B-spline tube model and pixel-wise posteriors. IEEE Autom. Robot. Lett. **1**, 303–308 (2016)
28. Dubuisson, M.P., Jain, A.K.: A modified Hausdorff distance for object matching. In: ICPR 1994, Jerusalem, Israel, pp. A:566–A:568 (1994)

29. Taha, A.A., Hanbury, A.: Metrics for evaluating 3D medical image segmentation: analysis, selection, and tool. BMC Med. Imaging **15**, 29 (2015)
30. Yang, H., Shan, C., Kolen, A., With, P.H.N.: Improving catheter segmentation and localization in 3D cardiac ultrasound using direction-fused FCN. In: Proceedings of the ISBI (2019)
31. Gherardini, M., Mazomenos, E., Menciassi, A., Stoyanov, D.: Catheter segmentation in X-ray fluoroscopy using synthetic data and transfer learning with light U-nets. Comput. Methods Programs Biomed. **192**, 105420 (2020)

Embedding Weighted Feature Aggregation Network with Domain Knowledge Integration for Breast Ultrasound Image Segmentation

Yuxi Liu, Xing An, Longfei Cong, Guohao Dong, and Lei Zhu(✉)

Shenzhen Mindray BioMedical Electronics, Co., Ltd., Shenzhen, China
zhulei@mindray.com

Abstract. Breast cancer is the most common cancer in women, and ultrasound imaging is one of the most widely used approaches for diagnosis due to its non-radioactive process, ease of operation and low cost. Moreover, image segmentation plays a great role in medical image analysis, since it affects the accuracy of computer aided diagnosis (CAD) results. However, the malignant mass of breast in ultrasound images often appears irregular boundary and indistinct margin which is difficult to distinguish from other surrounding tissues. Therefore, breast ultrasound images segmentation is significant for diagnosis, and it has attracted the attention of researchers for many years. In this paper, we propose a weighted feature aggregation network with fusing domain knowledge for two-dimensional breast ultrasound images segmentation. (I) We modify the U-Net by adding a classification branch, in which BI-RADS category information is applied as the classification label. (II) In order to deal with the artifacts in ultrasound, such as posterior shadowing, we conduct Squeeze-and-Excitation (SE) block and aggregation mechanism to compose the up-sampling part in U-Net. (III) We employ the conditional random field (CRF) to optimize segmentation to make the boundaries more continuous and integral after getting the output of U-Net. The experiment conducted on a challenging and representative dataset includes more than three thousand two-dimensional breast ultrasound images. Our method achieves Jaccard Index of 84.9%, Matthew correlation coefficient of 90.9%, and Dice Coefficient of 90.8% in testing which demonstrates the potential clinical value of our work.

Keywords: Segmentation · Breast ultrasound images · Convolutional Neural Network

1 Introduction

Breast cancer is the most common cancer in women, and has a very high mortality rate around the world. Early detection and diagnosis are of great significance for breast cancer treatment, which is beneficial to raise the survival rate. For breast cancer, ultrasound imaging is one of the most efficient and widely used diagnostic methods due to its non-radioactive process, ease of operation and low cost. Additionally, the Breast Imaging Reporting and Data System (BI-RADS) [1] provides standard terminology to describe

Y. Hu et al. (Eds.): ASMUS 2020/PIPPI 2020, LNCS 12437, pp. 66–74, 2020.
https://doi.org/10.1007/978-3-030-60334-2_7

breast mass as well as classification system for ultrasound. Moreover, it has been proved that BI-RADS is helpful to doctor's diagnosis and the following therapeutic plan.

Image segmentation is an important procedure in research and clinical practice. Accurate segmentation result benefits a lot to the tasks such as diagnosis and treatment planning. Recently, much attention has been paid to the field of deep learning based segmentation methods. For example, the aggregation methods are employed to boost information flow in proposal-based instance segmentation framework [2]. A fast scanning deep convolutional neural network is proposed to segment the breast tumor region in histopathological images [3]. Moreover, a number of research efforts have been devoted to breast ultrasound images segmentation so as to further improve the performance of computer aided diagnosis (CAD) system for breast cancer. We can broadly divide these works into three major types. Firstly, using convolutional neural network such as FCN and U-Net to segment the mass in breast ultrasound images directly [4]. Secondly, using traditional image processing techniques, i.e. thresholding, clustering and active contour model, to segment breast mass in ultrasound images [5, 6]. Thirdly, this type of method emphasizes on integrating domain knowledge to further improve the accuracy of results with Convolutional Neural Networks (CNN) or traditional methods [7].

It should be noticed that the diagnosis results of CAD are highly correlated with the accuracy of breast mass segmentation performance. However, segmentation for breast ultrasound images is still a challenging problem due to the following three reasons. (I) Recent works on CNN based segmentation methods usually consider breast cancer as benign and malignant, whereas it should be classified into four major types (BI-RADS 2, 3, 4 and 5). In other words, domain knowledge of clinical diagnosis in BI-RADS is not fully used and integrated. Another reason for using BI-RADS category instead of benign and malignant is that the lesions' grade lower than 4a are not recommended for biopsy so that there have no pathological diagnosis results for some cases. (II) Artifacts in breast ultrasound images misleads the algorithm in finding a real mass, especially for malignant mass with a shadow behind the posterior border. (III) The obtained mask of CNN always get a rough border, which is not exact enough to characterize the specific local representation of malignancy, such as microlobulated and spiculated.

In view of these issues, we proposed a U-Net [8] based network to segment breast mass accurately and effectively in ultrasound images. The main contributions of our work are three-fold. (I) A classification branch is added in U-Net with integrated domain knowledge to supervise the detection and segmentation of mass. (II) An embedding weighted aggregation module is introduced to fuse the multi-scale attention information in decoding layers, in order to improve the segmentation performance of malignant mass. (III) A fully connected conditional random field (CRF) module is appended at the end of network, which will further increase the segmentation accuracy of mass with indistinct boundaries.

2 Method

The architecture of the proposed framework is illustrated in Fig. 1. The proposed network is primarily based on U-Net, incorporated with a classification branch to integrate the clinical diagnosis knowledge. In the last fewer layers of the network, weighted feature aggregation module and CRF module are embedded. With the above methods, the presented work can not only increase the accuracy of mass segmentation with regular boundary and distinct margin, but also improve the performance to detect malignant mass with artifacts in ultrasound images.

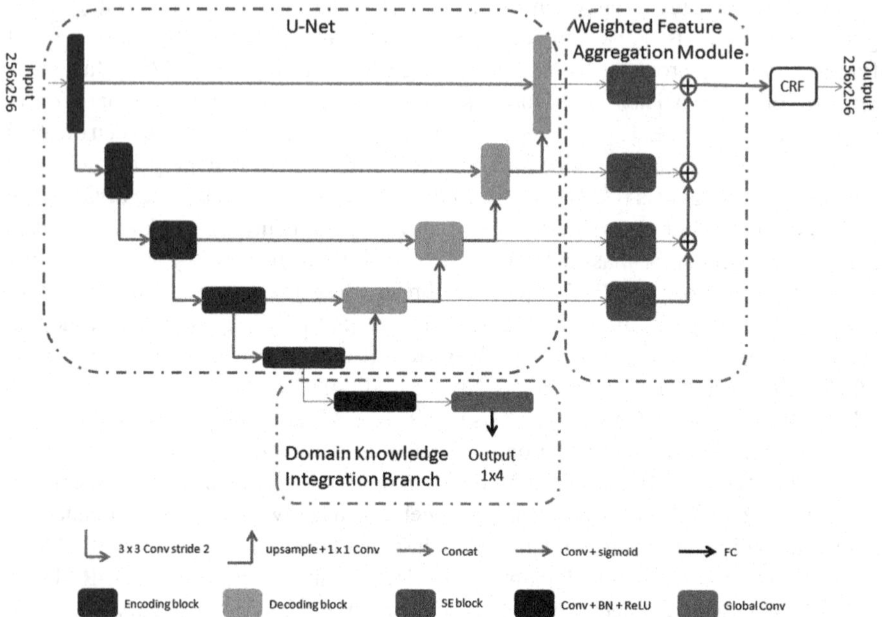

Fig. 1. Illustration of the proposed network, which includes a U-net based encoder-decoder part, a domain knowledge integration branch, a weighted feature aggregation module and a CRF module. 'Conv', 'BN', 'FC', and '+' denotes the convolutional, batch normalization, fully connected layers and addition operation, respectively.

2.1 Domain Knowledge Integration Branch

Inspired by multi-task leaning strategies [9], classification branch is introduced to the U-Net. The generalization ability of breast mass segmentation could be improved by adding a joint learning branch. It is worth noting that BI-RADS divide the mass in breast ultrasound images into several grades according to its possibility of malignancy. Different levels of mass have divergence on the symptom of boundary. Generally, the lower possibility of malignancy the mass is, the more regular and smoother the boundary will be. Therefore, to integrate this domain knowledge, we add a classification branch after the final convolution layer of the top-down path way to predict the BI-RADS category of the mass, instead of using the label of benign and malignant in [7]. As illustrated in Fig. 1, for this classification branch, the inputs go through a stack of 3×3 Conv + BatchNorm + ReLU layers, and then the global convolutional layer generates $1 \times 1 \times C$ feature vector. Finally, a fully connected layer with softmax activation is applied to get the probability for classification, and the softmax cross entropy is used as the loss function. With the BI-RADS information as the supervised label, breast mass detection and segmentation can achieve a better performance.

2.2 Weighted Feature Aggregation Module

Recently, Feature Pyramid Network (FPN) [10] is one of the most used approaches to solve the multi-scale problem in object detection and segmentation. Usually, feature maps of the same scale are summed up along the channel dimension in FPN module. However, not all features in high-level layers are effective for locating the objects. Moreover, artifacts in ultrasound images cause the boundary of mass unclear or invisible such as posterior shadowing where the area posterior to the mass appears darker. As a result, it is difficult for the CNN network even the clinical experts to find the correct edge of the malignant mass. A novel architectural unit called as Squeeze-and-Excitation (SE) block, which can distinguish the importance of different channels of the neural network is introduced in [11]. Inspired by this view, we propose a weighted feature aggregation module to extract and aggregate features and information from multi-scale layers to optimize the performance of mass segmentation. As illustrated in Fig. 1, output of the last four convolutional layers in the decoding path are fed into the SE block to extract the important information of each layer. The details of SE block can be seen in Fig. 2 and the reduction ratio r is set to be 16. The outputs of SE block in each layer are then passed to a 2×2 upsampling layer and a 3×3 convolutional layer with ReLU activation to keep the same dimension of output image as the feature maps in next stage. Finally, all feature maps are summed up along the channel dimension to form the final inputs of the last step. In short, our aggregation module can extracts useful information and combines it with features in each layer through multi-scale information fusion. Thus, region of the mass and its edge in the final feature maps are emphasized in the network.

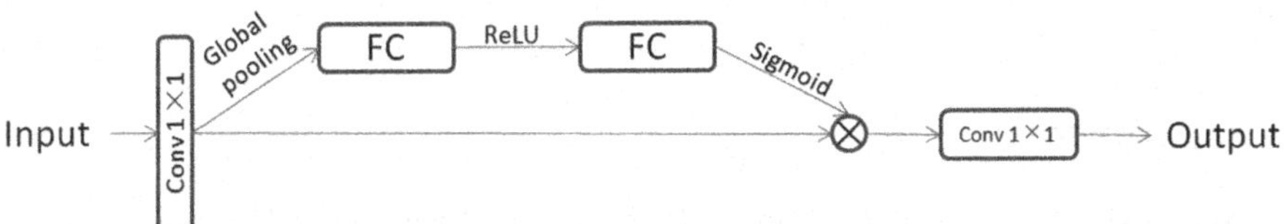

Fig. 2. Illustration of the SE block. '×' denotes multiplication operation.

Finally, a 1×1 convolutional layer followed by sigmoid activation is applied to generate the output. Instead of only using cross-entropy loss for segmentation, we jointly optimize the Dice loss and the cross entropy loss for segmentation task during the training stage, which is defined as:

$$\mathcal{L}_{\text{seg}} = \lambda_1 \mathcal{L}_{\text{Dice}} + \lambda_2 \mathcal{L}_{\text{CE}} \tag{1}$$

where λ_1 and λ_2 are the weights of $\mathcal{L}_{\text{Dice}}$ and $\mathcal{L}_{\text{CE}}$, satisfied with $\lambda_1 = 0.6$ and $\lambda_2 = 0.4$ in this paper. The cross-entropy loss function penalizes pixel classification errors while the dice loss function measures the overlap between the predicted areas and the ground truth. Finally, the training loss of the whole network is

$$\mathcal{L}_{\text{total}} = \mathcal{L}_{\text{cls}} + \alpha\mathcal{L}_{\text{seg}} \tag{2}$$

where α is the hyper-parameter balancing $\mathcal{L}_{\text{cls}}$ and $\mathcal{L}_{\text{seg}}$. In our experiment, weight α is set to 1.

2.3 CRF Refine Module

In fact, it is common that the malignant mass and tissues around it have similar appearance in breast ultrasound images. That is to say, the margin of the malignant mass often appears indistinct, hence it leads to a decrease in accuracy of the output mask of the mass generated by the network directly. To address this problem, we add a fully connected CRF module at the end of our proposed network. This can improve the continuity and integrity of the contour of the mass by allowing spatial constrains between different objects. Given the probability map from the U-Net and the same size of input ultrasound images, we formulate the final results as the inference from CRF model. The energy function of our CRF model is defined as:

$$\mathrm{E(x)} = \sum\nolimits_{\mathrm{i}} \psi_{\mathrm{u}}(x_{\mathrm{i}}) + \sum\nolimits_{\mathrm{i}<j} \psi_{\mathrm{p}}(x_{\mathrm{i}}, x_{\mathrm{j}}) \tag{3}$$

where $\psi_{\mathrm{u}}(x_{\mathrm{i}})$ is the unary potential term which computed independently for each pixel by a classifier that produces a distribution over the label assignment x_{i}. And $\psi_{\mathrm{p}}(x_{\mathrm{i}}, x_{\mathrm{j}}) = \mu(x_{\mathrm{i}}, x_{\mathrm{j}}) \sum_{\mathrm{m}=1}^{\mathrm{K}} \mathrm{w}^{(\mathrm{m})}\mathrm{k}^{(\mathrm{m})}(\mathrm{f_i}, \mathrm{f_j})$ is the pairwise energy term measuring likelihood of the neighboring pixel pair where $\mathrm{k}^{(\mathrm{m})}(\mathrm{f_i}, \mathrm{f_j})$ is a Gaussian kernel, $\mathrm{f_i}$, $\mathrm{f_j}$ is the feature vectors for pixel i and j, $\mathrm{w}^{(\mathrm{m})}$ are linear combination weights, and $\mu(x_{\mathrm{i}}, x_{\mathrm{j}})$ is the label compatibility function. We choose the label x_{i} as our final label and minimize the energy function with 5 iterations based on the mean field approximation algorithm [12].

3 Experiments

Datasets. We conducted experiments on 3341 two-dimensional breast ultrasound images which collected from different hospitals using Mindray Resona 7 Ultrasound Imaging System (Mindray, Shenzhen, China). All the data is reviewed by several experienced ultrasonic physicians and the final diagnosis is obtained by majority voting. There is at least one mass in each image in the dataset. The dataset is divided into six categories, i.e. category 2, category 3, category 4A, category 4B, category 4C, and category5, according to the BI-RADS guideline. There are 702, 883, 358, 356, 291, 753 data for each category, respectively. The data among grades 4A, 4B, and 4C are similar to each other in terms of texture and shape. In most cases, it is not easy to be distinguished even for clinical experts. Moreover, there has a critical imbalance problem of the data, and will cause the divergence in the training stage. Concerning the above problems, we separate the dataset into 4 categories, i.e. category 2, category 3, category 4, and category 5, and randomly split it as training and testing sets in the proportion of 80% and 20%, respectively.

Implementation Details. We automatically cropped all the images with Otsu's thresholding method and only remained the image content, in order to remove the useless regions such as background, probe information, and imaging parameters. Then data augmentations including rotation, shifting, cropping, zooming, and flipping were employed. And the input images were resized to 256 × 256. The initial weight of the backbone network in our proposed method is Resnet-50 [13], which was pre-trained on ImageNet [14], and the parameters of other layers were randomly initialized. The whole frame work was trained on a NVIDIA Titan Xp GPU with batch size of 16. Adam optimizer with a momentum of 0.9 and a weight decay of 0.001 were used to optimize our models. We trained the network for 100 epochs and stop when the validation loss does not decrease significantly and it took approximate 10 h to train the network on our breast dataset.

Evaluation Metrics. We choose U-Net as the baseline network and adopt Jaccard Index, Matthew correlation coefficient (Mcc), and Dice coefficient for quantitative evaluation. These three metrics are defined as

$$\text{Jaccard Index} = \frac{\text{TP}}{\text{FP} + \text{FN} + \text{TP}} \tag{4}$$

$$\text{Mcc} = \frac{\text{TP} \times \text{TN} - \text{FP} \times \text{FN}}{\sqrt[2]{(\text{TP} + \text{FP}) \times (\text{TP} + \text{FN}) \times (\text{TN} + \text{FP}) \times (\text{TN} + \text{FN})}} \tag{5}$$

$$\text{Dice coefficient} = \frac{2 \times \text{TP}}{2 \times \text{TP} + \text{FP} + \text{FN}} \tag{6}$$

where TP refers to true positives, FP refers to false positives, TN refers to true negatives, and FN refers to false negatives.

Quantitative Analysis. We report the segmentation results using the evaluation metrics in Table 1. Our model outperforms Mask R-CNN [15] and U-Net in all three evaluation metrics for breast ultrasound images segmentation task. We have trained and tested the model for three times with the same hyper-parameters to eliminate the influence of random factors. Moreover, Fig. 3 presents qualitative results of different methods on five ultrasound images. As shown in the figure, all methods have a great performance on the mass with a smooth and regular boundary in the first row. As for the mass has an irregular and indistinct border, from the second to fourth rows in Fig. 3, segmentation results of Mask R-CNN and U-Net have some parts of missing or over-segmentation in the indistinct areas. The first two methods cannot detect the small mass in the last row while our method detects and segments the mass accurately.

Ablation Study. We conducted a set of ablation experiments to evaluate the contributions and effectiveness of each component of the proposed methods: (i) U-Net (Baseline), (ii) U-Net equipped with domain knowledge branch, (iii) U-Net with domain knowledge branch and aggregation module, (iv) U-Net with aggregation and CRF modules, (v) our proposed method. The results are shown in Table 2. We choose U-Net as the baseline network, which achieves 80.29%, 86.89%, and 86.71% in terms of Jaccard Index, Mcc, and Dice Index, respectively. When we append the proposed domain knowledge

Table 1. Segmentation performance comparison on breast dataset

Method	Jaccard (%)	Mcc (%)	Dice (%)
Mask R-CNN [15]	79.6	86.2	86
U-Net [8]	80.3	86.9	86.7
Ours	**84.9**	**90.9**	**90.8**

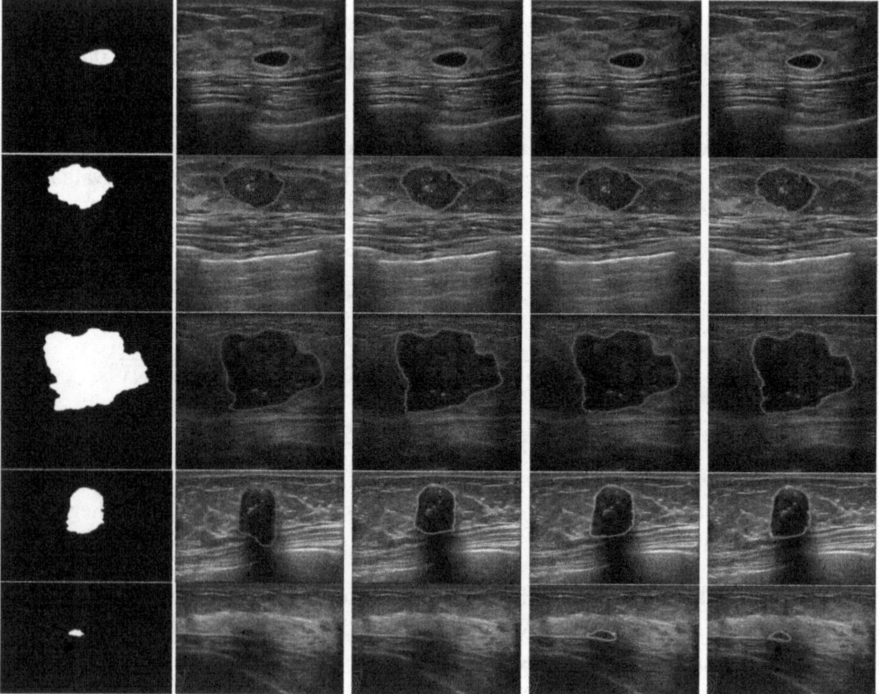

Fig. 3. Qualitative results of segmentation results. From left to right: Ground Truth, Mask R-CNN, U-Net, U-Net + Domain Knowledge and Ours.

integration, it yields results of 81.64%, 88.50%, and 88.59% (Jaccard, Mcc, and Dice). With the weighted aggregation module appended, it brings 0.86%, 0.74%, and 0.49% improvement for Jaccard, Mcc and Dice index. Furthermore, when we adopt all three methods, it significantly improves the performance by 4.56%, 4.04%, and 4.15% for the evaluation metrics compared with the baseline network, which shows the effectiveness of the proposed method.

Table 2. Ablation studies on our network measured by Jaccard Index, Matthew Correlation Coefficient (Mcc) and Dice coefficient.

	Method			Evaluation Metrics		
	DK	Aggregate	CRF	Jaccard (%)	Mcc (%)	Dice (%)
U-Net				80.3	86.9	86.7
	✓			81.6	88.5	88.6
	✓	✓		82.5	89.2	89.1
	✓		✓	83.7	90.0	89.9
		✓	✓	83.4	89.8	89.6
	✓	✓	✓	**84.9**	**90.9**	**90.8**

4 Conclusion

In this paper, we proposed a U-Net based approach for the challenging task of breast mass segmentation on breast ultrasound images. The proposed method takes advantage of both domain knowledge integration and weighted feature aggregation, and obtains an improved performance on malignant mass segmentation. The experiment results demonstrate that our techniques can tackle the segmentation problems of irregular boundary, indistinct margin, and posterior shadowing in breast ultrasound images. Our method provides a fast and accurate ultrasound images processing tool and can be applied to other instance segmentation task in medical field. In the future, the specific BI-RADS information and biopsy results will be investigated and utilized to fine-tune the network when more data is collected.

References

1. D'Orsi, C., et al.: ACR BI-RADS® Atlas, Breast Imaging Reporting and Data System (2013)
2. Liu, S., Qi, L., Qin, H., Shi, J., Jia, J.: Path aggregation network for instance segmentation. In: IEEE CVPR (2018)
3. Su, H., et al.: Region segmentation in histopathological breast cancer images using deep convolutional neural network. In: IEEE 12th International Symposium on Biomedical Imaging (ISBI), pp. 55–58 (2015)
4. Yap, M.H., Goyal, M., Osman, F., et al.: Automated breast ultrasound lesions detection using convolutional neural networks. IEEE J. Biomed. Health Inform., 1 (2017). https://doi.org/10.1109/jbhi.2017.2731873
5. Moon, W.K., et al.: Tumor detection in automated breast ultrasound images using quantitative tissue clustering. Med Phys. **41**(4), 042901 (2014)
6. Moraru, L., Moldovanu, S., Biswas, A.: Optimization of breast lesion segmentation in texture feature space approach. Med. Eng. Phys. **36**(1), 129–135 (2014)
7. Cao, Z., et al.: Breast tumor detection in ultrasound images using deep learning. In: Wu, G., Munsell, B.C., Zhan, Y., Bai, W., Sanroma, G., Coupé, P. (eds.) Patch-MI 2017. LNCS, vol. 10530, pp. 121–128. Springer, Cham (2017). https://doi.org/10.1007/978-3-319-67434-6_14

8. Ronneberger, O., Fischer, P., Brox, T.: U-Net: convolutional networks for biomedical image segmentation. In: Navab, N., Hornegger, J., Wells, W.M., Frangi, A.F. (eds.) MICCAI 2015. LNCS, vol. 9351, pp. 234–241. Springer, Cham (2015). https://doi.org/10.1007/978-3-319-24574-4_28
9. Caruana, R.: Multitask learning. Mach. Learn. **28**(1), 41–75 (1997)
10. Lin, T.Y., Dollár, P., Girshick, R., He, K., Hariharan, B., Belongie, S.: Feature pyramid networks for object detection. In: IEEE CVPR, pp. 2117–2125 (2017)
11. Hu, J., Shen, L., Albanie, S.: Squeeze-and-excitation networks, pp. 7132–7141 (2018). https://doi.org/10.1109/cvpr.2018.00745
12. Zheng, S., Jayasumana, S., Romera-Paredes, B., et al.: Conditional random fields as recurrent neural networks. In: ICCV, pp. 1529–1537 (2015)
13. He, K., Zhang, X., Ren, S., Sun, J.: Deep residual learning for image recognition. In: The IEEE Conference on Computer Vision and Pattern Recognition (CVPR), pp. 770–778 (2016)
14. Simonyan, K., Zisserman, A.: Very deep convolutional networks for large-scale image recognition. arXiv preprint arXiv:1409.1556 (2014)
15. He, K., Gkioxari, G., Dollár, P., Girshick, R.: Mask R-CNN. In: 2017 ICCV, pp. 2980–2988 (2017)

A Curriculum Learning Based Approach to Captioning Ultrasound Images

Mohammad Alsharid[1](✉), Rasheed El-Bouri[1], Harshita Sharma[1], Lior Drukker[2], Aris T. Papageorghiou[2], and J. Alison Noble[1]

[1] Institute of Biomedical Engineering, University of Oxford, Oxford, UK
mohammad.alsharid@eng.ox.ac.uk

[2] Nuffield Department of Women's and Reproductive Health, University of Oxford, Oxford, UK

Abstract. We present a novel curriculum learning approach to train a natural language processing (NLP) based fetal ultrasound image captioning model. Datasets containing medical images and corresponding textual descriptions are relatively rare and hence, smaller-sized when compared to the datasets of natural images and their captions. This fact inspired us to develop an approach to train a captioning model suitable for small-sized medical data. Our datasets are prepared using real-world ultrasound video along with synchronised and transcribed sonographer speech recordings. We propose a "dual-curriculum" method for the ultrasound image captioning problem. The method relies on building and learning from curricula of image and text information for the ultrasound image captioning problem. We compare several distance measures for creating the dual curriculum and observe the best performance using the Wasserstein distance for image information and tf-idf metric for text information. The evaluation results show an improvement in all performance metrics when using curriculum learning over stochastic mini-batch training for the individual task of image classification as well as using a dual curriculum for image captioning.

Keywords: Image captioning · Curriculum learning · Fetal ultrasound

1 Introduction

Image captioning involves the generation of words constituting a descriptive caption given an image of interest. Image captioning has proven to be popular in computer vision, and this fact is illustrated by the number of datasets consisting of natural images and their corresponding captions made available as large-scale datasets [4]. Medical image captioning is an area of growing interest because of the potential to automate reporting and assist non-experts in interpreting images. Generating clinically meaningful captions requires medical experts for the annotation process; however, such experts are an expensive and often scarce

M. Alsharid and R. El-Bouri—Equal contribution.

Y. Hu et al. (Eds.): ASMUS 2020/PIPPI 2020, LNCS 12437, pp. 75–84, 2020.
https://doi.org/10.1007/978-3-030-60334-2_8

resource. Using crowd-sourcing services, as used in some natural image captioning tasks, is not an option since laypeople do not possess the professional knowledge to describe clinical images. In addition, patient privacy and confidentiality prevent the widespread sharing of sensitive medical data. Unfortunately, these facts leave researchers with relatively small-sized datasets of medical images and their corresponding captions. Therefore, in this paper, we consider a training regimen more suited and tailored for small-sized multi-modal medical data of images and text. The contribution of this paper is the development of algorithms to prepare suitable curricula using curriculum learning techniques from a relatively small-sized training dataset and the demonstration of how this leads to improved deep learning-based image classification and captioning models for fetal ultrasound images. To the best of our knowledge, this is the first work to propose a curriculum learning technique to prepare curricula based on both medical image and text data concurrently for the task of medical image captioning.

Randomly shuffling the training dataset throughout the epochs of training is standard practice in deep learning. This randomness is meant to help regularise model training. The goal of regularisation is to prevent the values of model parameters from getting stuck in local minima of the optimisation function.

In curriculum learning, the defining concept is the order in which data samples are introduced. Thus, curriculum learning also attempts to perform regularisation but in a more organised, less random way. Curriculum learning was introduced in [3] to mimic the way that learning occurs in humans. Humans are trained with a curriculum that begins with easy concepts and progresses to harder, more 'complex' topics [9]. In the literature, a number of ways to approach and define curriculum learning have been proposed [5]. In this paper, curriculum learning is independent of any specifics of the model architecture or its hyperparameters that determine how it is trained. The only aspect under consideration is how the training batches are prepared and presented to the network. Curriculum learning techniques address the fact that optimising the parameters of a neural network is a non-convex problem. Therefore, a function's global minimum is not necessarily reachable, and the lowest possible error cannot be obtained during normal stochastic mini-batch gradient descent training [3,5].

Related Works. There have only been a few studies investigating the captioning of ultrasound images. A convolutional neural network (CNN) based captioning model for second trimester fetal ultrasound images that fuses text and image information for the next word generation is described in [2]. In that method, random shuffling of training data was used without any optimization based on sample complexity. We improve on the findings of [2] using a curriculum learning approach for small-sized datasets; however, a direct comparison with that paper is not possible due to the use of different datasets (details in Sect. 3). An image captioning framework to caption ultrasound images of the abdomen is built in [23]. Their framework begins with a classifier to identify the structure of interest in the given abdominal ultrasound image, before passing the ultrasound image to the encoding convolutional neural network (CNN) of the captioning model of that structure. In contrast, in the current paper, the classifier is effectively also responsible for encoding the image information for the captioning model. Examples of using curriculum learning exist in computer vision [18] and natural language processing [6,10,22] as well as a few in biomedical imaging applications, such as classification of lesions in chest X-rays [17] to address weakly labeled data and detection of cardiac MR motion artefacts [14] to deal with class imbalance. In this paper, we consider techniques to build curricula to aid in the captioning of second trimester fetal ultrasound images. To the best of our knowledge, this paper is the first work towards optimizing results in medical image captioning, a multi-modal task, for small-sized real-world datasets, by proposing the training of the deep neural network in an organised manner through a dual curriculum.

2 Methods

Curriculum Learning and Distance Measures. To understand curriculum learning, we first define a metric, H, that encodes some notion of complexity (examples of H are defined in the paragraphs below). We then split the training dataset into batches according to this complexity such that $H[B_i] < H[B_j]$, where B is a batch of data from our training set, i is an index of an earlier batch, and j is an index of a later batch. These batches are ordered for presentation to the network and training according to the choice of curriculum. There is no current consensus on what a general curriculum looks like as a curriculum is usually tailored to the problem at hand. For example, for some problems, models achieve greater performance when trained with 'anti-curricula' (presentation of data from high 'complexity' or entropy to low) [3,13]. In this paper, we experiment with various configurations and curriculum strategies.

It has been hypothesized that curriculum learning performs a similar function to numerical continuation methods [3], whereby a complex surface is approximated by a smooth version before increasing the complexity of that surface to become more similar to the original [1]. Entropy is a measure of randomness and uncertainty. Data samples with low entropy with respect to the mean of the samples are 'easier' to learn from. In terms of the curriculum, by optimising with a low entropy, 'easy' to learn batch, we provide a smoother version of the prediction error surface. By training sequentially with data in higher 'complexity' batches, we progressively increase the complexity of the surface while already having some parameters within the domain of a minimum which takes the solution closer to the global minimum, thus giving us model weights that can provide better results. In this work, when building an image-based curriculum, we experiment with the Mahalanobis distance [11], the cosine similarity and the Wasserstein distance as H metrics. We perform experiments using a forward curriculum (low H to high H). The data samples for image focused tasks are image feature vectors extracted through a finetuned VGG16 [21].

The Mahalanobis distance d_{ml} measures how far, or how different, an image feature vector $\boldsymbol{x}_n$ is from the mean of the samples $\boldsymbol{u}$. It is the multi-dimensional generalisation of standard deviation from the mean and given in Eq. 1,

$$d_{ml} = ((\boldsymbol{x}_n - \boldsymbol{u})^T S^{-1} (\boldsymbol{x}_n - \boldsymbol{u}))^{(1/2)} \tag{1}$$

where S is the covariance matrix.

The cosine similarity d_{cos} is defined in Eq. 2. We use a fixed reference (mean) vector to compare the dot products of model inputs with.

$$d_{cos} = \boldsymbol{x}_n \boldsymbol{u} / |\boldsymbol{x}_n||\boldsymbol{u}| \tag{2}$$

The Wasserstein distance d_{ws} is defined as the distance between two distributions and is mathematically defined in Eq. 3,

$$d_{ws} = \inf_{\pi \in \Gamma(\hat{x}_n, \hat{u})} \int_{R \times R} |m - n| d\pi(m, n) \tag{3}$$

where Γ denotes the collection of all measures on a space, $R \times R$, over all joint distributions of the random variables m and n with marginals $\hat{x}_n$ and $\hat{u}$ respectively. In this case, $\hat{x}_n$ and $\hat{u}$ are the softmaxed distributions of our features and the mean of the features respectively. The use of the Wasserstein distance arose to determine the optimal transport of piles of sand, represented by the distributions $\hat{x}_n$ and $\hat{u}$ [15]. To use a Wasserstein distance-based curriculum, we first apply a softmax function on the image feature vectors, representing them as distributions. Then, the distance between the distribution of every image vector and the distribution of the mean feature vector is computed.

For preparing text-focused curricula, we used term frequency–inverse document frequency (tf-idf) score [19], as calculated by Eq. 4:

$$d_{ti} = \frac{\#(w \in c)}{\Sigma_{w_i}^{W} \#(w_i \in c)} \ln \frac{\#(c \in C)}{\#(c \; if \; w \in c)} \tag{4}$$

where d_{ti} is a word's tf-idf score, $\#()$ is a count function, w is a word, c is a caption, W are all the words in caption c, and C are all the captions in the dataset. It provides a measure of the meaningfulness that a word possesses. For each caption, the tf-idf scores of its constituent words are summed, allowing us to incorporate the length of a caption into its complexity.

The dual curriculum, as used in the captioning task, uses two metrics of complexity, one for each data modality, namely, image H_1 and text H_2. Each metric ranks the data samples s in the dataset S differently. With dual curriculum, we combine these rankings. The scales used by the different metrics are not the same, so it was necessary to first normalise each metric before obtaining a combined measure of 'difficulty'. This allows us to take into account the difficulty associated with both images and text as shown in Eq. 5:

$$d_{dc} = \frac{H_{1s} - min(H_1)}{max(H_1) - min(H_1)} + \frac{H_{2s} - min(H_2)}{max(H_2) - min(H_2)} \tag{5}$$

Image Classification Model. Before considering the image captioning task, we first consider which distance metric works best for the simpler task of fetal ultrasound image classification. This image classification model is later used as the image information branch of the image captioning model shown in Fig. 1. In other words, the upper branch of the image captioning model serves as the

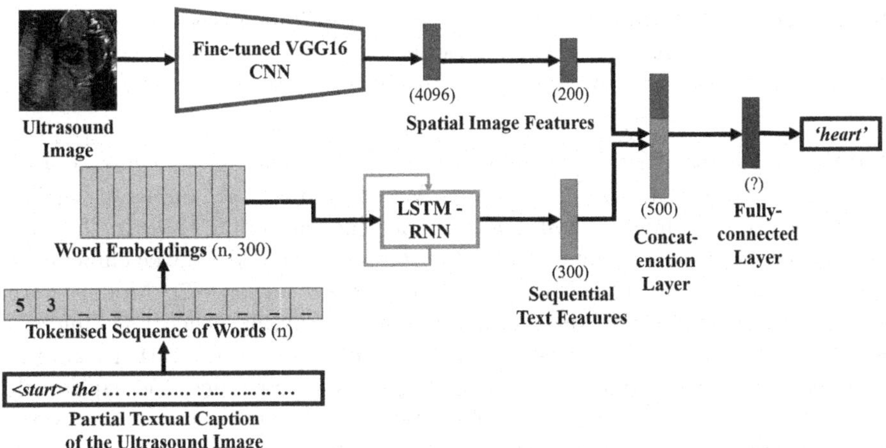

Fig. 1. The image captioning model. 'n' represents the maximum sequence length.

base of the image classification model. Specifically, the problem is to classify an ultrasound image given four classes; the abdomen, the head, the heart, and the spine. We consider a pre-trained VGG16 [21] that has been fine-tuned on fetal ultrasound images. The images and labels used in fine-tuning the VGG16 are obtained from video clips in the US scan videos that were manually labelled based on the viewed anatomies [20]. The VGG16 architecture provides image feature vectors that can serve as input for a shallow 3-layer image classifier. We compare four variants of the model for evaluation of distance measures trained using: 1) mini-batches with stochastic gradient descent and random sampling, 2) a Mahalanobis distance based image curriculum (MD-IC), 3) a cosine similarity based image curriculum (CD-IC), 4) a Wasserstein distance based image curriculum (WD-IC).

Image Captioning Model. Figure 1 shows the image captioning model. The image captioning model consists of two separate branches for image and text modalities, combined in a late fusion configuration using a concatenation layer followed by a fully-connected classification layer [2]. The upper branch followed by a fully-connected layer with softmax activation represents the image feature classifier model. '?' represents a varying number of words depending on the vocabulary of the anatomical structure that the specific captioning model would correspond to. For the image captioning task, we explored three different dual-curriculum options (MD-DC, CD-DC, WD-DC) that combine metrics discussed in the previous section with the tf-idf score. Four captioning models were trained, one for each anatomical structure. During training the partial caption comes from the ground truth caption, whereas at inference, the model would rely on its previously generated words. At inference, the US image was first classified using the trained US image classifier. Once the associated anatomical structure of the image was determined, the corresponding captioning model was deployed to caption the image. Posing the captioning problem this way places a high importance on first correctly identifying the structure.

Training Process. In all experiments, the loss function was categorical cross entropy, and Adam optimisation was used. When training, the number of batches was 32 for the classification task and eight for the captioning task. In the captioning tasks, the words were embedded with fine-tunable Word2vec embedding vectors that were pre-trained on the Google News corpus [12]. Models were trained for 150 epochs with early stopping. During training, teacher forcing was used where partial captions consisted of the ground truth words rather than the words the model generated at previous steps, but at inference, the captioning model had to rely on its previously generated words to generate the next word in the caption. Dropout was applied throughout with a rate between 0.4 and 0.5.

3 Experiments

Dataset and Data Preparation. The image-caption pairs were obtained from ten full-length fetal ultrasound scans as part of the PULSE study [8]. The mean length of the videos is 37 min. The UK Research Ethics Committee (Reference 18/WS/0051) approved this study. Written informed consent was given by all participating pregnant women and sonographers. The images were obtained from ultrasound video frames [8] with audio additionally recorded. The audio recordings were transcribed to provide the captions for the images in the dataset [2]. In this work, we use a total of ten full-length transcribed videos, as opposed to five videos in [2]. Seven video scans were used for training, two were used for validation, and one was used for testing. The training and validation data were subsampled to ensure an equal distribution of the four different anatomical structures in the dataset. A total of 12808 image-caption pairs were used for training and validation. The test set consisted of 9979 image-caption pairs. All images were cropped to remove the user interface, keeping only the ultrasound image, and then resized to 224×224 pixels. All punctuation was dropped from the text, and all letters made lowercase.

Performance Evaluation. To evaluate the model performance, we use the $F1$ score, *BLEU-1 (B1)* [16], *ROUGE-L (RL)* [7], and *ARS* (the Anatomical Relevance Score) as introduced in [2]. *BLEU-1* and *ROUGE-L* have been slightly modified for the task at hand as follows. Traditionally, both these metrics check that two captions are similar based on their constituent words with no regard to the actual semantic relevance of the generated words to those in the ground truth caption. In order to prevent relatively high scores being obtained when no relevant anatomical terminology is generated, we calculate *B1* and *RL* by modifying them according to the anatomical classification performance.

Table 1. Image classification

Metric	P	R	$F1$
No curriculum	0.83	0.76	0.73
CD-IC	0.63	0.73	0.67
MD-IC	0.94	0.95	0.95
WD-IC	**0.96**	**0.96**	**0.96**

Table 2. Image captioning

Metric	$B1$	RL	ARS	$F1$
No curriculum	0.18	0.37	0.23	0.77
CD-DC	0.22	0.34	0.22	0.73
MD-DC	0.25	**0.47**	0.40	0.96
WD-DC	**0.27**	0.42	**0.43**	**0.97**

Each image has a ground truth label (one of the four anatomical structures), hence, when evaluating a captioning model, the $B1$ and RL scores for the corpus (i.e the image-captioning test set of that structure) are multiplied by the percentage of images that are correctly classified by the image classification model of the same curriculum. If the percentage of correctly classified images is high (e.g. 90%) for that structure, the $B1$ and RL scores for that structure will only be slightly reduced. If the percentage of images that are misclassified is high, the $B1$ and RL scores will drop. This will penalise models for generating captions describing the wrong structure. We then take the mean of the scores for each structure.

4 Results and Discussion

The results for the image classification task are shown in Table 1 (P: Precision, R: Recall). We observe that the WD-IC trained model outperformed the traditionally trained (no curriculum) model and the CD-IC trained model. The latter two relatively struggled. The MD-IC trained model performed well and was only slightly inferior in terms of accuracy to the WD-IC model. For the classification problem, the WD-IC and MD-IC models both performed comparably well, and we see this behavior extended into the captioning problem.

Figure 2 shows the distribution of structures in ten batches prepared by an MD-IC, a CD-IC, and a WD-IC. For visualisation purposes, we assume that the data is split into ten batches. A higher batch number would mean 'harder' data samples in the batch. From this visualisation, we can observe class imbalance in the batches. Preliminary experiments in image classification showed that the curricula struggled when batches had a disproportionate number of samples of the different structures as in Fig. 2. Future work will investigate this observation. To alleviate this problem, for the rest of the experiments reported in this paper, batch preparation was done through the curricula as follows. Rather than having a single mean of the whole dataset from which a distance measure is calculated for each data sample, each structure had its own mean. In each of these balanced batches, for each structure, we had data samples with the lowest entropy relative to that structure's mean instead of the data samples with the lowest entropy relative to the mean of the whole dataset.

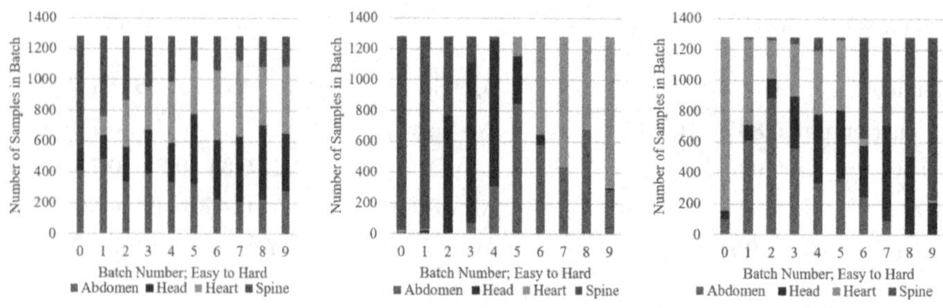

Fig. 2. Distribution of anatomical structures in an MD-IC (left), a CD-IC (center), and a WD-IC (right) with non-balanced batches (with respect to anatomy class).

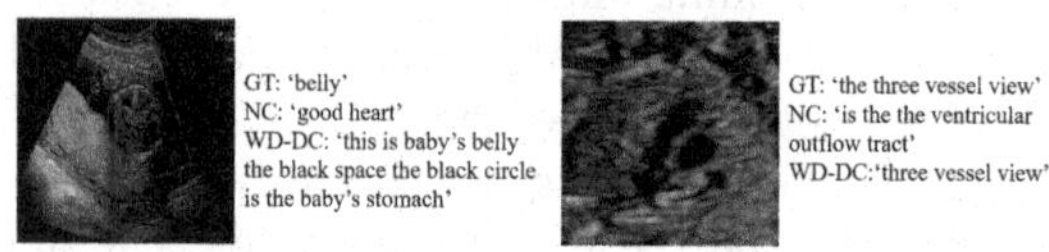

Fig. 3. Qualitative results for an abdomen image and a heart image. GT is for 'Ground Truth'. 'NC' is for 'No Curriculum'.

Qualitative results of the image captioning task are shown in Fig. 3. Quantitative results are summarized in Table 2. We notice an improvement when compared to the traditionally trained model. WD-DC is superior to other curricula for three out of four metrics. The reason RL is lower for WD-DC than for MD-DC is discussed as follows. RL looks for the longest common subsequence (series of words) between the ground truth and generated captions, whereas $B1$ looks for single words in common. There might be a certain multiple-word-long way to phrase captions that exists in the training set that the model trained with MD-DC seems to be better at emulating; however, not phrasing the captions in this way is not indicative of loss of relevant information because otherwise we would have noticed ARS and $F1$ to be lower for WD-DC than for MD-DC.

5 Conclusion and Future Work

Curriculum learning helps to train more accurate models than using a traditional stochastic mini-batch preparation process does for image captioning. We built curricula for image classification and image captioning tasks suitable for small-sized medical datasets. In particular, we found the Wasserstein-distance-based curriculum and the Mahalanobis-distance-based curriculum to be good options for automatic fetal ultrasound image captioning. In the future, we will investigate if curriculum learning could help obtain comparable results while using a simpler model with less trainable parameters for real time video captioning applications.

Acknowledgement. We acknowledge the ERC (ERC-ADG-2015 694 project PULSE), the EPSRC (EP/MO13774/1), the Rhodes Trust, and the NIHR BRC funding scheme. ReB is supported by an EPSRC Industrial Strategy Challenge Fund PhD studentship.

References

1. Allgower, E.L., Georg, K.: Numerical Continuation Methods: An Introduction. Springer Series in Computational Mathematics, vol. 13. Springer Science & Business Media, Berlin, Heidelberg (2012). https://doi.org/10.1007/978-3-642-61257-2
2. Alsharid, M., Sharma, H., Drukker, L., Chatelain, P., Papageorghiou, A.T., Noble, J.A.: Captioning ultrasound images automatically. In: Shen, D., et al. (eds.) MICCAI 2019. LNCS, vol. 11767, pp. 338–346. Springer, Cham (2019). https://doi.org/10.1007/978-3-030-32251-9_37
3. Bengio, Y., Louradour, J., Collobert, R., Weston, J.: Curriculum learning. In: Proceedings of the 26th Annual International Conference on Machine Learning, pp. 41–48 (2009)
4. Bernardi, R., et al.: Automatic description generation from images: a survey of models, datasets, and evaluation measures. J. Artif. Intell. Res. **55**, 409–442 (2016)
5. El Bouri, R., Eyre, D., Watkinson, P., Zhu, T., Clifton, D.: Student-teacher curriculum learning via reinforcement learning: predicting hospital inpatient admission location. arXiv preprint arXiv:2007.01135 (2020)
6. Cirik, V., Hovy, E., Morency, L.P.: Visualizing and understanding curriculum learning for long short-term memory networks. arXiv preprint arXiv:1611.06204 (2016)
7. Lin, C.-Y.: Rouge: a package for automatic evaluation of summaries. In: Proceedings of the Workshop on Text Summarization Branches Out, Barcelona, Spain, pp. 56–60 (2004)
8. Department of Engineering Science: Pulse (2019). https://www.eng.ox.ac.uk/pulse/. https://www.eng.ox.ac.uk/pulse/
9. El-Bouri, R., Eyre, D., Watkinson, P.J., Zhu, T., Clifton, D.: Hospital admission location prediction via deep interpretable networks for the year-round improvement of emergency patient care. IEEE J. Biomed. Health Inf. **PP**(99), 1 (2020)
10. Liu, C., He, S., Liu, K., Zhao, J.: Curriculum learning for natural answer generation. In: Proceedings of the 27th International Joint Conference on Artificial Intelligence, pp. 4223–4229 (2018)
11. Mahalanobis, P.C.: On the generalized distance in statistics. National Institute of Science of India (1936)
12. Mikolov, T., Chen, K., Corrado, G., Dean, J.: Efficient estimation of word representations in vector space. arXiv preprint arXiv:1301.3781 (2013)
13. Morerio, P., Cavazza, J., Volpi, R., Vidal, R., Murino, V.: Curriculum dropout. In: Proceedings of the IEEE International Conference on Computer Vision, pp. 3544–3552 (2017)
14. Oksuz, I., et al.: Automatic CNN-based detection of cardiac MR motion artefacts using k-space data augmentation and curriculum learning. Med. Image Anal. **55**, 136–147 (2019)
15. Panaretos, V.M., Zemel, Y.: Statistical aspects of Wasserstein distances. Ann. Rev. Stat. Appl. **6**, 405–431 (2019)

16. Papineni, K., Roukos, S., Ward, T., Zhu, W.J.: BLEU: a method for automatic evaluation of machine translation. In: Proceedings of the 40th Annual Meeting on Association for Computational Linguistics, pp. 311–318. Association for Computational Linguistics (2002)
17. Park, B., et al.: A curriculum learning strategy to enhance the accuracy of classification of various lesions in Chest-PA X-ray screening for pulmonary abnormalities. Sci. Rep. **9**(1), 1–9 (2019)
18. Ren, Z., Wang, X., Zhang, N., Lv, X., Li, L.J.: Deep reinforcement learning-based image captioning with embedding reward. In: Proceedings of the IEEE Conference on Computer Vision and Pattern Recognition, pp. 290–298 (2017)
19. Sammut, C., Webb, G.I. (eds.): TF-IDF, pp. 986–987. Springer, Boston (2010)
20. Sharma, H., Droste, R., Chatelain, P., Drukker, L., Papageorghiou, A., Noble, J.: Spatio-temporal partitioning and description of full-length routine fetal anomaly ultrasound scans. In: 2019 IEEE 16th International Symposium on Biomedical Imaging (ISBI 2019), pp. 987–990. IEEE (2019)
21. Simonyan, K., Zisserman, A.: Very deep convolutional networks for large-scale image recognition. arXiv preprint arXiv:1409.1556 (2014)
22. Tsvetkov, Y., Faruqui, M., Ling, W., MacWhinney, B., Dyer, C.: Learning the curriculum with Bayesian optimization for task-specific word representation learning. In: Proceedings of the 54th Annual Meeting of the Association for Computational Linguistics (vol. 1: Long Papers), pp. 130–139 (2016)
23. Zhu, X., Li, L., Liu, J., Peng, H., Niu, X.: Captioning transformer with stacked attention modules. Appl. Sci. **8**(5), 739 (2018)

Deep Image Translation for Enhancing Simulated Ultrasound Images

Lin Zhang[1(✉)], Tiziano Portenier[1], Christoph Paulus[2], and Orcun Goksel[1]

[1] Computer-assisted Applications in Medicine, ETH Zurich, Zürich, Switzerland
lin.zhang@vision.ee.ethz.ch
[2] VirtaMed AG, Schlieren, Switzerland

Abstract. Ultrasound simulation based on ray tracing enables the synthesis of highly realistic images. It can provide an interactive environment for training sonographers as an educational tool. However, due to high computational demand, there is a trade-off between image quality and interactivity, potentially leading to sub-optimal results at interactive rates. In this work we introduce a deep learning approach based on adversarial training that mitigates this trade-off by improving the quality of simulated images with constant computation time. An image-to-image translation framework is utilized to translate low quality images into high quality versions. To incorporate anatomical information potentially lost in low quality images, we additionally provide segmentation maps to image translation. Furthermore, we propose to leverage information from acoustic attenuation maps to better preserve acoustic shadows and directional artifacts, an invaluable feature for ultrasound image interpretation. The proposed method yields an improvement of 7.2% in Fréchet Inception Distance and 8.9% in patch-based Kullback-Leibler divergence.

Keywords: Ray tracing · Attenuation · Generative adversarial nets

1 Introduction

Ultrasound (US) is a low-cost, real-time, and portable diagnostic imaging technique without ionizing radiation, hence widely used in gynecology and obstetrics. Since its interpretation can be nontrivial due to ultrasound-specific artifacts such as acoustic shadows and tissue-specific speckle texture, sonographer training is crucial. For an education tool, ray tracing can be used for US simulation [3,14], where US wavefront is represented with rays on the GPU to simulate interaction with tissue layers, whereas speckle patterns are simulated with a convolutional model of tissue speckle noise. With stochastic Monte-Carlo sampling of rays [11], this can produce realistic looking images. However, interactive computational constraints often necessitate a compromise in image quality, e.g. with limited number of rays or by disabling or reducing essential simulation features.

Deep learning has achieved great success in various computer vision and graphics tasks. In particular, generative adversarial networks (GANs) [5] have been demonstrated as a powerful tool for image synthesis and translation [8,23].

Y. Hu et al. (Eds.): ASMUS 2020/PIPPI 2020, LNCS 12437, pp. 85–94, 2020.
https://doi.org/10.1007/978-3-030-60334-2_9

GANs have been widely adapted for various medical image synthesis tasks, such as image inpainting [2] and cross modality translation in both supervised [1,13] and unsupervised [20,22] settings. In US image synthesis, a two-stage stack GAN was introduced in [17] for simulating intravascular US imagery conditioned on tissue echogenicity map. In [7], freehand US images are generated conditioned on calibrated physical coordinates. Recently in [18], feasibility of improving the realism of ray-traced US images has been demonstrated using cycleGAN [23].

In this work we propose a deep learning based approach for improving the quality of simulated US images that are obtained using a ray tracing algorithm, such that computationally simpler (low quality) images can be used to generate higher quality images mimicking a computationally sophisticated simulation that may not be feasible at interactive frame rates. Access to a simulation framework together with comprehensive anatomical models allows us to obtain realistic paired images of differing quality aligned with anatomical models. Therefore, we tackle this problem in an image-to-image translation setting with paired low and high quality images. Our framework leverages conditional GANs [12] to recover image features that are missing in the low quality images. Since low quality images may have missing anatomical structures, which introduces ambiguities in the image translation process, we propose to additionally leverage information that is readily available from the underlying simulation algorithm. For this purpose, we use 2D segmentation map slices at given transducer locations, to provide any anatomical information missing from low quality images. Since major acoustic effects such as shadows are integral along wave path and hence global in nature, they would require large network receptive fields to model. Thus, we further propose to incorporate integral attenuation maps as additional input to the network. Such segmentation and attenuation maps can be easily obtained as by-products of ray-based simulation frameworks [3,11,14].

2 Materials and Methods

Data Generation. Simulated B-mode US images are generated using a Monte-Carlo ray tracing framework on a custom geometric fetal model for obstetric training [11]. US wave interactions are simulated using a surface ray tracing model to find the ray segments between tissue boundaries. Tissue properties such as acoustic impedance, attenuation and speed-of-sound are assigned to each tissue type from literature and based on sonographers' visual inspection. Along each extracted ray segment, a ray-marching algorithm is applied on the GPU to emulate US scatterer texture by convolving a locally changing point-spread-function with an underlying tissue scatterer representation generated randomly using Gaussian distributions per tissue type [10]. Simulated RF data is post-processed with envelope detection, time-gain compensation, log compression and scan-conversion into Cartesian coordinates, yielding a gray-scale B-mode image.

US Images. For each regularly-sampled key frame of a simulated US fetal exam, paired low and high quality images are generated using two simulation passes: low quality images using one primary ray per US scanline and one elevational

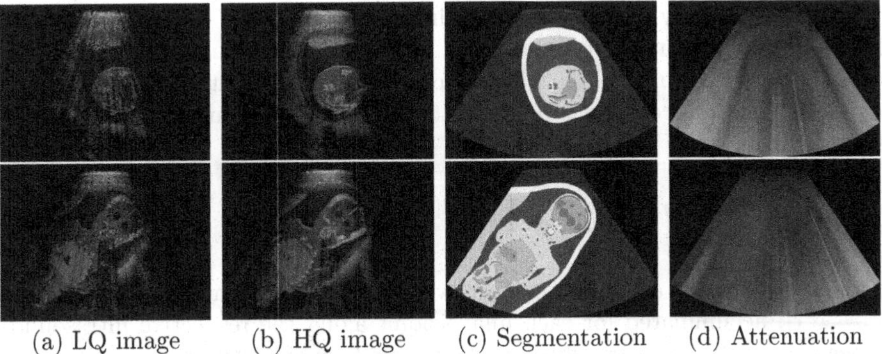

(a) LQ image (b) HQ image (c) Segmentation (d) Attenuation

Fig. 1. Low quality (a) and high quality (b) simulation outputs, with corresponding segmentation map (c) and integral attenuation map (d).

layer; and high quality images using 32 primary rays per scanline and three elevational layers [11]. Other simulation parameters are kept identical for both simulation passes, cf Table 1. Example B-mode images are shown in Fig. 1(a–b).

Image Mask. A fixed binary image mask demarcating the imaging region after scan-conversion for the convex probe is also provided as input to the network, in order to constrain the meaningful image translation region and help to save generator capacity.

Segmentation Maps. As additional input for our method, segmentation maps as the cross-section of input triangulated anatomical surfaces are also output by the simulation, corresponding to each low-/high-quality image, cf Fig. 1(c).

Attenuation Maps. A characteristic feature in real US images is the presence of directional artifacts, which is also valuable for the interpretation of images, for instance in diagnosis of pathology. It is therefore important to accurately simulate such artifacts for training purposes. Besides reflection and refraction effects, a major source of directional US artifacts is attenuation, which is caused by a reduction in acoustic intensity along the wave travel path due to local tissue effects such as absorption, scattering, and mode conversion. Since such artifacts are not only a function of local tissue properties but an integral function along the viewing direction, we propose to directly provide this integrated information to the translation network, hypothesized to improve the quality of translation.

Table 1. Simulation parameters

Parameter	Value
Triangles fetus	400k
Triangles mother	275k
Image depth	15.0 cm

Parameter	Value
Transducer frequency	8 MHz
Transducer field-of-view	70°
Axial samples	3072

Acoustic intensity arriving at a depth z can be modeled as $I(z) = I_0 e^{-\mu z}$, where μ is the attenuation constant at a given imaging frequency and I_0 is the initial intensity. Given that the waves travel through different tissue layers with varying attenuation constants $\mu(z)$, the total intensity arriving at a point z can be approximated by

$$I(z, \mu|_0^z) = I_0 \prod_{i=0}^{z} e^{-\mu[i]} = I_0 e^{-\sum_{i=0}^{z} \mu[i]}. \tag{1}$$

To approximate such attenuation effect, we create attenuation integral maps $a = e^{-\sum_{i=0}^{z} \mu[i]}$, accumulated for each image point along the respective ultrasound propagation path. For better dynamic range and to avoid outliers, these maps are normalized by the 98 %ile of image intensities and then scan-converted into the same Cartesian coordinate frame as the simulated B-mode images. Figure 1(d) shows sample integral attenuation maps.

Image Translation Network. Our image-to-image translation framework is based on the *pix2pix* network proposed in [8]. Simulated low and high quality US images are considered as source and target domain, respectively, where a translation network G learns a mapping from the source to the target domain. Specifically, G maps the low quality US image x, the binary mask m, the segmentation map s, and the attenuation integral map a to the high quality US image y, i.e.: $G : \{x, m, s, a\} \rightarrow \{y\}$. The discriminator D is trained to distinguish between real and fake high quality images conditioned on the corresponding inputs to the generator. The objective function of the conditional GAN consists of a weighted sum between a GAN loss L_{GAN} and a data fidelity term L_{F}, i.e.,

$$L = L_{\text{GAN}}(G, D) + \lambda L_{\text{F}}(G), \tag{2}$$

$$L_{\text{GAN}} = \mathbf{E}_{\tilde{x},y}[\log D(y|\tilde{x})] + \mathbf{E}_{\tilde{x}}[\log(1 - D(G(\tilde{x})|\tilde{x})], \tag{3}$$

$$L_{\text{F}} = \mathbf{E}_{\tilde{x},y}[||y - G(\tilde{x})||_1], \tag{4}$$

where $\tilde{x} = (x, m, s, a)$. Before computing the losses, the output is element-wise multiplied with the binary mask to restrict the loss to the relevant output regions.

Similarly to [8], we use a deterministic G parametrized using a 8-layer Unet with skip connections and D using a 4-layer convolutional network, i.e. a *patch-GAN* discriminator. Instance normalization is applied before nonlinear activation. The full field-of-view B-mode images from the simulation are of size 1000×1386 pixels. Applying pix2pix directly at such high resolution may lead to unsatisfactory results, as reported in [19]. We therefore use randomly cropped patches of a smaller size. A patch size of 512×512 pixels is found empirically to provide sufficient anatomical context, without degradation in image quality. Figure 2 shows an overview of our network architecture.

3 Experiments and Results

Implementation Details and Network Training. We use the Adam optimizer [9] with a learning rate of 0.0002 and exponential decay rates $\beta_1 = 0.5$

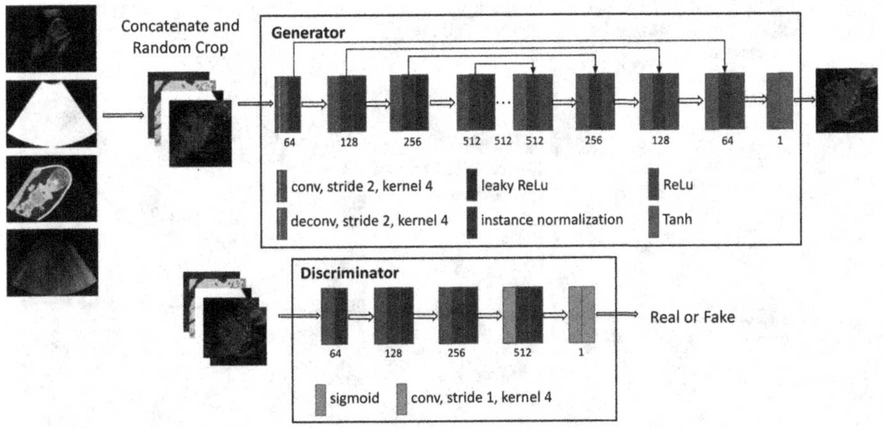

Fig. 2. Network architecture

and $\beta_2 = 0.999$. Since GANs in general underfit [21] and the Nash equilibrium is often not reached in practice, we early stop training at 50k iterations, by when FID of a randomly-sampled training subset saturates. We use a batch size of 16 and set $\lambda = 100$. Our dataset consists of 6669 4-tuples (x, y, s, a) and a constant binary mask m covering the beam shape for all samples. We use randomly-selected 6000 images for training and the rest for evaluation. To quantitatively evaluate our models, from each test image we randomly crop four patches of size 512×512, yielding an evaluation set of 2676 image patches that are not seen during training. Note that our original dataset consists of images that are temporally far apart, thus the test images cannot be temporally consecutive and thus inherently similar to any training images.

Comparative Evaluation. To demonstrate the effectiveness of the proposed additional inputs from the image formation process, we conduct an ablation study by considering different combinations of network inputs. We refer the pix2pix network with low quality image and binary mask in the input channel as our baseline $L2H_{\mathrm{M}}$. We compare this baseline with the following variants: 1) $L2H_{\mathrm{MS}}$: $L2H_{\mathrm{M}}$ with segmentation map s as additional input; 2) $L2H_{\mathrm{MSA}}$: $L2H_{\mathrm{MS}}$ with attenuation integral map a as additional input.

Qualitative Results. Figure 3 shows a visual comparison of the three model variants on four examples. The baseline $L2H_{\mathrm{M}}$ fails to preserve anatomical structures due to missing structural information in the input images. Resulting ambiguities in the network prediction cause artifacts such as blur in regions that feature fine details such as bones. Providing segmentation maps as additional input ($L2H_{\mathrm{MS}}$) greatly reduces such artifacts as shown in Fig. 3(c). However, $L2H_{\mathrm{MS}}$ still struggles in modeling complex non-local features such as directional occlusion artifacts, note the lack of acoustic shadows in Fig. 3(c). In contrast, our final model $L2H_{\mathrm{MSA}}$ is able to accurately synthesize these features and produces translations significantly closer to the target, as demonstrated in Fig. 3(d).

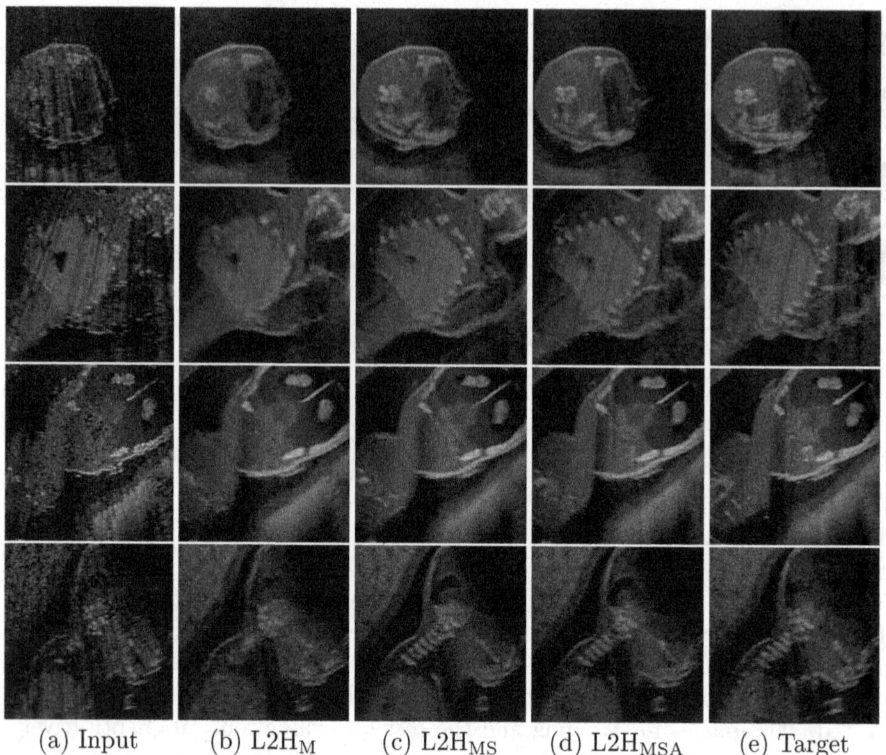

(a) Input (b) L2H_{M} (c) L2H_{MS} (d) L2H_{MSA} (e) Target

Fig. 3. Low-quality input (a), GAN outputs (b–d), and high-quality target (e).

In particular, our proposed model with segmentation and attenuation integral maps is able to recover both missing anatomical structures and directional artefacts.

Quantitative Results. The effectiveness of the proposed model is further evaluated using the following quantitative metrics:

1) PSNR: Peak signal-to-noise ratio between two images A and B is defined by $\text{PSNR} = 10\log_{10}(\frac{255}{\text{MSE}})$ with mean squared error MSE between A and B.
2) SSIM: Structural similarity index quantifies the visual changes in structural information as $\text{SSIM}(A, B) = \frac{(2\mu_A\mu_B+c_1)(2\sigma_{AB}+c_2)}{(\mu_A^2+\mu_B^2+c_1)(\sigma_A^2+\sigma_B^2+c_2)}$ with regularization constants c_1 and c_2, local means μ_A and μ_B, local standard deviations σ_A and σ_B, and cross covariance σ_{AB}. We use the default parameters of the MATLAB implementation to compute the metric.
3) pKL: Speckle appearance, relevant for tissue characterization in US images [15], affects image histogram statistics. Hence, discrepancy in histogram statistics can quantify differences in tissue-specific speckle patterns. Kullback-Leibler divergence compares normalized histograms h_A and h_B of two images A and B as: $\text{KL}(h_A||h_B) = \sum_{l=1..d} h_A[l] \log\left(\frac{h_A[l]}{h_B[l]}\right)$. We set the

number of histogram bins d to 50. To emphasize structural differences, we calculate KL divergence locally within 32×32 sized non-overlapping patches and report the metric mean, called *patch KL* (pKL) herein.

4) FID: Fréchet Inception Distance compares the distributions of generated samples and real samples by computing the distance between two multivariate Gaussians fitted to hidden activations of Inception network v3. This is a widely used metric to evaluate GAN performance, capturing both perceptual image quality and mode diversity. For this purpose, center crops of test images are sub-divided into four pieces of 299×299, to match Inception v3 input size.

Table 2 summarizes quantitative results for all models and all metrics, with the additional comparison to the discrepancy between low quality and high quality images as reference. A preliminary baseline experiment without GAN loss resulted in very blurry images with an FID score of 184.71. The results in Table 2 demonstrate that $L2H_{\mathrm{MSA}}$ achieves the best translation performance in terms of all proposed metrics. The effectiveness of providing informative inputs to the network is well demonstrated in the gradual improvement in PSNR, SSIM and pKL, showing higher fidelity in anatomical structures and directional shadow artifacts. The metric pKL gives further indication of closer speckle appearance achieved by $L2H_{\mathrm{MSA}}$. Based on Wilcoxon signed-rank tests, improvements of $L2H_{\mathrm{MSA}}$ over $L2H_{\mathrm{MS}}$ and those two over the baseline $L2H_{\mathrm{M}}$ are statistically significant ($p < 10^{-5}$) for all evaluation metrics. Moreover, FID score indicates higher statistical similarity between the target and generated images using the proposed final model, with an improvement of 7.2% compared to $L2H_{\mathrm{M}}$.

Full Field-of-View Images. Above image translation has been demonstrated on patches. For the entire field-of-view (FoV) US images, patch fusion from image translation of non-overlapping patches would cause artifacts at image seams. Averaging overlapping patches, on the other hand, would blur the essential US texture. Although seamless tiling of US images is possible using graphical models [4], this requires prohibitively long computation time. Herein, we instead directly apply our trained generator on full FoV low-quality images, since the generator is fully convolutional and thus can operate on images of arbitrary size. Figure 4 shows two examples of translated images by $L2H_{\mathrm{MS}}$ and $L2H_{\mathrm{MSA}}$, demonstrating direct inference on full FoV images. While anatomical structures

Table 2. Quantitative results. %ile refers to 5 percentile values for PSNR and SSIM and 95 percentile otherwise. Bold number indicates the best performance.

	PSNR			SSIM [%]			pKL ($\times 10^2$)			FID
	Mean	Std	%Ile	Mean	Std	%Ile	Mean	Std	%Ile	
Low quality	25.31	4.07	20.18	64.05	17.10	35.10	38.90	22.84	82.02	204.60
$L2H_{M}$	29.07	3.71	24.62	70.75	14.53	45.73	15.14	8.97	31.45	17.88
$L2H_{MS}$	29.26	3.71	24.78	71.22	14.27	46.37	14.57	9.20	31.41	17.62
$L2H_{MSA}$	**29.40**	3.71	**24.89**	**71.47**	14.20	**46.67**	**13.80**	8.73	**29.02**	**16.59**

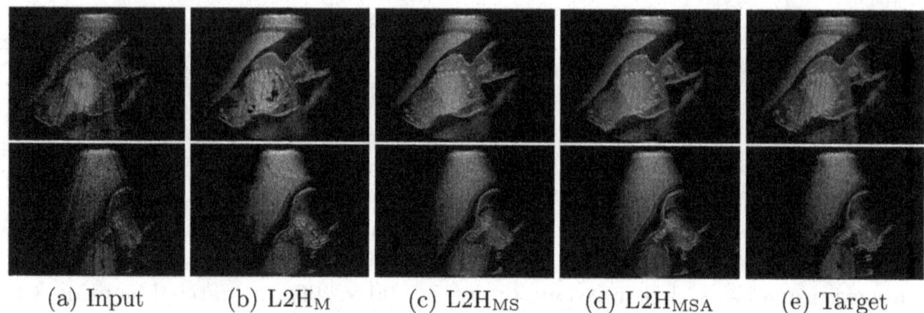

(a) Input (b) $L2H_{M}$ (c) $L2H_{MS}$ (d) $L2H_{MSA}$ (e) Target

Fig. 4. Inference on full field-of-view (FoV) images.

are well preserved and the effect of attenuation integral map is apparent, speckle texture appearance is seen to degrade slightly especially in the top image regions, where the ultrasound texture looking particularly different due to focusing difference and near-field effects.

4 Discussion and Conclusions

We have proposed a patch-based generative adversarial network for improving the quality of simulated US images, via image translation of computationally low-cost images to high quality simulation outputs. Providing segmentation and attenuation integral maps to the translation framework greatly improves preservation of anatomical structures and synthesis of important acoustic shadows. Continuous simulation parameters, such as transmit focus and depth-dependent lateral resolution, are implicitly captured by our framework thanks to training on image patches. For discrete simulation parameters such as imaging mode and transducer frequency that can take a handful of different values in typical clinical imaging, it is feasible to train a separate GAN for each such setting.

Image rendering time highly depends on chosen simulation parameters and 3D mesh model complexity. For instance, high framerates are reported for a simpler model in [16]. Rendering high and low quality images herein takes 75 ms and 40 ms, respectively. Our network inference time with a non-optimized code is 12.6 ms on average for full FoV images on a GTX 2080 Ti using TensorRT. This timing improvement is rather a lower-bound, since network inference can be further accelerated, e.g. with FPGAs [6]. Furthermore, since a pass through the network runs in constant time, potential time gain can be arbitrarily high depending on the desired complexity of the target simulation. With our proposed framework a trade-off between image quality and computational speed is obviated, thus enabling interactive framerates even with sophisticated anatomical scenes and computationally-taxing simulation settings. Although the convolutional network can process arbitrary sized image, translating full FoV images without any artifacts is still a challenge.

Acknowledgments. Funding was provided by the Swiss Innovation Agency Innosuisse.

References

1. Armanious, K., et al.: MedGAN: medical image translation using gans. Comput. Med. Imaging Graph. **79**, 101684 (2020)
2. Armanious, K., Mecky, Y., Gatidis, S., Yang, B.: Adversarial inpainting of medical image modalities. In: ICASSP 2019–2019 IEEE International Conference on Acoustics, Speech and Signal Processing (ICASSP), pp. 3267–3271. IEEE (2019)
3. Burger, B., Bettinghausen, S., Radle, M., Hesser, J.: Real-time GPU-based ultrasound simulation using deformable mesh models. IEEE Trans. Med. Imaging **32**(3), 609–618 (2013)
4. Flach, B., Makhinya, M., Goksel, O.: PURE: panoramic ultrasound reconstruction by seamless stitching of volumes. In: Tsaftaris, S.A., Gooya, A., Frangi, A.F., Prince, J.L. (eds.) SASHIMI 2016. LNCS, vol. 9968, pp. 75–84. Springer, Cham (2016). https://doi.org/10.1007/978-3-319-46630-9_8
5. Goodfellow, I., et al.: Generative adversarial nets. In: Advances in Neural Information Processing Systems, pp. 2672–2680 (2014)
6. Guo, K., Zeng, S., Yu, J., Wang, Y., Yang, H.: A survey of FPGA-based neural network accelerator. arXiv preprint arXiv:1712.08934 (2017)
7. Hu, Y., et al.: Freehand ultrasound image simulation with spatially-conditioned generative adversarial networks. In: Cardoso, M.J., et al. (eds.) CMMI/SWITCH/RAMBO -2017. LNCS, vol. 10555, pp. 105–115. Springer, Cham (2017). https://doi.org/10.1007/978-3-319-67564-0_11
8. Isola, P., Zhu, J.Y., Zhou, T., Efros, A.A.: Image-to-image translation with conditional adversarial networks. In: Proceedings of the IEEE Conference on Computer Vision and Pattern Recognition, pp. 1125–1134 (2017)
9. Kingma, D.P., Ba, J.: Adam: a method for stochastic optimization. arXiv preprint arXiv:1412.6980 (2014)
10. Mattausch, O., Goksel, O.: Scatterer reconstruction and parametrization of homogeneous tissue for ultrasound image simulation. In: 2015 37th Annual International Conference of the IEEE Engineering in Medicine and Biology Society (EMBC), pp. 6350–6353. IEEE (2015)
11. Mattausch, O., Makhinya, M., Goksel, O.: Realistic ultrasound simulation of complex surface models using interactive Monte-Carlo path tracing. Comput. Graph. Forum **37**, 202–213 (2018)
12. Mirza, M., Osindero, S.: Conditional generative adversarial nets. arXiv preprint arXiv:1411.1784 (2014)
13. Nie, D., et al.: Medical image synthesis with deep convolutional adversarial networks. IEEE Trans. Biomed. Eng. **65**(12), 2720–2730 (2018)
14. Salehi, M., Ahmadi, S.-A., Prevost, R., Navab, N., Wein, W.: Patient-specific 3D ultrasound simulation based on convolutional ray-tracing and appearance optimization. In: Navab, N., Hornegger, J., Wells, W.M., Frangi, A.F. (eds.) MICCAI 2015. LNCS, vol. 9350, pp. 510–518. Springer, Cham (2015). https://doi.org/10.1007/978-3-319-24571-3_61
15. Shankar, P.M., Reid, J.M., Ortega, H., Piccoli, C.W., Goldberg, B.B.: Use of non-rayleigh statistics for the identification of tumors in ultrasonic B-scans of the breast. IEEE Trans. Med. Imaging **12**(4), 687–692 (1993)

16. Starkov, R., Zhang, L., Bajka, M., Tanner, C., Goksel, O.: Ultrasound simulation with deformable and patient-specific scatterer maps. Int. J. Comput. Assist. Radiol. Surg. **14**(9), 1589–1599 (2019). https://doi.org/10.1007/s11548-019-02054-5
17. Tom, F., Sheet, D.: Simulating patho-realistic ultrasound images using deep generative networks with adversarial learning. In: 2018 IEEE 15th International Symposium on Biomedical Imaging (ISBI 2018), pp. 1174–1177. IEEE (2018)
18. Vitale, S., Orlando, J.I., Iarussi, E., Larrabide, I.: Improving realism in patient-specific abdominal ultrasound simulation using CycleGANs. Int. J. Comput. Assist. Radiol. Surg. **15**(2), 183–192 (2019). https://doi.org/10.1007/s11548-019-02046-5
19. Wang, T.C., Liu, M.Y., Zhu, J.Y., Tao, A., Kautz, J., Catanzaro, B.: High-resolution image synthesis and semantic manipulation with conditional gans. In: Proceedings of the IEEE Conference on Computer Vision and Pattern Recognition, pp. 8798–8807 (2018)
20. Wolterink, J.M., Dinkla, A.M., Savenije, M.H.F., Seevinck, P.R., van den Berg, C.A.T., Išgum, I.: Deep MR to CT synthesis using unpaired data. In: Tsaftaris, S.A., Gooya, A., Frangi, A.F., Prince, J.L. (eds.) SASHIMI 2017. LNCS, vol. 10557, pp. 14–23. Springer, Cham (2017). https://doi.org/10.1007/978-3-319-68127-6_2
21. Wu, Y., Burda, Y., Salakhutdinov, R., Grosse, R.: On the quantitative analysis of decoder-based generative models. arXiv preprint arXiv:1611.04273 (2016)
22. Zhang, Z., Yang, L., Zheng, Y.: Translating and segmenting multimodal medical volumes with cycle-and shape-consistency generative adversarial network. In: Proceedings of the IEEE Conference on Computer Vision and Pattern Recognition, pp. 9242–9251 (2018)
23. Zhu, J.Y., Park, T., Isola, P., Efros, A.A.: Unpaired image-to-image translation using cycle-consistent adversarial networks. In: Proceedings of the IEEE International Conference on Computer Vision, pp. 2223–2232 (2017)

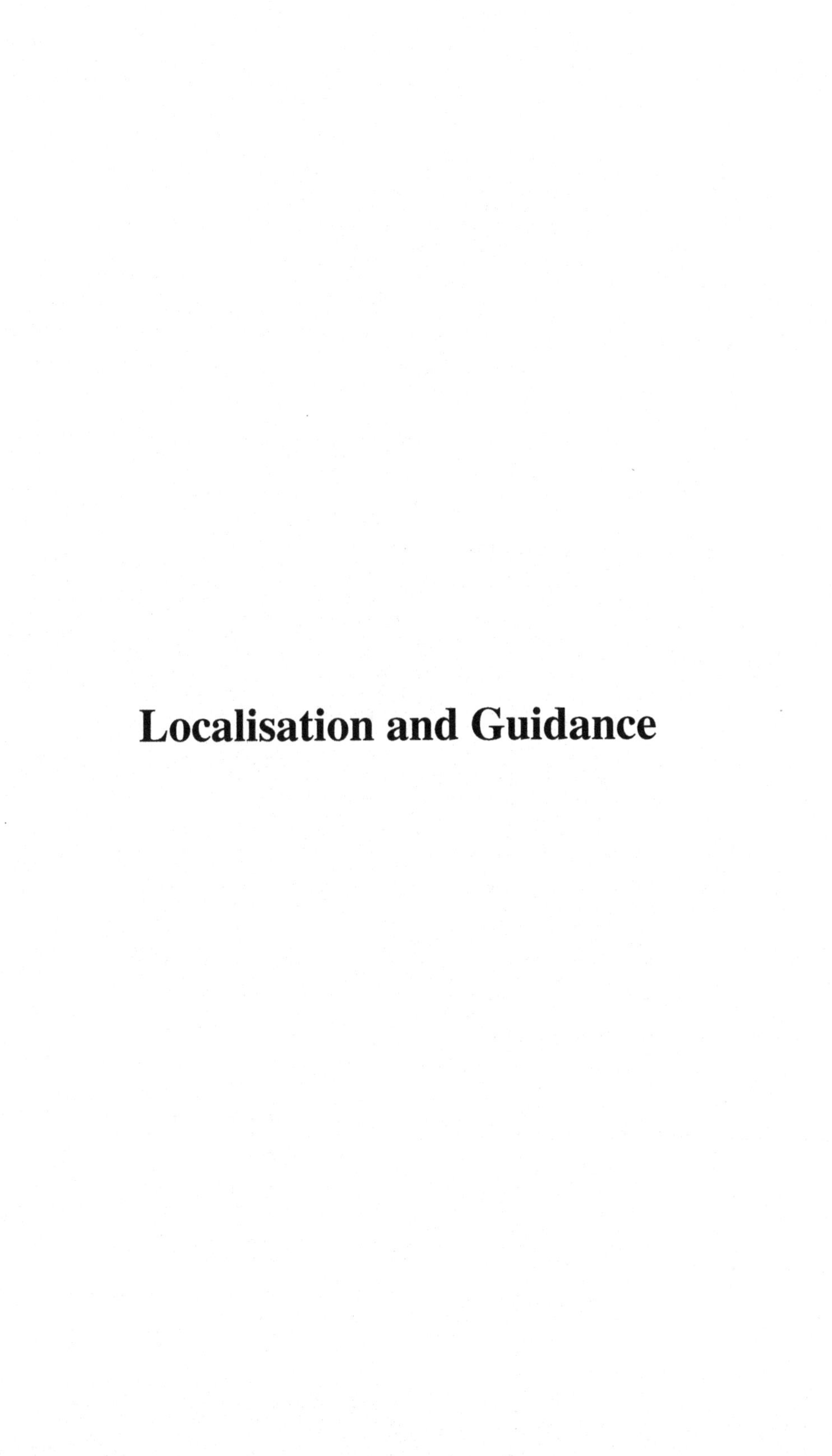

Localisation and Guidance

Localizing 2D Ultrasound Probe from Ultrasound Image Sequences Using Deep Learning for Volume Reconstruction

Kanta Miura[1(✉)], Koichi Ito[1], Takafumi Aoki[1], Jun Ohmiya[2], and Satoshi Kondo[2]

[1] Graduate School of Information Sciences, Tohoku University, 6-6-05, Aramaki Aza Aoba, Aoba-ku, Sendai-shi, Miyagi 9808579, Japan
kanta@aoki.ecei.tohoku.ac.jp

[2] AI Technology Development Division IoT Service Platform Development Operations, Konica Minolta, Inc., 1-2, Sakura-machi, Takatsuki-shi, Osaka 5698503, Japan

Abstract. This paper presents an ultrasound (US) volume reconstruction method only from US image sequences using deep learning. The proposed method employs the convolutional neural network (CNN) to estimate the position of a 2D US probe only from US images. Our CNN model consists of two networks: feature extraction and motion estimation. We also introduce the consistency loss function to enforce. Through a set of experiments using US image sequence datasets with ground-truth motion measured by a motion capture system, we demonstrate that the proposed method exhibits the efficient performance on probe localization and volume reconstruction compared with the conventional method.

Keywords: Ultrasound · Volume reconstruction · CNN · Probe localization

1 Introduction

Ultrasound (US) imaging has a number of advantages in medical diagnosis such as high spatial resolution, real-time imaging, and non-invasiveness. Recently, three-dimensional (3D) US [13] has attracted much attention as a valuable imaging tool for a diagnostic procedure because of the above advantages of US. If 3D US can be acquired using only the current US system with a 2D US probe, 3D US may be allowed to be used in place of other imaging modalities such as CT, MRI or PET, e.g., the point of care in an emergency situation requiring the rapid diagnosis, muscle and blood analysis in sports medicine, etc. Among 3D US acquisition protocols, we focus on the freehand protocol [4] because of its cost-effectiveness and flexibility. 3D volume data can be reconstructed from a 2D US image sequence by integrating a set of US images according to the position of the US probe. The quality of 3D volume data significantly depends on the

Y. Hu et al. (Eds.): ASMUS 2020/PIPPI 2020, LNCS 12437, pp. 97–105, 2020.
https://doi.org/10.1007/978-3-030-60334-2_10

accuracy of probe localization, i.e., 3D motion estimation of a 2D US probe in the acquisition protocol with freehand scanning.

The initial approach of localizing a 2D US probe is to use the special devices such as an electromagnetic tracking device [7,17] and an optical tracker [6,18]. The accuracy of probe localization is high, while such special devices require much cost and may sacrifice smooth scanning. The simple approach is to use markers to estimate the motion of a 2D US probe [9,12,16]. The cost of the system is cheap, while markers are attached on the skin surface, resulting in decreasing the flexibility and acceptability. Another approach is to use a camera, which is mounted on a 2D US probe. The motion of the probe is estimated from a video sequence of skin patterns captured by a camera using simultaneous localization and mapping (SLAM) [19] or structure from motion (SfM) [10,11]. This approach is cost-effective, while a camera may be intrusive for an operator. The challenging task is to estimate the motion of a US probe only from a US image sequence. Balakrinshnan et al. [1] proposed a similarity metric, which computes the similarity between two consecutive US images by correlating the parametric representation of image texture, to estimate out-of-plane motion in US probe sweeping. Prevost et al. [15] proposed a 2D US probe localization method using a convolutional neural network (CNN), which estimates the motion of a 2D US probe by image-based tracking. This method learns the relative 3D translations and rotations from a pair of images with additional information of optical flow, which is used to improve the accuracy of motion estimation. The CNN architecture of this method is relatively simple, which consists of 4 convolution layers, 2 pooling layers, and 2 fully-connected layers. Their latest work in [14] also used an inertial measurement unit (IMU), which was mounted on a US prove, to improve the accuracy of estimating 3D rotation.

In this paper, we propose a 2D US probe localization method only from US image sequences using deep learning. We consider a new CNN architecture for estimating the motion between two US images inspired by Prevost's work [14,15]. Our CNN architecture includes motion features obtained from FlowNetS [2]. We introduce the consistency loss function to improve the accuracy of motion estimation. We create a large-scale dataset of US image sequences with the ground-truth probe motion for evaluating the methods. The US image sequences are acquired by scanning forearm, breast phantom and hypogastric phantom, where the number of images of each target is 30,801, 8,940, and 6,242, respectively. The contribution of this work is summarized as follows:

1. propose a new CNN architecture for localizing a 2D US probe for volume reconstruction and
2. introduce a consistency loss function to improve the accuracy of probe localization.

2 Methods

This section describes our CNN architecture for estimating the motion between two US images and its loss functions to improve the accuracy of motion estimation.

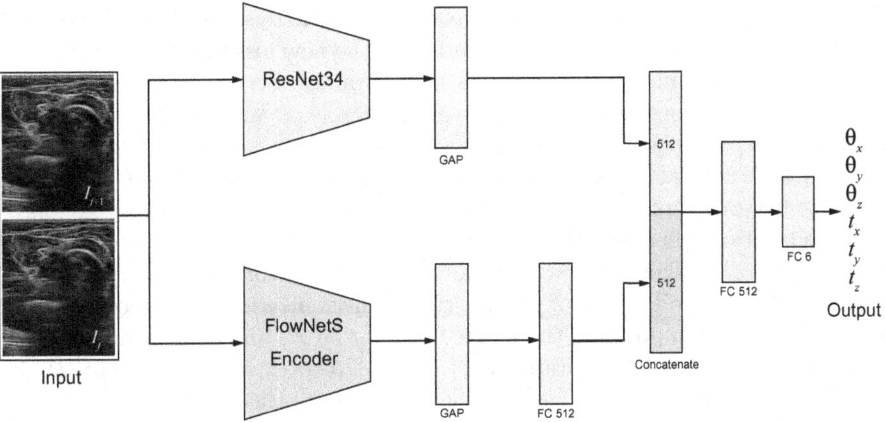

Fig. 1. Network architecture of our proposed CNN.

2.1 Network Architecture

In the previous work by Prevost et al. [14,15], they proposed a simple CNN architecture for estimating the motion between two US images, which consists of 4 convolution layers, 2 pooling layers, and 2 fully-connected layers. They used 4-channel input, which consists of the two US images and the two components of the vector field estimated by optical flow estimation [3]. The optical flow between the two US images is not always accurately estimated by [3] from our empirical observation. Figure 1 shows the network architecture of our proposed CNN for estimating the motion between two US images. This architecture consists of localization and optical flow estimation networks. In this paper, we employ ResNet34 [8] for localization network and the encoder of FlowNetS [2] for optical flow estimation network. The feature vector extracted from ResNet34 is reduced to a 512-dimensional feature vector by Global Average Pooling (GAP). The feature vector extracted from FlowNetS is also reduced to a 512-dimensional feature vector by GAP and the fully-connected layer. Then, two feature vectors are concatenated before the last two fully-connected layers. The output of CNN is 6 parameters consisting of 3 rotation angles $(\theta_x, \theta_y, \theta_z)$ and 3 translations (t_x, t_y, t_z), where $\boldsymbol{p} = \{\theta_x, \theta_y, \theta_z, t_x, t_y, t_z\}$. We employ FlowNetS pre-trained by the Flying Chairs dataset[1] and all the weight parameters are fixed in both training and test.

2.2 Loss Function

We employ the loss function defined by the Euclidean distance between estimated 6 parameters and the ground truth as well as the previous work [14,15], which is given by

$$L_{\text{Euc}} = ||\boldsymbol{P}^g - \hat{\boldsymbol{P}}||_2, \tag{1}$$

[1] https://lmb.informatik.uni-freiburg.de/resources/datasets/FlyingChairs.en.html.

where $\boldsymbol{P}^g$ indicates the ground-truth vector of parameters and $\hat{\boldsymbol{P}}$ indicates the estimated vector. We also consider introducing the new loss function to improve the accuracy of the motion between US image frames. Let the rotation and the translation from image frame I_f to I_{f+1} be $\boldsymbol{R}_{f\to f+1}$ and $\boldsymbol{t}_{f\to f+1}$, and their inverses be $\boldsymbol{R}_{f+1\to f}$ and $\boldsymbol{t}_{f+1\to f}$. $\boldsymbol{R}_{f\to f+1}$ and $\boldsymbol{t}_{f\to f+1}$ are estimated from I_f and I_{f+1} by CNN, and $\boldsymbol{R}_{f+1\to f}$ and $\boldsymbol{t}_{f+1\to f}$ are also estimated by CNN when reversing the order of the inputs. A point on I_f should be reprojected onto the same position when applying the transformation $[\boldsymbol{R}_{f\to f+1}|\boldsymbol{t}_{f\to f+1}]$ and then $[\boldsymbol{R}_{f+1\to f}|\boldsymbol{t}_{f+1\to f}]$. This is known as the reprojection error in stereo vision, and we can apply the similar idea of the left-right consistency loss in stereo vision [5] to our method. Let a point on the image frame I_f be $\boldsymbol{P}_f$ and a point reprojected from the consecutive image frame I_{f+1} be $\boldsymbol{P}'_f$, respectively. The point $\boldsymbol{P}'_f$ is calculated using the rotation and translation between the two image frames as follows:

$$\boldsymbol{P}'_f = \boldsymbol{R}_{f+1\to f}(\boldsymbol{R}_{f\to f+1}\boldsymbol{P}_{f1} + \boldsymbol{t}_{f\to f+1}) + \boldsymbol{t}_{f+1\to f}, \tag{2}$$

where We consider the following consistency loss function:

$$L_{\text{Cons}} = ||\boldsymbol{P}_f - \boldsymbol{P}'_f||_2. \tag{3}$$

3 Materials

We create a large-scale dataset of US image sequences with the ground-truth probe motion for evaluating the methods (Fig. 2). The target objects are forearm of 5 subjects, breast phantom and hypogastric phantom in the dataset. US image sequences are acquired by SONIMAGE HS1 (Konica Minolta, Inc.) with L18-4 linear probe (center frequency: 10 MHz) for forearm and breast phantom and with C5-2 convex probe (center frequency: 3.5 MHz) for hypogastric phantom, where the field of view (FOV) of US images is 40 × 38 mm, the frame rate is 30 fps, the recording time is about 6 s (180 frames), and the size of each US image frame is 442 × 526 pixels. The number of scans (image frames) is 190 (30,801) for forearm, 60 (8,940) for breast phantom, and 40 (6,242) for hypogastric phantom. The ground-truth position of the US probe is measured by V120:Trio (OptiTrack), where 5 markers are attached on the US probe to capture its motion.

4 Experiments

In the experiments, we separate the dataset into training, validation, and test data, where the training data is 180 scans (27,948 image frames) from forearm of 2 subjects and two phantoms, the validation data is 30 scans (5,176 image frames) from forearm of 1 subject, and the test data is 80 scans (12,859 frames) from forearm of 2 subjects. Each image frame with 442 × 526 pixels is cropped the center region with 442 × 442 pixels, and then is resized to 256 × 256 pixels. The pixel value of each resized image is normalized to have zero mean and the unit variance.

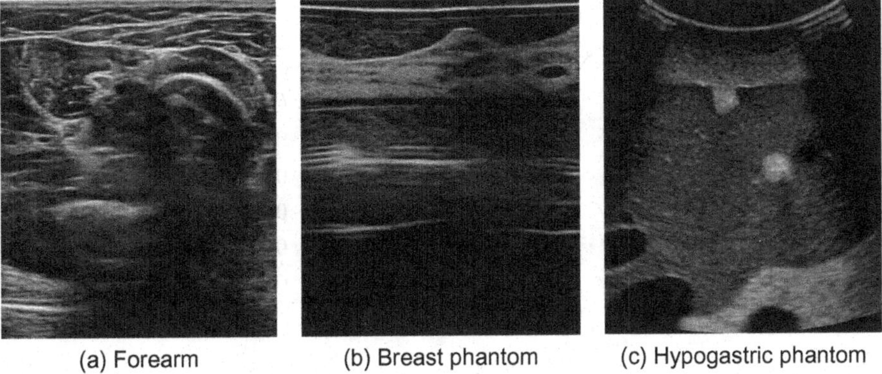

Fig. 2. Example of the US image frame acquired from (a) forearm, (b) breast phantom, and (c) hypogastric phantom.

The training parameters of our method are as follows: the optimizer is AdaGrad, the learning rate is 1e−3, the batch size is 64, the number of epochs is 30, and 25% dropout is added after the fully-connected layers except the last one. All the methods are implemented using PyTorch 1.0.0 on Intel(R) Xeon(R) W-2133 CPU 3.60 GHz with GeForce RTX 2080 Ti. We evaluate the accuracy of each parameter estimated by the conventional method [15] and our methods using mean absolute error (MAE), where we consider 4 combinations for the proposed method in the following ablation study. Note that we implemented the conventional method according to the paper [15] since an official implementation is not provided. The conventional method was trained and evaluated under the same experimental condition.

Table 1 shows the summary of the ablation study. There is no significant difference in estimation accuracy depending on the network architecture comparing the first and second rows of Table 1. The estimation accuracy is comparable when adding FlowNetS to the proposed method (i) comparing the second and third rows of Table 1. The estimation accuracy is improved when adding the consistency loss function to the proposed method (i) comparing the first and third rows of Table 1 The combination of loss functions can limit the search space of parameter optimization in CNN. The proposed method (iv), which employs all the techniques, exhibits the best estimation accuracy in the methods except for t_z as observed in the forth row of Table 1. Figure 3 shows the temporal variation of parameters estimated by each method. The conventional method cannot estimate large motion and therefore show the average temporal variation. The proposed method (i) shows a temporal variation close to the ground truth, while it may deviate significantly. The proposed method (iv) shows similar temporal variation to the ground truth for all the parameters except for t_z.

Table 1. Summary of the ablation study (OF: Optical flow, FN: FlowNetS).

Method		OF	FN	L_{Euc}	L_{Cons}	MAE (degree/mm)					
						θ_x	θ_y	θ_z	t_x	t_y	t_z
Prevost et al.	[14]	✓		✓		0.58	1.28	0.49	0.69	0.16	0.77
Ours	(i)	✓		✓		0.60	1.26	0.52	0.72	0.18	**0.76**
	(ii)	✓	✓	✓		0.61	1.28	0.52	0.74	0.18	0.78
	(iii)	✓		✓	✓	0.56	1.23	0.47	0.66	**0.15**	0.82
	(iv)	✓	✓	✓	✓	**0.53**	**1.21**	**0.47**	**0.64**	**0.15**	0.80

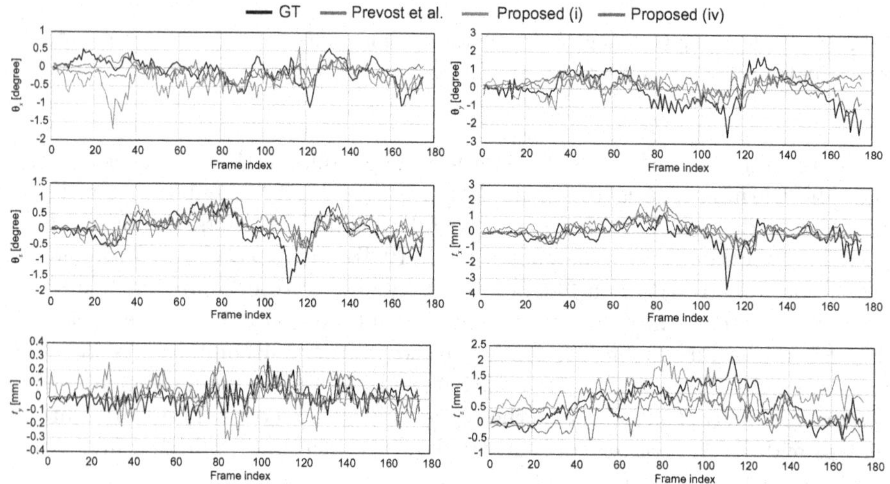

Fig. 3. Temporal variation of parameters estimated by each method.

Figure 4 shows the reconstructed US volume data using the probe location of the ground truth, the conventional method, and the proposed methods (i)–(iv). Each volume data is reconstructed using StradView[2]. The conventional method cannot handle the large motion of the US probe since the estimated motion is similar to the linear motion. Although the proposed methods (i) and (ii) attempt to estimate a large motion of the US probe, the estimated motion is rather large. The proposed methods (iii) and (iv) exhibit better performance than other methods since the shape of the reconstructed volume is similar to that of the ground truth.

[2] https://mi.eng.cam.ac.uk/Main/StradView.

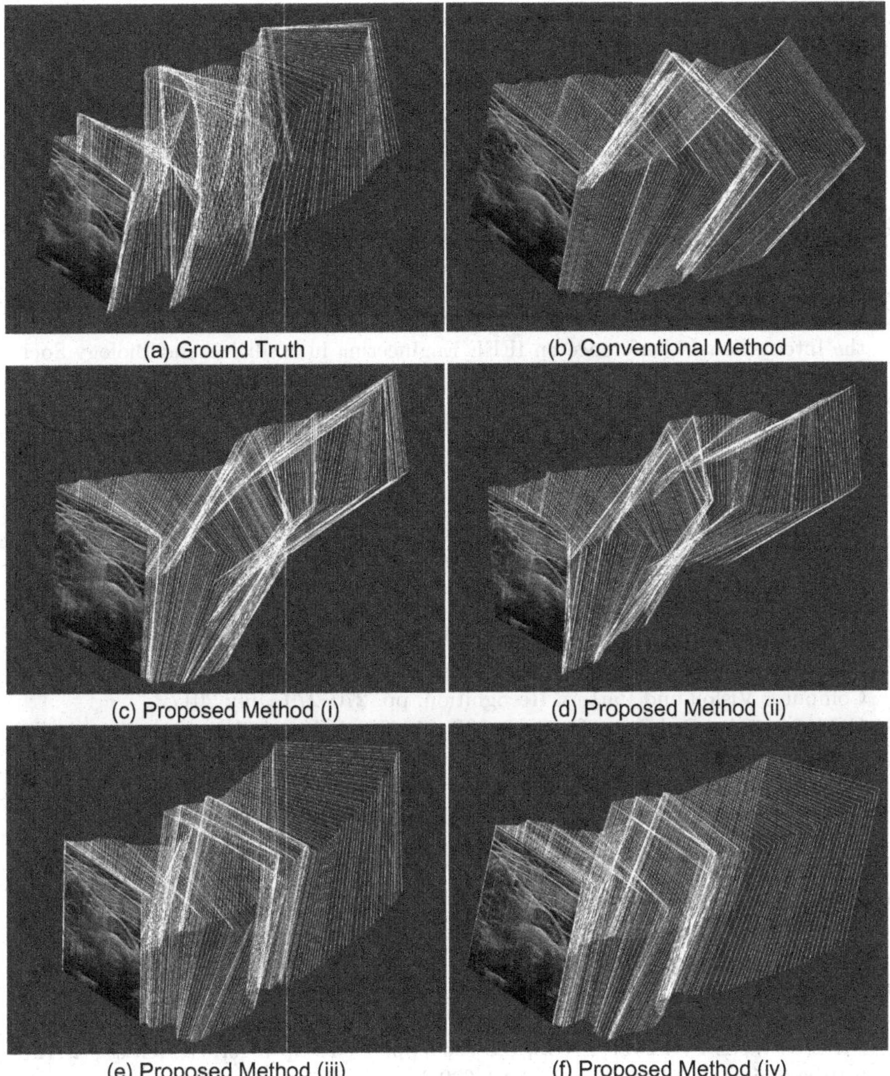

Fig. 4. Example of reconstructed US volume data: (a) ground truth, (b) conventional method, and (c)–(f) proposed method (i)–(iv).

5 Conclusion

In this paper, we proposed a 2D US probe localization method only from US image sequences using deep learning. Our CNN architecture extracts texture features and motion features, and estimate the motion between two US image frames. We considered the combination of loss functions to improve the accuracy of motion estimation. Through a set of experiments using our dataset of forearm, breast phantom, and hypogastric phantom, we demonstrated that our method exhibited better accuracy of probe localization than the conventional method. In future work, we will develop a 2D US probe with a small camera to support a large variety of probe motion to realize a free-hand 3D US reconstruction system for practical use.

References

1. Balakrishnan, S., Patel, R., Illanes, A., Friebe, M.: Novel similarity metric for image-based out-of-plane motion estimation in 3D ultrasound. In: Proceedings of the International Conference on IEEE Engineering in Medicine and Biology Society, pp. 5739–5742, July 2019
2. Dosovitskiy, A., et al.: FlowNet: learning optical flow with convolutional networks In: Proceedings of the International Conference on Computer Vision, pp. 2758–2766, December 2015
3. Farnebäck, G.: Two-frame motion estimation based on polynomial expansion. In: Bigun, J., Gustavsson, T. (eds.) SCIA 2003. LNCS, vol. 2749, pp. 363–370. Springer, Heidelberg (2003). https://doi.org/10.1007/3-540-45103-X_50
4. Gee, A., Prager, R., Treece, G., Berman, L.: Engineering a freehand 3D ultrasound system. Pattern Recognit. Lett. **24**(4–5), 757–777 (2003)
5. Godard, C., Aodha, O.M., Brostow, G.J.: Unsupervised monocular depth estimation with left-right consistency. In: Proceedings of the International Conference on Computer Vision and Pattern Recognition, pp. 270–279, July 2017
6. Goldsmith, A., Pedersen, P., Szabo, T.: An inertial-optical tracking system for portable, quantitative, 3D ultrasound. In: Proceedings of the IEEE International Ultrasonics Symposium, pp. 45–49, November 2008
7. Hastenteufel, M., Vetter, M., Meinzer, H.P., Wolf, I.: Effect of 3D ultrasound probes on the accuracy of electromagnetic tracking systems. Ultrasound Med. Biol. **32**(9), 1359–1368 (2006)
8. He, K., Zhang, X., Ren, S., Sun, J.: Deep residual learning for image recognition. In: Proceedings of the IEEE International Conference on Computer Vision and Pattern Recognition, pp. 770–778, June 2016
9. Horvath, S., et al.: Towards an ultrasound probe with vision: structured light to determine surface orientation. In: Linte, C.A., Moore, J.T., Chen, E.C.S., Holmes, D.R. (eds.) AE-CAI 2011. LNCS, vol. 7264, pp. 58–64. Springer, Heidelberg (2012). https://doi.org/10.1007/978-3-642-32630-1_6
10. Ito, K., Yodokawa, K., Aoki, T., Ohmiya, J., Kondo, S.: A probe-camera system for 3D ultrasound image reconstruction. In: Cardoso, M.J., et al. (eds.) BIVPCS/POCUS -2017. LNCS, vol. 10549, pp. 129–137. Springer, Cham (2017). https://doi.org/10.1007/978-3-319-67552-7_16
11. Ito, S., Ito, K., Aoki, T., Ohmiya, J., Kondo, S.: Probe localization using structure from motion for 3D ultrasound image reconstruction. In: Proceedings of the International Symposium on Biomedical Imaging, pp. 68–71, April 2017
12. Lange, T., Kraft, S., Eulenstein, S., Lamecker, H., Schlag, P.: Automatic calibration of 3D ultrasound probes. In: Proceedings of the Bildverarbeitung für die Medizin, pp. 169–173, March 2011
13. Nelson, T.R., Pretorius, D.H.: Three-dimensional ultrasound imaging. Ultrasound Med. Biol. **24**(9), 1243–1270 (1998)

14. Prevost, R.R., et al.: 3D freehand ultrasound without external tracking using deep learning. Med. Image Anal. **48**, 187–202 (2018)
15. Prevost, R., Salehi, M., Sprung, J., Ladikos, A., Bauer, R., Wein, W.: Deep learning for sensorless 3D freehand ultrasound imaging. In: Descoteaux, M., Maier-Hein, L., Franz, A., Jannin, P., Collins, D.L., Duchesne, S. (eds.) MICCAI 2017. LNCS, vol. 10434, pp. 628–636. Springer, Cham (2017). https://doi.org/10.1007/978-3-319-66185-8_71
16. Rafii-Tari, H., Abolmaesumi, P., Rohling, R.: Panorama ultrasound for guiding epidural anesthesia: a feasibility study. In: Taylor, R.H., Yang, G.-Z. (eds.) IPCAI 2011. LNCS, vol. 6689, pp. 179–189. Springer, Heidelberg (2011). https://doi.org/10.1007/978-3-642-21504-9_17
17. Rousseau, F., Hellier, P., Barillot, C.: A fully automatic calibration procedure for freehand 3D ultrasound. In: Proceedings of the IEEE International Symposium on Biomedical Imaging, pp. 985–988, July 2002
18. Stolka, P., Kang, H., Choti, M., Boctor, E.: Multi-DoF probe trajectory reconstruction with local sensors for 2D-to-3D ultrasound. In: Proceedings of the IEEE International Symposium on Biomedical Imaging, pp. 316–319, April 2010
19. Sun, S.-Y., Gilbertson, M., Anthony, B.W.: Probe localization for freehand 3D ultrasound by tracking skin features. In: Golland, P., Hata, N., Barillot, C., Hornegger, J., Howe, R. (eds.) MICCAI 2014. LNCS, vol. 8674, pp. 365–372. Springer, Cham (2014). https://doi.org/10.1007/978-3-319-10470-6_46

Augmented Reality-Based Lung Ultrasound Scanning Guidance

Keshav Bimbraw(✉), Xihan Ma, Ziming Zhang, and Haichong Zhang

Worcester Polytechnic Institute, Worcester, MA, USA
{kbimbraw,xma4,zzhang15,hzhang10}@wpi.edu

Abstract. Lung ultrasound (LUS) is an established non-invasive imaging method for diagnosing respiratory illnesses. With the rise of SARS-CoV-2 (COVID-19) as a global pandemic, LUS has been used to detect pneumopathy for triaging and monitoring patients who are diagnosed or suspected with COVID-19 infection. While LUS offers a cost-effective, radiation-free, and higher portability compared with chest X-ray and CT, its accessibility is limited due to its user dependency and the small number of physicians and sonographers who can perform appropriate scanning and diagnosis. In this paper, we propose a framework of guiding LUS scanning featuring augmented reality, in which the LUS procedure can be guided by projecting the scanning trajectory on the patient's body. To develop such a system, we implement a computer vision-based detection algorithm to classify different regions on the human body. The DensePose algorithm is used to obtain body mesh data for the upper body pictured with a mono-camera. Torso sub-mesh is used to extract and overlay the eight regions corresponding to anterior and lateral chests for LUS guidance. To minimize the instability of the DensePose mesh coordinates based on different frontal angles of the camera, a machine learning regression algorithm is applied to predict the angle-specific projection model for the chest. ArUco markers are utilized for training the ground truth chest regions to be scanned, and another single ArUco marker is used for detecting the center-line of the body. The augmented scanning regions are highlighted one by one to guide the scanning path to execute the LUS procedure. We demonstrate the feasibility of guiding the LUS scanning procedure through the combination of augmented reality, computer vision, and machine learning.

Keywords: Lung ultrasound · POCUS · COVID-19 · Coronavirus · Augmented reality · Computer vision · Machine learning · Image processing

1 Introduction

Lung ultrasound (LUS) is a non-invasive diagnostic exam that produces ultrasound images of various components of the chest such as the lungs and pleural spaces. Artifacts in the ultrasound images arising from LUS have been used for the diagnosis of respiratory illnesses such as pneumothorax [1]. SARS-CoV-2 coronavirus has caused a worldwide pandemic of highly communicable respiratory illness known as Coronavirus Disease 2019 (COVID-19) [2]. LUS has been suggested and used to detect pneumopathy

Y. Hu et al. (Eds.): ASMUS 2020/PIPPI 2020, LNCS 12437, pp. 106–115, 2020.
https://doi.org/10.1007/978-3-030-60334-2_11

for triaging and monitoring patients who are diagnosed or suspected with COVID-19 because of its high specificity and ease of use in resource-constrained environments [3]. With COVID-19 and related respiratory illnesses claiming hundreds of thousands of lives around the world, there is an imminent need to develop time and resource-constrained diagnosis and monitoring techniques. While LUS with the point-of-care ultrasound (POCUS) offers a cost-effective, radiation-free, and higher portability solution compared with chest X-ray and CT, its accessibility is limited due to its user dependency and the small number of physicians and sonographers who can perform scanning and diagnosis [4]. There is a need to develop systems that can assist the LUS procedure for diagnosis and monitoring of lung illnesses, and primarily COVID-19. In this work, we present a solution to address this need.

We introduce a framework of guiding LUS scanning with augmented reality (AR), in which the LUS procedure can be guided by projecting the scanning trajectory. To develop such a system, we implement a computer vision-based detection algorithm to classify different regions on the human body. While 2-D/3-D cameras and depth sensors are more common for human pose estimation, we focus on monocular human pose estimation (HPE) [5] considering the resource-limited environment. A single person's chest is pictured to detect the scanning regions which define AR overlay areas to be displayed in the pictures. In the literature, several regression-based algorithms have been proposed for 2D single person pose estimation [6–9]. These algorithms map the detected coordinates of body joints or the parameters of human body models over the input image. Besides, the detection-based methods treat the body parts as detection targets based on two widely used representations: image patches and heatmaps of joint locations [10–12]. For example, PoseNet is a widely utilized algorithm for human pose estimation with monocular images [13]. While it has a high detection accuracy, it is not suitable for lung region extraction because of a smaller number of torso data points segmented. On the contrary, DensePose is another real-time approach for mapping a 3D surface-based model of the body to human pixels from 2D RGB images [14]. DensePose generates a mesh data of the human body, from which several sub-meshes including a torso sub-mesh can be extracted. We utilize DensePose to obtain the torso mesh data and to augment the "overlay", the scanning region information for the ultrasound probe tracking and the LUS guidance and navigation. Further, ArUco markers [15] are used for the detection and guidance of an ultrasound probe for regions on the chest to facilitate an effective LUS.

In this paper, we present the AR-based LUS guidance with the outline described in the following order. First, Sect. 2 describes the implementation of the utilization of DensePose along with the ultrasound probe tracking using ArUco markers and the regression-based overlay region estimation. Next, Sect. 3 describes the experimental setup. Finally, Sect. 4 presents and discusses the results for overlay generation, probe tracking, and regression-based region estimation.

2 Materials and Methods

2.1 Lung Ultrasound Scanning Protocol

LUS is performed by scanning pre-defined regions of the chest. In a common clinical workflow, the operator scans 8 regions in a supine position with 4 locations on the front and 2 on each side of the chest [16, 18]. For the LUS procedure also including the prone position, an additional 2 to 6 regions are scanned on the back, increasing the total number of regions to be 10 to 14 [17, 19–23]. Table 1 summarizes the scanning regions of different LUS protocol. While more regions provide more information for the diagnosis, LUS in the supine position is more focused especially in emergency ultrasound because the prone position is not always accessible due to the immobility of patients. To avoid the complexity of guidance and workflow, this paper focuses on 4 anterior and 4 lateral chest regions for a corresponding AR overlay. The landmark method is used to obtain LUS data from specific landmarks on the chest.

Table 1. Regions and locations of different LUS protocols.

Ref. no.	# of regions	Region location	Guidance
[16]	8	4 anterior, 4 lateral	Landmark
[17]	12	12 zones	Rib
[18]	8	4 anterior, 4 lateral	Linear and curved
[19]	12	4 anterior, 4 lateral, 4 posterior	Exhaustive
[20]	12	Complex regions	Landmark
[21]	12	4 anterior, 4 lateral, 4 posterior	Landmark
[22]	14	4 anterior, 4 lateral, 6 posterior	Landmark
[23]	14	4 anterior, 4 lateral, 6 posterior	Exhaustive

2.2 DensePose-Based Upper Body Detection and Region Estimation

DensePose is a deep learning algorithm which establishes dense correspondences from 2D images to a 3D surface-based model of the human body using a single RGB image [20]. The algorithm uses the architecture of Mask-RCNN (Region-Based Convolutional Neural Network) [22] with FPN (Feature Pyramid Network) Features [23] and ROI (Region of Interest) Align pooling to obtain part labels and coordinates within each region. The supervised deep learning algorithm has the convolutional network on the top of the ROI pooling which generates per-pixel classification results for the selection of the surface part and regresses local coordinates within the part [20].

The region of interest for LUS is defined through the torso surface partition obtained after implementing the DensePose algorithm on a test image (Fig. 1(a)). The 2D surface partition thus obtained is partitioned into half to consider two hemithoraces (Fig. 1(c)). A new image is created by extracting all pixels with value 2 (relating to the torso region) in layer I. The U and V coordinates of this sub-region are used to draw an overlay based on [1] as shown in Fig. 1(b). The augmented scanning regions are used as a reference to assist the operator to perform the LUS based on a landmark-based method, as described in Sect. 2.1. Figure 1(c) shows I, U, and V layers.

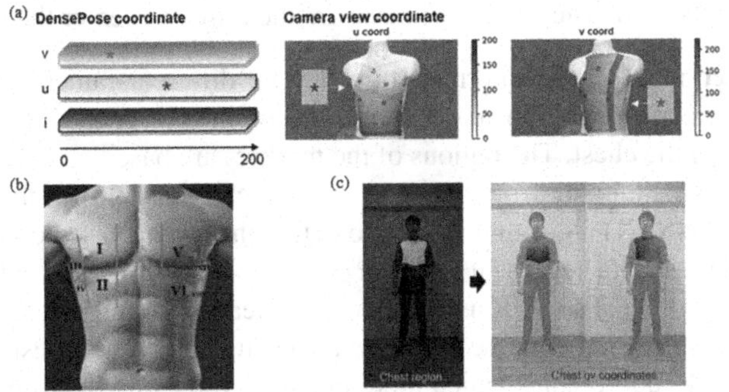

Fig. 1. DensePose-based torso region estimation: (a) DensePose Coordinates, (b) targeted LUS scanning regions augmented on the body based on the protocol presented in [16], & (c) post-processed IUV images for chest segmentation.

2.3 Probe Tracking and Scanning Region Training Using ArUco Markers

ArUco markers are binary square fiducial markers used to find correspondences to obtain the marker pose for the camera frame [21]. 6×6 marker dictionary is used which has 36 bits in the inner binary matrix. ArUco library is a part of the OpenCV python module cv2 which uses Numpy array data types. The *aruco.detectMarkers* function is used to detect the marker, its features, and identification information. Once the marker has been detected, the camera pose can be estimated given the internal camera matrix utilizing the *aruco.estimatePoseSingleMarkers* function.

To enable tracking of the ultrasound probe and to train the LUS scanning regions, 8 different ArUco markers were placed at 8 different locations on the chest based on regions shown in Fig. 1(b). Besides, an ArUco marker was also placed on top of the ultrasound probe, and the transformation matrix was calculated between the ArUco marker on the ultrasound probe and its tip. Then, based on the sequence of navigation to different regions on the chest, an arrow points towards the marker in the desired region to facilitate navigation of the markers. We obtained the 3 by 3 internal camera matrix, *cmat* for Logitech C920 webcam after calibrating with 20 different images of a checkerboard. This is used to obtain the tip position in *XYZ* coordinates as explained in Sect. 3.

2.4 Improving the Overlay Generation

While implementing the DensePose algorithm, there are two challenges: centering of torso mesh model irrespective of the camera angle, and inaccuracies in the mesh overlay (described in Fig. 1(b)) for varying camera angles (Fig. 2(b)). The angle was measured laterally assuming the anterior part of the body to be perpendicular to the testbed. In this subsection, we explain solutions to these issues.

Centering Torso Model. To center the torso overlay for varying camera angles, an ArUco marker was placed at the center of the torso near the neck. Center 'X' and 'Y' coordinates from the marker and the corresponding 'V' center coordinates given by DensePose are extracted. The 'V' coordinates are then used to center the torso overlay.

Overlay Correction. To have a corrected overlay for different camera angles, regression models are trained. The trained data are based on the 'U' and 'V' locations of the ArUco markers on the chest. The regions of the markers are based on Fig. 1(a). Models are trained for angles ranging from 40°–140° at an increment of 5° each. The Support Vector Regression (SVR) algorithm is used to define the model based on the data [24]. SVR is chosen for the data because it has been proven to be an effective tool in real-value function estimation [25]. The SVR uses a supervised learning approach and trains using a symmetrical loss function which equally penalizes high and low misestimates. Using SVR, the 'U' & 'V' coordinates which more precisely reflecting the true locations are predicted by using the camera angle as input to the machine learning model.

3 Experimental Implementation

The tracked ultrasound probe is used to navigate its scanning path from one region to the next through the combination with the AR-based guidance. Figure 2(a) shows the setup for probe tracking utilizing a camera. An ArUco marker is mounted on the top of the ultrasound probe for pose tracking.

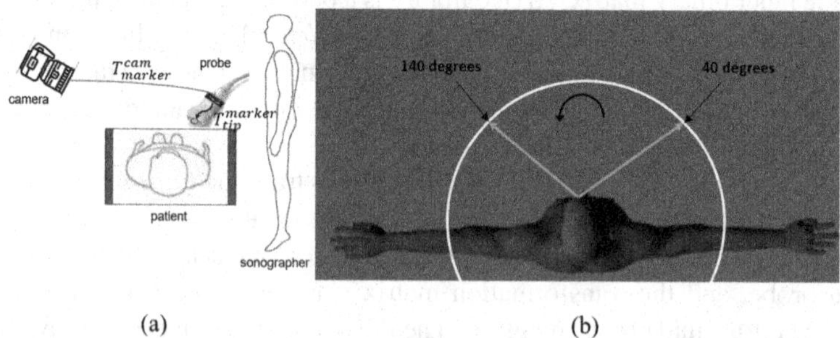

(a) (b)

Fig. 2. (a) Ultrasound probe tracking and guidance setup. (b) Angle measurement from 40°–140° at an increment of 5° with the camera along the circle in white.

Denoting the 4 by 4 homogeneous transformation matrix from camera frame to marker frame as T^{cam}_{marker} and from marker frame to transducer tip as T^{marker}_{tip}, T^{marker}_{cam} can be obtained using the *aruco.estimatePoseSingleMarkers* function. Equation 1 denotes the 3D coordinates of the tip location $tip_{xyz} = \left[tip_x, tip_y, tip_z\right]^T$ which is obtained as:

$$\begin{bmatrix} tip_{xyz} \\ 1 \end{bmatrix} = T^{cam}_{marker} \cdot T^{marker}_{tip}. \tag{1}$$

To determine the tip position $tip_{uv} = [tip_u, tip_v]^T$ for the regions, camera XYZ coordinates are converted to UV coordinates by applying the transformation defined in Eq. 2 as

$$\begin{bmatrix} tip_{uv} \\ 1 \end{bmatrix} = cmat.T^{world}_{cam}.\begin{bmatrix} tip_{xyz} \\ 1 \end{bmatrix}. \tag{2}$$

T^{world}_{cam} is the homogeneous transformation matrix from the world frame to the camera frame. Since the camera frame is defined as the world frame, T^{world}_{cam} is 3 by 3 identity matrix concatenated with $[0, 0, 0]^T$ to the right.

Figure 2(b) introduces the data collection process from the subjects. While laying in the supine position, the project member takes pictures of the human chest, with angles measured from 40°–140° at an increment of 5° with the camera along the circle in white.

4 Results and Discussion

Figure 3 presents the DensePose verification where the camera is set at the chest level to get the body images from 20 different angles. 8 ArUco markers (ID# from 1 to 8) were attached to the center of eight regions on the chest. An additional marker (ID# 9) was attached to the lower-neck region for locating the center of the overlay. 20 sub-figures corresponding to 20 angles were processed using DensePose and the overlay was generated.

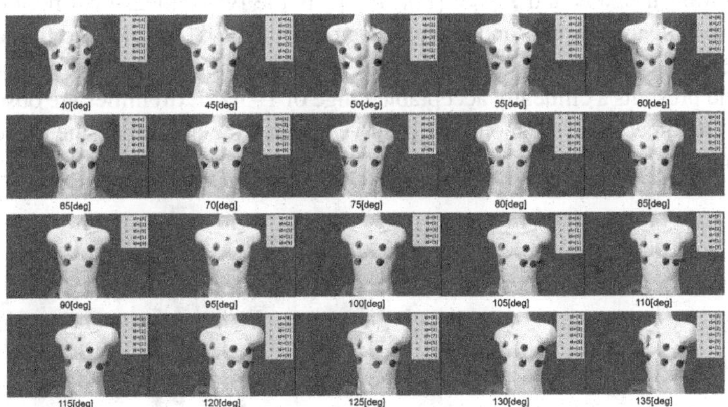

Fig. 3. DensePose verification for angles ranging from 40°–135° at an increment of 5°.

'U' and 'V' data corresponding to the different markers taken from camera angles from 40 to 140° at an increment of 5° were collected. To provide the best fit for the various streams of data (8 different u and v points), machine-learning based regression algorithms were utilized. Data preprocessing was done to eliminate the angles for which the marker 'U' and 'V' coordinates were zero. A total of 8 different pairs of regression models were trained, each pair corresponding to 'U' and 'V' coordinates per marker. R^2 score was utilized as a goodness of fit measure to quantify the performance of the machine learning models. Table 2 shows the R^2 score for 'U' and 'V' coordinate predictions for different camera angles for the 8 markers. Superscript 'w' has been used for 'U' predictions for marker 1 and 6 to denote the weighted data used to generate the final score. This was done to minimize the effect of outliers obtained during support vector regression modeling.

Table 2. R^2 score for U and V value predictions for the 8 markers.

Marker number	1	2	3	4	5	6	7	8
U	0.88^{w}	0.77	0.85	0.91	0.76	0.84^{w}	0.99	0.84
V	0.98	0.98	0.89	0.95	0.98	0.97	0.99	0.85

To evaluate whether the segmentation based on DensePose matches the desired segmentation, the error vector $e(i)$ in pixel space was defined as the Cartesian distance between the center of the overlay region and the center of the corresponding ArUco marker as defined in Eq. 4 as

$$e(i) = \frac{||P_m(i) - P_d(i)||}{\sqrt{w^2 + h^2}} \tag{4}$$

where $i \in [1, 8]$ is the region index, $P_m = \left[P_{mx}, P_{my}\right]^T$ is the two-dimensional marker center position in pixels and $P_d = \left[P_{dx}, P_{dy}\right]^T$ is the two-dimensional region center generated from DensePose. w and h are the frame width (1920 pixels) and frame height (1080 pixels) respectively. Figure 4 shows the region segmentation error for the marker position and presents a clinically acceptable range of 1–5%. Extremities are observed in markers 1 and 6 because of the outliers observed during the training of the model using the SVR algorithm.

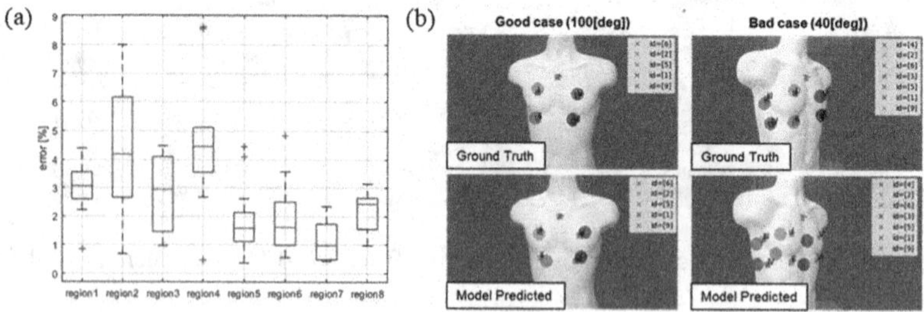

Fig. 4. (a) Scanning region segmentation error values from the true marker locations. Percentile errors were computed for the camera view dimension (frame size: 1080 * 1920 pixels). (b) Examples of the scanning region overlay with ground truth locations and locations predicted by the SVR model. (Color figure online)

The workflow of the real-time scanning procedure of the proposed guidance system is shown in Fig. 5. First, an overlay is generated using DensePose (area marked in red).

Due to high deploying requirements and relatively low running speed of DensePose, for 'real-time' scanning of the patient, assuming that the patient does not move during the ultrasound test, an overlay was generated once at the left and right sides, respectively. The distance between the ultrasound probe tip and the marker location is monitored and used to determine the switch of guidance from one region to another. The system guides the operator to move the probe from the center of the visible region (anterior chest) at the side to the center of the last visible region (lateral chest) using the green arrow. The developed system can be integrated with the head-mounted display or hand-held phone-based guidance for AR implementation. Future works include incorporation of LUS with the prone position as well as improving the pose estimation algorithms to achieve better region identification.

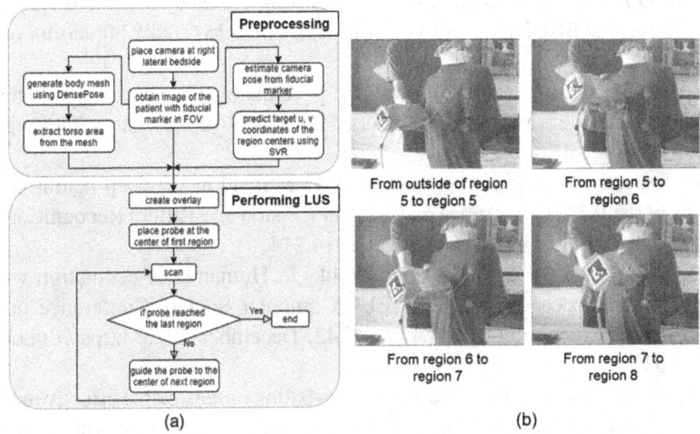

Fig. 5. (a) The workflow of the AR-based LUS guidance system. (b) Screenshots of real-time demonstration of the right chest as an example (right chest covers region 5 to 8).

5 Conclusions

In this paper, an AR-based LUS guidance framework is introduced by utilizing the scanning region identification through a combination of DensePose and ArUco markers for assisting diagnosis and subsequent monitoring of COVID-19 patients. An AR overlay can assist the sonographer to carry out the LUS for the diagnosis of respiratory illnesses such as COVID-19. Machine learning algorithms have been used to further improve the LUS region augmentation by minimizing the camera angle-associated inaccuracy. This system presents a demonstration of the capability to utilize AR, machine learning, and computer vision to help POCUS-based diagnosis and monitoring of lung-related illnesses such as COVID-19.

Acknowledgment. The financial support was provided through the Worcester Polytechnic Institute's internal fund; in part by the National Institute of Health (DP5 OD028162).

References

1. Lichtenstein, D., Mezière, G., Biderman, P., Gepner, A.: The comet-tail artifact: an ultrasound sign ruling out pneumothorax. Intensiv. Care Med. **25**(4), 383–388 (1999). https://doi.org/10.1007/s001340050862
2. WHO: Coronavirus Disease 2019 (COVID-19) Situation Reports, 1 April 2020. WHO Situation Report 2019(72), 1–19. https://www.who.int/docs/default-source/coronaviruse/situation-reports/20200324-sitrep-64-covid-19.pdf?sfvrsn=703b2c40_2%0Ahttps://www.who.int/docs/default-source/coronaviruse/situation-reports/20200401-sitrep-72-covid-19.pdf?sfvrsn=3dd8971b_2
3. Soldati, G., et al.: Is there a role for lung ultrasound during the COVID-19 pandemic? J. Ultrasound Med. Off. J. Am. Inst. Ultrasound Med., 1–4 (2020) https://doi.org/10.1002/jum.15284Ads
4. Lichtenstein, D.A., Mezière, G.A.: Relevance of lung ultrasound in the diagnosis of acute respiratory failure the BLUE protocol. Chest **134**(1), 117–125 (2008). https://doi.org/10.1378/chest.07-2800
5. Chen, Y., Tian, Y., He, M.: Monocular human pose estimation: a survey of deep learning-based methods. Comput. Vis. Image Underst. **192**, 1–23 (2020). https://doi.org/10.1016/j.cviu.2019.102897
6. Toshev, A., Szegedy, C.: DeepPose: Human pose estimation via deep neural networks. In: Proceedings of the IEEE Conference on Computer Vision and Pattern Recognition, pp. 1653–1660 (2014). https://doi.org/10.1109/CVPR.2014.214
7. Carreira, J., Agrawal, P., Fragkiadaki, K., Malik, J.: Human pose estimation with iterative error feedback. In: Proceedings of the IEEE Computer Society Conference on Computer Vision and Pattern Recognition, pp. 4733–4742, December 2016. https://doi.org/10.1109/CVPR.2016.512
8. Sun, C., Shrivastava, A., Singh, S., Gupta, A.: Revisiting unreasonable effectiveness of data in deep learning era. In: Proceedings of the IEEE International Conference on Computer Vision, pp. 843–852, October 2017. https://doi.org/10.1109/ICCV.2017.97
9. Luvizon, D.C., Tabia, H., Picard, D.: Human pose regression by combining indirect part detection and contextual information. Comput. Graph. (Pergamon) **85**, 15–22 (2019). https://doi.org/10.1016/j.cag.2019.09.002
10. Fourure, D., Emonet, R., Fromont, E., Muselet, D., Tremeau, A., Wolf, C.: Residual conv-deconv grid network for semantic segmentation. In: British Machine Vision Conference, BMVC 2017 (2017). https://arxiv.org/pdf/1707.07958.pdf
11. Sun, K., Xiao, B., Liu, D., Wang, J.: Deep high-resolution representation learning for human pose estimation. In: Proceedings of the IEEE Computer Society Conference on Computer Vision and Pattern Recognition, pp. 5686–5696, June 2019. https://doi.org/10.1109/CVPR.2019.00584
12. Tang, W., Wu, Y.: Does learning specific features for related parts help human pose estimation? In: Proceedings of the IEEE Computer Society Conference on Computer Vision and Pattern Recognition, pp. 1107–1116, June 2019. https://doi.org/10.1109/CVPR.2019.00120
13. Chen, Y., Shen, C., Wei, X.S., Liu, L., Yang, J.: Adversarial PoseNet: a structure-aware convolutional network for human pose estimation. In: Proceedings of the IEEE International Conference on Computer Vision, pp. 1221–1230, October 2017. https://doi.org/10.1109/ICCV.2017.137
14. Guler, R.A., Neverova, N., Kokkinos, I.: DensePose: dense human pose estimation in the wild. In: Proceedings of the IEEE Conference on Computer Vision and Pattern Recognition, pp. 7297–7306 (2016). https://doi.org/10.1109/CVPR.2017.280

15. Romero-Ramirez, F.J., Muñoz-Salinas, R., Medina-Carnicer, R.: Speeded up detection of squared fiducial markers. Image Vis. Comput. **76**, 38–47 (2018). https://doi.org/10.1016/j.imavis.2018.05.004
16. Volpicelli, G., et al.: Bedside lung ultrasound in the assessment of alveolar-interstitial syndrome. Am. J. Emerg. Med. **24**(6), 689–696 (2006). https://doi.org/10.1016/j.ajem.2006.02.013
17. Manivel, V., Lesnewski, A., Shamim, S., Carbonatto, G., Govindan, T.: CLUE: COVID-19 lung ultrasound in emergency department. Emerg. Med. Australas., EMA (2020). https://doi.org/10.1111/1742-6723.13546
18. Moore, S., Gardiner, E.: Point of care and intensive care lung ultrasound: a reference guide for practitioners during COVID-19. Radiography (2020). https://doi.org/10.1016/j.radi.2020.04.005
19. Bouhemad, B., Mongodi, S., Via, G., Rouquette, I.: Ultrasound for "lung monitoring" of ventilated patients. Anesthesiology **122**(2), 437–447 (2015). https://doi.org/10.1097/ALN.0000000000000558
20. Lee, F.C.Y.: Lung ultrasound-a primary survey of the acutely dyspneic patient. J. Intensiv. Care **4**(1) (2016). https://doi.org/10.1186/s40560-016-0180-1
21. Via, G., et al.: Instrument to Respiratory Monitoring Tool, August 2012
22. Soldati, G., et al.: Proposal for international standardization of the use of lung ultrasound for patients with COVID-19: a simple, quantitative, reproducible method. J. Ultrasound Med. (2020). https://doi.org/10.1002/jum.15285
23. Moro, F., Buonsenso, D., et al.: How to perform lung ultrasound in pregnant women with suspected COVID-19. Ultrasound Obstet. Gynecol. Off. J. Int. Soc. Ultrasound Obstet. Gynecol. **55**(5), 593–598 (2020). https://doi.org/10.1002/uog.22028
24. Cortes, C., Vapnik, V.: Support-vector networks. Mach. Learn. **20**(3), 273–297 (1995)
25. Awad, M., Khanna, R.: Support vector regression. In: Efficient learning machines, pp. 67–80. Apress, Berkeley (2015)

Multimodality Biomedical Image Registration Using Free Point Transformer Networks

Zachary M. C. Baum(✉), Yipeng Hu, and Dean C. Barratt

Centre for Medical Image Computing and Wellcome/EPSRC Centre for Interventional and Surgical Sciences, University College London, London, UK
zachary.baum.19@ucl.ac.uk

Abstract. We describe a point-set registration algorithm based on a novel free point transformer (FPT) network, designed for points extracted from multimodal biomedical images for registration tasks, such as those frequently encountered in ultrasound-guided interventional procedures. FPT is constructed with a global feature extractor which accepts unordered source and target point-sets of variable size. The extracted features are conditioned by a shared multilayer perceptron point transformer module to predict a displacement vector for each source point, transforming it into the target space. The point transformer module assumes no vicinity or smoothness in predicting spatial transformation and, together with the global feature extractor, is trained in a data-driven fashion with an unsupervised loss function. In a multimodal registration task using prostate MR and sparsely acquired ultrasound images, FPT yields comparable or improved results over other rigid and non-rigid registration methods. This demonstrates the versatility of FPT to learn registration directly from real, clinical training data and to generalize to a challenging task, such as the interventional application presented.

Keywords: Deep-learning · Point-set registration · Prostate cancer

1 Introduction

Ultrasound imaging (US) is a widely used intraoperatively where real-time imaging is required. Owing to the difficulties in obtaining good quality diagnostic imaging which are associated with US, methods for image fusion between US and a second, usually preoperative, imaging modality are widely incorporated into image-guided interventions [1]. One use of multimodality image fusion is to provide magnetic resonance/transrectal ultrasound (MR-TRUS) fusion imaging during targeted prostate gland biopsies. MR-TRUS fusion superimposes the diagnostic information of magnetic resonance (MR) imaging on the transrectal ultrasound (TRUS) images. This enables clinicians to acquire samples from predefined lesions within the prostate in MR imaging and provides a real-time and low-cost solution that outperforms the current reference standard of US-guided systematic biopsy [2]. Furthermore, MR-TRUS fusion has been shown to improve the detection of high-grade prostate cancers and reduce sampling errors [3, 4]. Improved sampling benefits patient management as higher-risk patients are more likely to be identified and offered appropriate treatment options [4].

Y. Hu et al. (Eds.): ASMUS 2020/PIPPI 2020, LNCS 12437, pp. 116–125, 2020.
https://doi.org/10.1007/978-3-030-60334-2_12

With its growing clinical use [5], the registration of pre-operative MR imaging to intraoperative TRUS persists as an active area of research [6–9]. Canonically, methods for MR-TRUS fusion must overcome the non-linear intensity differences between imaging modalities. Such methods must also be generalizable as to effectively handle inter- and intra-patient variation. Complete 3D US acquisition is often needed to obtain a full field of view that contains the prostate gland for registration [6–9]. While 3D US requires the probe to be held in place manually or with an additional robotic/mechanical device, 3D-to-2D registration methods utilize inherently 2D US, without the additional hardware requirements of 3D US acquisition [10, 11]. However, recent advances in automatic, well-validated, learning-based segmentation methods for MR [12] and TRUS [12, 13] permit real-time delineation of anatomical surfaces. Such surfaces may provide simplified representations for efficient and, perhaps more importantly, robust multimodal image registration in place of purely image-based methods.

Point-set registration is a widely-used and well-defined registration technique where a rigid or non-rigid spatial transformation model is defined and, subsequently, the optimal transformation is determined by a set of parameters for that model. Existing point-set registration algorithms, such as Iterative Closest Point (ICP) [14] and Coherent Point Drift (CPD) [15], use iterative optimization processes to determine the transformation for a given pair of point-sets [14–18]. In practice, the iterative nature of such methods may hinder their use in real-time registration tasks, leaving them unable to effectively take full advantage of the inherently real-time nature of US. Given the abilities for efficient inference and modeling complex, non-linear transformations, learning-based point-set registration can support rapid registration updates on-the-fly with sparse data – a task previously considered infeasible during time-critical interventional procedures with iterative registration methods.

In this work, we present a novel deep neural network architecture for data-driven, non-rigid point-set registration. The proposed Free Point Transformer (FPT) is trained in an unsupervised manner and therefore does not require ground-truth deformation data, which can be infeasible to obtain in interventional applications. FPT learns non-rigid transformation between multimodal images without any prior constraints such as displacement coherence or deformation smoothness. FPT also generalizes accurately to sparse point sets sampled from previously unseen patient data.

We present a quantitative analysis of FPT's performance in the MR-to-TRUS point-set registration task and compare it to other rigid and non-rigid registration methods. This work demonstrates FPT's feasibility for continual real-time MR-TRUS fusion in prostate biopsy using sparse data which may be generated from automatically segmented sagittal and transverse slices available from existing bi-plane TRUS probes.

2 Methods

2.1 Network Architecture

FPT is composed of two modules, a global feature extractor, and a point transformer, as illustrated in Fig. 1.

The first module, the global feature extractor, accepts two point-sets: the target point-set, P_T, and the source point-set, P_S and serves to extract permutation invariant and rotation invariant features from the point-sets. This module was composed of twin weight-sharing PointNets. PointNet is a previously-proposed neural network architecture that operates on a single point-set and allows permutation invariance [19], which has transformed how point-sets are represented and interpreted in many computer vision tasks, such as classification and segmentation. In this work, the 'input and feature transformation' and the 'global information aggregation' components of the original PointNet [19] are utilized as our global feature extractor. The global feature extractor module allows FPT to create a permutation and transformation invariant embedding function. Weights are shared between each PointNet to ensure that the inputs to the network pass through the same embedding function, which then aggregates each input into a 1024-dimensional source and target feature vector, respectively. PointNet's 'T-net' modules ensure FPT only learns transformations between point-sets which are relevant to the task, by applying a 3 × 3 transformation matrix to the coordinates of the input points [19]. The source and target feature vectors are concatenated into a 2048-dimensional global feature vector.

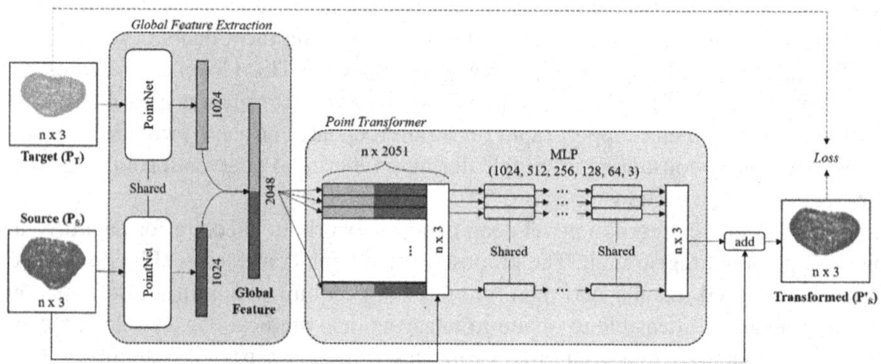

Fig. 1. Schematic representation of the FPT architecture for non-rigid point-set registration.

The second module, the point transformer, contains a series of weight-shared multilayer perceptrons (MLP). Each layer of the 6 layers consisted of a group of 2048 weight-shared fully connected layers with 1024, 512, 256, 128, 64, and 3 nodes per layer (Fig. 1). The first 5 layers used the ReLU activation function and the final layer used a linear activation function. This MLP is implemented as a series of 1D convolutions with a kernel size of one. This weight-sharing design choice allows potential regularization benefits for generalization, and ensures that each point passes through the point transformer via a common transformation function. The global feature vector is concatenated with each of the x, y, and z point location coordinates and passed through the MLP to produce an independent displacement vector for each point in P_S. This allows the global feature vector to be combined with all points in P_S, yet predict the displacements at individual locations independently using only the input point-sets. As such, the point transformer transforms each point without any constraints on smoothness or spatial coherence. The point transformer is only conditioned on the input feature vectors to determine a "model-free" transformation. Finally, the displacement vectors are added to P_S, to yield the transformed point-set, $P_S{}'$, upon which a loss may be computed.

2.2 Loss Function

Instead of an often-constrained spatial transformation model, FPT utilized a data-driven strategy to predict a displacement field on unstructured point locations. Prior knowledge regarding outliers, missing data and noise can be handled through data augmentation, reduction, and perturbation of the training data, respectively. Among distance metrics that do not require established correspondence, many require additional parameter tuning and explicit consideration of outliers or noise levels, such as those based on the likelihood or the divergence between point distributions.

In this work, we train using sparse data to illustrate the efficacy of our data-driven approach with a Chamfer distance [20]. We utilized the Chamfer distance as the basis for our loss function as it is simple to compute and easily parallelizable [20]. Our implementation has adapted the original Chamfer distance to a two-way formulation that minimizes mean distances between nearest neighbors in P_T and $P_S{}'$. However, other types of metrics and possible loss functions warrant investigation in future studies.

2.3 Implementation Details

FPT was trained using the ModelNet40 [21] dataset was used to pre-train FPT. This was done with a minibatch size of 32 and a learning rate of 10^{-3} with the Adam optimizer. By pre-training with a large dataset, we leverage what was learned with ModelNet40 to improve generalizability in another setting [22]. ModelNet40 contains meshes of 40 distinct shapes which are randomly split into a 9843 model training set and a 2468 model testing set. The point-sets are a collection of 2048 points uniformly sampled from these mesh surfaces. In training, the point-sets were augmented on-the-fly with scaling, deformation, and a transformation comprised of rotation and displacement. Point-sets were scaled, per-sample, between $[-1, 1]$. The scaled input is used as P_T. We simulated the non-rigid transformations on the scaled point-sets by TPS transformation. TPS deformation was defined by a perturbation of the control points by Gaussian random shift. Rotation angles for the transformation were randomly sampled from $[-45°, 45°]$ about each axis, with displacements randomly sampled from $[-1, 1]$ in each of the X, Y, and Z directions. The scaled, deformed, and transformed version of the input was used as P_S. The known transformations were only used for validation, as training was unsupervised.

3 Experiments

3.1 Data

The experimental dataset used in our evaluation was comprised of 108 pairs of pre-operative T2-weighted MR and intraoperative TRUS images from 76 patients which were acquired during the Smart Target clinical trials [23]. The dataset was split into training and testing sets, each containing 54 (50%) of the 108 patient pairs. Given its data-driven architecture, FPT was not defined by any hyperparameters beyond those described in Sect. 2.3. In this work, we did not use a hold-out set to prevent bias through an exhaustive hyperparameter search when fine-tuning the networks for the experiments described in Sect. 3.3. Therefore, this two-way random split experiment provided a non-overfitted estimate of registration performance, although data from different centers or differing acquisition protocols are still of value for future validation.

3.2 Implementation Details

In each experiment, the performance on the MR to TRUS registration task was evaluated using four different methods: center-alignment, ICP, CPD, and FPT. Center-alignment simply involved aligning the mean of each input point-set at the origin. ICP [14] is a widely-used, iterative method for rigid point-set registration. CPD [15] is a widely-validated, non-rigid, and iterative point-set registration algorithm.

As we sought to demonstrate the feasibility of FPT, we did not perform an exhaustive search of hyperparameter combinations for all methods to which ours is compared. All settings and implementation details that provided the best results in our search for each method are reported below. ICP was allowed to run for up to 25 iterations, all other parameters or initializations were performed as described in [14]. CPD was performed with $w = 0$, making the weight of the uniform distribution zero. We permitted CPD to run for up to 150 iterations. All other parameters remained as default [15]. The use of potentially non-optimized ICP and CPD also demonstrates the importance of initialization and parameter-tuning for such methods.

FPT was tested in two variations. First, where the network was only pre-trained on ModelNet40, as described in Sect. 2.3, and second, where the ModelNet40-trained network was fine-tuned on the MR-TRUS training dataset. Fine-tuning was performed with the same parameters which were used in pre-training. When fine-tuning, P_T was defined as the normalized TRUS prostate surface points, and P_S was defined as the normalized MR prostate surface points. No deformation, translation, or rotation was added to the surface points. No trainable weights of the networks were frozen.

3.3 Experimental Protocol

MR to TRUS Registration

In the first experiment, we presented each method with all TRUS and MR surface points to assess each method with complete data. For FPT, fine-tuning was performed with the training set. All evaluations were performed using only the testing set.

MR to Sparse TRUS Registration

In the second experiment, we assessed the performance of each method using sparse TRUS surface points to reflect a plausible clinical scenario, as described in Sect. 1. To simulate sparse TRUS data, we simulated TRUS surface points captured from one simultaneous acquisition from a biplane TRUS in the sagittal and transverse planes

(Fig. 2). This was done by removing the TRUS surface points which would not be visible in one simultaneous acquisition. As with our first experiment, fine-tuning was performed with the training set, and all evaluations were performed with the testing set.

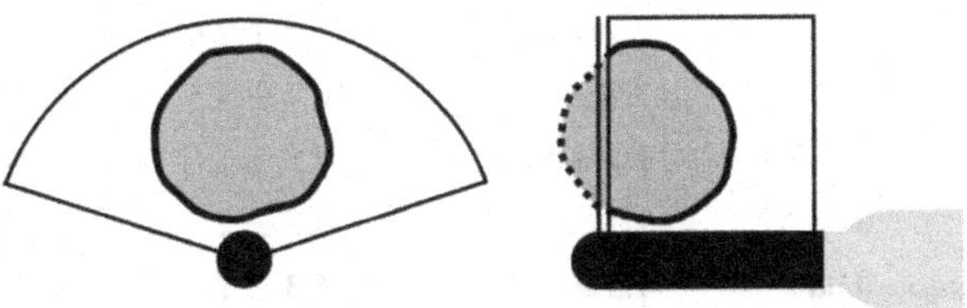

Fig. 2. Illustration of contours from which surface points would be extracted from a biplane TRUS transducer. Points from the transverse plane (left) and sagittal plane (right) that would be used are shown with solid lines. Dashed lines and other surface points are discarded.

Evaluation Metrics

All registrations were evaluated on their displacement predictions using Chamfer distance (D_C), Hausdorff distance (D_H), and registration time. We report registration accuracy on independent landmarks with target registration error (TRE) as has been used in many prior studies validation multimodal image registration [6–9], where its clinical relevance has been established. TRE is defined as the root-mean-square of the distances computed between all pairs of registered source and target landmarks for each patient. The landmarks comprised of 145 pairs of points included the apex and base of the prostate and patient-specific landmarks such as zonal structure boundaries, water-filled cysts, and calcifications, the spatial distribution of which is representative of the target registration distribution in this application. Landmarks were not included in any training, fine-tuning, or registration processes.

4 Results

Our quantitative results for the first experiment (Table 1) demonstrate a fine-tuned FPT's comparable or improved results to ICP and CPD in all metrics. Example qualitative results from the first experiment are provided in Fig. 3.

In the second experiment (Table 2), a fine-tuned FPT demonstrates improved results across all metrics, compared with those from ICP and CPD. Fine-tuning also further improves the registrations with respect to D_C and D_H. Comparing inference times, FPT requires, on average, 0.08 s per registration, compared with 0.14 s and 11 s, for ICP and CPD, respectively. Example qualitative results from the second experiment are provided in Fig. 4.

Table 1. Results from the first experiment, using complete TRUS data. STD: standard deviation.

Methods	Time (s)	D_C (mm)	D_H (mm)	TRE (mm)
	Mean	Mean ± STD	Mean ± STD	Mean ± STD
Center-aligned	–	2.7 ± 0.9	10.7 ± 2.6	5.1 ± 1.7
ICP [14]	0.15	2.5 ± 1.0	10.4 ± 2.5	4.9 ± 1.8
CPD [15]	13.77	**1.2 ± 0.2**	6.5 ± 1.6	4.8 ± 1.9
FPT	**0.08**	1.7 ± 0.3	8.2 ± 2.1	4.9 ± 1.9
FPT (fine tuned)	**0.08**	1.5 ± 0.2	**6.3 ± 1.6**	**4.7 ± 1.8**

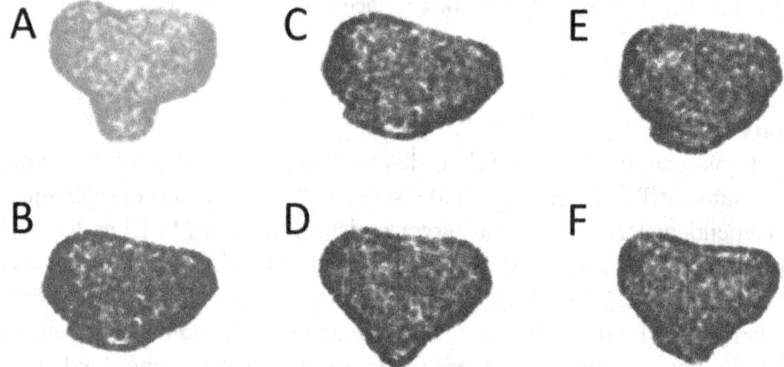

Fig. 3. Registration results from the first experiment on a target (a) and source (b) point-set using ICP (c), CPD (d), FPT (e), and FPT after fine-tuning (f).

Table 2. Results from the second experiment, using sparse TRUS data. STD: standard deviation.

Methods	Time (s)	D_C (mm)	D_H (mm)	TRE (mm)
	Mean	Mean ± STD	Mean ± STD	Mean ± STD
Center-aligned	–	2.9 ± 1.0	10.9 ± 2.7	5.3 ± 1.7
ICP [14]	0.13	2.6 ± 1.0	10.5 ± 2.4	5.0 ± 1.7
CPD [15]	11.08	7.2 ± 1.4	19.8 ± 4.5	6.9 ± 2.7
FPT	**0.08**	4.1 ± 0.8	11.3 ± 2.8	**4.4 ± 1.4**
FPT (fine tuned)	**0.08**	**1.9 ± 0.3**	**6.8 ± 1.4**	4.9 ± 1.7

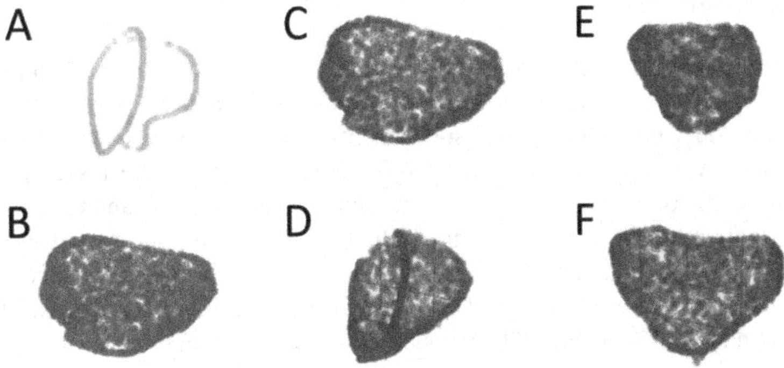

Fig. 4. Registration results from the second experiment on a sparse target (a) and source (b) point-set using ICP (c), CPD (d), FPT (e), and FPT after fine-tuning (f). The complete surface of (a) is identical to Fig. 3a.

5 Discussion

Conventional intensity-based registration algorithms for MR-TRUS fusion samples intensity information directly, whereas FPT receives only geometric and spatial information from the surface point-sets in the form of very limited and, potentially, easy-to-acquire data 2D US slices. Recently, conventional methods have obtained TREs of 1.5 mm [6], 2.4 mm [7], 1.9 mm [8], or 3.6 mm [9], validated on 16, 8, 8, and 76 patients respectively. Potentially, the robustness of point-set extraction from prostate gland segmentation may reduce variance in registration error, although additional validation is needed to draw further conclusions. However, comparing to other iterative or learning-based intensity-based registration methods may be considered outside of the scope of this work, due to the specific clinical scenarios of interest such as sparse slice availability. Nonetheless, our results demonstrate that FPT can directly learn descriptive and data-driven features from sparse data. From these features, FPT can efficiently compute a set of accurate displacements, as compared to conventional image-based registration methods. Further validation and investigation are required to assess FPT's ability to generalize on multi-center data, wherein there may be increased data heterogeneity.

Without fine-tuning, we see that FPT demonstrates the lowest TRE on the test dataset. It is possible that fine-tuning may result in FPT overfitting the training dataset, yielding a higher TRE. However, the fine-tuned FPT greatly outperforms the non-fine-tuned FPT in D_C, upon which it is trained to minimize, and D_H.

Given its rapid point-set registration approach, FPT may serve other multimodality registration applications, such as computed tomography/US (CT-US) fusion, well. As previously described with MR-TRUS fusion, CT-US fusion is an active area of research; with its use ranging from surgical interventions [24, 25] to radiotherapy planning [26]. As such, non-rigid point-set registration of surfaces extracted from US and CT may provide useful intraoperative visualizations which are of interest in future work, given the results in this work for prostate with MR-TRUS fusion.

6 Conclusion

We have presented Free Point Transformer (FPT), a deep neural network architecture for unsupervised data-driven point-set registration. FPT learns the displacement field required to produce individual point displacements using only the geometric information of its inputs. Evaluated on a real-world MR to TRUS registration task, FPT yields improvements or comparable performance to Iterative Closest Point and Coherent Point Drift. Most saliently, this work demonstrates that with a variable point-set sparsity, which may be generated from automatically segmented sagittal and transverse slices, readily available for all existing bi-plane TRUS probes in realistic clinical practices, FPT may enable continual real-time MR-TRUS fusion during prostate biopsies.

Acknowledgments. Z. Baum is supported by the Natural Sciences and Engineering Research Council of Canada Postgraduate Scholarships-Doctoral Program, the University College London Overseas and Graduate Research Scholarships. This work is also supported by the Wellcome/EPSRC Centre for Interventional and Surgical Sciences (203145Z/16/Z).

References

1. Maintz, J.B., Viergever, M.A.: A survey of medical image registration. Med. Image Anal. **2**(5), 1–36 (1998)
2. Costa, D.N., Pedrosa, I., Donato, F., Roehrborn, C.G., Rofsky, N.M.: MR imaging-transrectal US fusion for targeted prostate biopsies: implication for diagnosis and clinical management. RadioGraphics **35**(3), 696–708 (2015)
3. Puech, P., et al.: Prostate cancer diagnosis: multiparametric MR-targeted biopsy with cognitive and transrectal US-MR fusion guidance versus systematic biopsy – prospective multicenter study. Radiology **268**(2), 461–469 (2013)
4. Lavaerts, M., De Wever, L., Vanhoutte, E., De Keyzer, F., Oyen, R.: TRUS-MR fusion biopsy of the prostate: radiological and histological correlation. J. Belg. Soc. Radiol. **100**(1), 1–9 (2016)
5. Valerio, M., et al.: Detection of clinically significant prostate cancer using magnetic resonance imaging-ultrasound fusion targeted biopsy: a systematic review. Eur. Radiol. **68**(1), 8–19 (2015)
6. Karnik, V.V., et al.: Assessment of image registration accuracy in three-dimensional transrectal ultrasound guided prostate biopsy. Med. Phys. **37**(2), 802–813 (2010)
7. Hu, Y., et al.: MR to ultrasound registration for image-guided prostate interventions. Med. Image Anal. **16**(3), 687–703 (2012)
8. De Silva, T., et al.: 2D-3D rigid registration to compensate for prostate motion during 3D TRUS-guided biopsy. Med. Phys. **40**(2), 022904-1–022904-13 (2013)
9. Hu, Y., et al.: Weakly-supervised convolutional neural networks for multimodal image registration. Med. Image Anal. **49**, 1–13 (2018)
10. Zhang, S., Jiang, S., Yang, Z., Liu, R.: 2D ultrasound and 3D MR image reconstruction of the prostate for brachytherapy surgical navigation. Med. (Balt.) **94**(40), e1643 (2015)
11. Gilles, D.J., Gardi, L., De Silva, T., Zhao, S.R., Fenster, A.: Real-time registration of 3D to 2D ultrasound images for image-guided prostate biopsy. Med. Phys. **44**(9), 4708–4723 (2017)
12. van Sloun, R.J.G., et al.: Deep learning for real-time, automatic, and scanner adapted prostate (zone) segmentation of transrectal ultrasound, for example, magnetic resonance imaging-transrectal ultrasound fusion prostate biopsy. Eur. Urol. Focus. (2019). https://doi.org/10.1016/j.euf.2019.04.009

13. Ghavami, N., et al.: Integration of spatial information in convolutional neural networks for automatic segmentation of intraoperative transrectal ultrasound images. J. Med. Imaging **6**(1), 011003-1, 011003-6 (2018)
14. Besl, P.J., McKay, N.D.: A method for registration of 3-D shapes. IEEE Trans. Pattern Anal. Mach. Intell. **14**(2), 239–256 (1992)
15. Myronenko, A., Song, X.: Point set registration: coherent point drift. IEEE Trans. Pattern Anal. Mach. Intell. **32**(12), 2262–2275 (2010)
16. Jian, B., Vemuri, B.C.: Robust point set registration using gaussian mixture models. IEEE Trans. Pattern Anal. Mach. Intell. **33**(8), 1633–1645 (2010)
17. Chui, H., Rangarajan, A.: A new point matching algorithm for non-rigid registration. Comput. Vis. Image Underst. **89**(2–3), 114–141 (2003)
18. Aoki, Y., Goforth, H., Srivatsan, R.A., Lucey, S.: PointNetLK: robust and efficient point cloud registration using PointNet. In: The IEEE Conference on Computer Vision and Pattern Recognition, pp. 7163–7172. IEEE (2019)
19. Qi, C.R., Su, H., Mo, K., Guibas, L.J.: PointNet: deep learning on point sets for 3D classification and segmentation. In: The IEEE Conference on Computer Vision and Pattern Recognition, pp. 652–660. IEEE (2017)
20. Fan, H., Su, H., Guibas, L.J.: A point set generation network for 3D object reconstruction from a single image. In: The IEEE Conference on Computer Vision and Pattern Recognition, pp. 605–613. IEEE (2017)
21. Wu, Z., et al.: 3D ShapeNets: a deep representation for volumetric shapes. In: The IEEE Conference on Computer Vision and Pattern Recognition, pp. 1912–1920. IEEE (2015)
22. Pan, S.J., Yang, Q.: A survey on transfer learning. IEEE Trans. Knowl. Data Eng. **22**(10), 1345–1359 (2010)
23. Donaldson, I., et al.: MP33-20 the smart target biopsy trial: a prospective paired blinded trial with randomization to compare visual-estimation and image-fusion targeted prosate biopsies. J. Urol. **197**(4), e425 (2017)
24. Wein, W., Brunke, S., Khamene, A., Callstrom, M.R., Navab, N.: Automatic ct-ultrasound registration for diagnostic imaging and image-guided intervention. Med. Image Anal. **12**(5), 577–585 (2008)
25. Gueziri, H.-E., Drouin, S., Yan, C.X.B., Collins, D.L.: Toward real-time rigid registration of intra-operative ultrasound with preoperative ct images for lumbar spinal fusion surgery. Int. J. Comput. Assist. Radiol. Surg. **14**(11), 1933–1943 (2019)
26. Wein, W., Roper, B., Navab, N.: Automatic registration and fusion of ultrasound with ct for radiotherapy. In: International Conference on Medical Image Computing and Computer-Assisted Intervention, pp. 303–311 (2005)

Label Efficient Localization of Fetal Brain Biometry Planes in Ultrasound Through Metric Learning

Yuan Gao[1(✉)], Sridevi Beriwal[2], Rachel Craik[2,3], Aris T. Papageorghiou[2], and J. Alison Noble[1]

[1] Institute of Biomedical Engineering, University of Oxford, Oxford, UK
yuan.gao2@eng.ox.ac.uk

[2] Nuffield Department of Women's and Reproductive Health, University of Oxford, Oxford, UK

[3] King's College, London, UK

Abstract. For many emerging medical image analysis problems, there is limited data and associated annotations. Traditional deep learning is not well-designed for this scenario. In addition, for deploying deep models on a consumer-grade tablet, it requires models to be efficient computationally. In this paper, we describe a framework for automatic quality assessment of freehand fetal ultrasound video that has been designed and built subject to constraints such as those encountered in low-income settings: ultrasound data acquired by minimally trained users, using a low-cost ultrasound probe and android tablet. Here the goal is to ensure that each video contains good neurosonography biometry planes for estimating the head circumference (HC) and transcerebellar diameter (TCD). We propose a label efficient learning framework for this purpose that it turns out generalises well to unseen data. The framework is semi-supervised consisting of two major components: 1) a prototypical learning module that learns categorical embeddings implicitly to prevent the model from overfitting; and, 2) a semantic transfer module (to unlabelled data) that performs "temperature modulated" entropy minimization to encourage a low-density separation of clusters along categorical boundaries. The trained model is deployed on an Andriod tablet via TensorFlow Lite and we report on real-time inference with the deployed models in terms of model complexity and performance.

Keywords: Few-shot learning · Portable ultrasound · MobileNet

1 Introduction

Fetal brain biometry measurements, such as estimation of the head circumference (HC) and transcerebellar diameter (TCD), are of great clinical importance to assess fetal growth. In this study, we investigate automated identification of the relevant fetal biometry planes, namely the transthalamic (TT) and transcerebellar (TC) planes of the fetal head. Of note, fetal brain videos used in this

Y. Hu et al. (Eds.): ASMUS 2020/PIPPI 2020, LNCS 12437, pp. 126–135, 2020.
https://doi.org/10.1007/978-3-030-60334-2_13

study are acquired via a portable low-cost ultrasound probe and the solution is designed to be used by minimally trained healthcare staff. Such a system offers a number of benefits compared to a traditional ultrasound machine: it is affordable, flexible and, due to the limited training required, more scalable than traditional approaches. This may be of particular relevance to underserved regions where prenatal ultrasound may be limited or non-existent. However, one challenge this introduces is that video quality varies and the quality of the standardised biometry planes (TC and TT) may not be high. Other technical challenges presented by this application include that manual annotation of video is time-consuming and requires clinical expertise which is a scarce resource. Further, we are dealing with a dense labelling task (as shown in Fig. 1) with a few annotated training samples-only two planes (one transcerebellar (TC) and one transthalamic (TT)) per video are annotated from which the TCD and HC are measured, respectively.

Contributions: To cope with these challenges (1) we propose a new quality control protocol by adopting and adjusting the standard criteria [1] for characterising fetal brain biometry planes; (2) we introduce a metric learning based method to automatically identify and index the TC and TT planes which builds a model by learning from a few annotations; (3) finally, we deploy the trained models within a prototype ultrasound video acquisition system on an Android tablet and investigate the trade-off between model complexity and performance.

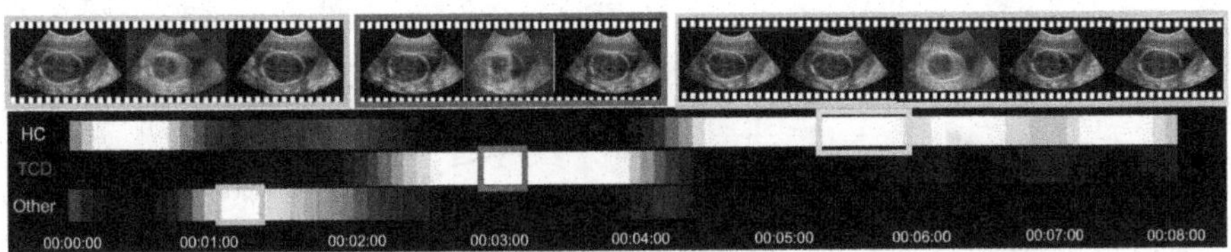

Fig. 1. Identifying and indexing good quality fetal brain biometry planes. Bottom "colorbars" depict the labelling confidence distributed over the whole video (8 s). The brighter the higher likelihood that a target plane is captured. HC: Planes good for measuring head circumference, TCD: Planes good for measuring transcerebellar diameter, Other: Planes not suitable for biometry.

Related Works: Recently, deep learning based approaches have shown success in recognition of fetal brain planes [2–5] and [6]. Baumgartner et al. [2] use a variant of VGG-Net, called SonoNet, for classification of 13 standardised fetal biometry planes, including TC and TV planes in fetal brain which was improved by [3] by introducing an attention mechanism. Gao et al. [5] model multi-scale spatial-temporal attention for detecting and tracking fetal structures, including the fetal head, but different to [2] and [3], does not specifically look at standard fetal biometry planes. Other works, such as [4] and [6], localize fetal brain standard planes in 3D ultrasound. Y. Li et al. [4] uses a CNN to regress a rigid transformation iteratively for localising TC and TV planes in 3D fetal ultrasound. Dou et al. [6] propose to localize TT and TV planes in 3D fetal ultrasound with a reinforcement learning framework, which can progressively interact with the volumes and modify the search trajectory towards the target planes. Yaqub et al. [7] consider automatic quality assurance of the TV plane when it has been acquired. In contrast to the above works considering standard fetal plane detection only, our concern is to detect planes and to explicitly verify that they are suitable for measurement. A further commonality of all the above methods is that they require supervision with a large amount of labelled training data. By contrast, we seek to learn how to select candidate image frames from a few annotated examples.

2 Method

We propose a semi-supervised learning framework, shown in Fig. 2, which consists of a feature extractor (CNN), a prototypical learning module and a semantic transfer module. We formulate the learning as a multi-way classification problem and the learned model is employed to automatically label unseen video frames in a dense manner. For each training iteration, we randomly sample a query set χ^Q and a small support set χ^S (few images per class) from n labelled frames, and an unlabelled set χ^U from m unlabelled frames (n $\ll$ m).

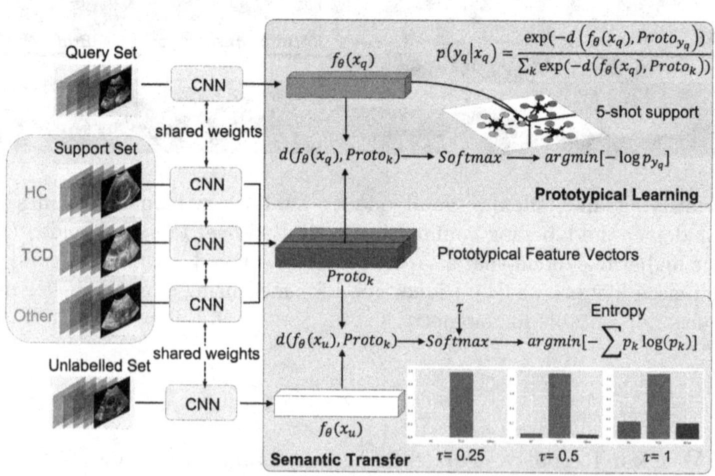

Fig. 2. Overview of our proposed learning framework. Notations: f_θ, feature descriptor; $d(\cdot)$, euclidean distance; k, class index; p, posterior probability; $Proto_k$, prototypes for k-th class; τ, temperature.

CNN Architecture: Considering the typical computational resources on a current consumer tablet, we employ current state-of-the-art light-weight deep CNNs, such as [10,11] and [12], in this study. For instance, MobileNet [10] introduces depth-wise separable convolution which significantly reduces the computational cost and the number of trainable parameters of convolution layers. This is achieved by applying a channel-wise convolution first followed by 1 × 1 point-wise convolution to linearly combine the feature maps across the channels. MobileNetV2 [11] improves on the MobileNet design by introducing inverted bottleneck layers and residual connection between the bottlenecks. The inverted bottleneck layers project features to a higher dimensional manifold that [11] argues prevents information loss from ReLU activation and the residual blocks facilitate the gradient back-propagation through a deep network. MobileNetV3 [12] upgrades the inverted bottleneck layers by introducing the squeeze and excitation in the residual layer which explicitly models channel interdependences and re-weights the feature importance.

Learning from Prototypes: As we only have a small number of labelled frames, the deep CNNs mentioned above are prone to overfitting when explicitly learning the classification. Instead, we sample few-shot examples (a support set) from each class and feed them through a CNN f_θ first to compute categorical prototypes [9]. Given a support set of N_S frames $x_s \epsilon \chi^{S_k}$ from the kth class, prototype $Proto_k$ is computed as the mean of the embedded D-dimensional feature vectors $f_\theta(x_s) \epsilon \mathbb{R}^D$:

$$Proto_k = \frac{1}{N_S} \sum_{x_s \epsilon \chi^{S_k}} f_\theta(x_s) \quad (1)$$

Then, we sample a query set of N_Q labelled frames (larger than the support set). For each query point (x_q, y_q), where $x_q \epsilon \chi^Q$ and $y_q \epsilon \{1, ..., K\}$ (K = 3 in this study), we measure its similarity to each prototype by the Euclidean distance and produce a probability distribution over all classes with a distance based softmax. We can then calculate the metric based cross-entropy loss:

$$L_{metric}(\chi^S, \chi^Q) = -\frac{1}{N_Q} \sum_{\{x_q, y_q\} \epsilon \chi^Q} log \frac{exp(-\left\|f_\theta(x_q) - Proto_{y_q}\right\|^2)}{\sum_{k=1}^{K} exp(-\left\|f_\theta(x_q) - Proto_k\right\|^2)} \quad (2)$$

With the loss, we introduce the constraint that data from the same class should be similar in the embedding space. Also, we find that this loss can provide a guidance to stabilize the unsupervised semantic transfer (described next).

Unsupervised Semantic Transfer: We define a new semantic transfer objective, $L_{ST}(\chi^U)$, which transfers information from the prototypes produced above to unlabelled datapoints by minimizing the entropy of a temperature-tuned softmax. Entropy minimization has been widely used for unsupervised [14,15] and semi-supervised [16] learning by encouraging low density separation between classes. At each training epoch, we sample an unlabelled set χ^U of N_U frames ($N_U = N_Q$), then for each datapoint in the unlabelled set $x_u \epsilon \chi^U$ we again compute the Euclidean distance between its feature embedding and each categorical prototype. Our semantic transfer loss is then defined as:

$$L_{ST}(\chi^U) = -\frac{1}{N_U} \sum_{x_u \epsilon \chi^U} \sum_{k \epsilon \{1...K\}} \tau^{-1} P(x_u, Proto_k) log \tau^{-1} P_\tau(x_u, Proto_k) \quad (3)$$

Where $P(x_u, Proto_k)$ is a softmax function that generates a probability distribution over all classes based on: $-\|f_\theta(x_u) - Proto_k\|^2$ and τ is the temperature of the softmax. We then tune the softmax temperature. As shown in Fig. 2, the distribution becomes one-hot when the temperature approaches 0, whereas becomes more uniformly distributed when increasing the temperature. Intuitively, a small temperature encourages each unlabelled frame to be very similar to one class, whereas a larger temperature will allow it to be similar to multiple classes.

Joint Learning: In addition to the above, we introduce another fully-connected layer that maps the feature vectors of query frames to class scores directly. This serves as an auxiliary classifier, trained with a cross-entropy (CE) loss, allowing us to investigate the interactions between direct learning and metric learning. To mitigate overfitting, we introduce training signal annealing (TSA) [17] to the cross-entropy loss:

$$L_{CE}(\chi^Q) = -\frac{1}{N_Q} \sum_{\{x_q, y_q\} \epsilon \chi^Q} [-I\{P_\theta(y_q|x_q) < \eta_t\}] \, log P_\theta(y_q|x_q) \quad (4)$$

Where $I\{.\}$ is the indicator function and $P_\theta(y_q|x_q)$ is the probability of x_q belonging to the class y_q. Specifically, the example (x_q, y_q) does not contribute to the loss function if the model predicted probability surpasses a threshold η_t, at training step t. We set $\eta_t = exp((\frac{t}{T} - 1) * 5) * (1 - \frac{1}{K}) + \frac{1}{K}$ that corresponds to the exponential schedule in [17] realising most of the supervised signal at the end of training. Intuitively, this is to prevent model from overfitting too quickly by penalizing over confident prediction in the early stage of training. Finally, our model jointly optimizes over the objective function as follows:

$$L(\chi^S, \chi^Q, \chi^U) = L_{ST}(\chi^U) + \alpha L_{metric}(\chi^S, \chi^Q) + \beta L_{CE}(\chi^Q) \quad (5)$$

where the hyperparameters α and β determine the influence of the metric learning and the direct learning, respectively.

3 Experiments and Results

Datasets and Annotation: The ultrasound videos used in this study are acquired by a wireless portable probe (Konted GEN 1 C10R) with which we acquire a set of three short fetal brain videos (8 s/video) for each subject.

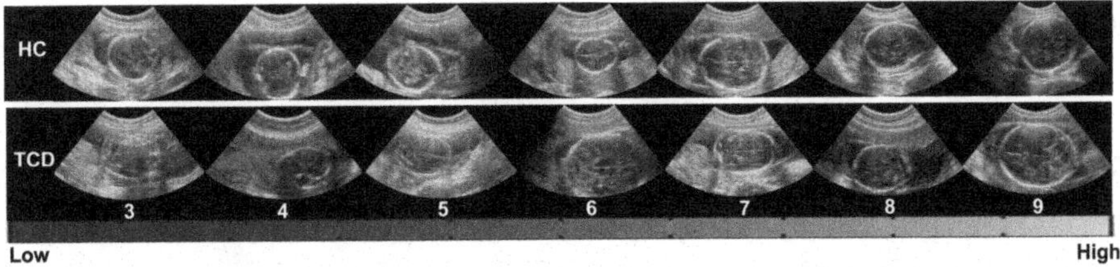

Fig. 3. Quality assessment. Scoring a **TCD** plane [1–9]: image horizontal* [1], 30% magnification† [1], symmetrical hemispheres† [1], CSP‡ (clear: [2], suspected: [1]), thalami‡ (clear: [2], suspected: [1]), cerebellum edge‡ (clear: [2], unclear: [1]). For a **HC** Plane [1–9]: all same as TCD except for No cerebellum visible† [1], HC oval* [1]. *: new criteria; †: existing criteria; ‡: revised criteria.

The goal is to identify the TT plane and TC planes that have good enough quality to measure the HC and TCD, respectively. However, we found that the standard criteria [1] for scoring plane quality do not apply well to our cases; for example, the appearance of key anatomies, such as cavum of the septum pellucidum (CSP), thalamus and cerebellum can be difficult to see. Therefore, we developed a revised criteria scoring system more customized to the appearance of typical video frames, as described in Fig. 3. Two experienced sonographers annotated three frames only per video (TCD, HC and background) and scored them. For training, we choose the annotated frames having a quality score ($\geqslant$6). This resulted in: 301 HC frames, 208 TCD frames, 120 Other (background) frames and 33,957 unlabelled frames from 441 training videos (147 subjects). For testing, a further 60 videos (20 subjects) were manually labelled frame by frame over the whole video for HC, TCD and background.

Implementation Details: Firstly, a MobileNetV1 [10] was trained as a baseline model with CE loss only, on all labelled training data (629 images). Secondly, we added TSA to the CE loss (Eq. 4) to derive a second model. Finally, we introduced the L_{metric} (Eq. 2) and the L_{ST} (Eq. refst) for joint learning and the number of support, query and unlabelled images was chosen as $N_S = 15$ (5 images/class), $N_Q = 45$ (15 images/class) and $N_U = 45$, respectively for each training iteration. We adjusted the signal weights α and β in this way: firstly, we set α to 1, and gradually reduce β from 1 to 0.5, 0.1 until 0 (no CE signal); then, we do the opposite and set β to 1, and gradually reduce the α to 0.5, 0.1 until 0 (no metric learning signal). We set the temperature $\tau = 0.5$ in Eq. 3 and the total number of training iterations (T) to 20,000. All models were trained using an Adam optimizer and with learning rate 10^{-4} and all the experiments were conducted with the TensorFlow 1.14.0. We also experiment with MobileNetV2 [11] and V3 [12] and study the trade-off between performance and capacity of models by adjusting the width multiplier (0.25, 0.5, 0.75 and 1 used). Finally, we deploy the trained models onto a Huawei tablet (MediaPad M5 lite10) via the TensorFlow Lite API to study its inference in terms of computational cost and performance. We firstly freeze the trained models and save the frozen graphs as .pb files. Then we convert the .pb files into .tflite for on device deployment.

Table 1. Performance measures over different learning configurations on the testset (CNN Backbone: MobileNetV1, Width multiplier: 1).

Categories	Models								
	Baselines		$\alpha{:}\beta$	$\alpha = 1$			$\beta = 1$		
	CE	CE_{TSA}	1:1	$\beta = 0.5$	$\beta = 0.1$	$\beta = 0$	$\alpha = 0.5$	$\alpha = 0.1$	$\alpha = 0$
TCD	0.459	0.547	0.673	0.735	**0.746**	0.740	0.639	0.614	0.611
HC	0.595	0.643	0.792	0.859	**0.897**	0.889	0.784	0.754	0.742
mAP	0.525	0.618	0.778	0.834	**0.869**	0.837	0.783	0.729	0.713

Effect of Metric Learning: We evaluate the models using Average Precision (AP) measured on frame level labels. For each class, we count a correct detection if it is a positive prediction with confidence above a certain thresholds (ranging from 0.1 to 0.9). We report AP for the individual classes as well as mean Average Precision (mAP) in Table 1. We found directly learning with CE loss can result in poor generalization to test data as indicated by the baseline model (CE) which is the worst among all models. Note that there is an improvement over all metrics after applying TSA to the CE loss but it is marginal. Moreover, we found that L_{metric} (Eq. 2) plays a crucial role in improving model generalization. When applying a full metric learning signal (i.e. fixing $\alpha = 1$), all metrics increase when reducing the contribution of the cross-entropy loss (i.e. reducing β) (Eq. 5).

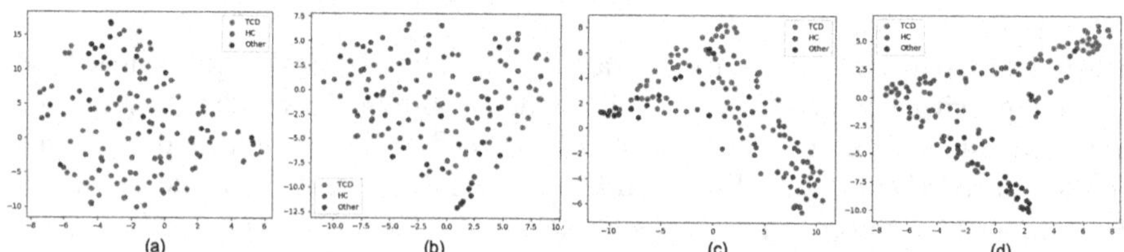

Fig. 4. t-SNE embeddings of global features (MobileNetV1 backbone) on test frames. (a): baseline (CE) (b): baseline (CE_{TSA}) (c): joint learning ($\alpha = 1$, $\beta = 0.5$) (d): joint learning ($\alpha = 1$, $\beta = 0.1$)

The best performance is achieved when β equals to 0.1. whereas, when applying a full cross-entropy signal (i.e. fixing $\beta = 1$), the performance of models overall is less superior than for models trained with a full metric learning signal. Of note, all metrics drop in value when gradually reducing the contribution of the metric learning loss from 0.5 to 0.1 to 0. We also found, overall, that there is a higher AP for the HC than TCD and this may be because some low quality

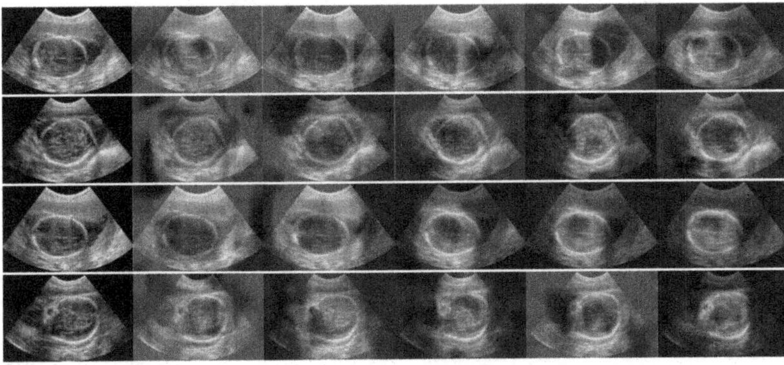

Fig. 5. Examples of TC (**Row 1 and 2**) and TT (**Row 3 and 4**) planes captured by different models. **Column 1**: example clips. **Column 2 to 6**: corresponding CAMs obtained from CE, CE_{TSA}, joint learning ($\alpha = 1$, $\beta = 1$), joint learning ($\alpha = 1$, $\beta = 0.5$), joint learning ($\alpha = 1$, $\beta = 0.1$), respectively. Best viewed in Adobe Reader. All videos should play automatically.

TCD frames (with unclear cerebellar edges) are prone to be confused as a HC frame. We have also performed t-SNE (t-Stochastic Neighbour Embedding) on the test dataset, summarized in Fig. 4: feature embedding (feature vectors after global pooling) visualisation. We found that the baseline model (CE) is severely overfitted as depicted in Fig. 4(a), that categorical clusters are not formed at all and datapoints are distributed randomly. Of note that in Fig. 4(b) a separation between classes can be seen after applying TSA to the CE loss. However, there is still no clear separation between the classes and all datapoints are still clustered together. In contrast, categorical clusters in Fig. 4 (c) and (d) are formed well with clear separation between the classes with the joint learning. We also observe that the stronger the metric learning signal, the stronger the "forces" that push the clusters away from each other.

In Fig. 5, we give examples of HC and TCD images that have been identified by different models and class activation mappings (CAMs). We linearly combine the feature maps before global pooling with score mapping weights to produce frame-wise class activation maps. We found that CAMs produced by CE and CE_{TSA} are extremely random indicating that the models do not learn where the discriminative features are. However, the joint learning models produce more discriminative CAMs and learn to highlight a variety of key anatomical structures, such as cerebellum on TC planes and thalamus on TT planes.

On-Device Inference: To evaluate models' on device performance, as shown in Fig. 6a, we estimate the NetScore metric $\Omega = 20log_{10}(mAP^{\gamma}p^{-\delta}c^{-\epsilon})$ [18] which measures model efficiency as a trade-off between mean average precision (mAP, percent), number of trainable parameters (p, millions) and number of float operations (FLOPs, billions). We set γ, δ and ϵ to be 2, 0.5 and 0.5 respectively, based on [18]. We construct smaller and less computationally expensive models by a width multiplier [10]. Of note, although mAP drops continuously when networks become thinner, higher netscores are achieved because models become more compact and efficient.

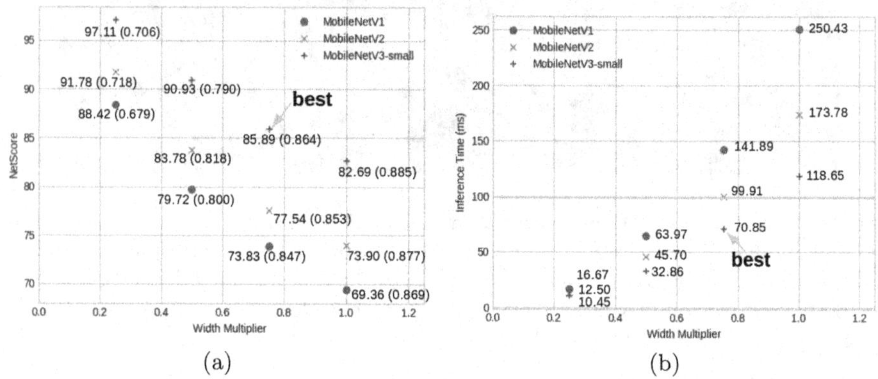

Fig. 6. Performance-model complexity trade-off. (a) NetScore (mAP). (b) Inference Time. All models trained with joint learning configured ($\alpha = 1$, $\beta = 0.1$).

Moreover, we also report inference times, as shown in Fig. 6b, for a single frame on the Huawei MediaPad equipped with KIRIN659 SoC. We found the thinner the networks, the faster the inference they achieved. As our videos are recorded at a rate of 10 frames/seconds (100 ms/frame), the models below the green line in Fig. 6b achieve real time inference. Considering jointly the NetScore, mAP and speed, the MobileNetV3-small with a width multiplier 0.75 (as indicated by green arrows) is the best and achieves comparable mAP (0.864) to a full capacity MobileNetV1 (0.869) but more than triple the inference speed (70.85 ms compared to 250.43 ms).

4 Conclusion

We have proposed a new quality control protocol for characterizing fetal brain biometry planes acquired by a low-cost portable probe. We have also demonstrated the success of learning from few labelled data and the metric learning module in this framework is the key to improve the model generalization. Finally, we deployed the trained models onto a mid-end consumer tablet and have studied the trade-off between models' performance and capacity.

Acknowledgements. We acknowledge the ERC (ERC-ADG-2015 694581, project PULSE) the EPSRC (EP/GO36861/1, EP/MO13774/1) and the NIHR Biomedical Research Centre funding scheme.

References

1. T. I. S. of Ultrasound in Obstetrics and Gynecology: Sono-graphic examination of the fetal central nervous system: guidelines for performing the basic examination and the fetal neurosonogram. Ultrasound in Obstetrics and Gynecology (2007)
2. Baumgartner, C.F., Kamnitsas, K., Smith, S., Koch, L.M., Kainz, B., Rueckert, D.: SonoNet: real-time detection and localisation of fetal standard scan planes in freehand ultrasound. In: IEEE TMI (2017)
3. Schlemper, J., et al.: Attention-gated networks for improving ultrasound scan plane detection. In: MIDL (2018)
4. Li, Y., et al.: Standard plane detection in 3D fetal ultrasound using an iterative transformation network. In: Frangi, A.F., Schnabel, J.A., Davatzikos, C., Alberola-López, C., Fichtinger, G. (eds.) MICCAI 2018. LNCS, vol. 11070, pp. 392–400. Springer, Cham (2018). https://doi.org/10.1007/978-3-030-00928-1_45
5. Gao, Y., Noble, J.A.: Learning and understanding deep spatio-temporal representations from free-hand fetal ultrasound sweeps. In: Shen, D., et al. (eds.) MICCAI 2019. LNCS, vol. 11768, pp. 299–308. Springer, Cham (2019). https://doi.org/10.1007/978-3-030-32254-0_34
6. Dou, H., et al.: Agent with warm start and active termination for plane localization in 3D ultrasound. In: Shen, D., et al. (eds.) MICCAI 2019. LNCS, vol. 11768, pp. 290–298. Springer, Cham (2019). https://doi.org/10.1007/978-3-030-32254-0_33
7. Yaqub, M., et al.: A deep learning solution for automatic fetal neurosonographic diagnostic plane verification using clinical standard constraints. In: Ultrasound in Medicine & Biology (2017)
8. Vinyals, O., Blundell, C., Lillicrap, T., Wierstra, D., et al.: Matching networks for one shot learning. In: NIPS (2016)
9. Snell, J., Swersky, K., Zemel, R.S.: Prototypical networks for few-shot learning. In: NIPS (2017)
10. Howard, A.G., et al.: MobileNets: efficient convolutional neural networks for mobile vision applications. arXiv preprint arXiv:1704.04861 (2017)
11. Sandler, M., et al.: MobileNetV2: inverted residuals and linear bottlenecks. In: CVPR (2018)
12. Howard, A., et al.: Searching for mobilenetv3. arXiv preprint arXiv:1905.02244 (2019)
13. Zhang, X., Zhou, X., Lin, M., Sun, J.: ShuffleNet: an extremely efficient convolutional neural network for mobile devices. arXiv:1707.01083 (2017)
14. Long, M., Zhu, H., Wang, J., Jordan, M.I.: Unsupervised domain adaptation with residual transfer networks. In: NIPS (2016)
15. Palubinskas, G., Descombes, X., Kruggel, F.: An unsupervised clustering method using the entropy minimization. In: AAAI (1999)
16. Grandvalet, Y., Bengio, Y., et al.: Semi-supervised learning by entropy minimization. In: NIPS (2004)
17. Xie, Q., Dai, Z., Hovy, E., Luong, M.T., Le, Q.V.: Unsupervised data augmentation for consistency training. arXiv preprint arXiv:1904.12848 (2019)
18. Wong, A.: NetScore: towards universal metrics for large-scale performance analysis of deep neural networks for practical usage. arXiv:1806.05512 (2018)

Automatic C-Plane Detection in Pelvic Floor Transperineal Volumetric Ultrasound

Helena Williams[1,2,4(✉)], Laura Cattani[1(✉)], Mohammad Yaqub[3], Carole Sudre[2(✉)], Tom Vercauteren[2(✉)], Jan Deprest[1(✉)], and Jan D'hooge[4(✉)]

[1] Department of Obstetrics and Gynaecology, University Hospitals Leuven, Leuven, Belgium
{helena.williams,laura.cattani}@kuleuven.be

[2] School of Biomedical Engineering and Imaging Sciences, King's College London, London, UK
{carole.sudre,Tom.vercauteren}@kcl.ac.uk

[3] Department of Computer Vision, Mohamed bin Zayed University of Artificial Intelligence, Abu Dhabi, United Arab Emirates

[4] Department of Cardiovascular Sciences, KU Leuven, Leuven, Belgium
{jan.deprest,jan.dhooge}@uzleuven.be

Abstract. Transperineal volumetric ultrasound (US) imaging has become routine practice for diagnosing pelvic floor disease (PFD). Hereto, clinical guidelines stipulate to make measurements in an anatomically defined 2D plane within a 3D volume, the so-called C-plane. This task is currently performed manually in clinical practice, which is labour-intensive and requires expert knowledge of pelvic floor anatomy, as no computer-aided C-plane method exists. To automate this process, we propose a novel, *guideline-driven* approach for automatic detection of the C-plane. The method uses a convolutional neural network (CNN) to identify extreme coordinates of the symphysis pubis and levator ani muscle (which define the C-plane) directly via landmark regression. The C-plane is identified in a postprocessing step. When evaluated on 100 US volumes, our best performing method (multi-task regression with UNet) achieved a mean error of 6.05 mm and 4.81° and took 20 s. Two experts blindly evaluated the quality of the automatically detected planes and manually defined the (gold standard) C-plane in terms of their clinical diagnostic quality. We show that the proposed method performs comparably to the manual definition. The automatic method reduces the average time to detect the C-plane by 100 s and reduces the need for high-level expertise in PFD US assessment.

1 Introduction

The Significance of the Levator Hiatus. Pelvic Floor Disease (PFD) refers to a group of conditions affecting the anatomy and function of pelvic organs. PFD consists of urinary and fecal incontinence, sexual dysfunction and pelvic

Y. Hu et al. (Eds.): ASMUS 2020/PIPPI 2020, LNCS 12437, pp. 136–145, 2020.
https://doi.org/10.1007/978-3-030-60334-2_14

organ prolapse (POP) [3,11]. PFD is assessed by observing the levator hiatus (LH) using 3D/4D ultrasound (US), in the plane of minimal hiatal dimensions (defined as the C-plane) as shown in Fig. 1. The C-plane is defined as the angled axial plane of shortest distance between the symphysis pubis (SP) and the pubovisceral muscle at the anorectal angle, referred to as the levator ani muscle (LAM) [7]. Assessments follow International Urogynecological Association (IUGA) and The American Institute of Ultrasound in Medicine (AIUM) standards [1]. Manual C-plane detection is prone to errors, labour intensive, and requires a high level of expertise. Thus, an automatic detection of the C-plane may reduce measurement variability, improve the clinical workflow, speed-up the detection process and possibly allows low-skilled clinicians to perform the procedure and hence may help a wide range of patients. Unfortunately, to date, no automatic solutions exist.

Automatic Plane Detection. Several studies investigated the extraction of 2D *standard* planes from 3D fetal and cardiac US volumes [4,9,10,14,15]. Chykeyuk et al. and Yaqub et al. used Regression Random Forests (RRF) to extract planes from US volumes [4,14]. Yaqub et al. [14] adopted an RRF and feature asymmetry to highlight informative voxels during training. Li et al. [9] proposed an iterative transformation network (ITN) for standard plane detection in 3D volumes. The ITN used a CNN to learn relationships between images of 2D planes and the transformation required to reach the ground-truth. These methods utilise clinical knowledge but not necessarily clinical guidelines. Zhu et al. [15] proposed a guideline-driven learning method to determine 2D planes using anatomical regularities according to guidelines. The use of guidelines improved results and running time on a variety of images. All methods performed well, but without the explicit use of clinical guidelines, the output of the networks will not necessarily produce an output that is clinically interpretable.

Contribution. We propose a novel guideline-driven methodology, that utilises CNNs to extract the C-plane automatically from a 3D US volume. This is a novel application of CNN landmark regression for plane detection, and, to the authors' knowledge, the first paper to present a fully automatic C-plane detection pipeline. The CNN identifies two coordinates (directly via landmark regression), that are sufficient to define the C-plane. These coordinates are well-known to clinicians; thus, the output of our proposed method is interpretable, unlike other plane detection methods. We determine the vector of minimal hiatal dimensions within the mid-sagittal (MS) plane, a direction transformation matrix and the mid-point of the plane. Our contributions consist of: a) a new methodological approach to identify the C-plane; b) the novel application of advances in landmark location for plane detection with clinical context; and c) a clinically viable blinded evaluation of C-plane detection.

2 Materials and Methods

2.1 Data and Manual Detection of the C-Plane

A dataset containing a training subset of 25 transperineal US volumes from 15 patients, and a validation subset of 100 transperineal US volumes from 43 patients was collected. The small training subset was due to the large clinical overhead required to generate the ground truth data used for training. The dataset was curated at UZ Leuven, Belgium, over the course of 6 months. It includes a high proportion of pathology cases, representing the true *clinical world*, with a variety of pathologies (minor to severe), and a range of image qualities. The volumes were acquired at rest, during Valsalva manoeuvre (i.e. forceful attempted exhalation against a closed airway), and during pelvic floor contraction [1].

To manually determine the C-plane, the acquired volume has been rotated such that the pubic rami are horizontally aligned in the coronal plane, following this stage there are two possible methods: the Multiplanar (MP) and the Omniview (OV) technique (GE Healthcare, Austria). In the MP technique, the MS plane is rotated until the SP and LAM are horizontally aligned. In the OV technique, the clinician draws a line of shortest distance between the SP and LAM to define the C-plane. In our study, volumes were annotated using the MP method, by one expert, resulting in Gold Standard (GS) C-plane orientations used for validation. In practice, manual determination of the C-plane from an US volume can take 2 min, which may increase depending on expertise and patient pathology.

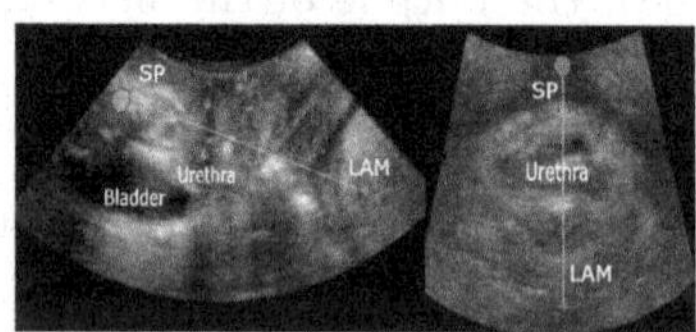

Fig. 1. US at rest, with identification of the C-plane in the MS (left) and oblique axial (right) planes. The yellow line shows the vector of minimal hiatal dimensions and the red contour delineates the hiatal area. (Color figure online)

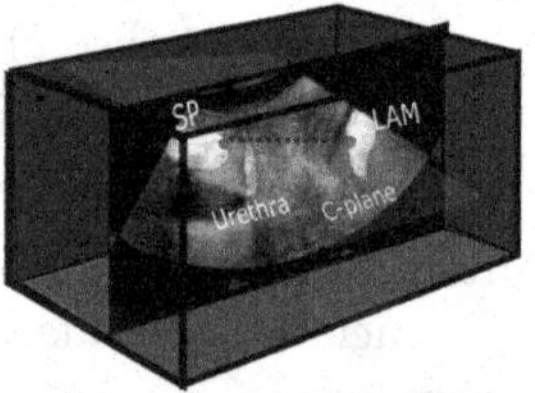

Fig. 2. Extreme coordinates shown as red dots define the C-plane bisecting the MS plane. The vector of minimal hiatal dimensions is shown as a blue line. (Color figure online)

2.2 Overall Framework

In this work we propose a pipeline to identify the C-plane from an US volume. This is the first time, to the author's knowledge, that localisation of anatomical landmarks has been used directly in the application of plane detection. The process utilises guidelines and automatically detects two extreme coordinates within the US volume; the LAM and the SP which define the C-plane, shown in Fig. 2. Figure 3 shows the pipeline that detects the extreme coordinates directly via landmark regression. These coordinates are known to clinicians, thus the output can be easily understood and interpreted as it follows the clinical guidelines.

Formation of the Direction Transformation Matrix and Mid-Point. Once SP and LAM extreme points are identified, as described in the following section, the transformation matrix can be determined. We define the vector of shortest Euclidean distance between the SP and the LAM within the MS plane, $\overrightarrow{AB}$. The C-plane is defined in the IUGA guidelines as the plane orthogonal to the depth direction of the US volume (i.e. $|0\ 0\ 1|$) and containing the vector $\overrightarrow{AB}$. The second orthogonal vector representing the plane can be defined as the cross product of the normal, and $\overrightarrow{AB}$, thus we define the final orthogonal vector, b_y, as $-AB_y\mathbf{i} + AB_x\mathbf{j} + 0\mathbf{k}$. $\overrightarrow{AB}$ only has magnitude within the x and y components as we restrict the extreme coordinates to lie within the same z slice, this ensures adherence to clinical guidelines. Thus, we have defined the bases of the C-plane and can formulate the following direction matrix

$$\left\|b_x\right\| \left\|b_y\right\| \left\|b_z\right\| = \begin{Vmatrix} AB_x & -AB_y & 0 \\ AB_y & AB_x & 0 \\ 0 & 0 & 1 \end{Vmatrix}. \tag{1}$$

To re-sample the volume, a midpoint, $\vec{O}$, to the C-plane is defined. We identify, $\vec{O}$, as the mid-point between LAM and SP extreme coordinates.

2.3 Regression of Extreme Coordinates

The method is based on 3D CNN landmark regression, in which we directly regress smooth, distance maps of the SP and LAM extreme coordinates to define the C-plane (see Fig. 3). The rationale for this approach is that regression of one coordinate from an average US volume of 450 × 500 × 450 voxels is hard to train. Hence, to make the regression model robust, we propose to regress a distance map of the SP/LAM extreme coordinates, and to use a combined distance map as a weighted sampler. We thus tackle plane detection via regression as a multi-task learning problem and compare two different CNN network architectures. The CNN architecture was adapted to have 2 inputs (i.e. SP and LAM distance maps) and multi-task learning ensuring that features are shared during training.

Determining Extreme Coordinates. The proposed method is based on following the IUGA guidelines. While the regression is performed in 3D, clinicians use 2D MS planes to determine these coordinates. Therefore, unlike other plane detection tasks, a 2D approach is also followed in the determination of the extreme coordinates. As the maximum pixel of the SP and LAM, may be in different MS plane positions within the volume, the combined local sub-pixel maxima of the SP and LAM distance maps are calculated for a small range of 2D MS planes. The range of MS planes remains limited to reduce computational load and is dependent on the overall pixel maxima position of SP and LAM distance maps. Hereto, the following are determined: SP and LAM combined overall maximum, corresponding SP and LAM extreme coordinates, the minimal hiatal vector, $\overrightarrow{AB}$, and mid-point, $\vec{O}$, of the C-plane.

2.4 Evaluation Methodology

Intra- and Inter-rater Variability. To evaluate the proposed method, we compare results against inter and intra-rater variability. The expert who determined the GS C-planes (Expert 1), determined the C-plane again a month later, on a subset of 37 volumes. We obtained intra-rater variability using the MP (same method as the GS) and the OV method. Inter-rater variability was obtained by a second expert (Expert 2) using the MP method on a subset of 23 volumes.

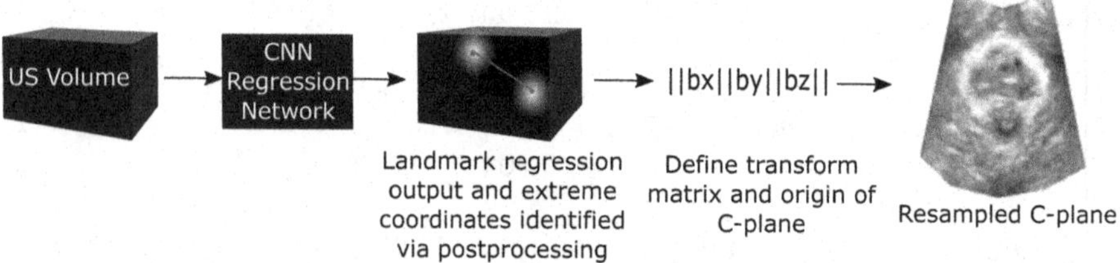

Fig. 3. Pipeline of the landmark regression approach to C-plane extraction.

Visual Turing Test. To evaluate clinical relevance, we performed what may be considered a visual *Turing Test* on 10 US volumes. We asked both experts to blindly rate each C-plane (GS and automatically detected), and the corresponding MS plane from 0–5 (5 being excellent, 4, above average, 3, average, 2, below average, 1, poor and 0, no clinical use). Based on the criteria: the minimal hiatal dimension line is placed in the MS plane (Test 1) and the C-plane is of sufficient quality for clinical diagnosis (Test 2). We did a paired Wilcoxon test to compare the proposed method performance against the GS.

Bio-Marker Analysis. The LH identified in the C-plane is a bio-marker used for PFD analysis. We manually segmented the LH in 35 C-planes extracted via the proposed method, 35 GS C-planes and 15 Expert 1 and 15 Expert 2 C-planes. Segmentations were checked and clinically accepted by Expert 1. The Hausdorff Distance (HD) and Robust 95th percentile HD between the segmentation of the GS and predicted C-planes were evaluated to assess the bio-marker quality.

3 Experiments, Results and Discussion

3.1 Implementation Details

The network was trained with 25 US volumes, from 12 patients, manually annotated for the SP and LAM positions. For validation, 100 US volumes were used in which C-planes had previously been extracted during clinical routine.

Experiments were implemented using NiftyNet [5] on a desktop with a 24 GB NVIDIA Quadro P6000. Two CNN architectures were compared. First an implementation of 3D UNet [16] by Isensee et al. [6], almost identical to the original 3D UNet, but due to high memory consumption of 3D convolutions with large patch sizes, the number of filters was reduced before up-sampling. This network was chosen due to its performance in LH segmentation [2]. The second network implemented was HighRes3DNet, proposed by Li et al. [8]. It has a large contextual field of view with little effect to parameter cost and was chosen due to its performance in 3D segmentation of the urethra from US volumes [12]. HighRes3DNet, has less trainable parameters than UNet, suggesting a faster inference time, which is beneficial for an *in-clinic* solution. Both multi-task Regression with UNet (mRegU) and multi-task Regression with HighRes3DNet (mRegHR) have a combined L2 loss of the SP and LAM distance maps with initial learning rate of 0.001. A smoother version of the combined distance maps was used for weighted sampling during training. Methods were optimised until network convergence, and data augmentation such as rotation and scaling were used.

3.2 Results and Discussion

Figure 4a compares the Euclidean distance of the mid-point of (manually and automatically) identified C-planes against the GS. From the proposed methods, mRegU showed to have the smallest distance to the GS, highlighting that UNet outperforms other CNN architectures in pelvic floor US landmark localisation tasks. The mean Euclidean distance of mRegU, mRegHR, Expert 1 (OV), Expert 1 (MP) and Expert 2 (MP), were 6.05 mm, 7.18 mm, 6.95 mm, 4.44 mm and 5.85 mm, respectively. This suggests that mRegU, is within a clinically acceptable error range, as the error is lower than inter-rater variability between experts. The outliers of mRegU and mRegHR were due to the CNN not identifying the true 'extreme coordinate'. In all cases, the network had correctly located a coordinate within the LAM and SP structures. However, it was not the true 'extreme coordinate' position. A contributing factor to the error was the severity of patient pathology. In misclassified cases, patients had one or more conditions such as severe hiatus ballooning, avulsion, bladder and/or vagina prolapse. In addition, poor US acquisition, stool and urine presence, poor acoustic coupling, and patient movement may have contributed to misclassification. In Fig. 4b the angular error is presented, showing that mRegU's interquartile range is smaller than the inter-rater variability. mRegU's mean angular difference was lower than Expert 1's (OV) and Expert 2's (MP), suggesting it is within the range of clinical acceptability. The worst angular mismatch of the detected C-plane was obtained in a patient with severe hiatal ballooning resulting in the LH not being fully within the axial plane due to its size, making it difficult for the network, as the SP was only partially visible in the MS plane. In extreme cases, the SP may not be present at all, clinicians face this problem but use a 4D cine-loop to estimate the SP projection and thereby its location. This is not exploited by the proposed regression network and thus a limitation of the proposed solution.

Figure 5 shows a visual comparison between the GS and the detected C and MS planes. Qualitatively, there is minimal difference; all show the same clinical diagnosis (symmetric and intact LH); and all structures are visible. The results of the *Turing test*, presented in Table 1, show that mRegHR outperformed all methods including the GS. In one case, the C-plane detected by mRegHR was voted the true minimum hiatal dimension on the MS plane, and the GS C-plane position was rated sub-optimal. This is due to the nature of pelvic floor US where occasionally the C-plane is placed slightly higher/lower than the true position. Although this results in an inaccurate C-plane position, clinicians obtain a better-quality image of the LH by avoiding the hyperechogenicity of the LAM and its associated shadow. This is a limitation to the proposed solution, as although it may determine the true position on the MS plane, the C-plane quality may be sub-optimal. We use a novel application of data and guidelines, to drive a hybrid approach to determine the C-plane, thus we can achieve relatively low errors with a small training dataset, as we utilise the geometry of the patient.

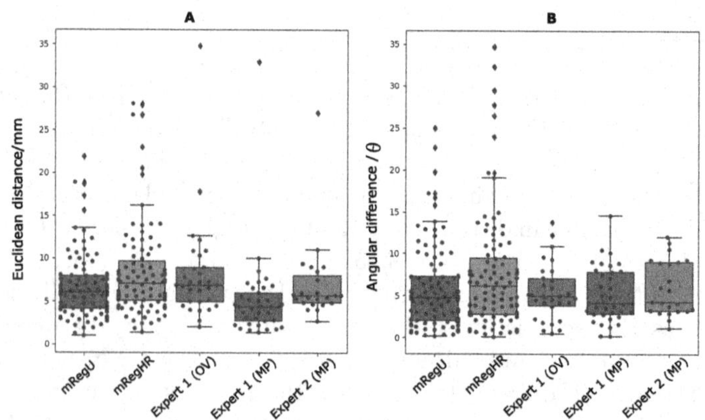

Fig. 4. a) Euclidean distance of the mid-point b) angular difference of the planes determined by the automatic method, Expert 1 (MP), Expert 1 (OV), and Expert 2 (MP) against the GS (generated using MP).

Results of Table 1 show the HD of LH segmentation compared to the GS, mRegU lies within inter-rater variability, thus clinically acceptable bio-markers can be extracted. mRegU and mRegHD perform C-plane detection in 20 s and 18 s respectively, independent of pathology and image quality. We believe this

Table 1. Hausdorff distance, *Turing test* results and time taken to determine the plane

Plane approach	HD/mm	Robust 95th percentile HD/mm	*Turing Test* 1	*Turing Test* 2	Time/s
mRegU	8.95 ± 4.20	6.13 ± 3.93	3	4	20
mRegHR	9.81 ± 4.31	6.53 ± 4.33	4	4	18
Intra-rater (MP)	8.30 ± 2.27	5.52 ± 2.99	–	–	120
Inter-rater (MP)	8.68 ± 3.83	5.99 ± 3.11	–	–	120

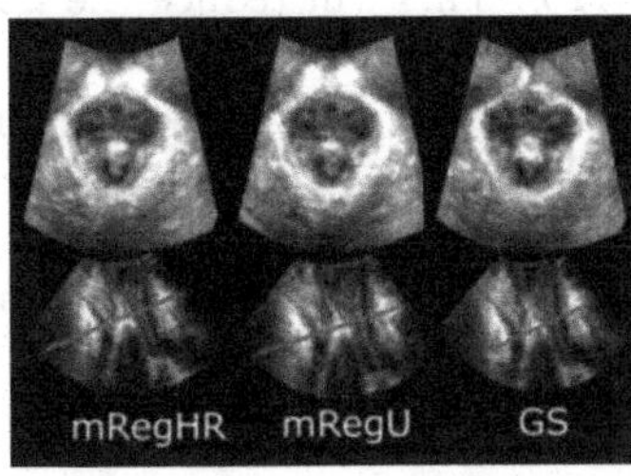

Fig. 5. Visualisation of axial (upper) and MS (lower) plane of minimal hiatal dimensions for automatic methods and GS.

might reduce with further code optimisation. The time difference, is due to UNet having more parameters than HighRes3DNet. Manually on average, Expert 1 and Expert 2 determine the C-plane in 2 min. However, this can vary greatly due to patient's exhibiting PFD, poor acquisition and limited clinical experience. To the author's knowledge, landmark regression of only two landmarks has not been used yet to localise a 2D plane from a 3D US volume, even though by practice this is how humans navigate a 3D volume. This method provides interpretability and can be developed to create a fully interactive plane detection application. Other plane detection tasks may be difficult for clinicians to understand why a specific plane was selected if incorrect, and more difficult to integrate into a clinical setting. The results presented in this paper are based on the training dataset of 25 volumes only. It seems plausible that with more training data the results will improve further. In future work, clinicians may be able to edit the C-plane position by re-selecting the extreme coordinate manually. We will expand this pipeline, by including 2D segmentation of the LH, to produce the first, fully automatic PFD bio-marker analysis pipeline.

4 Conclusion

We proposed an automatic plane detection method via CNN landmark regression, that is comparable to experts as demonstrated through validation on 100 US volumes. We automatically detect the plane from an US volume within 18–20 s compared to several minutes when performed manually. We discussed limitations to our solution, such as levator ballooning. However, by focusing on anatomy and clinical guidelines, we believe our method follows current clinical workflow, and produces results that are understandable to clinicians. Our hybrid method, which is data and guideline driven, allows our method to learn from a small set of examples, compared to a purely data-driven method. We identified that mRegU performed better than the mRegHR, suggesting the UNet architecture is favourable. In future work, the 2D segmentation of the LH will be included [2] to the pipeline. This will produce the first fully automatic bio-marker analysis pipeline, that can detect the C-plane, segment the LH, and indicate PFD disorders from an US volume [1,13]. This will reduce the need for high-level clinical expertise and decrease the time needed to perform PFD assessments. Finally, user interaction can be implemented, allowing clinicians to adapt the detected C-plane, by adjusting the SP and LAM coordinates if required.

Acknowledgments. We gratefully acknowledge the support of NVIDIA Corporation with the donation of the P6000 GPU and GE Healthcare Women's Health Ultrasound (Zipf, Austria) for their ongoing research and data support.

References

1. AIUM/IUGA practice parameter for the performance of urogynecological ultrasound examinations: developed in collaboration with the ACR, the AUGS, the AUA, and the SRU. J. Ultrasound Med. **38**(4), 851–864 (2019)
2. Bonmati, E., et al.: Automatic segmentation method of pelvic floor levator hiatus in ultrasound using a self-normalising neural network. J. Med. Imaging **5**, 12 (2017)
3. Cattani, L., et al.: Exo-anal imaging of the anal sphincter: a comparison between introital and transperineal image acquisition. Int. Urogynecology J. **31**(6), 1107–1113 (2019). https://doi.org/10.1007/s00192-019-04122-5
4. Chykeyuk, K., Yaqub, M., Alison Noble, J.: Class-specific regression random forest for accurate extraction of standard planes from 3D echocardiography. In: Menze, B., Langs, G., Montillo, A., Kelm, M., Müller, H., Tu, Z. (eds.) MCV 2013. LNCS, vol. 8331, pp. 53–62. Springer, Cham (2014). https://doi.org/10.1007/978-3-319-05530-5_6
5. Gibson, E., et al.: NiftyNet: a deep-learning platform for medical imaging. CoRR, abs/1709.03485 (2017)
6. Isensee, F., Kickingereder, P., Wick, W., Bendszus, M., Maier-Hein, K.H.: No new-net. CoRR, abs/1809.10483 (2018)
7. Lammers, K., Fütterer, J.J., Inthout, J., Prokop, M., Vierhout, M.E., Kluivers, K.B.: Correlating signs and symptoms with pubovisceral muscle avulsions on magnetic resonance imaging. Am. J. Obstet. Gynecol. **208**(2), 148.e1–148.e7 (2013)
8. Li, W., Wang, G., Fidon, L., Ourselin, S., Cardoso, M.J., Vercauteren, T.: On the compactness, efficiency, and representation of 3D convolutional networks: Brain parcellation as a pretext task. CoRR, abs/1707.01992 (2017)
9. Li, Y., et al.: Standard plane detection in 3D fetal ultrasound using an iterative transformation network. In: Frangi, A.F., Schnabel, J.A., Davatzikos, C., Alberola-López, C., Fichtinger, G. (eds.) MICCAI 2018. LNCS, vol. 11070, pp. 392–400. Springer, Cham (2018). https://doi.org/10.1007/978-3-030-00928-1_45

10. Lu, X., Georgescu, B., Zheng, Y., Otsuki, J., Comaniciu, D.: AutoMPR: automatic detection of standard planes in 3D echocardiography, pp. 1279–1282, June 2008
11. Whiteside, J.L., Muffly, T.: Chapter 26 overview of pelvic floor disorders: epidemiology, diagnosis, and treatment. In: Goldman, M.B., Troisi, R., Rexrode, K.M. (eds.) Women and Health, 2nd edn., pp. 389–403. Academic Press, Cambridge (2013)
12. Williams, H., et al.: 3D convolutional neural network for segmentation of the urethra in volumetric ultrasound of the pelvic floor. In: 2019 IEEE International Ultrasonics Symposium (IUS), pp. 1473–1476 (2019)
13. Xuan, Y., Friedman, T., Dietz, H.: Does levator ani hiatal area configuration affect pelvic organ prolapse? Ultrasound Obstet. Gynecol. Off. J. Int. Soc. Ultrasound Obstet. Gynecol. **54**(1), 124–127 (2019)
14. Yaqub, M., Kopuri, A., Rueda, S., Sullivan, P.B., McCormick, K., Noble, J.A.: A constrained regression forests solution to 3D fetal ultrasound plane localization for longitudinal analysis of brain growth and maturation. In: Wu, G., Zhang, D., Zhou, L. (eds.) MLMI 2014. LNCS, vol. 8679, pp. 109–116. Springer, Cham (2014). https://doi.org/10.1007/978-3-319-10581-9_14
15. Zhu, P., Li, Z.: Guideline-based machine learning for standard plane extraction in 3D cardiac ultrasound. In: Müller, H., et al. (eds.) MCV/BAMBI -2016. LNCS, vol. 10081, pp. 137–147. Springer, Cham (2017). https://doi.org/10.1007/978-3-319-61188-4_13
16. Çiçek, Ö., Abdulkadir, A., Lienkamp, S.S., Brox, T., Ronneberger, O.: 3D U-Net: learning dense volumetric segmentation from sparse annotation. In: Ourselin, S., Joskowicz, L., Sabuncu, M., Unal, G., Wells, W. (eds.) Medical Image Computing and Computer-Assisted Intervention, vol. 9901, pp. 424–432. Springer, Cham (2016). https://doi.org/10.1007/978-3-319-46723-8_49

Unsupervised Cross-domain Image Classification by Distance Metric Guided Feature Alignment

Qingjie Meng(✉), Daniel Rueckert, and Bernhard Kainz

Department of Computing, BioMedIA, Imperial College, London, UK
q.meng16@imperial.ac.uk

Abstract. Learning deep neural networks that are generalizable across different domains remains a challenge due to the problem of domain shift. Unsupervised domain adaptation is a promising avenue which transfers knowledge from a source domain to a target domain without using any labels in the target domain. Contemporary techniques focus on extracting domain-invariant features using domain adversarial training. However, these techniques neglect to learn discriminative class boundaries in the latent representation space on a target domain and yield limited adaptation performance. To address this problem, we propose distance metric guided feature alignment (MetFA) to extract discriminative as well as domain-invariant features on both source and target domains. The proposed MetFA method explicitly and directly learns the latent representation without using domain adversarial training. Our model integrates class distribution alignment to transfer semantic knowledge from a source domain to a target domain. We evaluate the proposed method on fetal ultrasound datasets for cross-device image classification. Experimental results demonstrate that the proposed method outperforms the state-of-the-art and enables model generalization.

1 Introduction

Despite the success of deep neural networks (DNNs) for medical imaging applications [4,11,21,26,27], learning a task-specific model which generalizes to various medical datasets remains a challenge. This is due to the difference of feature distributions between different datasets, which is known as domain shift [29]. In medical imaging, domain shift can result from different imaging modalities (*e.g.*, magnetic resonance imaging and ultrasound) or different image acquisition devices. In this paper, we focus on model generalization between different image acquisition devices, transferring knowledge from a source device domain to a target device domain.

Fine-tuning DNNs on labelled data from the target domain is a possible solution but is often infeasible due to the need for sufficient manual annotations. More importantly, fine-tuned models remain domain specific because performance gains do not propagate back to the source domain. Deep domain

Y. Hu et al. (Eds.): ASMUS 2020/PIPPI 2020, LNCS 12437, pp. 146–157, 2020.
https://doi.org/10.1007/978-3-030-60334-2_15

adaptation has been widely studied for tackling the problem of domain shift by extracting domain-invariant features [13,15,22]. Such approaches allow porting DNNs to the target domain without extensive annotation as well as preserving performance in both source and target domains. Unsupervised domain adaptation aims at transferring knowledge from a labeled source domain to an unlabeled target domain where both domains share a common label space [13,20,25]. This setting is important for real-world medical imaging scenarios, where data annotation is laborious, time consuming and requires rare expertise is available.

In this work, we propose distance metric guided feature alignment (MetFA) to learn a domain-invariant latent representations for model generalization in an unsupervised domain adaptation setting. We evaluate the proposed method on a challenging medical application, the classification of standardized diagnostic fetal ultrasound (US) view planes during prenatal screening. In many countries, fetal US is clinical routine for early detection of pathological development and informs subsequent decisions about treatment and delivery options [31]. However, domain shift caused by different acquisition devices and prohibitively expensive data annotation restricts the generalization of vanilla DNN classifiers. We show that MetFA enables unsupervised cross-device classification in fetal US.

Contribution. The main contributions of this paper are: (1) We propose distance metric guided feature alignment (MetFA), which learns a shared latent representation space between a labeled source domain and an unlabeled target domain; (2) we develop a framework that jointly learns class distribution alignment and MetFA, which further transfers semantic knowledge from a source domain to a target domain for model generalization; (3) we utilize the proposed method for cross-device anatomical classification in fetal US, which is an important medical imaging application that inherently requires knowledge transfer between different device domains to facilitate the use of DNNs for large scale population screening (Codes in https://github.com/qingjie99/MetFA).

Related Work. ***Unsupervised domain adaptation (UDA)*** mainly focuses on feature distribution alignment. Most UDA approaches explore an appropriate metric to measure the distance of feature distributions between two domains and subsequently train DNNs to minimize this distance [33]. Previous work such as Maximum Mean Discrepancy [22,35] utilizes kernels to measure the discrepancy between representations. Recent research explores domain adversarial training, where a domain discriminator is used to estimate this discrepancy while a feature extractor tries to deceive the discriminator by learning domain-invariant representations [2,23,24]. UDA has been applied to various medical imaging applications such as anatomical segmentation [3,6,9,17,28] and diagnostic classification [1,16]. Most of these works utilize domain adversarial training for feature alignment. In contrast to these works, we explicitly manipulate the latent space to learn discriminative features. Our work is inspired by MiniMax Entropy (MME) proposed in [30], which estimates domain-invariant prototypes and clusters target domain features around these prototypes in a *semi-supervised domain adaptation setting*. In contrast to [30], our method (1) embeds extracted features into a shared latent space with a fixed prior distribution before prototypes are estimated, and (2) simultaneously reduces intra-class variance while increasing inter-class variance across domains via cross-domain metric learning.

Metric learning aims at learning embedded representations that cluster similar samples while separating dissimilar samples in latent space [37]. Previous metric learning methods measure feature similarity by learning a linear Mahalanobis distance [19,36]. More recent works focus on deep metric learning, which learns non-linear relationships of data using DNNs with different losses, such as contrastive loss [8,14], triplet loss [5,36] and N-pair loss [32]. Deep metric learning has shown great benefits for domain adaptation. For example, Sohn et al. [33] proposed a deep metric learning method for unsupervised domain adaptation in disjoint label space. Dou et al. [10] introduced deep metric learning for domain generalization. Most existing metric-learning-based domain adaptation methods only utilize metric learning on the labeled source domain and neglect the relationship between intra-class samples. In contrast to these methods, we introduce cross-domain metric learning to (1) jointly measure the similarity between samples in a labeled source domain and an unlabeled target domain and (2) learn metrics between different groups of intra-class samples.

2 Method

We are given images and the corresponding labels from a source domain $\mathcal{D}_S = \{\mathcal{X}_S, \mathcal{Y}_S\}$ as well as unlabeled images from a target domain $\mathcal{D}_T = \{\mathcal{X}_T\}$. Both domains share a common label space and contain M classes. Our goal is to classify unlabeled target domain data by aligning latent features of both domains. The proposed method contains three main parts (see Fig. 1): (1) supervised classification on the labeled source domain, (2) distance metric guided feature alignment (MetFA) to transfer knowledge from the source domain to the target domain, and (3) class distribution alignment to preserve source domain class relationships in the target domain.

Classification. Classification in the unlabeled target domain is guided by the labeled source domain by sharing whole networks including an encoder E, a Gaussian embedding G and a classifier C. The cross-entropy loss is

$$\mathcal{L}_{ce} = -\mathbb{E}_{\{\mathbf{x},y\}\sim\{\mathcal{X}_S,\mathcal{Y}_S\}} \sum_{t=1}^{M} \mathbb{1}[y = t] log(C(G(E(\mathbf{x})))). \tag{1}$$

Classifier C simultaneously predicts class distributions for the target domain as $P_T(\hat{y}|\mathbf{x})|_{\mathbf{x}\in\mathcal{X}_T}$ (abbreviated as P_T). This prediction will be utilized in MetFA.

MetFA: Distance Metric Guided Feature Alignment. Feature embedding is used to constrain features from both domains to lie in a shared latent space. In this latent space, class representations (prototypes) are estimated to extract domain-invariant features in each class, while cross-domain metric learning is introduced to further separate clusters of different classes in both domains.

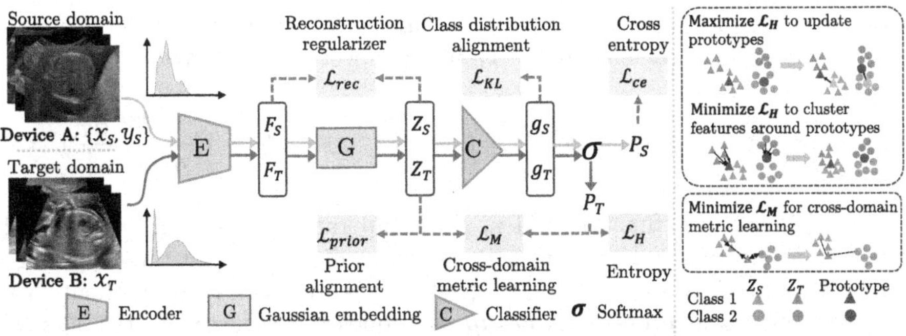

Fig. 1. Left: An overview of the proposed method. Our method consists of (1) supervised classification on the labeled source domain (optimize $\mathcal{L}_{ce}$), (2) distance metric guided feature alignment (MetFA), which aligns features between both domains (optimize $\mathcal{L}_{prior}$, $\mathcal{L}_H$, $\mathcal{L}_M$, $\mathcal{L}_{rec}$), and (3) class distribution alignment, which preserves class relationships in both domains (optimize $\mathcal{L}_{KL}$). Right: Schematic illustration of $\mathcal{L}_H$ and $\mathcal{L}_M$ optimization.

Feature embedding encourages features (F_S, F_T) extracted by an encoder E to share the same fixed prior distribution in a latent space $\mathcal{Z}$, which is similar to distribution matching in a variational autoencoder [18]. In our method, a Gaussian embedding G is built to model F_S and F_T by a standard Gaussian distribution $\mathcal{N}(0, I)$. Specifically, $Z_i \sim q(\mathcal{Z}|\mathcal{X}_i)|i \in \{S, T\}$ is sampled from $\mathcal{N}(\mu_i, \Sigma_i)|i \in \{S, T\}$ with the reparameterization trick [18], where $\{\mu_i, \Sigma_i\} = G(F_i)|i \in \{S, T\}$. The prior alignment loss is the Kullback-Leibler (KL) divergence between $\mathcal{N}(0, I)$ and $\mathcal{N}(\mu_i, \Sigma_i)|i \in \{S, T\}$, which is

$$\mathcal{L}_{prior} = D_{KL}(\mathcal{N}(\mu_S, \Sigma_S) \parallel \mathcal{N}(0, I)) + D_{KL}(\mathcal{N}(\mu_T, \Sigma_T)) \parallel \mathcal{N}(0, I)). \quad (2)$$

In order to guarantee that embedded features are representative of the extracted features, we add a feature reconstruction loss $\mathcal{L}_{rec}$ as a regularizer:

$$\mathcal{L}_{rec} = \|F_S - Z_S\|_2^2 + \|F_T - Z_T\|_2^2. \quad (3)$$

Feature embedding constrains distribution matching. In the absence of target domain labels, it is essential for subsequent feature alignment. However, feature embedding itself is unlikely to ensure that features are domain-invariant and discriminative between different classes. The rest of MetFA tackles this problem.

Domain-invariant feature extraction is motivated by Minimax Entropy (MME), proposed by Saito et al. [30]. Using unlabeled data in the target domain, MME learns a single domain-invariant prototype (a representation point) for each class in both domains and clusters target domain samples around these prototypes (see Fig. 1 upper right). We implement prototypes as the weights $\mathbf{W}$ of the last dense layer in the classifier C.

Training MME contains two iterative steps. The first step is to move prototypes from source domain to target domain, which is maximizing the similarity between $\mathbf{W}$ and its input features (H_T). This similarity maximization is equivalent to maximizing the entropy of $\mathcal{X}_T$ with respect to $\mathbf{W}$, using

$$\mathcal{L}_H = -\mathbb{E}_{\mathbf{x}\sim\mathcal{X}_T}\sum_{i=1}^{M} p_T(\hat{y}=i|\mathbf{x})\log p_T(\hat{y}=i|\mathbf{x}),\ \ p_T \in P_T = \sigma(\frac{1}{\tau_0}\frac{\mathbf{W}^T H_T}{\|H_T\|}), \quad (4)$$

where σ is a softmax function and τ_0 is a temperature parameter. The second step is to assign target domain features to the domain-invariant prototypes. To achieve this, $\mathcal{L}_H$ is minimized with respect to E, G and $C\setminus\mathbf{W}$ (C without $\mathbf{W}$).

Cross-domain metric learning is proposed to maximize the margin between different classes across domains. We define latent features of $\mathcal{X}_S$ and $\mathcal{X}_T$ (which are Z_S and Z_T) respectively as support samples and query samples. In cross-domain metric learning the distance between query and support samples is minimized when they are from the same class and simultaneously maximized when they are from different classes (see Fig. 1 lower right). The metric loss is

$$\mathcal{L}_M = \frac{1}{N}\sum_{i=1}^{M}\sum_{j=1}^{c_i^T}\log(1+\sum_{k\neq i}^{k\in[1,M]} e^{d_j^i - d_j^k}) = -\frac{1}{N}\sum_{i=1}^{M}\sum_{j=1}^{c_i^T}\log\frac{e^{d_j^i}}{e^{d_j^i}+\sum_{k\neq i}^{k\in[1,M]} e^{d_j^k}}, \quad (5)$$

where N and c_i^T are the number of all query samples and query samples from class i. Note that the labels of query samples are P_T in Eq. 4. d_j^i is the distance between a query sample q_j^i and a same class support sample s_t^i. d_j^k is the distance between q_j^i and s_t^k from different classes. Considering the relationship between intra-class samples and using a hard mining strategy [7], we define d_j^i and d_j^k as

$$\begin{aligned} d_j^i &= \max_t d(q_j^i, s_t^i),\ t\in[1,c_i^S],\ q_j^i \sim Z_T,\ s_t^i \sim Z_S, \\ d_j^k &= \min_t d(q_j^i, s_t^k),\ t\in[1,c_k^S],\ q_j^i \sim Z_T,\ s_t^k \sim Z_S, \end{aligned} \quad (6)$$

where c_i^S and c_k^S are the number of support samples from class i and class k. We use the squared Euclidean distance for $d(\cdot,\cdot)$ in Eq. 6.

Class Distribution Alignment. Apart from structuring a feature space for better class predictions, we want to further transfer semantic knowledge which is preserving class relationships between domains. Class distribution alignment is used for class relationship preservation between multiple labeled source domains in a domain generalization task [10]. In our method, we align class distributions between a labeled source domain and an unlabeled target domain. We utilize the symmetrized KL-divergence to define the class distribution alignment loss

$$\begin{aligned} \mathcal{L}_{KL} &= \frac{1}{M}\sum_{i=1}^{M}\Lambda[D_{KL}(\bar{p}_i^S \parallel \bar{p}_i^T) + D_{KL}(\bar{p}_i^T \parallel \bar{p}_i^S)], \\ \bar{p}_i^S = \sigma(\frac{1}{\tau_1}\frac{1}{c_i^S}\sum_{y=i} g_{\mathbf{x}}^S)&|_{(\mathbf{x},y)\sim\{\mathcal{X}_S,\mathcal{Y}_S\}},\ \bar{p}_i^T = \sigma(\frac{1}{\tau_1}\frac{1}{c_i^T}\sum_{\hat{y}=i} g_{\mathbf{x}}^T)|_{(\mathbf{x},\hat{y})\sim\{\mathcal{X}_T,P_T(\mathbf{x})\}}. \end{aligned} \quad (7)$$

Here, $\Lambda = [c_1^T, c_2^T, ..., c_M^T]$ contains the number of target domain samples predicted for each class. $\bar{p}_i^S$ and $\bar{p}_i^T$ are the ith class distributions in source and target domain. $g_{\mathbf{x}}^S$ and $g_{\mathbf{x}}^T$ are the pre-softmax activations from classifier C and τ_1 is a temperature parameter.

Optimization. The overall objective function of the proposed method is:

$$\min_{E,G,C\setminus\mathbf{W}} \{\mathcal{L} + \lambda_6 \mathcal{L}_H\}, \quad \min_{\mathbf{W}} \{\mathcal{L} - \lambda_6 \mathcal{L}_H\},$$
$$\text{with} \quad \mathcal{L} = \lambda_1 \mathcal{L}_{ce} + \lambda_2 \mathcal{L}_{prior} + \lambda_3 \mathcal{L}_M + \lambda_4 \mathcal{L}_{rec} + \lambda_5 \mathcal{L}_{KL}. \tag{8}$$

Here λ_1 to λ_6 are hyper-parameters chosen experimentally depending on the application. Our model is end-to-end trainable, with $\mathbf{W}$ and the rest of the networks are trained in an alternating fashion according to Eq. 8. We apply L2 regularization (scale $= 10^{-5}$) to all weights during training to prevent overfitting and apply random image flipping as data augmentation. Our model is trained on a Nvidia Titan X GPU.

3 Evaluation and Results

We evaluate the proposed method on 2D fetal US images acquired during routine prenatal screening. This US data is obtained by different imaging devices: Device A (GE Voluson E8) acquires $\sim$12k images and device B (Philips EPIQ V7 G) acquires unpaired $\sim$5.5k images. In both datasets, six anatomical standard planes have been selected by expert sonographers, including Four Chamber View (4CH), Abdominal, Left Ventricular Outflow Tract (LVOT), Right Ventricular Outflow Tract (RVOT), Femur and Lips. We evaluate our method in two scenarios where device A is the source domain while device B is the target domain, and vice versa. During training, the source domain is fully labeled and the target domain is unlabeled. In both scenarios, hyper-parameters λ_1 to λ_6 in Eq. 8 are $\lambda_1 = 10, \lambda_2 = 10^{-2}, \lambda_3 = 10^{-1}, \lambda_4 = 1, \lambda_5 = 10, \lambda_6 = 5$. τ_0 in Eq. 4 is 0.05 (same to [30]) and τ_1 in Eq. 7 is 2 (same to [10]). We use Stochastic Gradient Descent (SGD) with momentum optimizer to update our model.

Comparison Methods. We evaluate a VGG network which contains an encoder E and a classifier C from the proposed method as a baseline. This baseline is trained on data only from the source domain (*Source only*) to demonstrate the existence of domain shift. We compare the proposed method with the state-of-the-art domain-adaptation algorithms, including domain-adversarial training of neural networks (DANN) [13], adversarial discriminative domain adaptation (ADDA) [34] and semi-supervised domain adaptation via minimax entropy (MME) [30]. Note that for fair comparison, we use the MME model in an unsupervised learning paradigm. Additionally, given target domain labels, we show fine-tuned and fully-supervised classification on the target domain as references. Fine-tuned classification is pre-trained on the labeled source domain and fine-tuned on the labeled target domain. This fine-tuned model is evaluated on both source and target domains. Fully-supervised classification is trained from scratch on the labeled target domain and evaluated on the target domain.

Ablation Study. We further explore the effectiveness of different components in the proposed method by removing different loss components: UDA-MetFA-I: only contains $\mathcal{L}_{ce}$, $\mathcal{L}_{prior}$ and $\mathcal{L}_H$; UDA-MetFA-II: UDA-MetFA-I plus $\mathcal{L}_M$; UDA-MetFA-III: UDA-MetFA-II plus $\mathcal{L}_{KL}$; UDA-MetFA-IV: UDA-MetFA-II plus $\mathcal{L}_{rec}$; UDA-MetFA-V: contains all components.

Table 1. Comparison of *Source only*, the state-of-the-art and ablation study (UDA-MetFA- I to V) for fetal US anatomical classification with **device A as source domain and device B as target domain**. Fine-tuned and Fully-supervised are reference results given target domain labels. Best results in bold.

Methods	S: device A			T: device B		
	F1-score	Recall	Precision	F1-score	Recall	Precision
Source only	0.8782	0.8800	0.8786	0.2455	0.3400	0.3070
ADDA [34]	0.8841	0.8850	0.8860	0.1377	0.2050	0.1623
DANN [13]	0.8321	0.8350	0.8564	0.3390	0.3650	0.3756
MME [30]	0.8876	0.8900	0.8914	0.4398	0.5133	0.4565
UDA-MetFA-I	0.8894	0.8900	0.8911	0.5255	0.5550	0.5599
UDA-MetFA-II	0.8951	0.8967	0.8997	0.5959	0.6400	0.6359
UDA-MetFA-III	**0.9202**	**0.9200**	**0.9207**	0.6301	0.6850	0.6143
UDA-MetFA-IV	0.8970	0.8967	0.8986	0.6930	0.7067	0.7011
UDA-MetFA-V	0.8990	0.9000	0.9027	**0.7713**	**0.7717**	**0.7874**
Fine-tuned	0.7987	0.8050	0.8140	0.7114	0.7150	0.7373
Fully-supervised	–	–	–	0.5919	0.6100	0.6576

Results. Table 1 shows the experimental results of baselines and the ablation study where device A is the source domain and device B is the target domain. From this table, we observe that the UDA-MetFA-V model outperforms other baselines. In the target domain, UDA-MetFA-V achieves an average F1-score of 0.7713 while the highest average F1-score of other baselines is 0.4398 (MME [30]). UDA-MetFA-I greatly outperforms MME [30] in the target domain, demonstrating the importance of feature embedding in the proposed method. UDA-MetFA-V performs better than other ablation models in the target domain, illustrating the effectiveness of all components in the proposed method. Furthermore, the results of Fine-tuned and *source only* in the source domain indicate that the fine-tuned model remains less generalizable, whereas the proposed method (UDA-MetFA-V) enables model generalization with improved classification performance in both source and target domains.

We further compare MME (best baseline in Table 1) with the proposed method (UDA-MetFA-V) in confusion matrices and t-SNE plots. Figure 2(a) demonstrates that our method extracts more discriminative features for better classification, especially on easily confused anatomies (*e.g.*, LVOT vs. RVOT). Figure 2(b) shows that for UDA-MetFA-V, target features are closer to source features while features of different classes are more separated. This indicates that the proposed MetFA benefits the extraction of discriminative and domain-invariant features.

Table 2 shows the results of comparison methods and the proposed method (UDA-MetFA-V) on switched domains, where device B is the source domain and device A is the target domain. We observe that UDA-MetFA-V outperforms the state-of-the-art in both source and target domains, demonstrating that our method is capable of successfully transferring knowledge from source domain to target domain as well as improving model generalization.

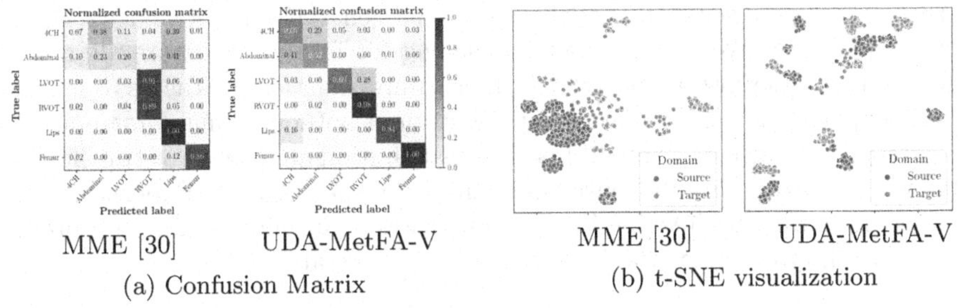

MME [30] UDA-MetFA-V

(a) Confusion Matrix

MME [30] UDA-MetFA-V

(b) t-SNE visualization

Fig. 2. Comparison of MME [30] and UDA-MetFA-V on (a) confusion matrix of target domain (device B) and (b) t-SNE plot of extracted test data features.

Table 2. Comparison of baselines and UDA-MetFA-V with **device B as source domain and device A as target domain**. Best results in bold.

Methods	S: device B			T: device A		
	F1-score	Recall	Precision	F1-score	Recall	Precision
Source only	0.5919	0.6100	0.6576	0.2854	0.3300	0.3555
DANN [13]	0.5198	0.5450	0.5451	0.3318	0.3500	0.3450
MME [30]	0.3776	0.4183	0.4500	0.1520	0.1883	0.2101
UDA-MetFA-V	**0.7101**	**0.7150**	**0.7441**	**0.5776**	**0.5550**	**0.6303**
Fully-supervised	–	–	–	0.8782	0.8800	0.8786

Discussion. Domain adaptation is commonly used to transfer a performant, task-specific model from a source domain to a target domain. However, the DNNs learning ability in a source domain can limit this ability in a target domain. This may explain the lower classification performance of the proposed method compared with a fully-supervised method in the target domain in Table 2. Current UDA methods rarely discuss the performance of DNNs in the source domain. From Table 2, we observe that tracking the source domain performance can be potentially used for data selection during model improvement in the source domain. A limitation of our method is the empirical hyper-parameters selection. For a specific application, we adjust hyper-parameters according to their importance and select the best combination with grid search. Meta-learning [12] will be explored in future work to allow automatic hyper-parameter selection.

4 Conclusion

In this paper, we discuss the problem of model generalization for unsupervised domain adaption. We propose metric learning for improved feature alignment (MetFA) to extract discriminative and domain-invariant features across domains. MetFA explicitly structures latent representations without using domain adversarial training. Our model integrates class distribution alignment for transferring semantic knowledge from a source domain to a target domain. Experiments on cross-device fetal US screening images demonstrate the effectiveness and practical applicability of our method compared with the state-of-the-art.

Acknowledgments. We thank the Welcome Trust IEH Award [102431] and Nvidia (GPU donations).

Appendices

A Examples of Ultrasound Images

We show more examples of ultrasound images acquired from different image acquisition devices (Fig. 3).

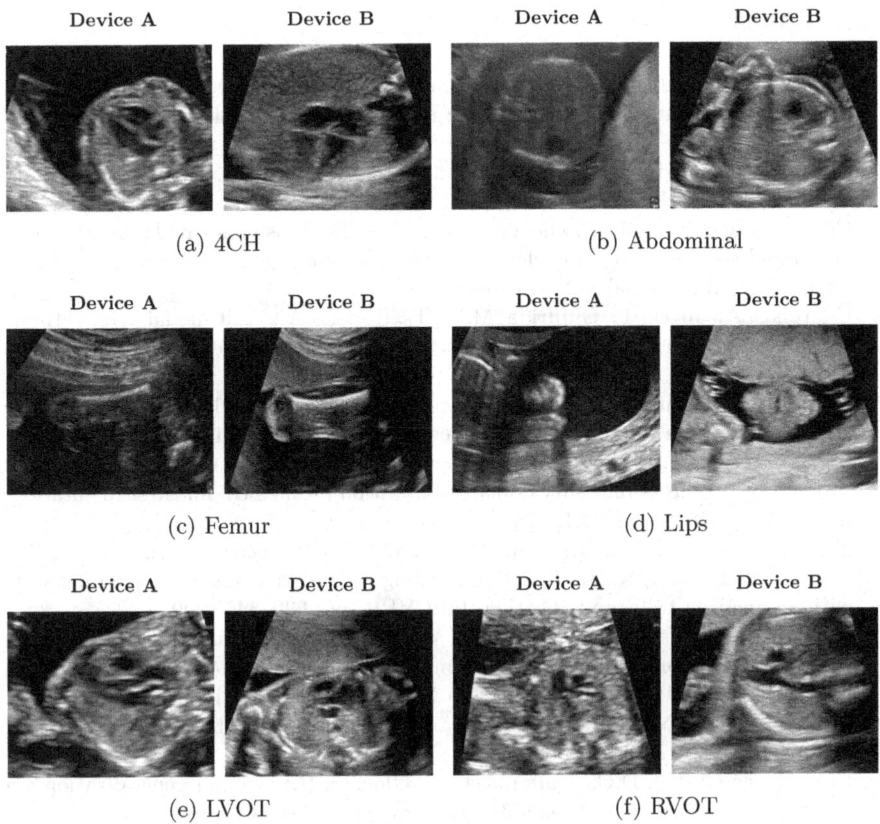

(a) 4CH (b) Abdominal

(c) Femur (d) Lips

(e) LVOT (f) RVOT

Fig. 3. Examples of ultrasound images acquired by different image acquisition devices. Device A is *GE Voluson E8* and device B is *Philips EPIQV7 G.*

B Split of Training Data

See Table 3.

Table 3. The number of images in each class for training. In the first scenario (S: device A, T: device B), images in device A are used as labeled data and images in device B are unlabeled. In the second scenario (S: device B, T: device A), images in device B are labeled and images in device A are unlabeled.

	4CH	Abdominal	Femur	Lips	LVOT	RVOT
Device A	700	700	700	700	700	700
Device B	828	728	815	600	328	559

References

1. Bernard, O., et al.: Deep learning techniques for automatic MRI cardiac multi-structures segmentation and diagnosis: is the problem solved? IEEE Trans. Med. Imaging **37**, 2514–2525 (2018)
2. Bousmalis, K., Trigeorgis, G., Silberman, N., Krishnan, D., Erhan, D.: Domain separation networks. In: NeurIPS, pp. 343–351 (2016)
3. Cai, J., Zhang, Z., Cui, L., Zheng, Y., Yang, L.: Towards cross-modal organ translation and segmentation: a cycle- and shape-consistent generative adversarial network. Med. Image Anal. **52**, 174–184 (2019)
4. Chartsias, A., Joyce, T., Giuffrida, M.V., Tsaftaris, S.A.: Multimodal MR synthesis via modality-invariant latent representation. IEEE Trans. Med. Imaging **37**, 803–814 (2017)
5. Chechik, G., Sharma, V., Shalit, U., Bengio, S.: Large scale online learning of image similarity through ranking. J. Mach. Learn. Res. **11**, 1109–1135 (2010)
6. Chen, C., Dou, Q., Chen, H., Qin, J., Heng, P.: Synergistic image and feature adaptation: towards cross-modality domain adaptation for medical image segmentation. In: AAAI, pp. 865–872 (2019)
7. Chen, G., Zhang, T., Lu, J., Zhou, J.: Deep meta metric learning. In: ICCV (2019)
8. Chopra, S., Hadsell, R., LeCun, Y.: Learning a similarity metric discriminatively, with application to face verification. In: CVPR, pp. 539–546 (2005)
9. Dong, N., Kampffmeyer, M., Liang, X., Wang, Z., Dai, W., Xing, E.: Unsupervised domain adaptation for automatic estimation of cardiothoracic ratio. In: Frangi, A.F., Schnabel, J.A., Davatzikos, C., Alberola-López, C., Fichtinger, G. (eds.) MICCAI 2018. LNCS, vol. 11071, pp. 544–552. Springer, Cham (2018). https://doi.org/10.1007/978-3-030-00934-2_61
10. Dou, Q., de Castro, D.C., Kamnitsas, K., Glocker, B.: Domain generalization via model-agnostic learning of semantic features. In: NeurIPS (2019)
11. Dou, Q., Liu, Q., Heng, P.A., Glocker, B.: Unpaired multi-modal segmentation via knowledge distillation. IEEE Trans. Med. Imaging **38** (2019)
12. Feurer, M., Klein, A., Eggensperger, K., Springenberg, J., Blum, M., Hutter, F.: Efficient and robust automated machine learning. In: NeurIPS, pp. 2962–2970 (2015)
13. Ganin, Y., et al.: Domain-adversarial training of neural networks. J. Mach. Learn. Res. **17**(1), 2030–2096 (2016)
14. Hadsell, R., Chopra, S., LeCun, Y.: Dimensionality reduction by learning an invariant mapping. In: CVPR, pp. 1735–1742 (2006)
15. Häusser, P., Frerix, T., Mordvintsev, A., Cremers, D.: Associative domain adaptation. In: ICCV, pp. 2784–2792 (2017)
16. Huang, Y., Zheng, H., Liu, C., Ding, X., Gustavo, R.K.: Epithelium-stroma classification via convolutional neural networks and unsupervised domain adaptation in histopathological images. IEEE J. Biomed. Health Inform. **21**, 1625–1632 (2017)
17. Kamnitsas, K., et al.: Unsupervised domain adaptation in brain lesion segmentation with adversarial networks. In: Niethammer, M., et al. (eds.) IPMI 2017. LNCS, vol. 10265, pp. 597–609. Springer, Cham (2017). https://doi.org/10.1007/978-3-319-59050-9_47
18. Kingma, D.P., Welling, M.: Auto-encoding variational bayes. In: Bengio, Y., LeCun, Y. (eds.) ICLR (2014)
19. Köstinger, M., Hirzer, M., Wohlhart, P., Roth, P.M., Bischof, H.: Large scale metric learning from equivalence constraints. In: CVPR, pp. 2288–2295 (2012)

20. Lee, C.Y., Batra, T., Baig, M.H., Ulbricht, D.: Sliced Wasserstein discrepancy for unsupervised domain adaptation. In: CVPR, pp, 10285–10295 (2019)
21. Liu, M., Zhang, J., Adeli, E., Shen, D.: Landmark-based deep multi-instance learning for brain disease diagnosis. Med. Image Anal. **43**, 157–168 (2018)
22. Long, M., Cao, Y., Wang, J., Jordan, M.I.: Learning transferable features with deep adaptation networks. In: ICML, pp. 97–105 (2015)
23. Long, M., CAO, Z., Wang, J., Jordan, M.I.: Conditional adversarial domain adaptation. In: NeurIPS, pp. 1640–1650 (2018)
24. Luo, Z., Zou, Y., Hoffman, J., Fei-Fei, L.F.: Label efficient learning of transferable representations across domains and tasks. In: NeurIPS, pp. 165–177 (2017)
25. Meng, Q., Rueckert, D., Kainz, B.: Learning cross-domain generalizable features by representation disentanglement. arXiv: 2003.00321 (2020)
26. Meng, Q., Sinclair, M., Zimmer, V., et al.: Weakly supervised estimation of shadow confidence maps in fetal ultrasound imaging. IEEE Trans. Med. Imaging **38**, 2755–2767 (2019)
27. Nie, D., Zhang, H., Adeli, E., Liu, L., Shen, D.: 3D deep learning for multi-modal imaging-guided survival time prediction of brain tumor patients. In: Ourselin, S., Joskowicz, L., Sabuncu, M.R., Unal, G., Wells, W. (eds.) MICCAI 2016. LNCS, vol. 9901, pp. 212–220. Springer, Cham (2016). https://doi.org/10.1007/978-3-319-46723-8_25
28. Ouyang, C., Kamnitsas, K., Biffi, C., Duan, J., Rueckert, D.: Data efficient unsupervised domain adaptation for cross-modality image segmentation. In: Shen, D., et al. (eds.) MICCAI 2019. LNCS, vol. 11765, pp. 669–677. Springer, Cham (2019). https://doi.org/10.1007/978-3-030-32245-8_74
29. Quinonero-Candela, J., Sugiyama, M., Schwaighofer, A., Lawrence, N.D.: Dataset Shift in Machine Learning. Neural Information Processing. MIT Press, Cambridge (2008)
30. Saito, K., Kim, D., Sclaroff, S., Darrell, T., Saenko, K.: Semi-supervised domain adaptation via minimax entropy. In: ICCV (2019)
31. Salomon, L.J., et al.: Practice guidelines for performance of the routine mid-trimester fetal ultrasound scan. Ultrasound Obstet. Gynecol. **37**, 116–126 (2011)
32. Sohn, K.: Improved deep metric learning with multi-class N-pair loss objective. In: Lee, D.D., Sugiyama, M., von Luxburg, U., Guyon, I., Garnett, R. (eds.) NeurIPS, pp. 1849–1857 (2016)
33. Sohn, K., Shang, W., Yu, X., Chandraker, M.: Unsupervised domain adaptation for distance metric learning. In: ICLR (2019)
34. Tzeng, E., Hoffman, J., Saenko, K., Darrell, T.: Adversarial discriminative domain adaptation. In: CVPR, pp. 2962–2971 (2017)
35. Tzeng, E., Hoffman, J., Zhang, N., Saenko, K., Darrell, T.: Deep domain confusion: maximizing for domain invariance. arXiv:1412.3474, December 2014
36. Weinberger, K.Q., Saul, L.K.: Distance metric learning for large margin nearest neighbor classification. JMLR, 207–244 (2009)
37. Xing, E.P., Jordan, M.I., Russell, S.J., Ng, A.Y.: Distance metric learning with application to clustering with side-information. In: NeurIPS, pp. 521–528 (2003)

Robotics and Skill Assessment

Dual-Robotic Ultrasound System for In Vivo Prostate Tomography

Kevin M. Gilboy[1(✉)], Yixuan Wu[1], Bradford J. Wood[2], Emad M. Boctor[1], and Russell H. Taylor[1]

[1] The Johns Hopkins University, Baltimore, MD 21218, USA
kgilboy1@jhu.edu
[2] National Institutes of Health, Bethesda, MD 20814, USA

Abstract. Ultrasound computed tomography (USCT) offers quantitative anatomical tissue characterization for cancer detection. While most research and commercial development has focused on submerging target anatomy in a transducer-lined cylindrical water tank, this is not practical for imaging deep anatomy and an alternative approach using aligned abdominal and endoluminal ultrasound probes is required. This work outlines and validates a clinical workflow and real-time motion framework for a novel dual-robotic approach specific to in vivo prostate imaging: one arm wielding a linear abdominal probe, the other wielding a linear transrectal ultrasound (TRUS) probe. After calibration, the robotic system works to keep the abdominal probe collinear with the physician-rotated TRUS probe using a convex contour tracking scheme, while also enforcing its gentle contact with the patient's pubic region to capture the ultrasound slices needed for limited-angle tomographic reconstruction. The repeatable and accurate robotic system presents feasibility for prostate USCT and future malignancy diagnosis and staging in vivo.

Keywords: Ultrasound tomography · Robotic ultrasound · Prostate imaging

1 Introduction

Prostate cancer is the second leading non-cutaneous cancer and the fifth leading cause of cancer death globally for males in 2018 [4]. Due to inaccuracies and limitations of prostate-specific antigen (PSA) testing and serial blind biopsies, modern diagnostics involve a combination of PSA and transrectal ultrasound (TRUS) followed by mpMRI if there is heightened concern for cancer [17]. MRI can also be fused with real-time TRUS data to guide targeted prostate biopsy [12] which, while the de facto gold standard in prostate cancer diagnosis, is only one factor in pathology determination and is usually costly and schedule-limited. This raises the question if the initial B-Mode TRUS scan can enhance sensitivity and specificity of cancer detection, despite only a 50%–60% detection accuracy and approximate 6% positive predictive value due to undetectable isoechoic

Y. Hu et al. (Eds.): ASMUS 2020/PIPPI 2020, LNCS 12437, pp. 161–170, 2020.
https://doi.org/10.1007/978-3-030-60334-2_16

or echopoor lesions [8]. Although qualitative ultrasound (US) imaging (e.g. B-mode) is limited in precision, quantitative imaging via US computed tomography (USCT) may be eligible for highly specific stratification. Past work on ultrasonic characterization of prostate biopsy samples demonstrated obvious attenuation and speed of sound (SoS) differences between normal and cancerous prostate tissue [16]. Work by [15] also showed that the SoS map of ex vivo prostate tissue submerged in a water tank correlates well with MRI-based pathology deduction.

Hardware and image reconstruction for USCT have improved since its debut in the 1970s. Recent research and commercial development have mainly utilized transducer-lined cylindrical water tanks for breast imaging. Two notable systems are the SoftVue by Delphinus [7] and QTScan by QT [14], which was FDA-approved for clinical use in 2017 [18]. Transmission US using these systems has succeeded in characterizing breast density and identifying masses comparable to mammography and tomosynthesis [13], suggesting the value of SoS as a clinical parameter. QT has additionally shown the effectiveness of using inverse scattering to image the human knee [19] and whole body piglet [10] immersed in a scanner tank. While a distal appendage can be easily submerged in a water tank, deep anatomy such as the prostate presents a technical challenge for imaging.

An alternative, dual-robotic approach to USCT of deep anatomy was proposed by Aalimifar, who suggested using software to align two robot-held linear US probes for slice acquisition [1]. This approach circumvents the need for anatomical submersion in a water tank thereby alleviating the size constraints of what can be imaged. While the work proved the feasibility of SoS reconstruction of an agar resected prostate phantom using aligned probes and outlined the calibrations necessary for a dual-robotic approach, it fell short of implementing a practical real-time system for in vivo USCT of the prostate with a TRUS probe. In this paper, we build upon the calibration methods from [1] and develop the first fully functional dual-robot system and clinical workflow to perform USCT of the prostate: one arm holding a physician guided linear TRUS probe for Tx and the other arm autonomously servoing a linear abdominal probe about the patient's pubic region for Rx. Concurrent convex contour tracking and alignment of the abdominal probe in response to TRUS rotations is enforced by our innovative real-time motion framework that works in any unconstrained environment.

2 Materials and Methods

2.1 Proposed General Workflow for Robotic Prostate Tomography

The general proposed clinical setup is shown in Fig. 1, and uses two robots for element-wise sequential Tx and Rx, respectively, and eventual tomographic reconstruction of the prostate: one to steadily hold a TRUS probe transrectally while allowing precise movement along and about the insertional axis (2-DoF), and one to hold a linear abdominal probe externally that autonomously servos (6-DoF) and tracks movement of the TRUS probe to maintain collinear line-of-sight between the probes while enforcing gentle contact with the patient's pubic region. The TRUS probe can either be controlled collaboratively through physician hand forces or operated with a joystick for precise control.

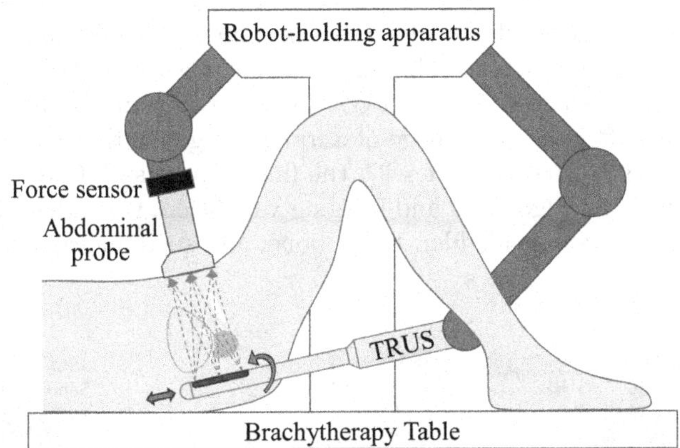

Fig. 1. General approach to dual-robotic USCT. Important anatomy shown in addition to the prostate (pink) includes the bladder (pink outline) which may contain air and the pubic bone (white) which may obfuscate the view of US transmission. (Color figure online)

The clinical workflow is (1) the patient (sedated, as is common for TRUS procedures) lies on a brachytherapy table surrounded by the two robot arms, (2) the physician guides the robotically-held TRUS probe into the rectum until the prostate can be seen on a B-Mode image, (3) coupling gel is generously applied to the pubic region, (4) the software autonomously lowers the robotically-held abdominal probe onto the patient's pubic region in alignment with the TRUS probe, (5) the physician manipulates the TRUS probe while the abdominal probe follows, allowing for continuous US transmission slice acquisition.

In this scheme, the TRUS probe must be the Tx transducer since it is closer to the prostate, allowing the prostate to be more insonated than if the prostate were closer to the Rx transducer, where the acoustic energy is reduced due to scatter. Additionally, the TRUS probe must be the physician controlled element while the abdominal probe is controlled autonomously. This decision was made since every 2-DoF TRUS probe pose has multiple corresponding 6-DoF abdominal probe poses that maintain alignment, whereas the inverse is not guaranteed. This is reasonable for safety and clinical liability since the TRUS probe is invasive.

2.2 Dual Robot Setup and Reference Frames

Two Universal Robots UR5 6-DoF robots were opposingly mounted at 45° on a custom 80/20 T-slot frame as shown in Fig. 2, and controlled by a central compute running software utilizing the open-source CISST/SAW real-time libraries [6]. The two robots used custom 3D printed adapters to hold a BPL9-5/55 linear

TRUS and L14-5W/60 linear abdominal probe respectively. The robot holding the abdominal probe additionally had a 6-DoF Robotiq FT150 force/torque sensor, which was filtered with a low-pass Kalman filter and used for enforcing probe contact against the patient's pubic region. The TRUS probe was connected to an Ultrasonix SonixTouch machine, which sent scanline triggers to a SonixDAQ US acquisition system to which the abdominal probe was connected. Synchronization logic was implemented on an FPGA to only transmit scanline triggers to the DAQ on and after the rising edge of a frame trigger so that US transmission acquisition always started capture with the first elements. A CIRS 048A pelvic phantom was used for algorithm and imaging validation, which had distinct SoS changes between prostate, bladder, pubic bone, and surrounding tissue.

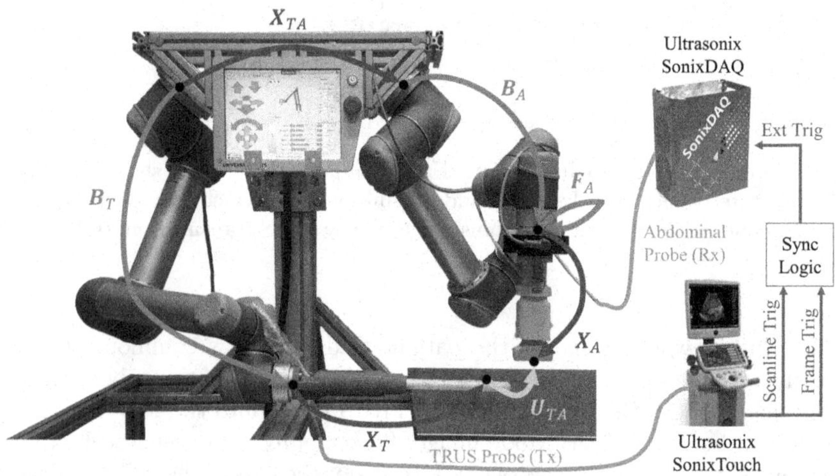

Fig. 2. Experimental setup and frames, including two UR5 robots and their respective US probes and control systems tied together by a synchronized scanline trigger. Transformations in green are known, red (named with X) are unknown and solved through calibration, and yellow are unknown and deduced from the complete kinematic chain. (Color figure online)

The pose of the abdominal probe relative to its robot base can be written $B_A F_A X_A$, where $B_A \in SE(3)$ is the retrievable robot pose, $F_A \in SE(3)$ is the rotational transformation of the robot end-effector to the force/torque sensor, and $X_A \in SE(3)$ is the calibrated transformation to US image-space. Similarly, the pose of the TRUS probe relative to its robot base can be written $B_T X_T$. The transformation from the TRUS probe robot to the abdominal probe robot was called X_{TA}, allowing the relative orientation from the TRUS image-space to the abdominal image-space to be written as $U_{TA} = X_T^{-1} B_T^{-1} X_{TA} B_A F_A X_A$.

2.3 Calibration

The three unknown frame transformations were sequentially calibrated similar to [1]. The transformations from each end effector to its US probe origin, X_A and X_T, were both off-line calibrated by solving separate BXp problems. Specifically, a cross-wire phantom fixed in a water tank was imaged under $N = 60$ independent poses of each robot arm represented by $B_A^{(i)}$ and $B_T^{(i)}$, where $i = 1, \ldots, N$. For each unique pose, the cross location was consistently imaged as a focused spot using each US probe and automatically segmented to get the position of the cross within the 2D US RF signal, $p_T^{(i)}$ and $p_A^{(i)}$. The general BXp problem is given as

$$\underset{X \in SE(3)}{\text{argmin}} \sum_{i=1}^{N-1} \sum_{j=i+1}^{N} \left\| B^{(i)} X p^{(i)} - B^{(j)} X p^{(j)} \right\|_2^2 \tag{1}$$

from which X_A and X_T were respectively optimized through an iterative gradient descent procedure proposed in [2] after algorithm initialization using values attained from measurement with calipers. We withheld $n = 0.1N$ samples of the data to assess calibration accuracy by calculating mean, standard deviation, and max of the Euclidean distance between each calculated cross location and the average cross location.

$$E^{(i)} = \left\| B^{(i)} X p^{(i)} - \frac{1}{n} \sum\nolimits_j B^{(j)} X p^{(j)} \right\|_2 \tag{2}$$

The calibration between robot bases, X_{TA}, was performed by moving the cross-wire phantom to multiple locations, collecting robot poses ($B_T^{(i)}$ and $B_A^{(i)}$) and cross locations ($p_T^{(i)}$ and $p_A^{(i)}$) recorded by each probe. The two point clouds of cross locations are related by $B_T^{(i)} X_T p_T^{(i)} = X_{TA} B_A^{(i)} F_A X_A p_A^{(i)}$, where X_{TA} was solved with Horn's quaternion-based method for $A = XB$ problems [9]. Five non-collinear points were collected to perform the calibration, which was assessed by mean, standard deviation, and max of the Euclidean distance

$$E^{(i)} = \left\| B_T^{(i)} X_T p_T^{(i)} - X_{TA} B_A^{(i)} F_A X_A p_A^{(i)} \right\|_2 \tag{3}$$

2.4 Robot Motion Framework

TRUS probe movements were chosen to be joystick controlled, and were constrained about and along the insertional axis. User-induced joystick movements were converted into commanded velocities via the admittance control algorithm $\boldsymbol{v} = k\boldsymbol{f}$, where k is the constant admittance gain matrix and $\boldsymbol{f}$ was the digitized positional readings from an analog joystick.

Abdominal probe lateral velocities corresponding to TRUS probe movements were calculated using an innovative formulation of hybrid force-position control [11] that achieved real-time, simultaneous abdominal probe alignment and gentle convex contour tracking along the patient's pubic region regardless of body habitus. Commanded robot velocities were the superposition of two velocity components, $\boldsymbol{v}_{cmd} = \boldsymbol{v}_{pose} + \boldsymbol{v}_{contact}$, as shown in Fig. 3. Robot Cartesian velocity $\boldsymbol{v}_{pose}$ was needed to reorient the abdominal probe to be collinear with the TRUS while not having any velocity in the y-direction (toward the patient). The velocity resulted from first calculating the goal transformation $U_{TA'}$ that defined what U_{TA} should approach for the two probes to be perfectly collinear without any probe y movement. $U_{TA'}$ was formulated in homogeneous coordinates as

$$U_{TA'} = \begin{bmatrix} 1 & 0 & 0 & \\ 0 & -1 & 0 & \boldsymbol{p}_I \\ 0 & 0 & -1 & \\ 0 & 0 & 0 & 1 \end{bmatrix} \tag{4}$$

which constitutes a 180° rotation about the x-axis (to preserve alignment) and a translation equal to the intersection point $\boldsymbol{p}_I$ of the TRUS line-of-sight vector with the plane formed by the abdominal probe transducer face (to nullify any y movement). Once calculated, the new desired abdominal probe robot orientation was calculated as $B_{A'} = X_{TA}^{-1} B_T X_T U_{TA'} X_A^{-1} F_A^{-1}$ from which $\boldsymbol{v}_{pose}$ was calculated through a PID loop for smoothing and scaling. Robot Cartesian velocity $\boldsymbol{v}_{contact}$ was needed to enforce probe coupling with the acoustic gel and accomplish convex contour tracking. It was calculated using impedance control

$$\boldsymbol{v}_{contact} = K(F_D - F) - D(\dot{F}) \tag{5}$$

with stiffness K, damping D, desired force F_D which was only nonzero for contact force, and Kalman-smoothed force measurements F arriving 125 Hz. The impedance control gains were manually tuned so that the probe "hovered" on the gel pad without applying excessive force to the phantom.

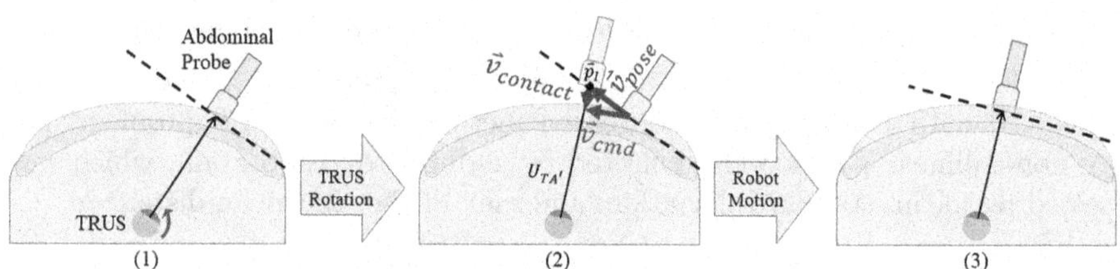

Fig. 3. Proposed robot motion framework for abdominal probe alignment and contour tracking following a TRUS movement, shown on an axial pelvic slice: (1) Initial setup. (2) Two distinct velocity vectors arising from the plane-axis intersection constraint and impedance control, and their superposition that was commanded to the robot. (3) Result of commanding velocities for a short duration.

3 Results

3.1 Calibration

The accuracy of X_A and X_T was assessed by (2) using withheld test data, resulting in $\overline{E}$ = 0.13 mm ± 0.08 mm, 0.52 mm ± 0.30 mm respectively, and

$\max\{E\} = 0.26\,\text{mm}$, 1.08 mm respectively. Repeating calibration and testing with shuffled datasets yielded similar results. The accuracy of X_{TA} was assessed by (3), resulting in $\overline{E} = 0.58\,\text{mm} \pm 0.32\,\text{mm}$ and $\max\{E\} = 1.01\,\text{mm}$.

These sub-millimeter individual calibration accuracies, also considering the repeatability of both robots (0.1 mm), exceeds the accuracy of [1] and is therefore acceptable for tomography by their proposed standard. The accuracy difference between the linear abdominal and TRUS probe calibrations is explained by the longer TRUS probe lever-arm and difficulty of maneuvering it into unique configurations within a water tank.

3.2 Robot Motion Framework

We validated our motion framework by collecting orientation and force metrics while rotating the TRUS probe within the pelvic phantom such that the abdominal probe laterally traversed the pelvic region once. An axial projection of abdominal probe Cartesian positions and orientations on the phantom surface with respect to a stationary coordinate frame (defined as the initial frame of the TRUS probe) is shown in Fig. 4a, where the probe is observed to smoothly trace a 2nd-degree polynomial approximation of the convex phantom pelvic region while successfully maintaining probe collinearity throughout. The subtle movement of the TRUS probe while rotating can be attributed to slight X_T calibration inaccuracy amplified over the length of the TRUS probe.

The detected force magnitudes during the traversal are shown in Fig. 4b, and averaged $2.15N \pm 0.15N$. Detected torque magnitudes were negligible and averaged $0.07N{\cdot}m \pm 0.03N{\cdot}m$. These results clearly indicate a stable motion framework, since the abdominal probe maintained continuous contact with the coupling gel while tracing the pubic contour and applied constant, gentle forces to the phantom without palpating. The abdominal probe was observed to "hover" on the generously applied gel pad during its traversal as designed without abraising, tugging, or indenting the phantom surface. This is desirable for patient comfort and air bubble avoidance, and ensures that our framework is robust to varying pubic region curvatures and subcutaneous fat compliances across patients. Our validated approach to real-time autonomous probe servoing in an unconstrained environment could also have implications for adding autonomy to any robot-assisted US procedure, such as remote lung imaging in the ICU.

3.3 Imaging

We tested the feasibility of collecting transmission US slices of our pelvic phantom for USCT using our novel dual-robotic rectum-to-abdomen imaging approach. Most importantly, we qualitatively verified that a suitable anatomical window through the prostate exists that is not obfuscated by the dense pelvic bone when the probes are aligned along the mid-sagittal plane. The window is illustrated in the manual overlay of two captured, opposing B-mode images in Fig. 4c. We also quantified the number of prostate slices that could be acquired by our tomographic setup, which is proportional to the attainable quality of SoS reconstruction. Figure 4a shows that the TRUS probe was only able to rotate about 23.3° total, which would theoretically allow 46 slices to be acquired for our 720 CPR motor encoder. It is difficult to deduce if this is sufficient for reconstruction and further verification is needed.

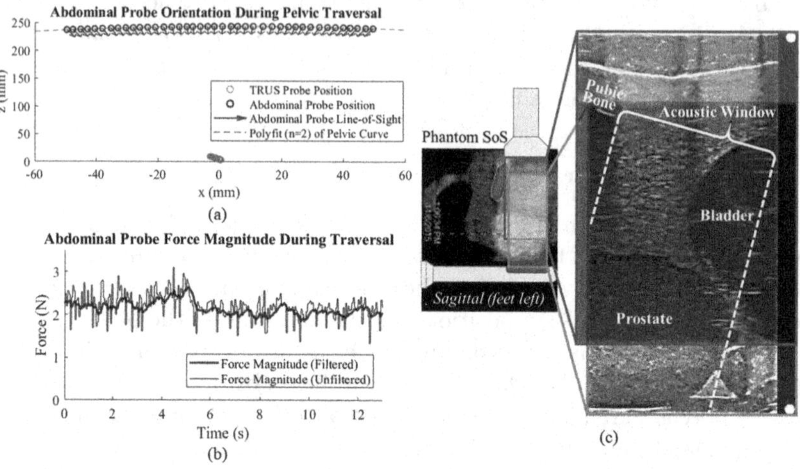

Fig. 4. (a) Abdominal probe Cartesian positions and orientations on the pubic region while rotating the TRUS probe, projected into 2-D and downsampled for clarity. Arrows show abdominal probe line-of-sight. (b) Abdominal probe force magnitudes while performing the lateral pelvic traversal in Fig. 4a. (c) Overlay of B-mode images acquired by both probes showing an acoustic window for transmission US of the prostate.

4 Discussion and Conclusions

The innovative dual-robotic setup, workflow, precise calibrations, and robot motion framework that we developed and validated is clinically feasible for US slice acquisition of the prostate towards tomographic reconstruction. Our evaluation methodology and reported metrics show proper functionality of the developed robot setup and motion framework, and confirm that an US transmission window through the prostate can be found without interference from the pubic bone. Additionally, while it is difficult to quantify the overall system accuracy needed for USCT since transmission US of the in vivo prostate by these means has not been attempted before, we believe that the sub-millimeter accuracy attained by our individual calibrations are sufficient for SoS mapping.

The main limitation of a dual-robotic USCT approach is the need for an accurate three-way calibration of the two probes and robots. Future work should include an improved active element calibration scheme for X_A and X_T, as well as an alternative calibration scheme for X_{TA} that isolates it from errors propagated by X_A and X_T, such as a pivot calibration about a fixed point. In-plane and out-of-plane accuracy should also be distinguished and exact angular error should be computed. We are additionally interested in a novel on-line calibration fine-tuning scheme for X_{TA}, in which the TRUS probe emits periodic pulses and the receiving abdominal probe, acting as a hydrophone, uses gradient descent guided motion to centralize itself directly within the TRUS probe's line-of-sight.

Using our system, future work should focus on implementing and enhancing limited-angle tomographic reconstruction methods to build accurate SoS maps from collected US data. Deep learning approaches [3,5] may greatly improve the image quality. It is our ultimate hope that, when applied in a human trial, the slices collected by our accurate dual-robotic US system will produce SoS mappings that significantly improve prostate cancer diagnosis and staging.

References

1. Aalamifar, F.: Co-robotic ultrasound tomography: a new paradigm for quantitative ultrasound imaging. Ph.D. thesis, Johns Hopkins University, October 2016
2. Ackerman, M.K., Cheng, A., Boctor, E., Chirikjian, G.: Online ultrasound sensor calibration using gradient descent on the Euclidean group. In: 2014 IEEE International Conference on Robotics and Automation (ICRA), pp. 4900–4905 (2014)
3. Anas, E.M.A., et al.: CNN and back-projection: limited angle ultrasound tomography for speed of sound estimation. In: Medical Imaging 2019: Ultrasonic Imaging and Tomography, vol. 10955, p. 109550M. International Society for Optics and Photonics (2019)
4. Bray, F., Ferlay, J., Soerjomataram, I., Siegel, R.L., Torre, L.A., Jemal, A.: Global cancer statistics 2018: GLOBOCAN estimates of incidence and mortality worldwide for 36 cancers in 185 countries. CA Cancer J. Clin. **68**(6), 394–424 (2018)
5. Cheng, A., et al.: Deep learning image reconstruction method for limited-angle ultrasound tomography in prostate cancer. In: Medical Imaging 2019: Ultrasonic Imaging and Tomography, vol. 10955, p. 1095516. International Society for Optics and Photonics (2019)
6. CISST libraries and Surgical Assistant Workstation (SAW). https://github.com/jhu-cisst/cisst/wiki
7. Delphinus Medical Technologies: Softvue system (2020). http://www.delphinusmt.com/technology/. Accessed 11 Mar 2020
8. Harvey, C., Pilcher, J., Richenberg, J., Patel, U., Frauscher, F.: Applications of transrectal ultrasound in prostate cancer. Br. J. Radiol. **85**(Spec. Issue 1), S3–S17 (2012)
9. Horn, B., Hilden, H., Negahdaripour, S.: Closed-form solution of absolute orientation using orthonormal matrices. J. Opt. Soc. Am. A **5**, 1127–1135 (1988). https://doi.org/10.1364/JOSAA.5.001127
10. Lenox, M., et al.: 3D inverse scattering in wholebody ultrasound applications (conference presentation). In: Medical Imaging 2019: Ultrasonic Imaging and Tomography, vol. 10955, p. 1095511. International Society for Optics and Photonics (2019)
11. Lozano, R., Brogliato, B.: Adaptive hybrid force-position control for redundant manipulators. In: 29th IEEE Conference on Decision and Control, vol. 3. pp. 1949–1950 (1990)

12. Marks, L., Young, S., Natarajan, S.: MRI-ultrasound fusion for guidance of targeted prostate biopsy. Curr. Opin. Urol. **23**(1), 43 (2013)
13. Natesan, R., Wiskin, J., Lee, S., Malik, B.H.: Quantitative assessment of breast density: transmission ultrasound is comparable to mammography with tomosynthesis. Cancer Prev. Res. **12**(12), 871–876 (2019)
14. QT Ultrasound: Quantitative transmission ultrasound: an evolution in breast imaging (2020). https://www.qtultrasound.com/about-us/. Accessed 11 Mar 2020
15. Seifabadi, R., et al.: Correlation of ultrasound tomography to MRI and pathology for the detection of prostate cancer. In: Medical Imaging 2019: Ultrasonic Imaging and Tomography, vol. 10955, p. 109550C. International Society for Optics and Photonics (2019)
16. Tanoue, H., Hagiwara, Y., Kobayashi, K., Saijo, Y.: Ultrasonic tissue characterization of prostate biopsy tissues by ultrasound speed microscope. In: 2011 Annual International Conference of the IEEE Engineering in Medicine and Biology Society, pp. 8499–8502. IEEE (2011)
17. Wallis, C.J., Haider, M.A., Nam, R.K.: Role of mpMRI of the prostate in screening for prostate cancer. Transl. Androl. Urol. **6**(3), 464 (2017)
18. Wiskin, J., et al.: Full wave 3D inverse scattering transmission ultrasound tomography: breast and whole body imaging. In: 2019 IEEE International Ultrasonics Symposium (IUS), pp. 951–958. IEEE (2019)
19. Wiskin, J.W., Malik, B., Natesan, R., Pirshafiey, N., Klock, J., Lenox, M.: 3D full inverse scattering ultrasound tomography of the human knee (conference presentation). In: Medical Imaging 2019: Ultrasonic Imaging and Tomography, vol. 10955, p. 109550K. International Society for Optics and Photonics (2019)

IoT-Based Remote Control Study of a Robotic Trans-Esophageal Ultrasound Probe via LAN and 5G

Shuangyi Wang[1(✉)], Xilong Hou[2], James Housden[3], Zengguang Hou[1], Davinder Singh[4], and Kawal Rhode[3]

[1] Chinese Academy of Sciences, Institute of Automation (CASIA), Beijing, China
shuangyi.wang@ia.ac.cn

[2] Peng Cheng Laboratory (PCL), Shenzhen, China

[3] School of Biomedical Engineering and Imaging Sciences, King's College London, London, UK

[4] Xtronics Ltd., Gravesend, UK

Abstract. A robotic trans-esophageal echocardiography (TEE) probe has been recently developed to address the problems with manual control in the X-ray environment when a conventional probe is used for interventional procedure guidance. However, the robot was exclusively to be used in local areas and the effectiveness of remote control has not been scientifically tested. In this study, we implemented an Internet-of-things (IoT)-based configuration to the TEE robot so the system can set up a local area network (LAN) or be configured to connect to an internet cloud over 5G. To investigate the remote control, backlash hysteresis effects were measured and analysed. A joystick-based device and a button-based gamepad were then employed and compared with the manual control in a target reaching experiment for the two steering axes. The results indicated different hysteresis curves for the left-right and up-down steering axes with the input wheel's dead-bands found to be 15° and 8°, respectively. Similar magnitudes of positioning errors at approximately 0.5° and maximum overshoots at around 2.5° were found when manually and robotically controlling the TEE probe. The amount of time to finish the task indicated a better performance using the button-based gamepad over joystick-based device, although both were worse than the manual control. It is concluded that the IoT-based remote control of the TEE probe is feasible and a trained user can accurately manipulate the probe. The main identified problem was the backlash hysteresis in the steering axes, which can result in continuous oscillations and overshoots.

1 Introduction

Trans-esophageal echocardiography (TEE) is a widely used imaging modality for diagnosing heart disease and guiding cardiac surgical procedures [1]. A TEE probe usually comprises an electronic interface, a control handle with two concentric wheels, a flexible endoscopic shaft, and a miniaturized ultrasound transducer mounted on the distal tip. During a procedure, the operator is required to manually hold and manipulate the TEE

Y. Hu et al. (Eds.): ASMUS 2020/PIPPI 2020, LNCS 12437, pp. 171–179, 2020.
https://doi.org/10.1007/978-3-030-60334-2_17

probe on site, which results in several challenges as many cardiac procedures where TEE is utilized are usually accompanied by X-ray fluoroscopy imaging. In this scenario, the operator is required to stand for long periods of time and wear heavy radiation-protection shielding. Evidences have suggested that up to 10% of the radiation from X-ray is still able to pass through the shielding [2]. Moreover, the protection aprons are heavy and can potentially cause orthopedic injuries to echocardiographers, e.g. various potential problems with the spine, hip, knee, and ankle due to the weight of the protective shielding [3]. Other studies also indicate that the sonographers may suffer from an unusually high incidence of musculoskeletal disorders, including eye strain, musculoskeletal pain or injury, repetitive strain injuries and other hazards [4, 5] as the result of holding the probe in one hand while adjusting scanning parameters with the other hand for prolonged periods of time.

Apart from the inconvenience and tedium of the manual control, the need for highly specialized skills is always a barrier for reliable and repeatable acquisition of ultrasound, especially in developing countries. Studies regarding the use of general ultrasound suggest that the lack of training is one of the biggest barriers to reliable image acquisition in low- and middle-income countries [6, 7]. The problem of skills and training for general ultrasound is made worse for TEE by the views of the heart being relatively complicated to understand. Moreover, as cardiac procedures requiring TEE need both a specialized surgeon and an echocardiographer to be available for the entire procedure, the procedures must be scheduled around both of their timetables.

A recently developed robotic system for TEE has made remote control possible [8, 9]. In the previous study, Bluetooth communication has been implemented, which allows the operator to manipulate the probe from a nearby area. However, the previous study has not scientifically demonstrated the validation experiments for doing this with the use of master control devices. Moreover, the configuration limits the use of the robot only in a local area. This meets the need for controlling the robot in the catheter lab environment but may not meet the future need when the robot is required to be used over a long distance. This was challenging in the past but now become feasible with the rapid developments of internet and 5G techniques. In this paper, we report the further developments of the robotic TEE system by implementing an Internet-of-things (IoT) based configuration so that the robot control and data transfer can be achieved over a network. The primary aim of the study is to test the feasibility of controlling the TEE probe remotely using the existing robot via local area internet (LAN) and current emerging 5G. To further understand the effectiveness of remote control, we also aim to investigate the use of gamepad and joystick as the master control device and study the associated problems identified from the user performances.

2 Materials and Methods

2.1 Robotic TEE Probe

An overview of the designed robotic system, as detailed in our previous publication [8], is shown in Fig. 1. The add-on TEE robot holds the probe handle and manipulates four degrees of freedom (DOFs) that are available in manual handling of the probe, including the rotation about and translation along the long axis of the TEE probe and additional manipulators with 2-DOFs to steer the probe head [10]. The overall rotation diameter of the handle control chamber is 110 mm. The dimensions of the whole robot are 500 × 210 × 40 mm. The robot is controlled by two microcontrollers with an operating frequency of 16 MHz (Arduino Nano, Adafruit Industries, New York, the United States).

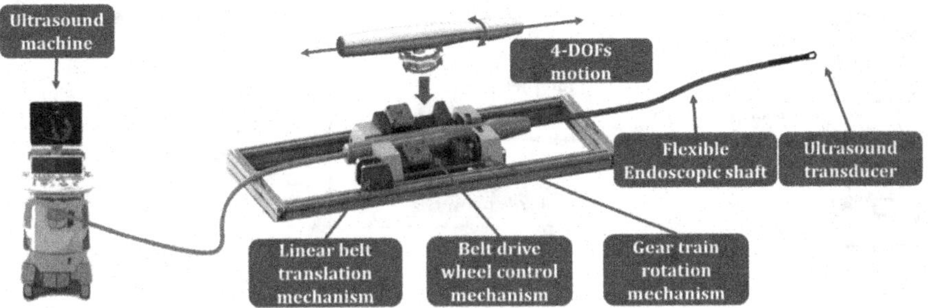

Fig. 1. Schematic drawing showing the overview of the proposed robotic TEE probe.

2.2 IoT-Based Remote Control

The proposed robotic TEE probe working as an IoT device when in clinical use would possibly include the following scenarios (Fig. 2): (1) The robot is placed in the surgical room and the echocardiographer sits in the adjacent control room. A local area network is required for the operator to remotely control the robot and stream the ultrasound images. (2) The echocardiographer can be in centralized hospitals, outpatient clinics, or home environments. In this setup, both the input devices controlled by the echocardiographer and the TEE robot need to be connected into the network and data can be transmitted via the internet cloud.

To enable the IoT-based control over internet, two TTL-WiFi converter modules (DT-06, Shenzhen Doctors of Intelligence & Technology Co., Ltd., Shenzhen, China) have been built into the robot. The module enables seamless transparent transmission between serial and WiFi and can be easily configured with the built-in HTTP web server. With further developments of the supporting hardware and software, the TEE robot can work in two different modes. In the station (STA) mode, the robot can connect to a WiFi network, e.g. one created by the wireless router or a 5G hotpot. In the access point (AP) mode, the robot can create its own network and have other devices connect to it. In the following experiments, 5G hotpot created by mobile phones are used to create a WiFi network when testing in the STA mode.

In the current study, we aim to test two different input devices. These include a joystick-based device (M5Stick JoyC, M5Stack, Shenzhen, China) which can be directly connected into the network and a button-based gamepad (SN30-G, 8BITDO Tech Co., Ltd., Shenzhen, China) which needs to be connected to a software interface (either on PC or microphone) via Bluetooth first before accessing the network. For both devices, each axis of movement is simply configured either to 'on' or 'off' state. By actuating certain axis on the devices at the master side, the corresponding axis of the TEE robot

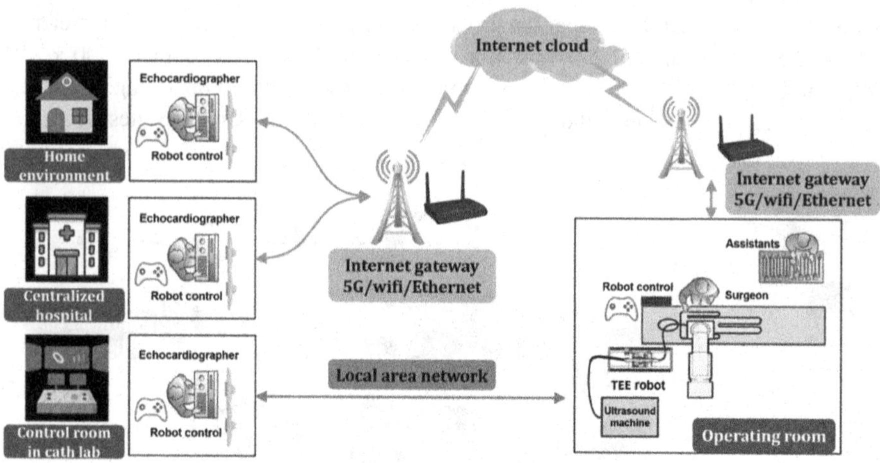

Fig. 2. Schematic diagram showing the potential long distance uses of the TEE robot.

would be actuated. When an axis on the device is released, the corresponding axis of the TEE robot would be disabled and stopped.

2.3 Experimental Design

To test the IoT-based remote control of the TEE robot and investigate the associated problems, an experimental setup has been designed (Fig. 3a).

On the robot side in the lab, the original TEE probe (x7-2t, Philips, The Netherlands) was attached to the add-on robot. A guide tube was fixed to a bench to constrain the shape and provide a path for the flexible endoscopic shaft of the TEE probe. On the tip of the TEE probe where the ultrasound transducer is mounted, an inertial measurement unit (IMU, JY901, Shenzhen Wit Intelligent Co., Ltd., Shenzhen, China) was attached using a 3D printed sensor holder to provide a feedback of the probe tip's pose for the following experiments in the test phase. A WiFi camera was utilized to provide the real-time video of the probe tip's movements when controlling remotely. On the control side in a separate nearby room, two different input control devices were investigated in the following experiments. The definitions of the motion are shown in Fig. 3b. Real-time video that monitors the probe tip's motion and the IMU readings in the format of three rotational angles were shown on the PC's screen. The following experiments were performed:

1. The first experiment aims to test whether there is a time difference between AP and STA mode when the robot completes a certain task. In this experiment, the AP mode set the robot as the sever while the STA mode utilized an internet cloud (Doit test cloud) as the server. Five different sequential movements of the robot were tested both in the AP and STA modes with each of them includes movements of all four axes of the robot. The amounts of time to finish the task were recorded. In the following experiments, STA mode was then utilized.

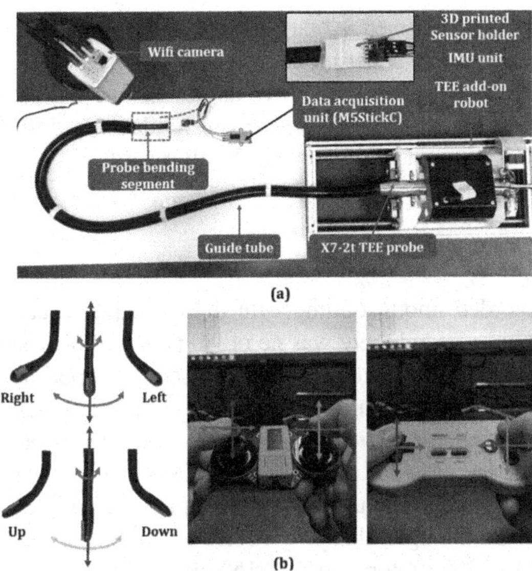

Fig. 3. Experimental setup for the remote-control tests: (a) configuration of the robot side setup in a lab; (b) configuration of the control side setup in a separate nearby office.

2. The second experiment aims to investigate the backlash hysteresis happening to the two steering axes. This is potentially the main influence on the remote control. The wire transmission between the navigation wheels and the bending section induces backlashes into the TEE probe. This can have an impact to the user's control as there are no output responses in the deadbands when reversing the direction. To quantify the size of the deadbands, the probe tip was steered to the leftmost and driven towards the rightmost with 400 motor steps interval. The probe tip was then steered back to the leftmost with the same interval. Same operation was applied to the up-down steering axis starting from the upmost location. IMU angles were recorded at each location and the measurement on each axis was repeated three times. The average angles were then calculated and used to form the hysteresis curves. It should be noted that the flexible endoscopes normally have a complex non-linear behavior [10, 11]. The deadbands of backlashes also depend on the configuration of the flexible endoscopic shaft. The current study measured the hysteresis with the flexible endoscopic shaft configured as the shape shown in Fig. 3.
3. The third experiment aims to explore the users' performances when controlling each steering axis moving towards targets. 10 expected poses in free space were defined as targets for each axis. These targets are within the realistic ranges that are used in the real TEE acquisition based on our previous analysis [9]. They are specially arranged to include small adjustments, movements passing through hysteresis zone, and directional change outside and within the hysteresis zone. In the experiment, three participants were involved. They are all non-TEE experts but have been very well trained to use the joystick-based device and the button-based gamepad to control the robot. They were asked to control the left-right and up-down steering axes

separately to reach the defined 10 targets following the designed sequence. Both devices were tested in this experiment and the participants were given three times for the trial of each axis. The recorded IMU angles and the WiFi camera's video were provided as the feedbacks. The participants were also asked to do manual control trials of the probe to complete the same tasks afterwards.

3 Results

By comparing the recorded amount of time to finish each sequence at AP and STA modes, the first experiment has verified there was no obvious time difference between the two working modes. The measured IMU angles in the second experiment were processed and the average hysteresis curves are shown in Fig. 4. The left-right steering axis has a deadband of 1200 motor steps (~15° wheel's rotation angle) that covers the whole steering iteration. The increase and decrease of the IMU angles are mostly linear when steering at a certain direction. The up-down steering axis has a deadband of 640 motor steps (~8° wheel's rotation angle) that only covers a region near the neutral position of the probe tip (1800 to 4200 motor steps; ~−15° to +15° wheel's rotation angle). The increase and decrease of the IMU angles are mostly linear when it is in the hysteresis zone with two different slopes. The angle changes have more complicated non-linear behaviors where the probe tip is steered out of the hysteresis zone.

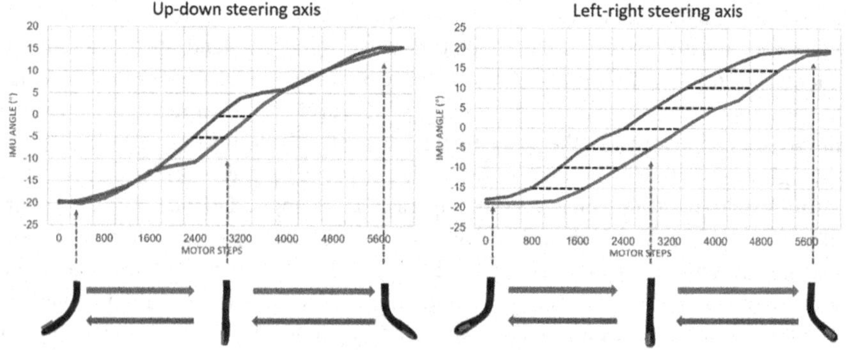

Fig. 4. Backlash hysteresis for the two steering axes in the same fixed configuration.

The participants' performances in the third experiment were analysed. An example performance for a single trial is shown in Fig. 5 as an example of the performance curves. In the figure, the blue line shows the recorded IMU angles, the yellow line shows the defined 10 targets, and the red zones highlight the oscillation experienced in the hysteresis deadbands. Although each volunteer's performances are different at each individual trail, several common findings were identified by analysing all three trials of the three participants over the 10 targets (N = 90) on each axis. The results are summarized in Table 1 with the position errors, the maximum overshoots, and the amounts of time to finish each individual task (from one target to the next) calculated.

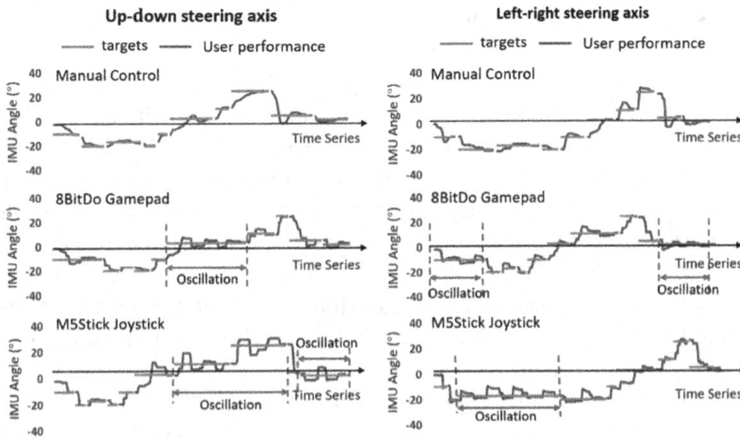

Fig. 5. Example participant performance curves for the target reaching experiments under the manual control, the button-based gamepad control, and the joystick-based device control. (Color figure online)

Table 1. Summary of the participants' performances using different control inputs

Control inputs	Error (Mean ± std, degree)		Maximum overshoot (Mean ± std, degree)		Time (Median ± IQR, sec)	
	U-D steering	L-R steering	U-D steering	L-R steering	U-D steering	L-R steering
Manual	0.4 ± 0.3°	0.4 ± 0.2°	1.1 ± 2.1°	2.6 ± 2.5°	6.8 ± 4.9 s	7.0 ± 2.6 s
Gamepad	0.5 ± 0.3°	0.5 ± 0.3°	2.7 ± 2.6°	2.3 ± 2.3°	11.5 ± 10.0 s	9.0 ± 4.0 s
Joystick	0.4 ± 0.3°	0.5 ± 0.3°	2.6 ± 3.3°	2.5 ± 3.0°	12.0 ± 15.5 s	12.5 ± 8.5 s

As can be seen in Table 1, similar magnitudes of positioning errors at around 0.5° and maximum overshoots at around 2.5° were found when manually and robotically controlling the probe. In terms of the amount of time to finish an individual task, a better performance using the button-based gamepad over joystick-based device has been found with certain level of differences identified ($p = 0.068$ for L-R and $p = 0.477$ for U-D axis, Welch's t-test), although both were clearly worse than the manual control ($p = 0.002$ for L-R and $p = 0.001$ for U-D axis, Welch's t-test). The left-right steering axis with a constant hysteresis zone has shown a better result in terms of the data variation compared to the up-down steering axis which has a relatively more complicated hysteresis (Coefficient of Variation = 0.72, 0.87, and 1.29 for U-D axis and 0.37, 0.44, and 0.68 for L-R axis with three different control inputs). By analyzing all the participant's performance curves, oscillation experienced in the hysteresis deadbands are more likely to happen in the up-down steering axes.

4 Discussion and Conclusion

In this paper, we introduce the development progress with an existing TEE robot by implementing an IoT-based control. It is generally believed that with the developments of internet and 5G techniques, controlling medical robots remotely over a long distance would have the potential to change the current approaches of diagnosis and surgery. For echocardiography, examples have been found in some recent clinical studies for transcatheter procedures guided solely by trans-thoracic echocardiography conducted in China [12, 13]. The clinical team, rather than staying in the centralized hospital in big cities, was routinely deployed to several small clinics in less developed areas to perform the procedure locally. This suggested the future use of echocardiography would need to be remotely over a long distance.

The backlash hysteresis effects and the deadbands are clearly identified as the main problem that would influence the user's performance for the steering axes. Those oscillations identified in the Fig. 5 can be interpreted as the user tried to reach certain targets but had small overshoots. When reversing the direction, the deadbands due to the backlash resulted in a short period of time that the user's inputs are not responded, which then result in further overshoots. Evidences shown in the Fig. 5 and Table 1 also clearly indicate the influence of the hysteresis, especially on the up-down steering axis. It is identified that the manual control of the probe can deal with the hysteresis in a much better way compared to the robotic control. This indicates better control algorithms which can smooth and optimize the speed of the motor when in the deadbands are important in the future developments.

For the joystick-based device and button-based gamepad, the results indicate that well trained users can manipulate the probe to reach a target with a small error and acceptable maximum overshoot. Considering the field of view of the ultrasound image, either in 2D or 3D, it is unlikely that these errors would cause problems to the acquisitions. As only IMU sensor was used in the current study and the combined steering and rotation motions can influence the measured results of IMU, the investigation for the user performances was limited only to the two steering axes. Meanwhile, we believe the rotation axis and translation axis would be easier to control as there are no hystereses. The IMU sensor used in this study is based on the Cortex-M0 core and incorporates novel on-board dynamic processing method with Kalman filter to achieve low-drifts sensing. The rated measurement accuracy is less than $0.1°$.

The current study was limited by the number of participants as we hope to only have the participants who are very well trained to use the control devices and the robots, so the results of the remote control are convincing. The study is also limited by not having realistic ultrasound images and TEE experts involved due to the current unavailability. The overall system lag is an important consideration in remote control scenario and a highly accurate method to measure the input and output signals' delay is yet to be developed. These are the problems to solve in our future studies.

To conclude, we implemented an Internet-of-things (IoT)-based configuration to the existing TEE robot so the system can set up a LAN or be configured to access an internet cloud over 5G in this study. The feasibility of the remote control over internet using a joystick-based device and a button-based gamepad has been verified. It is believed that a trained user can accurately manipulate the probe with tolerable overshoots. The main identified problem was the backlash hysteresis in the steering axes which can result in continuous oscillations and overshoots. The future work should focus on implementing advanced control algorithm to deal with the hysteresis and test the remote control with realistic ultrasound images and TEE experts involved.

References

1. Peterson, G.E., Brickner, M.E., Reimold, S.C.: Transesophageal echocardiography: clinical indications and applications. Circulation **107**, 2398–2402 (2003)
2. Brenner, D.J., et al.: Cancer risks attributable to low doses of ionizing radiation: assessing what we really know. Proc. Natl. Acad. Sci. **100**, 13761–13766 (2003)
3. Goldstein, J.A., Balter, S., Cowley, M., Hodgson, J., Klein, L.W.: Occupational hazards of interventional cardiologists: prevalence of orthopedic health problems in contemporary practice. Catheter Cardiovasc. Interv. **63**, 407–411 (2004)
4. Mercer, R.B., Marcella, C.P., Carney, D.K., McDonald, R.W.: Occupational health hazards to the ultrasonographer and their possible prevention. J. Am. Soc. Echocardiogr. **1**, 363–366 (1997)
5. Magnavita, N., Bevilacqua, L., Mirk, P., Fileni, A., Castellino, N.: Work-related musculoskeletal complaints in sonologists. J. Occup. Environ. Med. **41**, 981–988 (1999)
6. Shah, S., Bellows, B.A., Adedipe, A.A., Totten, J.E., Backlund, B.H., Sajed, D.: Perceived barriers in the use of ultrasound in developing countries. Crit. Ultrasound J. **7**(1), 1–5 (2015). https://doi.org/10.1186/s13089-015-0028-2
7. LaGrone, L.N., Sadasivam, V., Kushner, A.L., Groen, R.S.: A review of training opportunities for ultrasonography in low and middle income countries. Tropical Med. Int. Health **17**, 808–819 (2012)
8. Wang, S., Housden, J., Singh, D., Althoefer, K., Rhode, K.: Design, testing and modelling of a novel robotic system for trans-oesophageal ultrasound. Int. J. Med. Robot. Comput. Assist. Surg. **12**, 342–354 (2016)
9. Wang, S., Singh, D., Johnson, D., Althoefer, K., Rhode, K., Housden, J.: Robotic ultrasound: view planning, tracking, and automatic acquisition of trans-esophageal echocardiography. IEEE Robot. Autom. Mag. **23**, 118–127 (2016)
10. Ott, L., Nageotte, F., Zanne, P., de Mathelin, M.: Robotic assistance to flexible endoscopy by physiological-motion tracking. IEEE Trans. Rob. **27**, 346–359 (2011)
11. Do, T.N., Tjahjowidodo, T., Lau, M.W.S., Phee, S.J.: Nonlinear friction modelling and compensation control of hysteresis phenomena for a pair of tendon-sheath actuated surgical robots. Mech. Syst. Signal Process. **60**, 770–784 (2015)
12. Pan, X., et al.: Feasibility of transcatheter closure of atrial septal defect under the guidance of transthoracic echocardiography. Chin. J. Cardiovas. Dis. **42**, 744–747 (2014)
13. Wang, S., et al.: Transcatheter perimembranous ventricular septal defect closure under transthoracic echocardiographic guidance without fluoroscopy. J. Thorac. Dis. **10**, 5222 (2018)

Differentiating Operator Skill During Routine Fetal Ultrasound Scanning Using Probe Motion Tracking

Yipei Wang[1(✉)], Richard Droste[1], Jianbo Jiao[1], Harshita Sharma[1], Lior Drukker[2], Aris T. Papageorghiou[2], and J. Alison Noble[1]

[1] Institute of Biomedical Engineering, University of Oxford, Oxford, UK
yipei.wang@eng.ox.ac.uk

[2] Nuffield Department of Women's and Reproductive Health, University of Oxford, Oxford, UK

Abstract. In this paper, we consider differentiating operator skill during fetal ultrasound scanning using probe motion tracking. We present a novel convolutional neural network-based deep learning framework to model ultrasound probe motion in order to classify operator skill levels, that is invariant to operators' personal scanning styles. In this study, probe motion data during routine second-trimester fetal ultrasound scanning was acquired by operators of known experience levels (2 newly-qualified operators and 10 expert operators). The results demonstrate that the proposed model can successfully learn underlying probe motion features that distinguish operator skill levels during routine fetal ultrasound with 95% accuracy.

Keywords: Operator skill · Probe motion · Fetal ultrasound

1 Introduction

Ultrasound is a relatively low-cost medical imaging modality, convenient, non-invasive, yields real-time results and is widely considered to be safe. Therefore, it is the primary modality for pregnancy imaging used to assess the fetal anatomy, development and growth [5]. During an ultrasound scan, the operator is required to skillfully manipulate the ultrasound probe to acquire a series of standard anatomical planes for diagnostic interpretation or biometric measurements. Even minor probe movements could cause distortion of the viewed anatomy or largely influence the localization of the standard plane. Therefore, sonography is well recognized as a task that is difficult to learn. It takes a significant amount of time to train fetal ultrasound sonographers before reaching competency [15].

Despite the importance of ultrasound in obstetrics and difficulty in operator training, there is little quantitative research studying the process of operator training and operator skill assessment for obstetric scanning. Protocols and guidelines [11,12] exist for scanning but there is no universal objective sonographer skill assessment standard for fetal ultrasound scanning. Operators are

Y. Hu et al. (Eds.): ASMUS 2020/PIPPI 2020, LNCS 12437, pp. 180–188, 2020.
https://doi.org/10.1007/978-3-030-60334-2_18

trained and assessed under supervision and given feedback. Such a process is prone to human bias and might not be consistent across different settings [7]. Therefore, it would be practically useful to design new and automated objective approaches to support new trainees and inform them once they reach expert competency.

One approach recently introduced in the related area of surgical skill assessment is objective computer-aided technical skill evaluation [14]. Researchers have developed machine learning methods that use tool motion [2,9,18], surgeon/tool video [17,19,20], surgeons' eye-gaze [3], and the combination of these data to model a surgical procedure. In this study, we look at sonography from a similar perspective of surgical data science, where machine learning methods are used to classify skills and support training. We also factor in that ultrasound scanning is highly operator-dependent [4]. The underlying features of operator skill and personal style are entangled, which makes the model training process rather difficult. Therefore, recognising operator style-agnostic skills is crucial to building models that characterise operator skill.

Our contributions are as follows: (1) we propose a deep learning framework to differentiate operator skill based on probe motion data; (2) we constrain the training of networks to make the learnt models invariant to operators' personal scanning styles. Experiments show that the proposed framework is capable of learning operator-invariant features that distinguish different skill levels.

2 Method

2.1 Data Acquisition and Annotation

Probe motion data was acquired as part of the PULSE [13] study. This study was approved by the UK Research Ethics Committee (Reference 18/WS/0051), and written informed consent was given by all participating pregnant women. Sonographers also consented to participate in the study at the outset, but did not have any visual or other signal to know that the probe motion tracking device was functioning. The ultrasound scans were performed by qualified sonographers and fetal medicine doctors (collectively referred to as operators in this paper) using a General Electric Voluson E8 ultrasound machine. The ultrasound machine was equipped with a standard curvilinear (C2-9-D, C1-5-D) and 3D/4D (RAB6-D) probes. The selection of suitable motion tracking methods was limited. We could not use any electromagnetic trackers or optical trackers due to safety reasons in the scan room and not wide enough field of view, respectively. Hand motion video recording was also not possible because of privacy of patients. In this study, an inertial measurement unit was rigidly attached to the probe to record the probe motion data.

The research goal of this work was to understand what can be learned from motion alone independent of video. Ultrasound video was only used to identify the motion data segments corresponding to episodes of fetal brain scanning. We selected the collection of motion segments with the following criteria: 1) the video and motion data is well synchronized; 2) the scanner is not in image freeze mode during the segment; 3) the segment has been assigned an anatomy label (the brain). Scanning parameters were automatically extracted for each video frame in the full-length scan video using optical character recognition. This selection resulted in 396 motion segments of fetal brain scanning from 229 full-length scans performed by 12 operators. The original raw motion data was sampled at 400 Hz. To reduce the data dimension while preserving useful information, the data was downsampled to 30 Hz to match with the ultrasound video sampling rate.

We define operators with more than two years of experience of fetal anomaly screening ultrasound scanning as "expert" level, and those with less than two years of experience as "newly qualified". Data for 2 newly qualified and 10 expert operators was available. Operator years of experience and data contribution in terms of whole scans and selected motion segments are presented in Table 1.

Table 1. Operator experience and data contribution

Operator	S1	S2	S3	S4	S5	S6	S7	S8	S9	S10	S11	S12	Total
Experience (years)	0	1	14	10	2	6	3	5	8	15	10	7	–
Number of scans	116	23	39	18	13	8	4	1	1	3	1	2	229
Number of selected motion segments	214	35	67	26	20	12	7	3	2	3	2	5	396

2.2 Model Architecture

Our model needed to factor in that besides showing different proficiency levels during ultrasound scanning, operators also demonstrate personal scanning styles. Therefore, a naive network design might easily be biased to learn operator personal styles, in addition to the patterns that distinguish skill levels. One solution to this problem is to include a constraint in the network to reduce the influence of learned features from personal styles while preserving the influence of features from differentiating skill levels. To achieve this objective, we draw inspiration from recent success [6] in the domain adaptation field and introduce a domain classifier branch into our network.

As shown in Fig.1, our model consists of three parts; (1) a CNN feature extractor, (2) a skill level predictor, and (3) an operator classifier.

For motion feature extraction, we chose to implement a one-dimensional version of the 18-layer ResNet [8] for motion feature extraction. By introducing shortcut connections and residual blocks, ResNet [8] greatly alleviates gradient vanishing/exploding and has shown good performance on classification problems.

During the training phase, we expect the network to minimize the loss of skill level predictor while maximizing the loss of the operator classifier. Let $M = \{m_1, m_2, ..., m_N\}$ denote the probe motion dataset that has N motion segments. We use a neural network $f_v(m; \theta_v)$ with learnable parameters θ_v to learn a mapping from each motion data m_i to a feature vector v_i. The feature vector is mapped to the skill level s by a skill level predictor $f_s(v; \theta_s)$ with learnable parameters θ_s. The skill level predictor is trained with loss function

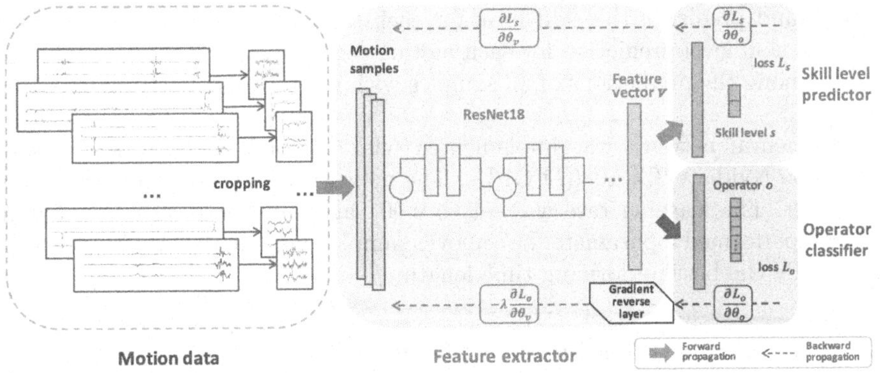

Fig. 1. The proposed framework for classifying operator skill levels. Motion segments are cropped into fixed sized samples before feeding into the feature extractor. During training, we minimize the loss of skill level predictor while at the same time maximize the loss of the operator classifier.

$L_s(f_s(f_v(m;\theta_v);\theta_s))$. For this we chose a binary cross-entropy loss. In the other branch, the operator classifier $f_o(v;\theta_o)$ tries to distinguish different operators $o_i \in O = \{o_1, o_2, ..., o_C\}$ from motion features where there are C operators. The parameters of the classifier are denoted as θ_o. The operator classifier is trained with loss function $L_o(f_o(f_v(m;\theta_v);\theta_o))$, which is a multinomial cross-entropy loss. Therefore, our model is trained with a joint loss function:

$$L(\theta_v, \theta_s, \theta_o) = L_s(f_s(f_v(m;\theta_v);\theta_s)) - \lambda L_o(f_o(f_v(m;\theta_v);\theta_o)), \tag{1}$$

where λ is the coefficient that balances the trade-off between two losses. During the training process, λ is gradually increased from 0 to 1 in order to limit the impact of operator loss at the early stage. We follow the strategy used in [6] to update λ:

$$\lambda = \frac{2}{1 + e^{-10p}} - 1, \tag{2}$$

where p represents the progress rate. Consider each training epoch $k \in \{1, 2, ..., K\}$, we feed a subset of motion data $M' = \{m_i, ..., m_j\}$ into the network. At the kth epoch, the progress p when feeding the motion data m_i is calculated by Eq. 3:

$$p = \frac{i + k \times (j - i + 1)}{K \times (j - i + 1)}. \tag{3}$$

2.3 Model Training

The duration of scanning varies from scan to scan. Therefore, for each epoch, we randomly cropped a fixed sized sample from each motion data segments and fed the samples into our network. In the testing phase, the operator classifier was removed. For each motion segment, we sequentially cropped the data into small samples and predicted the skill level for each sample with the trained model. The final skill level prediction for each motion segment was given by a majority voting among the predictions of all samples within the segment (the mode of all labels).

The neural network was implemented with PyTorch framework and was trained on Nvidia GTX 1080Ti GPUs. The network was optimized with Adam Optimizer. The learning rate was set to 0.001 and we choose 32 as the batch size. We performed a parameter sweep over sample length and chose $2s$ as it was empirically the best performing time length.

2.4 Comparative Classification Methods

Most prior work in sonographer skill assessment using hand motion uses predefined features (path length, completion time, and points scanned, etc.) [16,21]. Due to safety and privacy reasons in the pregnancy scan room, we could not use cameras or electromagnetic motion trackers as in some works. As a result, methods from prior work are not directly comparable to our data. Instead, we implemented an SVM which takes the statistical motion features as input to predict skill levels for comparison. We use the tsfresh [1] package to compute time series features and use the feature selection function to select the N most important features.

We also implemented an 18-layer 1D ResNet with skill level predictor only to show the effectiveness of our operator classifier branch.

3 Results and Discussion

We evaluated our proposed framework on the dataset mentioned in Sect. 2.1. Motion segments from the same subject could only be in one of the training, validation, or testing set. Detailed dataset partitioning is listed in Table 2.

Table 2. Dataset description

	S1	S2	S3	S4	S5	S6	S7	S8	S9	S10	S11	S12
Train	141	23	43	17	14	10	3	3	2	2	2	1
Validation	34	4	10	4	2	1	2	0	0	0	0	0
Test	39	8	14	5	4	1	2	0	0	1	0	4
Total	214	35	67	26	20	12	7	3	2	3	2	5

Operator skill classification results with comparison to a traditional SVM-based approach and an 18-layer 1D ResNet are presented in Table 3. We report model accuracy as well as precision, recall, and F1 score for expert group and newly qualified group. Mean and weighted mean for each metrics are also calculated. Our proposed framework achieves a 95% accuracy for classifying skill

Table 3. Results of operator skill level classification with different models using motion data when scanning the brain. "EX" and "NQ" denotes expert and newly qualified respectively. "Macro" and "Weighted" refers to the mean and weighted mean for each evaluation metric.

		Precision	Recall	F1 score	Accuracy
1D ResNet18	EX	0.88	0.71	0.79	0.85
	NQ	0.83	**0.94**	0.88	
	Macro	0.86	0.82	0.83	
	Weighted	0.85	0.85	0.84	
1D ResNet18 with operator loss	EX	**0.91**	**0.97**	**0.94**	**0.95**
	NQ	**0.98**	**0.94**	**0.96**	
	Macro	**0.94**	**0.95**	**0.95**	
	Weighted	**0.95**	**0.95**	**0.95**	
SVM	EX	0.67	0.65	0.66	0.75
	NQ	0.80	0.81	0.80	
	Macro	0.73	0.73	0.73	
	Weighted	0.75	0.75	0.75	

level groups. From the results we observe that convolutional neural networks obtain better prediction scores than SVM. By adding the operator classifier branch for domain adaptation during training, the model is constrained to learn operator-invariant skill related features of skill level prediction. The improvement is noticeable in all evaluation metrics.

To further explore the difference of feature embeddings between the model with or without operator classifier, we visualize the features from the last convolutional layer using t-distributed stochastic neighbor embedding (t-SNE) with same parameters [10]. In Fig. 2, newly qualified level and expert level are presented with dot markers and triangle markers respectively. The years of operator experience is mapped to a different color where blue shows fewer years of experience and red shows more years of experience. As shown in the figure, both models successfully divided the motion data into two skill level groups. Figure 2a also shows the trend that the projected motion features of less experienced to more experienced operators distributed from the top right corner to the bottom left corner. In the meantime, the projected motion features from the same operator are more scattered in Fig. 2b than in Fig. 2a, which demonstrates the effectiveness of the operator classifier.

We also perform a set of leave-one-operator-out experiments to test the model performance on the unseen sonographer's motion data. For the SVM, we report the test result on the model with the best validation accuracy. For 1D ResNet and our proposed framework, we took five models after converging, and report mean as well as the standard deviation of the accuracy. As listed in Table 4, the proposed model achieves the best mean accuracy on 5 out of 7 operators with

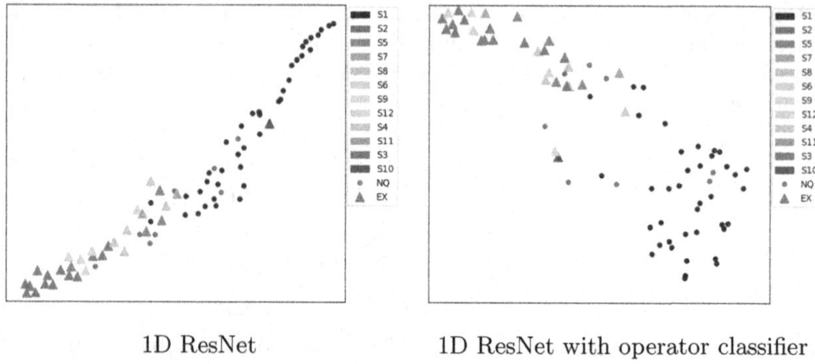

Fig. 2. tSNE visualization of feature embedding of the last convolutional layer (best viewed in color). (Color figure online)

Table 4. Leave one operator out experiment result

Leave one out operator	Accuracy (%)			Number of segments
	1D ResNet18	1D ResNet18 with operator loss	SVM	
S1	4.60 ± 1.46	**83.93** ± 16.11	25.70	214
S2	47.14 ± 9.86	**91.43** ± 6.52	34.29	35
S3	46.02 ± 6.06	**89.25** ± 8.09	41.79	67
S4	44.87 ± 9.84	46.92 ± 33.92	**50.00**	26
S5	**29.17** ± 6.07	26.00 ± 20.83	25.00	20
S6	56.94 ± 8.89	**66.67** ± 5.27	58.33	12
S7	7.14 ± 10.90	**82.85** ± 5.72	14.29	7
S8	38.89 ± 29.91	**86.67** ± 26.67	66.67	3
S9	25.00 ± 25.00	**40.00** ± 48.99	0.00	2
S10	0.00 ± 0.00	**73.34** ± 38.87	0.00	3
S11	**100.00** ± **0.00**	70.00 ± 40.00	50.00	2
S12	**86.67** ± **14.91**	60.00 ± 37.95	**80.00**	5

more than 5 available motion segments. The accuracy improvement is significant. Without the operator loss, the models learn features with a large amount of operator variance. As a result, the models perform badly on the unseen operator. For the newly qualified (NQ) group (S1 and S2), the proposed model achieves 83.93% and 91.43% of mean accuracy when leaving out each operator, with comparison to the baseline model of 4.60% and 47.14%. Note that S1 contributes 86% of the data to the NQ group and 54% of the data to the whole dataset. Although taking out S1 would significantly reduce the training data and result in large data imbalance between two skill levels, the model still gives prediction with high accuracy. Now we look at the expert (EX) group with more than 5 motion segments (S3 to S7). S3 contributes 45.6% of the data to EX group, although taking out S3 makes the training set even more unbalanced between the NQ and EX groups (from 62.9% vs. 37.1% to 75.7% vs. 24.3%), the model is still able to correctly predict an average of 89.25% of the S3 data as expert level. S4 is one experienced operator but classified as newly qualified more often, suggesting the scanning actions are similar to the latter category. This behavior, as an exception, needs to be further investigated in future work. For operator S5, the accuracy is low across all models, which may be caused by the fact that S5 only has 2 years of experience and the way that S5 scans is not yet approaching to the expert level. For the remaining operators (S8 to S12), their data contribution is very small therefore strong conclusions can not be drawn from the test results.

4 Conclusion and Future Work

We have presented a deep learning framework to model ultrasound probe motion for differentiating operator skill levels. The proposed model is evaluated on probe motion data that we collected from routine second-trimester fetal ultrasound scans undertaken by operators of different skill levels. The experiments show that the proposed model is capable of learning operator-invariant probe motion features that well distinguish operator skill levels and produce skill level prediction with high accuracy.

The proposed framework was designed as a model to support non-specialists or new trainees to assess their relative skill to an expert and could be used to establish when they reach expert competency in ultrasound scanning. It does not however identify areas of improvement which would be important for a trainee to progress. An interesting next step would be to see how to change the network to provide feedback on how to improve skills. The model might also be useful to assess the value of an assistive technology for a trainee, namely, when a trainee uses an assistive technology does their skill level approximate that of an expert. Our current work was limited by available data and data imbalance has been noted as an issue because we use data captured in a real-world setting. The model architecture is specifically designed to address data imbalance by forcing the model to learn operator-invariant features. However, it would be interesting to see how the model behaved on a larger balanced dataset.

Acknowledgement. We acknowledge the ERC (ERC-ADG-2015 694581, project PULSE), EPSRC (EP/M013774/1, Project Seebibyte), and the NIHR Oxford Biomedical Research Centre.

References

1. Tsfresh: Time series feature extraction based on scalable hypothesis tests. https://tsfresh.readthedocs.io/en/latest/
2. Ahmidi, N., et al.: String motif-based description of tool motion for detecting skill and gestures in robotic surgery. In: Mori, K., Sakuma, I., Sato, Y., Barillot, C., Navab, N. (eds.) MICCAI 2013. LNCS, vol. 8149, pp. 26–33. Springer, Heidelberg (2013). https://doi.org/10.1007/978-3-642-40811-3_4
3. Ahmidi, N., Ishii, M., Fichtinger, G., Gallia, G.L., Hager, G.D.: An objective and automated method for assessing surgical skill in endoscopic sinus surgery using eye-tracking and tool-motion data. In: International Forum of Allergy & Rhinology, vol. 2, pp. 507–515. Wiley Online Library (2012)

4. Chen, H., et al.: Standard plane localization in fetal ultrasound via domain transferred deep neural networks. IEEE J. Biomed. Health Inf. **19**(5), 1627–1636 (2015)
5. Cox, B., Beard, P.: Imaging techniques: super-resolution ultrasound. Nature **527**(7579), 451 (2015)
6. Ganin, Y., Lempitsky, V.: Unsupervised domain adaptation by backpropagation. arXiv preprint arXiv:1409.7495 (2014)
7. Hatala, R., Cook, D.A., Brydges, R., Hawkins, R.: Constructing a validity argument for the objective structured assessment of technical skills (OSATS): a systematic review of validity evidence. Adv. Health Sci. Educ. **20**(5), 1149–1175 (2015)
8. He, K., Zhang, X., Ren, S., Sun, J.: Deep residual learning for image recognition. In: Proceedings of the IEEE Conference on Computer Vision and Pattern Recognition, pp. 770–778 (2016)
9. Kumar, R., et al.: Assessing system operation skills in robotic surgery trainees. Inter. J. Med. Robot. Comput. Assist. Surg. **8**(1), 118–124 (2012)
10. Maaten, L., Hinton, G.: Visualizing data using t-SNE. J. Mach. Learn. Res. **9**, 2579–2605 (2008)
11. Salomon, L., et al.: Practice guidelines for performance of the routine mid-trimester fetal ultrasound scan. Ultrasound Obstet. Gynecol. **37**(1), 116–126 (2011)
12. Salomon, L., et al.: ISUOG practice guidelines: performance of first-trimester fetal ultrasound scan. Ultrasound Obstet. Gynecol. Official J. Int. Soc. Ultrasound Obstet. Gynecol. **41**(1), 102 (2013)
13. University of Oxford: PULSE: Perception ultrasound by learning sonographic experience. https://www.eng.ox.ac.uk/pulse/
14. Vedula, S.S., Ishii, M., Hager, G.D.: Objective assessment of surgical technical skill and competency in the operating room. Annu. Rev. Biomed. Eng. **19**, 301–325 (2017)
15. Vrachnis, N., et al.: International society of ultrasound in obstetrics and gynecology (ISUOG)-the propagation of knowledge in ultrasound for the improvement of OB/GYN care worldwide: experience of basic ultrasound training in Oman. BMC Med. Educ. **19**(1), 434 (2019)
16. Zago, M., et al.: Educational impact of hand motion analysis in the evaluation of fast examination skills. Eur. J. Trauma Emerg. Surg. 1–8 (2019). https://doi.org/10.1007/s00068-019-01112-6
17. Zappella, L., Béjar, B., Hager, G., Vidal, R.: Surgical gesture classification from video and kinematic data. Med. Image Anal. **17**(7), 732–745 (2013)
18. Zia, A., Essa, I.: Automated surgical skill assessment in RMIS training. Int. J. Comput. Assist. Radiol. Surg. **13**(5), 731–739 (2018)
19. Zia, A., Sharma, Y., Bettadapura, V., Sarin, E.L., Clements, M.A., Essa, I.: Automated assessment of surgical skills using frequency analysis. In: Navab, N., Hornegger, J., Wells, W.M., Frangi, A.F. (eds.) MICCAI 2015. LNCS, vol. 9349, pp. 430–438. Springer, Cham (2015). https://doi.org/10.1007/978-3-319-24553-9_53
20. Zia, A., et al.: Automated video-based assessment of surgical skills for training and evaluation in medical schools. Int. J. Comput. Assist. Radiol. Surg. **11**(9), 1623–1636 (2016)
21. Ziesmann, M.T., et al.: Validation of hand motion analysis as an objective assessment tool for the focused assessment with sonography for trauma examination. J. Trauma Acute Care Surg. **79**(4), 631–637 (2015)

Kinematics Data Representations for Skills Assessment in Ultrasound-Guided Needle Insertion

Robert Liu and Matthew S. Holden(✉)

School of Computer Science, Carleton University, Ottawa, Canada
matthew.holden@carleton.ca

Abstract. Ultrasound-guided needle insertion is a difficult skill to learn and, in the context of competency-based medical education, requires continual monitoring of trainees' performance. This work investigates two standard neural network architectures, temporal convolutional networks and long short-term memory networks, for automated classification of skill level based on kinematics data. It examines which data representations are optimal for skills assessment using the proposed architectures in low data scenarios. The data representation had significant effect on the computed results. But given the optimal data representation, the proposed architectures achieve skills classification on two simulated ultrasound-guided needle insertion tasks with better performance than summary statistics. Thus, neural networks can be an effective tool for skills assessment in ultrasound-guided interventions; however, it is recommended to search over the space of data representations when limited data is available.

Keywords: Surgical skills assessment · Machine learning · Ultrasound-guided interventions

1 Introduction

1.1 Motivation

Ultrasound-guided interventions are difficult to learn because the operator must simultaneously manipulate the ultrasound probe and one or more instruments, interpret the noisy ultrasound image in a rotated frame of reference, and guide the instrument to the target location. Mastering this skill takes considerable practice. This requires continual skills assessment and monitoring of learning curves, to ensure that trainees achieve a minimum level of proficiency prior to graduating to the next phase of training or practice.

As an alternative to direct observation of procedural skills or video-based skills assessment, automated skills assessment has been a growing field of study. This has held true for both surgeries and ultrasound-guided interventions, in particular. Automated skills assessment reduces time commitment and costs of human preceptors, improves standardization of assessment, and increases scalability of assessment.

Y. Hu et al. (Eds.): ASMUS 2020/PIPPI 2020, LNCS 12437, pp. 189–198, 2020.
https://doi.org/10.1007/978-3-030-60334-2_19

Recently, approaches for skills assessment have been undergoing a shift from using classical machine learning to using deep neural networks, following the ongoing trend of machine learning. While this obviates the need to extract domain-specific features, it has effectively replaced the problem with architecture engineering. The issue of architecture engineering is especially crucial in low-data scenarios. In particular, the way in which input data is represented becomes important.

The objective of this work is to identify the optimal representations for kinematics data for skills assessment in ultrasound-guided needle insertions. This work primarily seeks to understand which representations have the greatest added value when coupled with standard sequence modeling approaches (i.e. temporal convolution networks and long short-term memory networks). To our knowledge this is the first work that has used deep neural networks to assess skills in interventional ultrasound from kinematics data.

1.2 Previous Work

Traditionally, computer-assisted training for ultrasound-guided interventions has used performance metrics or summary statistics for skills assessment [1, 2]. This involves six degree-of-freedom tracking of the hands or instrument and the anatomy. From these trackers, performance metrics or summary statistics may be computed based upon clinically relevant quantities.

Previous work in skills assessment in ultrasound-guided interventions has explored spinal anesthesia [3, 4], peripheral nerve blockade [5], lumbar puncture [6], central venous catheterization [7], and generics targeting tasks [8, 9]. This prior work has focused on skills assessment in ultrasound-guided interventions in simulation-based training environments, rather than clinical environments [10].

Current work on skills assessment from kinematics or motion data uses modern deep neural network architectures. Indeed, most approaches using deep neural networks for skills assessment use temporal convolutional networks (TCN) or long short-term memory networks (LSTM). Wang et al. [11] proposed a TCN for skills assessment in robot-assisted minimally invasive surgery (RAMIS). Fawaz et al. [12] proposed a variant on a TCN by grouping channels into clusters for RAMIS; Castro et al. [13] proposed a variant on a TCN which uses quaternion convolution for RAMIS. Recent work from Kim et al. [14] has demonstrated the utility of standard TCNs in skills assessment from tool tip motion using different representations in a cataract surgery dataset. Ogul et al. [15] have investigated an LSTM architecture for pairwise ranking of surgical skills in an activity. Nguyen et al. [16] have demonstrated that a combined CNN+LSTM architecture with squeeze and excitation blocks accurately identifies skill in opens surgery using IMU data.

Many of these previous works have focused primarily on RAMIS and used the open-source JIGSAWS dataset [17]. These works report high performance, with accuracies, F1-scores, and AUCs up to and exceeding 0.90. Although, these previous works have all used a leave-one-trial-out validation protocol, rather than a leave-one-out-user protocol to determine how well their methods works on previously unseen operators.

2 Methods

2.1 Dataset

We use the ultrasound-guided needle insertion dataset originally presentation by Xia et al. [9] (Fig. 1). This dataset contains ultrasound-guided vascular access performed on a silicone model in a simulation-based training environment. There are 8 in-plane procedures and 7 out-of-plane procedures performed by 5 expert participants. There are 120 in-plane procedures performed by 20 novices and 114 out-of-plane procedures performed by 19 novices. Novices were medical students with no prior ultrasound-guided needle insertion experience; experts were attending emergency medicine physicians.

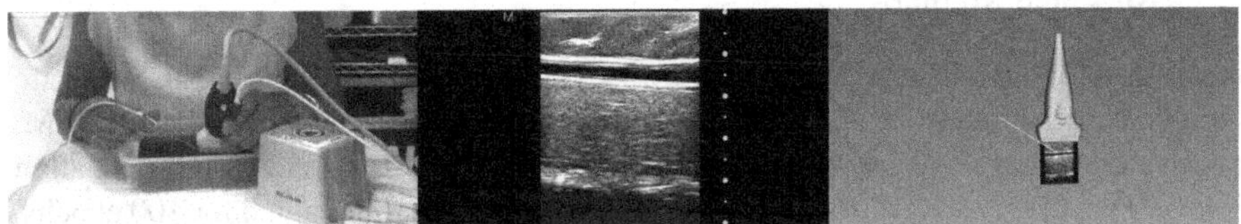

Fig. 1. Photograph, ultrasound image, and 3D visualization of participant performing ultrasound-guided needle insertion with electromagnetic trackers attached.

Kinematic data is collected through electromagnetic pose sensors (Ascension trakStar with Model 800 sensors, Northern Digital Inc., Waterloo, ON) rigidly attached to the needle, ultrasound probe, and phantom model (Fig. 1). Needle calibration was performed to find the needle tip's position using pivot and spin calibrations. Ultrasound calibration was performed to find the image's pose using the point-based method. Further details on the dataset may be found in the paper by Xia et al. [9].

2.2 Data Representations and Augmentation

We investigate skills assessment using four different transforms: (1) the Needle to Reference transform, (2) the Probe to Reference transform, (3) the Needle to Probe transform, and (4) the Needle Tip to Image transform. The former three transforms provide information about the needle's motion relative to the anatomy, the probe's motion relative to the anatomy, and the needle's motion relative to the probe, respectively. The latter transform, computed using the needle and probe calibration, provides information on how well the needle is visualized in ultrasound.

We investigate on four standard ways to represent the rotation of a transform. We consider (1) the Euler angle representation, (2) the axis-angle or rotation vector representation, (3) the quaternion representation, and (4) the rotation matrix representation. The Euler angle representation is a three-element vector, where we use the ZYX intrinsic rotation convention. The axis-angle or rotation vector representation is a three-element vector, where the vector's magnitude is the angle of rotation in radians. The quaternion representation is a four-element vector. The rotation matrix representation is a six-element vector, where we use the flattened first two columns of the rotation matrix [18].

We also investigate the value of the translation and rotation information. We simulate a scenario where we only have access to the translation information (e.g. single marker infrared tracker). We simulate a scenario where we only have access to the rotation information (e.g. inertial measurement unit). This is compared to using both the translation and rotation information.

Due to the small dataset size, we employ window slicing to cut each procedure into overlapping 60 frame snippets (approximately 8 s). Subsequently, we randomly resample snippets to ensure an equal number of novice and expert snippets (i.e. 10000 snippets for each class). We approximate that each snippet is representative of the whole trial, and thus, focus on classifying snippets of fixed length.

2.3 Assessment Methods

As a testbed for our data representations, we use two neural network architectures that are common across prior work on skills assessment from kinematic data: TCN and LSTM. In both architectures, we employed aggressive dropout ($p = 0.80$) and L2 regularization ($\lambda = 0.01$) to prevent overfitting on our dataset; each model was trained for 100 epochs. These values were determined empirically on a small validation set.

The TCN architecture we use treats the input time series data as a signal where each dimension (i.e. translation components and rotation components) is treated as a channel. Convolution is performed one-dimensionally across time. We employ two convolutional layers, followed by an average pooling layer, and several dense layers. The network's architecture is illustrated in Fig. 2.

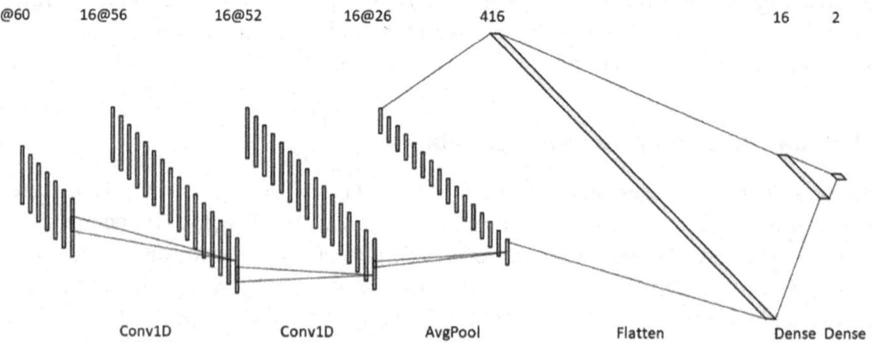

Fig. 2. Illustration of TCN architecture used for skills assessment. Top values indicate data size at each layer; bottom values indicate layer type. Input size is indicated as "number of channels @ number of frames" for each layer.

The LSTM architecture we use treats each translation component and rotation component as a feature. Recurrence is employed over time. We employ one LSTM layer, where the hidden output is used as the input to several dense layers. The network's architecture is shown in Fig. 3.

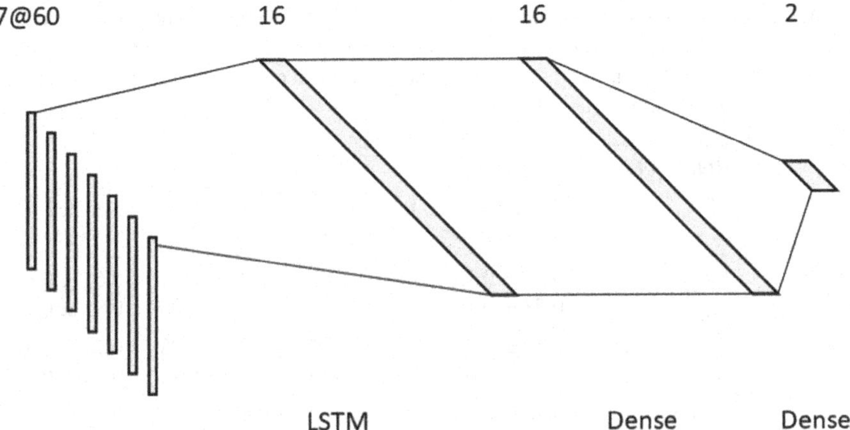

Fig. 3. Illustration of LSTM architecture used for skills assessment. Top values indicate data size at each layer; bottom values indicate layer type. Input size is indicated as "number of channels @ number of frames" for each layer.

2.4 Experimental Setup and Evaluation

To measure the performance of the assessment methods under different data representations, we performed user-out five-fold cross-validation for binary classification of novices vs. experts. We iterated over all five folds using each fold as the testing set, and randomly chose one fold from the training set as a validation set. Given there are only five expert users in the dataset, each fold contained data from exactly one expert. This cross-validation scheme best evaluates the proposed representations' generalizability to previously unseen users. Because there is class imbalance between the datasets, we report area under the curve (AUC) as the primary measure of performance. Networks for in-plane and out-of-plane data were trained separately.

3 Results

Results demonstrate that the highest performing data representation using the TCN is the NeedleTipToImage translation for in-plane insertions, with AUC of 0.83; the highest performing data representation is NeedleToReference translation for out-of-plane insertions, with AUC of 0.98. The highest performing data representation using the LSTM is the NeedleToProbe rotation matrix and translation for in-plane insertions, with AUC of 0.83; the highest performing data representation is ProbeToReference rotation matrix for out-of-plane insertions, with AUC of 0.70. Full results for all representations are reported using the TCN architecture (Table 1) and the LSTM architecture (Table 2).

By paired t-test, we found the skills assessment performance using the TCN was significantly better than using the LSTM for both in-plane ($p = 0.03$; mean 0.62 vs. 0.55, respectively) and out-of-plane ($p < 0.01$; mean 0.73 vs. 0.54, respectively) interventions.

Table 1. Area under the curve for skills classification using TCN architecture. For each cell, the top and bottom values indication performance for in-plane and out-of-plane insertions. Bolded results indicate best performance for each approach; underlined results indicate best performance for each transform per approach.

Rep.	Rotation Rep.	Transform			
		NeedleTo Reference	ProbeTo Reference	NeedleTo Probe	NeedleTip ToImage
Rotation + Translation	Euler	0.53 ± 0.13 0.77 ± 0.12	0.64 ± 0.15 0.74 ± 0.10	0.64 ± 0.13 0.83 ± 0.08	0.68 ± 0.09 0.81 ± 0.13
	Axis-Angle	0.71 ± 0.07 0.94 ± 0.02	0.76 ± 0.07 0.60 ± 0.11	0.43 ± 0.08 0.56 ± 0.12	0.70 ± 0.07 0.86 ± 0.11
	Quaternion	0.40 ± 0.14 0.49 ± 0.12	0.65 ± 0.14 0.78 ± 0.12	0.73 ± 0.12 0.76 ± 0.16	0.64 ± 0.13 0.73 ± 0.09
	Matrix	0.70 ± 0.13 0.76 ± 0.11	0.56 ± 0.14 0.73 ± 0.15	0.78 ± 0.10 0.50 ± 0.14	0.60 ± 0.08 0.69 ± 0.18
Rotation	Euler	0.66 ± 0.17 0.77 ± 0.07	0.51 ± 0.12 0.74 ± 0.10	0.43 ± 0.12 0.70 ± 0.10	0.66 ± 0.10 0.69 ± 0.09
	Axis-Angle	0.72 ± 0.07 0.59 ± 0.09	0.82 ± 0.05 0.43 ± 0.14	0.35 ± 0.10 0.73 ± 0.10	0.30 ± 0.09 0.82 ± 0.09
	Quaternion	0.51 ± 0.17 0.53 ± 0.13	0.55 ± 0.17 0.60 ± 0.11	0.69 ± 0.13 0.81 ± 0.10	0.55 ± 0.05 0.59 ± 0.17
	Matrix	0.79 ± 0.08 0.64 ± 0.11	0.74 ± 0.09 0.89 ± 0.06	0.60 ± 0.11 0.91 ± 0.05	0.44 ± 0.07 0.82 ± 0.12
Translation	–	0.56 ± 0.11 **0.98 ± 0.01**	0.64 ± 0.18 0.82 ± 0.09	0.81 ± 0.10 0.79 ± 0.13	**0.83 ± 0.07** 0.75 ± 0.12

By ANOVA we did not find a significant difference in skills assessment performance using any specific representation (mean AUC 0.62 for Euler & translation, 0.62 for axis-angle & translation, 0.61 for quaternion & translation, 0.64 for matrix & translation, 0.60 for Euler only, 0.58 for axis-angle only, 0.54 for quaternion only, 0.65 for matrix only, 0.64 for translation only). Nor was there any significant difference for rotation and translation, rotation only, and translation only (mean AUC 0.62, 0.59, 0.64, respectively). Likewise, we did not find a significant difference in skills assessment performance using the NeedleToReference, ProbeToReference, NeedleToProbe, or NeedleTipToImage transforms (mean AUC 0.62, 0.62, 0.61, 0.59, respectively).

Table 2. Area under the curve for skills classification using LSTM architecture. For each cell, the top and bottom values indication performance for in-plane and out-of-plane insertions. Bolded results indicate best performance for each approach; underlined results indicate best performance for each transform per approach.

Rep.	Rotation Rep.	Transform			
		NeedleTo Reference	ProbeTo Reference	NeedleTo Probe	NeedleTip ToImage
Rotation + Translation	Euler	0.62 ± 0.14 0.42 ± 0.10	0.64 ± 0.09 0.40 ± 0.13	0.59 ± 0.15 0.54 ± 0.15	0.55 ± 0.10 0.48 ± 0.13
	Axis-Angle	0.61 ± 0.06 0.60 ± 0.04	0.51 ± 0.13 0.48 ± 0.06	0.69 ± 0.07 0.60 ± 0.05	0.48 ± 0.12 0.35 ± 0.16
	Quaternion	0.60 ± 0.04 0.61 ± 0.14	0.59 ± 0.11 0.67 ± 0.08	0.52 ± 0.09 0.56 ± 0.12	0.38 ± 0.11 0.58 ± 0.12
	Matrix	$\underline{0.65 \pm 0.07}$ 0.62 ± 0.13	$\underline{0.65 \pm 0.09}$ 0.68 ± 0.12	$\underline{\mathbf{0.83 \pm 0.03}}$ 0.51 ± 0.10	0.41 ± 0.05 0.63 ± 0.13
Rotation	Euler	0.58 ± 0.12 $\underline{0.66 \pm 0.06}$	0.58 ± 0.08 0.65 ± 0.17	0.41 ± 0.15 $\underline{0.64 \pm 0.07}$	0.45 ± 0.07 0.42 ± 0.14
	Axis-Angle	0.53 ± 0.09 0.63 ± 0.06	0.56 ± 0.15 0.56 ± 0.09	0.58 ± 0.10 0.55 ± 0.14	0.58 ± 0.07 0.52 ± 0.15
	Quaternion	0.53 ± 0.10 0.41 ± 0.12	0.59 ± 0.09 0.48 ± 0.09	0.48 ± 0.12 0.34 ± 0.12	0.35 ± 0.09 $\underline{0.66 \pm 0.09}$
	Matrix	0.60 ± 0.07 0.56 ± 0.12	0.60 ± 0.13 $\underline{\mathbf{0.70 \pm 0.05}}$	0.50 ± 0.08 0.49 ± 0.15	$\underline{0.64 \pm 0.11}$ 0.50 ± 0.08
Translation	–	0.60 ± 0.12 0.52 ± 0.03	0.49 ± 0.07 0.45 ± 0.13	0.47 ± 0.06 0.56 ± 0.15	0.53 ± 0.08 0.43 ± 0.12

4 Discussion

Performance varies considerably due to representation, and the optimal representation varies depending on network architecture and task. Thus, we do not recommend an optimal data representation in general, but rather, searching over the space of data representations to find the optimal representation for a given task. This is crucial in tasks with small datasets, where deep neural networks do not generalize well.

The results show the proposed TCN outperforms the proposed LSTM across most data representations, although their results are not directly comparable due to different numbers of parameters used. Furthermore, assessment performance for the out-of-plane dataset exceeds assessment performance for the in-plane dataset.

This study has several limitations. Primarily, the sample size is small; thus, the uncertainty associated with the calculated measures of performance are high. This study also is limited by using operators' self-proclaimed appointment status (i.e. emergency medicine physicians or medical student). Ideally the ground-truth skill level should be determined by an expert rater using a scale with evidence of validity. This would account for variation in performance due to extraneous factors. Finally, the dataset comes from a simulation-based training situation, and therefore may not be directly applicable to a skills assessment in a clinical scenario.

The results shown here are consistent with the work from Kim et al. [14] which demonstrate that data representation of kinematics data for skills assessment important. Their work identifies that using tooltip velocities has benefit over using tooltip positions. The performance achieved for binary skills classification exceeds the results from Holden et al. [19] (0.83 vs. 0.82 AUC for in-plane insertions; 0.98 vs. 0.94 AUC for out-of-plane insertions), when the appropriate data representation is used. We highlight, however, that the numeric results reported in this comparison are not indicative of performance on a new dataset. These numeric results should be seen more like performance on a validation set, as the representation has been tuned on the testing set.

In many applications, it is desirable to use less expensive and less obtrusive hardware for data collection. For example, using an inertial measurement unit to determine rotation information or using a single marker optical tracker to determine translation information reduce the hardware needs. Results indicate that these setups may be possible in some cases without affecting skills assessment performance.

Future work involves using further data augmentation strategies (e.g. white noise, window warping, etc.) and representation strategies (e.g. multiple transforms with multiple representations) to determine their added value in skills assessment in scenarios with limited data. We also intend to collect a larger dataset so that we may get a more precise measure of performance for different representations. Finally, we wish to try more modern neural network architectures.

5 Conclusion

In this work, we have demonstrated that standard neural network architectures can be used for skills assessment in ultrasound-guided needle insertion. The proposed TCN outperforms previous work using machine learning on summary statistics for skills assessment [19], when the appropriate data representation is used. On the other hand, this work has found that data representation can significantly affect skills assessment performance. We found that the optimal representation can vary depending on the task and network architecture. Thus, it is recommended to search over the space of data representations when choosing a neural network architecture for skills assessment in interventional ultrasound when limited data is available.

Acknowledgement. This research was enabled in part by support provided by Compute Ontario (www.computeontario.ca) and Compute Canada (www.computecanada.ca).

References

1. Reiley, C.E., Lin, H.C., Yuh, D.D., Hager, G.D.: Review of methods for objective surgical skill evaluation. Surg. Endosc. **25**, 356–366 (2011). https://doi.org/10.1007/s00464-010-1190-z
2. Holden, M.S.: Computer-Assisted Assessment and Feedback for Image-Guided Interventions Training (2019)

3. Hayter, M.A., et al.: Validation of the imperial college surgical assessment device (ICSAD) for labour epidural placement. Can. J. Anesth. **56**, 419–426 (2009). https://doi.org/10.1007/s12630-009-9090-1
4. Corvetto, M.A., et al.: Validation of the imperial college surgical assessment device for spinal anesthesia. BMC Anesthesiol. **17** (2017). https://doi.org/10.1186/s12871-017-0422-3
5. Chin, K.J., Tse, C., Chan, V., Tan, J.S., Lupu, C.M., Hayter, M.: Hand motion analysis using the imperial college surgical assessment device: validation of a novel and objective performance measure in ultrasound-guided peripheral nerve blockade. Reg. Anesth. Pain Med. **36**, 213–219 (2011). https://doi.org/10.1097/AAP.0b013e31820d4305
6. Clinkard, D., et al.: Assessment of lumbar puncture skill in experts and nonexperts using checklists and quantitative tracking of needle trajectories: implications for competency-based medical education. Teach. Learn. Med. **27**, 51–56 (2015). https://doi.org/10.1080/10401334.2014.979184
7. Clinkard, D., et al.: The development and validation of hand motion analysis to evaluate competency in central line catheterization. Acad. Emerg. Med. **22**, 212–218 (2015). https://doi.org/10.1111/acem.12590
8. Tabriz, D.M., Street, M., Pilgram, T.K., Duncan, J.R.: Objective assessment of operator performance during ultrasound-guided procedures. Int. J. Comput. Assist. Radiol. Surg. **6**, 641–652 (2011). https://doi.org/10.1007/s11548-010-0541-5
9. Xia, S., et al.: A learning curve analysis of ultrasound-guided in-plane and out-of-plane vascular access training with Perk Tutor. In: Webster, R.J., Fei, B. (eds.) Medical Imaging 2018: Image-Guided Procedures, Robotic Interventions, and Modeling, p. 66. SPIE (2018). https://doi.org/10.1117/12.2293789
10. Vedula, S.S., Ishii, M., Hager, G.D.: Objective assessment of surgical technical skill and competency in the operating room. Annu. Rev. Biomed. Eng. **19**, 301–325 (2017). https://doi.org/10.1146/annurev-bioeng-071516-044435
11. Wang, Z., M.F., A.: Deep learning with convolutional neural network for objective skill evaluation in robot-assisted surgery. Int. J. Comput. Assist. Radiol. Surg. **13**(12), 1959–1970 (2018). https://doi.org/10.1007/s11548-018-1860-1
12. I.F., H., Forestier, G., Weber, J., Idoumghar, L., Muller, P.-A.: Accurate and interpretable evaluation of surgical skills from kinematic data using fully convolutional neural networks. Int. J. Comput. Assist. Radiol. Surg. **14**(9), 1611–1617 (2019). https://doi.org/10.1007/s11548-019-02039-4
13. Castro, D., Pereira, D., Zanchettin, C., MacEdo, D., Bezerra, B.L.D.: Towards optimizing convolutional neural networks for robotic surgery skill evaluation. In: Proceedings of the International Joint Conference on Neural Networks (2019). https://doi.org/10.1109/IJCNN.2019.8852341
14. Kim, T.S., O'Brien, M., Zafar, S., Hager, G.D., Sikder, S., Vedula, S.S.: Objective assessment of intraoperative technical skill in capsulorhexis using videos of cataract surgery. Int. J. Comput. Assist. Radiol. Surg. **14**(6), 1097–1105 (2019). https://doi.org/10.1007/s11548-019-01956-8
15. Oğul, B.B., Gilgien, M.F., Şahin, P.D.: Ranking robot-assisted surgery skills using kinematic sensors. In: Chatzigiannakis, I., De Ruyter, B., Mavrommati, I. (eds.) AmI 2019. LNCS, vol. 11912, pp. 330–336. Springer, Cham (2019). https://doi.org/10.1007/978-3-030-34255-5_24
16. Nguyen, X.A., Ljuhar, D., Pacilli, M., Nataraja, R.M., Chauhan, S.: Surgical skill levels: Classification and analysis using deep neural network model and motion signals. Comput. Methods Programs Biomed. (2019). https://doi.org/10.1016/j.cmpb.2019.05.008
17. Ahmidi, N., et al.: A dataset and benchmarks for segmentation and recognition of gestures in robotic surgery. IEEE Trans. Biomed. Eng. **64**, 2025–2041 (2017). https://doi.org/10.1109/TBME.2016.2647680

18. Zhou, Y., Barnes, C., Lu, J., Yang, J., Li, H.: On the continuity of rotation representations in neural networks. In: Proceedings of the IEEE Computer Society Conference on Computer Vision and Pattern Recognition (2019). https://doi.org/10.1109/CVPR.2019.00589
19. Holden, M.S., Lia, H., Xia, S., Keri, Z., Ungi, T., Fichtinger, G.: Configurable overall skill assessment in ultrasound-guided needle insertion. In: 16th Annual Imaging Network Ontario Symposium (ImNO) (2018)

PIPPI 2020

3D Fetal Pose Estimation with Adaptive Variance and Conditional Generative Adversarial Network

Junshen Xu[1(✉)], Molin Zhang[1], Esra Abaci Turk[2], P. Ellen Grant[2,3], Polina Golland[1,4], and Elfar Adalsteinsson[1,5]

[1] Department of Electrical Engineering and Computer Science, MIT, Cambridge, MA, USA
junshen@mit.edu
[2] Fetal-Neonatal Neuroimaging and Developmental Science Center, Boston Children's Hospital, Boston, MA, USA
[3] Harvard Medical School, Boston, MA, USA
[4] Computer Science and Artificial Intelligence Laboratory, MIT, Cambridge, MA, USA
[5] Institute for Medical Engineering and Science, MIT, Cambridge, MA, USA

Abstract. Fetal motion is the dominant challenge to reliable performance and diagnostic quality of fetal magnetic resonance imaging (MRI). The fetus can move unpredictably and rapidly, leading to severe image artifacts. Consequently, MR acquisitions are largely limited to so-called single-shot techniques in an attempt to "freeze" fetal motion through fast imaging, while the problem due to motion occur between slices still exists. In this work, we propose a deep learning method for fetal pose estimation from MR volumes using the paradigm of conditional generative adversarial network which consists of two networks, a generator and a discriminator. The generator is responsible for estimating keypoint heatmaps from input MRI and the discriminator tries to learn the features of plausible fetal pose and distinguish ground-truth heatmaps from generated ones. With this adversarial training scheme, the generator can robustly produce realistic heatmaps for fetal pose inference. Besides, we use adaptive variance to model the difference in intensity of motion of different keypoints. Evaluation shows that the proposed method can improve the performance of pose estimation in 3D MRI, achieving quantitatively an average error of 2.64 mm and 98.31% accuracy (with error less than 10 mm). The proposed method can process volumes with latency less than 300 ms, potentially enabling low-latency online tracking of fetal pose during MR scans.

Keywords: Pose estimation · Fetal magnetic resonance imaging (MRI) · Deep learning · Convolutional neural network (CNN) · Generative adversarial network (GAN)

Y. Hu et al. (Eds.): ASMUS 2020/PIPPI 2020, LNCS 12437, pp. 201–210, 2020.
https://doi.org/10.1007/978-3-030-60334-2_20

1 Introduction

Fetal magnetic resonance imaging (MRI) has been increasingly used in clinical practice for visualizing the fetus in utero [21] and monitoring placental function [15] as well. However, during fetal MR imaging, the motion of fetus is a major problem that severely affects image quality [11].

Prior research on fetal motion relied on simple indices for quantification and analysis of fetal movement, including the angle of the fetal body axes with respect to the maternal body [4], maternal perception of fetal motion [8] and score rated by radiologists [25]. Recently, Xu et al. [23] tried to access fetal motion in MRI by estimating the fetal pose from a series of MR volumes. Estimation of pose of fetus from volumetric MRI in pregnancy has a wide range of applications including motion correction [10] and monitoring fetal health [6].

Although human pose estimation is well-established in computer vision [12,19], few works have addressed the problem of fetal pose estimation in utero from medical images. In contrast to 2D human pose estimation, fetal pose estimation requires prediction of 3D pose from volumetric data, which highly increases the computational burden. Further complicating the task is the variable fetal orientation in utero [17], and change in fetal features over gestational age [1]. In the field of fetal pose estimation from medical images, different representations of fetal pose have been proposed. For example, Toussaint et al. [22] proposed a method for localization of fetus in ultrasound images based on six regions, including head, thorax, abdomen, spine, limbs and placenta. In [24], the authors extracted fetal pose by estimating several landmarks of fetus in 3D ultrasound using a deep learning method. As for MRI, Xu et al. [23] proposed a two-stage deep learning framework for estimating fetal pose from 3D MRI. The first stage is using a neural network to generate the heatmap of each keypoint from the MR volume, and the second stage is inferring keypoint locations from heatmaps using a Markov random field (MRF).

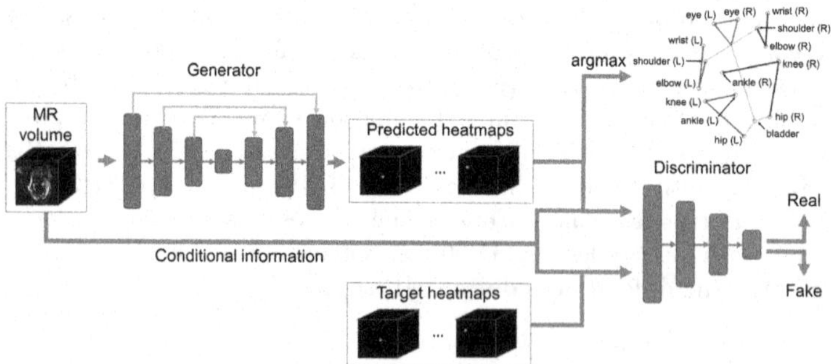

Fig. 1. Overall architecture of conditional generative adversarial network for 3D fetal pose estimation.

In the last few years, Generative Adversarial Network (GAN) [7] has achieved tremendous success in many fields of computer vision. One of the well-known problems is that the original GAN tends to have the unreliable gradient which make training unstable. To address this problem, several methods have been proposed. For example, Wasserstein GAN [3] minimizes the Wasserstein distance instead of cross entropy, which provides better estimation of the quality of the generated samples. Another work is the least squares GAN (LSGAN) [16] which removes the sigmoid function at output and adopts the least squares loss for the discriminator. The least squares loss solves the problem of gradient vanishing in the sigmoid cross entropy loss and therefore improves the stability of GAN. The concept of conditional GAN (cGAN) [18] was first introduced for image generation with class labels as prior information and further adopted in supervised learning problems where input images are treated as the conditional information [9].

In this paper, we propose a deep learning method to generate 3D fetal pose from MR volumes. We adopt the conditional generative adversarial network to improve the robustness of our model and also introduce adaptive variance to capture the difference in intensity of motion of different fetal body parts. Evaluation of the proposed method shows that our model can improve the accuracy in fetal pose estimation. Further, computation time of our method is less than 300 ms/volume, which potentially enables tracking fetal pose in MRI with low latency.

2 Methods

2.1 Fetal Pose Estimation in 3D MRI

Given a 3D MR volume $I \in \mathbb{R}^{H\times W\times D}$, the task of fetal pose estimation is to predict the location $p_j = (x_j, y_j, z_j), j = 1, 2, ..., J$ of a set of keypoints that describes the fetal body, where H, W, D is the size of volume and J is the number of keypoints of interest. Instead of estimating locations of keypoints directly, we aim to predict heatmaps that characterize the probabilities of observing each keypoint at different locations. We model each keypoint using a Gaussian distribution, i.e., the heatmap of the $j-$th keypoint is defined as $H_j(p_j;\sigma_j) = \sigma_j^{-3}\exp\{-(\|p_j - \overline{p}_j\|_2^2)/(2\sigma_j^2)\}$. Where $\overline{p}_j$ is the ground-truth location of the $j-$th keypoint, σ_j is the standard deviation of Gaussian distribution.

Using the heatmap representation, the task of fetal pose estimation becomes predicting heatmaps $H = [H_1, H_2, ..., H_J] \in \mathbb{R}^{H\times W\times D\times J}$ from MR volumes I using a network G, i.e., $\hat{H} = G(I)$. The location of keypoints is then estimated by finding the maximum in an aggregation of generated heatmaps.

2.2 Adaptive Heatmap and Variance Loss

One of the important observations from MR data is that the intensity of motion varies from keypoint to keypoint. For example, the motion of wrists is much more rapid than that of shoulders. Since the heatmap is a representation of the probability of observing each keypoint at different locations, the variance of heatmap is related to the motion of the corresponding keypoint.

However, In [23], the authors use a fixed variance for all keypoints, which is unable to capture the difference in intensity of motion of different keypoints. Inspired by [20], we make $\sigma_1, ..., \sigma_J$ trainable parameters, so that the network can learn an adaptive variance for each heatmap to model the volatility of motion of the corresponding keypoint. During the process of training, the network is optimized by minimizing the mean squared error (MSE) between generated heatmaps and target heatmaps, $\mathcal{L}_{\text{MSE}} = ||G(I) - H||_2^2$. However if we train the network with adaptive heatmaps using the MSE loss only, the output heatmaps will vanish and variances become infinity. To avoid model degeneration, regularizer for σ should be applied. Besides, it is worth noticing that the error due to discretization will increase as variance decrease and become unignorable. Inspired by the hinge loss, we propose the following variance loss for adaptive heatmap regression.

$$\mathcal{L}_{\text{var}} = \sum_{j=1}^{J} \max(\sigma_j^2 - \sigma_{\text{min}}^2, 0) \tag{1}$$

where σ_{min}^2 is the minimum variance of heatmaps.

2.3 Generative Adversarial Net for Pose Estimation

The architecture of conditional generative adversarial network for 3D fetal pose estimation is shown in Fig. 1, which consists of two networks, generator G and discriminator D. The generator is a fully convolutional neural network which takes MR volumes as input and predicts heatmaps. The second network D is a convolutional encoder trained to distinguish ground truth heatmaps from generated ones.

Generator. We adopt a 3D UNet architecture [5] for the generator whose goal is to learn a mapping from MR volume to heatmaps by minimizing the MSE loss. Besides, when training with adaptive heatmaps, variance loss should be employed to penalize large σ's to avoid heatmap vanishing, as mentioned in the previous section. In addition to the supervised loss, an adversarial loss from the discriminator is introduced to force the generator to produce heatmaps that look realistic and fool the discriminative network. Following LSGAN [16], we define the adversarial loss as the L2 loss between the output of discriminator $D([G(I), I])$ and 1 which is the indicator of real heatmaps.

$$\mathcal{L}_{\text{adv}} = ||D([G(I), I]) - 1||_2^2 \tag{2}$$

Therefore, the total loss function for generator can be written as

$$\mathcal{L}_G = \mathcal{L}_{\text{MSE}} + \lambda_1 \mathcal{L}_{\text{var}} + \lambda_2 \mathcal{L}_{\text{adv}} \tag{3}$$

where λ_1 and λ_2 are weight coefficients.

Discriminator. The discriminative network is similar to the encoding part of generator but with an extra 1×1 convolution as output layer. In contrast to the conventional GAN where the output of discriminator is the probability of the input being real heatmap, we adopted the idea of PatchGAN [9] in which the discriminator makes decision on each patch, rather than the whole heatmap. The input of the discriminator is either ground truth heatmaps or generated heatmaps concatenated with the corresponding MR volume and the output is a downscaled volume where each pixel is the classification result for the patch in the input heatmap defined by the receptive field. From the input pair, the discriminator should learn whether the pose described by the heatmaps is rational and corresponds to the fetus in the MR volume. The objective of the discriminator is to distinguish real heatmaps from generated ones. Similar to LSGAN, the loss of discriminator is the sum of the L2 loss for fake and real inputs.

$$\mathcal{L}_D = \mathcal{L}_{\text{fake}} + \mathcal{L}_{\text{real}} = ||D([G(I), I]) - 0||_2^2 + ||D([H, I]) - 1||_2^2 \tag{4}$$

Adversarial Training. The GAN is trained by minimizing $\mathcal{L}_G$ and $\mathcal{L}_D$ alternately which can be regarded as an adversarial two-player game. The generator tries to generate heatmaps realistic enough to fool the discriminator and make $D([G(I), I])$ close to 1, while the discriminator aims at distinguishing between true and fake heatmaps by pushing $D([G(I), I])$ to 0 and $D([H, I])$ to 1.

In [23], the authors adopted a MRF to model the restrictions on the connections between nearby keypoints explicitly. In this point of view, the discriminator tries to distinguish real data from generated data by learning features of plausible fetal pose configurations and imposes these constraints of rational fetal pose on the generator through the adversarial loss.

2.4 Datasets and Experiments Setup

The dataset consists of 3D MRI time series of 77 pregnant mothers at a gestational age ranging from 25 to 35 weeks. MR data were acquired on a 3T scanner. Multislice EPI sequence was used to acquire image of the whole uterus with resolution of $3 \times 3\text{mm}^2$, slice thickness of 3 mm and temporal resolution of 3.5 s. Each subject was scanned for 10 to 30 min. Fifteen keypoints are used to model the fetal pose [23], including ankles, knees, hips, shoulders, elbows, wrists, eyes and bladder. The whole dataset is divided into train (49 series, 12332 frames) validation (14 series, 3402 frames) and test (14 series, 4082 frames) sets.

We used the Adam optimizer [13] for training and employed the warm restart strategy [14]. Networks are trained for 200 epochs on a NVIDIA TITAN V GPU with initial learning rate of 1×10^{-4}. Besides, we set λ_1 to 1 and λ_2 to 1×10^{-3}.

As for evaluation, we compute the mean and median of error as well as Percentage of Correct Keypoint (PCK) [2] of each keypoint.

3 Results

3.1 Adaptive Variance

Figure 2a shows the PCK curves of model with adaptive variance and fixed variance ($\sigma = 2, 3, 4$ pixel) for the heatmaps. The adaptive variance method achieves better PCK performance than fixed variance. The idea of adaptive heatmap is motivated by the fact that different keypoints have different intensities of motion (see Fig. 3b). We plotted the adaptive variances learned by the network in Fig. 3a. Results show that ankles and wrists have the largest variance, followed by knees and elbows. Comparing the learned variance with the volatility of keypoints location in training labels, we found that keypoints with more rapid motion tend to have greater variance of heatmap (see Fig. 3c), which is consistent with our hypothesis.

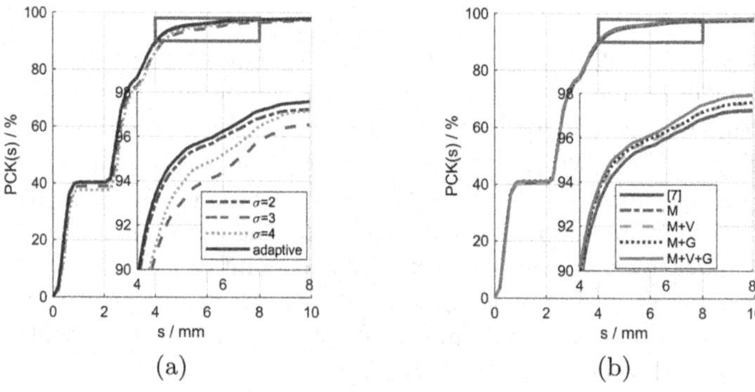

Fig. 2. (a) PCK curves of networks trained with adaptive and fixed variance. (b) PCK curves of different models. M: MSE, V: variance loss, G: GAN loss.

3.2 Conditional Generative Adversarial Net

We trained networks with four different loss function: a) MSE, b) MSE and variance loss, c) MSE and GAN loss, d) total loss function in Eq. 3 and compared the results with the method proposed in [23]. The PCK curves of different models in Fig. 2b show that the proposed method achieves the best PCK performance in our evaluation. Table 1 shows the quantitative metrics, including PCK at 5 and 10 mm as well as mean and median of errors.

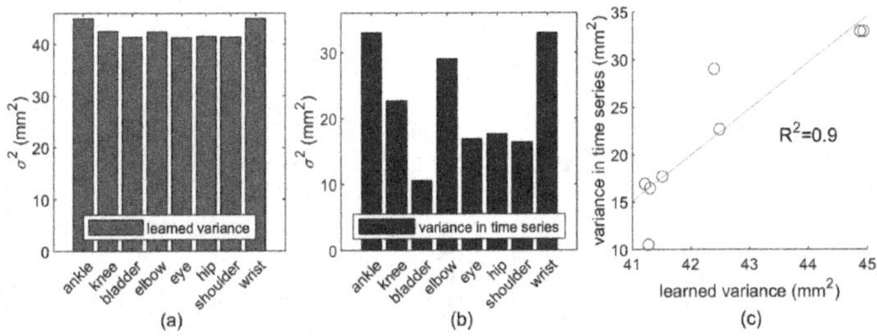

Fig. 3. (a): Variance of adaptive heatmap for each keypoint learned by the proposed method, which is the uncertainty of keypoint localization at each frame. (b): Variance of keypoints in training labels, i.e., the variance of keypoint location over the time series. (c): Scatter plot of variances of different keypoints.

To investigate the benefit of adversarial training in fetal pose estimation, we compared the proposed method with the model trained without GAN and plot the distribution of error of these two models in Fig. 4. The zoom-in view in Fig. 4 shows that the model with GAN has a lighter tailed distribution of error, which indicates that the gain in performance from GAN is mainly due to the reduction of cases with large error. Quantitative metrics in Table 1 lead to the same result, where the proposed method can reduce the mean of error but not the median of error. Examples of estimated fetal pose are displayed in Fig. 5a. The poses produced by the model without GAN (the bottom row) may have wrong configurations and look unrealistic. However, by competing with the discriminator, the generator is able to produce poses that are close to the subspace of plausible fetal pose (the top row). In addition, the change in local evidence due to random noise and change in contrast can affect the accuracy of the network, while training with GAN improves the robustness of the model and results in more stable estimation in the time series (see Fig. 5b).

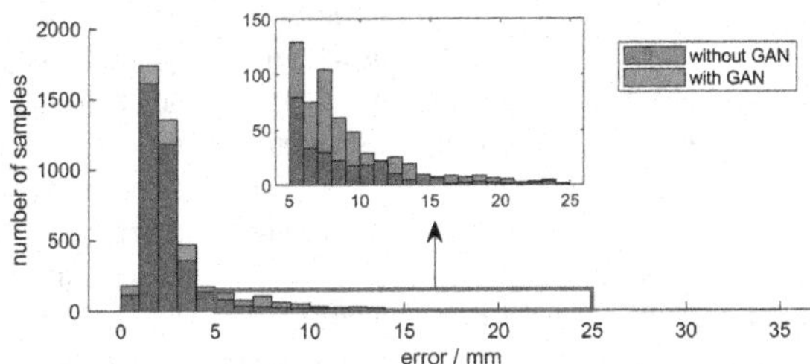

Fig. 4. Histograms of error for model with and without GAN.

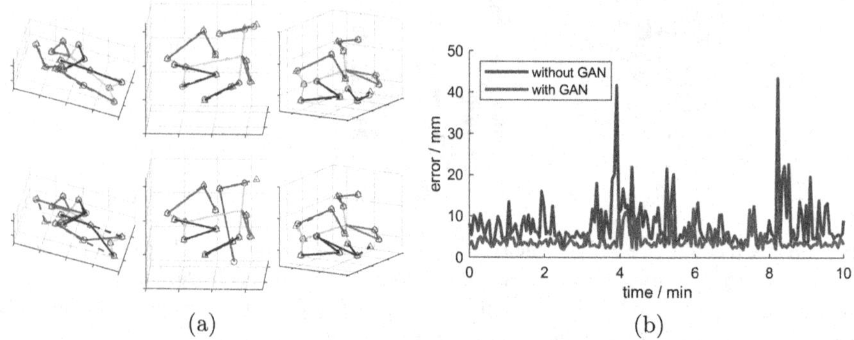

Fig. 5. (a) The top and bottom rows are examples of estimated fetal poses from models with and without GAN respectively. The circles and the solid lines are the predicted poses. The triangles and dashed lines are ground truth labels. The middle point of left and right shoulders are also shown for better visualization. (b) The error of pose estimation model with and without GAN in a time series.

Table 1. Quantitative metrics for different models, including PCK at 5 mm and 10 mm threshold as well as mean and median of error. M, V and G denote MSE loss, variance loss and GAN loss respectively.

Metric	Method	Wrist	Elbow	Shoulder	Eye	Bladder	Hip	Knee	Ankle	Total
PCK5 (%)	[23]	88.96	96.04	97.01	94.69	99.06	93.23	99.42	91.48	94.85
	M	88.96	96.00	96.98	94.88	99.06	93.01	99.42	91.48	94.84
	M+V	**89.73**	96.35	98.11	94.90	98.89	92.90	99.49	92.31	95.16
	M+G	89.12	**97.22**	**98.24**	93.12	98.84	**94.00**	99.51	93.56	95.27
	M+G+V	88.21	96.45	97.87	**96.03**	**98.91**	93.83	**99.52**	**93.85**	**95.43**
PCK10 (%)	[23]	95.63	99.82	99.73	98.18	99.25	95.28	99.94	94.05	97.60
	M	95.63	99.79	99.70	98.29	99.25	94.86	99.93	94.05	97.56
	M+V	96.61	99.82	99.77	98.43	**99.26**	95.40	99.93	95.16	97.93
	M+G	96.17	**99.87**	99.73	97.51	99.10	96.47	**99.95**	95.78	97.96
	M+G+V	**96.64**	99.83	**99.80**	**98.86**	99.24	**96.62**	99.93	**96.29**	**98.31**
Mean (mm)	[23]	4.357	2.313	2.146	3.341	2.064	2.938	1.615	4.990	3.020
	M	4.357	2.353	2.153	3.077	2.084	3.677	1.629	5.166	3.123
	M+V	3.867	2.289	2.152	2.713	2.265	3.432	1.692	4.900	2.965
	M+G	4.173	**2.204**	**1.957**	3.294	2.057	2.736	**1.614**	4.209	2.835
	M+G+V	**3.689**	2.282	2.035	**2.568**	**2.044**	**2.607**	1.754	**3.871**	**2.644**
Median (mm)	[23]	2.810	2.673	2.378	2.619	0.606	2.359	2.238	2.464	2.268
	M	2.810	2.673	2.378	2.605	0.606	2.361	2.238	2.464	2.268
	M+V	2.811	2.605	2.428	2.663	0.599	**2.311**	2.316	2.457	2.274
	M+G	2.820	**2.594**	**2.340**	**2.584**	**0.562**	2.357	**2.188**	**2.440**	**2.236**
	M+G+V	**2.725**	2.635	2.385	2.601	0.596	2.332	2.339	2.461	2.259

4 Conclusion

In this work, we propose a generative adversarial network for fetal pose estimation from 3D MRI. By competing with each other, the discriminator can implicitly model the constraints on plausible fetal pose configurations, while the generator is able to produce realistic fetal poses. Besides, we use adaptive heatmaps for keypoints to capture the difference in intensity of motion of different keypoints. Evaluation shows that the proposed method improves accuracy in fetal pose estimation and outperforms other state-of-the-art results. Since the discriminator is only used for training, it can be removed in inference, resulting in an end-to-end fetal pose estimation pipeline with processing time less than 300 ms/volume. In summary, the proposed method potentially enables low-latency fetal pose estimation in MRI with application to fetal health monitoring and prospective motion correction.

References

1. Alexander, G.R., Himes, J.H., Kaufman, R.B., Mor, J., Kogan, M.: A united states national reference for fetal growth. Obstet. Gynecol. **87**(2), 163–168 (1996)
2. Andriluka, M., Pishchulin, L., Gehler, P., Schiele, B.: 2D human pose estimation: new benchmark and state of the art analysis. In: Proceedings of the IEEE Conference on computer Vision and Pattern Recognition, pp. 3686–3693 (2014)
3. Arjovsky, M., Chintala, S., Bottou, L.: Wasserstein GAN. arXiv preprint arXiv:1701.07875 (2017)
4. Biglari, H., Sameni, R.: Fetal motion estimation from noninvasive cardiac signal recordings. Physiol. Meas. **37**(11), 2003 (2016)
5. Çiçek, Ö., Abdulkadir, A., Lienkamp, S.S., Brox, T., Ronneberger, O.: 3D U-Net: learning dense volumetric segmentation from sparse annotation. In: Ourselin, S., Joskowicz, L., Sabuncu, M., Unal, G., Wells, W. (eds.) MICCAI 2016. LNCS, vol. 9901, pp. 424–432. Springer, Cham (2016). https://doi.org/10.1007/978-3-319-46723-8_49
6. Fai, F.Y., Singh, K., Malcus, P., Biswas, A., Arulkumaran, S., Ratnam, S.: Assessment of fetal health should be based on maternal perception of clusters rather than episodes of fetal movements. J. Obstet. Gynaecol. Res. **22**(3), 299–304 (1996)
7. Goodfellow, I., et al.: Generative adversarial nets. In: Advances in Neural Information Processing Systems, pp. 2672–2680 (2014)
8. Heazell, A.P., Frøen, J.: Methods of fetal movement counting and the detection of fetal compromise. J. Obstet. Gynaecol. **28**(2), 147–154 (2008)
9. Isola, P., Zhu, J.Y., Zhou, T., Efros, A.A.: Image-to-image translation with conditional adversarial networks. In: Proceedings of the IEEE Conference on Computer Vision and Pattern Recognition, pp. 1125–1134 (2017)
10. Itti, L., Chang, L., Ernst, T.: Automatic scan prescription for brain MRI. Magn. Reson. Med. Off. J. Int. Soc. Magn. Reson. Med. **45**(3), 486–494 (2001)
11. Jokhi, R.P., Whitby, E.H.: Magnetic resonance imaging of the fetus. Dev. Med. Child Neurol. **53**(1), 18–28 (2011)
12. Khan, N.U., Wan, W.: A review of human pose estimation from single image. In: 2018 International Conference on Audio, Language and Image Processing (ICALIP), pp. 230–236. IEEE (2018)

13. Kingma, D.P., Ba, J.: Adam: a method for stochastic optimization. arXiv preprint arXiv:1412.6980 (2014)
14. Loshchilov, I., Hutter, F.: Fixing weight decay regularization in adam. arXiv preprint arXiv:1711.05101 (2017)
15. Luo, J., et al.: In vivo quantification of placental insufficiency by bold MRI: a human study. Sci. Rep. **7**(1), 3713 (2017)
16. Mao, X., Li, Q., Xie, H., Lau, R.Y., Wang, Z., Paul Smolley, S.: Least squares generative adversarial networks. In: Proceedings of the IEEE International Conference on Computer Vision, pp. 2794–2802 (2017)
17. Matsuo, K., Shimoya, K., Ushioda, N., Kimura, T.: Maternal positioning and fetal positioning in utero. J. Obstet. Gynaecol. Res. **33**(3), 279–282 (2007)
18. Mirza, M., Osindero, S.: Conditional generative adversarial nets. arXiv preprint arXiv:1411.1784 (2014)
19. Newell, A., Yang, K., Deng, J.: Stacked hourglass networks for human pose estimation. In: Leibe, B., Matas, J., Sebe, N., Welling, M. (eds.) ECCV 2016. LNCS, vol. 9912, pp. 483–499. Springer, Cham (2016). https://doi.org/10.1007/978-3-319-46484-8_29
20. Payer, C., Štern, D., Bischof, H., Urschler, M.: Integrating spatial configuration into heatmap regression based CNNs for landmark localization. Med. Image Anal. **54**, 207–219 (2019)
21. Saleem, S.N.: Fetal MRI: an approach to practice: a review. J. Adv. Res. **5**(5), 507–523 (2014)
22. Toussaint, N., et al.: Weakly supervised localisation for fetal ultrasound images. In: Stoyanov, D., et al. (eds.) DLMIA 2018, ML-CDS 2018. LNCS, vol. 11045, pp. 192–200. Springer, Cham (2018). https://doi.org/10.1007/978-3-030-00889-5_22
23. Xu, J., et al.: Fetal pose estimation in volumetric MRI using a 3D convolution neural network. In: Shen, D., et al. (eds.) MICCAI 2019. LNCS, vol. 11767, pp. 403–410. Springer, Cham (2019). https://doi.org/10.1007/978-3-030-32251-9_44
24. Yang, X., et al.: FetusMap: fetal pose estimation in 3D ultrasound. In: Shen, D., et al. (eds.) MICCAI 2019. LNCS, vol. 11768, pp. 281–289. Springer, Cham (2019)
25. Yen, C.J., Mehollin-Ray, A.R., Bernardo, F., Zhang, W., Cassady, C.I.: Correlation between maternal meal and fetal motion during fetal MRI. Pediatr. Radiol. **49**(1), 46–50 (2019)

Atlas-Based Segmentation of the Human Embryo Using Deep Learning with Minimal Supervision

Wietske A. P. Bastiaansen[1,2(✉)], Melek Rousian[2], Régine P. M. Steegers-Theunissen[2], Wiro J. Niessen[1], Anton Koning[3], and Stefan Klein[1]

[1] Department of Radiology and Nuclear Medicine, Biomedical Imaging Group Rotterdam, Erasmus MC, University Medical Center, Rotterdam, The Netherlands
[2] Department of Obstetrics and Gynecology, Erasmus MC, University Medical Center, Rotterdam, The Netherlands
[3] Department of Pathology, Erasmus MC, University Medical Center, Rotterdam, The Netherlands
w.bastiaansen@erasmusmc.nl

Abstract. We propose an atlas-based segmentation framework to achieve segmentation and spatial alignment of three-dimensional ultrasound images of the human embryo acquired during the first trimester of pregnancy. Our framework is based on deep learning with minimal supervision. The framework consists of two networks, one dedicated to learning an affine transformation and one dedicated to learning a nonrigid deformation. The affine registration network is trained in two stages, were the first stage is minimally supervised and the resulting transformation is refined in the second unsupervised stage. The nonrigid registration network is trained completely unsupervised and in one stage. The framework is trained, validated and tested on a dataset of ultrasound images of the human embryo acquired in the 9th week of pregnancy. We visually assessed the affine alignment, which was accurate in 77% of the images in the test set. For 14 out of 31 test images a manual segmentation was available and we achieved an average Dice similarity coefficient of 0.78. Therefore we conclude that our framework is a promising approach for segmentation and spatial alignment of the human embryo in three-dimensional ultrasound images with minimal supervision.

Keywords: Image registration · Segmentation · Alignment · Embryo · Ultrasound · Minimal supervision · Deep learning

1 Introduction

Nowadays there is an increasing interest in automatic analysis of prenatal ultrasound, since insight into this period is of crucial importance for current and future health and care [15]. Ultrasound is the most prominent tool used for

Y. Hu et al. (Eds.): ASMUS 2020/PIPPI 2020, LNCS 12437, pp. 211–221, 2020.
https://doi.org/10.1007/978-3-030-60334-2_21

prenatal screening and diagnostics, since it is noninvasive, real-time, safe, and has low cost compared to other imaging modalities [11]. However, first trimester ultrasound images present unique challenges for automatic analysis, such as low image quality, high variability of positions and orientations of the embryo, and the presence of the umbilical cord, placenta, and uterine wall. As a first step towards automatic analysis of first trimester ultrasound, we propose an atlas-based segmentation framework to achieve both segmentation and spatial alignment of the human embryo using deep learning with minimal supervision.

Many published studies focus on performing spatial alignment and segmentation separately; for a comprehensive overview see [16]. There are few studies focused on performing both tasks at once, using image registration techniques to achieve this [6,10,13]. Namburete et al. [13] developed a supervised multi-task deep learning approach for ultrasound images acquired between 22 and 30 weeks gestational age (GA), using knowledge of the orientation of the head, slice annotations, and manual segmentations. Chen et al. [6] used spatial features from eye detection to register and segment the head of fetuses of 19 till 22 week GA. Kuklisova-Murgasova et al. [10] used a MRI atlas and block matching to register ultrasound images of fetuses of 23 till 28 week GA. All work published until now focuses on ultrasound images acquired during the second or third trimester. Furthermore, these studies rely on the availability of a voxelwise ground truth in a large training set. This can be problematic since such a voxelwise ground truth is often not available and can be very laborious to obtain.

In line with the aforementioned studies, we also use image registration techniques. Recently, deep learning methods for image registration have been developed; for an extensive overview see [5]. In Bastiaansen et al. [4], we proposed an unsupervised deep learning approach (inspired by [3]) for atlas-based segmentation and spatial alignment of three-dimensional (3D) first trimester ultrasound images, using two separate networks for learning the affine and nonrigid deformations. Boveiri et al. [5] point out that for more challenging problems supervision using landmarks is often needed. As pointed out by Hu et al. [8], using landmarks offers a flexible framework to add minimal supervision. Here, we extended our previous work by training the networks sequentially instead of end-to-end, and adding a minimally supervised training stage using landmarks to initialize the network for affine registration. The crown and rump landmarks of the embryo are used, since the crown-rump length is relatively easy to obtain and well known in prenatal imaging [14]. Our main contribution is the development of a flexible framework for segmentation and alignment of challenging imaging datasets, such as (but not limited to) 3D ultrasound images of the human embryo in the first trimester of pregnancy.

2 Method

Framework. Let A be the atlas defined in the 3D domain $\Omega \subset \mathbb{R}^3$ and I, the image to be registered and segmented, henceforth called moving image defined in $\Omega \subset \mathbb{R}^3$. Assume both images contain single-channel gray scale data.

Furthermore, assume that the atlas A is in a standard orientation and the segmentation S_A is available. Now, our aim is to find a deformation ϕ such that:

$$A(x) \approx I(\phi(x)) \quad \forall x \in \Omega. \tag{1}$$

The deformation ϕ consists of an affine transformation ϕ_a and a nonrigid deformation ϕ_d, such that:

$$\phi(x) := \phi_a \circ \phi_d(x). \tag{2}$$

ϕ_a and ϕ_d are obtained using a convolutional neural network (CNN) to model the function g_θ: $(\phi_a, \phi_d) = g_\theta(I, A)$, with θ the network parameters. The affine transformation ϕ_a is learned as a 12-dimensional vector containing the coefficients of part of the affine transformation matrix $T \in \mathbb{R}^{4\times 4}$. The voxelwise nonrigid deformation is defined as a displacement field $u(x)$ with $\phi_d := x + u(x)$.

Training Strategy. In Fig. 1 an overview of our framework can be found. Our framework consists of two networks, one dedicated to learning an affine transformation and the other to learning a nonrigid deformation.

The input of the affine registration network is the atlas A and moving image I. During the first training stage the coordinates of the crown and rump landmarks are given, where x_c^A, x_c^I are the coordinates of the crown landmark, x_r^A and x_r^I the coordinates of the rump landmark, of the atlas A and respectively moving image I. After the first stage of training, the affine registration network gives as output the estimated affine transformation ϕ_a and the (roughly) affinely registered image $I(\phi_a(x))$.

During the second stage of training, the input is again the atlas A together with the (original) moving image I. The weights θ_{affine} learned in the first stage are used as initialization of the network. The result of the first stage is refined in a unsupervised manner, by minimizing the loss function based on similarity between the atlas and affinely registered image and the regularity of the affine transformation.

The input of the nonrigid registration network is an affinely registered image $I_{\phi_a(x)} := I(\phi_a(x))$ together with atlas A. Images that were not affinely aligned by the affine registration network are not expected to contribute to learning the nonrigid alignment. Therefore, before training the nonrigid registration network, we visually assess which images are correctly affinely aligned with the atlas; and these images are used for training. The output of the network consists of ϕ_d, along with the registered image $I(\phi_a \circ \phi_d(x))$. We call the weights of the nonrigid registration network θ_{nonrigid}.

Using ϕ_a and ϕ_d we can then obtain a segmentation of the moving image, by transforming the segmentation of the atlas image:

$$S_I(x) := S_A(\phi_d^{-1} \circ \phi_a^{-1}(x)). \tag{3}$$

Note that no ground truth deformations or segmentations are used for training; only two landmarks are used to guide the training in the first stage of the affine registration network. After training, a new image I, without annotated landmarks, can be given directly to both networks, together with the atlas, to obtain the registration in one go.

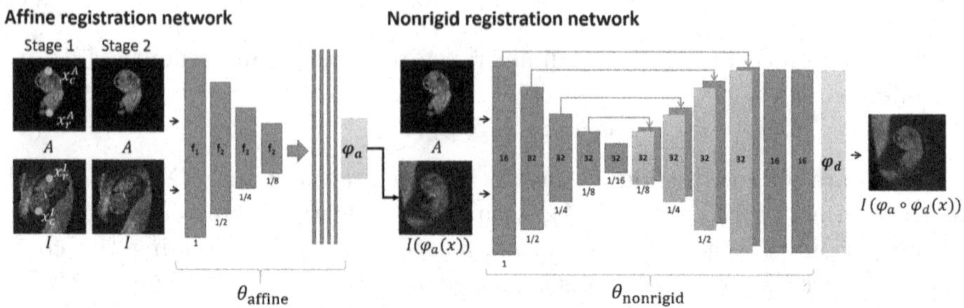

Fig. 1. Architecture of our framework. The affine registration network takes A and I as input and outputs ϕ_a. This network is trained in two stages. The first stage uses the crown and rump landmarks and the second stage uses θ_{affine} as initialization and refines the result. The nonrigid registration framework takes A and $I(\phi_a(x))$ as input and outputs ϕ_d.

Network Architecture. The affine registration network consists of an encoder, with convolutional layers with a stride of 2, where the images are down-sampled, followed by a global average pooling layer. The number of filters (f_1, f_2) in this encoder was varied during the experiments. The global average pooling layer gives as output one feature per feature map, which forces the network to encode position and orientation globally, followed by four fully connected layers with 1000 neurons and ReLu activation. The output layer consists of the entries of the affine transformation matrix T.

The architecture of the nonrigid registration network is the same as Voxelmorph [3] and consists of an encoder, again with convolutional layers with a stride of 2, a decoder with convolutional layers with a stride of 1, skip-connections, and an up-sampling layer. This is followed by convolutional layers at full resolution. The output layer contains the dense displacement field $u(x)$. In both networks, all convolutional layers have a kernel size of 3 and have a LeakyReLU activation with parameter 0.2.

Loss Function. In this section the loss function for each network and training stage is described per moving image I given to the network.

The loss function for the first training stage of the affine registration network is defined as:

$$\mathcal{L}\left(A, I, \phi_a, x^A, x^I\right) = \mathcal{L}_{\text{sim}}\left(A, I\left(\phi_a(x)\right)\right) + \lambda_l \mathcal{L}_{\text{landmark}}\left(\phi_a\left(x^A\right), x^I\right), \quad (4)$$

with x^A the coordinates of the landmarks in the A; and x^I in I. The first term of the loss function promotes similarity between the moving image after alignment and the atlas. The similarity loss is only calculated within the segmentation S_A, since there are other objects in the 3D ultrasound images besides the embryo. $\mathcal{L}_{\text{sim}}$ is chosen as the masked local (squared) normalized cross-correlation (NCC), which is defined as follows:

$$\text{NCC}(A,Y) = \frac{1}{M}\sum_{p\in\Omega} S_A(p)\frac{\left(\sum_q [A(q)-\bar{A}(p)][Y(q)-\bar{Y}(p)]\right)^2}{\left(\sum_q [A(q)-\bar{A}(p)]^2\right)\left(\sum_q [Y(q)-\bar{Y}(p)]^2\right)}, \quad (5)$$

with $Y = S_A(x)\cdot I(x)$, M is the number of nonzero elements in S_A, $\bar{A}$ (and $\bar{Y}$ similarly) denote: $\bar{A}(p) = A(p) - \frac{1}{j^3}\sum_q A(q)$, where q iterates over a j^3 volume around $p \in \Omega$ with $j = 9$ as in [3].

The second term minimizes the distance between the landmarks after registration and is defined as:

$$\mathcal{L}_{\text{landmark}}\left(\phi_a\left(x^A\right), x^I\right) = \frac{1}{n}\sum_{i=1}^{n}\left(x_i^I - \phi_a\left(x_i^A\right)\right)^2, \quad (6)$$

with n the number of annotated landmarks, with $n = 2$ in our case.

$$\mathcal{L}(A, I, \phi_a) = \mathcal{L}_{\text{sim}}\left(A, I\left(\phi_a(x)\right)\right) + \lambda_s \mathcal{L}_{\text{scaling}}\left(\phi_a(x)\right), \quad (7)$$

where $\mathcal{L}_{\text{sim}} = \text{NCC}(A, I(\phi_a(x)))$ as defined in Eq. (5). When objects in the background are present, penalizing extreme zooming is beneficial, as we showed in [4]. $\mathcal{L}_{\text{scaling}}$ is defined as:

$$\mathcal{L}_{\text{scaling}}\left(\phi_a\right) = \sum_{d=1}^{3}\log(s_d)^2, \quad (8)$$

following [2], with s_d the scaling factors of ϕ_a obtained using the Singular Value Decomposition.

The loss function for the nonrigid registration network is:

$$\mathcal{L}(A, I_{\phi_a}, \phi_d) = \mathcal{L}_{\text{sim}}\left(A, I_{\phi_a}\left(\phi_d(x)\right)\right) + \lambda_{\text{d}}\mathcal{L}_{\text{diffusion}}\left(\phi_d\right), \quad (9)$$

where $I_{\phi_a(x)} := I(\phi_a(x))$ is the output of the first network. $\mathcal{L}_{\text{sim}}$ is again defined as the NCC in Eq. 5.

Finally $\phi_d(x) = x + u(x)$ is regularized by:

$$\mathcal{L}_{\text{diffusion}}\left(\phi_d\right) = \frac{1}{|\Omega|}\sum_{p\in\Omega}\|\nabla u(p)\|^2, \quad (10)$$

with $|\Omega|$ the number of voxels in Ω. This loss term penalizes local spatial variations in ϕ_d to promote smooth local deformations [3].

Implementation. The framework is implemented using Keras [7] with Tensorflow backend [1]. The ADAM optimizer is used with a learning rate of 10^{-4}, as in [3]. For the second training stage of the affine registration network, we lower the learning rate to 10^{-5}, since the network has already largely converged in the first stage. By default we use 1000 epochs per stage with a batch size of one. Finally, ϕ_a^{-1} in Eq. (3) is calculated by inverting the matrix T and ϕ_d^{-1} in Eq. (3) is calculated using the Invert Displacement Field module of SimpleITK [12].

3 Data

The Rotterdam Periconceptional Cohort (Predict study) is a large hospital-based cohort study, conducted at the Erasmus, University Medical Center Rotterdam, the Netherlands. This prospective cohort focuses on the relationships between periconceptional maternal and paternal health and embryonic and fetal growth and development [15]. Between 6 and 13 weeks GA, 3D ultrasound images are acquired. The embryo develops rapidly during this period; therefore, as first a proof of concept, we only use data acquired in the 9th week of pregnancy.

The image chosen as atlas was put in a standard orientation and the embryo was manual segmented using virtual reality techniques [14]. There were 2239 3D ultrasound images of 1028 pregnancies available, 2119 images of 969 pregnancies were used for training, 89 images of 44 pregnancies for validation, and 31 images of 15 pregnancies for testing. The crown and rump landmarks of the embryo were annotated manually. All images were padded with zeros and re-scaled to $64 \times 64 \times 64$ voxels to speed up training.

In some experiments data augmentation was applied. Each scan in the training set was affinely transformed 8 times. The affine transformation consisted of a random rotation $\theta_x, \theta_y, \theta_z \in [10, 350]$ degrees along each axis, translation $t_x, t_y, t_z \in [-5, 5]$ pixels, and anisotropic zooming $z_x, z_y, z_z \in [0.9, 1.1]$.

In the Predict study the embryonic volume is measured using virtual reality techniques to monitor growth and development of the embryo [14]. For 40 of the 44 pregnancies in the validation set the volume in cm^3, referred to as EV_{gt}, was available. For a small subset, corresponding segmentations were saved. We use these segmentation, referred to as S_I^{gt}, for evaluation. In the training set 56 (3% of set) manual segmentations were available, in the validation set 40 (45% of set) and in the test set 14 (45% of set).

4 Experiments and Evaluation Measures

Experiments. To validate our framework, the following experiments were done:

1. *Tuning hyperparameters of affine registration network:* We evaluated how to choose λ_l in Eq. (4), λ_s in Eq. (7), the number of filters (f_1,f_2) in the encoder, and the usage of data augmentation.
2. *Tuning hyperparameter of nonrigid registration network:* The value for λ_d in Eq. (9) was evaluated.

3. *In-depth evaluation of final result:* The best result found for the validation set in experiment 1 and 2 was evaluated in depth using the available ground truth segmentations and visual assessment.

Evaluation Measures Experiment in 1 and 2. We compute the mean Euclidean distance between the landmarks after registration for the affine registration network, for image I in the validation set:

$$\text{Error}_\text{l} := \frac{1}{n}\sum_{i=1}^{n} \left\|x_i^I - \phi_a\left(x_i^A\right)\right\|_2, \tag{11}$$

with n the number of landmarks. In our experiments $n = 2$.

Secondly, we report the absolute difference between the volume calculated from $S_A(\phi^{-1}(x))$, referred to as $EV(I)$, and EV_{gt}:

$$\text{Error}_\text{EV} := |EV(I) - EV_{\text{gt}}| \tag{12}$$

with $\phi^{-1} := \phi_a^{-1}(x)$ for the affine registration network and $\phi^{-1} := \phi_d^{-1} \circ \phi_a^{-1}(x)$ for the nonrigid registration network.

In the results the mean and standard deviation over all images I in the validation set are reported for both Error_l and Error_EV.

Evaluation Measures in Experiment 3. For the best result found in experiment 1 and 2 for the validation set, we analyze the results in more detail on the validation set, and on the previously unused test set. The quality of the affine registration is assessed visually, by giving the following score to all images:

0 not aligned with the atlas,
1 crown and rump landmarks aligned with the atlas,
2 embryo correctly aligned with the atlas.

To address the quality of the segmentations found by our framework, we report the Dice similarity coefficient between the available manual segmentations S_I^{gt} and $S_A(\phi_a^{-1}(x))$ and $S_A(\phi_d^{-1} \circ \phi_a^{-1}(x))$.

5 Results

Experiment 1. In Table 1 the results can be found. We saw that for $\lambda_l = 0.001$, the landmark error was high, which illustrates that minimal supervision using landmarks was beneficial. The results deteriorated if $\lambda_l = 1$, since then the image similarity term in Eq. (4) is neglected in the optimization. For both evaluation measures we found that using data augmentation in combination with $(f_1, f_2) = (64, 128)$ and $\lambda_l = 0.01$ gave the best results. For the second training stage we concluded from Table 1 that λ_s has minor influence on the results. Note that Error_l increased a bit during the second stage of training, which is to

Table 1. Results for experiment 1 and 2. Mean and standard deviation over the validation set are reported. The results of the selected hyperparameter configurations are shown in bold.

Hyperparameters				No augmentation		Augmentation	
λ_l	λ_s	λ_d	(f_1, f_2)	Error_l	Error_EV	Error_l	Error_EV
	Affine						
Stage 1							
0.001	–	–	16,32	18.70 (4.12)	2.14 (0.71)	–	–
0.01	–	–	16,32	15.31 (8.30)	1.52 (0.87)	11.51 (7.39)	1.20 (0.85)
0.1	–	–	16,32	15.68 (10.04)	1.39 (0.83)	16.72 (9.21)	1.43 (0.80)
1	–	–	16,32	18.27 (10.55)	1.57 (0.86)	–	–
0.01	–	–	32,64	14.64 (7.79)	1.51 (0.83)	12.73 (7.99)	1.26 (0.79)
0.01	–	–	64,128	15.85 (8.80)	1.48 (0.86)	**11.50 (7.57)**	**1.08 (0.79)**
0.01	–	–	128,256	15.19 (6.93)	1.64 (0.92)	14.59 (9.20)	1.33 (0.72)
Stage 2							
–	0	–	64,128	11.77 (7.49)	0.98 (0.75)	12.05 (7.86)	1.09 (0.78)
–	0.005	–	64,128	11.93 (7.69)	0.96 (0.71)	12.13 (8.27)	1.01 (0.76)
–	0.05	–	64,128	**11.88 (8.13)**	**0.93 (0.71)**	**12.50 (9.00)**	**0.89 (0.71)**
–	0.5	–	64,128	12.63 (8.57)	0.92 (0.67)	18.35 (11.98)	0.94 (0.89)
	Nonrigid						
–	–	7.5	–	–	1.24 (0.62)	–	1.16 (0.45)
–	–	75	–	–	**0.78 (0.63)**	–	0.80 (0.64)
–	–	750	–	–	0.83 (0.62)	–	0.84 (0.66)

be expected, since the manually annotated landmarks have a limited precision and only measure the alignment at two positions. The best results were found for $\lambda_s = 0.05$. From Table 1 it is not clear if using data augmentation gave better results. Hence outputs of both configurations were evaluated as input for the nonrigid registration network. Without data augmentation 76% of the training set and 79% of the validation was correctly affinely aligned; with data augmentation we found 77% and 73% respectively.

Experiment 2. We evaluated hyperparameter settings for the nonrigid registration network. In Table 1 we saw that the best result in terms of both evaluation measures was found using the input with no data augmentation, and setting $\lambda_d = 75$. Setting $\lambda_d = 750$ resulted in too low flexibility of the deformation field, setting $\lambda_d = 7.5$ resulted in irregular deformation fields.

Experiment 3. Finally, we evaluated the performance of the best model in more detail. In Table 2 the result can be found. First of all note that the results for validation and test set were comparable. Furthermore, we saw that 77% of the test images were correctly affinely aligned with a mean Dice similarity coefficient of 0.71. After nonrigid alignment the mean Dice similarity coefficient became

0.78. Note that this was calculated only over images that were correctly affinely aligned, since the nonrigid registration network was only trained to register those images. Hence this number gives an impression of the performance over the correctly affinely aligned 77% of the test set. Figure 2 gives an impression of the results. The first two rows show successful segmentation and alignment. In the second row of the figure we observe the improved alignment between stage 1 and 2 of the affine registration network. The third row illustrates an unsuccessful case. The result of the affine registration failed, and the nonrigid registration network could not correct it.

Table 2. Results for experiment 3. Dice scores are only computed for images with correct affine registration. Standard deviation is reported between brackets.

		Training	Validation	Scores affine			Testing	Scores affine		
				0	1	2		0	1	2
Affine										
Stage 1	Correct	72%	67%	33%	51%	16%	77%	23%	48%	29%
	Dice	0.74 (0.10)	0.59 (0.14)				0.63(0.13)			
Stage 2	Correct	76%	79%	21%	52%	27%	77%	23%	42%	35%
	Dice	0.85 (0.10)	0.66 (0.11)				0.71 (0.10)			
Nonrigid	Dice	0.87 (0.10)	0.70 (0.12)	–	–	–	0.78 (0.09)	–	–	–

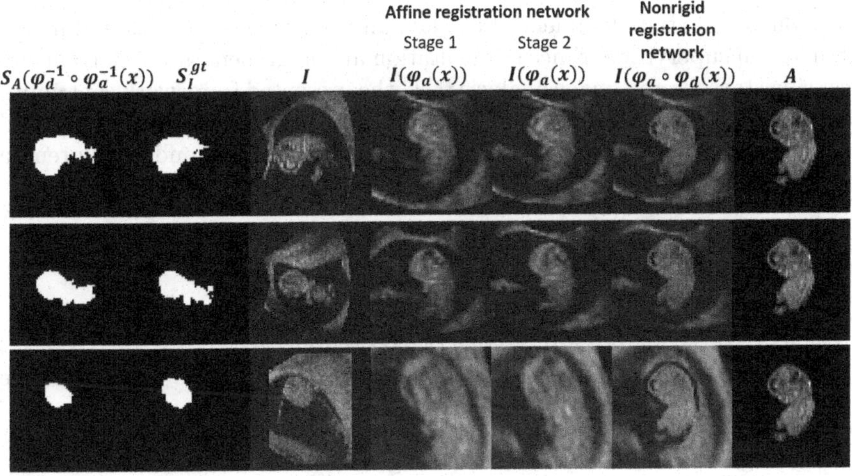

Fig. 2. Examples from the test set of results for the best model. For visualization only two-dimensional slices are shown. Dice similarity coefficient from top to bottom for $S_A(\phi_d^{-1} \circ \phi_a^{-1}(x))$ and S_I^{gt}: 0.89, 0.88, 0.52

6 Conclusion

We developed an atlas-based segmentation framework for 3D first trimester ultrasound images of the human embryo. Our framework consists of two networks, the first dedicated to learning an affine transformation and the second to learning a nonrigid deformation. Our framework is minimally supervised by using landmarks in the first training stage for the affine registration network. This resulting initial alignment is subsequently refined in the second unsupervised training stage. The nonrigid registration network is trained completely unsupervised. We used the crown and rump landmarks, but note that any landmark can be used. We trained the two networks for different hyperparameters and chose the best model based on the mean landmark error in Eq. (11) and mean absolute embryonic volume error in Eq. (12). The best model was studied in more detail using visual scoring and manual segmentations. For the test set we found that 77% of the images were affinely aligned with the atlas. We found a mean Dice similarity coefficient of 0.71 for $S_A(\phi_a^{-1}(x))$ and 0.78 for $S_A(\phi_d^{-1} \circ \phi_a^{-1}(x))$.

The main drawback of our current approach is that if affine registration fails, these images cannot be nonrigidly registered, since the nonrigid registration framework is not trained for this case. Moreover, small mistakes can propagate as well, see Fig. 2. To overcome this, we will explore multi-atlas segmentation [9]. It is well known that this leads to more robust results. Moreover, this technique could also be employed to make our framework applicable to the full first trimester, by adding atlases covering the entire period.

We conclude that the presented framework is a promising approach for segmentation and spatial alignment of the human embryo in 3D ultrasound images with minimal supervision. Since segmentation and alignment are important preprocessing steps for any image analysis task, the presented framework contributes to development of methods for automatic analysis of early prenatal ultrasound, which will stimulate further research onto the human embryo and early prenatal care.

References

1. Abadi, M., et al.: TensorFlow: large-scale machine learning on heterogeneous distributed systems (2016). http://arxiv.org/abs/1603.04467
2. Ashburner, J., et al.: Image registration using a symmetric prior- in three-dimensions. NeuroImage **9**, 212–225 (1999)
3. Balakrishnan, G., et al.: VoxelMorph: a learning framework for deformable medical image registration. IEEE Trans. Med. Imaging **38**(8), 1788–1800 (2019)
4. Bastiaansen, W.A.P., Rousian, M., Steegers-Theunissen, R.P.M., Niessen, W.J., Koning, A., Klein, S.: Towards segmentation and spatial alignment of the human embryonic brain using deep learning for atlas-based registration. In: Špiclin, Ž., McClelland, J., Kybic, J., Goksel, O. (eds.) WBIR 2020. LNCS, vol. 12120, pp. 34–43. Springer, Cham (2020). https://doi.org/10.1007/978-3-030-50120-4_4
5. Boveiri, H.R., et al.: Medical image registration using deep neural networks: a comprehensive review (2020). http://arxiv.org/abs/2002.03401

6. Chen, H., et al.: Registration-based segmentation of three-dimensional ultrasound images for quantitative measurement of fetal craniofacial structure. US Med. Biol. **38**(5), 811–823 (2012)
7. Chollet, F., et al. https://github.com/keras-team/keras (2015)
8. Hu, Y., et al.: Weakly-supervised convolutional neural networks for multimodal image registration. Med. Image Anal. **49**, 1–13 (2018)
9. Iglesias, J.E., et al.: Multi-atlas segmentation of biomedical images: a survey. Med. Image Anal. **24**(1), 205–219 (2015)
10. Kuklisova-Murgasova, M., et al.: Registration of 3D fetal neurosonography and MRI. Med. Image Anal. **17**(8), 1137–1150 (2013)
11. Liu, S., et al.: Deep learning in medical ultrasound analysis: a review. Engineering **5**(2), 261–275 (2019)
12. Lowekamp, B., et al.: The design of SimpleITK. Front. Neuroinform. **7**, 45 (2013)
13. Namburete, A., et al.: Fully-automated alignment of 3D fetal brain ultrasound to a canonical reference space using multi-task learning. Med. Image Anal. **46**, 1–14 (2018)
14. Rousian, M., et al.: Virtual reality imaging techniques in the study of embryonic and early placental health. Placenta **64**, S29–S35 (2018)
15. Steegers-Theunissen, R., et al.: Cohort profile: the Rotterdam periconceptional cohort (predict study). Int. J. Epidemiol. **45**, 374–381 (2016)
16. Torrents-Barrena, J., et al.: Segmentation and classification in MRI and US fetal imaging: recent trends and future prospects. Med. Image Anal. **51**, 61–88 (2019)

Deformable Slice-to-Volume Registration for Reconstruction of Quantitative T2* Placental and Fetal MRI

Alena Uus[1(✉)], Johannes K. Steinweg[1], Alison Ho[2], Laurence H. Jackson[1], Joseph V. Hajnal[1], Mary A. Rutherford[1], Maria Deprez[1], and Jana Hutter[1]

[1] School of Imaging Sciences and Biomedical Engineering, King's College London, St. Thomas' Hospital, London SE1 7EH, UK
alena.uus@kcl.ac.uk

[2] Academic Women's Health Department, King's College London, London, UK

Abstract. In 4D T2* placental MRI studies, motion correction is generally considered a prerequisite for quantitative analysis. However, the existing approaches use only global spatio-temporal alignment based on the classical 3D nonrigid registration and do not correct inter-slice motion. Alignment of T2* and T2 volumes in one reference space could also address the limitation of low resolution of T2* stacks and allow analysis of finer anatomical features. This work introduces a novel pipeline for motion correction in 4D T2* and 3D T2*+T2 placental MRI datasets based on the deformable slice-to-volume registration (DSVR) method. The pipelines are evaluated on 60 T2* placental MRI datasets.

Keywords: Motion correction · Placental and fetal MRI · Deformable slice-to-volume registration · Multi-modal reconstruction

1 Introduction

T2*-weighted MRI is widely used for placental studies and is now starting to emerge as a promising clinical test for placental dysfunction [15]. It includes individual T2* volumes and longer time series, often while medical oxygen is administered to evaluate the dynamics of the placenta. These acquisitions are; however, typically affected by maternal respiratory and fetal motion leading to the loss of structural continuity between consecutive 2D slices and/or 3D dynamics in time. Therefore, post-processing motion correction based on spatio-temporal alignment is generally considered a prerequisite for quantitative analysis.

The recent T2* and diffusion placental MRI studies have been routinely employing classical 3D nonrigid registration methods for alignment of all dynamics in 4D time series [4,6,11,18] or multi-modal 5D [5,12] volumes to a common template space. Outlier rejection methods for exclusion of motion corrupted 3D

M. Deprez and J. Hutter—Maria Deprez and Jana Hutter are co-senior authors.

Y. Hu et al. (Eds.): ASMUS 2020/PIPPI 2020, LNCS 12437, pp. 222–232, 2020.
https://doi.org/10.1007/978-3-030-60334-2_22

dynamics (e.g., affected by contractions) and correction of signal nonuniformities are another essential post-processing steps [17]. In [10], the template-based registration was extended with a temporal model while [17] proposed to divide dynamics into subvolumes based on interleaved slice acquisition model. In [6], registration was guided by one T2* echo with the highest contrast for structural features. There are also two approaches to the definition of a reference space: generation of a template from multiple dynamics [5] or selection of the dynamic with the highest similarity to the rest [18]. More recently, model-driven registration for placental diffusion MRI was proposed in [3]. However, the challenge of correction of through plane inter-slice motion in T2* volumes remains open.

In [7], a pipeline for reconstruction of 4D MRI respiration-resolved volumes of placenta was proposed for SWEEP acquisitions. The challenge of reconstruction of 3D isotropic volumes of placenta from multiple T2 stacks acquired under different orientations was addressed by using rigid slice-to-volume registration (SVR) [8] in [16], rigid patch-to-volume registration (PVR) [2] and deformable SVR (DSVR) [19] methods. In [9], non-rigid registration with Laplacian constraint in combination with SVR was used for distortion correction in fetal brain EPI and reconstruction in T2 space. Furthermore, placenta flattening techniques were employed to achieve a representation in a common space [1,13].

In addition to the analysis of mean placental T2*, spatially resolved analysis techniques are emerging to study placental heterogeneity. These however require more detailed anatomical information to localize (e.g., the cord insertion, vasculature), which are limited on the T2* maps due to the inherently lower resolution. Spatially co-registered higher resolution T2 and T2* scans would be an important step towards more detailed insights into placental function.

Contributions

This work introduces a novel pipeline for motion-correction of quantitaive 3D T2*+T2 and 4D T2* placental and fetal MRI based on the DSVR method [19] designed for motion correction for fetal body and placenta in T2-weighted MRI. The main new elements include: template-guided DSVR reconstruction, decoupling of fetal and maternal motion, multi-channel reconstruction for T2* volumes (DSVR guided by a specific echo) and reconstruction of 4D series.

The proposed multi-modal template-based DSVR pipeline with decoupled fetal and maternal motion allows reconstruction of the entire uterus with isotropic 3D T2* maps in the space of T2w volumes that can be reoriented in any plane. For 4D T2* datasets, DSVR reconstruction of all dynamics in the template space with correction of through-plane inter-slice motion showed to improve the consistency of quantitative evaluation of changes of local T2* values in time and thus constitutes an important steps towards studies of placental dynamics.

The pipeline was evaluated on 60 placental and fetal MRI datasets.

2 Methods

2.1 Datasets, Acquisition and Pre-processing

This study employed data acquired under the Placental Imaging Project (PIP, REC 14/LO/1169)[1]and the CARdiac and Placental Project (CARP, REC 19/LO/0852)[2] including 20 3D T2+T2* datasets and 40 4D T2* datasets. The acquisitions were performed on a clinical 1.5T Ingenia scanner (Philips, Best, The Netherlands) with a 28-channel torso coil. The mothers were scanned in supine position at 20 + 2–36 + 3 weeks GA with the scan time not exceeding 60minutes in two blocks of 30minutes. Structural T2-weighted Turbo Spin Echo acquisitions and Single-shot Multi-Echo Gradient Echo acquisitions were performed. The T2-weighted datasets were acquired in four different orientations, the parameters include (TE = 100 ms, resolution = 1.25 mm, slice thickness = 2.5 mm) The quantitative T2* datasets (TE = [7–160] ms, TR = [8–14] s, resolution = 2.5 mm isotropic) included 3D datasets and 4D datasets with 4 echoes and 30–80 dynamics. The T2 and T2* acquisitions were performed in a sequential order without global changes to the mother's position. T2* fitting was performed prior to motion correction and 3D masks of the placenta, fetal brain and body were manually drawn on the selected template stacks followed by label propagation.

The 4D T2* datasets were divided into 3 groups with respect to the severity of motion: 12 minor, 14 moderate and 14 severe motion cases. The motion was estimated similarly to the approach used in [19] in terms of normalised cross-correlation (NCC) between adjacent slices NCC between adjacent 3D dynamics and NCC with a 3D template for the placenta ROI. Table 1 presents the average NCC values for minor, moderate and severe motion datasets. The primary causes of motion included maternal breathing and fetal movement. A proportion of 4D T2* datasets was also affected by uterine contraction motion.

Table 1. Assessment of motion corruption for 40 4D T2* datasets for placenta ROI: average adjacent slice NCC, NCC between the adjacent 3D dynamics and global NCC between the 3D dynamics and the template.

	Slice NCC	Adjacent NCC	Template NCC
Minor motion (12)	0.878 ± 0.035	0.860 ± 0.058	0.810 ± 0.044
Moderate motion (14)	0.849 ± 0.034	0.799 ± 0.078	0.732 ± 0.071
Severe motion (14)	0.820 ± 0.042	0.741 ± 0.076	0.622 ± 0.090

The assessment of motion corruption of 20 3D T2+T2* datasets in summarised in Table 2 in terms of adjacent slice NCC for fetal brain, trunk and placenta ROIs. It can be observed that the fetal brain is affected by more severe motion patterns in T2 stacks than the other two ROIs. While in T2* stacks, the structural continuity between slices is preserved and is similar for all ROIs.

[1] PIP project: https://placentaimagingproject.org.

[2] CARP project: https://heartmeetsplacenta.org.

Table 2. Assessment of motion corruption for 20 3D T2+T2* datasets: adjacent slice NCC for fetal brain, trunk and placenta ROIs.

Metric	Fetal brain	Fetal trunk	Placenta
T2 stacks: slice NCC	0.438 ± 0.082	0.519 ± 0.083	0.499 ± 0.096
T2* stacks: slice NCC	0.624 ± 0.074	0.621 ± 0.058	0.631 ± 0.088

2.2 Motion Correction for Multimodal 3D Datasets

The proposed pipeline for 3D multi-modal reconstruction of T2+T2* volumes is shown in Fig. 1. Following selection of a T2 template stack $S^{T2}_{template}$, three masks defining the global regions of the fetal body, head and placenta are used for splitting the rest of the N T2 stacks into smaller ROIs $\{S^{T2}_i\}$ (including the background). This effectively decouples the motion patters of different objects. E.g., placenta is affected by breathing motion and shape deformations, the brain undergoes only rigid transformations while trunk is also affected by bending (see Table 2). The template stack is not decoupled. Then, the 3D T2 volume X^{T2} of the entire uterus is reconstructed following the standard DSVR pipeline with $S^{T2}_{template}$ as a reference.

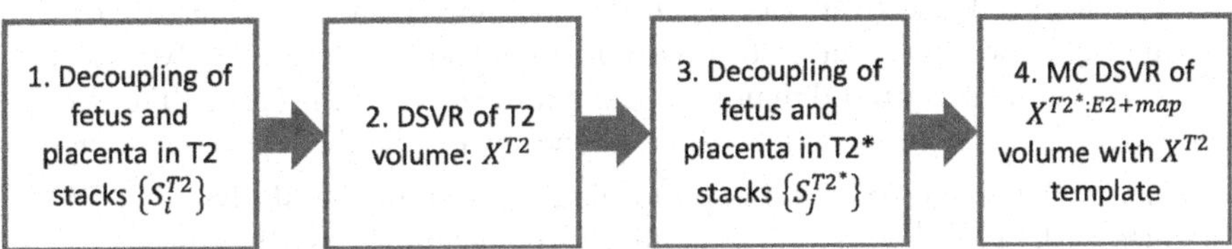

Fig. 1. The proposed MC DSVR pipeline for 3D T2+T2* reconstruction of the uterus.

The input T2* stacks consist of five channels: four echoes and the corresponding fitted T2* map. At first, the T2* stacks are decoupled into a subset $\{S^{T2*}_j\}$ using rigid propagation of the original global ROI masks. Similarly to the single T2* echo-guided registration approach in [6], the DSVR reconstruction of the T2* volume is based on using only the second echo (E2) channel ($\{S^{T2*:E2}_j\}$) for guiding registrations. It has the higher similarity with the contrast of the T2 X^{T2} volume used as a template for the first iteration. The slice-to-volume transformations are then transferred to the channel with T2* fitted map slices from $\{S^{T2*:map}_j\}$. We use NMI similarity metric for all registration steps and don't apply intensity matching from the original SVR pipeline [8,19] in order to avoid changes to quantitative data. The output multi-channel (MC) X^{T2*} volume includes E2 and fitted T2* map components. In addition, we employ global 3D free-form deformation (FFD) [14] registration of the reconstructed $X^{T2*:E2+map}$ volume to X^{T2} for correction of any remaining misalignments.

2.3 Motion Correction for 4D Datasets

The pipeline for 4D T2* MC DSVR reconstruction (Fig. 2) is also driven only by the second echo (E2) since it has the highest contrast for structural features and then the output stack and slice transformation from $\{S_i^{T2*:E2}\}$ are automatically propagated to the fitted T2* map $\{S_i^{T2*:map}\}$ channel.

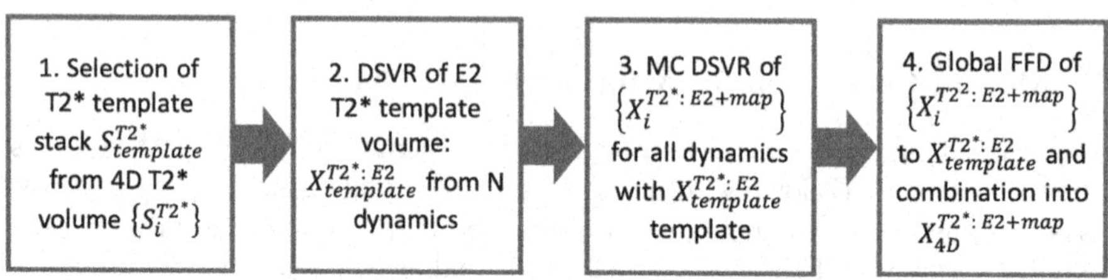

Fig. 2. The proposed MC DSVR pipeline for reconstruction of 4D T2* series.

At first, a template T2* volume ($X_{template}^{T2*:E2}$) is reconstructed from a subset of N (e.g., 6) stacks $\{S_i^{T2*} : E2\}$ adjacent to the selected dynamic volume using the classical DSVR method without intensity matching. Similarly to the approach used in [18], it was identified experimentally that the template dynamic $S_{template}^{T2*:E2}$ should be selected based on the highest global similarity with the rest of the dynamics and the lowest inter-slice motion corruption. In this case, we selected the least motion corrupted dynamic in the middle of the time series. The reconstructed $X_{template}^{T2*:E2}$ volume defines the reference space for the rest of the dynamics. Next, DSVR reconstruction is performed for each of the 3D $\{S_i^{T2*:E2+map}\}$ dynamics with $X_{template}^{T2*:E2}$ template similarly to the steps described in Sect. 2.2. We use only a single stack $S_i^{T2*:E2+map}$ for each reconstruction in order to preserve local T2* values. At the final step, additional global 3D FFD registration of reconstructed T2* dynamic volumes $\{X_i^{T2*:E2+map}\}$ to the T2* template is applied for additional correction of remaining misalignments and the outputs are combined into the 4D volume $X_{4D}^{T2*:E2+map}$.

2.4 Implementation Details

The proposed pipelines were implemented based on C++ SVRTK[3] MIRTK[4] -based package for motion correction in fetal MRI. We employ the main pipeline of DSVR method [19] with the additional implemented modules for multi-channel reconstruction, fetal/maternal decoupling, automated template stack selection, 4D alignment and optimisation for T2* reconstruction. The code is available online after as a part of SVRTK package. A typical reconstruction time for the entire uterus for 3D T2+T2* or 4D T2* can vary within 1–2 h depending on the system configuration, data resolution and the ROI size.

[3] SVRTK: https://github.com/SVRTK/SVRTK.
[4] MIRTK: https://github.com/BioMedIA/MIRTK.

3 Experiments and Results

3.1 Motion Correction for Multimodal 3D Datasets

Following the structure of the proposed pipeline, for each of the investigated 20 T2+T2* cases, T2 volumes of the entire uterus were reconstructed from four T2 $\{S_i^{T2}\}$ stacks decoupled into ROIs using DSVR with 1.25 mm output resolution. Next, the T2* volumes X^{T2*} were reconstructed in the X^{T2} template space with 1.85 mm isotropic resolution using the MC DSVR approach (Sect. 2.2).

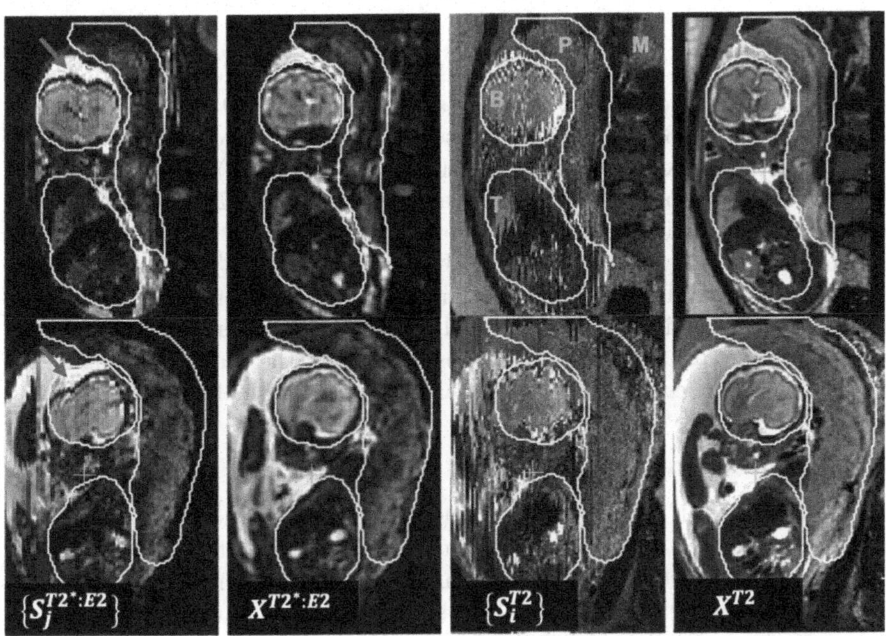

Fig. 3. An example of MC DSVR reconstruction of the entire uterus for a 3D T2+T2* dataset with decoupling of fetal and maternal motion: the original motion-corrupted $\{S_i^{T2*:E2}\}$ and $\{S_i^{T2}\}$ stacks with highlighted decoupling ROIs (M - maternal tissue, P - placenta, B - brain, T - trunk) and the corresponding reconstructed $X^{T2*:E2}$ and X^{T2} volumes (sagittal and coronal views). (Color figure online)

Figure 3 shows a typical example of DSVR reconstructed T2* volume $X^{T2*:E2}$ (2nd echo) and the corresponding X^{T2} template along with the examples of the original motion-corrupted $\{S_i^{T2}\}$ and $\{S_j^{T2*:E2}\}$ stacks with highlighted decoupling ROIs. In addition to the non-uniform ROI specific inter-slice misalignments in T2 stacks (see Table 2), there is a noticeable unrealistic change of the brain shape in the original T2* stack $\{S_E^{T2*:}2j\}$ (highlighted by the red arrow). These types of motion artefacts cannot be fully corrected by the non-rigid slice-to-volume registration of the whole region of interest.

Table 3. Quantitative assessment of motion correction for 20 3D T2+T2* datasets using T2 template-guided MC DSVR with (WD) and without (WTD) decoupling and classical 3D FFD registration. The metric is NCC between $X^{T2*:E3}$ and X^{T2}. The results are statistically significant with $p < 0.01$. The right column shows % difference in mean T2* values in the approximate fetal brain ROI before and after motion correction.

Method	T2 vs. T2*:E2 NCC	T2* diff [%]
3D FFD	0.401 ± 0.135	$1.435 \pm 1.003\%$
MC DSVR: WTD	0.429 ± 0.115	$2.407 \pm 1.906\%$
MC DSVR: WD	0.488 ± 0.090	$2.223 \pm 1.786\%$

The results of T2-guided T2* MC DSVR reconstructions of the entire uterus are compared to the original DSVR [19] and the classical 3D non-rigid registration (MIRTK-based 3D FFD [14]). We use NCC between the output T2 and T2* volumes for the masked placenta and fetus (trunk and brain) ROIs as a metric. Furthermore, we also assessed the difference in the mean T2* values measured for the approximate fetal brain ROI before and after motion correction. Table 3 summarises the analysis of the results. It shows that using T2 template-based T2* MC DSVR and ROI decoupling improves the T2-T2* correlation while preserving quantitative information (<5% difference). The differences in the mean brain T2* values are caused by the changed shape of the brain after alignment to T2, while the reference value was measured in the original T2* space.

3.2 Motion Correction for 4D Datasets

The proposed 4D MC DSVR pipeline was used for reconstruction of 40 4D T2* datasets (with 30–80 dynamics) to 1.85 mm isotropic resolution. We compared the proposed 4D reconstruction to 3D nonrigid registration of dynamics to a template (in our case MIRTK FFD [14]) since it has been routinely employed in the recent placental MRI studies [4,6,12,18]. We used the isotropic 3D template obtained from the 4D MC DSVR pipeline as the target for FFD registration.

An example of the processing outputs for one of the severe motion 4D T2* datasets with 80 dynamics is given Fig. 4. It shows temporal profiles in the placenta ROI of the original and 3D FFD and MC DSVR motion corrected volumes together with mean T2* and Jacobian values computed in the placenta ROI. This dataset was affected by a severe contraction (around t = [10; 40] s) and while 3D FFD corrected the global displacement of the 3D dynamics, the impact of inter-slice motion could not be resolved. Visual assessment shows that DSVR significantly improves the consistency of the volume in 4D. The higher mean Jacobian values during the contraction are expected due to the reduction in the volume and the lower T2* values due to the reduced inflow of oxygenated blood [18]. Both 3D FFD and MC DSVR showed similar T2* trends.

The consistency of the output 4D volumes is evaluated for the masked placenta ROI in terms of NCC between the reconstructed T2* E2 template and motion corrected E2 dynamics and NCC between the adjacent dynamics. In

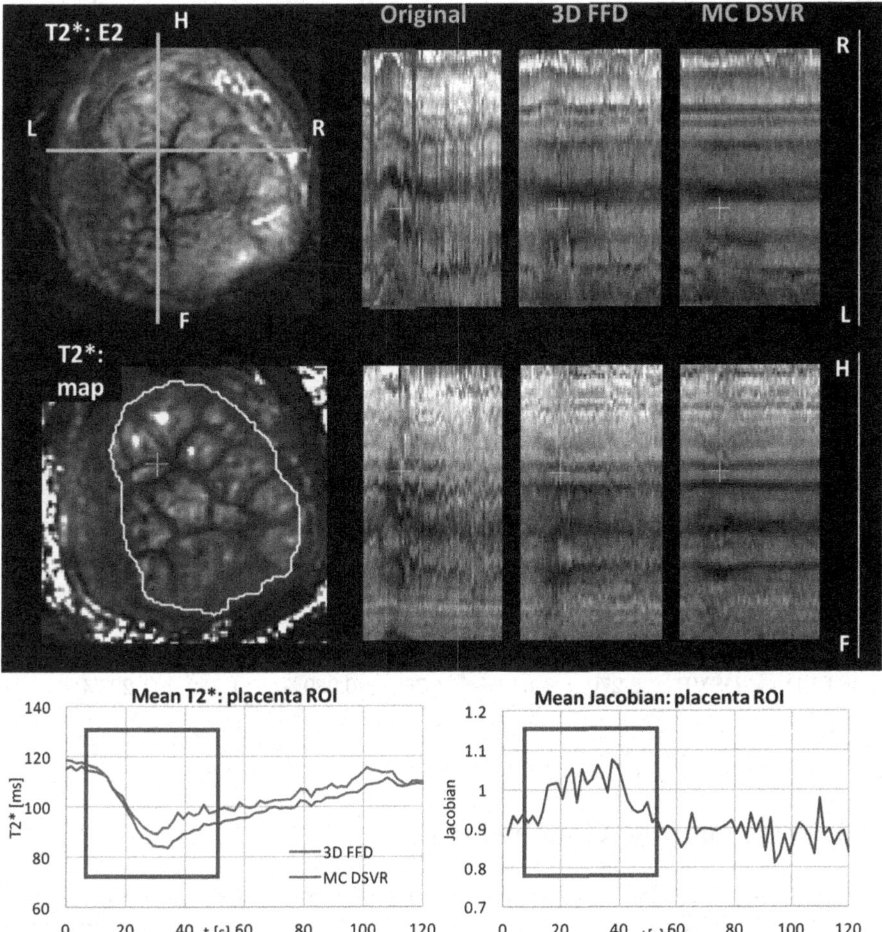

Fig. 4. An example of MC DSVR reconstruction for motion correction of a 4D T2* dataset with 80 dynamics affected by uterine contraction (around t = [10; 40] s time period - highlighted by red). The original 4D T2* (E2) and motion corrected volumes using 3D FFD and MC DSVR are shown as HF and RL profiles along the selected planes shown in the 2D view. The graphs demonstrate mean T2* and Jacobian values of global transformations between the dynamics and the template measured in the masked 3D placenta ROI vs. acquisition time. (Color figure online)

addition, in order to confirm that DSVR-reconstructed volumes result in similar quantitative T2* values as the 3D registration-based approach, we assessed the mean relative difference of T2* values computed for the same placental ROIs.

The results presented in Table 4 demonstrate that using the proposed DSVR-based pipeline improves the output image quality in terms of temporal consistency and shows <5% difference with the mean T2* values produced by the classical approach. Only a small proportion (<1%) of individual dynamics was affected by the larger differences (7–11%). This was caused by severely deformed shape of placenta that could not be resolved by 3D FFD registration.

Table 4. Quantitative assessment of MC DSVR vs. 3D FFD for 40 4D T2* datasets: mean NCC between $X_i^{T2*:E2}$ and $X_{template}^{T2*:E2}$ and mean NCC between the adjacent $X_i^{T2*:E2}$ and $X_{i+1}^{T2*:E2}$ dynamics in placenta ROI. The comparison results are statistically significant with $p < 0.01$. In addition, the last row shows the relative difference in mean placenta T2* values between 3D FFD and MC DSVR output 4D volumes.

Method	Minor motion	Moderate motion	Severe motion
Adjacent dynamic NCC			
3D FFD	0.906 ± 0.044	0.861 ± 0.066	0.813 ± 0.072
MC DSVR	0.938 ± 0.026	0.895 ± 0.052	0.871 ± 0.058
Template NCC			
3D FFD	0.913 ± 0.029	0.872 ± 0.041	0.831 ± 0.055
MC DSVR	0.952 ± 0.019	0.916 ± 0.037	0.887 ± 0.047
Relative difference in mean T2 values in the placenta ROI*			
FFD vs. DSVR	2.270 ± 1.642%	1.780 ± 0.989%	1.752 ± 1.228%

4 Discussion and Conclusions

This work introduced a novel DSVR-based pipeline for motion correction and multi-modal reconstruction of quantitative 4D T2* and multi-modal T2*+T2w placental and fetal MRI. Unlike the existing 3D nonrigid registration-based approaches routinely used in placental MRI studies, DSVR-based reconstruction allows correction of through-plane inter-slice motion thus improving accuracy of T2* quantitative analysis for local features in isotropic 3D and 4D volumes.

The pipelines were evaluated on 60 placental MRI datasets. The reconstructed multi-modal 3D datasets of the whole uterus showed that MC DSVR with ROI-based decoupling of fetal and maternal motion improved correlation between T2 and T2* volumes while preserving quantitative information. For the 4D T2* datasets, DSVR reconstruction of all dynamics in the template space showed improved results in terms of consistency of volumetric information in comparison to the classical registration-based approach. Furthermore, the structural consistency of isotropic reconstructed volumes facilitates 3D segmentation.

Our future work will focus on incorporation of model-based ROI-specific deformation constrains into registration for correction of large deformations.

Acknowledgments. We thank everyone who was involved in acquisition of the datasets and all participating mothers. This work was supported by the NIH (Human Placenta Project–grant 1U01HD087202-01), Welcome Trust Sir Henry Wellcome Fellowship (201374/Z/16/Z and 201374/Z/16/B), Wellcome-EPSRC Center for Medical Engineering, the NIHR Clinical Research Facility (CRF) at Guy's and St Thomas' and by the National Institute for Health Research Biomedical Research Centre based at Guy's and St Thomas' NHS Foundation Trust and King's College London. The views expressed are those of the authors and not necessarily those of the NHS, the NIHR or the Department of Health.

References

1. Abulnaga, S.M., Abaci Turk, E., Bessmeltsev, M., Grant, P.E., Solomon, J., Golland, P.: Placental Flattening via Volumetric Parameterization. In: Shen, D., et al. (eds.) MICCAI 2019. LNCS, vol. 11767, pp. 39–47. Springer, Cham (2019). https://doi.org/10.1007/978-3-030-32251-9_5
2. Alansary, A., et al.: PVR: patch-to-volume reconstruction for large area motion correction of fetal MRI. IEEE TMI **36**(10), 2031–2044 (2017)
3. Flouri, D., et al.: Improved fetal blood oxygenation and placental estimated measurements of diffusion-weighted MRI using data-driven Bayesian modeling. MRM **83**, 2160–2172 (2019)
4. Harteveld, A.A., et al.: Systematic evaluation of velocity-selective arterial spin labeling settings for placental perfusion measurement. MRM **84**, 1828–1843 (2020)
5. Hutter, J., et al.: Multi-modal functional MRI to explore placental function over gestation. MRM **81**(2), 1191–1204 (2019)
6. Hutter, J., et al.: Perfusion and apparent oxygenation in the human placenta (PERFOX). MRM **83**(2), 549–560 (2020)
7. Jackson, L.H., et al.: Respiration resolved imaging with continuous stable state 2D acquisition using linear frequency SWEEP. MRM **82**(5), 1631–1645 (2019)
8. Kuklisova-Murgasova, M., et al.: Reconstruction of fetal brain MRI with intensity matching and complete outlier removal. MediAN **16**(8), 1550–1564 (2012)
9. Kuklisova-Murgasova, M., et al.: Distortion correction in fetal EPI using non-rigid registration with a Laplacian constraint. IEEE TMI **37**(1), 12–19 (2018)
10. Liao, R., et al.: Temporal registration in in-utero volumetric MRI time series. MICCAI **9902**, 54–62 (2016)
11. Luo, J., et al.: In vivo quantification of placental insufficiency by BOLD MRI: a human study. Sci. Rep. **7**(1), 1–10 (2017)
12. Melbourne, A., et al.: Separating fetal and maternal placenta circulations using multiparametric MRI. MRM **81**(1), 350–361 (2019)
13. Miao, H., et al.: Placenta maps: in utero placental health assessment of the human fetus. IEEE TVCG **23**(6), 1612–1623 (2017)
14. Rueckert, D., et al.: Nonrigid registration using free-form deformations: application to breast MR images. IEEE TMI **18**(8), 712–721 (1999)
15. Sørensen, A., Hutter, J., Seed, M., Grant, P.E., Gowland, P.: T2*-weighted placental MRI: basic research tool or emerging clinical test for placental dysfunction? Ultrasound Obstet. Gynecol. **55**(3), 293–302 (2020)

16. Torrents-Barrena, J., et al.: Fully automatic 3D reconstruction of the placenta and its peripheral vasculature in intrauterine fetal MRI. MediAN **54**, 263–279 (2019)
17. Turk, E.A., et al.: Spatiotemporal alignment of in utero BOLD-MRI series. J. MRI **46**(2), 403–412 (2017)
18. Turk, E.A., et al.: Placental MRI: effect of maternal position and uterine contractions on placental BOLD MRI measurements. Placenta **95**, 69–77 (2020)
19. Uus, A., et al.: Deformable slice-to-volume registration for motion correction of fetal body and placenta MRI. IEEE TMI **39**, 2750–2759 (2020, in press)

A Smartphone-Based System for Real-Time Early Childhood Caries Diagnosis

Yipeng Zhang[1(✉)], Haofu Liao[1], Jin Xiao[2], Nisreen Al Jallad[2], Oriana Ly-Mapes[2], and Jiebo Luo[1]

[1] Department of Computer Science, University of Rochester, Rochester, USA
yzh232@u.rochester.edu

[2] Eastman Institute for Oral Health, University of Rochester Medical Center, Rochester, USA

Abstract. Early childhood caries (ECC) is the most common, yet preventable chronic disease in children under the age of 6. Treatments on severe ECC are extremely expensive and unaffordable for socioeconomically disadvantaged families. The identification of ECC in an early stage usually requires expertise in the field, and hence is often ignored by parents. Therefore, early prevention strategies and easy-to-adopt diagnosis techniques are desired. In this study, we propose a multistage deep learning-based system for cavity detection. We create a dataset containing RGB oral images labeled manually by dental practitioners. We then investigate the effectiveness of different deep learning models on the dataset. Furthermore, we integrate the deep learning system into an easy-to-use mobile application that can diagnose ECC from an early stage and provide real-time results to untrained users.

Keywords: Cavity diagnosis · Deep learning · Mobile deployment

1 Introduction

Early childhood caries (ECC) is defined as the presence of ≥1 decayed, missing (due to caries), or filled tooth surface in primary teeth in a child 71 months of age or younger [5]. ECC is by far the most common chronic childhood disease, with nearly 1.8 billion new cases per year globally [6,7,26]. In the US, it afflicts approximately 28% of children aged 2–5 years while disproportionately affecting up to 54% of low-income and minority children [6,18]. If not treated properly in time, the decay may become more severe, where usually a total oral rehabilitation treatment (TOR) under general anesthesia [13] with multiple tooth extractions and restorations/crowns is required, at a cost of nearly $7,000 per child (2009–2011 data) [20], leading to a USD 1.5 billion expense on the treatment per year in USA [27]. Further, almost 40% of children experience recurrent caries 6-month post TOR [3,9]. Untreated ECC often leads to higher risk of caries lesions in

Y. Hu et al. (Eds.): ASMUS 2020/PIPPI 2020, LNCS 12437, pp. 233–242, 2020.
https://doi.org/10.1007/978-3-030-60334-2_23

permanent teeth, diminished oral health-related quality of life, hospitalizations and emergency room visits due to systemic infection, and even death [2,4].

Continued use of these expensive restorative methods is a drain on the health care system. Despite years of clinical and research endeavors, the challenge remains, primarily due to the fact that, without training, it is hard for the general population to identify the disease from its appearance at its early stages. The current biomedical approach to control the ECC pandemic primarily focuses on individual-level restorative procedures rather than population-wide preventive strategies. Many US preschool children from low-income family often have poor access to pediatric dental services, leaving them in a situation that dental caries often are not diagnosed until at the late stages. Moreover, ECC is a multifactorial disease with host, microorganisms, diet and oral hygiene practice as the factors that determine the risks, children's caregivers need to be educated extensively about these risk factors that can be self-managed and altered in order to reduce children's risk for ECC.

In recent years, deep convolutional neural networks (CNN) have demonstrated supra-human level performance in many classification and object detection tasks [11,29]. Previous studies have also shown the efficacy of CNNs on the task of classifying dental caries on per-tooth periapical radiographs [14]. However, to the best of our knowledge, no deep learning-based method has been proposed for detecting dental caries from RGB images captured by regular cameras, as well as any suitable dataset for this task. In this study, we adopt an object detection approach. There are currently many one-stage object detection algorithms that are capable of performing fast, real-time inference while maintaining comparable accuracy [16,21] in company with light-weight feature extractor networks [17,23]. Multistage object detectors [22] with larger feature extractor networks [12,25] often yield better accuracy but require longer inference time. In this study, we compare the performance of selected frameworks on the cavity detection task.

The training of fully supervised object detection models requires a large amount of fully labeled image data. However, the collection of medical data is challenging considering the number of cases and sensitive information. Nevertheless, we collect 1,000 oral images to aid the training. We classify each tooth into 8 distinct categories and create a reasonably large-scale intraoral image dataset that includes the oral images with a total of 15,692 bounding boxes. All images in the dataset are annotated manually by dental practitioners. To account for the multifactorial nature of ECC, we propose a multistage deep learning-based diagnostic system that utilizes both analysis of user habits and symptoms and detection results from a cavity detector trained on our dataset. Further, we deploy the deep learning system onto Android devices to provide the highest ease of use. The deployed system provides caregivers, especially among the underserved population, a first-hand tool to detect early stages of ECC. The system also contains an interactive education module to provide caregivers extensive knowledge on ECC prevention. Experimental results demonstrate that the system proposed has the capability and potential to break the current ECC prevention deadlock.

In summary, our main contributions are four folds:

- We propose a multistage deep learning-based diagnostic method that employs both analysis of user habits and symptoms and detection results by a cavity detector trained on a large-scale expert-annotated intraoral image dataset.
- We integrate image capture assistance and automated image analysis into a streamlined process on Android devices to provide the highest ease of use to family caregivers who are untrained and not technology-savvy.
- We incorporate an interactive education module to provide family caregivers extensive knowledge on ECC prevention.
- We obtain experimental results to demonstrate that the entire smartphone-based system has the capability and potential to break the bottleneck in current ECC prevention.

2 Method

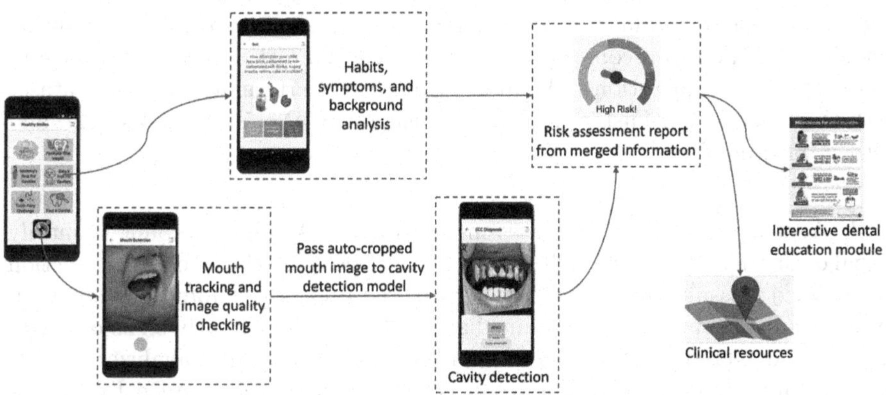

Fig. 1. Overview of the smartphone-based caries diagnosis system. Note that the interface pictures are actual screenshots from Android devices. (icon source: [1,19])

The proposed diagnostic system consists of two main modules: a 2-stage visual cavity detection module and a multifactorial analyzer module as shown in Fig. 1. The cavity detection module detects the visual signs of dental caries from a user-taken photo by a standard smartphone. The multifactorial analyzer module gathers information about the various factors that might affect the formation of caries, including the patient's habits, diet, and symptoms through interactive question answering and calculates the potential risk. Then, the risk assessment module takes into account results from both modules and generates an informative report. From there the user can choose to view the nearby certificated dentists' information and other clinical resources, or to enter an interactive education module that incorporates dental knowledge into a textual mini-game that aims to increase the family caregivers' knowledge about early signs and preventative methods of ECC.

Mouth Tracker. We deploy a real-time facial landmark detector to perform mouth tracking when the user is in the camera page. Based on the landmark points, our model visualizes a mouth bounding box and calculates the orientation of the mouth and quality of the image. The device will notify the user if the bounded mouth is not satisfactory for the following cavity detection (e.g. image quality is too low ($<224\times224$), mouth is tilted too much ($>5^\circ$), etc.). Otherwise, the user is prompted to take the photo. The mouth detected is then cropped and passed to the cavity detector.

Cavity Detector. We choose the Single Shot Multibox Detector (SSD) [16] using a MobileNetV2 backbone [23] as our cavity detection model. MobileNetV2 is an efficient CNN architecture that utilizes depth-wise separable convolutions to increase the speed of inference. This architecture is suitable for our task of performing real-time inference on smartphones, since those devices usually do not have very powerful computing hardware (e.g. GPUs) that we can utilize to accelerate tensor operations. We also compare its performance on our dataset with the much larger Faster R-CNN [22] using a ResNet50 backbone [12], and with trained dentists.

Risk Assessment. The risk assessment module takes into account primarily visual cavity detection results. If severe cavity (*level2*, see the Experiment section for detailed classification rules) is detected, the user is prompted to seek guidance from dental professionals immediately. If no cavity or early signs of cavity (*level1*) is detected, we take the result from the multifactorial analyzer module and inform the user as such. The result is based on the American Dental Association Caries Risk Assessment system [28]. We modify the elements in the system to accommodate the less health-literate individuals.

Education and Clinical Resources. We assembled a series of informative educational materials that provide appropriately timed information specific to pregnant women's oral health importance (as they may affect oral healthy conditions of the to-be-born child), children's tooth development, children's oral hygiene and diet recommendations. The educational information is built into forms of interactive mini-games like scored question answering, literacy bubble shooter, and son. We also provide a list of available dental clinics near the current location that accept dental insurance for low-income group (e.g. Medicaid).

Mobile Deployment. Our goal is to help the low-income families that have limited access to regular dental check-up. Therefore, we build the proposed deep learning system into an Android application in order to maximize both the coverage and accessibility. We use the light-weight SSD+MobileNetV2 model in the application for best user experience in real-time. Currently, the application functionality is successfully tested on Google Pixel 2 and OnePlus 5T with Android version $\geq$8.1. The deep learning models (mouth and cavity detector) perform inference at the speed of on the average 10 FPS on the tested devices.

3 Experiment

3.1 Dataset

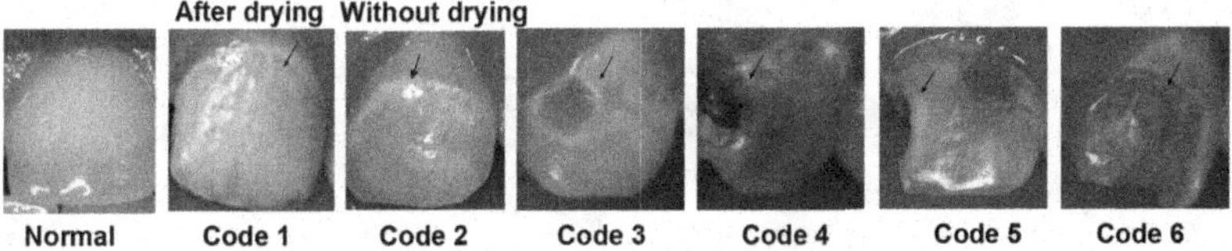

Fig. 2. Example images that demonstrate the ICDAS visual diagnostic criteria. Tooth hard surface is composed of the outer enamel and inner dentin layers. Codes 1 and 2 indicate the initiation of white spots on non-cavitated tooth enamel indicated by the arrows, with or without air-drying. Codes 3 and 4 indicate caries on cavitated tooth enamel. Code 4 reveals the gray shadow around and underneath the enamel. Codes 5 and 6 indicate caries involving dentin, with ascending extensiveness from 5 to 6.

We adopt the International Caries Diagnosis System (ICDAS) [10] as the reference on the severity of cavity. ICDAS is the gold standard caries diagnostic index for scoring caries severity and routinely used in caries research and epidemiological studies [24]. Following the criteria, we create the intraoral image dataset that consists of 1,000 fully labeled high resolution RGB oral images from consented patients, each containing around 15 tooth bounding boxes.

Our current work focuses on the anterior teeth since the anterior teeth erupt earlier than the posterior teeth and the maxillary anterior teeth are the most affected by ECC. Moreover, it is less technically challenging for parents to take front teeth photos using smartphones. Of the teeth photos in our dataset, 90% were obtained from children younger than 18 years of age, including 80% permanent anterior teeth and 10% primary anterior teeth. The enamel texture and shape of the permanent and primary teeth are similar, which do not introduce bias in caries detection and categorization using the ICDAS standard, whose categories are based on lesion color and size.

Besides the ICDAS categories, we add an *other* label to include human-imposed devices that block the teeth surface (e.g. braces, steel crowns). In total, there are 15,692 bounding boxes from 8 classes (numbers in the parentheses denote the number of each type in the dataset): *normal*(6,825), *code1*(0), *code2*(6,832), *code3*(990), *code4*(33), *code5*(382), *code6*(189), *other*(441). There are no tooth labeled as code 1 because code 1 requires drying of the tooth surface, which is not indicated by the image. Due to the similarity of codes 1 and 2, we labeled all the teeth with code 1 or 2 symptoms as code 2. The usage of this dataset can be generalized to general cavity diagnosis studies since the symptoms of childhood caries and caries at other ages are very similar.

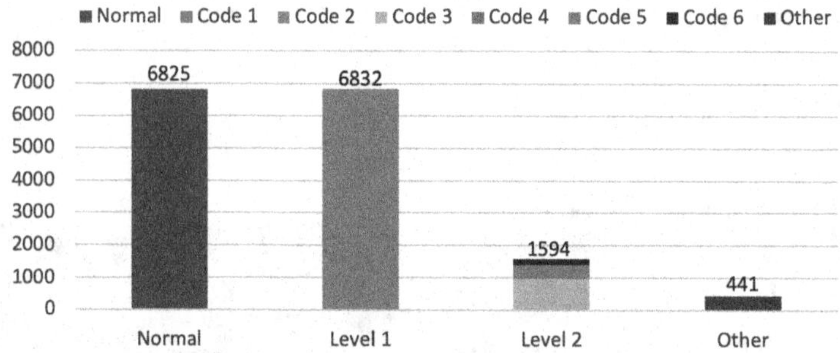

Fig. 3. Class distribution and the grouping schema of the intraoral dataset.

As shown in Fig. 2, most people are able to identify the cavity once the teeth surface starts to decay at code 3 and onward. However, it is challenging for the untrained general population to spot the cavity at codes 1 and 2. Therefore, in our task, it is sufficient to group codes 1 and 2 as category *level1* that consists of teeth at early stages of cavity, and codes 3–6 as category *level2* that consists of heavily cavitated teeth. The remaining 2 categories (*normal* and *other*) remain the same. The resulting distribution is shown in Fig. 3. We use the new 4-category dataset to train our object detection models and apply class weighting to deal with the imbalance.

3.2 Evaluation

We resize the images in our dataset to size 224 × 224 and split the dataset into training-validation set (80%) and test set (20%). We train both SSD and Faster R-CNN models using the SGD optimizer with a learning rate of $2e^{-4}$ and batch size of 8. The models are trained for 150 epochs of the training data. We evaluate the performance of the 2 models qualitatively and quantitatively. We also evaluate the performance of the deployed SSD-MobileNetV2 model with trained dentists.

Qualitative Comparison. Figure 4 shows the representative qualitative detection result comparison on the test set. We choose the images containing a wide

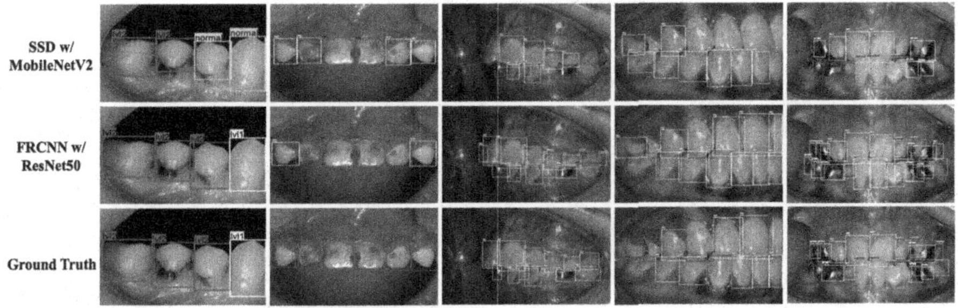

Fig. 4. Qualitative comparison between the cavity detection results by SSD and Faster R-CNN. Green boxes denote normal teeth; yellow boxes denote level 1 cavity; red boxes denote level 2 cavity; and white boxes denote human-imposed oral devices. (Color figure online)

Table 1. Quantitative detection results on our dataset (MSCOCO metrics).

	mAP	AP_{50}	AP_{75}	AR	Speed (ms)
SSD-MobileNetV2	0.303	0.522	0.320	0.562	22.45
Faster-RCNN-ResNet50	0.473	0.665	0.543	0.716	91.66

range of teeth categories to visualize the models' performance on all categories. It is clear that both models are able to correctly detect and classify most of the teeth in each image. We find the Faster R-CNN model performs significantly better than the SSD model; it successfully locates almost all the teeth and the misclassified teeth are sometimes those that are ambiguous in terms of severity levels. This is possible due to the different lighting conditions of the images. For example, the white spots in the signal *level1* cavity class can be caused by flashlight from the camera. We observe that the SSD model sometimes cannot detect all the teeth in an image when the number of teeth is large. However, it also shows the capability of detecting most teeth that contain caries.

Quantitative Comparison. Table 1 shows the performance scores of the two models using the MSCOCO metrics [15]. We also measure the average inference time per image on a Tesla K80 GPU. We present 4 major score fields: mean average precision (mAP), average precision at 0.5 and 0.75 intersection over union(IoU) thresholds (AP_{50}, AP_{75} respectively), and average recall (AR). We focus mostly on AR and AP_{50}. Since our goal is to spot the cavity and prompt the user to seek help from dentists, a high IoU score is much less important compared to ability of detecting the disease. Faster R-CNN still outperforms the SSD model in all the score fields, while taking much longer for inference.

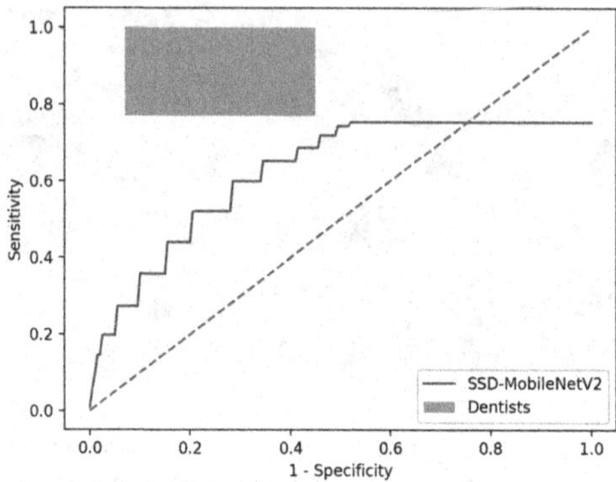

Fig. 5. ROC curve of cavity detection by the SSD-MobileNetV2 model. The red box denotes the average performance of dentists. The curve does not reach the upper right corner because we take into account the undetected teeth and incorrect detections. (Color figure online)

Model-Dentist Comparison. Currently, we incorporate the SSD model into the mobile application since it is fast and lightweight, thus not requiring high-end computational-expensive devices that our targeted audiences cannot afford. We then evaluate the performance of our system on medical metrics using the ROC curve. We evaluate the model by deriving an $(K+1)\times(K+1)$ detection confusion matrix (K denotes number of classes, 4 in our case) from the detection results on the test set. The extra row and column take into account the undetected teeth and incorrect detections (detected unlabeled areas). We then plot the ROC curve in Fig. 5 by calculating from the confusion matrix the sensitivity and specificity scores with respect to cavity detection instead of per category detection. We achieve this by grouping *level1* and *level2* as one category namely *cavity* and the rest as another. Previous studies have estimated the average performance of dentists on identification of dental caries: 0.77 to 1.00 for sensitivity and 0.45 to 0.93 for specificity [8]. The performance of dentists is visualized on the plot. We notice that there is still some distance between the performance of our deployed SSD model and that of trained dentists, but the gap is expected to shrink if we deploy a larger model or label more data for training.

We believe that the current system already offers a good addition to the current dental healthcare practice by allowing untrained family caregivers to participate, with the help of computerize image recognition, in the effort to break the bottleneck in ECC diagnosis and prevention. With the status quo, many ECC cases are simply undetected until it is too late and too costly to treat.

4 Conclusion and Future Work

We present a smartphone-based system for real-time early childhood caries diagnosis to fill in a major gap in ECC diagnosis and prevention in the current health care system. We create a first-ever large-scale intraoral dataset labeled manually by dental practitioners. The dataset can be used for future research not only on ECC but also on the general cavity diagnosis. We design a multistage deep learning system that uses object detection models supported by multifactorial user information analysis to perform both risk assessment and dental education. Furthermore, we deploy the system on Android devices to test its functionality and feasibility. In the future, we will perform clinical testing to evaluate the impact of the deployed system, while investigating ways to further improve the performance and deployability of other deep learning models. We will also extend the detection model to posterior teeth diagnosis using our archived images.

References

1. American Academy of Pediatrics: Provider Toolkit. https://www.aap.org/en-us/about-the-aap/aap-press-room/campaigns/tiny-teeth/Pages/default.aspx. Accessed 17 Mar 2020
2. American Academy on Pediatric Dentistry Clinical Affairs Committee-Pulp Therapy subcommittee: American academy on pediatric dentistry council on clinical affairs: guideline on pulp therapy for primary and young permanent teeth. Pediatr. Dent. **30**(7), 170–174 (2009)
3. Berkowitz, R.J., Amante, A., Kopycka-Kedzierawski, D.T., Billings, R.J., Feng, C.: Dental caries recurrence following clinical treatment for severe early childhood caries. Pediatr. Dent. **33**(7), 510–514 (2011)
4. Casamassimo, P.S., Thikkurissy, S., Edelstein, B.L., Maiorini, E.: Beyond the DMFT: the human and economic cost of early childhood caries. J. Am. Dent. Assoc. **140**(6), 650–657 (2009)
5. Çolak, H., Dülgergil, Ç.T., Dalli, M., Hamidi, M.M.: Early childhood caries update: a review of causes, diagnoses, and treatments. J. Nat. Sci. Biol. Med. **4**(1), 29 (2013)
6. Dye, B., et al.: Trends in oral health status: united states, 1988–1994 and 1999–2004. Vital Health Stat. Ser. 11 Data Natl. Health Surv. (248), 1–92 (2007)
7. Dye, B.A., Li, X., Thornton-Evans, G.: Oral health disparities as determined by selected healthy people 2020 oral health objectives for the United States, 2009–2010. No. 100, US Department of Health and Human Services, Centers for Disease Control and Prevention, National Center for Health Statistics (2012)
8. Gordan, V.V., et al.: Methods used by dental practice-based research network (DPBRN) dentists to diagnose dental caries. Oper. Dent. **36**(1), 2–11 (2011)
9. Graves, C., Berkowitz, R., Proskin, H., Chase, I., Weinstein, P., Billings, R.: Clinical outcomes for early childhood caries: influence of aggressive dental surgery. J. Dent. Child. **71**(2), 114–117 (2004)
10. Gugnani, N., Pandit, I., Srivastava, N., Gupta, M., Sharma, M.: International caries detection and assessment system (ICDAS): a new concept. Int. J. Clin. Pediatr. Dent. **4**(2), 93 (2011)
11. He, K., Zhang, X., Ren, S., Sun, J.: Delving deep into rectifiers: surpassing human-level performance on ImageNet classification. In: Proceedings of the IEEE International Conference on Computer Vision, pp. 1026–1034 (2015)
12. He, K., Zhang, X., Ren, S., Sun, J.: Deep residual learning for image recognition. In: Proceedings of the IEEE Conference on Computer Vision and Pattern Recognition, pp. 770–778 (2016)

13. Koo, H., Bowen, W.H.: Candida albicans and streptococcus mutans: a potential synergistic alliance to cause virulent tooth decay in children. Future Microbiol. **9**(12), 1295–1297 (2014)
14. Lee, J.H., Kim, D.H., Jeong, S.N., Choi, S.H.: Detection and diagnosis of dental caries using a deep learning-based convolutional neural network algorithm. J. Dent. **77**, 106–111 (2018)
15. Lin, T.-Y., et al.: Microsoft COCO: common objects in context. In: Fleet, D., Pajdla, T., Schiele, B., Tuytelaars, T. (eds.) ECCV 2014. LNCS, vol. 8693, pp. 740–755. Springer, Cham (2014). https://doi.org/10.1007/978-3-319-10602-1_48
16. Liu, W., et al.: SSD: single shot multibox detector. In: Leibe, B., Matas, J., Sebe, N., Welling, M. (eds.) ECCV 2016. LNCS, vol. 9905, pp. 21–37. Springer, Cham (2016). https://doi.org/10.1007/978-3-319-46448-0_2
17. Ma, N., Zhang, X., Zheng, H.-T., Sun, J.: ShuffleNet V2: practical guidelines for efficient CNN architecture design. In: Ferrari, V., Hebert, M., Sminchisescu, C., Weiss, Y. (eds.) Computer Vision – ECCV 2018. LNCS, vol. 11218, pp. 122–138. Springer, Cham (2018). https://doi.org/10.1007/978-3-030-01264-9_8
18. Office of Disease Prevention and Health Promotion: Us department of health and human services: healthy people 2010 (2000). https://www.health/gov/healthypeople/
19. Pixabay: Map Pin Icon. https://pixabay.com/vectors/map-pin-icon-map-pin-travel-1272165. Accessed 17 Mar 2020
20. Rashewsky, S., Parameswaran, A., Sloane, C., Ferguson, F., Epstein, R.: Time and cost analysis: pediatric dental rehabilitation with general anesthesia in the office and the hospital settings. Anesth. Prog. **59**(4), 147–153 (2012)
21. Redmon, J., Farhadi, A.: Yolov3: an incremental improvement. arXiv preprint arXiv:1804.02767 (2018)
22. Ren, S., He, K., Girshick, R., Sun, J.: Faster R-CNN: towards real-time object detection with region proposal networks. In: Advances in Neural Information Processing Systems, pp. 91–99 (2015)
23. Sandler, M., Howard, A., Zhu, M., Zhmoginov, A., Chen, L.C.: Mobilenetv 2: inverted residuals and linear bottlenecks. In: Proceedings of the IEEE Conference on Computer Vision and Pattern Recognition, pp. 4510–4520 (2018)
24. Shoaib, L., Deery, C., Ricketts, D., Nugent, Z.: Validity and reproducibility of ICDAS II in primary teeth. Caries Res. **43**(6), 442–448 (2009)
25. Simonyan, K., Zisserman, A.: Very deep convolutional networks for large-scale image recognition. arXiv preprint arXiv:1409.1556 (2014)
26. Vos, T., et al.: Global, regional, and national incidence, prevalence, and years lived with disability for 328 diseases and injuries for 195 countries, 1990–2016: a systematic analysis for the global burden of disease study 2016. Lancet **390**(10100), 1211–1259 (2017)
27. Xiao, J., et al.: Prenatal oral health care and early childhood caries prevention: a systematic review and meta-analysis. Caries Res. **53**(4), 412–422 (2019)
28. Young, D.A., et al.: The American dental association caries classification system for clinical practice: a report of the American dental association council on scientific affairs. J. Am. Dent. Assoc. **146**(2), 79–86 (2015)
29. Zhao, Z.Q., Zheng, P., Xu, S.t., Wu, X.: Object detection with deep learning: a review. IEEE Trans. Neural Netw. Learn. Syst. **30**(11), 3212–3232 (2019)

Automated Detection of Congenital Heart Disease in Fetal Ultrasound Screening

Jeremy Tan[1(✉)], Anselm Au[1(✉)], Qingjie Meng[1], Sandy FinesilverSmith[2], John Simpson[2], Daniel Rueckert[1], Reza Razavi[2], Thomas Day[2], David Lloyd[2], and Bernhard Kainz[1]

[1] Imperial College London, London SW7 2AZ, UK
{j.tan17,anselm.au}@imperial.ac.uk
[2] King's College London, St Thomas' Hospital, London SE1 7EH, UK

Abstract. Prenatal screening with ultrasound can lower neonatal mortality significantly for selected cardiac abnormalities. However, the need for human expertise, coupled with the high volume of screening cases, limits the practically achievable detection rates. In this paper we discuss the potential for deep learning techniques to aid in the detection of congenital heart disease (CHD) in fetal ultrasound. We propose a pipeline for automated data curation and classification. During both training and inference, we exploit an auxiliary view classification task to bias features toward relevant cardiac structures. This bias helps to improve in F1-scores from 0.72 and 0.77 to 0.87 and 0.85 for healthy and CHD classes respectively.

Keywords: Congenital heart disease · Fetal ultrasound

1 Introduction

Ultrasound is the foremost modality for fetal screening. Its portability, low cost, and fast imaging make it one of the easiest imaging modalities to deploy. This gives front-line sonographers the tools to perform screening at a *population* level. In each fetal examination, sonographers must inspect a wide range of anatomical features including but not limited to the spine, brain, and heart. The breadth of this task makes it difficult for sonographers to develop specialized expertise for every anatomical feature. Unfortunately, this can lead to some conditions going undiagnosed. The most fatal of which is congenital heart disease (CHD) which is associated with over 47% of perinatal deaths and over 35% of infant deaths (only considering deaths related to congenital abnormalities) [13].

Experts can detect CHD's with over 98% sensitivity and near 90% specificity [3,22]. However, shortage of specialists means that over 96% of examinations are performed by generalist sonographers [20]. As a result, *population*-based studies consistently report detection rates around 39% [15] (with one exception reaching 59% [20]). Machine learning methods could help close this gap and provide sonographers with assistance for more difficult diagnoses.

Y. Hu et al. (Eds.): ASMUS 2020/PIPPI 2020, LNCS 12437, pp. 243–252, 2020.
https://doi.org/10.1007/978-3-030-60334-2_24

Deep learning has been used in many fetal ultrasound applications including standard plane detection [2,4,7,11], extrapolation of 3D structure from 2D images [6], and biometric measurements for developmental assessment [10,18]. However, there have been relatively few works on diagnostic assistance in fetal screening. Some of the major challenges in this application are i) data curation and ii) disease variance. Data curation is crucial because only certain "standard planes" are considered diagnostic [14]. Extracting relevant frames for CHD is particularly challenging because pathological cases *by definition* deviate from the description of these standard planes. The high variation of the manifestation of CHD's also make diagnosis difficult.

In this work we propose a pipeline to perform automated diagnosis of hypoplastic left heart syndrome (HLHS), a term which encompasses a spectrum of malformations in the left ventricle and its outflow tract [17]. A standard plane detector is first used to extract relevant frames from the healthy and pathological cases. This data is then used to train a classifier to distinguish between normal control (NC) cases and HLHS patients.

2 Related Work

Most successful applications of deep learning in fetal ultrasound have been in pre-diagnostic tasks. In particular, standard plane detection has been studied extensively [2,4,7,11]. Standard plane detection is also involved in the proposed pipeline and is based on the SonoNet architecture [2].

Most closely related to our work is a recent study on diagnosing HLHS and Tetralogy of Fallot (TOF) in fetal ultrasound [1]. In their methodology, images are labelled based on standard planes allowing for extraction of relevant images with high diagnostic quality. Using these images, they train a series of binary classifiers to distinguish between healthy and pathological cases. Each classifier is trained using images from only one standard plane. The predictions from each plane are then summed and a threshold is used to determine the final diagnosis.

They achieve high sensitivity and specificity demonstrating that neural networks can learn to identify CHD. In their study, the training images are of high diagnostic quality and come from a diverse dataset including about 600 patients (for normal vs. HLHS). These favorable conditions are not always possible because of a lack of expert annotations and the rarity of CHD conditions. As such, we aim to investigate the feasibility of CHD detection in the low data regime, using a total of 100 patients. We also study the impact of automated and manual data curation.

The design of [1] is also dependent on data curation. Training individual networks for each standard plane means that training data must be accurately sorted into the correct planes. It also means that test data must be accurately sorted for inference because each network is only trained to recognize pathology in a single view. Furthermore, using individual networks for each plane leads to larger memory requirements. Instead, we train a single network for all views and explore the use of plane labels as an auxiliary task for multitask learning [5].

3 Method

The proposed pipeline consists of two key stages, plane extraction and pathology classification. Given uncurated data, this automated workflow allows for a model to be trained for CHD classification. Figure 1 depicts the overall workflow.

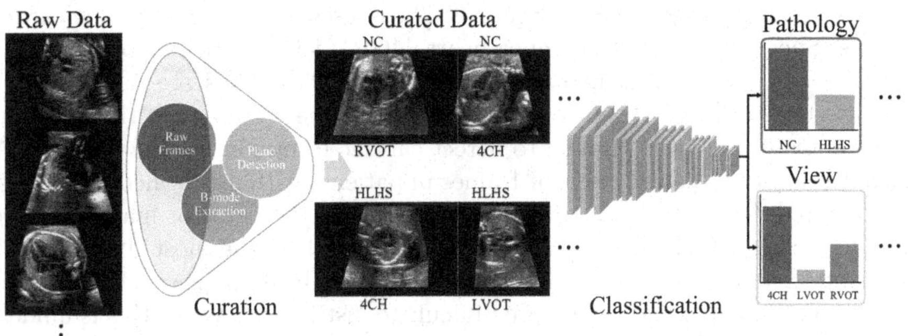

Fig. 1. Automated curation and classification pipeline.

3.1 Data Characteristics

Data was collected from 39 healthy patients and 61 patients diagnosed with HLHS, for a total of 100 patients. Each patient's data is collected as raw ultrasound DICOM videos. These videos are unannotated, meaning they contain i) frames of irrelevant anatomy, ii) frames in the vicinity of the heart, and iii) precise standard planes which are typically used for diagnosis. Table 1 summarizes the distribution of frames. The final extracted frames used for training are greyscale images of dimensions 224 $\times$ 188 pixels. The curation process used to go from raw videos to extracted frames is described in the following section.

Table 1. Distribution of patients, clean cardiac frames, and different cardiac views.

	NC			HLHS		
Unique patients	39			61		
Total frames in DICOM files	354867			741290		
Clean frames after curation	189000			376337		
Clean frames (cardiac views)	102993			143468		
View	4CH	LVOT	RVOT	4CH	LVOT	RVOT
Extracted frames	31938	62195	8452	49176	73203	19959

3.2 Plane Extraction

The data curation pipeline involves i) extraction of B-mode frames, and ii) standard plane extraction. In the B-mode extraction phase, frames are run through a series of tests which detect the presence of certain colors, user interface elements, or particular histogram characteristics. These help remove Doppler, split-view, and M-mode frames respectively.

A standard plane detector, SonoNet [2], is used to extract relevant cardiac frames. Specifically, the 4 chamber heart (4CH), left ventricular outflow tract (LVOT) and right ventricular outflow tract (RVOT) views are used. Table 1 displays the number of frames extracted for each view. Note that this standard plane detector has been trained to detect cardiac frames in *healthy* patients. As such, its ability to detect relevant frames in patients with malformed hearts may be impaired. Given the bias toward normal hearts, the detector may not recognize frames which show gross defects, which would be the most diagnostically relevant. Instead it may favor instances where the heart appears closer to normal, potentially making them more difficult to distinguish. While this is unideal, it represents the most general case where we do not have access to annotations which highlight the most diagnostic frames. This circumvents the need to train individual plane detectors for every pathology. To test whether diagnostic information can be gleaned from these images, we train a classifier as described in the following section.

3.3 CHD Classification

We train a single classifier to discriminate between healthy and HLHS patients. All three cardiac views are used for training within the same network. The network architecture is the same as SonoNet [2] which has been inspired by the staple VGG network [16]. A standard binary cross-entropy loss (Eq. 1) is used for optimization.

In the low data regime (particularly when the number of unique patients is low) it is difficult to ensure that the classifier learns features that are genuinely related to pathology. Instead, the network might learn extraneous features that are reliable within the training data but are not robust within the test set. It is also prohibitively expensive to annotate which regions are important in each image. As such, we exploit the view labels which come for free from the data curation pipeline. Discriminating between the 4CH, LVOT and RVOT views requires the network to identify cardiac structures. It is also an intra-patient task, meaning that patient-specific features are not reliable. View classification is thus added as auxiliary task to bias the network toward cardiac structures and away from memorization of patient-specific characteristics that do not generalize to test data. The auxiliary loss and combined multitask [5] loss are given in Eq. 2 and Eq. 3 respectively.

$$\mathcal{L}_{\text{CHD}}(x_i, y_i, f) = -\sum_{c=1}^{N=2} y_{i,c}\log(f(x_{i,c})) \tag{1}$$

$$\mathcal{L}_{\text{view}}(x_i, v_i, f) = -\sum_{c=1}^{N=3} v_{i,c}\log(f(x_{i,c})) \quad (2)$$

$$\mathcal{L}_{\text{Multitask}}(x_i, y_i, v_i, f) = \mathcal{L}_{\text{CHD}} + \lambda\mathcal{L}_{\text{view}} \quad (3)$$

$$\lambda_i = 1 - 0.5\mathcal{L}'_{\text{CHD}}(x_i, y_i, f) \quad (4)$$

The weight of the view loss, λ, is computed individually for each instance (Eq. 4). It is based on the minmax-scaled CHD loss values, $\mathcal{L}'_{\text{CHD}} \in [0, 1]$, of each sample within a batch. The view loss only increases when a sample has a lower CHD loss, making CHD the network's priority. There are more sophisticated ways of finding the optimal weighting between tasks, e.g. [9], but this simplistic approach has little overhead and demonstrates an improvement over a naive setting of $\lambda = 1$.

3.4 Assessing Diagnostic Quality During Inference

The automated curation pipeline helps to reduce manual data processing. However, it may extract low quality frames which have less diagnostic information. Including predictions on such frames adds noise to the overall diagnosis. As such, we aim to identify and remove unreliable predictions. Note that even if *all* frames from a patient are rejected, it is better than providing a diagnosis which is unreliable.

A reliable prediction for cardiac disease should depend on the cardiac structures themselves, rather than extraneous features in the background. Such a prediction should be robust to small perturbations as long as the cardiac structures are kept intact. Our aim is to generate these perturbations and use them to identify which predictions are reliable.

Generating perturbations that preserve the cardiac structures requires knowledge of the location of the cardiac structures. However, annotating these structures is expensive. As such, we exploit the auxiliary view task as a proxy. The view classification task determines which cardiac plane is presented in the image, which depends heavily on the cardiac structures. To generate a perturbation we use the gradient from the view task to distort the image in a way that does not change the view prediction (i.e. the cardiac structures). This is similar to adversarial examples [19], except we keep the prediction the same (Eq. 5) by following the negative gradient (Eq. 6 [12]). Multiple perturbation steps, δ, can be taken; each time using a step size of $\alpha = 2$ up to a maximum perturbation of ± 8 from a pixel's original value $p \in [0, 300]$.

$$\min_{\delta \in \Delta} \mathcal{L}_{\text{view}}(x_i + \delta, v_i^*, f) \text{ , where } v_i^* = f(x_i) \quad (5)$$

$$\delta = -\alpha\text{sgn}(\nabla_x \mathcal{L}_{\text{view}}(x_i, v_i^*, f)) \quad (6)$$

3.5 Evaluation

After automatically extracting the relevant frames for all patients, *manual* curation was performed on images from roughly 20% of the patients. In manual curation, the images are sorted into three groups based on their diagnostic quality (high, medium, and low) by expert clinicians. Half of these patients are used for testing and the other half are used for validation. Evaluation on the test data measures how well the model is able to learn generalizable features from the automatically curated data. The quality of the automated curation can also be measured by comparing results on test sets with and without manual curation. We report precision, recall, F1-scores and the area under curve for the receiver operator characteristic curve (ROC-AUC).

4 Results

An overview of the results is presented in Table 2. The test data produced by automated curation contains images with varying levels of diagnostic quality. Testing on all levels (low-high quality) results in poor performance. Using medium-high quality immediately improves all metrics. The multitask loss provides a considerable improvement and the weighted multitask approach ($\lambda \propto \mathcal{L}_{\text{CHD}}$, Eq. 4) further improves performance. Using robust inference (described in Sect. 3.4) helps to remove predictions that are deemed less reliable. The fact that performance increases indicates that robust inference is effective in identifying and excluding predictions that are less accurate.

Table 2. Pathology classification results for different models using testing data with different diagnostic quality.

Loss	Test quality	Precision (NC:CHD)	Recall (NC:CHD)	F1-score (NC:CHD)	ROC-AUC
CHD	All	0.72 0.64	0.59 0.76	0.65 0.70	0.75
CHD	Med-High	0.72 0.77	0.71 0.77	0.72 0.77	0.82
Multitask ($\lambda = 1$)	Med-High	0.77 0.81	0.77 0.81	0.77 0.81	0.87
Multitask ($\lambda \propto \mathcal{L}_{\text{CHD}}$)	Med-High	0.80 0.80	0.74 0.85	0.77 0.83	0.89
Multitask ($\lambda \propto \mathcal{L}_{\text{CHD}}$)	Robust frames	0.83 0.89	0.90 0.82	0.87 0.85	0.93

A closer examination of robust inference is given in Fig. 2. Using regular inference (blue), the ROC-AUC becomes severely compromised when including low quality images. However, the performance can be recovered by using robust inference (green) to automatically determine when a prediction is less reliable.

The white hatched bars (Fig. 2) indicate the percentage of images which are deemed reliable in each set. The percentage of reliable images increases as the expert-rated quality increases. This indicates that the proposed reliability rating corresponds to expert judgement to some extent. Ideally 100% of the high quality images should be retained; however 73% are deemed reliable. Nonetheless

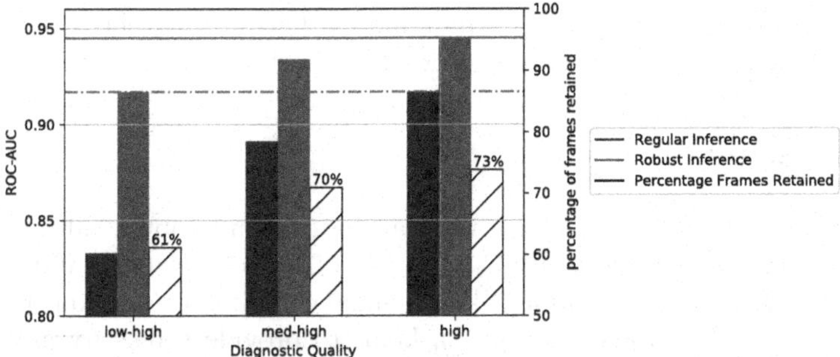

Fig. 2. ROC-AUC comparison of regular and robust inference. Including low quality frames quickly leads to a sharp decline in performance (blue). Robust inference can help to identify frames that are more reliable (white hatch, right y-axis). Evaluating only reliable frames leads to more accurate overall predictions (green). (Color figure online)

the excluded predictions were indeed unreliable and their exclusion results in an improvement of almost 0.03 (solid and dotted red lines). In the low-high set, only 61% of frames are retained. To put this in perspective, experts only considered 39% of the low-high set as being of acceptable quality (medium or above).

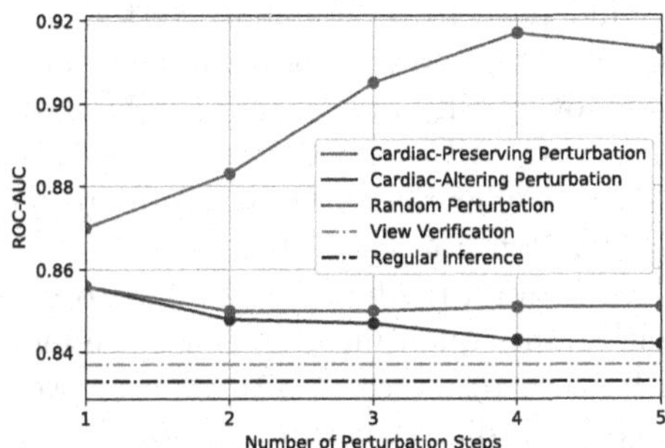

Fig. 3. ROC-AUC using different approaches of frame quality assessment. All methods improve upon regular inference (black). Cardiac-preserving perturbations stand out as being considerably better at removing unreliable predictions (green). (Color figure online)

We also compare different approaches to robust inference in Fig. 3. The view verification approach excludes any images which produce an incorrect view prediction (based on 'ground truth' view labels provided by the plane detector in the curation pipeline). This gives very limited improvement (grey).

The proposed cardiac-preserving perturbations are able to find and remove inaccurate predictions, which consistently improves ROC-AUC (Fig. 3, green). In fact, increasing the number of perturbation steps actually leads to better results. In comparison, random (purple) and cardiac-altering perturbations (i.e. adversarial examples - blue) do not provide as much improvement.

5 Discussion

Various elements, including multitask learning [5] and robust inference, contribute toward improving the ROC-AUC from 0.75 to over 0.91. With a small number of unique patients and a lack of manual curation, the standard classifier performs poorly. Multitask learning [5] helps to provide a bias toward cardiac structures that are relevant for the view classification task. These features are also helpful for pathology classification and lead to an increase in performance (Table 2).

Robust inference also helps to improve the scores by filtering out unreliable predictions. Predictions are considered less reliable if they change when the image is perturbed in a way that preserves cardiac features. Stronger perturbations (using more steps) are more likely to alter predictions. However, predictions that rely on cardiac features should remain unaffected. Figure 3 demonstrates that strong cardiac-preserving perturbations are the most adept at finding unreliable predictions. In comparison, random and cardiac-altering (adversarial) perturbations are not able to tease apart reliable and unreliable predictions.

We find that robust inference is an important component because the automated curation pipeline includes many images of low diagnostic quality. Typically, these frames would have to be manually vetted in order to reduce the noise in the overall prediction. However, robust inference can serve as a filter to remove predictions from low quality images. For low-high quality images, robust inference improves the ROC-AUC from 0.83 to 0.92. This is on par with the ROC-AUC achieved with regular inference on *only* high quality images (0.92). This is highlighted in Fig. 2 with a red dotted line.

Measuring the reliability of a prediction is similar to uncertainty estimation (e.g. [8]). However, uncertainty quantification is a much more complex task and is not always straightforward to interpret [21]. Instead, we simply measure the prediction's dependence on cardiac structures (which should hold key diagnostic information). With this prior knowledge we can estimate *our* confidence in the prediction, rather than the network's intrinsic uncertainty.

We demonstrate that it is possible to train a classifier to identify CHD from standard B-mode images. In the future, temporal information or Doppler images could be used to provide more diagnostic information. Nevertheless, this work represents a step toward the goal of assisting front-line sonographers with CHD diagnosis at a population level.

6 Conclusion

We propose an automated pipeline for curating and classifying CHD in fetal ultrasound. The curation step extracts relevant frames which makes training possible. Automated curation includes many images with poor diagnostic quality.

Noisy predictions on such images can lead to a reduction in overall performance. As such, robust inference is introduced in this work to exclude predictions which may be less trustworthy. This helps to achieve a F1-score of 0.87 and 0.85 for NC and CHD classes respectively and an ROC-AUC of 0.93.

Acknowledgements. Support from Wellcome Trust IEH Award iFind project [102431]. JT is supported by the ICL President's Scholarship.

References

1. Arnaout, R., Curran, L., Chinn, E., Zhao, Y., Moon-Grady, A.: Deep-learning models improve on community-level diagnosis for common congenital heart disease lesions. arXiv preprint arXiv:1809.06993 (2018)
2. Baumgartner, C.F., et al.: SonoNet: real-time detection and localisation of fetal standard scan planes in freehand ultrasound. IEEE Trans. Med. Imaging **36**(11), 2204–2215 (2017)
3. Bennasar, M., et al.: Accuracy of four-dimensional spatiotemporal image correlation echocardiography in the prenatal diagnosis of congenital heart defects. Ultrasound Obstet. Gynecol. **36**(4), 458–464 (2010)
4. Cai, Y., Sharma, H., Chatelain, P., Noble, J.A.: Multi-task SonoEyeNet: detection of fetal standardized planes assisted by generated sonographer attention maps. In: Frangi, A.F., Schnabel, J.A., Davatzikos, C., Alberola-López, C., Fichtinger, G. (eds.) MICCAI 2018. LNCS, vol. 11070, pp. 871–879. Springer, Cham (2018). https://doi.org/10.1007/978-3-030-00928-1_98
5. Caruana, R.: Multitask learning. Mach. Learn. **28**(1), 41–75 (1997)
6. Cerrolaza, J., et al.: 3D fetal skull reconstruction from 2DUS via deep conditional generative networks. In: Frangi, A.F., Schnabel, J.A., Davatzikos, C., Alberola-López, C., Fichtinger, G. (eds.) MICCAI 2018. LNCS, vol. 11070, pp. 383–391. Springer, Cham (2018). https://doi.org/10.1007/978-3-030-00928-1_44
7. Chen, H., et al.: Standard plane localization in fetal ultrasound via domain transferred deep neural networks. IEEE J. Biomed. Health Inform. **19**(5), 1627–1636 (2015)
8. Gal, Y., Ghahramani, Z.: Dropout as a Bayesian approximation: representing model uncertainty in deep learning. In: International Conference on Machine Learning, pp. 1050–1059 (2016)
9. Kendall, A., Gal, Y., Cipolla, R.: Multi-task learning using uncertainty to weigh losses for scene geometry and semantics. In: Proceedings of the IEEE Conference on Computer Vision and Pattern Recognition, pp. 7482–7491 (2018)
10. Kim, B., Kim, K.C., Park, Y., Kwon, J.Y., Jang, J., Seo, J.K.: Machine-learning-based automatic identification of fetal abdominal circumference from ultrasound images. Physiol. Measur. **39**(10), 105007 (2018)
11. Kong, P., Ni, D., Chen, S., Li, S., Wang, T., Lei, B.: Automatic and efficient standard plane recognition in fetal ultrasound images via multi-scale dense networks. In: Melbourne, A., et al. (eds.) PIPPI/DATRA -2018. LNCS, vol. 11076, pp. 160–168. Springer, Cham (2018). https://doi.org/10.1007/978-3-030-00807-9_16
12. Madry, A., Makelov, A., Schmidt, L., Tsipras, D., Vladu, A.: Towards deep learning models resistant to adversarial attacks. In: International Conference on Learning Representations (2018)

13. National Congenital Anomaly and Rare Disease Registration Service: Congenital anomaly statistics 2017 (2017)
14. National Health Service and Public Health England: NHS Fetal Anomaly Screening Programme Handbook Valid from August 2018. Technical report (2018). https://www.gov.uk/government/publications/fetal-anomaly-screening-programme-handbook
15. Pinto, N., Keenan, H., Minich, L., Puchalski, M., Heywood, M., Botto, L.: Barriers to prenatal detection of congenital heart disease: a population-based study. Ultrasound Obstet. Gynecol. **40**(4), 418–425 (2012)
16. Simonyan, K., Zisserman, A.: Very deep convolutional networks for large-scale image recognition. arXiv preprint arXiv:1409.1556 (2014)
17. Simpson, J.: Hypoplastic left heart syndrome. Ultrasound Obstet. Gynecol. Official J. Int. Soc. Ultrasound Obstet. Gynecol. **15**(4), 271–278 (2000)
18. Sinclair, M., et al.: Human-level performance on automatic head biometrics in fetal ultrasound using fully convolutional neural networks. In: 2018 40th Annual International Conference of the IEEE Engineering in Medicine and Biology Society (EMBC), pp. 714–717. IEEE (2018)
19. Szegedy, C., et al.: Intriguing properties of neural networks. In: International Conference on Learning Representations (2014). http://arxiv.org/abs/1312.6199
20. Van Velzen, C., et al.: Prenatal detection of congenital heart disease-results of a national screening programme. BJOG Int. J. Obstet. Gynaecol. **123**(3), 400–407 (2016)
21. Yao, J., Pan, W., Ghosh, S., Doshi-Velez, F.: Quality of uncertainty quantification for Bayesian neural network inference. arXiv preprint arXiv:1906.09686 (2019)
22. Yeo, L., Luewan, S., Romero, R.: Fetal intelligent navigation echocardiography (fine) detects 98% of congenital heart disease. J. Ultrasound Med. **37**(11), 2577–2593 (2018)

Harmonised Segmentation of Neonatal Brain MRI: A Domain Adaptation Approach

Irina Grigorescu(✉), Lucilio Cordero-Grande, Dafnis Batalle, A. David Edwards, Joseph V. Hajnal, Marc Modat, and Maria Deprez

School of Biomedical Engineering and Imaging Sciences, King's College London, London, UK
irina.grigorescu@kcl.ac.uk

Abstract. Medical image deep learning segmentation has shown great potential in becoming an ubiquitous part of the clinical analysis pipeline. However, these methods cannot guarantee high quality predictions when the source and target domains are dissimilar due to different acquisition protocols, or biases in patient cohorts. Recently, unsupervised domain adaptation techniques have shown great potential in alleviating this problem by minimizing the shift between the source and target distributions. In this work, we aim to predict tissue segmentation maps on an unseen dataset, which has both different acquisition parameters and population bias when compared to our training data. We achieve this by investigating two unsupervised domain adaptation (UDA) techniques with the objective of finding the best solution for our problem. We compare the two methods with a baseline fully-supervised segmentation network in terms of cortical thickness measures.

Keywords: Segmentation · Domain adaptation

1 Introduction

In medical imaging, deep learning methods have recently shown great success in solving a wide range of scientific problems, including tissue segmentation or image classification [11]. However, most methods rely on the assumption that the training and testing datasets are drawn from the same distribution. This means that the performance of these models will drop when applied to images which were acquired with acquisition protocols different than the ones used to train the models. Unsupervised domain adaptation techniques [3] offer a solution to this problem by minimizing the disparity between a source and a target domain, without requiring the use of labelled data in the target domain. In this work, we investigate two unsupervised domain adaptation methods with the aim of predicting brain tissue segmentations on axial slices of T_2-weighted (T_2w) magnetic resonance imaging (MRI) data of an unseen preterm-born neonatal population. The key contributions of this work are:

Y. Hu et al. (Eds.): ASMUS 2020/PIPPI 2020, LNCS 12437, pp. 253–263, 2020.
https://doi.org/10.1007/978-3-030-60334-2_25

- We study the application and viability of unsupervised domain adaptation methods in terms of harmonising two neonatal datasets.
- We propose an additional loss term in one of the methods, in order to constrain the network to more realistic reconstructions.
- We compare the three unsupervised domain adaptation methods with a fully-supervised baseline and report our results in terms of Dice scores obtained on the holdout dataset. We do this in order to show that all four methods were able to generalise well on unseen source domain data.
- Finally, we calculate mean cortical thickness measures for every subject in the two datasets and we perform an ANCOVA analysis in order to find group differences between the predicted source and target domains.

2 Method

Data Acquisition. The T_2w MRI data used in this study was collected as part of two independent projects: the developing Human Connectome Project (dHCP[1]), and the evaluation of Magnetic Resonance Imaging to Predict Neurodevelopmental Impairment in Preterm Infants study (ePrime[2]). The dHCP data was acquired using a Philips 3T scanner and a 32-channels neonatal head coil [5], using a a T_2w turbo spin echo (TSE) sequence with parameters: $T_R = 12$ s, $T_E = 156$ ms, and overlapping slices with resolution $0.8 \times 0.8 \times 1.6$ mm^3. All data was motion corrected [2,8] and resampled to an isotropic voxel size of 0.5 mm^3. The ePrime dataset was acquired with a Philips 3T system and an 8-channel phased array head coil, using a T_2w fast-spin echo (FSE) sequence with parameters: $T_R = 14.73$ s, $T_E = 160$ ms [1]. Images were acquired with a voxel size of $0.86 \times 0.86 \times 2$ mm, with 1 mm overlap.

Image Selection. In this work we use two datasets, one comprising of 396 MRI scans of infants born between 23–42 weeks gestational age (GA) and scanned at term-equivalent age (after 37 weeks GA) as part of the dHCP pipeline, and a dataset of 428 MRI scans of infants born between 23–33 weeks gestational age (GA) and scanned at term-equivalent age as part of the ePrime project. Their age distribution is shown in Fig. 1.

Image Preprocessing. In order to allow for a fair comparison between the two datasets, we performed a series of pre-processing steps. First, we rigidly registered all of our data to a common 40 weeks gestational age atlas space [14] using the MIRTK [13] software toolbox. Then, we linearly upsampled the ePrime images to 0.5 mm^3 isotropic resolution in order to match the resolution of our dHCP dataset. For both of our datasets, we performed skull-stripping using the available brain masks [9] and we selected the middle axial slices. Finally, we cropped the images to a 256×256 size.

[1] http://www.developingconnectome.org/.
[2] https://www.npeu.ox.ac.uk/prumhc/eprime-mr-imaging-177.

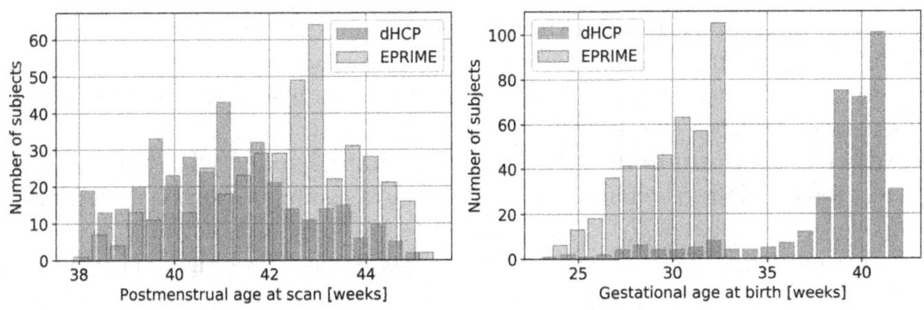

Fig. 1. Age distribution of subjects in our datasets.

Data Preprocessing. We divided both of our datasets into 80% training, 10% validation and 10% test, keeping the distribution of ages at scan as close to the original as possible. The validation sets were used to inform us about our models' performance during training, while the holdout set was used to report our final models' results and showcase their capability to generalize. A full description of the dataset partition is shown in Table 1.

Table 1. Number of scans in different datasets used for training, validation and testing the models. The numbers reported inside the brackets represent the number of term-born neonates (t) and the number of preterm-born neonates (pt).

Dataset	Train	Validate	Holdout
dHCP	312 (253t + 59pt)	43 (37t + 6pt)	41 (37t + 4pt)
ePrime	337 (0t + 337pt)	45 (0t + 45pt)	46 (0t + 46pt)

Unsupervised Domain Adaptation Models. In order to investigate the best solution for segmenting our target dataset (ePrime), we compared four independently trained deep learning models:

- **Baseline.** First, a 2D U-Net [12] is used as a baseline segmentation network and therefore trained on the source dataset (dHCP) only (see Fig. 2).
- **Adversarial domain adaptation in the latent space.** Second, an adversarial (DA) solution, similar to Kamnitsas et al. [7], is trained such that the learnt feature representations of the segmentation network become agnostic to the data domain (see Fig. 3). When training the segmentation network, source (dHCP) images together with their ground truth labels are used to compute the loss function. On the other hand, when training the discriminator network, source (dHCP) and target (ePrime) images are fed as one batch to the segmentation network and the features at each layer of the decoding branch are collected, upsampled and concatenated in order to be fed as input into the discriminator.

- **Adversarial domain adaptation in the image space.** The third solution consists of an image-based adversarial DA method, where the segmentation network is trained to segment synthesised ePrime-like images produced by a generator network (see Fig. 4).
- **Adversarial domain adaptation in the image space with reconstruction loss.** Finally, the fourth model consists of a similar solution as presented above, with an extra (NCC) loss added to the generator network to enforce image similarity between real and synthesised images (see Fig. 4 dashed black line).

Network Architectures. The segmentation network has the same architecture in all three setups and contains 5 encoding-decoding branches with 16, 32, 64, 128 and 256 channels, respectively. Each encoder block consists of 3×3 convolutions (with a stride of 1), instance normalisation [18] and LeakyReLU activations. The first down-sampling block contains a 2×2 average pooling layer, while the others use 2×2 max pooling layers. Each decoder block consists of 3×3 convolutions (with a stride of 1), instance normalisation [18], LeakyReLU activations, and 3×3 transposed convolutions. The model outputs a 5-channel 2D image (of the same size as the input image), corresponding to our 5 classes: background, cerebrospinal fluid (CSF), white matter (WM), cortical gray matter (cGM) and deep gray matter (dGM).

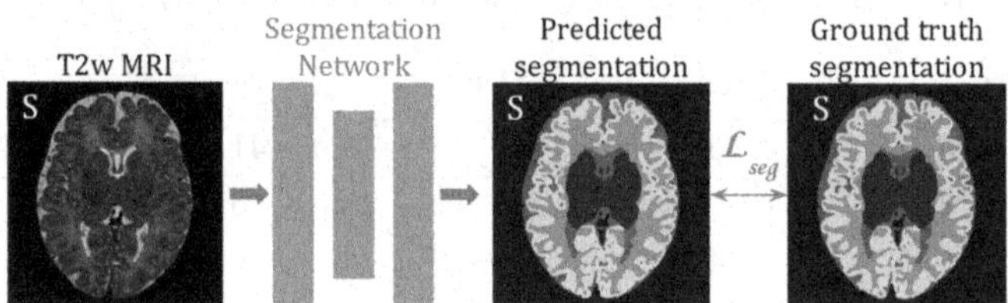

Fig. 2. The baseline model consists of a single 2D U-Net trained to segment the source (dHCP) axial slices. The input T2w MRI images, the predicted segmentation and the ground truth segmentations are marked with S to remind the reader that the network is trained using source (dHCP) images only.

The discriminator network used in the second and third methods (see Figs. 3 and 4) is a PatchGAN discriminator as proposed in [6]. It is made up of repeated blocks of 2D convolutions (with 64, 128, 256 and 512 channels), instance normalisation layers and LeakyReLU activations. The generator network used in the third method (see Fig. 4) is a 2D U-Net similar to the segmentation network used in all three setups. The main difference between the two is the last convolutional layer which is followed by a Tanh activation and which outputs a single channel image.

Training. In the first setup (see Fig. 2) the segmentation network was trained by minimizing a generalised Dice loss (see Eq. 1) [16] using the Adam optimizer with the default parameters ($\beta_1 = 0.9$ and $\beta_2 = 0.999$).

$$\mathcal{L}_{method_1} = \mathcal{L}_{seg} = 1 - 2\frac{\sum_{l=1}^{M} w_l \sum_n p_{ln} t_{ln}}{\sum_{l=1}^{M} w_l \sum_n p_{ln} + t_{ln}} \tag{1}$$

where $w_l = 1/(\sum_n t_{ln})^2$ is the weight of the lth tissue type, p_{ln} is the predicted probabilistic map of the lth tissue type at voxel n, t_{ln} is the target label map of the lth tissue type at voxel n, and M is the number of tissue classes which, in our case, is equal to 5. During training, the learning rate was varied in a decaying cyclical fashion [15] with a base learning rate of $2 \cdot 10^{-6}$ and a maximum learning rate of $2 \cdot 10^{-3}$.

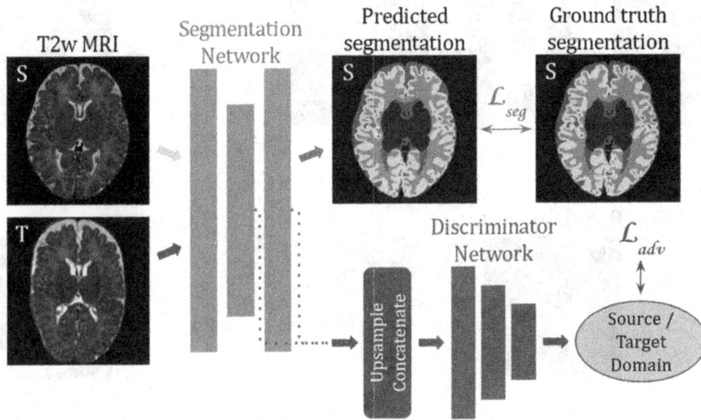

Fig. 3. The latent space domain adaptation setup consists of a 2D U-Net trained to segment the source (dHCP) slices, coupled with a discriminator network which forces the segmentation network to learn domain-invariant features. Source domain images are marked with S. Target domain images are marked with T.

The second method was trained as proposed by [7]. Batches of both source (dHCP) and target (ePrime) images are fed to the segmentation network, while the activations of the feature maps from every level of the decoder arm of the 2D U-Net are passed to the discriminator network. This is performed after the low resolution feature maps are up-sampled and the high resolution maps are down-sampled to match the size of the second deepest layer. Finally, these are concatenated and passed through the discriminator network which acts as a domain classifier. This network is trained by minimizing the Cross-Entropy loss by comparing the predicted class values with assigned target labels representing the two domains. As proposed in [7], the loss for the second method (see Eq. 2) is a combination of the generalised Dice loss and the adversarial loss:

$$\mathcal{L}_{method_2} = \mathcal{L}_{seg} - \alpha \mathcal{L}_{adv} \tag{2}$$

where α is a hyperparameter which is increased linearly from 0 to 0.05 starting at epoch 20, and remains equal to 0.05 from epoch 50 onward. This approach aims to concomitantly maximize the domain classification loss, while minimizing the segmentation loss. Furthermore, setting $\alpha = 0$ for the first 20 epochs allows both networks to train independently so that the discriminator does not wrongly influence the segmentation network with initial poor adversarial gradients. We train the segmentation network in the same way as the baseline network, while the discriminator network is trained using the Adam optimiser with $\beta_1 = 0.5$ and $\beta_2 = 0.999$ and a learning rate of $2 \cdot 10^{-3}$ with a linearly decaying scheduler.

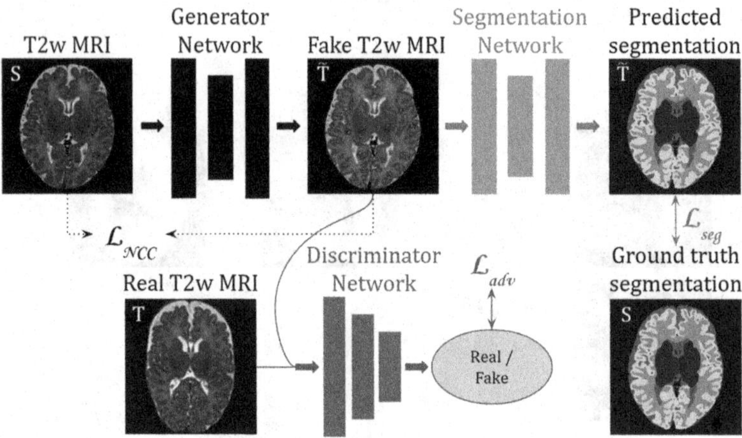

Fig. 4. The image space domain adaptation setup uses a generator network to produce ePrime-like T_2w MRI images (marked with $\widetilde{\mathrm{T}}$), which are then used as input into the segmentation network.

The third method uses an additional generator network which is trained to produce synthetic ePrime-like images. The segmentation network is trained similarly to the other two methods, using both fake ePrime-like and real dHCP images. The generator and the discriminator networks are trained using the Adam optimiser with $\beta_1 = 0.5$ and $\beta_2 = 0.999$ and a learning rate of $2 \cdot 10^{-3}$ with a linearly decaying scheduler. When training the discriminator, we use a loss function similar to Least Squares GAN [10]: $\mathcal{L}_D = \mathbb{E}_{x \sim T}[(D(x) - b)^2] + \mathbb{E}_{x \sim S}[(D(G(x)) - a)^2]$ where a represents the label for fake images and b is the label for real images.

The generator and the segmentation network are trained together using the following loss:

$$\mathcal{L}_{method_3} = \mathcal{L}_{seg} + \mathcal{L}_{adv} \tag{3}$$

where $\mathcal{L}_{adv} = \mathbb{E}_{x \sim S}[(D(G(x)) - b)^2]$. This loss function aims to simultaneously minimize the segmentation loss and the adversarial loss. An additional normalised cross-correlation loss is used between the real and the generated images, and the two methods (with and without the additional loss) are compared.

All four methods are trained for 100 epochs during which we use the validation sets to inform us about our models' performance and to decide on the best performing models. We use the holdout set to report our final models' results and showcase their capability to generalize on the source domain. Finally, we produce tissue segmentation maps for all 824 subjects in our datasets, and use them as input into ANT's DiReCT algorithm [17] (using its default parameters) to compute cortical thickness measures. In order to analyse our results and to determine if there is a statistically significant difference between the two predicted groups, we conduct a one-way ANCOVA between dHCP and ePrime datasets on the calculated mean cortical thickness measures, controlling for gestational age at birth.

3 Results

Results on dHCP Test Dataset. Figure 5 summarizes the results of our trained models when applied on the holdout dataset of the source domain (dHCP) for which we have ground truth segmentations. The figure shows the mean Dice scores computed between the predicted tissue segmentation maps and the ground truth labels (obtained using the Draw-EM pipeline for automatic brain MRI segmentation of the developing neonatal brain [9]) for each of the four proposed models. The image space domain adaptation method (image space DA) obtained Dice scores which were significantly higher when compared to the baseline for cGM, WM and dGM tissue types. On the other hand, the latent space DA and the image space DA with the extra NCC loss showed no statistically significant difference ($p > 0.05$) in terms of reported Dice scores when compared to the baseline. These results show that our trained models were able to generalise to unseen source domain data, and that the performance on the dHCP dataset was not compromised by using domain adaption techniques.

Cortical Thickness. Figure 6 summarizes the results of applying the cortical thickness algorithm on the predicted segmentation maps for all four methods. While the dHCP results are similar across all methods, only the image space domain adaptation techniques brought the mean cortical thickness measures for the ePrime dataset down to comparable values.

As our dHCP dataset contains both term and preterm neonates, while the ePrime dataset contains only preterm babies, we conducted a one-way ANCOVA to determine whether the differences between the two groups are significant in terms of mean cortical thickness when controlling for the gestational age at birth. Our results showed that only the fourth method (image space DA + NCC) results in no significant difference in cortical thickness in dHCP and ePrime datasets. As postmenstrual age at scan (PMA) is also associated with cortical thickness [9], we conducted an ANCOVA analysis when controlling for PMA and obtained similar results, meaning no significant differences between groups for the fourth method only.

Example Predictions. Finally, Fig. 7 shows example predictions on both the source and target domains, for all four methods. For the ePrime example, the

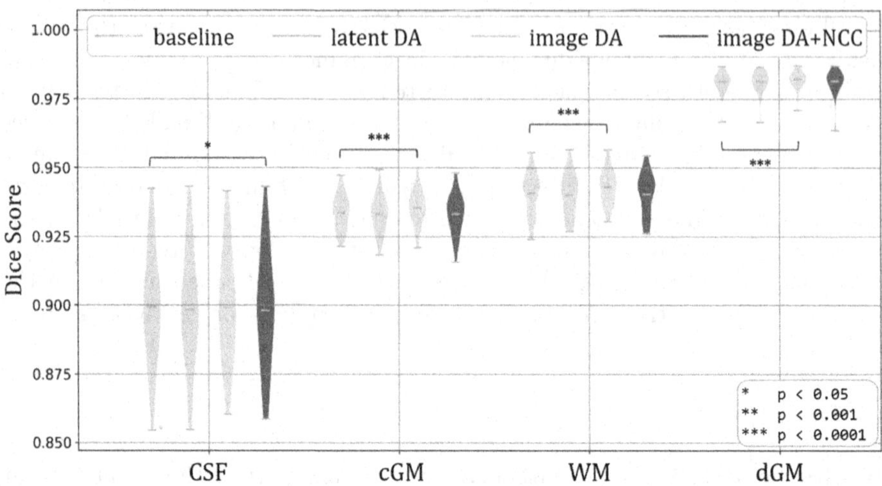

Fig. 5. The results on our dHCP holdout dataset for all four methods. Methods which are significantly different when compared to the baseline method are shown above each pair.

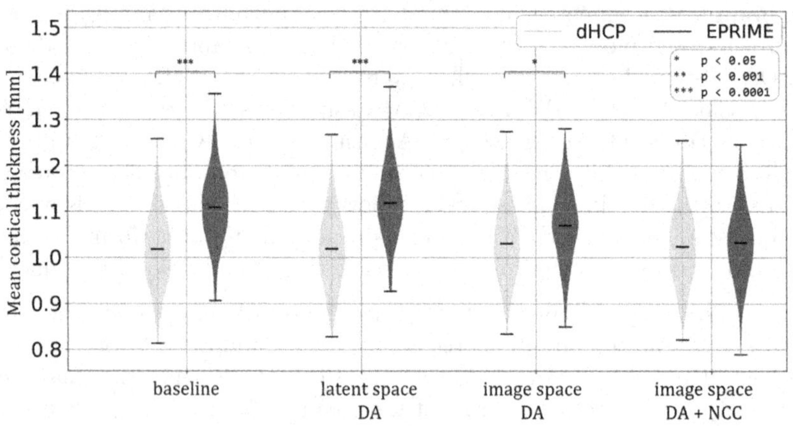

Fig. 6. Mean cortical thickness measures computed for all the images in our source and target datasets. The results of the one-way ANCOVA (controlling for gestational age at birth) are reported above each group in terms of *p-values.*

yellow arrow points to an error that can be observed in the image space DA method which underestimates the CSF boundary. This is because the ePrime dataset contains only preterm-born neonates which, as reported in [4], have more CSF than the term-born neonates when compared at term-equivalent age. The generator in the image space DA method will therefore try to produce realistic looking preterm babies, which will end up having an enlarged CSF boundary. This problem is ameliorated when adding the extra NCC loss which aims to constrain the generator to produce ePrime-like contrasts while keeping the overall shape of anatomy the same. The white arrow points to an area of the brain where the baseline method did not segment the cortical gray/white matter boundary well, while the unsupervised domain adaptation methods correctly identified the structure. Finally, the circle is showing an area where the latent space DA misclassified the structure as WM, when, in fact, it was supposed to be CSF.

4 Discussion and Future Work

In this work we showed for the first time the application of unsupervised domain adaptation techniques for the purpose of harmonising tissue segmentation maps of two independent neonatal cohorts (dHCP and ePrime) acquired with different scanning protocols. We compared these methods with a fully-supervised segmentation network, and proposed the use of an extra NCC loss to constrain the image generator network to produce more realistic ePrime-like images. Our cortical thickness analysis showed that the proposed method achieved harmonisation of our two datasets in terms of cortical gray matter tissue segmentation maps. For future work we plan to adapt our work to 3D structural MRI scans, and extend it to harmonise diffusion MRI datasets.

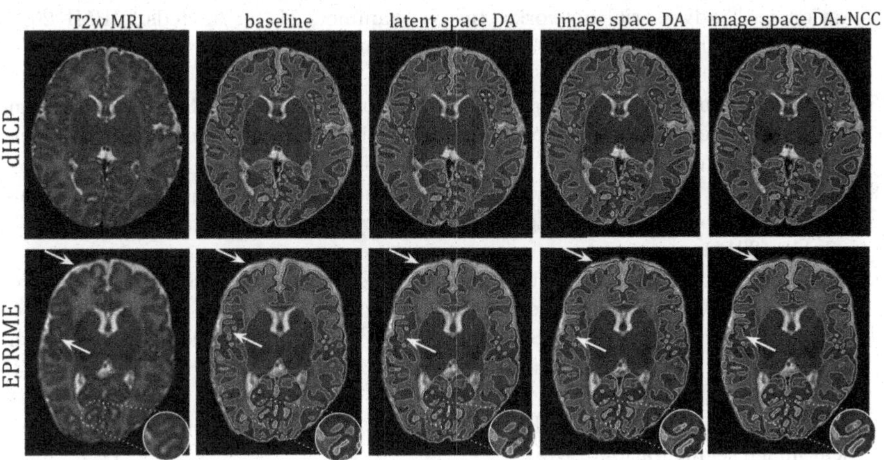

Fig. 7. Example predictions for all four methods. The first line shows a T2w MRI axial slice from the dHCP dataset together with the predicted maps for all four methods. The second line shows an example from the ePrime dataset. (Color figure online)

Acknowledgments. This work was supported by the Academy of Medical Sciences Springboard Award (SBF004\1040), European Research Council under the European Union's Seventh Framework Programme (FP7/ 20072013)/ERC grant agreement no. 319456 dHCP project, the Wellcome/EPSRC Centre for Medical Engineering at King's

College London (WT 203148/Z/16/Z), the NIHR Clinical Research Facility (CRF) at Guy's and St Thomas' and by the National Institute for Health Research Biomedical Research Centre based at Guy's and St Thomas' NHS Foundation Trust and King's College London. The views expressed are those of the authors and not necessarily those of the NHS, the NIHR or the Department of Health.

References

1. Ball, G., et al.: Multimodal image analysis of clinical influences on preterm brain development. Ann. Neurol. **82**, 233–246 (2017)
2. Cordero-Grande, L., Hughes, E.J., Hutter, J., Price, A.N., Hajnal, J.V.: Three-dimensional motion corrected sensitivity encoding reconstruction for multi-shot multi-slice MRI: application to neonatal brain imaging. Magn. Reson. Med. **79**, 1365–1376 (2018)
3. Ganin, Y., Lempitsky, V.: Unsupervised domain adaptation by backpropagation (2014)
4. Georgios, A., Hugo, L., Ulrika, A., Nelly, P., Mats, B.: Brain growth gains and losses in extremely preterm infants at term. Cereb. Cortex **25**, 1897–1905 (2014)
5. Hughes, E.J., et al.: A dedicated neonatal brain imaging system. Magn. Reson. Med. **78**, 794–804 (2017)
6. Isola, P., Zhu, J.Y., Zhou, T., Efros, A.A.: Image-to-image translation with conditional adversarial networks (2016)
7. Kamnitsas, K., et al.: Unsupervised domain adaptation in brain lesion segmentation with adversarial networks. In: Niethammer, M., et al. (eds.) IPMI 2017. LNCS, vol. 10265, pp. 597–609. Springer, Cham (2017). https://doi.org/10.1007/978-3-319-59050-9_47
8. Kuklisova-Murgasova, M., Quaghebeur, G., Rutherford, M.A., Hajnal, J.V., Schnabel, J.A.: Reconstruction of fetal brain MRI with intensity matching and complete outlier removal. Med. Image Anal. **16**, 1550–1564 (2012)
9. Makropoulos, A., et al.: The developing human connectome project: a minimal processing pipeline for neonatal cortical surface reconstruction. Neuroimage **173**, 88–112 (2018)
10. Mao, X., Li, Q., Xie, H., Lau, R.Y.K., Wang, Z., Smolley, S.P.: Least squares generative adversarial networks (2016)
11. Miotto, R., Wang, F., Wang, S., Jiang, X., Dudley, J.T.: Deep learning for healthcare: review, opportunities and challenges. Briefings Bioinform. **19**, 1236–1246 (2018)
12. Ronneberger, O., Fischer, P., Brox, T.: U-Net: convolutional networks for biomedical image segmentation (2015)
13. Rueckert, D., Sonoda, L.I., Hayes, C., Hill, D.L.G., Leach, M.O., Hawkes, D.J.: Nonrigid registration using free-form deformations: application to breast MR images. IEEE Trans. Med. Imaging **18**, 712–721 (1999)
14. Schuh, A., et al. : Unbiased construction of a temporally consistent morphological atlas of neonatal brain development. bioRxiv (2018)
15. Smith, L.N.: No more pesky learning rate guessing games. CoRR (2015)
16. Sudre, C.H., Li, W., Vercauteren, T., Ourselin, S., Jorge Cardoso, M.: Generalised dice overlap as a deep learning loss function for highly unbalanced segmentations. In: Cardoso, M.J., et al. (eds.) DLMIA/ML-CDS -2017. LNCS, vol. 10553, pp. 240–248. Springer, Cham (2017). https://doi.org/10.1007/978-3-319-67558-9_28

17. Tustison, N.J., et al.: The ANTs cortical thickness processing pipeline. In: Medical Imaging 2013: Biomedical Applications in Molecular, Structural, and Functional Imaging (2013)
18. Ulyanov, D., Vedaldi, A., Lempitsky, V.: Instance normalization: the missing ingredient for fast stylization (2016)

A Multi-task Approach Using Positional Information for Ultrasound Placenta Segmentation

Veronika A. Zimmer[1(✉)], Alberto Gomez[1], Emily Skelton[1], Nooshin Ghavami[1], Robert Wright[1], Lei Li[1,2,3], Jacqueline Matthew[1], Joseph V. Hajnal[1], and Julia A. Schnabel[1]

[1] School of Biomedical Engineering and Imaging Sciences, King's College London, London, UK
veronika.zimmer@kcl.ac.uk

[2] School of Biomedical Engineering, Shanghai Jiao Tong University, Shanghai, China

[3] School of Data Science, Fudan University, Shanghai, China

Abstract. Automatic segmentation of the placenta in fetal ultrasound (US) is challenging due to its high variations in shape, position and appearance. Convolutional neural networks (CNN) are the state-of-the-art in medical image segmentation and have already been applied successfully to extract the placenta in US. However, the performance of CNNs depends highly on the availability of large training sets which also need to be representative for new unseen data. In this work, we propose to inform the network about the variability in the data distribution via an auxiliary task to improve performances for under representative training sets. The auxiliary task has two objectives: (i) enlarging of the training set with easily obtainable labels, and (ii) including more information about the variability of the data in the training process. In particular, we use transfer learning and multi-task learning to incorporate the placental position in a U-Net architecture. We test different models for the segmentation of anterior and posterior placentas in fetal US. Our results suggest that these placenta types represent different distributions. By including the position of the placenta as an auxiliary task, the segmentation accuracy for both anterior and posterior placentas is improved when the specific type of placenta is not included in the training set.

1 Introduction

Fetal ultrasound (US) is used globally as the main imaging modality to monitor fetal health. Routine clinical scans focus on the fetal body and its development, while the placenta, an organ that connects the blood supply of mother and fetus, is rarely studied in the literature. The placenta is known to influence fetal health, but only its position is routinely assessed. The main factors limiting a more thorough routine assessment of size and morphology are the high variations in shape and position of the placenta and the lack of contrast in US. Automatic

Y. Hu et al. (Eds.): ASMUS 2020/PIPPI 2020, LNCS 12437, pp. 264–273, 2020.
https://doi.org/10.1007/978-3-030-60334-2_26

extraction of placental position, shape and function potentially provides valuable information during pregnancy. This work focuses on the segmentation of the placenta specifically considering its position in the womb - anterior or posterior. Anterior placentas grow at the front of the uterus towards the mother's abdomen (Fig. 1, top row) and posterior placentas grow at the back of the uterus towards the mother's spine (Fig. 1, bottom row). Anterior placentas are closer to the US probe, yielding higher contrast between placental and other tissues. On the other hand, the appearance of posterior placentas in US often suffers from shadows (the fetus can lie between the US probe and placenta) and attenuation artifacts. The placenta can be sited in any position between the anterior or posterior of the uterine wall, however these are the largest difference in site and therefore the rationale behind assessing the segmentation task in the two locations.

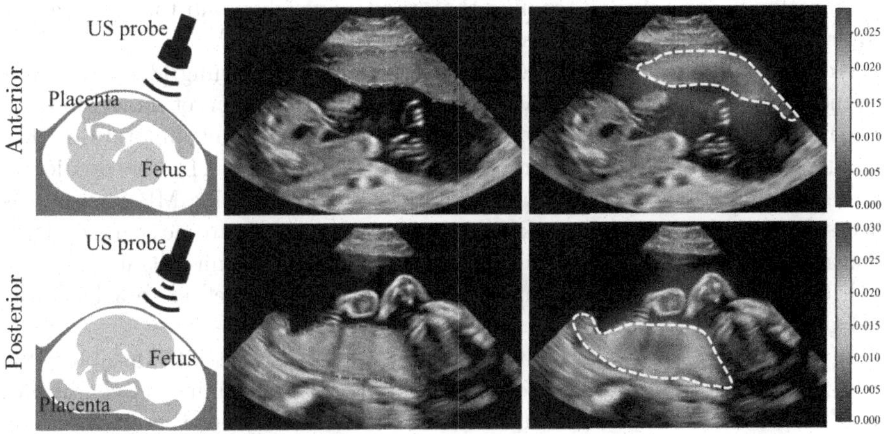

Fig. 1. Examples of anterior (top row) and posterior (bottom row) placentas in US. The placenta is delineated by the red (middle column) and white (right column) dashed line. Attention maps generated by a classification model are shown in the right column. (Color figure online)

Early works in placenta segmentation in US images have focused on the segmentation of anterior placentas [1,2]. To generalize the segmentation, semi-automatic methods have been proposed in [2,3]. Both methods need a manual initialization to find the position of the placenta in the image. In [4], an ensemble of methods is proposed to increase robustness: First, an initial segmentation of the placenta is predicted using a 2D slice, and then a multi-atlas label fusion algorithm is used to provide the full segmentation in 3D. In recent years, convolutional neural networks (CNNs) have become the state-of-the-art methods for medical image segmentation and have also shown good performance for segmenting structures in US images, including the placenta [5–7]. One major drawback of the use of CNNs in medical imaging is their requirement of a large amount of annotated data, which is expensive and time-consuming to acquire. In addition, the training data has to be selected carefully to represent the true data distribution in order to create a model which can generalize to unseen data. Some segmentation tasks can have great variability in the data which is difficult to capture with limited training data. To relate this to our problem at hand: we hypothesize that a segmentation model only trained on placentas at a certain position (e.g. anterior) is likely to underperform for the segmentation of placentas on other positions (e.g. posterior).

To deal with the lack of large annotated data sets, transfer learning is a common strategy in many (medical and non-medical) applications, where information and/or features can be transferred from another image domain, or another task. For the former, one starts with pre-trained models [8] (e.g., pre-trained on large natural image datasets such as ImageNet) and then fine-tune the model weights on the new data. The assumption is that the pre-trained weights, even when trained on a different data domain, provide a better initialization for the optimization process during training than random weights, and that less data is required to achieve good performance for the final model [9].

Another approach is to use self-supervised transfer learning [8,10] to adapt the model to a new task. This involves pre-training on the target image domain, but training for a task (the pretext task) which uses different annotations that are already part of the data (or very easy to obtain). In [11], the prediction of the location of multiple anatomical positions in 2D cardiac MR images was successfully used as a pretext task to boost the accuracy of cardiac segmentation. The transfer learning has been enhanced by a multi-task training strategy, where both the pretext task and the main task are optimized together to achieve the best performance.

In this work, we propose to inform the network about the data variability via an auxiliary task to improve performance in unfavorable training set conditions. For this, we use transfer and multi-task learning. We choose the classification of the position of the placenta as a pretext task and the segmentation as the downstream task. We hypothesize that the appearance of the placenta is related to its position and therefore prior knowledge about the placental position can improve segmentation accuracy. Since the position of the placenta is typically recorded in fetal screening, the pretext task does not require any additional manual labeling and many more images can be used for pre-training than for the segmentation task. We incorporate the classification task in the encoder part of a segmentation U-Net for pre-training and show that by using transfer and multi-task learning, the segmentation accuracy for both anterior and posterior placentas is improved when the training set does not contain the specific type of placenta.

2 Methods

We present and compare four placenta segmentation frameworks including: a baseline UNet segmentation network (UNet), a pre-trained UNet (Pre-Unet) using transfer learning, a multi-task UNet (MT-UNet) and a pre-trained, multi-task UNet (PreMT-UNet). For both the pre-training and the multi-task, a placenta position classification task is defined in addition to the placenta segmentation task. These two tasks can be combined subsequently or trained end-to-end in a single network, as described below.

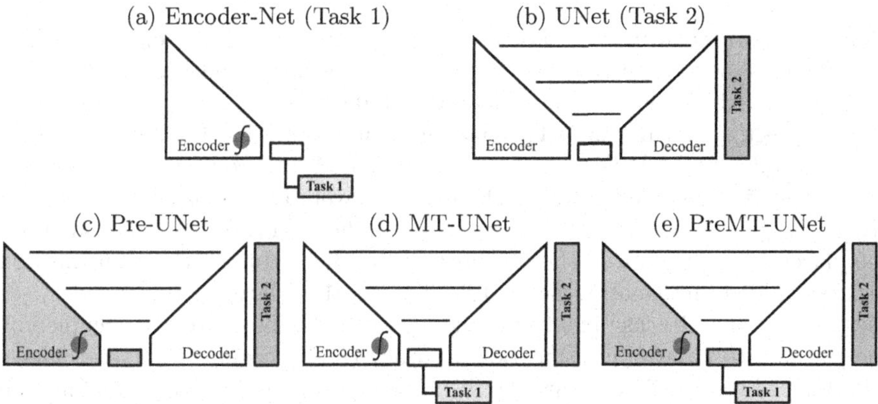

Fig. 2. Network architectures for placenta segmentation (Task 2) incorporating information from placental position classification (Task 1) in different ways: (a) Classification network with attention mechanism (blue circle); (b) Vanilla U-net for segmentation; (c) Pretraining of the encoder on Task 1, followed by a fine-tuning on Task 2; (d) Multi-task learning on both tasks simultaneously; (e) Like (d), but with pretrained weights on Task 1. Pretrained parts are colored in gray. The horizontal lines refer to the skip connections. (Color figure online)

In a supervised CNN approach, the classification or segmentation of an object is learned only driven by the data from a training set $\mathcal{T} = \{(I_n, L_n), n = 1, \ldots, N\}$ with images $I_n : \mathbb{R}^d \rightarrow \mathbb{R}$. The reference labels L_n are class memberships for classification and manual pixel-wise annotations for segmentation, respectively. The model f is trained to estimate for an unseen input image I its label $\tilde{L} = f(I, \Theta)$. The training aims to optimize a loss function $\mathcal{L}$, which measures the agreement between reference and estimated labels, for the training set $\mathcal{T}$ with respect to the model parameters Θ.

Image Segmentation. For segmentation, $L_n = S_n : \mathbb{R}^d \rightarrow \{0, 1\}$ is the pixel-wise manual annotation of placental tissue in image I_n. Our segmentation network $f_{\text{Seg}}(I, \Theta_{\text{Seg}})$ is based on the widely used U-net architecture [12] and predicts a segmentation $\tilde{S}$ for image I with network parameters Θ_{Seg}. The network has a fully convolutional encoder-decoder structure with 4 layers (strided convolutions using max pooling for downsampling, ReLUs and dropout in the encoder layers for regularization with $(32, 64, 128, 256)$ feature maps per layer), a bottleneck layer in between and skip connections from encoder to decoder (see

Fig. 2(b)). The U-net is trained by minimizing the sum of the binary cross-entropy loss and Dice loss between the output $\tilde{S}$ of the network and the manual reference segmentations S. We denote the loss for image segmentation as $\mathcal{L}_{\text{Segm}}(\tilde{S}, S)$.

Image Classification. For classification, the labels are $L_n = \mathbf{c}_n = \mathbf{e}_c \in \mathbb{R}^C$ with the c-th unit vector $\mathbf{e}_c$ and $c = 0, \ldots, C-1$ denoting the class membership of image I_n with C classes. The model is denoted by $f_{\text{Class}}(I, \Theta_{\text{Class}})$ and predicts the class vector $\tilde{\mathbf{c}}$ for image I. The classification network has the same structure as the encoder of the U-net (see Fig. 2(a)) followed by a convolutional, a linear and a sigmoid layer. We refer to these extra layers as the pretext branch. In order to implicitly introduce, through this classification task, information about the placenta localization in the images that can be useful for the segmentation task, we added an attention layer [13] after the third layer of the encoder (see Fig. 2). This layer learns pixel-wise weights that highlight the region occupied by the placenta to improve classification accuracy (Fig. 1, right). An unseen image I is assigned to class $\tilde{c}$ if $\tilde{c} = \text{argmax}(\tilde{\mathbf{c}})$. Cross entropy is used as a loss function for classification, denoted by $\mathcal{L}_{\text{Class}}(\tilde{\mathbf{c}}, \mathbf{c})$.

Transfer and Multi-task Learning. The classification of the placenta position ($c = 0$: anterior, $c = 1$: no placenta tissue in image, or $c = 2$: posterior) is used as a pretext task (task 1). In order to optimize both tasks in one single network, we added the pretext branch after the encoder in the U-Net, and added also the attention mechanism to the encoder, as shown in Fig. 2. We propose three different models to incorporate the pretext task in a segmentation network:

- *Pre-UNet:* In the first strategy, both tasks are optimized sequentially as typically done in transfer learning. First, the encoder of the U-Net and the pretext branch are trained on task 1. After convergence, the U-Net is fine-tuned on task 2, the segmentation (see Fig. 2(c)).
- *MT-UNet:* In the second strategy, both tasks are optimized simultaneously (Fig. 2(d)). The loss functions $\mathcal{L}_{\text{Class}}(\tilde{\mathbf{c}}, \mathbf{c})$ and $\mathcal{L}_{\text{Segm}}(\tilde{S}, S)$ are combined in a multi-task loss function $\mathcal{L}_{\text{MT}}(\tilde{S}, \tilde{\mathbf{c}}, S, \mathbf{c})$ as

$$\mathcal{L}_{\text{MT}}(\tilde{S}, \tilde{\mathbf{c}}, S, \mathbf{c}) = \mathcal{L}_{\text{Class}}(\tilde{\mathbf{c}}, \mathbf{c}) + \beta \mathcal{L}_{\text{Segm}}(\tilde{S}, S). \quad (1)$$

  The parameter $\beta > 1$ emphasizes the downstream task (placental segmentation) in the training.
- *PreMT-UNet* The last strategy is to initialize the weights of the encoder and pretext branch with the pre-trained weights on task 1, and fine-tune the weights of the U-Net using both tasks simultaneously using the loss function in Eq. (1) (see Fig. 2(e)).

3 Experiments and Results

Dataset. To evaluate our methods, we used a dataset of real-time 3D US image streams sweeping over the placenta from 67 patients. The gestational age (GA) is 19–33 weeks, with 37 patients in the second and 30 patients in the third trimester of pregnancy. The position of the placentas is anterior for 35 patients and posterior for 32 patients. For each patient, 5-30 3D US images were selected, which resulted in 1054 images in total. An expert sonographer manually segmented the placenta in a subset of 269 images, from now on referred to as the segmentation dataset, from 56 patients.

We train the networks in 2D. Therefore, we extracted $17 - 48$ slices from each 3D volume covering the elevation angles with a step size of 2°. In the following, we report the number of images x of which y have manual segmentations as x/y. We split the images into training (41 patients in total), validation (12 patients) and test sets (12 patients), which resulted in 21,274/5,370 2D images for training, 5,807/2,167 images for validation and 5,149/1,718 images for testing. This is equivalent to 694/150 (training), 186/65 (validation) and 172/54 (testing) images in 3D. To test the generalization ability of our models to different placental position, we divided the training data into three sets:

- *Set A* contains only manual segmentations of anterior placentas. Total number of images in set A: 21,274 images with 2,632 manual segmentations.
- *Set P* contains only manual segmentations of posterior placentas. Total number of images in set P: 21,274 images with 2,738 manual segmentations.
- *Set AP* contains manual segmentation from both anterior and posterior placentas. To ensure a fair comparison to training set A and set P, we included only half of the images from these sets. This results in a total number of images for set AP of 21,274/2,669.

For evaluation, the segmented slices are reconstructed to a volume and segmentation accuracy according to the Dice score and Hausdorff distance is computed in 3D. To check whether the results are significantly different, we performed the Wilcoxon Signed-Rank Test between the UNet and each of the proposed models on the corresponding training set.

Implementation. The models were implemented using PyTorch. We resampled the images to 128×128 pixels. The loss function is optimized using the Adam optimizer with a learning rate of $1 \cdot 10^5$ for pre-training on task 1 and $1 \cdot 10^4$ for segmentation and multi-task learning. We cut off the 0.1 and 99.9 percentile of intensities and performed contrast stretching before normalizing the intensity values between 0 and 1. We augmented the data set by flipping the image around the x-axis (image is not flipped upside down to keep a correct positioning of the frustum), and affine transformations (translation range of 30 pixels and rotation range of 25°). Those training parameters and the U-Net architecture as described in Sect. 2 were selected using the validation set.

The baseline UNet and Pre-UNet were trained for 500 epochs. For multi-task learning, we followed the training procedure described in [11]. Since the number of training data for task 1 and task 2 was not consistent (task 1 > 20,000, task 2 $\approx$ 2,700), a training procedure alternating between the two different tasks at each epoch was employed. At each epoch, task 1 was optimized for one and task 2 for $\beta = 8$ (chosen empirically) sub-iterations. Here, $\beta > 1$ was chosen to give a higher weight to task 2. To ensure that task 2 was trained for approximately the same sub-iterations as for models UNet and Pre-UNet, the models MT-UNet and PreMT-UNet were only trained for 20 epochs.

Experimental Results. The encoder and the pretext branch are pretrained on the full training dataset of 21,274 images. This yielded a balanced accuracy of 0.89 for anterior placentas, 0.87 for posterior placentas and 0.84 for no placenta. As illustrated in Fig. 1, right column, and Fig. 3, second row, the resulting attention maps localize the placenta in the image.

Table 1. Segmentation accuracy measured using the Dice coefficient and the Hausdorff distance. A baseline U-Net (UNet) is compared to three models (Pre-UNet, MT-UNet, PreMT-UNet) incorporating the auxiliary task of placenta position classification in different ways. All models are trained with three training sets: set A (only anterior), set P (only posterior), set AP (both anterior and posterior). Significant different results with $p < 0.05$ between a model and the corresponding UNet are marked with *.

Training		Dice coefficient		Hausdorff distance (mm)	
Set		Anterior	Posterior	Anterior	Posterior
A	UNet	0.86 ± 0.06	0.37 ± 0.27	36.88 ± 17.23	60.25 ± 23.65
A	Pre-UNet	$\mathbf{0.87 \pm 0.06}^*$	$0.46 \pm 0.24^*$	$\mathbf{26.79 \pm 14.37}^*$	59.34 ± 19.22
A	MT-UNet	0.86 ± 0.06	$0.51 \pm 0.27^*$	34.23 ± 16.62	57.19 ± 24.77
A	PreMT-UNet	0.86 ± 0.06	$\mathbf{0.53 \pm 0.23}^*$	34.14 ± 16.47	$\mathbf{55.50 \pm 24.50}$
P	UNet	0.61 ± 0.22	$\mathbf{0.83 \pm 0.07}$	56.34 ± 27.61	31.12 ± 10.94
P	Pre-UNet	0.63 ± 0.23	0.82 ± 0.08	$\mathbf{51.48 \pm 29.00}$	$\mathbf{29.72 \pm 14.35}$
P	MT-UNet	0.59 ± 0.23	$0.81 \pm 0.07^*$	57.03 ± 30.00	$37.63 \pm 14.48^*$
P	PreMT-UNet	$\mathbf{0.70 \pm 0.18}^*$	0.82 ± 0.07	53.64 ± 27.84	36.44 ± 15.67
AP	UNet	$\mathbf{0.87 \pm 0.07}$	$\mathbf{0.81 \pm 0.09}$	29.41 ± 23.53	$\mathbf{33.69 \pm 14.98}$
AP	Pre-UNet	$\mathbf{0.87 \pm 0.07}$	$\mathbf{0.81 \pm 0.08}$	30.09 ± 20.73	38.73 ± 17.10
AP	MT-UNet	0.86 ± 0.07	$0.77 \pm 0.11^*$	$\mathbf{24.37 \pm 14.16}$	40.98 ± 21.39
AP	PreMT-UNet	0.86 ± 0.08	$0.78 \pm 0.12^*$	28.66 ± 24.77	35.02 ± 15.22

The proposed models Pre-UNet, MT-UNet and PreMT-UNet are compared to a baseline UNet architecture, and the segmentation results for anterior and posterior placentas, trained on the three training sets A, P and AP are shown in Table 1 and Fig. 3.

A first observation is that anterior and posterior placentas represent two different distributions in the data. The vanilla UNet trained only on anterior placentas (set A) achieves a high Dice score of 0.86, but performs badly on posterior placentas with a Dice score of 0.37. When trained only on posterior placentas (set P), the Dice is higher for anterior (0.61) and a bit lower for posterior placentas (0.83), confirming that it is easier to segment anterior placentas.

With the incorporation of the auxiliary task on additional training data (task 1), the performance of the models Pre-UNet, MT-UNet and PreMT-UNet increase both for posterior placentas when trained on set A, and anterior placentas when trained on set P. Model PreMT-UNet improves significantly ($p < 0.05$) the baseline UNet to a Dice of 0.53 for posterior on set A, and to a Dice of 0.70 for anterior on set P (see also Fig. 3, columns three and four). Interestingly, the best Hausdorff distance is obtained more often with model Pre-UNet.

When trained on set AP, which is representative for both anterior and posterior placentas, the additional information of placental position does not add much and all models perform comparably, only significantly slightly worse results for MT-UNet and PreMT-UNet on posterior placentas measured using Dice.

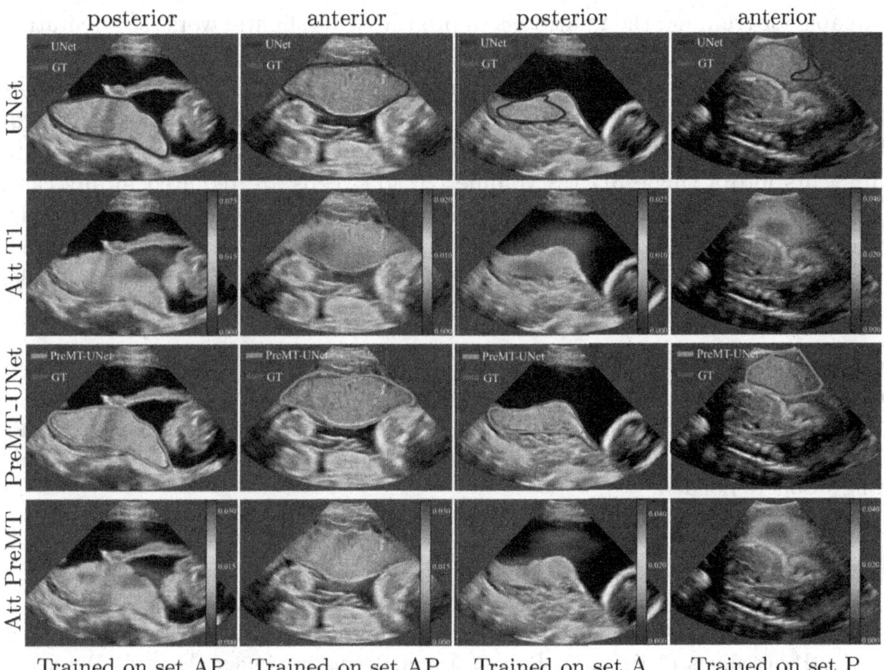

Fig. 3. 2D slice of placenta segmentation with vanilla UNet in blue (top row) and PreMT-UNet in green (third row). Manual reference segmentations are shown in red. Attention maps localize the placenta and are generated by pretraining on task 1 (second row) and by PreMT-UNet (bottom row). First and second columns are results when trained on set AP (both anterior and posterior placentas), the third column when trained on set A (only anterior placentas) and last column when trained on set P (only posterior placentas). (Color figure online)

4 Conclusion

In this work, we explored the effect of transfer and multi-task learning on the segmentation of anterior and posterior placentas in 3D US. Generating a large amount of manually annotated training data is time-consuming and requires a high level of expertise. We propose to use different annotations (already available or easier to produce) in a pre-training and multi-task fashion to improve performance. We compare three architectures, which incorporate this task in a segmentation U-Net in different ways and our results show that the models can improve segmentation accuracy. In addition, we showed that anterior and posterior placentas represent different distributions and that the information of placental position yields much better segmentation results, when the specific type of placenta is lacking in the training set. When both placental types are available for training, the multi-task approach yields slightly worse segmentation accuracy than a vanilla UNet. We will investigate this effect in the future.

This study addresses a 3D segmentation by stacking 2D segmentations. This limits the amount of 3D context that can be learned by the networks, but introduces some advantages: image quality is superior in 2D US; the entire placenta rarely fits into a single 3D US volume [7], so sweeps are required in any case; the volumes obtained for sweeps need to be stitched for which registration (particularly challenging for placenta which lacks features) or tracking is required. If tracking is used, then reconstructing 3D volumes from 2D slices is possible. Last, 3D volumes can also be processed slice-wise, as we demonstrate here.

Acknowledgments. This work was supported by the Wellcome Trust IEH Award [102431], by the Wellcome/EPSRC Centre for Medical Engineering [WT203148/Z/16/Z] and by the National Institute for Health Research (NIHR) Biomedical Research Centre at Guy's and St Thomas' NHS Foundation Trust and King's College London.

References

1. Oguz, I, et al.: Automated placenta segmentation from 3D ultrasound images. In: Proceedings of Preterm, Perinatal and Paediatric Image Analysis Workshop (PIPPI), pp. 1–10 (2016)
2. Stevenson, G.N., Collins, S.L., Ding, J., Impey, L., Noble, J.A.: 3-D ultrasound segmentation of the placenta using the random walker algorithm: reliability and agreement. Ultrasound Med. Biol. **41**(12), 3182–3193 (2015)
3. Oguz, I., et al.: Minimally interactive placenta segmentation from three-dimensional ultrasound images. J. Med. Imaging **7**(1), 014004 (2020)
4. Oguz, B.U., et al.: Combining deep learning and multi-atlas label fusion for automated placenta segmentation from 3D US. In: Proceedings DATRA/Preterm, Perinatal and Paediatric Image Analysis Workshop (PIPPI), pp. 138–148 (2018)
5. Looney, P., et al.: Fully automated, real-time 3D ultrasound segmentation to estimate first trimester placental volume using deep learning. JCI Insight **3**(11), e120178 (2018)

6. Yang, X., et al.: Towards automated semantic segmentation in prenatal volumetric ultrasound. IEEE Trans. Med. Imaging **38**(1), 180–193 (2018)
7. Zimmer, V.A., et al.: Towards whole placenta segmentation at late gestation using multi-view ultrasound images. In: Shen, D., et al. (eds.) MICCAI 2019. LNCS, vol. 11768, pp. 628–636. Springer, Cham (2019). https://doi.org/10.1007/978-3-030-32254-0_70
8. Shin, H., et al.: Deep convolutional neural networks for computer-aided detection: CNN architectures, dataset characteristics and transfer learning. IEEE Trans. Med. Imaging **35**(5), 1285–1298 (2016)
9. Rajpurkar, P., et al.: AppendiXnet: deep learning for diagnosis of appendicitis from a small dataset of CT exams using video pretraining. Sci. Rep. **10**(1), 1–7 (2020)
10. Raghu, M., Zhang, C., Kleinberg, J., Bengio, S.: Transfusion: understanding transfer learning for medical imaging. In: Proceedings of NeurIPS, pp. 3342–3352 (2019)
11. Bai, W., et al.: Self-supervised learning for cardiac MR image segmentation by anatomical position prediction. In: Shen, D., et al. (eds.) MICCAI 2019. LNCS, vol. 11765, pp. 541–549. Springer, Cham (2019). https://doi.org/10.1007/978-3-030-32245-8_60
12. Ronneberger, O., Fischer, P., Brox, T.: U-Net: convolutional networks for biomedical image segmentation. In: Navab, N., Hornegger, J., Wells, W.M., Frangi, A.F. (eds.) MICCAI 2015. LNCS, vol. 9351, pp. 234–241. Springer, Cham (2015). https://doi.org/10.1007/978-3-319-24574-4_28
13. Jetley, S., Lord, N.A., Lee, N., Torr, P.H.: Learn to pay attention. In: Proceedings of ICLR (2018)

Spontaneous Preterm Birth Prediction Using Convolutional Neural Networks

Tomasz Włodarczyk[1,4](✉), Szymon Płotka[1,4], Przemysław Rokita[1], Nicole Sochacki-Wójcicka[2,3], Jakub Wójcicki[2,3], Michał Lipa[2,3], and Tomasz Trzciński[1,5]

[1] Warsaw University of Technology, Warsaw, Poland
wlodarczyk.tomasz@gmail.com
[2] Medical University of Warsaw, Warsaw, Poland
[3] Ernest Wójcicki Prenatal Medicine Foundation, Warsaw, Poland
[4] Fetai Health Ltd., Warsaw, Poland
[5] Tooploox, Warsaw, Poland

Abstract. An estimated 15 million babies are born too early every year. Approximately 1 million children die each year due to complications of preterm birth (PTB). Many survivors face a lifetime of disability, including learning disabilities and visual and hearing problems. Although manual analysis of ultrasound images (US) is still prevalent, it is prone to errors due to its subjective component and complex variations in the shape and position of organs across patients. In this work, we introduce a conceptually simple convolutional neural network (CNN) trained for segmenting prenatal ultrasound images and classifying task for the purpose of preterm birth detection. Our method efficiently segments different types of cervixes in transvaginal ultrasound images while simultaneously predicting a preterm birth based on extracted image features without human oversight. We employed three popular network models: U-Net, Fully Convolutional Network, and Deeplabv3 for the cervix segmentation task. Based on the conducted results and model efficiency, we decided to extend U-Net by adding a parallel branch for classification task. The proposed model is trained and evaluated on a dataset consisting of 354 2D transvaginal ultrasound images and achieved a segmentation accuracy with a mean Jaccard coefficient index of 0.923 ± 0.081 and a classification sensitivity of 0.677 ± 0.042 with a 3.49% false positive rate. Our method obtained better results in the prediction of preterm birth based on transvaginal ultrasound images compared to state-of-the-art methods.

Keywords: Classification · Convolutional Neural Networks (CNNs) · Spontaneous preterm birth prediction (sPTB)

1 Introduction

Preterm birth (PTB), defined as birth before 37 weeks of gestation, affects 5–18% of pregnancies worldwide, which is equivalent to 15 million preterm neonates each

Y. Hu et al. (Eds.): ASMUS 2020/PIPPI 2020, LNCS 12437, pp. 274–283, 2020.
https://doi.org/10.1007/978-3-030-60334-2_27

year [1]. Despite major advances in perinatal care, preterm birth still accounts for 75% of neonatal deaths and over 50% of neurological handicap in children. Prediction and early detection of women at high risk of PTB are crucial as it allows timely intervention. Current diagnostic methods involve the collection of maternal characteristics and transvaginal ultrasound imaging conducted in the first and second trimester of pregnancy. Analysis of the ultrasound data is based on visual inspection of images by a gynaecologist, sometimes supported by hand-designed image features such as cervical length. Apart from that, it can be difficult, even for an expert, to identify relevant structures within the image. Due to the complexity of this process and its subjective component, approximately 30% of spontaneous preterm deliveries are not correctly predicted. We gave an overview of the current state-of-art models for semantic segmentation, especially applied in the recent research on medical image segmentation [5]. We introduced the major, popular network structures used for image segmentation: Fully Convolutional Network, U-Net and Deeplabv3 for cervix segmentation task. We evaluated all three proposed models against cervix segmentation task, compared its results and decided to proceed with U-Net as the one obtained best segmentation results. Recently, several works showed how quantitative methods based on U-Net-like architecture can successfully be used to perform a joint segmentation and classification task [6,7]. However, none of those methods are dedicated to preterm birth classification tasks.

In this paper, we address the problem of spontaneous preterm birth prediction. We introduce a novel approach in the context of preterm birth, that is inspired by linking classification and segmentation together. As a contribution, we propose a deep-learning preterm prediction and cervix segmentation framework for ultrasound images. We show that extracted cervix features in the U-Net contracting path contains valid information for preterm classification task. To the best of our knowledge, this is the first one-stage work which employs deep convolutional neural networks (CNNs) for detecting preterm birth using transvaginal ultrasounds images.

Our method introduces objectively the obtained result, in contrast to the gynaecologist's manual approach, based solely on his knowledge. Unlike U-Net, our network is capable of detecting a preterm pregnancy and segmenting the cervix in an US image simultaneously. The preterm *vs.* control type classification is implemented by feeding a part of the features in U-Net to a sequence of fully-connected layers followed by a sigmoid layer.

2 Methods

In this section, we first discuss dataset and preprocessing used in training and testing. Secondly, we present multi-task loss function for segmentation and classification task. Then, we propose an extension for one of neural network architecture for simultaneous segmentation and classification preterm *vs.* control. Finally, we present Grad-CAM as visualization to increase understanding of the classification spontaneous preterm birth by a convolutional neural network.

Dataset: The original dataset consists of 354 two-dimensional transvaginal cervical ultrasound images. Data were collected from female volunteers during check-ups conducted in the first and second trimesters of pregnancy. Data includes 319 images of the pregnancy control group and 35 images of premature deliveries which reflects the statistical occurrence of this phenomenon in reality. Note that to get information about image labels, we waited for the pregnancy result of each patient. The data was provided by two different clinics: King's College London and Medical University of Warsaw. All images have been annotated by several independent gynecologist experts via our own annotation tool. Sample images from the data set are depicted in Fig. 1.

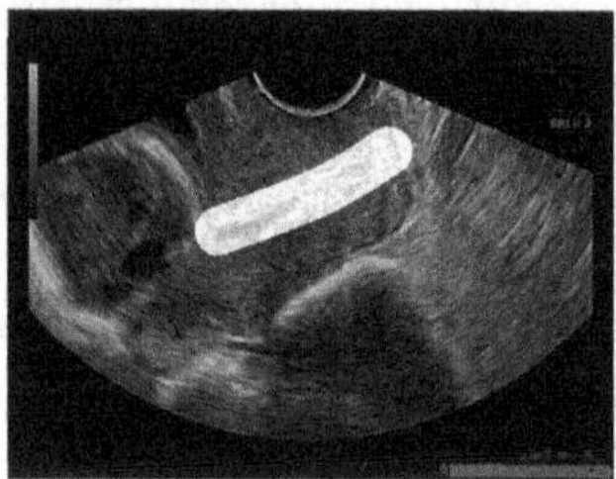

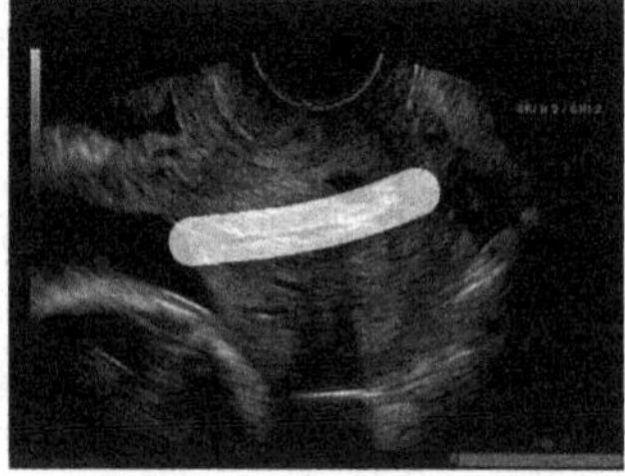

Fig. 1. Example of our 2D transvaginal ultrasound images used as a part of dataset. Input images and their masks showing the location and shape of the cervix

The annotations received contained the study identifier and four control points which allowed for the drawing of cubic Bézier curves that outlined the shape and position of the cervix in the image. Bézier curves were used to create masks for cervical segmentation.

Preprocessing: We first removed the manually embedded annotations in the form of yellow and green crosses placed by gynecologists during routine ultrasound examinations. For this purpose, we used the inpainting algorithm proposed by Telea [8], which was used in a similar case by [9]. This allowed our algorithm to learn from the images rather than learning manually embedded annotations. Note, these annotations were unrelated to the task we were doing. In order to improve model generalization we divided the dataset into three parts: training, test, and validation. Then we did a 50:50 data augmentation between the preterm class and control on each subset to avoid heavily focusing on the majority class by classification algorithm. We applied various types of data augmentation techniques such as cropping, random rotation in the range of -15 to $+15$ degrees and adding contrast, brightness or noise. As a result the set was expand to 6354 images. On the dataset, based on created annotations for each examination by several gynecological experts, we created segmentation masks, which were used to train the neural network in the segmentation task.

Loss Function: We define a multi-task total loss as

$$\mathcal{L} = \mathcal{L}_{Seg} + \mathcal{L}_{Cls} \tag{1}$$

where $\mathcal{L}_{Seg}$ and $\mathcal{L}_{Cls}$ are the binary cross-entropy loss (BCE) functions for the segmentation and classification tasks, respectively. Where y is the ground truth label, $\hat{y}$ is the prediction, BCE is defined as follows:

$$BCE(y, \hat{y}) = y \cdot log\hat{y} + (1 - y) \cdot log(1 - \hat{y}) \tag{2}$$

In order to improve the segmentation accuracy, we use the negative value of Dice coefficient (called Dice loss) as well as the criterion to optimize the model parameters. The Dice score coefficient (DSC) is a measure of overlap widely used to assess segmentation performance. Proposed in Milletari et al. [10] as a loss function, it can be expressed as

$$\mathcal{L}_{Dice} = 1 - \frac{2\sum y\hat{y}}{\sum y^2 + \sum \hat{y}^2 + \epsilon} \tag{3}$$

The ϵ term is used here to ensure the loss function stability by avoiding the numerical issue of dividing by 0.
Total segmentation loss is defined as:

$$\mathcal{L}_{Seg} = \alpha \cdot BCE + (1 - \alpha) \cdot \mathcal{L}_{Dice} \tag{4}$$

The BCE loss itself tries to match the background and foreground pixels in the prediction to the ground truth masks. BCE loss does not emphasize on keeping the object together while Dice loss considers the entire object by computing the overlap between predicted and ground truth objects. Thus combining both BCE loss and the Dice loss will give us the advantages of both. For the classification task, to account for the class imbalance between the *preterm* and *term* classes, we introduced a stronger weight in the loss function for the under-represented class (*preterm*).

$$\mathcal{L}_{Cls} = \beta \cdot BCE_w \tag{5}$$

In the experiment, α is set to 0.5, and β to 0.8.

Training: In the experiment, we selected 3812 images (60%) for training, 1271 images (20%) for validating and 1271 images (20%) for testing. Note, after augmentation, all images of a given patient were in the same set: either training, test or validation. We resized all images into 256 px × 256 px. We trained a network on a machine with AMD FX-8320 @ 3.5 GHz CPU and NVIDIA TITAN X 12 GB GPU and implemented our models using the PyTorch library with CUDA support.

We trained all networks for 500 epochs with a batch size of 4. We chose Adam optimizer with the default parameters ($\beta_1 = 0.9$ and $\beta_2 = 0.999$), learning rate of 10^{-4} and weight decay of $5 \cdot 10^{-4}$. The training took 15 h.

Visualization: In order to increase the understanding of the predictions of spontaneous preterm births performed by the convolutional neural network on ultrasound images, we have visualized them by using the gradient weighted class activation mapping (Grad-CAM) method. This method is used for visual interpretation of deep neural networks through a gradient-based location, highlighting

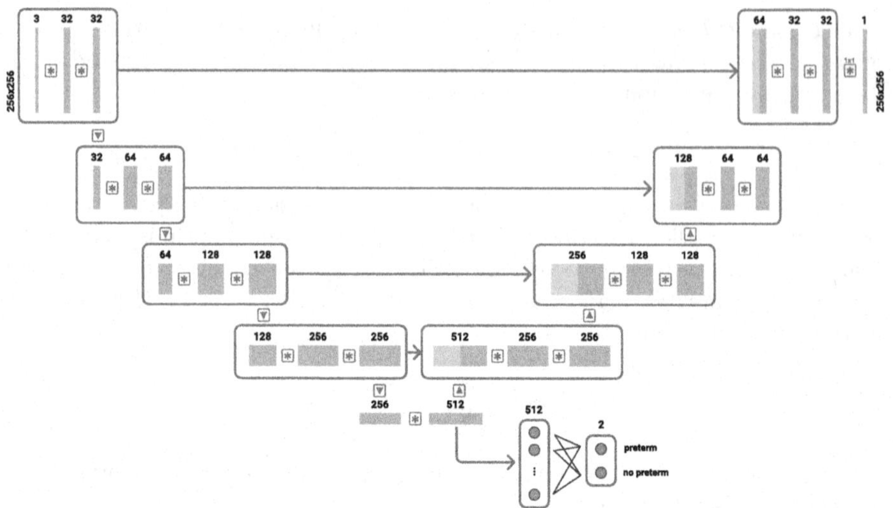

Fig. 2. Neural network architecture for simultaneous segmentation and classification for end-to-end spontaneous birth preterm classification.

the most interesting regions in the image for prediction. Grad-CAM uses gradient information provided to the last layer of the CNN to allow the viewer a greater understanding of the importance of each neuron's region of interest. By using Grad-CAM, it is possible to visualize which features in the cross section contribute to judging the class. For this purpose, we used the original implementation of the work of Selvaraju et al. [13].

3 Results

In this section, we evaluate three described neural network models and check how they perform in the task of cervix segmentation. Then, based on obtained results, the best performing model is selected, extended and evaluated for classification task.

3.1 Image Segmentation

We validated three models against the cervix segmentation task applied to transvaginal ultrasounds images: FCN, DeepLab and U-Net. Visualization of results for segmentation are presented on Fig. 3. As shown in Table 1, the best performing results were achieved by U-Net. U-Net is built upon the architecture of FCN. Besides the increased network depth to 19 layers, U-Net benefits from a superior design of skip connections between different stages of the network. The most important advancement of U-Net over FCN is the shortcut connections between layers of equal resolution in the analysis path to expansion path. This gives U-Net better performance because it has multiple upsampling layers along with more skip connections which make it more robust to scale variations as compared to FCN.

DeepLab, on the contrary, uses convolutions with upsampled filters - dilated convolutions - to achieve better control over the feature response resolution and to incorporate larger context without increasing the computational cost. However, the discontinuity between the dilated convolution kernel leads to the omission of some pixels, which may lead to the neglect of the continuity information on the image [11]. This means that whereas increasing dilation factors is important in terms of resolution and context, it can be detrimental to small objects, especially on noisy ultrasound images.

We chose the U-Net based network for the classification task for several reasons. First, we obtained the best segmentation result qualitatively. The U-Net network best predicts edges that help us classify images based on the shape of the cervix. In addition, the U-net network contains the least parameters among the other networks tested, without requiring a large number of images and length of training to get a good performance.

Table 1. Mean IoU and std scores of U-net, Fully Convolutional Network and DeepLab Net. The three models were trained for 500 epochs and use the same loss function (4)

	U-Net	FCN	DeepLab
Train	**0.975** (0.041)	0.848 (0.062)	0.813 (0.056)
Val	**0.921** (0.042)	0.770 (0.023)	0.791 (0.086)
Test	**0.913** (0.041)	0.755 (0.042)	0.756 (0.087)

3.2 Classification

We achieved good segmentation results due to the easy structure of the cervix, which is relatively large in the ultrasound image. In Fig. 4 we show examples of retrieved cervix segmentation masks for each of the classes. From these examples, it can be seen that our proposed method was able to localise cervixes which are subject to variability in scale and appearance. Table 2 shows the quantitative performance of the proposed method in terms of mean ± std of IoU coefficient, precision, recall and AUC.

Our method obtained better results according to Intersection over Union (IoU) in segmentation, recall and precision for the classification task than [12]. Table 3 presents a comparison of our results with the baseline - IoU for segmentation and recall, precision, AUC for the classification task. The confusion matrix for the preterm birth classification is shown in Table 4. We obtained specificity of 0.951 and sensitivity of 0.68 with a 3.49% false positive rate.

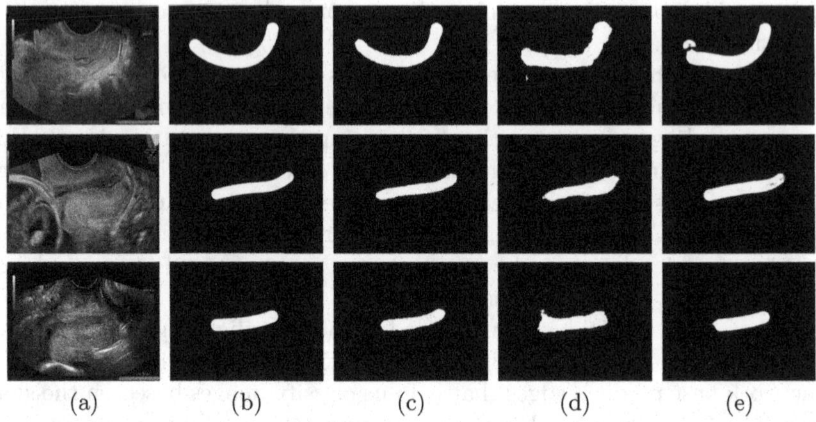

Fig. 3. Visualization of results for segmentation: a) Input image b) Ground truth mask c) U-Net d) FCN e) Deeplabv3

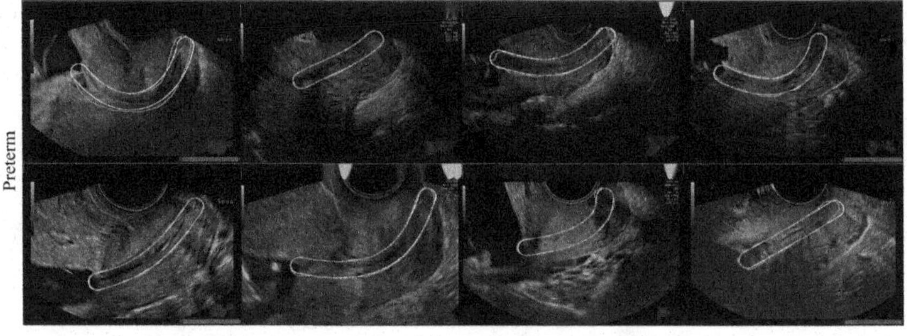

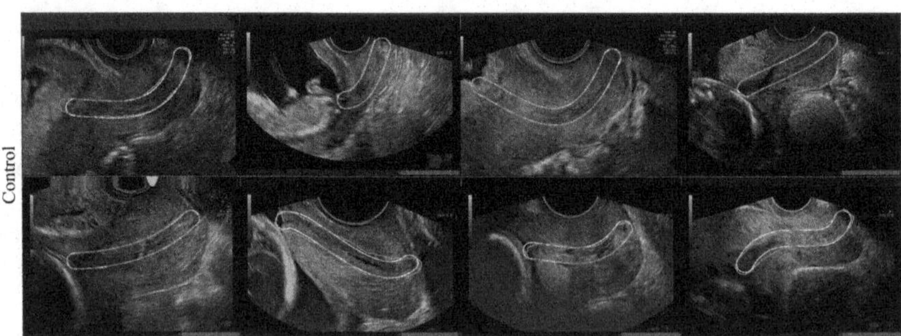

Fig. 4. Results of cervical segmentation on transvaginal ultrasound images using the segmentation part of the neural network architecture. White represents ground truth, while green represents our predictions. We obtained an average Jaccard index of 92.3, with a standard deviation of 0.081 (Color figure online)

Table 2. Segmentation (mIoU) and classification results (Recall, Precision, AUC) (mean and std) for train, validation and test dataset

	IoU	Recall	Precision	AUC
Train	0.972 (0.047)	0.781 (0.092)	0.772 (0.096)	0.782 (0.108)
Val	0.925 (0.072)	0.698 (0.023)	0.698 (0.086)	0.757 (0.156)
Test	0.923 (0.081)	0.677 (0.042)	0.683 (0.087)	0.723 (0.134)

Table 3. Comparison of the results obtained between state-of-the-art [12] and ours

	IoU	Recall	Precision	AUC
Włodarczyk et al.	0.91	0.596	0.659	0.78
Our	**0.923**	**0.677**	**0.683**	0.723

Table 4. The confusion matrix for the preterm birth classification task.

		Predicted	
		Control	Preterm
Actual	Control	1105	40
	Preterm	41	85

3.3 Grad-CAM

It was found by Baños et al. [14] that information extracted from the region along the length of the anterior cervical stroma is relevant to control vs preterm classification. In addition, Pachtman et al. [15] proved that the region along the length of the anterior cervical stroma and the analysis of its relative organization of cervical collagen fibers may have the capacity to identify preterm birth. To the contrary, Grad-CAM shows the preterm class is classified based on the lower segment of the cervix, close to the ectocervix. We can note that during classification, the neural network focuses on the heterogeneity of the density of tissues around the cervix. For the control class, our model is focusing on the top part of the largest homogeneous region in middle part of anterior cervical lip, which is the part of the cervix closest to the transducer. Examples of Grad-CAM results can be seen in Fig. 5 for the preterm and control class.

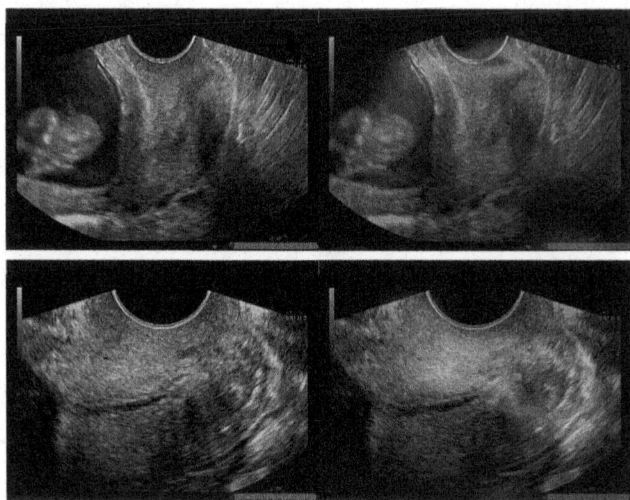

Fig. 5. Visual interpretation of CNNs through a gradient-based location, highlighting the most interesting regions in the image for prediction control (top) and preterm (bottom) class. The decision of the classifier is made based on the central parts of the ultrasound image which is similar to the analysis done manually by the physicians

4 Conclusions

The goal of this paper was to evaluate whether convolutional neural networks can be successfully applied to preterm birth prediction tasks, especially considering analysis of transvaginal ultrasound images. Conducted experiments show that a convolutional model outperforms common approaches based on manually engineered features [16] and achieves a similar level as other feature learning methods.

The proposed method achieves a segmentation accuracy with a mean Jaccard coefficient index of 0.923 ± 0.081 and a classification sensitivity of 0.68 ± 0.042. To the best of our knowledge, this is the best result of a segmentation and classification method for spontaneous preterm birth prediction using transvaginal ultrasound images. The results presented in this paper show that methods based on deep neural networks can provide automatic, quantitative analysis of ultrasound images. This, in turn, can lead to significant time savings and increase the efficiency of current diagnostic methods without losing its precision.

Our proposal, an objective method for detection preterm birth, may help to identify patients at risk for sPTB before any changes reflected by CL measurement. Although our results are encouraging, a prospective, longitudinal study is necessary to validate this technique, allow us to avoid selection bias at enrollment and control for potential confounding variables related to treatment nonuniformity. In the future, we want to reduce the size of false negative error by increasing the size of the dataset and employing UNet-3D for deeper analyses of ultrasound images.

References

1. Howson, C.P., Kinney, M.V., Mcdougall, L., Lawn, J.E.: Born too soon: preterm birth matters. Reprod. Health. **10** (2013)
2. Ronneberger, O., Fischer, P., Brox, T.: U-Net: convolutional networks for biomedical image segmentation. In: Navab, N., Hornegger, J., Wells, W.M., Frangi, A.F. (eds.) MICCAI 2015. LNCS, vol. 9351, pp. 234–241. Springer, Cham (2015). https://doi.org/10.1007/978-3-319-24574-4_28
3. Long, J., Shelhamer, E., Darrell, T.: Fully convolutional networks for semantic segmentation. In: 2015 IEEE Conference on Computer Vision and Pattern Recognition (CVPR) (2015)
4. Chen, L. C., Papandreou, G., Schroff, F., Adam, H.: Rethinking atrous convolution for semantic image segmentation. arXiv preprint arXiv:1706.05587 (2017)
5. Hesamian, M.H., Jia, W., He, X., Kennedy, P.: Deep learning techniques for medical image segmentation: achievements and challenges. J. Digit. Imaging **32**(4), 582–596 (2019). https://doi.org/10.1007/s10278-019-00227-x
6. Wang, P., Patel, V.M., Hacihaliloglu, I.: Simultaneous segmentation and classification of bone surfaces from ultrasound using a multi-feature guided CNN. In: Frangi, A.F., Schnabel, J.A., Davatzikos, C., Alberola-López, C., Fichtinger, G. (eds.) MICCAI 2018. LNCS, vol. 11073, pp. 134–142. Springer, Cham (2018). https://doi.org/10.1007/978-3-030-00937-3_16
7. Mehta, S., Mercan, E., Bartlett, J., Weaver, D., Elmore, J.G., Shapiro, L.: Y-Net: joint segmentation and classification for diagnosis of breast biopsy images. In: Frangi, A.F., Schnabel, J.A., Davatzikos, C., Alberola-López, C., Fichtinger, G. (eds.) MICCAI 2018. LNCS, vol. 11071, pp. 893–901. Springer, Cham (2018). https://doi.org/10.1007/978-3-030-00934-2_99
8. Telea, A.: An image inpainting technique based on the fast marching method. J. Graph. Tools **9**, 23–34 (2004)
9. Baumgartner, C.F., et al.: SonoNet: real-time detection and localisation of fetal standard scan planes in freehand ultrasound. IEEE Trans. Med. Imaging **36**, 2204–2215 (2017)
10. Milletari, F., Navab, N., Ahmadi, S.-A.: V-Net: fully convolutional neural networks for volumetric medical image segmentation. 2016 Fourth International Conference on 3D Vision (3DV) (2016)
11. Lei, X., Pan, H., Huang, X.: A dilated CNN model for image classification. IEEE Access **7**, 124087–124095 (2019)
12. Włodarczyk, T., et al.: Estimation of preterm birth markers with U-Net segmentation network. In: Wang, Q., et al. (eds.) PIPPI/SUSI -2019. LNCS, vol. 11798, pp. 95–103. Springer, Cham (2019). https://doi.org/10.1007/978-3-030-32875-7_11
13. Selvaraju, R.R., Cogswell, M., Das, A., Vedantam, R., Parikh, D., Batra, D.: Grad-CAM: visual explanations from deep networks via gradient-based localization. In: 2017 IEEE International Conference on Computer Vision (ICCV) (2017)
14. Baños, N., et al.: Quantitative analysis of cervical texture by ultrasound in mid-pregnancy and association with spontaneous preterm birth. Ultrasound Obstet. Gynecol. **51**, 637–643 (2018)
15. Pachtman, S.L., et al.: Ultrasonic assessment of cervical heterogeneity for prediction of spontaneous preterm birth. Am. J. Obstet. Gynecol. **216** (2017)
16. Sochacki-Wójcicka, N., Wójcicki, J., Bomba-Opon, D., Wielgos, M.: Anterior cervical angle as a new biophysical ultrasound marker for prediction of spontaneous preterm birth. Ultrasound Obstet. Gynecol. **46**, 377–378 (2015)

Multi-modal Perceptual Adversarial Learning for Longitudinal Prediction of Infant MR Images

Liying Peng[1,2](✉), Lanfen Lin[1](✉), Yusen Lin[3], Yue Zhang[1], Roza M. Vlasova[2], Juan Prieto[2], Yen-wei Chen[4], Guido Gerig[5], and Martin Styner[2,6]

[1] Department of Computer Science, Zhejiang University, Hangzhou, Zhejiang, China
{liyingpeng,llf}@zju.edu.cn

[2] Department of Psychiatry, UNC School of Medicine, University of North Carolina, Chapel Hill, NC, USA

[3] Department of Electrical and Computer Engineering, University of Maryland, College Park, MD, USA

[4] Department of Information Science and Engineering, Ritsumeikan University, Shiga, Japan

[5] Department of Computer Science and Engineering, New York University, New York, NY, USA

[6] Department of Computer Science, University of North Carolina, Chapel Hill, NC, USA

Abstract. Longitudinal magnetic resonance imaging (MRI) is essential in neuroimaging studies of early brain development. However, incomplete data is an inevitable problem in longitudinal studies because of participant attrition and scan failure. Data imputation is a possible way to address such missing data. Here, we propose a novel 3D multi-modal perceptual adversarial network (MPGAN) to predict a missing MR image from an existing longitudinal image of the same subject. To the best of our knowledge, this is the first application of deep generative methods for longitudinal image prediction of structural MRI in the first year of life, where brain volume and image intensities are changing dramatically. In order to produce sharper and more realistic images, we incorporate the perceptual loss into the adversarial training process. To leverage complementary information contained in the multi-modality data, MPGAN predicts T1w and T2w images jointly in the prediction process. We evaluated MPGAN versus six alternative approaches based on visual as well as quantitative assessment. The results indicate that our MPGAN predicts missing MR images in an accurate and visually realistic fashion, and shows better performance than the alternative methods.

Keywords: Generative adversarial networks · MRI · Prediction

Electronic supplementary material The online version of this chapter (https://doi.org/10.1007/978-3-030-60334-2_28) contains supplementary material, which is available to authorized users.

Y. Hu et al. (Eds.): ASMUS 2020/PIPPI 2020, LNCS 12437, pp. 284–294, 2020.
https://doi.org/10.1007/978-3-030-60334-2_28

1 Introduction

Early childhood (0–1 year of age) is a period of dynamic and rapid brain development resulting in MR images that display a dramatic change in appearance. This period is associated with early atypical developmental trajectories in neuropsychiatric disorders, such as autism spectrum disorder (ASD) and schizophrenia [1,2]. Longitudinal magnetic resonance imaging (MRI) allows the quantification of developmental changes in the same individual over time and plays a critical role in neuroimaging studies of early brain development. However, missing data is a major issue in longitudinal studies due to scan failure and participant attrition. To tackle this problem, missing data is often imputed either at the image or measurement level. In this paper, we focus on image-level approaches for infant longitudinal MRI prediction/imputation, which can be regarded as an image synthesis problem.

Generative adversarial networks (GANs) [3] have been explored in various medical image synthesis tasks, e.g., cross-modality synthesis (MR-to-CT [4], MR-to-PET [5], and 3T-to-7T [6]), and cross-site synthesis [7]. Recently, several studies have suggested the use of GANs for longitudinal MRI prediction. For example, Xia et al. [8] proposed an age-conditioned GAN to predict brain images at an older age. Ravi et al. [9] presented a GAN framework to generate images incorporating neurodegeneration. However, these longitudinal prediction methods are limited to 2D T1w MRI and designed for adult images.

In this work, we aim at a longitudinal prediction of infant MR images in the first year of life. Due to large scale size and shape changes in the first year of life, 2D approaches are not appropriate in our task. Hence, we propose a 3D GAN-based method for infant MRI prediction. Another difficulty in our task is the handling of the large variation in appearance, mainly due to the myelination process. One possible way to address this issue is to add a voxel-wise constraint, e.g., an L1 loss, to explicitly guide the generator to produce images that match ground-truth images at the voxel level. However, L1 loss often leads to blurred results [10]. Thus, to alleviate this problem, we also propose the use of the perceptual loss [11], which maintains the appearance consistency at the feature level by computing perceptual differences based on high-level image features extracted from pretrained networks. Here, we propose to use Model Genesis [12], which is directly built on 3D medical images, for feature extraction. In order to handle the reduced tissue contrast during the first year of life, particularly at about 6 months of age, we further propose the joint use of T1w and T2w images so that both modalities can provide complementary information. Our main contributions are summarized as follows:

- To the best of our knowledge, this is the first application of deep generative methods for longitudinal prediction of structural MRI in the first year of life.
- Our approach is based on a 3D MRI prediction, unlike previous 2D-based approaches that are inappropriate for our setting.
- To produce sharper and more realistic images, we employ the perceptual loss in the adversarial training process. The perceptual loss is computed via an application-specific model to extract features appropriate for medical images.

- To leverage complementary information from multi-modality data, we propose a novel multi-modal framework to jointly predict T1w and T2w images.

2 Methods

In this section, we describe our multi-modal perceptual adversarial network for longitudinal prediction of infant MRI. First, let us recap generative adversarial networks (GANs). GANs are composed of a generator G and a discriminator D. The goal of GANs on image-to-image translation tasks is to learn a mapping from the input image x to the target image y. During training, G aims to fool D by generating image $G(x)$ that looks similar to real target image y, whereas D tries to distinguish between real image y and fake image $G(x)$. This two-player *minmax* setting can be defined as: $\min_G \max_D \mathcal{L}_{adv}(G, D)$, where the adversarial loss $\mathcal{L}_{adv}$ is formulated as $\mathcal{L}_{adv}(G, D) = \mathbb{E}_x[(1 - D(G(x)))^2] + \mathbb{E}_y[D(y)^2]$.

2.1 Problem Formulation

We consider two situations in our task. One is a single-input-single-output setting and the other is a multi-input-multi-output setting. In the former case, we assume $\{x_i, y_i\}_{i=1}^N$ is a set of paired subjects, where x_i is the T1w or T2w image at age a_1, y_i is the corresponding T1w or T2w image at age a_2, and N is the number of paired instances in the training set. Our target is to learn the mapping $G : x \rightarrow y$. In the latter case, suppose $\{x_i^{T1}, x_i^{T2}, y_i^{T1}, y_i^{T2}\}_{i=1}^N$ is a set of paired instances, where x_i^{T1}, x_i^{T2} denote the T1w and T2w images at age a_1, and y_i^{T1}, y_i^{T2} represent the corresponding T1w and T2w images at age a_2. The goal is then to learn two mapping functions: $G_{T1} : \{x^{T1}, x^{T2}\} \rightarrow y^{T1}$ and $G_{T2} : \{x^{T1}, x^{T2}\} \rightarrow y^{T2}$.

2.2 Objective

Adversarial Loss. In the single-input-single-output setting, to learn the mapping $G : x \rightarrow y$, we can use the adversarial loss function of the original GAN. In the multi-input-multi-output setting, two generators $G_{T1} : \{x^{T1}, x^{T2}\} \rightarrow y^{T1}$ and $G_{T2} : \{x^{T1}, x^{T2}\} \rightarrow y^{T2}$ are defined. The goal of G_{T1} and G_{T2} is to generate fake T1w and T2w images close to real images, respectively. Two discriminators D_{T1} and D_{T2} are defined, where D_{T1} aims to distinguish the real T1w image y^{T1} from the generated T1w image $G_{T1}(x^{T1}, x^{T2})$. Similarly, D_{T2} tries to distinguish between y^{T2} and $G_{T2}(x^{T1}, x^{T2})$. For generator G_{T1} and its discriminator D_{T1}, the adversarial loss can be written as

$$\mathcal{L}_{adv}(G_{T1}, D_{T1}) = \mathbb{E}_{x^{T1}, x^{T2}}[(1 - D_{T1}(G_{T1}(x^{T1}, x^{T2})))^2] + \mathbb{E}_{y^{T1}}[D_{T1}(y^{T1})^2] \quad (1)$$

The adversarial loss $\mathcal{L}_{adv}(G_{T2}, D_{T2})$ can be defined in the same way.

Voxel-Wise Reconstruction Loss. We employ L1 loss on the generator to enforce the voxel-wise consistency between generated and real images. For single-input-single-output, the voxel-wise reconstruction loss is formulated as $\mathcal{L}_{vr}(G) = \mathbb{E}_{x,y}[\|y - G(x)\|_1]$. For multi-input-multi-output, the voxel-wise reconstruction loss is expressed as $\mathcal{L}_{vr}(G_{T1}, G_{T2}) = \mathbb{E}_{x^{T1},x^{T2},y^{T1}}[\|y^{T1} - G_{T1}(x^{T1}, x^{T2})\|_1] + \mathbb{E}_{x^{T1},x^{T2},y^{T2}}[\|y^{T2} - G_{T2}(x^{T1}, x^{T2})\|_1]$.

Perceptual Loss. While the voxel-wise reconstruction loss enforces the consistency between real and generated images, it prefers an over-smoothed solution [10]. To alleviate this problem, we add a perceptual loss [11] term on the generator, which leads to sharper and more visually realistic images. The perceptual loss computes the difference between two images in the feature space in place of the voxel space. Thus, it forces the generated images to be perceptually similar to the real images, instead of driving them to match intensities exactly at the voxel level. Assume $\phi_m(x)$ is the output from the m-th layer of a feature extractor ϕ when processing the image x. For single-input-single-output, the perceptual loss is defined as $\mathcal{L}_p(G) = \mathbb{E}_{x,y}[\|\phi_m(y) - \phi_m(G(x))\|_1]$. For multi-input-multi-output, the perceptual loss is defined as

$$\begin{aligned}\mathcal{L}_p(G_{T1}, G_{T2}) = &\mathbb{E}_{x^{T1},x^{T2},y^{T1}}[\|\phi_m(y^{T1}) - \phi_m(G_{T1}(x^{T1}, x^{T2}))\|_1] \\ &+ \mathbb{E}_{x^{T1},x^{T2},y^{T2}}[\|\phi_m(y^{T2}) - \phi_m(G_{T2}(x^{T1}, x^{T2}))\|_1]\end{aligned} \tag{2}$$

Overall Objective. The overall objective in the single-input-single-output setting is defined as

$$\min_G \max_D \mathcal{L}(G, D) = \mathcal{L}_{adv}(G, D) + \alpha\mathcal{L}_{vr}(G) + \beta\mathcal{L}_p(G) \tag{3}$$

The overall objective in the multi-input-multi-output setting is expressed as

$$\begin{aligned}\min_{G_{T1},G_{T2}} \max_{D_{T1},D_{T2}} &\mathcal{L}(G_{T1}, G_{T2}, D_{T1}, D_{T2}) = \mathcal{L}_{adv}(G_{T1}, D_{T1}) \\ &+ \mathcal{L}_{adv}(G_{T2}, D_{T2}) + \alpha\mathcal{L}_{vr}(G_{T1}, G_{T2}) + \beta\mathcal{L}_p(G_{T1}, G_{T2})\end{aligned} \tag{4}$$

where α and β are the coefficients to weight the loss contributions.

2.3 Network Architectures

Perceptual Adversarial Network. Shown in Fig. 1(a), the perceptual adversarial network (PGAN) is the base for the multi-modal perceptual adversarial network (MPGAN). The PGAN includes a generator G, a discriminator D and a feature extractor ϕ. The traditional 3D-Unet [13] is used as the generator. The discriminator D consists of four stride-2 convolutional layers, with 64, 128, 256, and 512 channels, respectively. The output layer is a stride-1 convolutional layer with one channel, followed by a *sigmoid* activation function. Instance normalization is applied to the convolutional layers in both generator and discriminator.

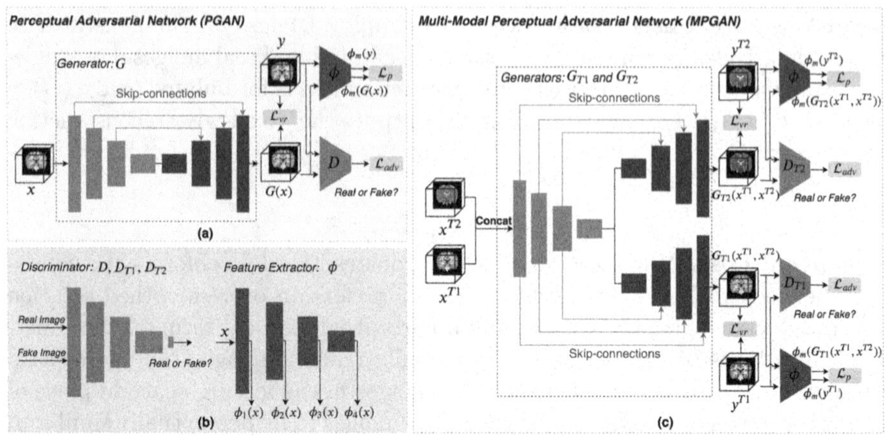

Fig. 1. Overview of the proposed methods. (a) and (c) are the architectures of PGAN and MPGAN, respectively. (b) shows the structures of the discriminators and the feature extractor for the perceptual loss computation.

Moreover, we use Model Genesis [12] as our feature extractor ϕ. Since Model Genesis is directly pretrained on 3D medical images, it is more suitable for medical image tasks compared to pretrained VGG networks [19], which are often used as feature extractors for natural images. The encoder part of Model Genesis is employed for feature extraction here.

Multi-modal Perceptual Adversarial Network. As shown in Fig. 1(c), MPGAN contains two generators G_{T1} and G_{T2}, two discriminators D_{T1} and D_{T2} and one feature extractor ϕ. The feature extractor ϕ and the architectures of D_{T1} and D_{T2} are the same as for PGAN. G_{T1} and G_{T2} are both based on 3D-Unets that utilize a shared encoder and two independent decoders with skip-connections. The shared encoder learns complementary information from both T1w and T2w images and skip connections are used to transfer this information from the shared encoder to different decoders. We combine the T1w and T2w images before feeding them into the generators by applying a channel-wise concatenation.

3 Experiments and Results

3.1 Experimental Setup

Materials. A set of 289 subjects were collected from 'Infant Brain Imaging Study' (IBIS) database. Each subject in our study has two completed scans at 6 and 12 months that passed quality control. MR imaging parameters are as follows: (1) 3T Siemens Tim Trio at 5 sites; (2) T1w MRI: TR/TE = 2400/3.16 ms, 256 × 256 × 160, 1 mm^3 resolution; (3) T2w MRI: TR/TE = 3200/499 ms, same matrix and resolution as T1w. Several preprocessing steps were applied, i.e., ICBM alignment, skull stripping, bias correction and intensity normalization to range (−1,1). In order to fit the networks into the GPU memory (NVIDIA TITAN X/V, 12 GB), all scans were cropped and downsampled by factor 2 along each axis. The final image size is $72 \times 96 \times 80$. The dataset was split into three sets: training set (231 subjects), validation set (29 subjects), and test set (29 subjects).

Implementation. All the networks were implemented in Python with Tensorflow and optimized using Adam algorithm with a batch size of 2. The learning rate was initially set to 2e−4 for the first 85 epochs and decayed every 45 epochs with a base of 0.5 for an additional 345 epochs. In Eq. 3 and Eq. 4, α and β were set to 25 based on a grid search ranging from 0 to 50. We empirically observe that the model performance is not very sensitive to α and β. Perceptual loss $\mathcal{L}_p$ was calculated based on $\phi_1(x)$, i.e., the output from the first layer of the feature extractor ϕ. Details regarding the choice $\phi_1(x)$ are shown in Fig. 2.

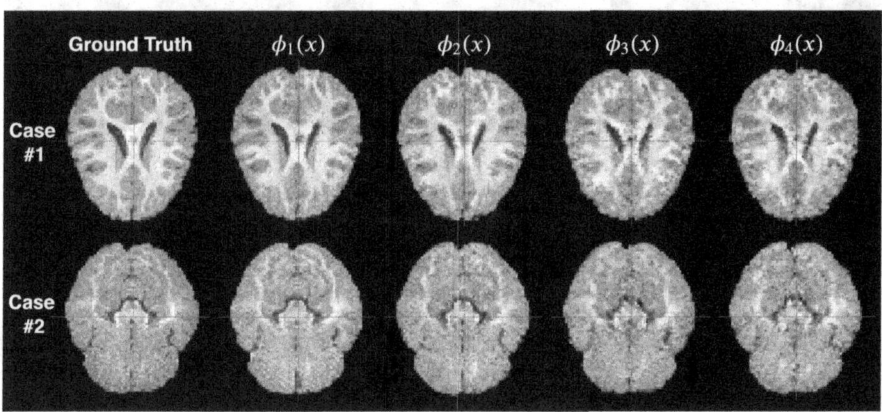

Fig. 2. Examples of predicted MR images of our method using different feature maps when calculating perceptual loss, showing that employing the 1-th feature map ($\phi_1(x)$) as feature extractor ϕ can generate images with finer anatomical detail.

Alternative Networks for Comparison. We trained six additional networks: (1) CycleGAN: 3D extension of original CycleGAN [14]. (2) Unet($\mathcal{L}_{vr}$): 3D-Unet trained with $\mathcal{L}_{vr}$. (3) Unet($\mathcal{L}_p$): 3D-Unet trained with $\mathcal{L}_p$. (4) Unet ($\mathcal{L}_{vr} + \mathcal{L}_p$): 3D-Unet trained with both $\mathcal{L}_p$ and $\mathcal{L}_{vr}$. (5) GAN: original GAN. (6) GAN+$\mathcal{L}_{vr}$: original GAN with additional $\mathcal{L}_{vr}$ term. The generators of (5) and (6) are based on the 3D-Unet and the discriminators are the same as for our MPGAN method.

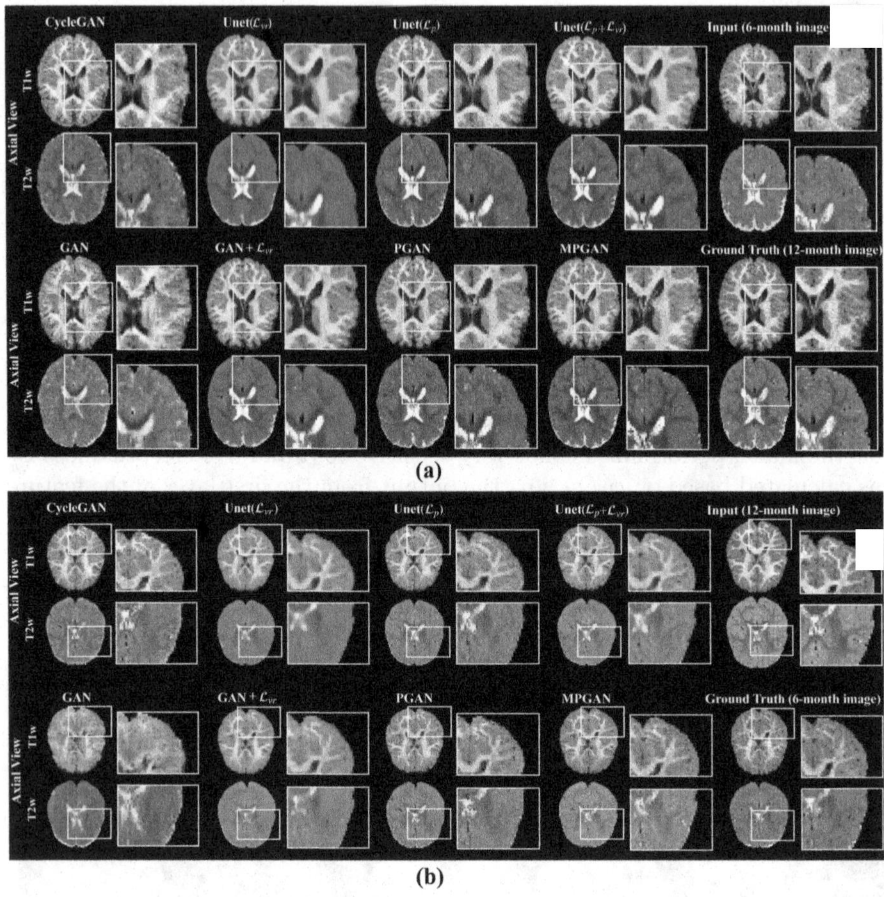

Fig. 3. Examples of predicted MR images. (a) 6 to 12 prediction. (b) 12 to 6 prediction.

3.2 Evaluation via Visual Inspection

We performed experiments for two prediction tasks: prediction from 6-month to 12-month images and prediction from 12-month to 6-month images. Note that although structural similarity index measure (SSIM) and peak signal-to-noise ratio (PSNR) are traditional metrics used to evaluate the image quality in generative image tasks, both metrics have been found to correlate poorly with human assessments of visual quality [11,15,16,18], as over-smoothed/blurry images tend to get high values of PSNR and SSIM, while easily dismissed as bad results by visual inspection. We strongly concur here based on our experimental results and choose to compare methods via two alternative ways: a) visual inspection and b) segmentation-based quantitative measurement (Sect. 3.3).

The visual results on axial and sagittal views for the different approaches are shown in Fig. 3 and Fig. 4, respectively. We have the following common

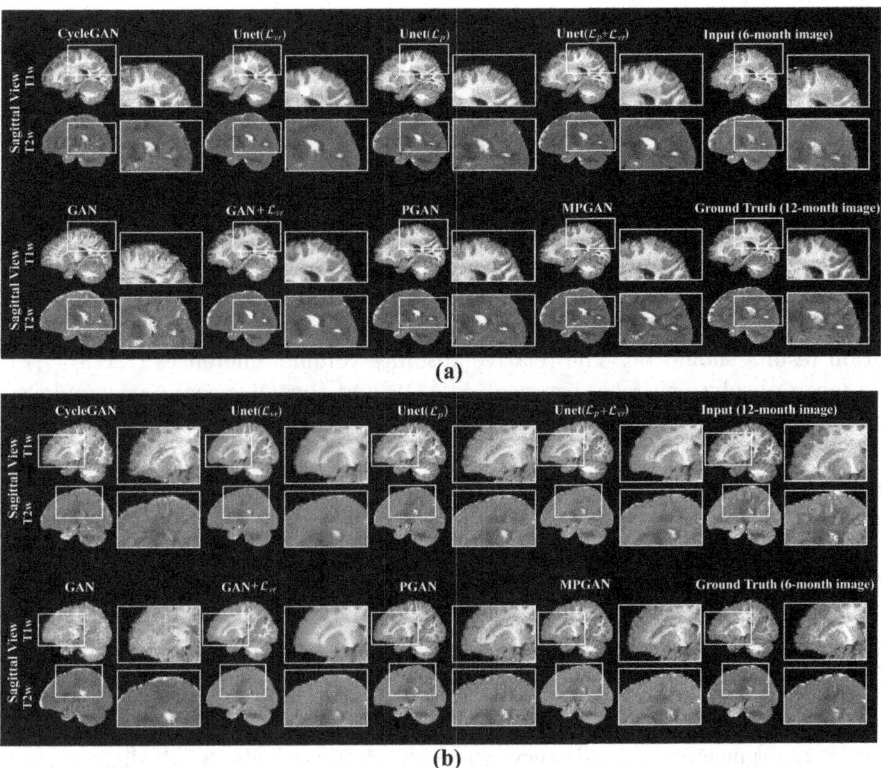

Fig. 4. Examples of predicted MR images on sagittal view. (a) 6 to 12 prediction. (b) 12 to 6 prediction.

findings in both 6-to-12 and 12-to-6 month prediction tasks. (1) Unet($\mathcal{L}_{vr}$), Unet($\mathcal{L}_p + \mathcal{L}_{vr}$) and GAN+$\mathcal{L}_{vr}$ generate images that are overly smoothed and lack high-frequency detail. (2) The images generated from Unet($\mathcal{L}_p$) have grid-like artifacts at the voxel level, which leads to an unsatisfactory visual quality. (3) The images predicted by GAN and CycleGAN are the least anatomically accurate of the tested methods. A possible explanation is that they are trained without any additional constraints to enforce appearance consistency between predicted and ground-truth images. (4) Compared to other methods, our PGAN and MPGAN produce visually realistic images with more accurate detail as compared to the other methods. In addition, for the 6-to-12 month prediction, MPGAN predicts finer details particularly on T2w images. We believe that the multi-modal learning helps MPGAN to predict more accurate images by incorporating rich information from both T1w and T2w images.

3.3 Evaluation on Segmentation Task

In order to evaluate the predicted images with respect to a potential image analysis task, we performed a subcortical segmentation on both predicted and ground-truth images. Quantitative assessment of the segmentation differences allows us to assess the quality of the predicted images for a segmentation task. Here, a multi-atlas segmentation method [17] was applied to 12-month images in our test set. We evaluated the prediction quality by assessing how close the automatic segmentation of the predicted image is to the one of the ground-truth image. The intuition is that if two images are segmented by the same algorithm, the more similar the two images are, the more similar their segmentation results should be. The relative absolute volume differences ($|\Delta V|/V_{GT}$), the mean absolute surface distance (MAD), and the $Dice$ score are employed as evaluation metrics (see Table 1).

Table 1 provides the segmentation task results. For $|\Delta V|/V_{GT}$, CycleGAN performs very poorly (14% error) as compared to other methods and there is no significant difference among the other methods ($p > 0.05$). MPGAN achieves a significantly better performance on MAD and $Dice$ score ($p < 0.05$), when compared to Unet($\mathcal{L}_{vr} + \mathcal{L}_p$) and PGAN. With exception of CycleGAN (due to its large $|\Delta V|/V_{GT}$ error), all methods performed decently with an MAD that is close to half of the original image's voxelsize, and a $Dice$ score above 80%. Yet overall our MPGAN performed better than all other methods.

Table 1. Segmentation consistency across different methods. SegPredict$_{CycleGAN}$, SegPredict$^{\text{Unet}(\mathcal{L}_p+\mathcal{L}_{vr})}$, SegPredict$_{PGAN}$, and SegPredict$_{MPGAN}$ denote automatic segmentations on the predicted images from CycleGAN, Unet($\mathcal{L}_p + \mathcal{L}_{vr}$), PGAN, and MPGAN, respectively. SegGT is automatic segmentation on the ground-truth image. *: Significantly different compared to MPGAN ($p < 0.05$). $^{\Delta}$: Significantly different compared to PGAN ($p < 0.05$). ↓: lower is better. ↑: higher is better.

	$\|\Delta V\|/V_{GT}$ ↓	MAD ↓	$Dice$ ↑
SegPredict$_{\text{CycleGAN}}$ vs SegGT	$^{*\Delta}14.594 \pm 6.873$	0.496 ± 0.108	0.832 ± 0.045
SegPredict$_{\text{Unet}(\mathcal{L}_{vr}+\mathcal{L}_p)}$ vs SegGT	4.240 ± 2.063	$^{*}0.577 \pm 0.097$	$^{*}0.809 \pm 0.053$
SegPredict$_{\text{PGAN}}$ vs SegGT	5.327 ± 0.045	$^{*}0.590 \pm 0.084$	$^{*}0.805 \pm 0.049$
SegPredict$_{\text{MPGAN}}$ vs SegGT	4.952 ± 2.193	$^{\Delta}0.534 \pm 0.062$	$^{\Delta}0.821 \pm 0.041$

4 Conclusion

We proposed a 3D deep generative method, named MPGAN, for longitudinal prediction of Infant MRI for the purpose of image data imputation. Our method can jointly produce accurate and visually-satisfactory T1w and T2w images by incorporating the perceptual loss into the adversarial training process and considering complementary information from both T1w and T2w images. Visual examination and segmentation-based quantitative evaluation were applied to assessing the quality of predicted images. The results show that our method overall performs better than the alternative methods studied in this paper.

Acknowledgement. This study was supported by grants from the Major Scientific Project of Zhejiang Lab (No. 2018DG0ZX01), the National Institutes of Health (R01-HD055741, T32-HD040127, U54-HD079124, U54-HD086984, R01-EB021391), Autism Speaks, and the Simons Foundation (140209). MDS is supported by a U.S. National Institutes of Health (NIH) career development award (K12-HD001441). The sponsors had no role in the design and conduct of the study; collection, management, analysis, and interpretation of the data; preparation, review, or approval of the manuscript; and decision to submit the manuscript for publication.

References

1. Gilmore, J.H., et al.: Imaging structural and functional brain development in early childhood. Nat. Rev. Neurosci. **19**(3), 123–137 (2018)
2. Hazlett, H.C., et al.: Early brain development in infants at high risk for autism spectrum disorder. Nature **542**(7641), 348–351 (2017)
3. Goodfellow, I., et al.: Generative adversarial nets. In: Advances in Neural Information Processing Systems, pp. 2672–2680 (2014)
4. Wolterink, J.M., Dinkla, A.M., Savenije, M.H.F., Seevinck, P.R., van den Berg, C.A.T., Išgum, I.: Deep MR to CT synthesis using unpaired data. In: Tsaftaris, S.A., Gooya, A., Frangi, A.F., Prince, J.L. (eds.) SASHIMI 2017. LNCS, vol. 10557, pp. 14–23. Springer, Cham (2017). https://doi.org/10.1007/978-3-319-68127-6_2
5. Pan, Y., Liu, M., Lian, C., Zhou, T., Xia, Y., Shen, D.: Synthesizing missing PET from MRI with cycle-consistent generative adversarial networks for Alzheimer's disease Diagnosis. In: Frangi, A.F., Schnabel, J.A., Davatzikos, C., Alberola-López, C., Fichtinger, G. (eds.) MICCAI 2018. LNCS, vol. 11072, pp. 455–463. Springer, Cham (2018). https://doi.org/10.1007/978-3-030-00931-1_52
6. Qu, L., Wang, S., Yap, P.-T., Shen, D.: Wavelet-based semi-supervised adversarial learning for synthesizing realistic 7T from 3T MRI. In: Shen, D., et al. (eds.) MICCAI 2019. LNCS, vol. 11767, pp. 786–794. Springer, Cham (2019). https://doi.org/10.1007/978-3-030-32251-9_86
7. Zhao, F., et al.: Harmonization of infant cortical thickness using surface-to-surface cycle-consistent adversarial networks. In: Shen, D., et al. (eds.) MICCAI 2019. LNCS, vol. 11767, pp. 475–483. Springer, Cham (2019). https://doi.org/10.1007/978-3-030-32251-9_52
8. Xia, T., Chartsias, A., Tsaftaris, S.A.: Consistent brain ageing synthesis. In: Shen, D., et al. (eds.) MICCAI 2019. LNCS, vol. 11767, pp. 750–758. Springer, Cham (2019). https://doi.org/10.1007/978-3-030-32251-9_82
9. Ravi, D., Alexander, D.C., Oxtoby, N.P.: Degenerative adversarial NeuroImage nets: generating images that mimic disease progression. In: Shen, D., et al. (eds.) MICCAI 2019. LNCS, vol. 11766, pp. 164–172. Springer, Cham (2019). https://doi.org/10.1007/978-3-030-32248-9_19
10. Pathak, D., et al.: Context encoders: feature learning by inpainting. In: CVPR, pp. 2536–2544 (2016)
11. Johnson, J., Alahi, A., Fei-Fei, L.: Perceptual losses for real-time style transfer and super-resolution. In: Leibe, B., Matas, J., Sebe, N., Welling, M. (eds.) ECCV 2016. LNCS, vol. 9906, pp. 694–711. Springer, Cham (2016). https://doi.org/10.1007/978-3-319-46475-6_43

12. Zhou, Z., et al.: Models genesis: generic autodidactic models for 3D medical image analysis. In: Shen, D., et al. (eds.) MICCAI 2019. LNCS, vol. 11767, pp. 384–393. Springer, Cham (2019). https://doi.org/10.1007/978-3-030-32251-9_42
13. Çiçek, Ö., Abdulkadir, A., Lienkamp, S.S., Brox, T., Ronneberger, O.: 3D U-Net: learning dense volumetric segmentation from sparse annotation. In: Ourselin, S., Joskowicz, L., Sabuncu, M.R., Unal, G., Wells, W. (eds.) MICCAI 2016. LNCS, vol. 9901, pp. 424–432. Springer, Cham (2016). https://doi.org/10.1007/978-3-319-46723-8_49
14. Zhu, J.Y., et al.: Unpaired image-to-image translation using cycle-consistent adversarial networks. In: ICCV, pp. 2223–2232 (2017)
15. Wang, Z., et al.: Mean squared error: love it or leave it? A new look at signal fidelity measures. Signal Process. Mag. **26**(1), 98–117 (2009)
16. Huynh-Thu, Q., et al.: Scope of validity of PSNR in image/video quality assessment. Electron. Lett. **44**(13), 800–801 (2008)
17. Wang, J., et al.: Multi-atlas segmentation of subcortical brain structures via the AutoSeg software pipeline. Front. Neuroinformatics **8**, 7 (2014)
18. Zhang, R., et al.: The unreasonable effectiveness of deep features as a perceptual metric. In: CVPR, pp. 586–595 (2018)
19. Simonyan K., et al.: Very deep convolutional networks for large-scale image recognition. In: ICLR (2015)

Efficient Multi-class Fetal Brain Segmentation in High Resolution MRI Reconstructions with Noisy Labels

Kelly Payette[1](✉), Raimund Kottke[2], and Andras Jakab[1]

[1] Center for MR-Research, University Children's Hospital Zurich, Zurich, Switzerland
kelly.payette@kispi.uzh.ch

[2] Diagnostic Imaging and Intervention, University Children's Hospital Zurich, Zurich, Switzerland

Abstract. Segmentation of the developing fetal brain is an important step in quantitative analyses. However, manual segmentation is a very time-consuming task which is prone to error and must be completed by highly specialized individuals. Super-resolution reconstruction of fetal MRI has become standard for processing such data as it improves image quality and resolution. However, different pipelines result in slightly different outputs, further complicating the generalization of segmentation methods aiming to segment super-resolution data. Therefore, we propose using transfer learning with noisy multi-class labels to automatically segment high resolution fetal brain MRIs using a single set of segmentations created with one reconstruction method and tested for generalizability across other reconstruction methods. Our results show that the network can automatically segment fetal brain reconstructions into 7 different tissue types, regardless of reconstruction method used. Transfer learning offers some advantages when compared to training without pre-initialized weights, but the network trained on clean labels had more accurate segmentations overall. No additional manual segmentations were required. Therefore, the proposed network has the potential to eliminate the need for manual segmentations needed in quantitative analyses of the fetal brain independent of reconstruction method used, offering an unbiased way to quantify normal and pathological neurodevelopment.

Keywords: Segmentation · Fetal MRI · Transfer learning

1 Introduction

Fetal MRI is a useful modality for prenatal diagnostics and has a proven clinical value for the assessment of intracranial structures. Quantitative analysis potentially provides added diagnostic value and helps the understanding of normal and pathological fetal brain development. However, the quantitative assessment of fetal brain volumes requires

Electronic supplementary material The online version of this chapter (https://doi.org/10.1007/978-3-030-60334-2_29) contains supplementary material, which is available to authorized users.

Y. Hu et al. (Eds.): ASMUS 2020/PIPPI 2020, LNCS 12437, pp. 295–304, 2020.
https://doi.org/10.1007/978-3-030-60334-2_29

accurate segmentation of fetal brain tissues, which can be a challenging task. Artifacts resulting from fetal and maternal movement are present, leading to difficulty in differentiating tissue types. Recently, advances have been made in the processing and super-resolution (SR) reconstruction of motion-corrupted low resolution fetal brain scans into high resolution volumes [1–7]. The enhanced resolution and improved image quality of the SR data in comparison to the native low-resolution scans has in turn resulted in greatly improved volumetric fetal brain data, the segmentation of which has not been assessed in detail.

Segmentation of the fetal brain from maternal tissue in the original scans has been explored [3, 8–11]. Methods to segment the original low resolution MR scans into different brain tissues have also been evaluated [12], as well as for a single tissue type within a high resolution volume [13, 14]. MRI atlases of the fetal brain have been generated with the intent of being used for atlas based-segmentation methods [9, 15, 16]. However, atlas-based methods are not easily expandable to pathological fetal brains, as currently no publicly available pathological fetal brain atlases exist. To overcome this, we propose using a multi-class U-Net for the segmentation of different types of fetal brain tissues in high resolution SR volumes.

The network should be able to work with SR reconstructions, regardless of the method used to create the fetal brain volume without requiring new manual segmentations. This can be challenging, as there are differences in shape, structure boundaries, textures, and intensities between volumes created by different reconstruction methods. Therefore, a network trained with one reconstruction method is not necessarily generalizable to other SR reconstruction methods, even when the same input data is used. To overcome this, the original labels can be rigidly registered to the alternate SR volume, creating 'noisy' labels, where noisy labels refer to incorrect labelling of the fetal brain volume as opposed to noise or artifact within the image itself. A network can then be trained using these noisy labels, thereby eliminating the need for further time consuming, manual brain segmentations.

Noisy labels have been shown to be a challenge for neural networks, where more noise results in performance degradation [17, 18]. Considerable research has been devoted to developing effective methods for handling noise, such as transfer learning, alternate loss functions, data re-weighting, changes to network architecture, and label cleaning, among others [19]. As the proposed method falls under the category of 'same task, different domain', transfer learning will be explored, as well as an alternate loss function (mean absolute error, MAE) that has been shown to be robust in the presence of noisy labels [20, 21]. Through transfer learning, the weights from the first network with 'clean' labels will be used for the initialization of a network with noisy labels, providing an automatic, objective segmentation of the fetal brains that is independent of SR method used.

Our proposed method aims to overcome these limitations (anatomical variability, the challenge of generalizability across SR methods, and the lack of noise-free, unambiguous anatomical annotations) and allow for multi-class fetal brain tissue segmentation across multiple SR reconstruction methods. Improvements to SR reconstruction methods can then be easily utilized for the quantitative analysis of the development of fetal brains with no new time-consuming manual segmentations required.

2 Methods

2.1 Image Acquisition

Multiple low-resolution orthogonal MR sequences of the brain were acquired on 1.5T and 3T clinical GE whole-body scanners at the University Children's Hospital Zurich using a T2-weighted single-shot fast spin echo sequence (ssFSE), with an in-plane resolution of 0.5 × 0.5 mm and a slice thickness of 3–5 mm for 15 subjects. Each subject underwent a fetal MRI for a clinical indication and were determined to have unaffected neurodevelopment. The average gestational age in weeks (GA) of the subjects at the time of scanning was 28.7 ± 3.5 weeks (range: 22.6–33.4 GA).

2.2 Super-Resolution Reconstruction

For each subject's set of images, SR reconstruction was performed using three different methods: mialSRTK [4], Simple IRTK [1], and NiftyMIC [3] using the following steps:

Preprocessing: The acquired images were bias corrected and de-noised prior to reconstruction using the tools included within each pipeline where applicable.

Masking: Each reconstruction method had different masking requirements. For the mialSRTK method, we reoriented and masked the fetal brains in each low-resolution image using a semi-automated atlas-based custom MeVisLab module [22]. For Simple IRTK and NiftyMIC, re-orientation of the input images was not required. For Simple IRTK, a brain mask was needed for the reference low-resolution image only, and this was generated using the network from [11], re-trained on the masks created with the aforementioned MeVisLab module. For NiftyMIC, the masking method available within the software was used.

SR Reconstruction: After pre-processing and masking, each SR reconstruction method was performed for each subject's low-resolution scans (mialSRTK, Simple IRTK, and NiftyMIC), resulting in three different fetal brain SR reconstructions with a resolution of 0.5 × 0.5 × 0.5 mm, created with the same set of low-resolution input scans. Each SR volume was rigidly registered to the atlas space using FSL's flirt [23]. See Fig. 1 for examples of each SR reconstruction.

2.3 Image Segmentation

A 2D U-Net was chosen as the basis for image segmentation [24] with an adam optimizer, a learning rate of 10E-5, L2 regularization, ReLu activation, and batch normalization after each convolutional layer, and a dropout layer after each block of convolutional layers (see supplementary materials). The network was programmed in Keras and trained on an Nvidia Quadro P6000. The network was trained for 100 epochs with early stopping. The training data was histogram-matched and normalized prior to training. The 2D U-Net was trained in the axial orientation. The generalized Dice coefficient and the mean absolute error (MAE) were used as a loss functions [25]. The initial network was trained on a set of n images $\{r_i, l_i\}$, where r_i is a reconstructed image using the mialSRTK method, and l_i is the corresponding manually annotated label map (The mialSRTK method was chosen due to availability of manual annotations). In order to create l_i, the SR volume using the mialSRTK method was segmented into 7 tissue types (white matter (WM), grey matter (GM), external cerebrospinal fluid (eCSF), ventricles, cerebellum, deep GM, brain stem). Two volumes (GA: 26.6, 31.2) were retained for validation. The remaining 13 volumes were used for training and testing. Data augmentation (flipping, 360° rotation, adding Gaussian noise) was also utilized. In addition, we registered the manual label maps to the Simple IRTK and NiftyMIC SR volumes using ants and an age-matched label map in order to compare a simple atlas-based method to the U-Net [26].

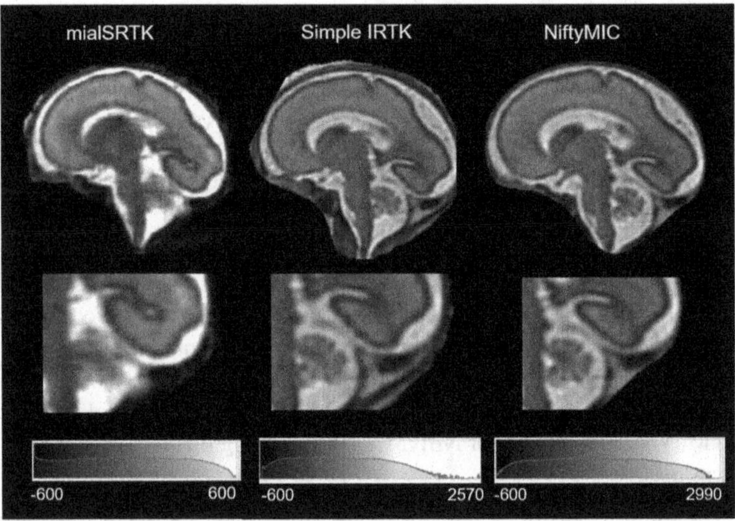

Fig. 1. SR reconstructions with each method. Top row: Complete SR reconstruction; middle row: enlarged area of the SR method; bottom row: intensity histogram of each reconstruction (27.7 GA). Each method has variations in shape, structure boundaries, texture, image contrast, and they retain different amounts of non-brain tissue for the same subject.

For each alternate reconstruction method, a set of n images $\{z_i', l_i\}$ was generated, where z_i denotes the ith reconstruction created with the alternate method, and l_i de notes the original labels. The noisy labels were created by rigidly registering the new reconstruction (z_i') to the existing label map using flirt [23]. Errors in the registration, plus the difference between the reconstruction methods cause the original labels to only be an approximate match to the new reconstruction (the so-called 'noisy' labels), as shown in Fig. 2.

The weights generated in the initial mialSRTK U-Net (Network 1) were used as weight initializations for training segmentation networks for the other reconstruction methods. See Table 1 for a detailed overview of the networks trained.

In addition, volumes created with NiftyMIC and Simple IRTK were segmented with Network 1 as comparison. The volumes retained for validation in Simple IRTK and NiftyMIC were manually annotated for validation purposes. The networks were evaluated by comparing the individual labels of the newly segmented label and the original annotation using the Dice coefficient (DC) and the 95% percentile of the Hausdorff distance (HD) [27].

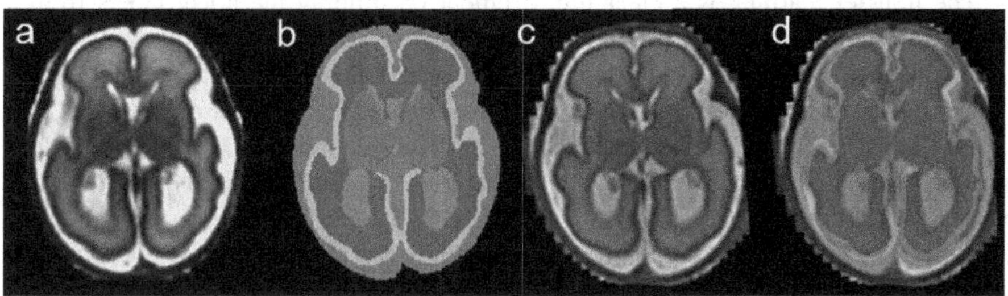

Fig. 2. a) mialSRTK reconstruction; b) manually annotated label; c) Simple IRTK reconstruction registered to the original mialSRTK image and corresponding label; d) the label displayed in b) overlaid on the SR volume shown in c), showing that the same label overlaid on Simple IRTK volume is noisy, leading to mislabeling in the anterior GM and ventricles, and posterior external CSF space in this slice.

Table 1. Overview of the networks. Note: networks 2–6 were created for each alternate SR method (Simple IRTK, NiftyMIC)

Network number	Images	Labels	Weight initialization	Loss function
1	r_i: SR volume created with mialSRTK	l_i	Glorot uniform	Generalized dice
2	z_i': SR volume created with alternate SR method, registered to labels l_i	l_i	Glorot uniform	Generalized dice
3	z_i': SR volume created with alternate SR method, registered to labels l_i	l_i	Transfer Learning (from Network 1)	Generalized dice
4	z_i': SR volume created with alternate SR method, registered to labels l_i	l_i	Glorot uniform	MAE
5	z_i': SR volume created with alternate SR method, registered to labels l_i	l_i	Transfer Learning (from Network 1)	MAE
6	r_i and z_i', registered to labels l_i	l_i	Glorot uniform	Generalized dice

3 Results

The network with the original labels and SR method 1 (mialSRTK) performs with an average Dice coefficient of 0.86 for all tissue types, with values ranging from 0.672 (GM) to 0.928 (cerebellum). When the SR methods 2 (Simple IRTK) and 3 (NiftyMIC) are run through the same network (Network 1), all labels perform on average 0.04–0.05 DC points lower, while the HD results seem to vary label to label (see Fig. 4, 5). Interestingly, the ventricles and cerebellum in the Simple IRTK SR reconstruction are segmented more accurately than in the mialSRTK volume, potentially due to stronger intensity differences between tissue and CSF.

The transfer learning is a clear improvement on training the noisy labels from a standard weight initialization (from an average DC of 0.62 to 0.79 with the generalized dice loss function, as well as improving the average HD from 34.4 to 25.2), but it fails to outperform the original network (based on the average DC: 0.81). Using the MAE loss with the transfer learning is not as accurate as with the generalized Dice coefficient loss (average DC: 0.70, average HD: 26.6) as the network is unable to classify the brainstem in one of the SR methods. It is also unable to detect all required classes in both alternate SR methods when trained without transfer learning. The is potentially due to the class imbalance (the network fails to find the smaller classes by number of voxels such as the brainstem and cerebellum but can detect the larger classes such as GM and WM). Within each SR volume method, some tissue classes are segmented more accurately than those within the reference SR volume trained in Network 1, even if the average across all tissues for each network is lower. Combining all volumes together in one network training set (Network 6) resulted in high dice scores in the cerebellum, deep GM, and the brainstem, but the overall average of the Dice scores across all labels was lower when compared to other networks. The ants registration segmentation did not perform as well when looking at the DC (average DC: 0.78), but it drastically out-performed all of the networks when looking at the HD (average HD: 14.7). Example segmentations of each SR method can be found in Fig. 3.

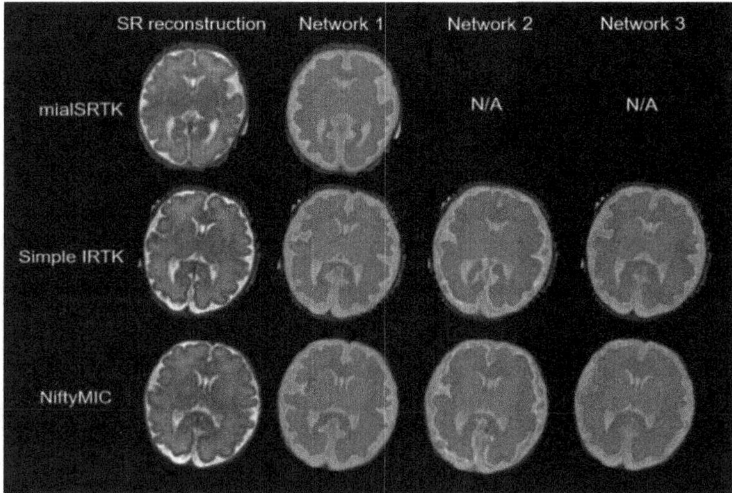

Fig. 3. Automatic segmentations created by Networks 1, 2, and 3 for each SR method. Network 2 (noisy labels without transfer learning) has difficulty delineating the GM, and the midline is shifted. These segmentation errors are resolved in Network 3 (with transfer learning), however the cortex is thinner.

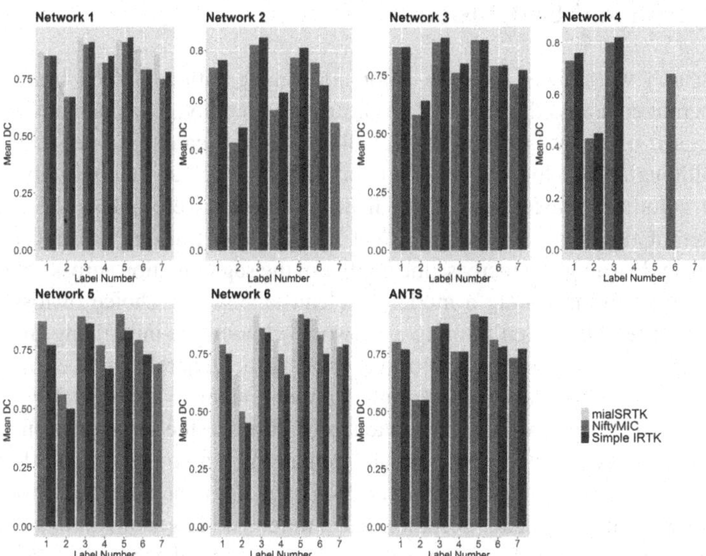

Fig. 4. Average DC for each label in each network. The mialSRTK volumes have the highest scoring DC. The networks that use transfer learning (3 and 5) perform as well as Network 1 for SR methods NiftyMIC and Simple IRTK, but do not reach the same value as mialSRTK in Network 1. There was no overlap for labels 4, 5, and 7 in the NiftyMIC method, and none for labels 4–7 in Simple IRTK in Network 4.

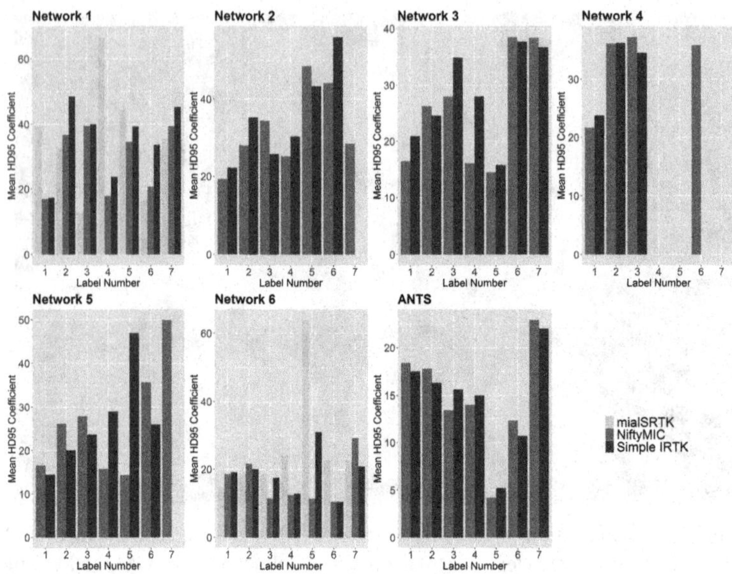

Fig. 5. Average HD (95 percentile) for all classes for each network.

4 Discussion and Conclusion

In this research we showed that the automatic segmentation of fetal brain volumes can be generalized across different SR reconstruction methods. Segmentation accuracy in the presence of noisy labels is very challenging, and can be helped with transfer learning, although not to the level of a network trained on clean labels. High resolution fetal brain volumes created from three distinct methods were able to be segmented into 7 different tissue types using a U-Net trained with transfer learning and noisy labels. Transfer learning can increase the quality of the segmentation across SR methods, but cannot outperform training a model on clean labels. The choice of loss function is important, especially when training a network without pre-initializing the weights. The MAE loss function does not perform as well as the generalized dice loss function in the presence of noisy labels. A potential improvement to the model would be to expand it to a 3D model, which may potentially improve the segmentation accuracy, but would require either increased data augmentation or a larger training dataset. We expect further increase of segmentation performance after including additional cases, potentially representing broader gestational age range and larger anatomical variability including pathological fetal brains, thus increasing the generalizability of our approach. The atlas-based segmentation method performed incredibly well when looking at the HD values. This is potentially because in atlas-based segmentations, existing shape data exists, which improves the shape of the segmentation, even if the overlap is not as correct as in the U-Net. However, the SR reconstructions used here are considered to be neuro-developmentally normal brains, so the effectiveness of this method is unknown for pathological brain structures.

This method will limit the amount of manual segmentation needed for future quantitative analyses of fetal brain volumes. It could also potentially be used as an automated segmentation training strategy for when new SR algorithms are developed in the future. In addition, this could potentially be used to further investigate the differences between the various SR methods in order to understand the quantitative differences between the methods, and how the method chosen could impact analyses. In the future, this method can potentially be used to expand the network's applicability for use with data from other MR scanners, across study centers, or with new SR algorithms.

Acknowledgements. Financial support was provided by the OPO Foundation, Anna Müller Grocholski Foundation, the Foundation for Research in Science and the Humanities at the University of Zurich, EMDO Foundation, Hasler Foundation, the Forschungszentrum für das Kind Grant (FZK) and the PhD Grant from the Neuroscience Center Zurich.

References

1. Kuklisova-Murgasova, M., Quaghebeur, G., Rutherford, M.A., Hajnal, J.V., Schnabel, J.A.: Reconstruction of fetal brain MRI with intensity matching and complete outlier removal. Med. Image Anal. **16**, 1550–1564 (2012). https://doi.org/10.1016/j.media.2012.07.004
2. Kainz, B., et al.: Fast volume reconstruction from motion corrupted stacks of 2D slices. IEEE Trans. Med. Imaging **34**, 1901–1913 (2015). https://doi.org/10.1109/TMI.2015.2415453
3. Ebner, M., et al.: An automated framework for localization, segmentation and super-resolution reconstruction of fetal brain MRI. NeuroImage **206**, 116324 (2020). https://doi.org/10.1016/j.neuroimage.2019.116324
4. Tourbier, S., Bresson, X., Hagmann, P., Thiran, J.-P., Meuli, R., Cuadra, M.B.: An efficient total variation algorithm for super-resolution in fetal brain MRI with adaptive regularization. NeuroImage **118**, 584–597 (2015). https://doi.org/10.1016/j.neuroimage.2015.06.018
5. Jiang, S., Xue, H., Glover, A., Rutherford, M., Rueckert, D., Hajnal, J.V.: MRI of moving subjects using multislice snapshot images with volume reconstruction (SVR): application to fetal, neonatal, and adult brain studies. IEEE Trans. Med. Imaging **26**, 967–980 (2007). https://doi.org/10.1109/TMI.2007.895456
6. Rousseau, F., et al.: Registration-based approach for reconstruction of high-resolution in utero fetal MR brain images. Acad. Radiol. **13**, 1072–1081 (2006). https://doi.org/10.1016/j.acra.2006.05.003
7. Kim, K., Habas, P.A., Rousseau, F., Glenn, O.A., Barkovich, A.J., Studholme, C.: Intersection based motion correction of multislice MRI for 3-D in utero fetal brain image formation. IEEE Trans. Med. Imaging **29**, 146–158 (2010). https://doi.org/10.1109/TMI.2009.2030679
8. Tourbier, S., et al.: Automated template-based brain localization and extraction for fetal brain MRI reconstruction. NeuroImage **155**, 460–472 (2017). https://doi.org/10.1016/j.neuroimage.2017.04.004
9. Wright, R., et al.: Automatic quantification of normal cortical folding patterns from fetal brain MRI. NeuroImage **91**, 21–32 (2014). https://doi.org/10.1016/j.neuroimage.2014.01.034
10. Keraudren, K., et al.: Automated fetal brain segmentation from 2D MRI slices for motion correction. NeuroImage. **101**, 633–643 (2014). https://doi.org/10.1016/j.neuroimage.2014.07.023
11. Salehi, S.S.M., et al.: Real-time automatic fetal brain extraction in fetal MRI by deep learning. In: 2018 IEEE 15th International Symposium on Biomedical Imaging (ISBI 2018), pp. 720–724 (2018). https://doi.org/10.1109/ISBI.2018.8363675

12. Khalili, N., et al.: Automatic brain tissue segmentation in fetal MRI using convolutional neural networks. Magn. Reson. Imaging (2019). https://doi.org/10.1016/j.mri.2019.05.020
13. Gholipour, A., Akhondi-Asl, A., Estroff, J.A., Warfield, S.K.: Multi-atlas multi-shape segmentation of fetal brain MRI for volumetric and morphometric analysis of ventriculomegaly. NeuroImage **60**, 1819–1831 (2012). https://doi.org/10.1016/j.neuroimage.2012.01.128
14. Payette, K., et al.: Longitudinal analysis of fetal MRI in patients with prenatal spina bifida repair. In: Wang, Q., et al. (eds.) PIPPI/SUSI - 2019. LNCS, vol. 11798, pp. 161–170. Springer, Cham (2019). https://doi.org/10.1007/978-3-030-32875-7_18
15. Gholipour, A., et al.: A normative spatiotemporal MRI atlas of the fetal brain for automatic segmentation and analysis of early brain growth. Sci. Rep. **7** (2017). https://doi.org/10.1038/s41598-017-00525-w
16. Habas, P.A., Kim, K., Rousseau, F., Glenn, O.A., Barkovich, A.J., Studholme, C.: Atlas-based segmentation of developing tissues in the human brain with quantitative validation in young fetuses. Hum. Brain Mapp. **31**, 1348–1358 (2010). https://doi.org/10.1002/hbm.20935
17. Yu, X., Liu, T., Gong, M., Zhang, K., Batmanghelich, K., Tao, D.: Transfer Learning with Label Noise (2017)
18. Moosavi-Dezfooli, S., Fawzi, A., Fawzi, O., Frossard, P.: Universal adversarial perturbations. In: 2017 IEEE Conference on Computer Vision and Pattern Recognition (CVPR), pp. 86–94 (2017). https://doi.org/10.1109/CVPR.2017.17
19. Karimi, D., Dou, H., Warfield, S.K., Gholipour, A.: Deep learning with noisy labels: exploring techniques and remedies in medical image analysis (2019)
20. Ghosh, A., Kumar, H., Sastry, P.S.: Robust loss functions under label noise for deep neural networks. In: AAAI. AAAI Publications (2017)
21. Cheplygina, V., de Bruijne, M., Pluim, J.P.W.: Not-so-supervised: a survey of semi-supervised, multi-instance, and transfer learning in medical image analysis. Med. Image Anal. **54**, 280–296 (2019). https://doi.org/10.1016/j.media.2019.03.009
22. Deman, P., Tourbier, S., Meuli, R., Cuadra, M.B.: meribach/mevislabFetalMRI: MEVISLAB MIAL Super-Resolution Reconstruction of Fetal Brain MRI v1.0. Zenodo (2020). https://doi.org/10.5281/zenodo.3878564
23. Jenkinson, M., Bannister, P., Brady, M., Smith, S.: Improved optimization for the robust and accurate linear registration and motion correction of brain images. NeuroImage **17**, 825–841 (2002). https://doi.org/10.1016/s1053-8119(02)91132-8
24. Ronneberger, O., Fischer, P., Brox, T.: U-Net: convolutional networks for biomedical image segmentation. In: Navab, N., Hornegger, J., Wells, W.M., Frangi, A.F. (eds.) MICCAI 2015. LNCS, vol. 9351, pp. 234–241. Springer, Cham (2015). https://doi.org/10.1007/978-3-319-24574-4_28
25. Sudre, C.H., Li, W., Vercauteren, T., Ourselin, S., Jorge Cardoso, M.: Generalised dice overlap as a deep learning loss function for highly unbalanced segmentations. In: Cardoso, M.J., et al. (eds.) DLMIA/ML-CDS - 2017. LNCS, vol. 10553, pp. 240–248. Springer, Cham (2017). https://doi.org/10.1007/978-3-319-67558-9_28
26. Avants, B.B., Tustison, N., Song, G.: Advanced normalization tools (ANTS). Insight J. **2**, 1–35 (2009)
27. Taha, A.A., Hanbury, A.: Metrics for evaluating 3D medical image segmentation: analysis, selection, and tool. BMC Med. Imaging **15** (2015). https://doi.org/10.1186/s12880-015-0068-x

Deep Learning Spatial Compounding from Multiple Fetal Head Ultrasound Acquisitions

Jorge Perez-Gonzalez[1(✉)], Nidiyare Hevia Montiel[1], and Verónica Medina Bañuelos[2]

[1] Unidad Académica del Instituto de Investigaciones en Matemáticas Aplicadas y en Sistemas en el Estado de Yucatán, Universidad Nacional Autónoma de México, 97302 Mérida, Yucatán, Mexico
{jorge.perez,nidiyare.hevia}@iimas.unam.mx

[2] Neuroimaging Laboratory, Electrical Engineering Department, Universidad Autónoma Metropolitana, 09340 Iztapalapa, Mexico
vera@xanum.uam.mx

Abstract. 3D ultrasound systems have been widely used for fetal brain structures' analysis. However, the obtained images present several artifacts such as multiplicative noise and acoustic shadows appearing as a function of acquisition angle. The purpose of this research is to merge several partially occluded ultrasound volumes, acquired by placing the transducer at different projections of the fetal head, to compound a new US volume containing the whole brain anatomy. To achieve this, the proposed methodology consists on the pipeline of four convolutional neural networks (CNN). Two CNNs are used to carry out fetal skull segmentations, by incorporating an incidence angle map and the segmented structures are then described with a Gaussian mixture model (GMM). For multiple US volumes registration, a feature set, based on distance maps computed from the GMM centroids is proposed. The third CNN learns the relation between distance maps of the volumes to be registered and estimates optimal rotation and translation parameters. Finally, the weighted root mean square is proposed as composition operator and weighting factors are estimated with the last CNN, which assigns a higher weight to those regions containing brain tissue and less ponderation to acoustic shadowed areas. The procedure was qualitatively and quantitatively validated in a set of fetal volumes obtained during gestation's second trimester. Results show registration errors of 1.31 ± 0.2 mm and an increase of image sharpness of 34.9% compared to a single acquisition and of 25.2% compared to root mean square compounding.

Keywords: Image registration · Image fusion · Fetal brain

1 Introduction

Ultrasound (US) systems have been widely used to assess maternal and fetal well-being, because they are non-invasive, work in real-time and are easily portable.

Y. Hu et al. (Eds.): ASMUS 2020/PIPPI 2020, LNCS 12437, pp. 305–314, 2020.
https://doi.org/10.1007/978-3-030-60334-2_30

Particularly, head biometry and brain structures' analysis are crucial to evaluate fetal health. However, US image acquisition is challenging because it requires an adequate transducer orientation to obtain definite borders between brain tissues and to avoid multiplicative noise and acoustic shadows [6]. This latter phenomenon is mainly present during gestation's second trimester and is caused by non-uniform calcification of the fetal skull, which originates considerable differences of acoustic impedances between cranium and brain tissue. To solve this problem, several authors [11,16] have reported that it is possible to acquire partial information from images obtained at different projections and that they can be complemented to observe the whole brain structures. Therefore, methods to efficiently combine multiple information from US images acquired at different angles become necessary. The goal of this research consisted on developing a methodology for the fusion or "composition" of US fetal head volumes acquired at different angles, with the purpose of generating a new enhanced 3D US study with increased quality, having less shadowed regions and therefore with best defined structures without occlusion artifacts.

Spatial composition is a technique that combines US volumes acquired at different transducer orientations, to generate a higher quality single volume [13]. Several researchers have proposed compounding algorithms based on the mean as combination operator, in order to enhance Signal to Noise Ratio (SNR) [12,15], to widen the field of vision or to attenuate those regions affected by acoustic shadows [7]. Specifically for fetal heads, several automatic and semi-automatic algorithms have been proposed to align and combine brain information, using probabilistic approaches or multiple-scale fusion methods [10,11,16].

Fusion of multiple fetal head volumes is challenging because the fetal exact position with respect to the transducer is unknown and because the positions of mother and fetus change after each US acquisition. This provokes that the alignment of US volumes to be compounded becomes difficult. Besides, due to the non-uniform skull calcification, each volume can contain different but complementary information depending on acquisition angles. Therefore, it is necessary to propose adequate registration strategies as a step previous to compounding. For instance, in [2,3] the registration of volumes using shape and texture patterns extracted from a Gabor filter bank has been reported. Also, in [5] an algorithm for fetal head registration of US phantom volumes was proposed. It is based on previously matching segmented features such as the eyes or the fetal head using feature-based registration. However, these algorithms were tested on phantom images or on US 2D studies without occlusion artifacts. Other authors have proposed rigid registration algorithms, based on the alignment of point sets using variations of the Coherent Point Drift method [9]. This approach can be useful, because given a set of fiduciary salient points, mono or multimodal registrations can be carried out and it can also perform properly in the presence of noise or occlusion artifacts. However, it assumes closeness between pair of points to be registered, which affects the alignment of those point sets completely misaligned.

The main contribution of this research is the design and evaluation of a Convolutional Neural Network (CNN)-based architecture for the registration and composition of multiple noisy and occluded US fetal volumes, with the purpose of obtaining a higher quality, less shadowed single volume. For the registration step a novel method is proposed, that consists on getting a feature set of distance maps obtained from the centroids of a Gaussian mixture that model the fetal skull previously segmented through the algorithm proposed in [4]. A CNN learns the relation of distance maps between volumes to be registered and estimates optimal rotation and translation parameters. The weighted root mean square is proposed as composition operator of multiple volumes, where ponderation factors are estimated with another CNN that assigns a higher weight to those regions containing brain tissue and lesser weight to occluded areas. This is a novel registration and composition method able to generate a single US volume of the whole fetal brain with enhanced quality, obtained from multiple noisy acquisitions obtained at different transducer angles.

2 Methodology

The proposed methodology is composed of four stages (Fig. 1): (a) Acquisition of multiple US volume of the fetal head, taken at axial, coronal and sagittal projections. (b) Complete segmentation of fetal skull using two U-Net neural networks and incidence angle maps (IAM). (c) Alignment of fetal heads using a CNN fed by a set of distance maps computed from the previous segmentations. This CNN estimates registration parameters $\mathcal{T}$, which are iteratively adjusted with a finer alignment using Normalized Mutual Information (NMI) Block Matching. From the registered volumes, a last CNN predicts weighting factors to carry out the final composition by applying the Weighted Root Mean Square (WRMS) operator. Each step is detailed in the following subsections.

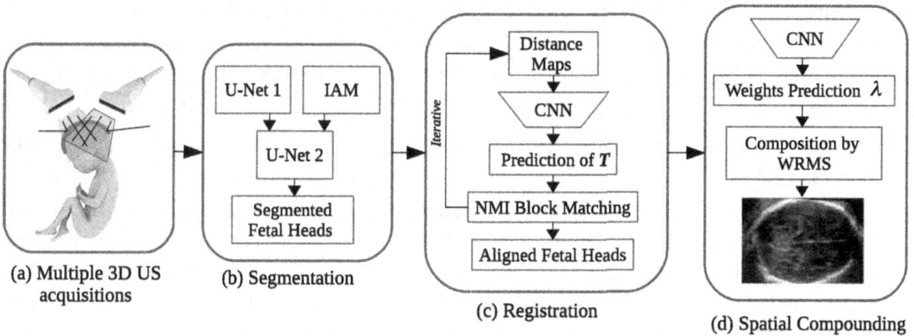

Fig. 1. Overall diagram of the proposed methodology for fetal head composition.

2.1 Data Set

Data used in this research consist on 18 US fetal head studies, obtained at pregnancies' second trimester. For each case, an obstetrics expert acquired a pair of volumes at axial-coronal and axial-sagittal projections, which contain complementary information useful during the composition process. Images were taken in B-mode, using a motorized curvilinear transducer with a frequency of 8–20 MHz and isotropic resolution. All subjects gave their written informed consent and agreed with the declaration of Helsinki. For assessment purposes, eight of these volumes were manually segmented by an expert obstetrician to delineate the corresponding fetal skulls. The same expert also aligned manually the 18 pairs of US volumes, taking as reference several fiduciary points of each fetal brain.

2.2 Fetal Head Segmentation

As a step previous to registration, the fetal skull must be segmented. This was accomplished following the methodology reported by Cerrolaza et al. [4], that consists on a two-stage cascade deep convolutional neural network (2S-CNN), both based on the U-Net architecture. The first CNN is used to pre-segment the fetal skull from all visible regions on US volumes. The second CNN is fed with a combination of the probability map obtained from the pre-segmentation step and an IAM (architecture details are in [4]). For both CNNs it was necessary to increase the number of training cases by applying random affine transformations. Results obtained were validated with manual segmentations delineated by an obstetrics expert, using Dice, Area under the ROC Curve (AUC) and Symmetric Surface Distance as performance metrics. A 4-fold cross-validation in a total of eight volumes (75% for training and 25% for testing) was applied.

2.3 CNN-Based Registration by Distance Maps

For registration purposes, the obtained fetal head segmentation is modeled as a points' set distributed in a coordinate space $\{x, y, z\}$. Given that, consider two point sets to be registered denoted by $\mathbf{P_F} \in \mathcal{R}^3$ and $\mathbf{P_D} \in \mathcal{R}^3$, where $\mathbf{P_F}$ is a fixed set (reference fetal head) and $\mathbf{P_D}$ is a displaced point cloud (fetal head to be registered). The purpose is to find a homogeneous transformation matrix $\mathcal{T}$, that satisfies $\mathbf{P_F} - \mathcal{T}\{\mathbf{R}\mathbf{P_D} + \mathbf{T}\}$. Thus, the problem consists on finding two rotation angles $\mathbf{R} \in \mathbb{R}^2$ (corresponding to azimuth and zenith in spherical coordinates) and translation displacements $\mathbf{T} \in \mathbb{R}^3$ in cartesian coordinates, that optimally align both sets of points $\mathbf{P_F}$ and $\mathbf{P_D}$.

Unlike other point cloud registration approaches, such as Iterative Closest Point [1] or Deep Closest Point [14], the proposed method does not assume closeness between point pairs to be aligned. In this research the distance relationship between points to be aligned is characterized with the help of distance maps, represented by a matrix $\mathbf{M}$ of size $f \times d$, where f and d correspond to the number of points that compose the reference (fixed) and the displaced point clouds respectively (in this case $f = d$). For instance, the Euclidean distance map (**EM**) between points $\mathbf{P_F} = \{P_1, P_2, P_3, \ldots, P_f\}$ and $\mathbf{P_D} = \{P_1, P_2, P_3, \ldots, P_d\}$ is computed as:

$$\mathbf{EM}_{(f,d)} = \|\mathbf{P_F} - \mathbf{P_D}\|_2^2 = \begin{pmatrix} e_{11} & e_{12} & e_{13} & \cdots & e_{1d} \\ e_{21} & e_{22} & e_{23} & \cdots & e_{2d} \\ e_{31} & e_{32} & e_{33} & \cdots & e_{3d} \\ \vdots & \vdots & & \ddots & \vdots \\ e_{f1} & e_{f2} & e_{f3} & \cdots & e_{fd} \end{pmatrix}, \tag{1}$$

where $\|.\|$ represents 2-norm on $\mathbb{R}^3$ and e is the Euclidean distance between a pair of points. Figure 2 shows a graphical example of the described procedure.

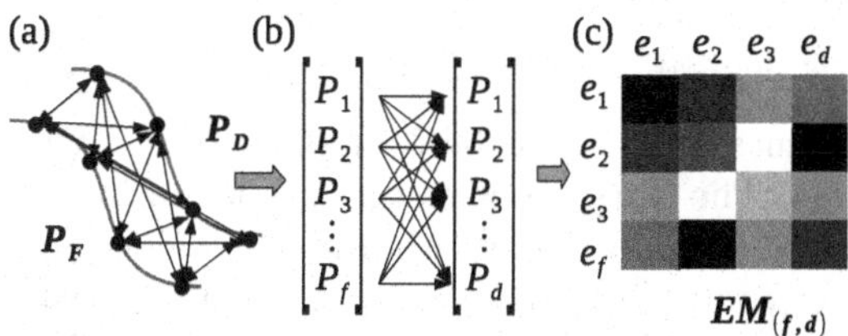

Fig. 2. Example of Euclidean distance maps computation. (a) Sets of points to be aligned, (b) Pairing of points and (c) Distance map represented as an image.

Five distance maps are proposed in this work: Chebyshev (**CM**), Mahalanobis (**AM**), Manhattan (**NM**), Hamming (**HM**) and Euclidean (**EM**), to constitute a set of maps $\mathbf{M} = \{\mathbf{CM}, \mathbf{AM}, \mathbf{NM}, \mathbf{HM}, \mathbf{EM}\}$. Each of these maps provides relevant information about distance relationships between the point sets being registered and all of them are used as input to the CNN that will estimate the optimal parameters of transformation $\mathcal{T}$. The architecture consists of three convolutional filters of $3 \times 3 \times 3$, three max-pooling layers of $2 \times 2 \times 2$ and a fully connected layer trained by sparse autoencoders (the input data size depends on the number of points to be registered). The number of data used to train the CNN by sparse autoencoders is increased by applying affine transformations. To reduce maps' size, each points cloud is modeled with a Gaussian mixture (GMM) having isotropic covariance matrix. New point subsets $\mathbf{P}'_\mathbf{F}$ and $\mathbf{P}'_\mathbf{D}$ are generated taking the centroids of the GMM (CGMM).

Finally, a more precise adjustment is carried out applying NMI Block Matching between intensity levels of each US volume [8]. Cumulated NMI (CNMI) is computed by $CNMI = \sum_{b=1}^{B} NMI(\mathbf{V}_{\mathbf{F}_b}, \mathbf{V}_{\mathbf{D}_b})$, where B is the total number of blocks b, and $\mathbf{V_F}$, $\mathbf{V_D}$ correspond to US volumes to be registered. CNMI is calculated only considering intensity information of the fetal cranium and brain structures, which presents the advantage of attaining a finer registration adjustment without considering information external to fetal skull. The complete registration procedure works iteratively until optimal alignment of multiple studies is obtained and its performance is assessed by measuring the Root Mean Square

Error (RMSE) between the automatically obtained result and the manual alignment made by an obstetrics expert, with a 6-fold cross-validation (considering 18 volume pairs: 83.3% for training and 16.7% for testing). Furthermore, performance validation regarding subsampling with CGMM, was carried out by varying the number of Gaussians considered in the model in a range of 50% to 95% of the total number of points.

2.4 Spatial Compounding

After US volumes have been aligned, their composition using WRMS is carried out. This operator is defined as $WRMS = \sqrt{\frac{1}{N}\sum_{n=1}^{N} \boldsymbol{\lambda}_n \cdot \mathbf{V}_n}$, where N is the total number of volumes $\mathbf{V} \in \mathcal{R}^3$ to be compounded and $\boldsymbol{\lambda} \in \mathcal{R}^3 \rightarrow [0, 1]$ are the weighting factors. The purpose of factor $\boldsymbol{\lambda}$ is to optimally highlight those regions containing visible brain tissue with a higher weight and to decrease the contribution of zones contaminated by noise or having acoustic occlusion artifacts, by lowering their weight. Previous to weight estimation, an echography expert manually selected different types of volumes of interest (VOIs) with different assigned factors: acoustic occlusion artifacts (0), anechogenic VOIs (0.25), hypoechogenic VOIs (0.5), isoechogenic VOIs (0.75) and hyperechogenic VOIs (1). A CNN was trained by sparse autoencoders with information extracted from a single fetal head US volume (it contains 2,184,530 voxels) and the annotated regions were used in the regression process. The architecture consists of three convolutional filters ($128 - 3 \times 3 \times 3$, $256 - 3 \times 3 \times 3$ and $512 - 3 \times 3 \times 3$), three max-pooling layers of $2 \times 2 \times 2$ and a fully connected layer. In this way, the CNN predicts optimal factors $\boldsymbol{\lambda}$ to weight each voxel of a new given US volume, depending on its echogenicity. To validate the CNN prediction capability, the Mean Absolute Percentage Error (MAPE) between the estimated and the real values with a 6–fold cross-validation was carried out. In addition, composition quality was assessed by measuring $SNR = \mu_{VOI}/\sigma_{VOI}$, where μ_{VOI} is the mean and σ_{VOI} standard deviation. Besides, Sharpness (SH) computed as the variance of LoG filter ($\sigma = 2$) on normalized images (unit variance, zero mean) was also determined: $SH = Var(LoG(X))[10^{-3}]$. Both parameters were measured only on fetal brain tissue and skull regions.

3 Results and Discussion

Performance of the fetal skull segmentation stage resulted in a Dice similarity index of $81.1 \pm 1.4\%$, AUC of $82.4 \pm 2.7\%$ and an SSD of 1.03 ± 0.2 mm, after 4-fold cross-validation. It is important to note the consistence of these results reflected by a very low variance. A comparison of registration results obtained with the CNN fed only with distance maps and those obtained by combining the CNN with a finer adjustment by Block Matching, are shown in Fig. 3. They are reported as a function of subsampling using CGMM. It can be observed that the incorporation of NMI block matching for a finer alignment helps to reduce registration errors in all cases. It can also be noted that CGMMs subsampling shows a performance between 85% and 95%, which correspond to acceptable average errors below 2 mm (between 95% and 100%, no differences were found according to RMSE). As the subsampling percentage increases, RMSE also shows an exponential growing which indicates that a reduced number of Gaussian centroids does not model adequately the fetal skull and therefore affects the algorithm's performance; in contrast, with a lower number of GMM the computational time decreases. The lowest obtained error was 1.31 ± 0.2 mm when applying the CNN, NMI Block Matching and 95% subsampling combination. These results outperform registration errors of 2.5 mm and 6.38 mm reported by [9,16]; however the reported registration results were obtained with a reduced number of volumes compared to [16]. It is important to highlight that the proposed method can work with non-predefined views (freehand). When comparing registration methods such as Iterative Closest Points and block matching individually, the RMS errors are very high (greater than 20 mm). This may happen because these methods depend on pairs of close volumes; however for fetal brain registration, angle differences between 70° and 110°, and translations in a rank of 30 to 80 mm are expected.

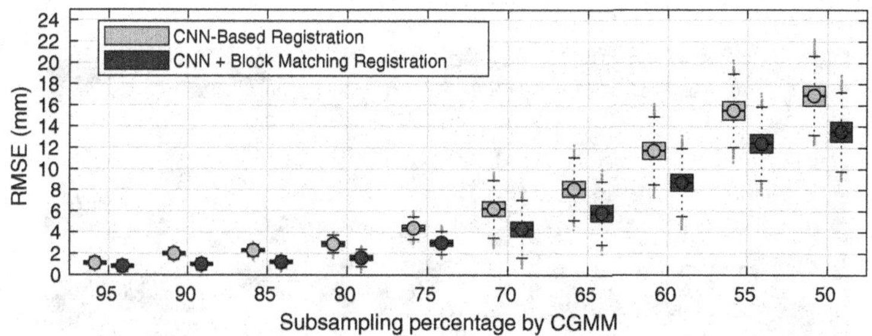

Fig. 3. Registration algorithm's performance measured by RMSE. X-axis corresponds to subsampling percentages extracted from point clouds, using GMM centroids. Light blue squares indicate CNN-based estimation while dark blue correspond to the combination of CNN and NMI block matching.

The CNN proposed for composition showed a MAPE of $2 \pm 1.1\%$, which reflects a good capability to estimate the values used in the composition. Visual composition results can be observed in Fig. 4, where columns correspond to three examples of the processed US fetal head volumes. The first row shows results obtained with the proposed method: WRMS weighted with CNN-estimated factors (WRMS-CNN). The second row corresponds to RMS-based composition while the last shows a single US acquisition. Volumes were compounded only considering two projections in axial-coronal and axial-sagittal views. It can be noticed that a single acquisition presents several acoustic occlusion artifacts reflected in a low SNR, thus impeding the clear observation of internal brain structures. Visual analysis of results obtained with RMS reveal an echogenicity attenuation of some areas such as the cerebellum (subject 2), cranium and middle line (all subjects), which are fundamental structures in fetal biometrics. Finally, for the three cases, a qualitative analysis with the proposed method shows hyperechogenicity or bright intensity in fetal skull, allowing a better contour definition of several structures, such as brain's middle line. This is reflected quantitatively in SH values obtained from the three shown examples, following a 6-fold cross-validation: WRMS-CNN (SNR $= 10.7 \pm 2.2$ and SH $= 10.9 \pm 3.4$), RMS (SNR $= 9.8 \pm 3.4$ and SH $= 8.7 \pm 2.3$) and single acquisition (SNR $= 7.7 \pm 2.7$ and SH $= 8.3 \pm 2.5$), thus showing that the proposed methodology outperforms the RMS-based composition.

Although quantitatively the proposed method showed a better performance, SNR and SH metrics do not reflect the high quality of brain structures definition. As a complementary assessment, an echography expert visually compared the obtained results and reported a clear enhancement of fetal cranium and a higher definition of structures such as cerebellum, peduncles and middle line. Furthermore, the proposed WRMS-CNN allows a better recovery of occluded brain tissue compared to a single acquisition. This can be due to the optimal weighting of different regions made by the CNN, that assigns a lower prevalence to acoustic shadows and a higher weight to brain tissue areas.

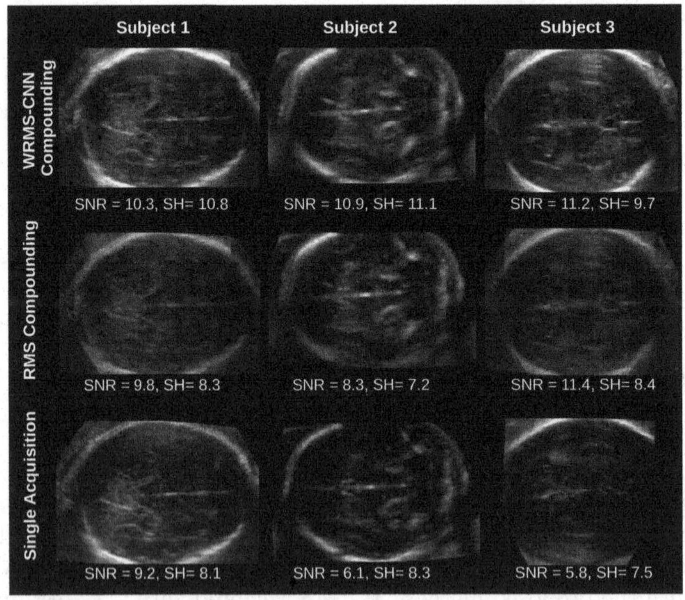

Fig. 4. Composition results obtained with: WRMS-CNN (first row), Root Mean Square (RMS) operator (second row) and a single acquisition of the fetal head (last row).

4 Conclusions

Fetal US biometrics presents a challenge during pregnancy's second trimester, due to skull non-homogeneous calcification, that provokes acoustic occlusion and impedes the adequate assessment of brain structures development. Unlike other reported researches, in this paper we address this challenge by proposing a novel composition method applied to multiple second trimester US volumes, with the purpose of generating a single, higher quality fetal head volume, useful for clinical diagnosis.

The developed methodology allows the fusion or composition of multiple projections to reduce the percentage of acoustic shadows in a single higher quality volume and to increase the definition of brain tissue contours. The main contributions of this research are: (1) a novel rigid registration method, based on distance maps that are fed to a CNN, which estimates the optimal rotation and translation parameters that adequately align multiple US volumes; (2) a new composition scheme based on optimal weighting factors' estimation, made also by a CNN, where higher weights are assigned to brain tissue regions and lower prevalences to acoustically occluded areas. The obtained results outperform previous researches reported in the literature, which can be due to the optimal estimation of transformation matrix and to the finer tuning of alignment through block matching during registration. Also, the incorporation of distance maps could allow this method to register volumes with larger displacements. On the other hand, volumes composed with the proposed compounding method show a higher quality compared to single US acquisitions and to previously reported RMS-based approaches, determined by quantitative and qualitative analyses. The generated volume presents an increased definition of different structures, such as cranium, cerebellum and middle line. Besides, the weighting factors help to mitigate shadowed regions, thus preserving brain tissue recovered from the multiple composed volumes. Therefore, the proposed methodology contributes also to increase the diagnostic usefulness of the generated US volumes and to clinical assessment of fetal wellbeing during this stage of pregnancy.

Acknowledgment. This work was supported by UNAM–PAPIIT IA102920 and IT100220. The authors also acknowledge the National Institute of Perinatology of Mexico (INPer) for sharing the Ultrasound images.

References

1. Besl, P., McKay, H.: A method for registration of 3-D shapes. IEEE Trans. Pattern Anal. Mach. Intell. **14**(2), 239–256 (1992)
2. Cen, F., Jiang, Y., Zhang, Z., Tsui, H.T., Lau, T.K., Xie, H.: Robust registration of 3-D ultrasound images based on Gabor filter and mean-shift method. In: Sonka, M., Kakadiaris, I.A., Kybic, J. (eds.) CVAMIA/MMBIA - 2004. LNCS, vol. 3117, pp. 304–316. Springer, Heidelberg (2004). https://doi.org/10.1007/978-3-540-27816-0_26

3. Cen, F., Jiang, Y., Zhang, Z., Tsui, H.T.: Shape and pixel-property based automatic affine registration between ultrasound images of different fetal head. In: Yang, G.-Z., Jiang, T.-Z. (eds.) MIAR 2004. LNCS, vol. 3150, pp. 261–269. Springer, Heidelberg (2004). https://doi.org/10.1007/978-3-540-28626-4_32
4. Cerrolaza, J.J., et al.: Deep learning with ultrasound physics for fetal skull segmentation. In: 2018 IEEE 15th International Symposium on Biomedical Imaging (ISBI 2018), pp. 564–567, April 2018. https://doi.org/10.1109/ISBI.2018.8363639
5. Chen, H.C., et al.: Registration-based segmentation of three-dimensional ultrasound images for quantitative measurement of fetal craniofacial structure. Ultrasound Med. Biol. **38**(5), 811–823 (2012)
6. Contreras Ortiz, S.H., Chiu, T., Fox, M.D.: Ultrasound image enhancement: a review. Biomed. Signal Process. Control **7**(5), 419–428 (2012)
7. Gooding, M.J., Rajpoot, K., Mitchell, S., Chamberlain, P., Kennedy, S.H., Noble, J.A.: Investigation into the fusion of multiple 4-D fetal echocardiography images to improve image quality. Ultrasound Med. Biol. **36**(6), 957–966 (2010)
8. Modat, M., et al.: Global image registration using a symmetric block-matching approach. J. Med. Imaging **1**(2), 1–6 (2014)
9. Perez-Gonzalez, J., Arámbula Cosío, F., Huegel, J., Medina-Bañuelos, V.: Probabilistic learning coherent point drift for 3D ultrasound fetal head registration. Comput. Math. Methods Med. **2020** (2020). https://doi.org/10.1155/2020/4271519
10. Perez-Gonzalez, J.L., Arámbula Cosío, F., Medina-Bañuelos, V.: Spatial composition of US images using probabilistic weighted means. In: 11th International Symposium on Medical Information Processing and Analysis, International Society for Optics and Photonics, SPIE, vol. 9681, pp. 288–294 (2015). https://doi.org/10.1117/12.2207958
11. Perez-Gonzalez, J., et al.: Spatial compounding of 3-D fetal brain ultrasound using probabilistic maps. Ultrasound Med. Biol. **44**(1), 278–291 (2018). https://doi.org/10.1016/j.ultrasmedbio.2017.09.001
12. Rajpoot, K., Grau, V., Noble, J.A., Szmigielski, C., Becher, H.: Multiview fusion 3-d echocardiography: improving the information and quality of real-time 3-D echocardiography. Ultrasound Med. Biol. **37**(7), 1056–1072 (2011)
13. Rohling, R., Gee, A., Berman, L.: Three-dimensional spatial compounding of ultrasound images. Med. Image Anal. **1**(3), 177–193 (1997)
14. Wang, Y., Solomon, J.M.: Deep closest point: learning representations for point cloud registration. In: IEEE 15th International Symposium on Biomedical Imaging (ISBI 2018), pp. 564–567, April 2019. https://doi.org/10.1109/ISBI.2018.8363639
15. Wilhjelm, J., Jensen, M., Jespersen, S., Sahl, B., Falk, E.: Visual and quantitative evaluation of selected image combination schemes in ultrasound spatial compound scanning. IEEE Trans. Med. Imaging **23**(2), 181–190 (2004)
16. Wright, R., et al.: Complete fetal head compounding from multi-view 3D ultrasound. In: Shen, D., et al. (eds.) MICCAI 2019. LNCS, vol. 11766, pp. 384–392. Springer, Cham (2019). https://doi.org/10.1007/978-3-030-32248-9_43

Brain Volume and Neuropsychological Differences in Extremely Preterm Adolescents

Hassna Irzan[1,2(✉)], Helen O'Reilly[3], Sebastien Ourselin[2], Neil Marlow[3], and Andrew Melbourne[1,2]

[1] Department of Medical Physics and Biomedical Engineering, University College London, Gower Street, Kings Cross, London WC1E 6BS, UK
hassna.irzan.17@ucl.ac.uk
[2] School of Biomedical Engineering and Imaging Sciences, Kings College London, Strand, London WC2R 2LS, UK
[3] Institute for Women's Health, University College London, 84-86 Chenies Mews, Bloomsbury, London WC1E 6HU, UK

Abstract. Although findings have revealed that preterm subjects are at higher risk of brain abnormalities and adverse cognitive outcome, very few studies have investigated the long-term effects of extreme prematurity on regional brain structures, especially in adolescence. The current study aims to investigate the volume of brain structures of 88 extremely preterm born 19-year old adolescents and 54 age- and socioeconomically-matched full-term born subjects. In addition, we examine the hypothesis that the volume of grey matter regions where a significant group or group-sex differences are found would be connected with the neurodevelopmental outcome. The results of the analysis show regional brain difference linked to extreme prematurity with reduced grey matter content in the subcortical regions and larger grey matter volumes distributed around the medial prefrontal cortex and anterior medial cortex. Premature birth and the volume of the left precuneus and the right posterior cingulate gyrus accounts for 34% of the variance in FSIQ. The outcome of this analysis reveals that structural brain differences persist into adolescence in extremely preterm subjects and that they correlate with cognitive functions.

Keywords: Prematurity · Brain volume · T1-weighted MRI · Grey matter

1 Introduction

The number of newborns surviving preterm birth is growing worldwide [8]; however, the outcome of their general health extends from physical impairments such

Electronic supplementary material The online version of this chapter (https://doi.org/10.1007/978-3-030-60334-2_31) contains supplementary material, which is available to authorized users.

Y. Hu et al. (Eds.): ASMUS 2020/PIPPI 2020, LNCS 12437, pp. 315–323, 2020.
https://doi.org/10.1007/978-3-030-60334-2_31

as brain abnormality [1,9,14] and cardiovascular diseases [12] to psychological and cognitive function disabilities [6,15]. While the normal period of gestation before birth is at least 37 weeks, preterm born subjects are born before this period [8]. Extremely preterm born subjects are born before 28 weeks of gestation [8].

Previous neuroimaging studies on preterm adolescents [9,13,14] have regularly reported developmental abnormalities throughout the brain volume and the grey matter in particular. The grey matter differences might have risen from premature exposure to the extra-uterine environment and the consequent interruption of normal cortical maturation, which takes place mainly after the 29th week of gestation [17]. Differences in brain structural volume have been described in preterm newborns and adolescents, particularly in the prefrontal cortex, deep grey matter regions and cerebellum [1,14]. Research has revealed that preterm subjects, across infancy and adolescence, are at higher risk of adverse neurodevelopmental outcome [12,15]. Establishing links between regional brain volume and cognitive outcome could pave the way to better define specific risks in preterm subjects of enduring neurodevelopmental deficits [9,13,14].

Despite the researchers' efforts in investigating preterm infants cohorts [1], very few studies have investigated structural brain alteration in extremely preterm (EP) subjects, especially in adolescence. The long-term impact of extreme prematurity later in life is less examined, and the adolescent brain phenotype of extreme prematurity is not extensively explored. Neuroimaging data and neurodevelopmental measurements of EP adolescents are now available, and the measurement of brain structures can be linked with neurocognitive performance. This study aims to estimate the difference between the expected regional brain volume for EP subjects and full-term (FT) subjects once variation in regional brain volume linked to total brain volume has been regressed out. Besides, we test the hypothesis that the effect of premature birth on brain volume depends on whether one is male or female. Moreover, we investigate the hypothesis that the volume of grey matter regions where the significant group or sex-group differences are found would be connected with neurodevelopmental outcome.

2 Methods

2.1 Data

The Magnetic Resonance Imaging (MRI) data include a group of 88 (53/35 female/male) 19-year old adolescents born extremely preterm, and 54 (32/22 female/male) FT individuals matched for the socioeconomic status and the age at which the MRI scans were acquired. Table 1 reports further details about the cohort.

T1-weighted MRI acquisitions were performed on a 3T Philips Achieva system at a repetition time (TR) of 6.93 ms, an echo time (TE) of 3.14 ms and a 1 mm isotropic resolution. T1-weighted volumes were bias-corrected using the N4ITK algorithm [16]. Tissue parcellations were obtained using the Geodesic

Information Flow method (GIF) [3]. GIF produces 144 brain regions, 121 of which are grey matter regions, cerebellum, and brainstem.

Overall cognitive ability was evaluated using the Wechsler Abbreviated Scale of Intelligence, Second Edition (WASI-II) [11]. Full-scale IQ (FSIQ) was obtained by combining scores from block design, matrix reasoning, vocabulary, and similarities tasks [15].

Table 1. Demographic features of the extremely preterm (EP) born females and males and the full-term (FT) females and males. The table reports the sample size, the age at which the MRI scans were acquired (Age at scan) in years, and the gestational age (GA) at birth in weeks (w).

Data-set features	EP females	EP males	FT females	FT males
Sample size	53	35	32	22
Age at scan [years]	19	19	19	19
GA [w] μ, (95% CI)	25.0 (23.3–25.9)	25.3 (25.9–23.4)	40 (36–42)	40 (36–42)

2.2 General Linear Model with Interaction Effects

The following linear model interprets the relationship between the volume of a brain region (RBV), the total brain volume (TBV), sex, and birth condition.

$$\log(\text{RBV}) = \alpha + \beta_1 * \text{group} + \beta_2 * \text{sex} + \beta_3 * \text{group} * \text{sex} + \beta_4 * \log(\text{TBV}) \quad (1)$$

The increase in TBV is linked to an increase in the volume of RBV. RBV and TBV are log-transformed to account for potential non-linearities. Dummy variables are used to moderate the effect of other explanatory variables such as sex and preterm birth. Specifically, α is the intercept, β_1 is the coefficient of the dummy variable group (EP $= 1$, FT $= 0$), β_2 the coefficient of the dummy variable for male/female (male $= 1$, female $= 0$), β_3 the coefficient for the interaction effect, and β_4 is the contribution of TBV.

The gap in expected regional brain volume between EP and FT females is estimated by β_1; while the gap in expected regional brain volume between EP and FT males is $\beta_1 + \beta_3$. The coefficient β_1 estimates the difference between the expected RBV for FT subjects and EP born subjects once variation in RBV caused by sex and TBV has been regressed out. The product variable group $*$ sex is coded 1 if the respondent is both male and EP subject. Hence the increment or decrement to average regional brain volume estimated for group $*$ sex applies only to this distinct subset. Therefore, the coefficient β_3 for the interaction term estimates the extent to which the effect of being preterm born differs for male and female sample members.

For the sake of our analysis, we are interested in the gap between the groups and the interactions effect. By using the natural logarithmic transformation of the RBV, the relationship between the independent variables and the dummy variables from β_1 to β_3 is in proportional terms [7]. The difference in percentage associated with β_i is $100 * [\exp(\beta_i) - 1]$ [7]. The t test associated with the regression coefficients of the dummy variable β_1 tests the significance of the effect of being EP female rather than FT female (reference group). To assess the effect of being EP female rather than EP male, the t test associated with the difference in regression coefficients is [7]: $t = [(\beta_1 + \beta_3) - \beta_1]/[\mathrm{var}((\beta_1 + \beta_3) - \beta_1)]^{1/2}$, using a *p-value* threshold of 0.05.

2.3 Cognitive Outcome and Grey Matter Volumes

The contribution of the regional brain volumes with significant between-group (or sex) differences to the neurodevelopmental outcome is analysed using stepwise linear regression. The FSIQ scores denote the dependant variable, while the grey matter volume and group (or sex) membership are the regressors.

3 Results

Overall the TBV of the EP born males (1074.82 cm^3) is significantly lower ($p = 1.96e^{-5}$) than the TBV of FT born males (1198.74^3). Similarly the TBV of EP born females (988.09 cm^3) is significantly lower ($p = 7.26e^{-4}$) than the TBV of FT born females (1054.24 cm^3).

Group differences in grey matter regions are mostly bilaterally distributed. Figure 1 shows the amount by which the volume of each brain region has changed in the EP subjects (encoded in β_1) and the additional difference due to male sex (encoded in β_3). The values are in proportion to the reference group (FT born females). Figure 2 shows the statistics of the coefficients β_1 and β_3. Overall the subcortical structures, including bilateral thalamus, pallidum, caudate, amygdala, hippocampus, ententorhinal area, left parahippocampal gyrus, and right subcallosal area are significantly reduced by $8.23\% \pm 1.89\%$ on average. Bilateral central operculum is reduced by 8.17%, superior occipital gyrus by 6.75%, post-central gyrus medial segment by 19.99%, left posterior orbital gyrus by 6.95%, right gyrus rectus by 7.97%, right middle temporal gyrus by 8.36%, right superior parietal lobule by 7.27%, and brainstem by 3.77%.

The brain regions that are significantly increased in the EP are distributed in the medial prefrontal cortex with an average increase of $10.26\% \pm 3.55\%$, anterior medial cortex with mean rise of $10.25\% \pm 1.96\%$, bilateral middle frontal cortex a mean rise of 8.43%, and regions in the occipital lobe with an mean rise of $10.00\% \pm 5.88\%$.

The coefficient β_3 of the interaction effect shows that the bilateral temporal pole (L: −8.61%, R: −6.98%), cerebellum (L: −14.37%, R: −13.56%), cerebellar vermal lobules I-V (−15.71%), cerebellar vermal lobules VIII-X (−11.80%), and left fusiform gyrus (−6.34%) are significantly ($p < 0.05$) reduced in EP males. Left hippocampus (6.71%), left ententorhinal area (7.36%), and right parietal operculum (17.45%) are significantly ($p < 0.05$) increased in EP males.

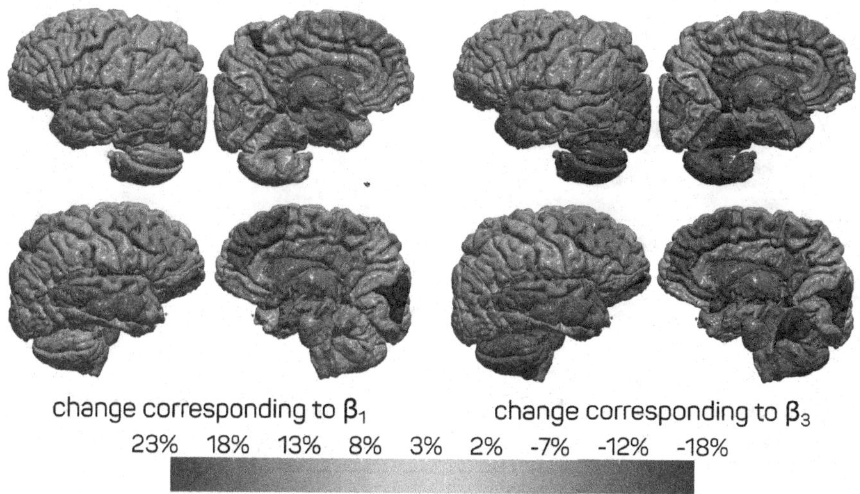

Fig. 1. The left side shows the change in the volume of being EP subject regardless of sex, while the right side illustrates the additional effect of being a male subject born extremely premature. The regions in blue colours are reduced and the regions in red are increased. The darker the colour, the greater the change. (Color figure online)

There is a significant difference ($p = 7.57e^{-11}$) between EP subjects (mean = 88.11, SD = 14.18) and FT participants (mean = 103.98, SD = 10.03) on FSIQ. Although, there is no statistically significant ($p > 0.05$) difference between males and females in each group, the EP males (mean = 85.94, SD = 14.04) achieved lower mean score than the EP female individuals (mean = 89.70, SD = 14.07).

Results of the stepwise linear regression comparing EP and FT revealed that the premature birth and the volume of the left precuneus and the right posterior cingulate gyrus (in which EP showed greater regional volume than FT) accounts for 34% of the variance of FSIQ (F = 22.96 $p = 4.67e^{-12}$). Group membership ($p = 1.76e^{-7}$) accounted for most of the variance (21.8%) and the volume of the right posterior cingulate gyrus accounted for the least (2.5%). The stepwise linear regression comparing EP males and females showed that the sex differences in the EP subjects and the volume of the cerebellar vermal lobules IV and right temporal pole account for 23.5% of the variance in FSIQ (F = 8.27 $p = 7.26e^{-5}$).

4 Discussion

We examined regional brain volume differences in a cohort of extremely preterm adolescents compared to their age- and socioeconomically-matched peers. We controlled for total brain volume and sex and investigated the impact of extremely preterm birth on the volume of grey matter structures. We further examined the hypotheses that differences in regional brain volume associated with extreme prematurity would be more substantial for male than female individuals, and that there is an association between the volume of grey matter

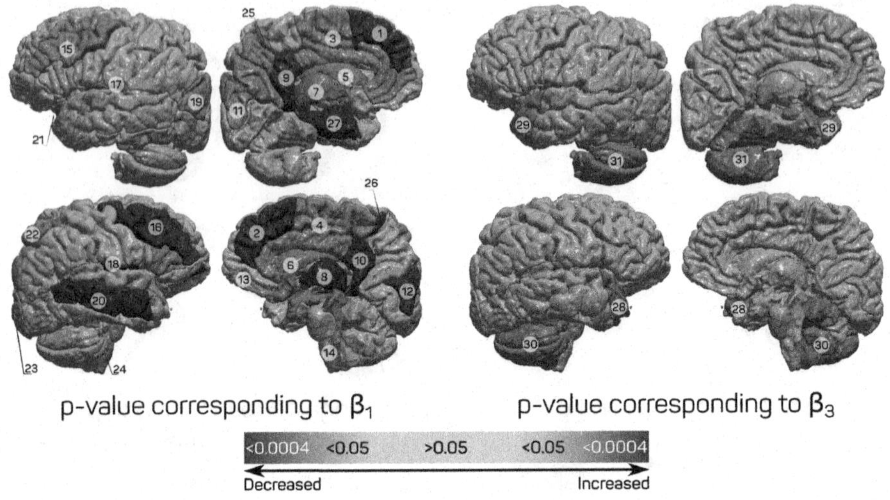

Fig. 2. Statistics of the difference in regional brain volume in EP born subjects. The regions in grey colour do not exhibit a significant difference ($p > 0.05$). Darker colour indicates that the region is significantly different after Bonferroni correction ($\alpha = 0.0004$) and lighter colour shows that the region is lower than the standard threshold $p = 0.05$ but above the critical Bonferroni threshold. Red colours indicate increased volume in EP subjects and blue colours display decreased volume in EP subjects. The significant regions are: 1 : 2 R-L superior frontal gyrus medial segment, 3 : 4 L-R supplementary motor cortex, 5 : 6 R-L caudate, 7 : 8 R-L thalamus, 9 : 10 R-L posterior cingulate gyrus, 11 : 12 R-L cuncuneus, 13 R gyrus rectus, 14 brainstem, 15 : 16 R-L middle frontal gyrus, 17 : 18 R-L hippocampus, 19 L middle occipital gyrus, 20 middle temporal gyrus,28 : 29 R-L temporal pole, 30 : 31 R-L cerebellum (Color figure online).

regions where significant between-group (or sex) differences are found and neurodevelopmental outcome.

The findings of the present analysis suggests that EP adolescents lag behind their peers as the brain differences and poor cognitive outcome persist at adolescence. Similar to other studies on very preterm individuals in mid-adolescence [13], our analysis showed both smaller and larger brain structures. The decrease in the volume of subcortical regions observed in the present analysis has been reported by many preterm studies on newborns [1] and mid-adolescents [14]. The consistency of these findings suggests that these regions might be especially vulnerable to damage and that the EP subjects would endure long-lasting or permanent brain alterations. The loss in grey matter content in the deep grey matter might be a secondary effect of white matter injury, as white matter damage is linked to grey matter growth failure [2]. Larger grey matter volumes in EP subjects are distributed around the medial prefrontal cortex and anterior medial cortex. Such a result might reflect a paucity of white matter content;

alternatively, as proposed by some authors [14], this might indicate a delayed pruning process specific to these regions.

The interaction term investigates whether the effect of being extremely preterm born differed for males and females. The results showed that the status of being male and born extremely preterm results in a significant reduction in the bilateral cerebellum and temporal pole. Although this result did not persist after adjustment for multiple comparisons was made, it is worth considering for further analysis in view of other studies describing sex-specific brain alterations [13] and sex-specific cognitive impairments [15]. As the incidence of cerebellar haemorrhage [10] and white matter injury [5] is higher in preterm born males, it is plausible that the reduced volume in the cerebellum and temporal pole is due to grey matter loss attributable to complex pathophysiological mechanisms triggered by either cerebellar haemorrhage [4] or white matter injury [2].

In line with previous findings [14,15], EP subjects achieved lower scores than FT subjects on Full-scale IQ measurements. Our results suggest involvement of the precuneus and posterior cingulate gyrus in explaining the variance in the IQ scores although this does not rule out important influences from other connected brain regions.

The assumption of homogeneity of variance might not hold due to either the *a priori* variable impact of prematurity on EP subjects or the unequal sample sizes of the groups. The change in brain structures in the EP cohort is variable with EP subjects reporting from normal to very divergent brain volume. Besides, the dataset contains more EP than FT individuals and more females than males subjects. Although Levene's test suggests that all input samples are from populations with equal variances ($p = 0.1$), the factors as mentioned earlier might present a limitation in the present analysis. The linear model presented here can capture the average group effect; however, it is clear that there is an individual variability that this kind of analysis ignores. As mentioned above, since the extreme prematurity has a variable effect on EP subjects, an analysis targeted to tackle this might lead to richer findings. Future work on this dataset will develop a framework to investigate this opportunity.

The present analysis has been carried out on a unique dataset of EP 19-year old adolescents with no differences in gestational age, age at which the MRI scans were acquired, and socio-economic status; moreover, the control group are matched with EP in age at MRI scan and socio-economic status. These characteristics of the data allow the analysis to rule out some hidden factors that affect other studies. Furthermore, the volume of brain structures has been measured in the subjects space, removing from the workflow additional uncertainty due to registration error.

The grey matter of the EP adolescent brain shows long-term developmental differences, especially in subcortical structures, medial prefrontal, and anterior medial cortex. The variations in the regional brain volume are linked with neurodevelopmental outcome. The main outcome of this analysis is that the extremely preterm brain at adolescence remains affected by early-life injuries; however, it is hard to conclude if the observed volume abnormalities are growth lag or permanent changes. To investigate this further, future investigations on this cohort or similar cohorts need to take place at later stages of life of the subjects.

Acknowledgement. This work is supported by the EPSRC-funded UCL Centre for Doctoral Training in Medical Imaging (EP/L016478/1). We would like to acknowledge the MRC (MR/J01107X/1) and the National Institute for Health Research (NIHR).

References

1. Ball, G., et al.: The effect of preterm birth on thalamic and cortical development. Cereb. Cortex **22**(5), 1016–1024 (2012). https://doi.org/10.1093/cercor/bhr176
2. Boardman, J.P., et al.: A common neonatal image phenotype predicts adverse neurodevelopmental outcome in children born preterm. NeuroImage **52**(2), 409–414 (2010). https://doi.org/10.1016/j.neuroimage.2010.04.261. http://www.sciencedirect.com/science/article/pii/S1053811910006889
3. Cardoso, M.J., et al.: Geodesic information flows: spatially-variant graphs and their application to segmentation and fusion. IEEE Trans. Med. Imaging **34**(9), 1976–1988 (2015). https://doi.org/10.1109/TMI.2015.2418298
4. Chen, X., Chen, X., Chen, Y., Xu, M., Yu, T., Li, J.: The impact of intracerebral hemorrhage on the progression of white matter hyperintensity. Front. Hum. Neurosci. **12**, 471 (2018). https://doi.org/10.3389/fnhum.2018.00471. https://www.frontiersin.org/article/10.3389/fnhum.2018.00471
5. Constable, R.T., et al.: Prematurely born children demonstrate white matter microstructural differences at 12 years of age, relative to term control subjects: an investigation of group and gender effects. Pediatrics **121**(2), 306 (2008). https://doi.org/10.1542/peds.2007-0414. http://pediatrics.aappublications.org/content/121/2/306.abstract
6. Costeloe, K.L., Hennessy, E.M., Haider, S., Stacey, F., Marlow, N., Draper, E.S.: Short term outcomes after extreme preterm birth in England: comparison of two birth cohorts in 1995 and 2006 (the epicure studies). BMJ Br. Med. J. **345**, e7976 (2012). https://doi.org/10.1136/bmj.e7976. http://www.bmj.com/content/345/bmj.e7976.abstract
7. Hardy, M.A.: Regression with Dummy Variables. SAGE Publications Inc. (1993). https://methods.sagepub.com/book/regression-with-dummy-variables
8. Howson, M.V. Kinney, J.L.: March of dimes, PMNCH, save the children, WHO. Born too soon: the global action report on preterm birth, Geneva (2012)
9. Irzan, H., O'Reilly, H., Ourselin, S., Marlow, N., Melbourne, A.: A framework for memory performance prediction from brain volume in preterm-born adolescents. In: 2019 IEEE 16th International Symposium on Biomedical Imaging (ISBI 2019), pp. 400–403 (2019)
10. Limperopoulos, C., Chilingaryan, G., Sullivan, N., Guizard, N., Robertson, R.L., du Plessis, A.: Injury to the premature cerebellum: outcome is related to remote cortical development. Cereb. Cortex **24**(3), 728–736 (2014). https://doi.org/10.1093/cercor/bhs354. https://pubmed.ncbi.nlm.nih.gov/23146968
11. McCrimmon, A.W., Smith, A.D.: Review of the Wechsler abbreviated scale of intelligence, second edition (WASI-II). J. Psychoeduc. Assess. **31**(3), 337–341 (2012). https://doi.org/10.1177/0734282912467756

12. McEniery, C.M., et al.: Cardiovascular consequences of extreme prematurity: the epicure study. J. Hypertens. **29**, 1367–1373 (2011)
13. Nosarti, C., et al.: Preterm birth and structural brain alterations in early adulthood. NeuroImage Clin. **6**, 180–191 (2014). https://doi.org/10.1016/j.nicl.2014.08.005. http://www.sciencedirect.com/science/article/pii/S2213158214001144
14. Nosarti, C., et al.: Grey and white matter distribution in very preterm adolescents mediates neurodevelopmental outcome. Brain **131**, 205–217 (2008)
15. O'Reilly, H., Johnson, S., Ni, Y., Wolke, D., Marlow, N.: Neuropsychological outcomes at 19 years of age following extremely preterm birth. Pediatrics **145**(2), e20192087 (2020). https://doi.org/10.1542/peds.2019-2087. http://pediatrics.aappublications.org/content/145/2/e20192087.abstract
16. Tustison, N.J., et al.: N4itk: improved N3 bias correction. IEEE Trans. Med. Imaging **29**(6), 1310–1320 (2010). https://doi.org/10.1109/TMI.2010.2046908
17. Van Der Knaap, M.S., van Wezel-Meijler, G., Barth, P.G., Barkhof, F., Adèr, H.J., Valk, J.: Normal gyration and sulcation in preterm and term neonates: appearance on MR images. Radiology **200**(2), 389–396 (1996). https://doi.org/10.1148/radiology.200.2.8685331

Automatic Detection of Neonatal Brain Injury on MRI

Russell Macleod[1(✉)], Jonathan O'Muircheartaigh[1,3,4], A. David Edwards[1], David Carmichael[2], Mary Rutherford[1], and Serena J. Counsell[1]

[1] Centre for the Developing Brain, School of Biomedical Engineering and Imaging Sciences, King's College London, London, UK
russell.macleod@kcl.ac.uk

[2] Department of Bioengineering, School of Biomedical Engineering and Imaging Sciences, King's College London, London, UK

[3] Department of Forensic and Neurodevelopmental Sciences, King's College London, London, UK

[4] MRC Centre for Neurodevelopmental Disorders, King's College London, London, UK

Abstract. Identification of neonatal brain abnormalities on MRI requires expert knowledge of both brain development and pathologies particular to this age group. To aid this process we propose an automated technique to highlight abnormal brain tissue while accommodating normal developmental changes. To train a developmental model, we used 185 T2 weighted neuroimaging datasets from healthy controls and preterm infants without obvious lesions on MRI age range = 27 + 5 − 51 (median = 40 + 5) weeks + days post menstrual age (PMA). We then tested the model on 39 preterm subjects with known pathology age range = 25 + 1 − 37 + 5 (median = 33) weeks PMA + days. We used voxel-wise Gaussian processes (GP) to model age (PMA) and sex against voxel intensity, where each GP outputs a predicted mean intensity and variance for that location. All GP outputs were combined to synthesize a 'normal' T2 image and corresponding variance map for age and sex. A Z-score map was created by calculating the difference between the neonate's actual image and their synthesized image and scaling by the standard deviation (SD). With a threshold of 3 SD the model highlighted pathologies including germinal matrix, intraventricular and cerebellar hemorrhage, cystic periventricular leukomalacia and punctate lesions. Statistical analysis of the abnormality detection produces an average AUC value of 0.956 and 0.943 against two raters' manual segmentations. The proposed method is effective at highlighting different abnormalities across the whole brain in the perinatal period while limiting false positives.

Keywords: Abnormality detection · Neonatal imaging · Gaussian processes · Normative modeling

1 Introduction

Magnetic resonance imaging (MRI) is increasingly used to assess neonatal brain injury [1–3]. MRI provides images with both high resolution and signal to noise thereby allowing detection of small, subtle brain abnormalities. When present, early and accurate

Y. Hu et al. (Eds.): ASMUS 2020/PIPPI 2020, LNCS 12437, pp. 324–333, 2020.
https://doi.org/10.1007/978-3-030-60334-2_32

detection of these abnormalities can often be vital to guide clinical interventions and improve outcomes. However, examining these images requires expert knowledge of potential abnormalities and their appearance on MRI images. As both the neonatal brain and brain injuries are highly heterogeneous, detection and interpretation of MRI findings are subject to inter and intra-rater inconsistencies [4]. Radiological interpretation is also time-consuming so an automated method that could highlight areas of suspected abnormality could assist and streamline this process and potentially improving identification consistency.

A first broad approach to abnormality detection in adults is to detect specific pathology such as multiple sclerosis lesions, tumors, etc. Of these, several use dual systems that detect abnormality with one method (e.g. random forests [5]) then regularizing using a second (conditional random fields [5]) to remove noise. Alternatively, they first shift data into some plane that better separates pathology (Berkley wavelet transform [6]) then a second highlights the abnormalities (support vector machine (SVM) [6]). More recently methods tend towards single pass deep-learning methods (neural networks [7]) which are often highly accurate but require large datasets and training times. Common factors of these techniques are that they detect only a single or a limited number of pathologies and require labelled training data (sometimes large amounts).

An alternative approach is to model normal brain structure and look for any outliers. While using different inputs (extension and junction maps [8] or synthesized 'healthy' images [9, 10]), several methods calculate the difference between averaged 'normal' measures and specific subject measures, either directly [9, 10] or as Z-scores [8]. These can be combined with additional techniques (gaussian mixture models [10]), used as inputs for additional classifiers (SVM [8, 10]), or by applying a threshold to the raw difference [9] to detect these outliers. Recent work from our group [11] used a similar technique based on Gaussian processes (GP). They constructed a model of a 'normal' neonatal brain using an expected range of intensity values at each voxel then compared each subjects brain to this model. Areas that were outside of the expected range were highlighted to detect punctate white matter lesions (PWML).

We propose an adaption of this method, evaluating its ability to detect a range of pathologies seen on T2 weighted images in preterm neonates (minimizing dataset requirements for training and testing as well as reducing computational load) and investigate the influence of image preprocessing on performance.

2 Methods

2.1 Sample and Dataset

We use an MRI dataset of 423 preterm neonates acquired at Hammersmith Hospital on a Philips 3T scanner. From this dataset, 48 were discarded due to high levels of motion, incomplete dataset or severe artifacts leaving 375 usable images. Ethical approval was granted by a research ethics committee and written informed parental consent was obtained in each case. Two acquisitions were used (Table 1).

From the 375 images we selected 185 term and preterm neonates for our training set. Datasets with major pathology (including cystic PVL and hemorrhagic parenchymal infarction) were excluded from the training set though some neonates with punctate

Table 1. Acquisition parameters.

Scan	TR	TE	Voxel size	Subjects
T2 FSE	7000 < 8000 ms	160 ms	0.859 × 0.859 × 1 mm	347
T2 dynamic	20000 < 30000 ms	160 ms	0.859 × 0.859 × 1 mm	28

lesions were still included. This also has the benefit of being more representative of data available in hospital environments. Of the remaining 190 images with pathologies we selected 39 preterm neonates, with a range of tissue injuries, for manual segmented by two independent raters as ground truth. For manual labels, we included a range of representative pathologies seen in the neonatal and preterm brain. These included the following neonatal pathologies: Germinal matrix hemorrhage (N = 14), inter-ventricular hemorrhage (N = 7), cerebellar hemorrhage (N = 11), hemorrhagic parenchymal infarct (N = 4), temporal horn cysts (N = 1), sub-arachnoid cysts (N = 2), pseudocysts (N = 1), cystic periventricular leukomalacia (N = 3), large/many punctate white matter lesions (PWML) (N = 8) and few/single PWML (N = 10). Subject information is displayed in Table 2.

2.2 Pre-processing

Pre-processing consisted of 4 steps; MRI B0 inhomogeneity was corrected using ANTs N4BiasCorrection [12]. Extra cortical tissue was removed using FSL brain extraction technique (BET) [13]. Affine registration between the MRI images and a 36-week template [14] using FSL FLIRT [15, 16] followed by nonlinear registration using ANTs Registration [12] to the same template. No image smoothing was performed to ensure sensitivity to smaller lesions.

Table 2. Subject information.

Parameter	Value
Total subjects (female)	375 (179)
Post menstrual age (PMA) range (weeks + days) [median]	25 + 1 to 55 + 0 [37 + 1]
Gestational age (GA) range [median]	23 + 2 to 42 + 0 [29 + 5]
Healthy & preterm neonates without lesions (training)	185
PMA range [median]	27 + 5 to 51 + 0 [40 + 5]
GA range [median]	23 + 2 to 42 + 0 [30 + 3]
Neonates with brain injury (manually labelled)	39
PMA range [median]	25 + 2 to 37 + 5 [33 + 0]
GA range [median]	24 + 3 to 35 + 2 [30 + 0]

2.3 Modelling Tissue Intensity Using Gaussian Processes

Gaussian process regression [17] is a Bayesian non-parametric method that models a distribution over all possible functions that fit the data. This is constrained by an initial mean (usually 0) and variance where functions close to a mean function are most likely to fit the data and those further away less likely.

$$\varepsilon \sim N\left(0, \sigma_n^2\right) \tag{1}$$

A covariance matrix Σ is constructed from the datapoints using a kernel function that quantifies the similarity between the different points to act as a prior.

$$\Sigma = K(x, x) \tag{2}$$

In this instance the kernel used for our covariance matrix is the radial basis function (RBF).

$$K(x, x) = \exp\left(-\frac{x - x'}{2\sigma^2}\right) \tag{3}$$

This is initially applied to an individual datapoint where $\mathrm{x}_1 - \mathrm{x}_\mathrm{i}$ each represent a single parameter but is then repeated with $\mathrm{x}_1 - \mathrm{x}_\mathrm{i}$ represent individual datapoints. The GP is fit by allowing the covariance matrix to alter the mean such that it passes through or near these points but will be closer to the a priori mean in areas with few or no points. We the optimize the variance, using the Adam optimizer [18], which has the effect of increasing the model confidence close to areas with observed training data.

Predictions are made based on the joint conditional probability of the data seen in training and the new unseen points.

$$\begin{bmatrix} f \\ f^* \end{bmatrix} \sim \left(0, \begin{bmatrix} k\ (x, x) & k\ (x, x^*) \\ k\ (x^*, x) & k\ (x^*, x^*) \end{bmatrix}\right) \tag{4}$$

Where k(x,x) is the covariance matrix training data, k(x*,x*) is the covariance matrix of the testing data and k(x*,x) (k(x,x*) being equal to k(x*,x) transposed) being the covariance matrix between the training and testing data.

Here, we used voxel-wise GPs coded with the GPyTorch library [19] to model and predict the most likely intensities in the control neonatal MRI brain volume for a range of ages between 25–55 weeks PMA. In this model, each individual voxel has its own GP modelling PMA and sex and outputs the expected mean intensity value and variance based on the data in the training set. The age distribution of the neonatal cohort along with examples of a simplified GP are given in Fig. 1.

2.4 Detecting Pathology

In addition to the main aim of modelling tissue intensity development, we tested alternative approaches to intensity scaling the input images and different SD thresholds on detection accuracy of manually labelled tissue pathology. In all cases, abnormality detection is achieved by creating an absolute Z-map of the difference between the subject's

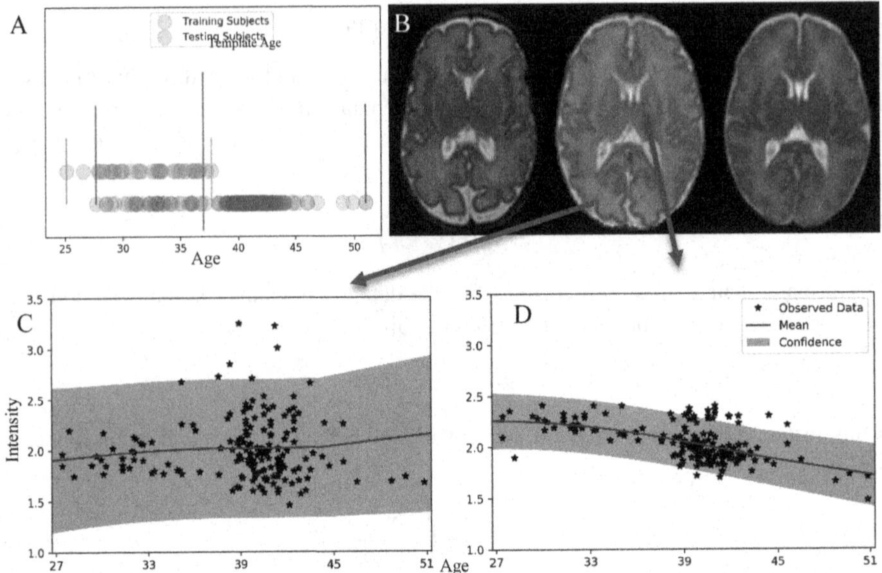

Fig. 1. A: Subject distribution, bars show min/max age of train/test set and template age. B: Raw subject image, subject image in template space, template. C and D show two Gaussian processes C for a voxel with high variance and D a voxel with low variance. Each image shows all training points as well as the mean (blue line) and standard deviation (shaded area). (Color figure online)

actual image and the predicted, scaled by the model standard deviation map, thresholding at fixed Z to indicate clinical utility. We compared the effect of the following different types of image scaling. Normalization: voxel intensity value minus image intensity Mean or Median divided by the image intensity range. Standardization: image intensity values Z scaled with the Mean or Median intensity value standard deviation. As a uninformed baseline we calculated the simple voxel-wise Z-scores using the same training data to compare model performance.

We calculated the following criteria for each approach: specificity, sensitivity (recall), precision, receiver operating characteristic (ROC), area under curve (AUC) and precision recall curve (PRC). The resulting AUCs were compared pairwise using non-parametric Wilcoxon tests. Control GP model accuracy was tested using 5-fold cross-validation and measured with mean absolute error (MAE) and false positive rate.

3 Results

After training, the model demonstrated accurate prediction of a 'normal' image based on the mean voxel intensities in the training data. Figure 2A shows a mean absolute error map (MAE) of the differences between the observed and predicted control images where high intensity represents areas of high cortical variability and poorer model performance. Qualitatively, there was smoothing around highly variable areas of cortex.

Using median standardization and a threshold of $Z > 3$, Fig. 2B–E demonstrates the result of using model deviations to highlight abnormalities in 4 cases. Using this

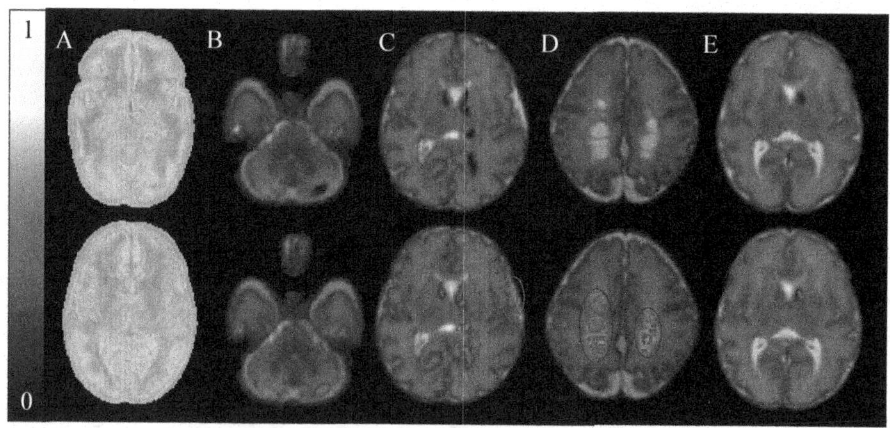

Fig. 2. A: Mean Absolute Error map. Row 1 (B–E): Raw images. Row 2 (B–E): GP detection. B: Cerebellar hemorrhage. C: Intraventricular hemorrhage. D: Cystic periventricular leukomalacia. E: Germinal matrix hemorrhage. Red circle: incorrectly highlighted normal voxels. Blue circles: abnormalities core highlighted but edges missed. (Color figure online)

measure, we can highlight multiple types of tissue injury (such as intraventricular hemorrhage and cystic periventricular leukomalacia). However, in areas of high inter-subject heterogeneity (e.g. cortical surface) there were false positives, Fig. 2C red circle. This is likely due to inaccurate image registration to different cortical folding patterns across individuals and development. The statistical results are shown in Table 3.

Table 3. Average specificity, sensitivity and precision of our models and simple Z-score for both raters with a threshold of 3 SD.

Test	Specificity	Sensitivity/Recall (Range)	Precision
Median standard	0.997	**0.372 (0.967)**	**0.110**
Median normal	**0.999**	0.049 (0.592)	0.065
Mean standard	0.997	**0.372 (0.967)**	**0.110**
Mean normal	**0.999**	0.049 (0.592)	0.065
Z-scores	0.997	0.291 (0.954)	0.095

When testing the effect of different Z-score thresholds on abnormality detection. We found that for an absolute Z of 2 we achieved an mean average of 0.989, an average sensitivity of 0.533 and an average precision of 0.036 for both raters. These change to an average specificity of 0.999 an average of 0.204; and an average precision of 0.205 for an absolute Z value of 4.5. If we do the same comparison, but from one rater to the other, we find a specificity of 0.979, sensitivity of 0.675 and precision of 0.487. For the cross-validation of healthy controls we used the found that false positive rate decreases

Table 4. Area under curve of receiver operating characteristic.

Preprocessing type	AUC Rater1	AUC Rater2
Median standard	**0.961**	**0.947**
Median normal	0.927	0.907
Mean standard	**0.961**	**0.947**
Mean normal	0.927	0.907
Z-Score	0.934	0.915

from 0.013 to < 0.001 when the absolute Z value changes from 2 to 4.5 representing a reduced number of voxels being erroneously identified as abnormal although given the large overall number of voxels this is still large.

We can see that all models have high levels of specificity and only by lowering the SD threshold to 2 do we get values lower than 0.99. The sensitivity appears to be relatively low with only a threshold of 2 SD being able to detect over 50% of the abnormal voxels. Precision was mostly low being 0.110 for Median standard (best result) and rising to 0.241 when the SD threshold is raised to 4.5. The model was insensitive to Mean and Median scaling as both produced the same results.

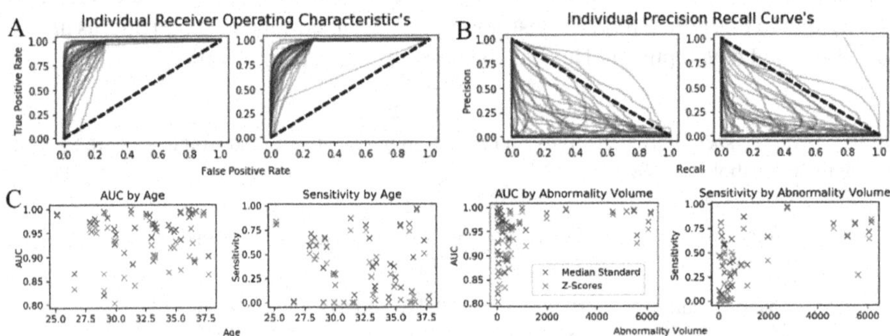

Fig. 3. A: Overlay of individual Median standard ROC curves of both manual segmentations. B: Overlay of individual Median standard PRC's of both manual segmentations. C: AUC score difference between simple Z-score outlier (Orange) and Median standard (Blue) detection both at a SD threshold of 3 by age and by lesion size. (Color figure online)

We produced ROC curves and PRC for each model including all tested methods as well as simple Z-score outlier detection for comparison. We also calculated the AUC for each of these ROC curves shown in Table 4. Wilcoxon p scores of 1.196e−6 (Median standard-simple Z), 0.295 (Median normal-simple Z) and 3.617e−5 (Median standard-Median normal) demonstrating significant statistical difference between the outputs of the different methods. Figure 3A shows our median standard ROC curves and Fig. 3B the PRC for all individuals against both manual segmentations. Figure 3C shows the AUC score difference between simple Z-score outlier detection and our Median standard detection by age and by lesion size. Standardization methods both outperformed simple Z-scores having greater AUC scores while both of the normalization methods scored lower.

4 Discussion

We used voxel-wise Gaussian Processes trained on healthy controls and preterm neonates with no overt pathology to synthesize approximations of normal neonatal brains. We highlighted abnormalities in a held-out testing set of neonates with pathology using the absolute deviation between the subject and subject equivalent synthesized imaged.

While sensitivity appears low this is due to the effect of averaging over all images and the individual sensitivities range from 0.967 to 0 at a threshold of 3 SD. The sensitivity scores of 0 (not detected by our system) were recorded in 5 images, 4 were single PWMLs, 1 was a cerebellar hemorrhage and all were very small lesions with minimal differences between abnormal and normal tissue intensity. Investigation into outcome would be useful here as, due to their small size, these missed lesions may have minimal effect of development and therefore their detection is less relevant for abnormality screening. In all other cases this approach successfully highlights the central area of the abnormality but can underestimate total volume. This is due to voxels at the edge of a lesion that can be partially normalized to expected intensified due to partial volume (Fig. 2D blue circle). Lowering the SD threshold can assist lesion coverage but at the cost of a higher number of false positives. The highly variable nature of the cortical surface resulted in a number of false positives in these areas when CSF is present in the subject image (Fig. 3C red circle) and is responsible for our relatively low precision. Specificity remains high due to the fact that the number of voxels in an MRI image is large compared to the noisy voxels and overpowers their effect.

In future we will incorporate noise suppression approaches, improve small/subtle lesion detection and increasing coverage of large lesions. Noise suppression could use similar regularization methods as those seen in [5] while detection of small/subtle abnormalities (e.g. PWML) could include incorporating a second modality (T1) in which lesions appear more obvious. Improving large lesion coverage could be achieved by applying a second pass at a lower SD threshold around areas with a number of highlighted voxels. At present, we calculate sensitivity and specificity measures in a voxel-wise manner but will include a second measure based on the highlighting of a sufficiently large part of a tissue injury (coincidence as opposed to spatial overlap). Future work will also incorporate local neighborhood information (patch) into the GP models.

5 Conclusion

Our goal was to detect a range of pathologies in preterm neonates using only T2 weighted images. Using voxel-wise Gaussian Processes, we modeled these typical intensity values in the brain throughout the preterm and term neonatal period. By detecting tissue intensity values outside of a typical range, we provide an automatic approach to detect a wide range of brain abnormalities and injuries observed in the preterm neonatal brain.

Acknowledgments. This work was supported by The Wellcome/EPSRC Centre for Medical Engineering at Kings College London (WT 203148/Z/16/Z), the NIHR Clinical Research Facility (CRF) at Guy's and St Thomas' and by the National Institute for Health Research Biomedical Research Centres based at Guy's and St Thomas' NHS Foundation Trust, and South London, Maudsley NHS Foundation Trust. The views expressed are those of the authors and not necessarily those of the NHS, the NIHR or the Department of Health. R.M's PhD is supported by the EPSRC Centre for Doctoral Training in Smart Medical Imaging at King's College London. J.O. is supported by a Sir Henry Dale Fellowship jointly funded by the Wellcome Trust and the Royal Society (grant 206675/Z/17/Z). J.O. received support from the Medical Research Council Centre for Neurodevelopmental Disorders, King's College London (grant MR/N026063/1). The project includes data from a programme of research funded by the NIHR Programme Grants for Applied Research Programme (RP-PG-0707-10154). The views and opinions expressed by authors in this publication are those of the authors and do not necessarily reflect those of the NHS, the NIHR, MRIC, CCF, NETSCC, the Programme Grants for Applied Research programme or the Department of Health.

References

1. Imai, K., et al.: MRI changes in the thalamus and basal ganglia of full-term neonates with perinatal asphyxia. Neonatology **114**, 253–260 (2018)
2. Kline-Fath, B.M., et al.: Conventional MRI scan and DTI imaging show more severe brain injury in neonates with hypoxic-ischemic encephalopathy and seizures. Early Hum. Dev. **122**, 8–14 (2018)
3. Chaturvedi, A., et al.: Mechanical birth-related trauma to the neonate: an imaging perspective. Insights Imaging **9**(1), 103–118 (2018). https://doi.org/10.1007/s13244-017-0586-x
4. Bogner, M.S.: Human Error in Medicine. CRC Press, Boca Raton (2018)
5. Pereira, S., et al.: Automatic brain tissue segmentation in MR images using random forests and conditional random fields. J. Neurosci. Methods **270**, 111–123 (2016)
6. Bahadure, N.B., et al.: Image analysis for MRI based brain tumor detection and feature extraction using biologically inspired BWT and SVM. Int. J. Biomed. Imaging **2017**, 12 pages (2017)
7. Rezaei, M., et al.: Brain abnormality detection by deep convolutional neural network. arXiv preprint arXiv:1708.05206(2017)
8. El Azami, M., et al.: Detection of lesions underlying intractable epilepsy on T1-weighted MRI as an outlier detection problem. PLoS ONE **11**(9), e0161498 (2016)
9. Chen, X., et al.: Unsupervised detection of lesions in brain MRI using constrained adversarial auto-encoders. arXiv preprint arXiv:1806.04972(2018)
10. Bowles, C., et al.: Brain lesion segmentation through image synthesis and outlier detection. NeuroImage Clin. **16**, 643–658 (2017)
11. O'Muircheartaigh, J., et al. "Modelling brain development to detect white matter injury in term and preterm born neonates. Brain, **143**, 467–479 (2020)
12. Avants, B.B., et al.: Advanced normalization tools (ANTS). Insight J. **2**, 1–35 (2009)
13. Smith, S.M.: Fast robust automated brain extraction. Hum. Brain Mapp. **17**(3), 143–155 (2002)
14. Makropoulos, A., et al.: The developing human connectome project: a minimal processing pipeline for neonatal cortical surface reconstruction. Neuroimage **173**, 88–112 (2018)
15. Jenkinson, M.: A global optimisation method for robust affine registration of brain images. Med. Image Anal. **5**(2), 143–156 (2001)

16. Jenkinson, M., et al.: Improved optimisation for the robust and accurate linear registration and motion correction of brain images. NeuroImage **17**(2), 825–841 (2002)
17. Rasmussen, C.E.: Gaussian processes in machine learning. In: Bousquet, O., von Luxburg, U., Rätsch, G. (eds.) ML-2003. LNCS (LNAI), vol. 3176, pp. 63–71. Springer, Heidelberg (2004). https://doi.org/10.1007/978-3-540-28650-9_4
18. Kingma, D.P., et al.: Adam: a method for stochastic optimization. arXiv preprint arXiv:1412.6980 (2014)
19. Gardner, J., et al.: GPyTorch: blackbox matrix-matrix Gaussian process inference with GPU acceleration. In: Advances in Neural Information Processing Systems (2018)

Unbiased Atlas Construction for Neonatal Cortical Surfaces via Unsupervised Learning

Jieyu Cheng[1], Adrian V. Dalca[1,2], and Lilla Zöllei[1(✉)]

[1] A. A. Martinos Center for Biomedical Imaging, Harvard Medical School, Massachusetts General Hospital, Boston, USA
lzollei@mgh.harvard.edu

[2] Computer Science and Artificial Intelligence Laboratory, Massachusetts Institute of Technology, Cambridge, USA

Abstract. Due to the dynamic cortical development of neonates after birth, existing cortical surface atlases for adults are not suitable for representing neonatal brains. It has been proposed that pediatric spatio-temporal atlases are more appropriate to characterize the neural development. We present a novel network comprised of an atlas inference module and a non-linear surface registration module, SphereMorph, to construct a continuous neonatal cortical surface atlas with respect to post-menstrual age. We explicitly aim to diminish bias in the constructed atlas by regularizing the mean displacement field. We trained the network on 445 neonatal cortical surfaces from the developing Human Connectome Project (dHCP). We assessed the quality of the constructed atlas by evaluating the accuracy of the spatial normalization of another 100 dHCP surfaces as well as the parcellation accuracy of 10 subjects from an independent dataset that included manual parcellations. We also compared the network's performance to that of existing spatio-temporal cortical surface atlases, i.e. the 4D University of North Carolina (UNC) neonatal atlases. The proposed network provides continuous spatial-temporal atlases rather than other 4D atlases at discrete time points and we demonstrate that our representation preserves better alignment in cortical folding patterns across subjects than the 4D UNC neonatal atlases.

1 Introduction

Considering the rapid evolution of the cerebral cortex during early brain development, it is essential to construct a spatio-temporal representation to model its dynamic changes. Spatio-temporal surface atlases provide a reference for spatial normalization within a group and facilitate a better understanding of the neonatal brain development process over time.

Classical strategies for the construction of cortical spatio-temporal models [3,8,13,14] mostly rely on an age threshold to create sub-populations and use

Y. Hu et al. (Eds.): ASMUS 2020/PIPPI 2020, LNCS 12437, pp. 334–342, 2020.
https://doi.org/10.1007/978-3-030-60334-2_33

kernel regression to formulate atlases from each of those [8,11]. Some of the methods select a representative or the mean surface [3] as the initial template and then run several iterative steps of repeated registration of the individuals to the current template, incurring an extremely high runtime. Group registration methods [10,14] do find the global optimum, but their performance is limited by the nature of the sub-populations.

In this paper, we build on recent deep learning based developments [6,7,12] and propose a novel deep neural network, which is capable of achieving group-wise registration of neonatal brain surfaces and simultaneously producing continuous spatio-temporal atlases. The network consists of an atlas inference and a spherical surface registration module. It requires neonatal surfaces as input and solves the registration problem in the polar coordinate space. We encode neighboring via a spherical kernel in all convolution and pooling operations and derive an objective function that maximizes the data likelihood on the spherical surface as well as regularizes the geodesic displacement field.

2 Methods

We adapt a conditional template learning framework [7] to the spherical domain and use geometric features of cortical surfaces to drive the alignment in our experiments. Let $S = \{s_1, s_2, \cdots, s_N\}$ denote a group of N spherical signals, one for each input brain surface, that are parameterized by longitude $\theta \in [0, 2\pi)$ and latitude $\varphi \in [0, \pi)$, as well as $A = \{a_i\}$ indicate the ages of the corresponding subjects. Our goal is to find a spatial-temporal atlas and a group of N optimal deformation fields $\Phi = \{\phi_i\}$ that maximize the posterior likelihood of $p(\Phi|S, A)$. We model the spatial-temporal atlas as a function of age $f_w(A)$ with parameters w. The proposed model is designed to find optimal parameters w^* in atlas inference function and deformation field Φ^* that maximizes:

$$L = \log p_w(\Phi|S, A) = \log p_w(S|\Phi; A) + \log p(\Phi). \quad (1)$$

where the first term encourages data similarity between an individual and the warped atlas and the second regularizes the deformation field.

We model each training spherical signal $s_i(\theta, \varphi)$ with attribute a_i as a noisy observation of the atlas after warping, $s_i(\theta, \varphi) = \mathcal{N}(f_w(a_i) \circ \phi_i, \sigma^2 I)$, where $\circ$ is the spatial warp operator and σ is the standard deviation. Assuming a fixed signal sampling rate $r = \frac{1}{d\theta d\varphi}$ on the unit spherical surface area, where $d\theta$ and $d\varphi$ are the respective differential elements of θ and ϕ, the number of sampled vertices at an infinitely small region centered at (θ, φ) is $n = r * \sin\varphi d\theta d\varphi = \sin\varphi$. The joint log-likelihood for all sampled vertices on the sphere can be written as:

$$\begin{aligned}\log p_w(s_i|\phi_i;a_i) &= \sum_{\theta,\varphi} \sin\varphi \log p_w(s_i(\theta,\varphi)|\phi_i;a_i) \\ &= \sum_{\theta,\varphi} \sin\varphi \left[-1/2\log(2\pi) - \log\sigma - \frac{1}{2\sigma^2}(s_i - f_w(a_i)\circ\phi_i)^2\right] \\ &= -\sum_{\theta,\varphi} \frac{\sin\varphi}{2\sigma^2}(s_i - f_w(a_i)\circ\phi_i)^2 + const.\end{aligned} \tag{2}$$

In our implementation, we discretize θ and φ to 512 and 256 elements, that is $d\theta = d\phi = \pi/256$.

To diminish bias in the constructed atlas, we encourage the average deformation across the data set to be close to the identity deformation. Additionally, we assume each deformation field to be smooth. Given these two constraints, we model the prior probability of the deformation as:

$$p(\Phi) \propto e^{(-\lambda|\bar{u}|^2)} \prod_i \mathcal{N}(0,\Sigma_i), \tag{3}$$

where $u_i = \mathcal{N}(0,\Sigma_i)$ is the displacement field of $\phi_i = Id + u_i$ for s_i and $\bar{u}$ is the average displacement field. Then we arrive at:

$$\log p(\Phi) = -\lambda|\bar{u}|^2 + \sum_i \log\mathcal{N}(0,\Sigma_i) + const. \tag{4}$$

2.1 Spherical Regularization

In the Euclidean space, a conventional solution for obtaining a smooth deformation field results from Laplacian regularization, by letting $\Sigma_i^{-1} = \gamma L$, where L is the Laplacian matrix of a neighborhood graph, defined on the Euclidean grid. However, we have shown that on the spherical surface the smoothness of its corresponding warp field in the parameter space, i.e. (θ,φ), does not hold, especially for regions near the poles [4]. We compute the geodesic displacement $g(u)$ instead of the displacement in parameter space and apply Laplacian regularization on $g(u)$. Considering that the distance between two adjacent vertices in parameter space might be different, we set the weight of the connecting edge as $w_{jk} = \exp(-d^2)$, where $d = |ver_j - ver_k|$ is the distance between vertices ver_j and ver_k, and compute the Laplacian matrix L_S for the weighted graph. We then compute the regularization term on the prior probability of the deformation field as:

$$\begin{aligned}\log p(\Phi) &= -\lambda|\bar{u}|^2 + \sum_i \log p(g(u_i)) + const \\ &= -\lambda|\bar{u}|^2 + \gamma\sum_i\sum_j \sum_{k\in Neighbor(j)} w_{jk}|g_j(u_i) - g_k(u_i)|^2 + const.\end{aligned} \tag{5}$$

2.2 Network Structure

Our proposed construction follows the conditional template learning framework of [7] and is associated with a spherical kernel as proposed in SphereNet [5]. Specifically, the network consists of an atlas inference module, which produces an atlas given a particular age, and a SphereMorph module, which registers the atlas to the input surface signal. Figure 1(a) illustrates the difference between a spherical and a 2D rectangular kernel. Briefly, for a given vertex at location (θ, ϕ), we utilize inverse gnomonic projection to obtain the corresponding locations on the parameterized image for the neighboring vertex on its tangent plane. All the convolution and pooling operations of the network take information from 3×3 local tangent patches. Figure 1(b) illustrates our detailed network structure. In our implementation, we assume diffeomorphic deformation with stationary velocity field v and use scaling and squaring layer to obtain the deformation ϕ.

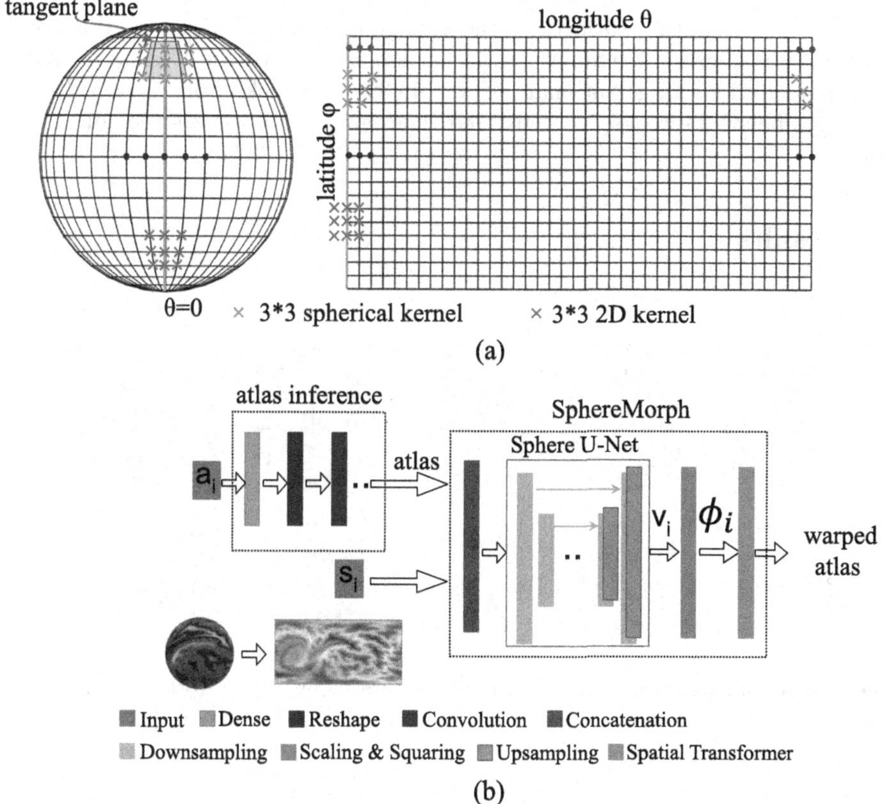

Fig. 1. (a) Illustration of the spherical and the 2D conventional kernels over a spherical mesh and its corresponding 2D rectangular grids by planar projection; (b) The proposed atlas construction framework with an atlas inference module and a non-linear surface registration module (SphereMorph).

3 Experiments

We used MRI brain images of 545 neonatal subjects aged between 35 and 44 weeks (39.89 ± 2.14 weeks) at the time of scan from the 2nd release of the Developing Human Connectome Project (dHCP)[1]. The corresponding cortical surfaces were generated by the dHCP minimal processing pipeline [9]. Furthermore we also relied on imaging data from 10 subjects (41.7 ± 0.8 weeks) from the Melbourne Children's Regional Infant Brain (M-CRIB) atlas [2] that all had manual annotations. We reconstructed their surfaces using the M-CRIB-S pipeline [1].

In order to train our proposed network, we randomly selected 445 surfaces from the dHCP dataset. We then evaluated the resulting atlases using two sets of experiments. First we examined the accuracy of the spatial normalization using the remaining 100 subjects from the dHCP dataset as test subjects. Second we analyzed the outcome of a surface parcellation experiment with the 10 M-CRIB subjects, relying on their manual annotations as ground truth. We also registered these testing surfaces to the 4D age-matched UNC neonatal atlases. Their atlases consist of template surfaces associated with the Desikan-Killiany (DK) parcellations for gestational ages within 39 to 44 weeks. For testing subjects with ages below 39 weeks, we registered their surfaces to the 39-week-old UNC atlas.

4 Results

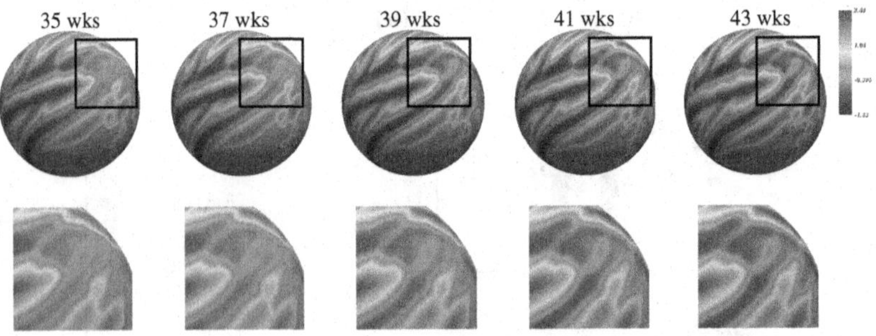

Fig. 2. A set of age-specific convexity atlases generated by our network. The lower row provides a closer view of the selected regions as marked in the upper row.

[1] http://www.developingconnectome.org.

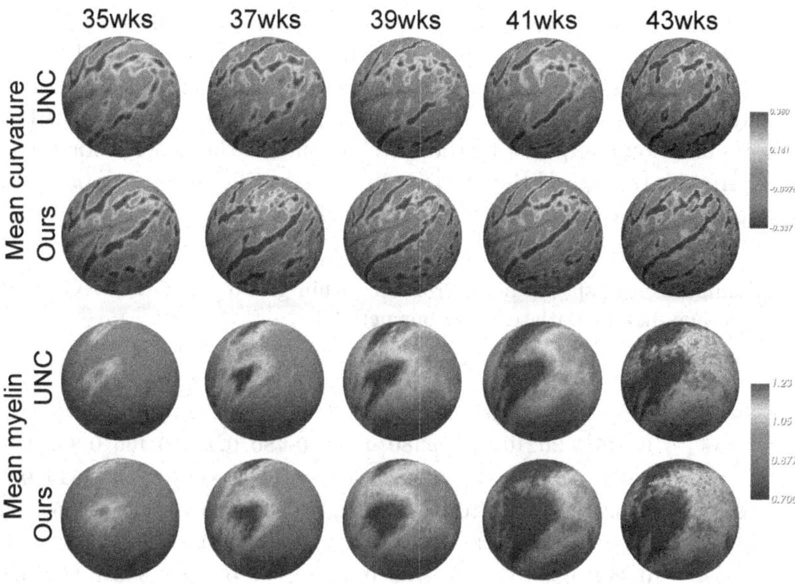

Fig. 3. Mean curvature and myelin maps associated with 35, 37, 39, 41 and 43 weeks, a subset of all ages, after aligning with the age-matched UNC neonatal and our atlases. The learnt atlases are continuous.

4.1 Spatial Normalization

Figure 2 displays the age-specific convexity atlases constructed using our network, with the lower row zooming in on the marked regions. The resulting patterns suggest longitudinal consistency. Figure 3 shows an extensive comparison of group mean curvature and myelin features between the 4D UNC and our network-generated atlases at a selected set of ages. We divided our test subjects by age into a total of 10 groups, corresponding to $35, 36, ..., 44$ weeks. For both of the surface features, all age groups exhibit sharper patterns using the proposed atlases, indicating better alignment across subjects when compared to the UNC atlases.

Since there is no ground truth for newborn surface atlases, we performed the quantitative evaluation of the atlas quality by calculating the within-group spatial normalization accuracy. We further divided the 100 test subjects into two subgroups, with equal numbers of subjects at each week. We compared the convexity, curvature as well as the myelin content maps after alignment in a pairwise manner between the two subsets, by computing the correlation coefficients (CC). Using convexity values, sulcal and gyral regions could be obtained for each aligned surface. Then for each week, we calculated average information entropy (Entropy) [14] of all aligned surfaces and respective Dice overlap ratios of sulcal and gyral regions between the two subsets. Table 1 provides an overview of all the above-mentioned metrics using the 4D UNC neonatal and our network-generated atlases. Except for the average information entropy, higher values of the metrics indicate better alignment of the registered surfaces. The proposed atlases yield lower within-group entropy, higher correlations of all feature maps in the two subsets and higher overlap in both sulcal and gyral regions. This suggests better spatial normalization compared to the UNC neonatal atlases, even for the ages exactly covered by these, and therefore an increased utility of our proposed atlas regarding population comparison of cortical surfaces.

Table 1. Comparison of spatial normalization within group using 4D UNC neonatal and generated age-matched atlases from our network.

Age(wks)		35	36	37	38	39	40	41	42	43	44
Entropy	4D UNC	0.550	0.337	0.512	0.596	0.576	0.595	0.572	0.604	0.413	0.422
	Ours	**0.335**	**0.202**	**0.354**	**0.380**	**0.440**	**0.480**	**0.454**	**0.466**	**0.399**	**0.406**
CC_{myelin}	4D UNC	0.891	0.698	0.875	**0.936**	0.928	0.953	0.949	**0.913**	**0.814**	**0.846**
	Ours	**0.902**	**0.769**	**0.910**	0.911	**0.929**	**0.953**	**0.964**	0.912	0.789	0.813
CC_{curv}	4D UNC	0.437	0.129	0.442	0.604	0.535	0.729	0.748	0.464	0.487	0.424
	Ours	**0.659**	**0.364**	**0.579**	**0.730**	**0.666**	**0.777**	**0.803**	**0.593**	**0.507**	**0.445**
CC_{sulc}	4D UNC	0.839	0.497	0.856	0.926	0.887	0.948	0.958	**0.869**	0.867	**0.853**
	Ours	**0.922**	**0.759**	**0.892**	**0.945**	**0.915**	**0.954**	**0.963**	0.869	**0.873**	0.833
$Dice_{sulc}$	4D UNC	0.813	0.651	0.814	0.878	0.850	0.885	0.909	0.821	0.824	0.826
	Ours	**0.902**	**0.806**	**0.894**	**0.934**	**0.900**	**0.927**	**0.918**	**0.860**	**0.874**	**0.848**
$Dice_{gyri}$	4D UNC	0.831	0.675	0.829	0.888	0.861	0.891	**0.918**	**0.830**	0.839	**0.841**
	Ours	**0.886**	**0.789**	**0.868**	**0.922**	**0.876**	**0.908**	0.901	0.828	**0.850**	0.818

4.2 Parcellation Accuracy

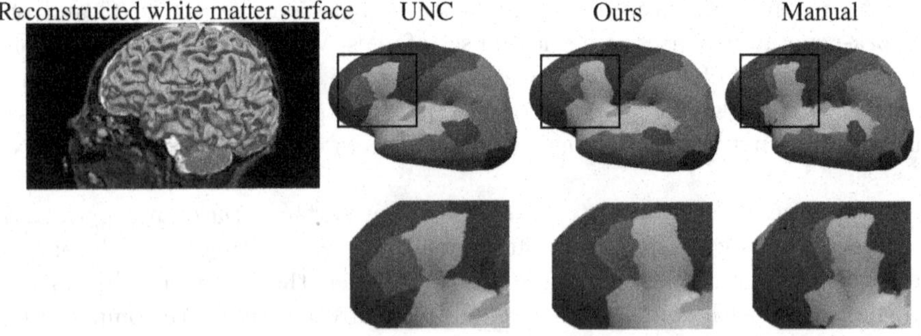

Fig. 4. Different parcellation results superimposed on the inflated surface for an example subject from the M-CRIB data set.

We performed a registration between individual spherical surfaces from the M-CRIB-S pipeline and the age-matched UNC atlas and then propagated the atlas parcellations to the individual. For our atlases, given the limited number of subjects, we used leave-one-out cross-validation to train a probabilistic parcellation atlas using the 9 selected subjects and obtained the parcellation on the remaining subject. Figure 4 displays the white matter surface reconstruction resulting from a T2-weighted image and the various parcellation solutions superimposed on the inflated surface representation of one of the subjects. When compared with manual annotations, the 4D UNC atlas yields 0.76 ± 0.03 and our atlas 0.78 ± 0.06 of Dice overlap coefficient.

5 Conclusions

In this work we proposed a novel framework for the construction of an unbiased and continuous spatio-temporal atlas of neonatal cortical surfaces. We characterized its performance by evaluating the resulting spatial alignment quality, the accuracy of cortical segmentations enabled by it as well as its representation to the UNC spatio-temporal cortical neonatal atlases. We found that both the registration and parcellation results suggest high potential of the proposed framework an demonstrated that our representation preserves better alignment in cortical folding patterns than the 4D UNC ones.

References

1. Adamson, C.L., et al.: Parcellation of the neonatal cortex using Surface-based Melbourne Children's Regional Infant Brain atlases (M-CRIB-S). Sci. Rep. **10**(1), 1–11 (2020)
2. Alexander, B., et al.: A new neonatal cortical and subcortical brain atlas: the Melbourne Children's Regional Infant Brain (M-CRIB) atlas. NeuroImage **147**, 841–851 (2017)
3. Bozek, J., et al.: Construction of a neonatal cortical surface atlas using multimodal surface matching in the developing human connectome project. NeuroImage **179**, 11–29 (2018)
4. Cheng, J., Dalca, A.V., Fischl, B., Zöllei, L.: Cortical surface registration using unsupervised learning. NeuroImage **221**, 117161 (2020). https://doi.org/10.1016/j.neuroimage.2020.117161, http://www.sciencedirect.com/science/article/pii/S1053811920306479
5. Coors, B., Paul Condurache, A., Geiger, A.: SphereNet: learning spherical representations for detection and classification in omnidirectional images. In: Proceedings of the European Conference on Computer Vision (ECCV), pp. 518–533 (2018)
6. Dalca, A.V., Balakrishnan, G., Guttag, J., Sabuncu, M.: Unsupervised learning of probabilistic diffeomorphic registration for images and surfaces. Med. Image Anal. **57**, 226–236 (2019)
7. Dalca, A.V., Rakic, M., Guttag, J., Sabuncu, M.R.: Learning conditional deformable templates with convolutional networks. In: Neural Information Processing Systems, NeurIPS (2019)
8. Li, G., Wang, L., Shi, F., Gilmore, J.H., Lin, W., Shen, D.: Construction of 4D high-definition cortical surface atlases of infants: methods and applications. Med Image Anal. **25**(1), 22–36 (2015)

9. Makropoulos, A., et al.: The developing human connectome project: a minimal processing pipeline for neonatal cortical surface reconstruction. NeuroImage **173**, 88–112 (2018)
10. Robinson, E.C., Glocker, B., Rajchl, M., Rueckert, D.: Discrete optimisation for group-wise cortical surface atlasing. In: Proceedings of the IEEE Conference on Computer Vision and Pattern Recognition Workshops, pp. 2–8 (2016)
11. Serag, A., et al.: Construction of a consistent high-definition spatio-temporal atlas of the developing brain using adaptive kernel regression. NeuroImage **59**(3), 2255–2265 (2012). https://doi.org/10.1016/j.neuroimage.2011.09.062, http://www.sciencedirect.com/science/article/pii/S1053811911011360
12. de Vos, B.D., Berendsen, F.F., Viergever, M.A., Sokooti, H., Staring, M., Išgum, I.: A deep learning framework for unsupervised affine and deformable image registration. Med. Image Anal. **52**, 128–143 (2019)
13. Wright, R., et al.: Construction of a fetal spatio-temporal cortical surface atlas from in utero MRI: application of spectral surface matching. NeuroImage **120**, 467–480 (2015)
14. Wu, Z., Wang, L., Lin, W., Gilmore, J.H., Li, G., Shen, D.: Construction of 4D infant cortical surface atlases with sharp folding patterns via spherical patch-based group-wise sparse representation. Hum. Brain Mapp. **40**, 3860–3880 (2019)

Author Index

Printed in the United States
By Bookmasters